THE COMPREHENSIVE
CATALOG
AND
ENCYCLOPEDIA
OF U.S. COINS

2ND EDITION

BY THE EDITORS OF COIN WORLD

The CONFIDENT
COLLECTOR™

AVON BOOKS NEW YORK

THE CONFIDENT COLLECTOR: THE COMPREHENSIVE CATALOG AND ENCYCLOPEDIA OF U.S. COINS, 2nd EDITION is an original publication of Avon Books.

AVON BOOKS
A division of
The Hearst Corporation
1350 Avenue of the Americas
New York, New York 10019

Acknowledgements

We wish to acknowledge the efforts of those many who helped in ways large and small, but in no case insignificant. We especially thank Project Editor David T. Alexander and Technical Editor Thomas K. DeLorey for their superb and exacting work. David A. Novoselsky has added a new dimension to the Patterns section with his insight and expertise.

Accumulating the necessary photographs for this book proved to be a monumental task, and it is only with the generous cooperation of many organizations that it has succeeded. Many photographs come from *Coin World* files. Other sources are named with each photograph.

We would like to single out the firms of Stack's, New York; Harlan J. Berk Ltd., Chicago; Bowers and Merena Galleries, Wolfeboro, N.H.; and Superior Galleries, Beverly Hills, Calif. These firms actually handle as a routine most of the coins cataloged in this book. It is their attention to detail in their excellent auction catalogs that provide much of the raw material for works such as this book. Each of these firms supplied many photographs, in some instances of very rare or even unique pieces. The importance of their contribution cannot be overstated, and their assistance in greatly appreciated.

Many photographs, particularly in the Patterns section, are from the Smithsonian Institution, National Numismatic Collection. The Smithsonian's unparalleled storehouse of numismatic items is essential to continuing research in the field.

While it is not the intent of the editors for this book to be a price guide, market values and auction results are important bits of information, and are therefore included. Values for federal issues — half cents through double eagles, including commemoratives and bullion coins — are adapted from *Coin World Trends*.

The study of numismatics is a vigorous field of endeavor. Many areas have been explored in exacting detail, while others remain dark caves waiting for an intrepid explorer. Any published research must therefore be no more than a snapshot in time; continuing discoveries will be incorporated into the body of knowledge that is numismatics, and into future editions of this book.

We respectfully acknowledge the efforts of those researchers who have gone before for their contributions contained herein, and gladly encourage all who will follow.

Brad Reed
Coordinating Editor

Sidney, Ohio
Oct. 30, 1997

Dedication

To Pat, whose computer wizardry made this book possible; to Jean, whose patience and support carried the task through; and to the coin collectors, whose hunger for information has made this book necessary.

Contents

Pattern, Experimental & Trial Pieces — 345

Judd Reference Concordance — 478

Philippine Coinage 1903-1947 — 485

Introduction & Overview

Numismatics, the study and collecting of coins, medals, tokens and paper money, had its beginning in the Renaissance, when men of leisure rediscovered the art and history of the ancient world. Then as now, coins offered a unique insight into vanished worlds of the past, and coin collecting was the fashionable pursuit of the affluent and educated in European society.

For centuries, numismatics was literally the hobby of kings.

The Habsburg rulers of Austria, Britain's King Charles I, German and Italian princes were among the most avid collectors. The vast fortune of the Rothschild family had its seeds in the rare coins sold under the "Red Shield" which hung over a little shop in Frankfurt's 18th century Judengasse.

Hessian Landgrave Friedrich II financed his coin collecting in part by sale of his subjects as mercenary soldiers to the forces of British King George III. In more recent times, Russian Grand Duke George Mikhailovitch amassed a great collection of his country's coins and medals. Italy's King Victor Emanuel III emerged as one of the greatest numismatists of all time. The collection of Egyptian King Farouk seized the headlines when it was sold at auction after his ouster.

Coin collecting blossomed in the United States in the first half of the 19th century. Early collectors such as Matthew Stickney, Joseph J. Mickley, Montroville W. Dickeson, Lorin G. Parmelee, Charles I. Bushnell, R. Coulton Davis, Sylvester S. Crosby and others laid the foundation of systematic collecting of American material.

Early dealers and auctioneers such as Edward Cogan, Augustus Sage, Ebenezer Mason, Capt. John Haseltine, William Idler, Edouard Frossard, J.W. Scott, Lyman Low, W. Elliott Woodward, Henry and Samuel Hudson Chapman created the world of American commercial numismatics. A later generation would include Thomas L. Elder, Wayte Raymond, B. Max Mehl and many more.

United States Mint Director James Ross Snowden launched the Washington Cabinet of Medals and began restriking various rare coins to use as trading stock in his quest for rare Washington items, then the hottest things in U.S. numismatics. Throughout much of that century, the Mint was a major force in the world of coin collecting.

Collectors of that era sought American Colonial coins and tokens, early United States copper coins, Indian Peace and Washington medals, Hard Times and temperance tokens, political items, world and ancient coins with the same avidity. Local and national organization sprang up, including the New York-based American Numismatic Society in 1858.

Publication of Augustus G. Heaton's book *Mint Marks* in 1893 led to a fundamental shift in collecting toward regular issue U.S. coins by date and Mint mark. Wayte Raymond confirmed this trend by introducing his National coin albums in the early 1930s, making it possible to store coins in an orderly manned and have them available for easy display at the same time.

In the 1885-1930 era, great collections were amassed by such figures as the Garrett family of Baltimore, H.O. Granberg, Virgil Brand of Chicago, Col. E.H.R. Green, William H. Woodin, the Norwebs of Cleveland.

A more popular type of numismatics was served by the American Numismatic Association (ANA), founded by Dr. George Heath in 1891. Popular numismatics swept the field dramatically in the Depression years with the appearance of the first of the "penny boards," invented by J.K. Post of Neenah, Wis., and marketed by R.S. Yeoman of Whitman Publishing Co. of Racine. Inexpensive albums made assembling sets of Lincoln cents from circulation a national craze and brought millions of Americans into coin collecting.

Lee F. Hewitt of Chicago introduced the influential monthly magazine *Numismatic Scrapbook* in 1935. Raymond's *Standard Catalogue of United States Coins* made accurate information available, freeing collectors of reliance on widely distributed but self-serving dealer house organs such as Mehl's *Star Rare Coin Encyclopedia*.

The continuing post-war information explosion began when Yeoman's new *Guide Book of United States Coins* first appeared in 1946. The arrival of numismatic newspapers, *Numismatic News*, which began as a biweekly in 1952, and *Coin World* as a weekly in 1960, transformed the marketplace.

The fast-developing coin market saw many cycles. One of the first was the 1939 commemorative coin boom, followed at length by booms in Proof sets in the 1950s, rolls and bags in the 1960s.

During the 1970s a new class of active coin investor entered the market. Many established coin firms served such investors, but more were reached by telemarketers, aggressive sellers of coin via telephone solicitation.

Grading has been an intrinsic part of the coin market since the beginning and has remained a controversial area ever since. Strictly speaking, grading should be a description of the amount of wear, if any, that a coin has received since leaving the Mint.

Most frequently used terms and their abbreviations are Poor, Fair, About Good (AG), Good (G), Very Good, (VG), Fine (F), Very Fine (VF), Extremely Fine (EF), About Uncirculated (AU) and Uncirculated (Unc.). Proofs are specially prepared coins, struck on polished blanks between polished dies. Proof (Prf.) is a method of manufacture, not a condition.

Today, grading and price have become so closely interwoven that the statement of a coin's grade has a determining effect on its price. After decades of wrangling, the ANA attempted to standardize grading terms in 1977, when numismatist Abe Kosoff adapted the Sheldon numerical grading scale to all U.S. coins through the book *Official ANA Grading Standards for United States Coins*.

This system had been created by Dr. William H. Sheldon in 1945 to grade early American coppers such as the 1794 large cents by condition and color. A value of 1 was given a "basal state" coin, worn virtually smooth. A Mint State 70 coin was a perfect coin that had never seen circulation. Mint State or Uncirculated coins were given numerical grades of MS-60 or better.

The American Numismatic Association Certification Service, ANACS, began third-party grading in 1979, after some years of authenticating coins for the numismatic community. ANACS applied the Sheldon scale to all U.S. coins it graded and showed that a profitable market for independent grading existed.

Early in 1986, the Professional Coin Grading Service (PCGS) was born, offering what it termed precision grading by professional numismatists, including 11 grades of

Uncirculated from MS-60 to MS-70. Sonically sealing the coins it graded in rigid plastic holders soon known as "slabs," PCGS made possible sight-unseen trading in coins bearing its assigned grades through a nation-wide network of participating dealers pledged to accept all PCGS grades without question.

Some time later, the Numismatic Guaranty Corporation of America, NGC, began its precision, third-party grading and "slabs" became the basis of a whole new wave of numismatic investment marketing.

Today, the most widely used grades and numbers include Good-4, Very Good-8, Fine-12 and 15, Very Fine-20 and 30, Extremely fine-40, Choice Extremely Fine-45, About Uncirculated- 50, Choice About Uncirculated-55. Mint State or Uncirculated grades begin with MS-60. Most often encountered are MS-63, Choice Uncirculated (sometimes called Select); MS-65, Gem Uncirculated (sometimes called Choice); MS-67, Superb Uncirculated; MS-70, the theoretically perfect coin, struck from perfect dies on a perfect planchet.

Using this book

Included in this book are all Colonial and Early State coins, associated coins and tokens traditionally collected as part of the U.S. series, regular issue U.S. coins in all metals, private and territorial gold coins and patterns of 1830-1861, as well as the pattern and trial pieces that are a vital part of American numismatic history.

Coins are listed in chronological order. Whenever possible, the number struck of each date will be given. These numbers are as accurate as may be possible, based on the editors' research and the figures published in *The 1998 Coin World Guide to U.S. Coins, Prices & Value Trends.*

It must be emphasized that the passage of time, melting and accident give mintage figures very limited value in determining rarity. Nor does the figure necessarily mean that all these coins bear the date listed. For many years, the Mint used steel dies until they crumbled, and these often bore earlier dates. Thus the Mint report stated that 19,570 silver dollars were struck during 1804, but did not note that these bore the actual date 1803.

A hypothetical listing 1867/6 (4,400,000) (902) indicates that 4.4 million coins of all varieties were reportedly struck in 1867. In addition, 902 pieces were struck as Proofs on polished blanks between polished dies. Proof describes a method of manufacture, not a condition, although such coins are graded according to the Sheldon scale as Proof-60, Proof-65, etc.

Below this listing may appear 1867 Normal date, 1867 doubled reverse, 1867 inverted G in AMERICA. These are all varieties of the 1867 date. The first listing is an overdate, with 7 punched into the die over an earlier 6. The mintage figure does not mean that 4.4 million overdates were struck, but rather that 4.4 million coins were struck during the 1867 reporting period, some of which are overdates, some bear normal dates, others show doubled die or an inverted G in AMERICA.

Abbreviations used in this book include Obv. and Rev. for Obverse and Reverse, the "heads" and "tails" side of a coin. R.E. indicates a reeded edge, P.E. a plain edge, L.E. a lettered edge.

In describing rarity, the word Rare will generally mean that 31 to 75 pieces are believed to exist; Very Rare will indicate 13 to 30 pieces; Extremely Rare, four to 12 pieces known; Excessively Rare, three or fewer; Unique coins are those of which one specimen is known to exist.

Rarity and high market value do not always got hand in hand. A reasonably common Morgan silver dollar in MS-65 (Gem. Uncirculated) that is sought by thousands of collectors will sell for more than a rare Washington medal that only interests a few. A common coin in MS-65 may command a far greater price than a coin of far greater absolute rarity that is only Very Good (VG-8).

Nor is age the key determinant of value. Thousands of ancient Roman silver coins sell for less than a 1909-S VDB U.S. Lincoln cent. The real key to market value is current demand, how many collectors actually want a coin enough to pay a high price to own it.

About the editors

Scott Publishing Co. of New York released the first edition of the *Comprehensive Catalog and Encyclopedia of United States Coins* in 1971, edited by numismatic author Don Taxay. The 1976 edition was revised by Joseph H. Rose and Howard Hazelcorn in a different size and internal format. Both books were widely acclaimed for their completeness and represented a major breakthrough in U.S. numismatics.

The 1989 edition was so completely revised that it was, in effect, a different book. In preparing the new edition, no effort has been spared to update all numismatic information, include new discoveries and all U.S. coins that have been issued since 1989.

Project editor for editions since 1989 is David T. Alexander, numismatic writer, cataloger and appraiser. A coin collector since age nine, Alexander directed the Historical Museum of Southern Florida in Miami, Fla., before joining the staff of *Coin World* in Sidney, Ohio, in 1974. He was staff writer and later international editor of *Coin World*, as well as executive editor of *Numismatic Scrapbook* magazine between 1974 and 1976.

He has worked as cataloger for several major auction firms and has handled most of the great rarities in the U.S. field, including colonial, regular Federal, pattern and pioneer coinages. In 1984 he founded his own independent consulting firm, Alexander Numismatic Services Inc. Since early 1990 he has been a cataloger at Stack's in New York City.

A life member of the American Numismatic Association, Alexander's byline appears regularly in leading numismatic publications. He is a long-time member and past executive director of the Numismatic Literary Guild and received its Clemy Award in 1987. He belongs to the New York Numismatic Club and received the Society for International Numismatics' Silver Medal of Merit for writing and research in 1990.

Also a collector from an early age, Technical Editor Thomas K. DeLorey was a member of the *Coin World* staff from 1973 to 1978. He wrote for the newspaper's Collectors Clearinghouse section and served as its third editor. He possesses in-depth knowledge of all U.S. coins, Mint errors and the minting process. Joining the ANACS staff in 1978, DeLorey launched ANACS grading and was Senior Authenticator Grader. He currently is senior U.S. numismatist for Harlan J. Berk Ltd. in Chicago, Illinois.

Deeply interested in numismatic research, DeLorey has received the ANA's Heath Award and its Wayte and Olga Raymond Awards several times for articles appearing in *The Numismatist*.

Evolution of United States Coins
Coins in use in America before 1793

The first coins in circulation in non-Spanish North America were standard French and English issues used in a variety of unsuccessful colonies ranging from the St. Lawrence River to the Caribbean. The colonists were not likely to have too much specie left after they purchased their supplies for the voyage, but what was left most certainly did come along, as the travelers did not dare to leave anything of value in a land to which they were likely never to return.

With the establishment of successful colonies in the early 1600s, the colonists began to trade both with their parent companies and the Spanish colonies of the Caribbean. The trade with England was highly restricted, and most English gold and silver that reached these shores soon returned to Europe in the form of taxes, custom duties, and profit for the companies. The trade with Latin America was much less formal (thanks to smuggling), and provided much of the circulating coinage for the Colonies.

Because the Colonies could never acquire enough coinage of the homeland to fulfill their needs, they were eventually forced to produce some themselves. The General Court of the Massachusetts Bay Colony authorized production of silver shillings, sixpence, and threepence, of lighter weight to assure that they would remain in the colony. All bore the authorization date 1652 except the 1662 Oak Tree twopence, specifically authorized and dated 1662.

There would be a number of attempts to provide colonial coinage through contracts or patents from the Crown, as well as purely local, private issues of varying weight and quality. Dr. Samuel Higley of Granby, Connecticut, operated a copper mine, smelting metal in defiance of British policy. He struck his own threepence tokens, and after criticism of this high face value, candidly modified the legends to read VALUE ME AS YOU PLEASE. All of these will be described in detail with each type listed under Colonial, Early State and Associated issues below.

After the Revolution, several prominent merchants issued private tokens which provided needed small change and also publicized their businesses. A number of these were made in England and were of better quality than the majority of the various state issues. Incuse edge inscriptions made some tokens payable at the issuers' stores, but others were payable only at London or Liverpool or other equally distant places. These tokens circulated for several years after the establishment of the Philadelphia Mint, and some provided ready-made planchets for recoining into U.S. copper coins.

The Articles of Confederation, adopted in 1781, permitted the states to issue their own coinages, with Congress fixing a uniform "standard of weights and measures." Only three of the 13 states struck coins for circulation under the Articles of Confederation: Connecticut, Massachusetts and New Jersey. Vermont, the 14th state, struck coinage before it entered the union. Most of the state coinages were produced by private manufacturers under contract to the states, although Massachusetts operated its own Mint in 1787 and 1788. Connecticut authorized a Mint, but most of its coinage was struck privately.

The U.S. Constitution, however, brought an end to the state coinage. Article 1, Section 10, Paragraph 1 of the Constitution reads, "No state shall . . . coin money, emit bills of credit, make anything but gold or silver coin a tender in payment of debts." The sole right to coin money was granted to the federal government (although until 1864 a loophole permitted private coinage) by the ratification of the Constitution in 1788.

Federal coinage studies

A federal coinage system had been under study since the early 1780s. Two plans merit attention here. The first was submitted to Congress Jan. 15, 1782, by Superintendent of Finance Robert Morris. The proposal was written by Assistant Financier of the Confederation Gouverneur Morris (no relation to Robert Morris). This proposal was a complicated one, designed to unify nearly all existing (and conflicting) state currencies. Morris proposed substituting a decimal system based on the familiar Spanish Milled Dollar or Piece of Eight for the British system of pounds, shillings and pence. The basic "Unit" would be equal to 1/1,440 of the Spanish dollar, a sum arrived at by determining the largest common divisor by which state currencies could be divided without a fraction. The denominations would have been copper 5-unit and 8-unit pieces, plus a silver bit worth 100 units, a silver quint worth 500 units and a mark worth 1,000 units. The cumbersome Morris system failed to receive Congressional approval, though rare patterns exist of all but one of its denominations.

Meanwhile, as Congress debated various monetary plans, it took one concrete step and authorized a copper coinage in 1787. At this time, three states were still producing copper coinage. Congress met in Philadelphia and authorized a copper coinage on April 21, "agreeable to the Federal standard," to be struck by private contractor under the general supervision of Congress.

The result was the Fugio cent, the first coin authorized by the United States government. It is named for the Latin legend FUGIO ("I Fly") that appears above a sundial on the the coin's obverse with the legend MIND YOUR BUSINESS, in other words, "Time flies, attend to your business." The reverse bore 13 linked rings and name UNITED STATES with the then more hopeful than accurate motto, WE ARE ONE. All these devices were plainly derived from the enigmatic 1776 Continental "Dollar." James Jarvis, a Connecticut businessman, received a contract to strike 300 tons of the copper coins, or about 26,666,666 pieces, by paying a massive bribe demanded by Superintendent of Finance Col. William Duer. Jarvis began coinage of the cents in New Haven, Conn., while he sought a way to obtain supplies of planchets and necessary dies in Europe. The Fugio venture ended in embezzlement and the flight of Jarvis and his confederates, who had struck fewer than 400,000 Fugio cents by June 1, 1787. The federal government voided Jarvis' contract for missing the December 1787 delivery date (the coins were not delivered until beginning in May 1788). The Fugio cents actually delivered were generally underweight and unpopular with the public. Thus failed the Federal government's first experiment in coinage.

The second plan warranting attention was submitted to Congress by Alexander Hamilton, Secretary of the Treasury, on Jan. 21, 1791, also based on the existing Spanish

Milled Dollar. Hamilton recommended denominations including gold $10 coin, a gold dollar, a silver dollar, a silver tenth-dollar, a copper coin valued at one hundred to the dollar, and a second copper coin, valued at 200 to the dollar.

The Hamilton proposal was very similar to what Congress would approve in April 1792. Following Hamilton's proposal, Congress passed a resolution March 3, 1791, that a Federal Mint be built, and President Washington in his third State of the Union speech agreed. Then, on April 2, 1792, Congress passed a law authorizing both a Federal Mint and coinage. Ten denominations of coins, more than recommended by Hamilton, were approved: gold $10 eagle, $5 half eagle and $2.50 quarter eagle; silver dollar, half dollar, quarter dollar, disme (the "s" was dropped by 1793, with the 10-cent piece called a dime) and half disme; copper cent and half cent, neither of which would have legal tender status.

History of U.S. Coinage Denominations

Since coinage began at the Philadelphia Mint in 1793, 21 denominations have appeared on the circulating and commemorative coins of the United States. Gold coins have been the $50 (commemorative, Gold Rush Assay Office and bullion pieces), the $25 (on the American Eagle bullion coins), $20, $10, $5, $3, $2.50 and $1. Among silver coins (many later changed to copper-nickel clad copper by the Mint Act of 1965), have been the silver dollar, the Trade dollar, the 50-cent coin, the quarter dollar, 20-cent coin, dime, half dime and 3-cent coin. There have also been copper-nickel 5-cent, 3-cent and 1-cent coins; a bronze 2-cent coin; cents in six different alloys; and a copper half cent.

Production of U.S. coinage began in earnest in 1793 with the production of copper half cents and cents. The striking of the first silver coins began one year after copper coinage production. The Mint began striking silver half dollars and dollars in 1794; silver half dimes (dated 1794) in 1795; and silver dimes and quarter dollars in 1796. Gold coinage began in 1795 with the half eagle and the eagle, followed by the quarter eagle in 1796.

During the earlier years of the U.S. Mint, not all denominations were struck in all years. In 1804, coinage of the silver dollar ceased with the striking of 1803-dated coins; dollar coinage was not resumed until 1836. A few gold eagles were struck in 1804, but coinage then ceased until 1838. No quarter eagles were struck from 1809 through 1820. Production of the other denominations was sporadic except for the cent; the War of 1812 prevented any 1815-dated cents from being produced, but otherwise the chain has been unbroken since 1793.

Meanwhile, as the country's borders and population grew, the monetary system grew with them. The denominations authorized in 1792 were no longer sufficient to meet the country's monetary needs. New denominations were authorized at the century's midpoint. In 1849, Congress authorized a gold dollar and a gold $20 double eagle (both under the Act of March 3, 1849). In 1851, a silver 3-cent coin, supposedly to facilitate the purchase of 3-cent postage stamps (Act of March 3, 1851). A gold $3 coin was introduced in 1854 (Act of Feb. 21, 1853), again to help in the purchase of 3-cent stamps (in sheets of 100). A smaller copper-nickel cent was approved in 1857 to replace the cumbersome copper large cent. The half cent was also eliminated in 1857.

The American Civil War opened in 1861, causing massive hoarding of coinage and the necessity of coinage substitutes like encased postage stamps, privately produced copper-alloy cent-like tokens and finally, the first federal paper money since the Revolutionary War. More changes to U.S. coins began in 1864, when the composition of the cent was changed to "French bronze," an alloy of 95 percent copper and

5 percent tin and zinc, and when a bronze 2-cent coin was introduced (both under the Act of April 22, 1864). A copper-nickel 3-cent coin was issued beginning in 1865 (Act of March 3, 1865) to replace the silver 3-cent coins (which was struck in decreasing numbers until the last coins were produced in 1873). In 1866, a copper-nickel 5-cent piece was introduced (Act of May 16, 1866); the silver half dime was eliminated after 1873.

The year 1873 brought many changes to the U.S. coinage system, because of a law denounced by the silver interests as the "Crime of 1873." The Act of Feb. 12, 1873, is called by numismatic historian Don Taxay "the most exhaustive [coinage act] in our history." Four denominations were abolished by the act: the 2-cent coin, the silver 3-cent coin, the half dime and the silver dollar. A Trade silver dollar was authorized for use by merchants in the Orient; a year later, Congress revoked the coin's legal tender status in the United States. The weights of the silver half dime, dime, quarter dollar and half dollar were increased. In effect, the law demonetized silver and placed the United States on a gold standard, triggering a national debate that would last for the next quarter century.

Another new denomination was authorized under the Act of March 3, 1875 — the silver 20-cent piece. The coin was struck for circulation in 1875-76, setting an early record for the shortest-lived silver denomination in U.S. coinage history. Coinage of Proof 20-cent pieces continued in 1877-78, but for collectors only.

Meanwhile, the powerful silver interests in the United States, faced with the demonetization of silver left by the Crime of '73, fought in Congress. The resulting Act of Feb, 28, 1878, reinstituted the standard silver dollar abolished by the Act of Feb. 12, 1873. The specifications were unchanged from the silver dollar of 1837-73: an alloy 90 percent silver and 10 percent copper, weighing 26.73 grams. Obverse and reverse designs created by newly arrived, British-born Mint Engraver George T. Morgan were selected for the dollar, today generally called the Morgan dollar, though long known as the Bland-Allison dollar after the congressmen responsible for the bill. Coinage of the Morgan dollar continued through 1904.

Coinage denominations in use continued unchanged through 1889, when the copper-nickel 3 cents, the gold dollar and gold $3 denominations were struck for the last time.

The silver dollar was resurrected twice for circulation: in 1921, to continue through 1935; and in 1964, when several hundred thousand silver Peace silver dollars were struck. These coins were reportedly destroyed before entering circulation, after government support for them was withdrawn. The copper-nickel Eisenhower dollar was introduced in 1971, and the smaller Susan B. Anthony dollar was issued briefly from 1979-81.

Since the Mint Act of 1875, three new denominations have been authorized, none for circulation. In 1915, a gold $50 coin was approved to commemorate the Panama-Pacific Exposition being held in San Francisco that year. More than 70 years later, in 1986, the $50 denomination was revived for the American Eagle bullion program. That same legislation (Act of Dec. 17, 1986, Public Law 99-185) also approved the United States' first $25 coin, the American Eagle half-ounce coin. In 1997 came the introduction of the highest denomination: $100 for the 1-ounce platinum bullion coin. The platinum half ounce is $50, and the quarter-ounce $25.

Designs

The story behind the designs of U.S. coinage is one of artistic experimentation and drone-like uniformity; of political necessity and political favoritism; of beauty tempered by the realities of the coining process.

The senators and representatives who approved the U.S. monetary system created design parameters that affect new U.S. coin designs even today, more than 200 years after that initial legislation. The Mint Act of April 2, 1792, specified that certain design features and legends appear on the coins which were authorized. On one side of all coins was to be an impression symbolic of Liberty, plus the word LIBERTY and the year of coinage. For the silver and gold coins, an eagle and UNITED STATES OF AMERICA were to appear on the reverse. The denomination was to appear on the reverses of the half cents and cents.

For more than 115 years in the history of U.S. coinage, Liberty was portrayed by allegorical female figures, either a bust or a full-length portrait. Liberty's changing face through the years says a lot about the artistic abilities of the craftsmen employed on the Mint staff and the artists hired from outside to design certain coins. Some of the most attractive U.S. coins were designed by non-Mint employees, often in opposition to a jealous Mint engraving staff who seemed more concerned about whether the coin would stack than its physical beauty. Many beautiful designs created by Mint's own staff engravers never went beyond the pattern stage. Drone-like uniformity characterized U.S. designs from the mid-1830s into the early 20th century.

The changing portrait of Liberty also reveals the embodiment of the "ideal woman" by the physical standards set by the American men of the time, and men have always dominated U.S. coinage design. The first coinage portraits of Liberty are "Rubenesque" by modern standards. The most recent allegorical figure of Liberty to appear on U.S. coins is on American Eagle gold bullion coins. They depict a reproduction of an 80-year-old design, "slimmed down" to resemble the trimmer woman championed by American advertising and dietary standards in the 1980s.

The 1793 half cents and cents introduced the allegorical themes used on U.S. coins: The half cent depicts a bust of Liberty with her hair flowing free. A Liberty Cap on a pole, a familiar symbol of Liberty in the American and French revolutions of the latter 18th century, rests on her right shoulder, giving the design its name: the Liberty Cap. On the first cents of 1793, another Flowing Hair Liberty appears. Contemporary reports claim Liberty looks frightened on the cent. The designs are somewhat crude by modern standards. However, the Liberty busts were cut directly into steel by hand. Mint technicians had none of the modern equipment and techniques available to their counterparts today.

Since the Mint Act of 1792 required only the denomination to appear on the reverses of the copper coins, the Mint engravers had a free rein. The first half cents have a wreath on the reverse, a device used as late as 1958 on the reverse of the Lincoln cent in the form of two ears of wheat. The reverse device on the first cents lasted only months. A 15-link chain meant to represent the unity of the 15 states appears on the first 1793 cents. The chain was believed by the public to be a symbol of enslavement perceived to represent "a bad omen for Liberty." Changes in the design of both sides of the cent came rapidly. The Chain reverse was replaced by a wreath, then the obverse design of the "frightened Liberty" was replaced with a Liberty Cap design similar to that on the half cent. Thus, three distinct cents were struck with the 1793 date: the Flowing Hair Liberty, Chain cent; the Flowing Hair, Wreath cent; and the Liberty Cap, Wreath cent.

Additional design changes were instituted for the cent in 1796, when a Draped Bust design was introduced and used through 1807. Liberty appears without a cap, her hair falling over bare shoulders. Loose drapery covers Liberty's bust. Another Liberty Head design called the Classic Head design was used on the cent from 1808-14. It differs considerably from the earlier allegorical motifs, with Liberty wearing a ribbon inscribed with LIBERTY around her hair.

The Coronet design was introduced in 1816 on the large cent. This design would prove one of the more versatile of the 19th century. A variation of the Coronet design would appear on both copper coins until 1857, and on most of gold denominations from the 1830s to the first decade of the 20th century. The design is similar on all of the coins, depicting a classic-featured female wearing a coronet inscribed with the word LIBERTY.

Designs for the half cent were generally similar to the cent's designs, although the timetable for introduction was often different. The half cent used a Liberty Cap design until 1797, and from 1800-08 a Draped Bust design was used. The Classic Head design was used on the half cent from 1809-36 and the Coronet design was introduced in 1840.

Silver coins

The silver coins of the 18th century feature designs generally similar to those on the copper coins. The silver coins used a Flowing Hair design in 1794-95, and in 1795-96 a Draped Bust design was introduced on all silver coins. The Capped Bust design was used first for the half dollar in 1807, with the dime following in 1809, the quarter dollar in 1815 and the half dime in 1829. The eagles appearing on the reverse of the silver coins appeared in several forms, first in a Small Eagle design that some critics likened to a pigeon, then a Heraldic Eagle which was used on the dollar beginning in 1798, the half dollar in 1801 and the quarter dollar in 1804.

Allegorical Liberty figures with similar themes but somewhat different details were used on the early gold coins. A Capped Bust, Heraldic Eagle design was used from 1796-1807 for the quarter eagle, then replaced in 1808 with the one-year-only Capped Bust type. The Capped Head quarter eagle was struck between 1821-34. On the half eagle, the Capped Bust design was used from 1795-1807; the Small Eagle reverse was used from 1795-98, and a Heraldic Eagle design was used from 1798-1807, though pieces are known dated as early as 1795 due to the practice of reusing outdated obverse dies. The Capped Draped Bust was used on the half eagle from 1807-12, and the Capped Head, from 1813-34. The Classic Head design was used briefly, from 1834-38. For the $10 eagle, the Capped Bust design was used from 1795 to 1804, when the denomination ceased coinage. On the reverse of the $10 coin, the Small Eagle was used from 1795-97, and the Heraldic Eagle design was used from 1797 to 1804.

Several things took place in the mid-1830s that were to affect coinage designs for decades. Among them was the Act of Jan. 18, 1837, which eliminated the need for an eagle on the reverses of the half dime and dime. The other event was the resumption of coinage of the silver dollar in 1836, and the adoption of a new design that eventually would appear on six different denominations, on some of them for more than half a century.

Production of the silver dollar resumed in 1836 with the Gobrecht design. The obverse depicts a Seated Liberty figure sitting on a rock, her body wrapped in robes. The reverse depicts a Flying Eagle design.

With the creation of the Seated Liberty design, a new age of uniformity ensued on

U.S. coins. The Seated Liberty obverse design was introduced on the half dime and dime in 1837, the quarter dollar in 1838 and the half dollar in 1839. Wreaths were placed on the half dime and dime in 1837; eagles appeared on the new quarter dollar and half dollar; and the dollar received a new eagle design in 1840, with the Flying Eagle replaced by an eagle similar to those on the quarter and half dollar.

Gold coins, too, entered the uniform age of coin designs when the Coronet (sometimes called Liberty Head on gold coins) design was introduced in 1838 for the eagle, 1839 for the half eagle and 1840 for the quarter eagle. When the gold dollar and double eagle were introduced in 1849, a different Coronet design was used for both. Like the silver coins, the gold coins would not break out of uniformity until the early 20th century, except for the dollar.

New theme

A new theme was introduced in 1854 on the gold dollar, replacing the Coronet figure. An Indian Head portrait by James B. Longacre was introduced, the first in a series of medallic tributes to the first native Americans that would last until shortly before the beginning of World War II. Ironically, the Indian was being used as a symbol of Liberty even as the American movement to push the Indians into increasingly smaller portions of the West grew. However, the gold dollar portrait was not a true Indian; Longacre simply placed an Indian headdress on the same Liberty head (now believed based on the facial features of his own family, complete with the meticulous nose) he would use in many different versions. A slightly larger Indian Head was used beginning in 1856 on the gold dollar. The gold $3 coin of 1854 depicts an Indian Head portrait, and the reverse depicts not an eagle but a wreath.

When the large cent was abandoned in 1857 for a smaller cent, a Flying Eagle design was placed on the obverse (the 1856 Flying Eagle cents are patterns, struck before Congress authorized a change in composition). This was the first non-human portrayal of Liberty, and the only time an eagle would appear on the cent. The obverse design was changed to an Indian Head design in 1859. Wreaths of various types appear on the two smaller cents.

Several non-allegorical designs began to appear on U.S. coins in the 1850s. On the silver 3-cent piece, a six-point star appears as the central obverse design; the reverse depicts the Roman numeral III inside a large letter "C." Shields appear on the obverses of the 2-cent piece and the first copper-nickel 5-cent piece. A Liberty Head design replaced the Shield design on the 5-cent coin in 1883. The silver dollar, abandoned in 1873 and reinstated in 1878, depicts a Liberty Head and an eagle (called the Morgan dollar).

The Seated Liberty coinage design was dusted off and placed on the short-lived 20-cent coin of 1875-78. However, the Seated Liberty design, used on most of the silver coins since 1836, was finally abandoned at the end of 1891. By this time, it was in use only on the dime, quarter dollar and half dollar. It was replaced in 1892 with a Liberty Head design by Mint Chief Engraver Charles Barber, who also created a Heraldic Eagle for use on the reverse of the quarter dollar and half dollar; the reverse wreath appearing on the Seated Liberty dime was maintained on the reverse of the "Barber" dime. The Barber designs remained in use through mid-1916.

The first two decades of the 20th century resulted in two major design trends for U.S. coins. One, beginning in 1907, resulted in what can be called the "Golden Age of U.S. Coin Designs." The other, beginning in 1909, was the first step away from the allegorical depictions that had characterized U.S. coins since 1793 in favor of medallic tributes to prominent political figures from American history.

The "golden age" began with the election of Theodore Roosevelt as president of the United States. Roosevelt, best-known among non-numismatists as a vibrant president who built the Panama Canal and advocated the carrying of a "big stick," did more to improve the aesthetics of U.S. coins than any other politician since Washington. He invited Augustus Saint-Gaudens, the premier U.S. sculptor of the day, to create coin designs Roosevelt hoped would suggest the beauty of ancient Greece. Saint-Gaudens submitted designs for the cent, $10 eagle and $20 double eagle. Roosevelt chose from the submissions the designs for the two gold coins: The $10 coin depicts an allegorical Liberty Head wearing an Indian headdress on the obverse, and a standing eagle on the reverse; the double eagle depicts a Standing Liberty facing the viewer on the obverse, and a Flying Eagle design for the reverse.

The Mint's Chief Engraver Charles E. Barber was not happy with the hiring of outside talent, even though Saint-Gaudens' double eagle is considered by many collectors to be the finest U.S. coin design ever. The first $20 coins struck in 1907 feature exceptionally high relief features, an artistic creation that created problems in production. The coins required too many strikings of the press for efficient production, so the relief was lowered later in 1907. Saint-Gaudens, who had been in ill-health, was dead by this time and unable to protest the changes in the design.

The "golden age" continued in 1908, with Bela Lyon Pratt's new designs for the $2.50 quarter eagle and $5 eagle: an American Indian on the obverse, and a Standing Eagle on the reverse. These were the first true Indians to appear on U.S. coins. What made the designs so unusual, however, was their placement on the coin. The designs were created in the oxymoronic "incused relief." Often incorrectly referred to as incused, the designs resemble ancient Egyptian art with raised devices sunken into the fields so their highest points are level with the flat fields. This design feature was criticized, with some suggesting that the "incused" portions would permit enough germs to accumulate to prove a health hazard. The experiment also displeased Barber.

In 1913, the designs for the 5-cent coin were changed. An American Indian was placed on the obverse, and an American bison was placed on the reverse. The coin, known variously as the Indian Head, Bison or Buffalo 5-cent coin, is considered the most American of U.S. designs because of the two themes portrayed. The Indian design appearing on the obverse is probably the finest to be placed on a U.S. coin. Three Native Americans — Iron Tail, Two Moons and Chief John Big Tree — posed for designer James Earle Fraser, who created a composite portrait.

More design changes were made in 1916, when the Barber designs for the dime, quarter dollar and half dollar were replaced in mid-year (although no 1916 Barber half dollars were struck). The dime features a Winged Liberty Head on the obverse; the design is often called the "Mercury" dime, but Mercury was a Roman male god with wings on his ankles, while the figure on the dime is female and wears a winged cap. The reverse depicts a fasces in a branch of laurel adapted from the wall decoration of the House of Representatives chamber.

The quarter dollar design introduced in 1916 proved controversial. The Standing Liberty figure had an exposed right breast, an anatomical feature which had also appeared on the allegorical figure of Electricity on the Series 1896 $5 silver certificate until it was replaced in 1899 with a less prurient American Indian vignette. Some citizens of the period deemed the design too revealing on the quarter dollar as well, so in 1917 the offending breast was covered with a coat of mail (both varieties of 1917 design exist). The reverse depicts a Flying Eagle; its position was modified slightly in 1917 when Liberty was given additional clothing. Amusingly, correspondence between Mint officials and designer Hermon MacNeil refer to changes in the placement of the eagle but apparently do not mention the unclad Liberty. The coat of mail was added very quietly.

The Walking Liberty half dollar was also introduced in 1916. The obverse depicts a Walking Liberty figure inspired by French designer Louis Oscar Roty's figure of Liberty as "The Sower," while the reverse depicts one of the most attractive eagles placed on a regular issue of U.S. coins.

In 1921, the Peace dollar replaced the Morgan, which had been briefly resurrected in 1921 (coinage ceased in 1904). This dollar commemorates the peace which followed the end of World War I. Silver coinage ceased in 1935, the dollar denomination was abandoned.

The second coinage trend to begin in the early 20th century occurred in 1909 when a bust of Abraham Lincoln by Victor D. Brenner replaced the Indian Head on the cent. For the first time, a historical, non-allegorical figure was used on a circulating coin of the United States. Lincoln's 100th birthday was celebrated in 1909. His 150th birthday in 1959 resulted in the Lincoln Memorial replacing the two ears of wheat found on the Lincoln cents of 1909-58.

The trend continued in 1932, when the Standing Liberty quarter dollar was replaced with the Washington design on the bicentennial of Washington's birth. Felix Schlag's portrait of Thomas Jefferson replaced the American Indian in 1938, after the Treasury Department held a design contest that attracted some 400 participants. Recently deceased President Franklin D. Roosevelt was placed on the dime in 1946, a year after his death. Benjamin Franklin and the Liberty Bell were placed on the half dollar in 1948 by John R. Sinnock, replacing the Walking Liberty designs. He was replaced in turn in 1964 by John F. Kennedy and the Presidential Seal, designed by Gilroy Roberts and Frank Gasparro in a numismatic tribute to the assassinated president.

In 1971, a copper-nickel dollar coin was introduced bearing President Dwight D. Eisenhower's portrait on the obverse and allegorical figure of an eagle landing on Earth's moon, commemorating the Apollo moon landings.

The Bicentennial of the Declaration of Independence in 1976 brought changes to the reverses of the quarter dollar, half dollar and dollar. The reverse of the 1976 quarter dollar depicts a Revolutionary War drummer; the half dollar depicts Independence Hall in Philadelphia; and the dollar depicts the Liberty Bell superimposed over the moon. The designs reverted to their original versions in 1977.

In 1979, a new copper-nickel clad dollar sized between the quarter dollar and half dollar was introduced, replacing the Eisenhower dollar. The new design depicts feminist Susan B. Anthony and a reduced version of the moon-landing design. Anthony was the first non-allegorical U.S. woman to appear on a circulating coin. The choice was not a popular one, since many collectors had hoped a reincarnation of the Flowing Hair Liberty, designed by Chief Sculptor-Engraver Frank Gasparro especially for the smaller dollar would appear. Letters from collectors focused on the supposed unattractiveness of Anthony, although those same writers apparently had never criticized the physical attributes of Lincoln (who, after all, was referred to as an ape in the press of his time before his assassination) and Washington.

Ironically, a descendant of Anthony was critical of an early version of Gasparro's Anthony portrait as too "pretty" and not at all indicative of the woman's strong character; Gasparro modified the design before it was placed on the coin. However, the coin did not circulate well, mainly because of its similarity in size and color to the quarter dollar (many found the two denominations too close to each other in diameter). Poor public usage of the smaller dollar resulted in none being struck after 1981 (the 1979-80 coins were struck for circulation, and the 1981 coins were struck for collectors only).

The reintroduction of commemorative coins and the American Eagle bullion coins have brought renewed interest in coinage designs, and renewed controversy. Collectors and others have been critical of some of the designs on the commemorative coins (the two torchbearers on an early version of the 1984 Olympic $10 eagle were lampooned as "Dick and Jane running" by congressional members). Others, most notably the obverse of the 1986-W Statue of Liberty half eagle, designed by Chief Sculptor-Engraver Elizabeth Jones, have been praised. Internationally acclaimed medallic sculptor Jones, incidentally, helped to end the male domination of U.S. coinage designs as the first woman to serve as Chief Sculptor-Engraver of the U.S. Mint.

The reintroduction of two older designs on the American Eagle coins has proven controversial. The obverse of the silver dollar depicts the Walking Liberty half dollar obverse, enlarged for placement on the larger coin. A new Heraldic Eagle appears on the reverse.

The designs chosen for the gold bullion coins were even more controversial. Saint-Gaudens' obverse Liberty for the double eagle was chosen, but not until Treasury Secretary James A. Baker III ordered Liberty on a diet. The Mint engraver assigned to the project was ordered to reduce Liberty's apparent weight, by giving her slimmer arms and legs. Members of the Commission of Fine Arts decried the changes to what is considered a classic design. Members were also critical of the reverse, a Family of Eagles design by Dallas sculptor Miley Busiek. The legislation authorizing the gold coins mandated the Busiek design. Busiek had been an untiring champion of her work, which shows two adult eagles and two younger birds. She lobbied in Congress and the Treasury Department for months in a politically successful attempt to have her design placed on the bullion coins. She says the design reflects the values of the American family.

Currently, hobbyists are calling for new designs on circulating coins, which the Treasury Secretary may change without congressional approval after they have been in use 25 years. The 25-year limitation was placed on the coinage system in the Act of Sept. 26, 1890. Until then, there were no limitations concerning the life of a coin design. This act is now a part of Title 31 of the U.S. Code, but general Treasury opposition to redesign seems immovable.

One-time Commission of Fine Arts member Diane Wolfe fought unsuccessfully for redesign, pointing out that the Lincoln cent has been in use since 1909 (the reverse, since 1959). The Jefferson 5-cent coin has been around since 1938, and the Roosevelt dime, since 1946. The Kennedy half dollar was introduced in 1964. Mint officials, however, have publicly stated that to change coinage designs would cause hoarding of the old designs, thus generating a coinage shortage.

Specifications

The physical specifications of U.S. coins — metallic content, weights, diameters — have been ever changing. Changes were in response to increases and decreases in the prices of the metals contained in them; public unpopularity of large-diameter coins; and other factors.

Even before the first copper coins were struck in 1793, their weights were reduced under the Act of May 8, 1792. The modified weights are 6.74 grams for the half cent, and 13.48 grams for the cent (weights are given in grams for modern convenience; the early coinage laws specified the weights in grains). Weights for both copper coins were reduced in 1795, to 5.44 grams for the half cent, and to 10.89 grams for the cent.

The 1794-95 silver coinage was struck in a composition of 90 percent silver and 10 percent copper. When additional silver denominations were added in 1796, the composition for all five coins was changed to 892.427 silver and 107.572 copper, until additional change came in 1836-37.

Composition of the first gold coins is 916.667 gold and 83.333 copper and silver.

The only changes made to U.S. coins between the first decade of the 19th century and 1834 were to the designs. Then, on June 28, 1834, the weight of gold coins was reduced and the alloy changed for two years to 899.225 percent gold and 100.775 copper and silver. In 1836, the gold alloy was changed again, to 90 percent gold and 10 percent copper and silver, an alloy unchanged until 1873. Changes were made to silver coins in 1836 as well, when the silver content was changed to 90 percent silver and 10 percent copper, an alloy not abandoned until the mid-1960s.

The rising price of silver resulted in a reduction in weights for the silver coins during 1853 (except for the silver dollar). Arrows were added to both sides of the dates on the reduced weight half dimes, dimes, quarter dollars and half dollars, a design feature used for 1853-55. The arrows were removed in 1856 although the weights of the silver coins remained the same.

Major changes to the country's copper coinage were made in 1857. The half cent was eliminated and the large copper cent was replaced during the year with a smaller cent composed of 88 percent copper and 12 percent nickel (Act of Feb. 21, 1857). Diameter of the old cent is approximately 29 millimeters; the new cent has a diameter of 19mm.

The weights of the fractional Seated Liberty silver coinage increased slightly in 1873 to round them off to even fractions of grams, and once again arrows were placed at either side of the date for two years to signify the increased weight. At the same time, silver was virtually dropped from the gold-coin alloy; the coins were now composed of 90 percent gold and 10 percent copper with just a trace of silver.

The next major compositional changes in U.S. coins were made during World War II. At the beginning of the United States' entry into World War II, several metals used in coinage became in critical supply. The first to change was the 5-cent coin, which had nickel removed in mid-1942 after some copper-nickel specimens were struck. The new composition was 56 percent copper, 35 percent silver and 9 percent manganese. The old alloy was resumed in 1946.

Also during the war, the composition of the cent changed. First, tin was removed late in 1942. Then, in 1943, a zinc-plated steel cent was introduced to conserve copper. The brass alloy of 95 percent copper and 5 percent zinc was resumed in 1944 through 1946. The 95 percent copper, 5 percent tin and zinc composition resumed in 1947 and continued until late 1962. Once again, tin was removed from the bronze alloy, turning the alloy into the same brass composition used in 1944-46.

The 175-year-old history of United States coinage was changed with the stroke of a pen on July 23, 1965. On that day President Lyndon Johnson signed into law the Coinage Act of 1965, the most sweeping changes to the U.S. coinage system since the Mint Act of 1873. The 1965 act eliminated silver in dimes and quarter dollars and reduced the silver content of the half dollars to 40 percent.

Special congressional hearings relative to the nationwide coin shortage were first held in 1964. Coin shortages had continually worsened in the decade prior to 1965 as a result of the population growth, expanding vending machine businesses, popularity of Kennedy half dollars and the worldwide silver shortage.

In the face of the worldwide shortage of silver, it was essential that dependence on silver for the production of coins be reduced. Otherwise the country would be faced with a chronic coin shortage. As a result of studies conducted by both the Treasury and the Battelle Memorial Institute, a clad metal composed of three layers of metal bonded together was selected for the new coinage.

The dimes and quarter dollars were to be composed of two layers of 75 percent copper and 25 percent nickel bonded to a core of pure copper. The half dollars were to be composed of two layers of 80 percent silver and 20 percent copper bonded to a core of approximately 21 percent silver and 79 percent copper, such that the entire coin is composed of 40 percent silver.

The combination of copper-nickel and copper gave the new coins the required electrical conductivity, a necessary property for vending machines. The copper-nickel surfaces also continued the traditional silvery color of the coins. In addition, a clad metal would be much harder to counterfeit.

The legal weights of the coins were affected by the change in alloy. The new clad dime weight is 2.27 grams, the quarter dollar weighs 5.67 grams and the silver clad half dollar weighed 11.5 grams. With the elimination of silver from half dollars in 1971 and the introduction of a copper-nickel clad version, the weight was changed to 11.34 grams. The cladding of all coins constitutes approximately 30 percent of the coin by weight.

At first all of the strip was produced at the Olin Brass Division of Olin Mathison Chemical Corp. in East Alton, Ill. From there it was shipped to the U.S. Mints at Philadelphia and Denver and to the San Francisco Assay Office. As time had passed and the Mints built new facilities, more and more of the cladding was produced at the Mints. However, the Mint now buys all strip from outside manufacturers. Mint officials claim it is more efficient and less expensive to do so. In addition, the Mint buys some of its planchets from private contractors, including all of the copper-plated zinc cent planchets and all of the precious metals planchets for special programs like commemorative coins and the American Eagle bullion coins.

In an effort to maximize production of coinage and discourage hoarding, 1964-dated silver coins were struck as late as April 1966. The Coinage Act of 1965 also made it mandatory that clad coins be dated not earlier than 1965. The first clad dimes were struck in late December 1965 and were released March 8, 1966. The first clad quarter dollars were struck Aug. 23, 1965, and released Nov. 1, 1965. The first clad half dollars were released March 8, 1966, but were struck starting Dec. 30, 1965. The 1965 date was retained until July 31, 1966, when the date was changed to 1966. Normal dating was resumed on Jan. 1, 1967.

The last great compositional change to U.S. circulating coinage came in mid-1982, when the brass cent was replaced with a cent of nearly pure zinc, "barrel plated" with a thin layer of pure copper to retain its copper appearance. Rising copper prices were the cause. The switchover to the copper-plated zinc cent was made with few non-numismatists noting the difference.

When the American Eagle bullion coins were introduced in 1986, some numismatists were critical of the .9167 gold content, a composition they deemed "non-traditional"; there was some preference for a .900 gold content. However, the chosen composition is virtually identical to the alloy first used for U.S. gold coins, from 1795 to 1834. A new silver composition was introduced with the production of the .999 fine silver American Eagle dollar. Mint officials have been toying with the idea of releasing gold American Eagles in .9999 fine to directly compete with the Canadian Maple Leaf. The platinum bullion coins are .9995 fine, a metallurgically pure state, but so hard that up to nine impressions were needed to strike up the initial Proofs.

Pioneer gold coins

These issues are an interesting combination of private enterprise and pioneer necessity. Most were produced privately and legally, since the Constitution prohibited the states but not individuals from striking gold coins. However, "pioneer" is a better adjective to describe the gold coins than "private" and "territorial." Some of the coins in California were struck by the official U.S. Assayer, Augustus Humbert, and thus are of Federal issue and are not truely private; some of the gold coins were struck in states, not U.S. territories, thus "territorial" is incorrect for many of the issues. "Pioneer" describes the spirit in which the coins were struck: as necessity issues, brought about by the inability of the Federal government to provide sufficient quantities of coinage in areas of the country newly opened to settlement.

The pioneer gold coins can best be classified by the region in which they were made, as the years in which they were struck often overlap. These regions are the southern Appalachians, the western Rockies (including Utah, which was much larger then) and Colorado. The scarcity of these coins is primarily due to their often having an intrinsic value less than the face value. The coins were often unaccepted and eventually melted.

The first significant gold mines in the United States were in the mountainous backwoods of North Carolina and Georgia. Transporting the gold overland to the Philadelphia Mint was slow and dangerous, whereas shipping it around Cape Hatteras was fast but expensive and not without risk. As the miners wished to have the convenience of coined gold without the expense of shipping the raw gold to the Philadelphia Mint, two private mints were established in 1830 and 1831.

The first mint was opened by Templeton Reid at Gainesville, Ga. Probably because he had no competition he charged a high fee for processing the bullion into coins. Reid handled a large quantity of gold during his first and only year, but after adverse newspaper publicity attacked his accuracy and reliability, most of his coins were eventually melted down as were regular U.S. gold coins, due to the prevailing price ratio of gold to silver. He was forced out of business amid charges that he had misrepresented the purity and value of his coins.

The following year a second mint was opened by the Bechtler family, at Rutherfordton in southwestern North Carolina. For years the company produced coins equal in value to regular U.S. gold, although little of it circulated as the bullion value of the gold was greater than the face value of the coins.

This situation improved after 1834 (ultimately the coinage was accepted), and the new weight coins were temporarily marked with the date Aug. 1, 1834. The founder of the firm Christopher Bechtler Sr. died in 1842, and his son August and nephew Christopher the younger carried on until 1852, but by then the standard of quality had declined and they could no longer compete with the two federal branch Mints in Georgia and North Carolina.

While it was difficult to go from northern Georgia to Philadelphia in 1849, it was virtually impossible to get there from California. The quickest route from San Francisco to Philadelphia or New Orleans was by ship to Mexico or Central America and then overland to a second ship for the voyage north. Although the situation clearly called for a branch Mint in California, one was not officially opened until 1854. In the meantime more than a dozen companies were engaged at various times in the production of gold coins.

A relic of this shipping route is the *S.S. Central America*, discovered off the South Carolina coast in 1989. Early in the salvage of the gold treasure carried by the steamship, several discovery pieces of pioneer gold were discovered. As the full cargo is recovered and cataloged, many chapters of this colorful history of American numismatics will have to be rewritten.

The most popular issues were the $5 and $10 denominations, as these were needed for use in daily commerce. Later, $20 coins and $50 slugs were made for use in large business dealings, this being an era when the value of a check was dependent not only upon the solvency of the issuer but of the bank as well.

In addition to the questionable coins from the do-it-yourself mints, there were also in circulation legal tender coins struck by either the U.S. Assayer or the U.S. Assay Office. The first of these were octagonal $50 coins (officially called ingots) struck by the firm of Moffat & Co. but bearing both the legend UNITED STATES OF AMERICA and the name and title of AUGUSTUS HUMBERT, UNITED STATES ASSAYER OF GOLD, CALIFORNIA, 1851 or 1852. Eagles and double eagles were produced in 1852 before the Moffat & Co. firm dissolved.

The government contract was taken over by a new private firm which was called the United States Assay Office of Gold, managed by Curtis, Perry and Ward. This semi-official Mint produced eagles, double eagles and $50 "ingots" until December 1853, at which time its facilities were closed for reorganization as the official San Francisco Mint. Because the new official Mint could not at first produce coins as fast as the old semi-official one, several private companies opened to compete with the new federal Mint through 1854 and 1855.

In addition to the shortage of large denomination coins there was always a shortage of small change for use in retail stores. Several small, anonymous companies therefore produced gold dollars, half dollars, and even quarter dollars using a number of different designs, primarily Liberty or Indian head types on either round or octagonal planchets. These fractional coins were struck from 1852 to 1882; federal law in 1864 finally forbid private coinage of any sort. It has been suggested that the later strikes were never intended for circulation but were merely souvenirs of California.

A number of eagles and half eagles were struck by the Oregon Trading Company, composed of several leading men of this pioneer community in 1849, despite the objections of the new territorial governor. The issue was short-lived and the coins are excessively rare today.

The Church of Jesus Christ of Latter-Day Saints, the Mormons, issued $2.50, $5, $10 and $20 pieces in 1849, as well as half eagles in 1850 and 1860. This last issue was made of Colorado gold from the Pikes Peak area. Most of the early issues of Mormon gold did not receive widespread acceptance, as they were underweight by as much as 15 percent.

The last period of "legal" pioneer gold coins (i.e., issued before 1864), was the Pikes Peak gold rush of 1860-61. Only three major firms produced coins in these two years, although several unverified patterns are known. It is interesting to note that in 1862 the largest of these companies, Clark, Gruber and Co., sold its equipment to the federal government, which intended to open a branch Mint in Denver at this time. The specie hoarding of the Civil War presumably doomed this project, and a Denver Mint did not open until 1906.

Other pioneer gold issues are known for Alaska and the northwestern states, but these were primarily made as souvenirs and did not circulate as coinage.

Just like regular coinage, pioneer gold coins are subject to Gresham's Law. Those which are of full weight and value or better will be hoarded and probably melted, while those that are undervalued are spent as soon as possible so as to avoid getting stuck with the coin.

Current coins

Lincoln cent

When the Lincoln cent made its appearance in 1909, it marked a radical departure from accepted styling, introducing as it did for the first time a portrait coin in the regular series. A strong feeling had prevailed against the use of portraits on the coins of the country but public sentiment stemming from the 100th anniversary celebration of Abraham Lincoln's birthday proved stronger than the long-standing prejudice.

The only person invited to participate in the formulation of the new design was Victor David Brenner. President Theodore Roosevelt was so impressed with the talents of this outstanding sculptor that Brenner was singled out by the president for the commission.

The likeness of Lincoln on the obverse is an adaption of a plaque Brenner executed which had come to the attention of President Roosevelt. In addition to prescribed elements — LIBERTY and the date — the motto IN GOD WE TRUST appeared for the first time on a U.S. cent. Of interest is that the Congress passed the Act of March 3, 1865, authorizing the use of this expression on U.S. coins during Lincoln's tenure of office.

A study of three models for the reverse resulted in the approval of a very simple design bearing two ears of wheat in memorial style. Between these, in the center of the coin, are the denomination and UNITED STATES OF AMERICA, while curving around the upper border is the national motto, E PLURIBUS UNUM.

Even though no legislation was required for a new design, approval of the Treasury Secretary was necessary. Franklin MacVeagh gave his approval July 14, 1909, and not quite three weeks later, on Aug. 2, the new cent was released to the public.

The original model bore the full name BRENNER. Prior to issuance, however, the initials VDB were substituted on the lower reverse because Mint officials felt the name was too prominent. After the coin was released, many protested that even the initials were conspicuous and detracted from the design. Because the coin was in great demand, and because making a change in size would have required halting production, the decision was made to eliminate the initials entirely, a simple engraving process. They were restored in 1918, and are to be found in minute form on Lincoln's shoulder.

More cents are produced than any other denomination, which makes the Lincoln cent a familiar item. In its life span this little coin has weathered two world wars, one of which was to change it materially. Metals play a vital part in any war effort. At the time of World War II the cent was composed of 95 percent copper and 5 percent tin and zinc. These metals were denied the Mint for the duration of the emergency, making it necessary to seek a substitute. After much deliberation, even including consideration of plastics, zinc-plated steel was chosen as the best in a limited range of suitable materials.

Production of this wartime cent was provided for in the act approved Dec. 18, 1942, which also set as the expiration date of the authority Dec. 31, 1946. Low-grade carbon steel formed the base, to which a zinc plating .005 inch thick was deposited on each side electrolytically as a rust preventative. The same size was maintained but the weight was reduced from the standard 48 grains to 42 grains, due to the use of a lighter alloy. Operations commenced Feb. 27, 1943, and by Dec. 31 of that year the three Mints then functioning had struck an almost record-breaking number of cents, with the total reaching 1,093,838,670 pieces. The copper released was enough to meet the combined needs of two cruisers, two destroyers, 1,243 B-17 Flying Fortresses, 120 field guns and 120 howitzers; or enough for 1.25 million shells for the U.S. big field guns.

On Jan. 1, 1944, the Mints were able to adopt a modified alloy, the supply being derived from expended shell casings which when melted furnished a composition similar to the original but with only a faint trace of tin; the 6 grains dropped from the total weight were restored. The original alloy was resumed in 1947.

On Feb. 12, 1959, a revised reverse was introduced as a part of the 150th anniversary celebration of the Great Emancipator's birth. No formal competition was held. Frank Gasparro, then Assistant Sculptor-Engraver at the Mint in Philadelphia, prepared the winning entry, selected from a group of 23 models the engraving staff at the Mint had been asked to present for consideration. Again, only the Treasury Secretary's approval was necessary to make the change because the design had been in force for more than the required 25 years.

The imposing marble Lincoln Memorial in Washington, D.C., provides the central motif; the legends E PLURIBUS UNUM and UNITED STATES OF AMERICA form the rest of the design, together with the denomination. Gasparro's initials, FG, appear on the right near the shrubbery.

The composition of the smallest U.S. denomination was changed once more in 1962. Mint officials felt that deletion of the tin content would have no adverse effect upon the wearing qualities of the coin, whereas, the manufacturing advantages to be gained with the alloy stabilized at 95 percent copper and 5 percent zinc would be of much benefit. Congressional authority for this modification is contained in the Act of Sept. 5, 1962.

As the price of copper rose along with the demand for cents, a resolution was introduced Dec. 7, 1973, giving the Treasury Secretary power to change the 1-cent alloy. It appeared the new alloy would be aluminum.

The bill met opposition from the vending machine industry and the medical profession, and when the price of copper took a downhill turn, Mint Director Mary Brooks announced aluminum cents would not be necessary. There was no change in the 1-cent alloy. However, 1,579,324 1974-dated aluminum cents were struck in 1973 as experimental pieces. Most were melted, although a few specimens given to congressional members and staff disappeared. One coin is housed in the National Numismatic Collection of the Smithsonian Institution, where it was given by a congressional staff member.

In a report made public in September 1976, the Research Triangle Institute recommended that cent production be terminated by 1980, due to increasing costs of manufacturing the cent and the poor circulation of the coin. However, in making the study public the Mint said that it did not endorse the recommendations of the report, nor did it plan to adopt the recommendations at that time.

In 1982, feeling the pressure of rising copper prices again, Mint officials decided to switch to a new alloy composed of a core of 99.2 zinc and 0.8 percent copper plated by pure copper (total composition, 97.5 percent zinc, 2.5 percent copper). Both the old alloy and new alloy were produced during the year at all minting facilities striking cents. Copper and brass producers sued the federal government, claiming the Treasury Secretary did not have the authority to alter the composition despite the earlier legislation. A federal judge ruled against the producers, however, and the cent remains composed of copper-plated zinc.

Jefferson 5 cents

The Thomas Jefferson 5-cent coin was released to the public Nov. 15, 1938, after a national contest for the obverse and reverse designs.

The coin was designed by Felix Schlag of Chicago, Ill. Born in Frankfurt, Germany, in September 1891, Schlag had won numerous prizes in nationwide competitions. He began his art studies in the Munich Academy in Germany and became an American citizen in 1929. The competition rules stipulated that the obverse of the coin would carry a profile of Thomas Jefferson. The reverse was to bear a view of Monticello, the president's historic home near Charlottesville, Va. Some 400 entries were received.

President Franklin D. Roosevelt was personally interested in the design of the Jefferson 5-cent coin. It was a result of his suggestion that the chosen sculptor altered his original design so as to emphasize certain architectural features, particularly the two wings of the building at Monticello.

Although the law did not then require that the phrase IN GOD WE TRUST appear on the coin, it was placed there at the request of the Director of the Mint. This was the first time this motto had reappeared on the United States 5-cent coin since 1883.

In the years following the release of the coin, there was considerable interest nationally, and particularly on the part of the Michigan congressional delegation, to place on the Jefferson coin the initials of the sculptor, Felix Schlag. (Schlag died in Owosso, Mich., March 9, 1974. He was 82.)

The failure of the sculptor to "sign" his work is said to have been due to the fact that he didn't know he could. All other current issues of United States coins bear the initials of their sculptors. Placing of the initials on the coin was an administrative decision of the Secretary of the Treasury, at the request of Assistant Secretary Wallace and Mint Director Eva Adams. The initials appear on the 5-cent pieces dated 1966 and subsequent issues.

Roosevelt dime

Almost immediately after President Franklin D. Roosevelt's death in the spring of 1945, letters came to the Treasury Department from all over the country in advocacy of his portrait being placed on a coin of the United States. The dime was most frequently suggested by reason of his having been identified with that coin through the March of Dimes drives for the Infantile Paralysis Fund.

The coinage laws prohibit the changing of a coin design more often than once every 25 years. The same laws empower the Director of the Mint with the approval of the Secretary of the Treasury, to cause new designs to be prepared and adopted at any time after the expiration of said 25-year period. The Winged Liberty Head design having been in use for more than the required time, the Treasury officials acceded to public sentiment and placed the likeness of President Roosevelt on the 10-cent piece. The new Roosevelt dime was released Jan. 30, 1946, the late president's birthday.

The obverse bears a portrait of Roosevelt, facing left and LIBERTY to his left. In the left field is IN GOD WE TRUST and in the lower right field the date. On the reverse, in the center, is a torch with an olive branch on the left and an oak branch on the right. At the border is UNITED STATES OF AMERICA with ONE DIME below and across the lower field is E PLURIBUS UNUM.

The designer was John R. Sinnock, at that time the Mint's Chief Engraver. Known as one of the country's great artists in this highly specialized field, Sinnock produced outstanding medals of the presidential series, various commemorative medals and coins, and designs used on several of the medals for the nation's war heroes, including the Purple Heart.

Some researchers believe that Sinnock's profile was inspired by the bas relief plaque of Roosevelt sculpted by Dr. Selma Burke, an African-American woman artist and educator. Dr. Burke apparently was commissioned to design a plaque of Roosevelt from life in 1943. The president died before the third sitting, and Dr. Burke executed the sculpture from two sittings. Sinnock did not credit Burke, however, and the numerous photographs of Roosevelt make a sculpture from life somewhat unnecessary for a coin design.

Washington quarter

The Washington quarter dollar replaced the Standing Liberty quarter dollar in 1932. The Standing Liberty had not been issued for the 25 years required by law, thereby making an act of Congress necessary to issue the Washington quarter. Congress passed the authorization act March 4, 1931, to commemorate the 200th birthday of the first president.

John Flanagan, a noted New York sculptor, designed the coin. His work was chosen from approximately 100 models that were submitted. The Treasury Department worked in close cooperation with the Commission of Fine Arts in selecting the design.

The commission did not agree with the Treasury Department on the final selection, advocating instead the design by Laura Gardin Fraser, which had twice been chosen as the finest entry. Secretary of the Treasury Mellon and his successor Ogden Mills insisted on giving the Flanagan models the official nod. The first coins were issued for general circulation Aug. 1, 1932. The designer's initials, J.F., appear on the obverse.

The obverse side shows the head of Washington with LIBERTY around the top of the coin. The date is directly under the head and the motto IN GOD WE TRUST is to the lower left of the head.

The reverse side shows an eagle with wings spread standing on a bundle of arrows. Beneath the eagle are two sprays of olive leaves. Over the top are the words UNITED STATES OF AMERICA and centered directly under these words and above the head of the eagle are the words E PLURIBUS UNUM. The inscription QUARTER DOLLAR is at the bottom under the olive spray.

New plaster models were made for both sides of the quarter in 1977, altering the relief slightly so as to increase die life.

Kennedy half dollar

John Fitzgerald Kennedy was inaugurated president of the United States Jan. 20, 1961, and served not quite three full years of his term of office. His assassination Nov. 22, 1963, resulted in such an outpouring of public sentiment that President Lyndon Johnson, on Dec. 10, 1963, sent to Congress a request for legislation to authorize the Treasury Department to mint new 50-cent pieces bearing the likeness of his predecessor.

Congress gave its overwhelming approval to the president's recommendation and on Dec. 30, 1963, Public Law No. 88-256 was enacted directing the Mint to proceed with the production of the new design. The first of the John F. Kennedy half dollars for general circulation purposes were struck at the Mints in Philadelphia and Denver on Feb. 11, 1964. The half dollar was selected because this would add another presidential portrait to a coin of regular issue.

In the center of the obverse, or face of the coin, is a strong but simple bust of the late president. Above, and around the border is LIBERTY. Just below the bust is IN GOD WE TRUST, which appears on all United States coins of current issue. The date is at the bottom around the border.

The presidential coat of arms forms the motif for the reverse. It is the central part of the presidential seal, the only difference being that the words SEAL OF THE PRESIDENT OF THE UNITED STATES have been removed and in their place are inscriptions required by law to appear on all coins: the words UNITED STATES OF AMERICA, above, around the border, and the denomination, HALF DOL-LAR, around the bottom border. Other requirements already incorporated in the coat of arms are the eagle, and E PLURIBUS UNUM, which appears on the ribbon above the eagle's head.

The Kennedy coin had its beginnings when official sculptors were engaged in preparing a new medal for the historic series of presidential pieces manufactured in bronze for sale to the public. Gilroy Roberts, nationally known Chief Sculptor-Engraver of the Mint, and a member of the Philadelphia staff for many years, worked on the likeness of the president, studying first many photographs to capture the character and personality of his subject. He then selected a single portrait and commenced placing his concept in a preliminary model. During the final stages, Roberts called at the White House and studied the president at work, at which time he completed the model.

After the president's death, when the decision was reached to honor him on a United States coin, the Roberts' portrait was adapted from the medal, lowered in relief and simplified for use on a smaller scale necessary for a coin. His initials G.R. appear on the truncated bust.

Frank Gasparro, himself a veteran member of the Philadelphia staff, executed the reverse of the presidential medal. The coat of arms of the president of the United States, an integral part of this design, was chosen as the companion side for the half dollar. Gasparro's initials F.G. appear at the lower right edge of the shield.

The presidential seal originated during the administration of President Rutherford B. Hayes, apparently as a rendering of the Great Seal of the United States. There was no known basis in law for the coat of arms and the seal which had been used by presidents since 1880 and which was reproduced on the presidential flag. President Truman, when he signed the Executive Order of Oct. 25, 1945, containing the official description, established for the first time a legal definition of the president's coat of arms and his seal. According to heraldic custom, the eagle on a coat of arms, unless otherwise specified in the heraldic description, is always made to face to its own right. There is no explanation for the eagle facing to its own left in the case of the president's coat of arms. To conform to heraldic custom, and since there was no authority other than usage for the former coat of arms, President Franklin Roosevelt had asked that it be redesigned. The designs reached Washington after the president's death.

In the new coat of arms, seal and flag, the eagle not only faces to its right — the direction of honor — but also toward the olive branches for peace which it holds in its right talon. Formerly, the eagle faced toward the arrows in its left talon — symbolic of war.

Initial distribution of this newly designed coin took place on March 24, 1964, in the usual manner, when 26 million were released by the Mints directly to the Federal Reserve Banks and Branches for simultaneous distribution through the commercial banking system.

The Research Triangle Institute report of 1976 recommended the elimination of the half dollar from the U.S. coinage system.

Mint officials reported in 1986 that no half dollars would be struck for circulation in 1987; the coin was only to be struck for use in Proof, Uncirculated and Souvenir Mint sets.

Eisenhower dollar

On Dec. 31, 1970, President Richard M. Nixon signed into law the Bank Holding Company Act. Appended to the legislation were important amendments relating to coinage. Pertinent to this narrative is one which concerns the reissuance of the dollar denomination. Section 203 of the Act reads:

"The dollars initially minted under authority of Section 101 of the Coinage Act of 1965 shall bear the likeness of the late President of the United States Dwight David Eisenhower, and on the other side thereof a design which is emblematic of the symbolic eagle of the Apollo 11 landing on the moon."

The act further provided for the removal of all silver from the dollar denomination and its coinage in the copper-nickel clad composition. The language was qualified, however, to permit the Secretary of the Treasury to mint and issue not more than 150 million dollar pieces composed of 40 percent silver. Of these, 130 million were to be manufactured and sold in Uncirculated condition, and 20 million processed as Proof coins, with the widest possible distribution among citizens interested in acquiring a few each. Production of this denomination for general circulation was in the copper-nickel clad metal.

The coin was designed by the Mint's Chief Sculptor-Engraver, Frank Gasparro, whose initials appear on both sides of the coin. Reverse of the coin shows the bald eagle, symbolic of the Apollo 11 spacecraft christened Eagle landing on the cratered surface of the moon, clutching an olive branch in both claws. The Earth appears above the eagle's head. The 13 stars circling the eagle represent the first states of the Union.

Gasparro began working on the obverse drawing for the coin in spring 1969. He settled on using a profile of the former president and general of the army because of an image Gasparro saw of the supreme commander of the allied armies in Europe as Eisenhower rode through New York City June 20, 1945.

Gasparro made a profile drawing immediately suitable to cut directly in steel and capture the facial features that had impressed him. When he was asked to design the Eisenhower dollar coin, he studied his first drawing of Eisenhower and some 30 other pictures before sketching his design for the obverse of the coin. He began working on the reverse of the coin in October 1969. On Nov. 1, 1971, the first Eisenhower dollars were released for circulation.

The Research Triangle Institute report of 1976 recommended a reduction in the size of the dollar coin. Several designs for a smaller coin were tested in 1976, but none was accepted at that time.

Bicentennial dollar varieties

Almost as soon as the first 1776-1976 Bicentennial Eisenhower dollars were struck, Mint officials realized that the design did not lend itself well to high-speed mass production. Minor changes were made on the obverse and major changes on the reverse to facilitate that mode of production. The changes created two varieties of dollars.

Variety 1 dollars have thick, block-style lettering with nearly closed E's and straight tails on the R's. Variety 2 dollars have thinner, more contoured lettering with more open E's and curved tails on the R's.

Two of the reverse details which, if memorized, will enable anyone to tell the variety without having both varieties for comparison are the last S in STATES and the relationship of the first U in UNUM to the first U in PLURIBUS.

On Variety 1 the tail of the last S in STATES is level with the center bar of the E. On Variety 2 the tail of the S barely reaches the top of the bottom bar of the E. On Variety 1 the first U of UNUM is almost directly below the first U of PLURIBUS while on Variety 2 it is between the L and U.

The Denver Mint Variety 1 dollars outnumber the Philadelphia coins by a ratio of approximately six to one.

Anthony dollar

President Jimmy Carter signed the Susan B. Anthony Dollar Act into law Oct. 10, 1978, but not until after a long fight over the design. A smaller dollar coin, sized between the quarter dollar and the half dollar, was recommended by the Research Triangle Institute report in 1976. The same report recommended that the introduction of a smaller dollar coin coincide with the elimination of the half dollar.

The first design submitted for the dollar was an adaption by Frank Gasparro of the Flowing Hair large cent design, with a Flying Eagle design of Gasparro's creation on the reverse. Collectors almost universally panned the design at first, although supporters welcomed a return to more traditional, non-partisan coinage designs. Meanwhile, in Congress in 1978, a movement toward placing feminist Susan B. Anthony's portrait on the coin was growing as the legislation for a smaller dollar advanced through both houses.

Many hobbyists lobbied against the Anthony proposal in favor of a more traditional, allegorical portrait. Ironically, Gasparro's Flowing Hair Liberty design became the darling of the hobby as support for the Anthony design grew in Congress.

The Senate passed the Anthony dollar bill Aug. 22, 1978, without dissent; the House passed the bill Sept. 26 with a vote of 368 to 38. The first coins were struck at the Philadelphia Mint Dec. 13, 1978, with 1979 dates. The Mint mark "P" was used for the first time since the Wartime 5-cent coins of World War II. Denver strikes were produced Jan. 9, 1979, and the San Francisco Assay Office began producing business strikes Feb. 2, 1979.

Despite Treasury hopes to save $30 million a year by reducing demand for the $1 Federal Reserve note, the Anthony dollar never caught on with the public, which claimed the coin was too similar in size to the quarter dollar. The vending industry, which had supported the change in size but fought against a more distinctive multi-sided coin, never fully converted vending machines to accept the new, smaller dollar. The coins were produced for circulation and collectors' sets in 1979 and 1980, and only for collectors in 1981. None have been produced since 1981 although the law authorizing the Anthony dollar is still valid.

In the fall of 1985 the Mint began offering Anthony dollar sets through its catalog of products. The response surprised many, as the Anthony dollars were among the most popular items in the catalog.

History of Mint marks

A Mint mark on U.S. coins is a small letter added to the design of the coin to show which Mint manufactured it. Mint marks on United States coins began with the act of March 3, 1835, establishing the first branch Mints: in New Orleans, La., Charlotte, N.C., and Dahlonega, Ga. The first Mint marks appeared in 1838.

When other branch Mints were established, coins struck there bore an appropriate Mint mark. The letters used to signify the various Mints are as follows:

"C" for Charlotte, N.C., (gold coins only), 1838-1861
"CC" for Carson City, Nev., 1870-1893
"D" for Dahlonega, Ga. (gold coins only), 1838-1861
"D" for Denver, Colo., 1906-present
"O" for New Orleans, La., 1838-1861; 1879-1909
"P" for Philadelphia, Pa., 1942-45; 1979-present
"S" for San Francisco, Calif., 1854-1955; 1968-present
"W" for West Point Mint 1984-present

With one four-year exception, U.S. coins struck at the Philadelphia Mint bore no Mint marks until 1979. The initial use of the "P" appears on the Jefferson, Wartime 5-cent pieces, struck from 1942 to 1945 in a silver alloy. The "P" Mint mark on these issues was designed to distinguish the silver alloy issues from regular copper-nickel 5-cent pieces; during the war, silver was less important strategically than copper or nickel.

With the passage of the Coinage Act of 1965, which gave the United States copper-nickel clad coinage, Mint marks were removed from coins dated 1965 and from subsequent issues until 1968. The move was designed to help alleviate a coin shortage by removing the distinction between coins struck at branch Mints and those struck in Philadelphia so collectors could not determine which were the more limited strikes.

Since the San Francisco Assay Office opened in 1965 for coinage purposes, after 10 years of inactivity, no coins struck there after 1965 bear Mint marks until 1968, when they were returned to all coinage.

With the announcement Jan. 4, 1968, that Mint marks would return to coinage, Mint Director Eva Adams made several changes in Mint mark application. First, to achieve uniformity, she directed that all Mint marks be placed on the obverse of the coins. The Mint mark, she announced, on the cent, 5-cent piece, dime and quarter dollar would be to the right of the portraits, while on the half dollar it would appear in the center under the portrait of Kennedy.

Second, she announced Proof coin sets would be manufactured at the San Francisco Assay Office and would bear an "S" Mint mark. Previously, all Proof sets were produced at Philadelphia and so had no Mint mark, except for some 1942 5-cent pieces. Proof sets were discontinued altogether after 1964 because of the coin shortage and revived in 1968.

Mint marks were again omitted from certain U.S. coins when cents were struck at the West Point Bullion Depository in 1974 and later, and when dimes were struck in San Francisco in 1975.

Major changes were made in Mint mark policy beginning in 1978. Mint officials in 1978 announced that the 1979 Susan B. Anthony dollar would bear the "P" Mint mark for Philadelphia business strikes. The list of coins to bear the "P" Mint mark grew in 1980, when all other denominations but the 1-cent piece received the new Mint mark.

A new Mint mark, a "W," the eighth, was added to the U.S. inventory in September 1983, when the West Point Bullion Depository (now the West Point Mint) began striking 1984-dated $10 gold eagles commemorating the Los Angeles Olympic Games. Although other coins were being struck at West Point, the Mint mark was not added to circulation coins, but has appeared on later commemorative issues.

Additional changes were announced in 1984 when it was reported that beginning in 1985, the Mint mark would be placed on the master die instead of the working dies for all Proof coinage. This was to forestall production of errors similar to the Proof 1983 No S Roosevelt dime and the 1971 No S 5 cents. Mint officials denied that business strike master dies would be Mint marked as well. But in 1989, Mint officials acknowledged that the procedure would be phased in for circulating coinage, ending a 150-year-old tradition of individually punching Mint marks into each working die.

In 1986, Mint officials decided to add the Mint marks on all commemorative and Proof coins at the plasticene model stage. Thus, on these special collectors' coins, the Mint mark appears on all stages of models, hubs and dies.

Location of Mint marks

Half cents — All coined at Philadelphia, no Mint mark.

Large cents — All coined at Philadelphia, no Mint mark.

Flying Eagle cents — All coined at Philadelphia, no Mint mark.

Indian cents — 1908 and 1909, under the wreath on reverse side.

Lincoln cents — Under the date.

Two cents, Three cents (copper-nickel) — All coined at Philadelphia, no Mint mark.

Three cents (silver) — All coined at Philadelphia, except 1851 New Orleans Mint — reverse side, at right.

Shield 5-cent pieces — All coined at Philadelphia, no Mint mark.

Liberty 5-cent pieces — All coined at Philadelphia except 1912-S and -D — reverse side to left of word CENTS.

Indian 5-cent pieces — Reverse side under words FIVE CENTS.

Jefferson 5-cent pieces until 1964 — Reverse side at right of the building.

Jefferson 5-cent pieces (1942-1945, silver) — above dome on the reverse side.

Jefferson 5-cent pieces from 1968 to present — on obverse under Jefferson's queue.

Half dimes — Reverse side either within or below the wreath.

Dimes — Old types, reverse side below or within wreath; Winged Liberty Head type (1916-1945) on the reverse to left of base of fasces; Roosevelt type to 1964, left of bottom of torch on reverse; Roosevelt type from 1968 to present, obverse above date.

Twenty cents — Reverse side under the eagle.

Quarter dollars — Old types, on reverse side under eagle; Standing Liberty type, on obverse to left of date; Washington type to 1964, on reverse under wreath; Washington type from 1968 to present, on obverse to right of Washington's queue.

Half dollars — 1838 and 1839 "O" Mint mark above date; other dates to 1915 on reverse under eagle; 1916 on obverse below motto, 1917 on obverse below motto and on reverse. After 1917 on lower left reverse. Franklin type, above bell beam; Kennedy type in 1964, near claw and laurel at left on reverse; Kennedy type from 1968 to present, on obverse under Kennedy portrait.

Dollars — Old types, on reverse under eagle; Peace type, on reverse at lower tip of the eagle's wing; Eisenhower, on obverse above the date. Anthony, on obverse to left of bust.

Trade dollars — On reverse under eagle.

Gold dollars — On reverse under wreath.

Quarter eagles — 1838 and 1839, over the date; other dates prior to 1907, on reverse under the eagle; Indian type (1908-1929), on reverse lower left.

Three dollar pieces — Reverse under the wreath.

Half eagles — Same as quarter eagles.

Eagles — Reverse under eagle; after 1907 at left of value, either above or below olive branch.

Double eagles — Old types on reverse under eagle; Saint-Gaudens (after 1907) above the date.

American Eagle — gold bullion coin, Proof version only, on obverse between second and third rays at right, below date. Silver bullion coin, Proof version only, on reverse to left of eagle's tail. Platinum bullion coin, Proof version only, left, between rays.

Coinage manufacturing processes

United States coins have their beginnings in the private sector, where a number of companies produce some coinage planchets and all coils of strip metal the Mint purchases. The Mint produced its own strip metal as late as fiscal year 1982 at the Philadelphia Mint, but the operations were closed officially in fiscal 1983.

Basically, the coinage metals are assayed, melted and formed into slabs which are then rolled to the proper thickness. For clad coinage, bonding operations are required to bond the two layers of copper-nickel to the core of pure copper. The strip is then coiled and shipped to the Mint for blanking.

Some of the purchased material arrives in planchet form, ready to be coined, including the copper-plated zinc cent planchets used since 1982.

The blanking presses are simply punch presses similar to those found in any machine shop. They have a bank of punches (or rams) which travel downward through the strip and into a steel bedplate which has holes corresponding to the punches. The presses punch out planchets each time the punches make their downward cycle. The planchets made at this stage are slightly larger than the finished coins. Because of the shearing action of the punches, the planchets have rough edges. Most of the rough edges (or burrs) are removed during succeeding operations.

The planchets (also called flans or blanks) are next passed over sorting screens, called riddlers, which are supposed to eliminate all of the defective planchets. Thin and incomplete planchets will fall through the screens. These rejected planchets are remelted.

During the finish rolling and blanking press operations the planchets have again been hardened and must now be softened, or annealed. The planchets are passed through a cylinder which has spiral grooves in its walls. As the cylinder turns, the planchets are forced from one end to the other by the spirals. As they move along the cylinder walls, the planchets are heated to controlled temperatures, approximately 1400 degrees, changing their crystal structure to a softer state. Planchets are "frozen" into that state by a water quench bath. This annealing process prolongs the life of the coining dies by ensuring well-struck coins with lower striking pressures.

Type I planchets

Despite a protective atmosphere, annealing causes some discoloration on the surfaces of the planchets which must be removed. The planchets are tumbled against each other and passed through a chemical bath. Then they are dried by forced hot air. The planchets are now completed Type I planchets and if they happen to bypass the coining presses you will see them as flat disks.

The upsetting mill consists of a rotating wheel with a groove on its edge. The grooved edge of the wheel fits into a curved section (or shoe) which has a corresponding groove. The distance between the wheel and the shoe gets progressively narrower so that, as the planchet is rolled along the groove, a raised rim is formed on both sides of the planchet. This raised rim serves several purposes. It sizes and shapes the planchet for better feed at the press and it work-hardens the edge to prevent escape of metal between the obverse die and the collar.

The planchets are now called Type II planchets and are ready to be struck into coins.

Die preparation

The dies used for striking coins start out as an approved sketch of the coin in the Engraving Department at the Philadelphia Mint. The sculptor-engraver makes a plasticene (modeling wax) model in bas-relief from the sketch. The model will be anywhere from three to 12 times as large as the finished coin. Next, a plaster-of-paris negative is cast from the model. The negative is touched up and details are added. Then a plaster-of-paris positive is made. The positive is used as the model to be approved by the Mint Director and the Secretary of the Treasury. If pictures are required for such approval, they are taken of this positive.

When final approval is received another negative is made and a hard epoxy positive model is prepared. The epoxy model replaces the copper galvano once used by the U.S. Mint.

Epoxy to hub

The completed epoxy is then mounted on a Janvier transfer engraving machine. This machine cuts the design in a soft tool steel blank to the exact size of the coin, following the exact details of the epoxy, producing a positive replica of the model. This positive is called a "hub." The hub is then heat treated to harden it and is used in a hydraulic press to prepare a master die. The original hub is carefully stored in a safe place to ensure against loss of the original reduction.

Working hubs are made from the master die in the hydraulic press, and similarly hardened in the same way.

Working dies are made from the working hub in the same way. Pressing an image into a piece of soft tool steel hardens the metal, so annealing is usually needed to fully form the image. Two to three cycles may be required to properly impress all details into the steel, although the Mint has been working to cut this down to one cycle, to eliminate multiple die image errors.

Coinage operations are performed in the coin press room. It is here that the little disks take on their final identity. They go into the presses as blanks and come out bearing the devices and inscriptions which make them coins of the realm.

Coining presses

Coining presses are general purpose machines, and are not designed for a specific denomination of coin. Dies and collars are interchangeable and striking pressures are adjustable for the various denominations and metals. The collar forms the wall of the coining chamber and one die forms the base. The dies impress the various designs and devices on the obverse and reverse for the coin while the collar forms the edge of the coin, square and smooth on cents and 5-cent pieces and reeded on the larger denominations. The collar, which is minutely larger in diameter than the dies, is mounted on springs which allows slight movement.

It is generally assumed that the reverse die is the lower (or anvil) die while the obverse die is the upper (or hammer) die; however, there are exceptions to this general rule. Both dies can be adjusted both horizontally and vertically. Horizontal adjustments center the design of the coin on the planchet. Vertical adjustments determine how well the dies are impressed into the planchet. [In recent years, the Mint has been installing high-speed, single-die Schuler coining presses. These presses differ from the other presses in the Mint in that the striking is horizontal, rather than vertical.]

Planchets are fed through a tube by gravity from a basin attached to the press. The tube will stack 20 or so planchets and from this stack the bottom planchet is fed into the press by the feed fingers or a rotating disc with holes to carry the planchets. The dial-feed system can increase the capacity of a press by 20 to 30 percent, according to Mint tests, and older presses are being fitted with the new delivery systems.

Feed fingers are two parallel pieces of metal joined in such a way that they can open and close. On one end of the two pieces is a covered recessed slot and in the center is a hole. Feed fingers shove a finished piece out of the way while depositing a fresh planchet; dial feeders are an "indexed" system, in that the planchet/coin is moved in relative position to others in the machine.

At frequent times, while a press is in operation, the press attendant will pick up a finished coin for inspection. He makes the inspection under a magnifier and it reveals any defects made in the die during operation.

After the coins have been struck they are ready for a final inspection. After passing the inspection, they are counted in automatic machines, weighed and bagged. The bags are sewn shut and are ready for shipment to the Federal Reserve Banks for distribution.

The first coining presses in the Mint were hand operated which severely limited their output. Later presses were powered by steam boilers and capable of 55 strokes per minute. Still later presses, speeded up to 140 strokes per minute, were converted to accept dual dies which doubled the output. And still later some were converted to quadro, four dies, increasing capacity up to 560 per minute. The high-speed Schuler presses can operate at about 600 strikes per minute, but only one coin at a time. Their greatest advantage is in the production of quarter dollars, which require too much pressure for the older presses to produce dual or quad strikes. Cents can be struck four at a time on older presses at about the same coins-per-minute rate as the Schuler.

Colonial & Early State Issues

In this section are listed coins struck under royal authority for circulation in American colonies now forming part of the United States, coinages struck under the authority of colonial legislatures or proprietors and private tokens of the era that were struck in or imported into the colonies. These compose the Colonial series as that term should be properly applied.

Under the heading of Associated and Quasi-Colonial Coins are issues used in the colonies although initially struck for use elsewhere, circulating medalets and tokens made before the War of Independence. It must be remembered that American collectors of the mid-19th century were aggressively seeking material that could be somehow declared "American" to make it collectible. Therefore, such categories as Wood's Hibernia coins and Saint Patrick "farthings" were eagerly embraced. Traditionally, these and other items of uncertain provenance have been collected as part of the Colonial series.

Before the new Federal government took control of coinage, "coppers" (not cents) were struck under the authority of the states of Connecticut, Vermont, Massachusetts, and New Jersey. A variety of speculative coins and tokens were also struck resembling state or national coins, as were private tokens bearing post-independence dates and designs. Once carelessly lumped under the heading Colonial, these post-Independence pieces are more accurately grouped as early state issues.

It should be remembered that from the beginning of settlement, Mercantile economics fostered an unfavorable balance of trade and depleted the supply of coins in Britain's American colonies. Nearly all gold and silver coins were drained from the colonies to pay for manufactured goods supplied by British merchants. Unlike the Spanish provinces to the south, the British dominions were forbidden to strike their own coins.

Coins were seldom seen by many American colonists, and daily transactions were more often conducted by barter, with commodities taking the place of coins. Tobacco filled this role in Virginia until overproduction and adulteration forced its elimination as legal tender in 1633. Virginia's continuing coin shortage led the colony to abolish money debts in 1641 and to fix legal values on goods of various kinds the following year.

Munitions were another common currency. In both Virginia and Maryland, powder and shot were a common medium for paying ship's duties. Massachusetts Bay passed the first act regulating small currency in 1634, decreeing circulation of musket balls "of a full boare" at a farthing each.

A long-enduring medium of exchange was wampum, (a word derived from the Algonquin *wampumpeage*, string of white beads) strings of small blue, white, black or purple shell beads made by the Indians from clam and conch shells. Colored beads were valued more highly than white, and the practice of dyeing white ones may represent the first currency alteration in American history.

In 1648, a law was passed by Massachusetts requiring beads to be strung in fixed denominations, the white in values of a penny, threepence, sixpence, one shilling, two and one half shilling and five shillings. In 1650 the beads were made a legal tender up to 40 shillings, but this regulation was revoked in 1661. Between 1652 and 1682 Massachusetts struck its own silver coinage, but barter soon returned, and by 1690 wheat, barley, Indian corn, peas, oats, pork and beef were all serving as currency.

Neighboring Connecticut drafted labor in lieu of taxes for projects "that do concern the whole" such as building bridges, improving harbors and clearing land. Wheat, corn and rye were favored commodities and the General Court at Hartford provided in 1642 "that no man within these liberties shall refuse merchantable Indian corn at the rate of 2s. per bushel. for any contracte made for the labor of men or cattell or commodityes sold after the publishing of this order."

Wool served as the principal commodity in Rhode Island, fish and lumber in New Hampshire. The Carolinas depended on tobacco, wheat, corn, beef, pork and tar. Toward the end of the 17th century, New Jersey saw circulation of wheat, corn, butter, pork, beef, and tobacco; Pennsylvania added flax and hemp.

A large majority of judgments in colonial New York lawsuits were rendered in tobacco and beaver skins. Imported Dutch bricks were sold in New York at $4.16 per thousand, payable in beaver skins. By 1675, taxes had become payable in beef and pork. In the same year, winter wheat was made a legal tender at five shillings and summer wheat at four shillings sixpence per bushel.

As late as the 18th century, American merchants reckoned their goods at different prices, depending on whether they were to receive "pay," "money," "pay as money," or "trust." "Pay" was grain, pork, beef and other commodities whose values were fixed by law.

"Money" included Spanish colonial gold and silver coins entering the colonies through widespread smuggling, "Boston" or "Bay" shillings or other available specie, with wampum for small change. "Pay as money" was provisions of any kind taken at a discount of one-third the legal price, while "trust" was, of course, credit. A popular tavern-owner's saying recalls the latter, "My liquor's good, my measures just. But, honest sirs, I will not TRUST."

Madam Knight observed during her 1704 journey from Boston to New York, "When the buyer comes to ask for a commodity, sometimes before the merchant answers that he has it he says, 'is your pay ready?' Perhaps the chap replied 'Yes.' 'What do you pay in?' says the merchant. The buyer having answered, then the price is set; as suppose he wants a sixpenny knife, in pay it is twelvepence,— in pay as money eight pence, and in hard money at its own price, viz. sixpence."

Spanish colonial coins dominated colonial finance, but virtually any gold or silver coin from whatever source was welcomed; there were probably few current denominations that did not in some small measure find their way to America.

Another pivotal element of early American money was Colonial paper currency. As Eric P. Newman has pointed out, paper was far more familiar to the colonists than the scanty Colonial coinage. Paper money lies outside the scope of this book, but collectors wishing to grasp the full picture of money in early America should consult the basic works on Colonial paper currency.

Colonial coins were favorites of most pioneer collectors in the earliest years of American collecting. They gradually yielded pride of place to Federal decimal coins, collected by date and Mint with added enthusiasm after publication of Augustus Heaton's treatise, *Mint Marks* in 1893. After the great American Numismatic Society exhibition of U.S. coins in 1914, interest in this field dwindled . Since the late 1980's, Colonial and early State coins have enjoyed a remarkable renaissance.

James Spilman's *Colonial Newsletter*, the recently organized Colonial Coin Collectors Club (publishers of the *C-4 Newsletter*) , and the American Numismatic Society's Coinage of the Americas Conferences have provided much needed forums for sharing the results of new research and the restudy of many old assumptions about this complex field. Auction realizations since 1990 confirm this remarkable rebirth of interest in America's earliest coins. We are particularly indebted to Michael J. Hodder of Wolfeboro, N.H. for updating of information, especially for New Jersey issues.

A note on pricing

It is not this book's purpose to provide a definitive price guide to all types, dates and varieties. Whenever possible, significant auction records of the last decade or so are given for as many coins as possible. Collectors should note, however, that such auction records are generally those attained by higher-grade coins. Low-grade examples sell for a fraction of these prices, both in retail trade and at auction. Pieces which have not appeared at auction are not priced. Most unpriced coins are excessively rare, but this is not necessarily true for all. Please see the bibliography for the names of firms conducting many pre-1990 auctions which established many records reproduced here. For post-1990 citations, simplified abbreviations have been used, ST for Stack's of New York City; BM for Bower & Merena, Wolfeboro, N.H.

Massachusetts Bay silver coinage

Massachusetts never had royal permission to coin money, but took advantage of the chaotic situation of Britain's Civil War to begin coining its own silver money. Believing that the Puritan regicide Cromwell would not object, the colony's General Court appointed Boston silver smith John Hull as Mint master on May 26, 1652. The only two dates appearing on Massachusetts silver coins, 1652 and 1662, are those of the enabling legislation passed by the colony's General Court.

Hull and his partner Robert Sanderson were authorized to strike sterling silver shillings, sixpence and threepence at the weight of 72 grains per shilling. This was 22 1/2 percent below the weight of the existing British shilling, assuring that the lighter weight coins would remain in the colony.

The Mint was set up on Hull's Boston property, using silver imported quietly from the Spanish colonies. Many surviving Massachusetts silver pieces show indentations from use as teething rings. The story that bent or creased coins were "witch pieces" carried as protection against evil spells during the Salem witch hysteria of 1692 is purely legendary.

N E COINAGE

The first issue was inscribed N(ew) E(ngland) on the upper obverse, Roman numeral denomination at the opposite end of the reverse. Struck with a hammer, this simple design invited clipping and counterfeiting and was discontinued in October 1652.

Massachusetts Bay coinage continued

N E shilling (Bowers & Merena)

C.1. **N E Shilling:** Six varieties exist from three obv. and four rev. punches, all very rare. Garrett (Noe I-D) EF $47,500; Picker, ST 5/91 (Noe 2-A) EF, $34,000; Robison (Noe 3-B) $18,000; Norweb (Noe 3-C) VF-30, $13,200; Eliasberg 5/96 VF-30 $63,800.

N E sixpence (Bowers & Merena)

C.2. **N E Sixpence:** Thick lettering, seven known; the two or three Thin Lettering examples may be contemporary counterfeits. Garrett VF, $75,000.

C.3. **N E Threepence:** Single variety used NE punch of shilling, three known.

WILLOW TREE COINAGE

On Oct. 19, 1652, the General Court ordered that a tree replace the simple NE. It is uncertain what kind of tree was depicted, but the name Willow was applied by 19th century numismatists. The reverse die rotated with each hammer blow, causing multiple impressions of the crudely engraved design. This coinage continued until 1660 with the date 1652.

Willow Tree shilling (Bowers & Merena)

C.4. **1652 Shilling:** Six varieties from three obv. and five rev. dies. Very rare, perhaps 40 survive. Garrett (dies of Noe 1-A) Superb AU, $35,000; Norweb (Noe 2-A) VF-20, $52,800; (Noe 2-B) BM 9/90, EF-40, $29,700; (Noe 3-D) EF-40/VF-30, $44,000.

Willow Tree sixpence (Bowers & Merena)

C.5. **1652 Sixpence:** One variety, perhaps 15 known. Garrett EF-AU, $46,000.

C.6. **1652 Threepence:** One variety, three known.

OAK TREE COINAGE

About 1660, an Oak Tree replaced the Willow and continued until 1667. A screw press came into use, accounting for the vastly improved striking characteristics of this new coinage. A twopence was authorized in 1662 and actually bears that date instead of 1652.

A venerable numismatic fable alleges that Sir Thomas Temple showed specimens of this design to the restored King Charles II, tactfully remarking that the tree was the "Royall Oake which had preserved His Majesty's life" from Cromwell's victorious troops after the disastrous battle of Worcester. The unreliability of such charming tales calls to mind the remark of Sir Thomas De Quincy, "History, being composed largely of anecdotes, must necessarily be a tissue of lies."

Oak Tree shilling (Bowers & Merena)

C.7. **1652 Shilling:** NEW ENGLAND AN DOM reverse, many varieties. Garrett (Noe 1) AU, $7,500; Norweb (Noe 5) EF-45, $6,820; (Noe 6) ST 3/93, Ch.VF, $6,700.

Oak Tree shilling (Stack's)

C.8. **1652 Shilling:** NEW ENGLAND AN DO reverse, two varieties, Noe 2 and 3. Noe 2 is the only Oak Tree shilling with a rosette after O. Norweb (Noe 2) without specific grade, $5,060.

Oak Tree sixpence (Bowers & Merena)

C.9. **1652 Sixpence:** MASATHVSETS/IN NEW ENGLAND ANO. Noe 16. Roper EF, $3,300.
C.10. **1652 Sixpence:** NEW ENGLAND AN DOM. Noe 15, 17, 18. The Garrett example of Noe 15 was struck over a cut-down shilling, Choice AU, $21,000; Hydra Tree var., (Noe 14) Norweb AU-50, $18,700.

Oak Tree sixpence (Stack's)

C.11. **1652 Sixpence:** MASATHVSETS IN/NEW ENGLAND ANO. Noe 20-22; some known struck over Oak Tree shillings. Norweb (Noe 21) VF-30, $6,160; (Noe 22); AU-55, $6,160; ST 3/94 (Noe 20 over 14), Fine, $2,500.

Massachusetts Bay coinage continued

*Oak Tree threepence, S's reversed
(Bowers & Merena)*

C.12. **1652 Threepence:** MASATHVSETS IN. Noe 23, all S's reversed, Norweb VF-20, $1,980.

Oak Tree threepence

C.13. **1652 Threepence:** MASATHVSETS. Most varieties are recuttings, Noe 24 shows reversed first S, Norweb VF-30, $11,000.

Oak Tree twopence (Stack's)

C.14. **1662 Twopence:** Large or small 2 in date, several varieties and reworkings. Norweb (Noe 20) MS-60, $5,280; ST 9/93, (Noe 34) Ch. AU, $6,000.

PINE TREE COINAGE

In 1667 and again in 1675, new coinage contracts were drawn up between the General Court, Hull and Sanderson. These resulted in the many varieties of Pine Tree shillings: large planchet (27-31 mm) and small planchet (22-26 mm); and lesser numbers of sixpence and threepence pieces. Die life was increased by the smaller size shillings, and production was vastly increased by coiners certain that their project was soon to be closed down by the Crown.

Pine Tree shilling (Bowers & Merena)

C.15. **1652 Shilling:** Large planchet, MASATHVSETS IN (N's often backward). Many vars., most common is Noe 1, only variety with berries or pellets at sides of trunk, ST 12/93, AU, $4,500; Eliasberg 5/96 MS-60 $16,500. Noe 2 is the Straight Branch variety, Garrett VF-EF, $4,250; Eliasberg 5/96 MS-60 $24,200. Noe 3 displays largest tree and large letters, Garrett AU, $11,000; Noe 4, ST 9/94, EF, $2,800; Noe 5, ST 6/91, EF, $1,950; Noe 6, CU, Rarcoa Auction '81, $20,500; Noe 7 has M centered below tree, Norweb MS-60, $26,400.

Massachusetts Bay coinage continued

Pine Tree shilling (Stack's)

C.16. **1652 Shilling:** Large planchet, MASATHVSETS IN (sic). Noe 11, ST 9/94, VF, $1,600; unique Noe 11a has reworked tree and colons added. Garrett EF, $4,750.

Pine Tree shilling (Bowers & Merena)

C.17. **1652 Shilling:** Large dies, struck on small planchet, Noe 13-14; Noe 31 is the Nested Bowls variety, Roper VF, $1,045. All are possibly contemporary counterfeits made to simulate genuine clipped coins.

Pine Tree shilling (Stack's)

C.18. **1652 Shilling:** Small planchet, many rare varieties based on lettering size, punctuation, size of tree. The unique "scrawny tree" Noe 12 is a possible contemporary counterfeit. Garrett (Noe 16) Choice AU, $8,000; Norweb (Noe 17) MS-60, $10,450; BM 5/92, (Noe 23) VF-25, $1,8770 Norweb (Noe 24) VF-30, $24,200.

Pine Tree sixpence, "Spiny Tree"
(Bowers & Merena)

C.19. **1652 Sixpence:** Spiny Tree variety, Noe 32, stiff branches without berries or pellets at trunk. Norweb EF-40, $2,860.

Pine Tree sixpence (Stack's)

C.20. **1652 Sixpence:** Flexible branches and one berry on either side of trunk; all of this type without berries are later forgeries. Garrett (Noe 33) AU, $5,500.

Pine Tree threepence (Bowers & Merena)

C.21. **1652 Threepence:** NEW ENGLAND, tree with berries, Noe 34. Garrett AU, $5,500.

Massachusetts Bay coinage continued

Pine Tree threepence, "Berries" (Bowers & Merena)

C.22.   1652 Threepence: NEW ENGLAND ANO, tree with berries, Noe 35. Garrett EF-AU, $5,000.

Pine Tree threepence, "No berries" (Stack's)

C.23.   1652 Threepence: NEW ENGLAND, no berries, Noe 36-37. Garrett (Noe 36) AU, $5,500; BM 6/90 (Noe 37) VF-20, $1,650.

Maryland

LORD BALTIMORE'S COINAGE

The first colony to guarantee religious freedom, Maryland was settled in 1633 as a refuge for English Catholics. The royal charter granted the same rights once exercised by the Bishops of Durham to Proprietor George Calvert, first Lord Baltimore. Problems arising from the use of tobacco as money led Cecil Calvert, second Lord Baltimore to exercise his charter right to issue his own colonial coinage in 1658.

Puritan enemies denounced the coinage and brought legal action charging the proprietor with illegally exporting bullion from the mother country. The firmly anti-Catholic government of regicide Protector Oliver Cromwell rather surprisingly backed Lord Baltimore in the matter. After the Restoration of Charles II, Maryland passed an act establishing its own Mint on May 1, 1661, but no actual coinage resulted from this action.

Shilling

C.24.   Shilling: Large Bust, colon after MARIAE, point of shield at right base of M. About 66 grains (4.2 grams). Garrett EF, 68.1 grains, $11,000 ST James A. Stack, 11/89, AU, $16,000; Eliasberg 5/96 Unc. $17,600.

C.25.   Shilling: No colon after MARIAE, shield point touches V. Norweb AU-55 to MS-60, 73.3 grains, $9,350.

C.26.   Shilling: Same as last but copper pattern, five known. Norweb EF-45 to AU-50, $12,100.

C.27.   Shilling: Reverse arms quartered with Lady Baltimore's cross botony, as it appears on the Maryland commemorative half dollar of 1934, supposedly in collection of Sir Frederick Morton Eden.

Maryland coinage continued

Sixpence (Stack's)

C.28. **Sixpence:** Small bust, dash before MARIAE, no period after MVLTIPLICAMINI. About 34 grains. Robison AU, $5,500; Eliasberg 5/96 AU-55 $17,600.

C.29. **Sixpence:** Small bust, no hyphen before MARIAE. Rarcoa Auction '81 VF, $3,250.

C.30. **Sixpence:** Small bust, no period after MVLTIPLICAMINI. Norweb VF-30, $4,400.

C.31. **Sixpence:** Copper pattern, two known.

C.32. **Sixpence:** Small bust, motto misspelling MVLTILICAMINI, two known: Garrett VF, $13,500; Norweb AU-55 to MS-60, $27,500.

Sixpence (Bowers & Merena)

C.33. **Sixpence:** Large bust, period after MVLTIPLICAMINI. Norweb EF-45, $19,800.

C.34. **Sixpence:** Copper pattern similar to last, British Museum, unique?

Groat (Bowers & Merena)

C.35. **Groat (four pence):** Small bust and shield, faint periods (not colons) surrounding ET, no hyphen before MARIAE. Unique. Norweb EF-40, planchet crack, $26,400.

Groat (Stack's)

C.36. **Groat (four pence):** Large bust and shield, about 25 grains (1.61 grams). ST Starr 1/93, EF, $6,500. Piefort, 40.1 grains, ex S.S. Crosby, Richard Winsor, holed AG/Good, ST 3/93, $2,300; Eliasberg 5/96 Ch. AU $25,300.

Denarium (Stack's)

C.37. **Denarium (penny):** Copper, five known with R in MARIA first punched upside down, then corrected. Roper VF, $13,200.
(Not to be confused with William Idler's 19th century store card, Rulau Pa215B ff).

Richard Holt Plantation Tokens

In August 1688, Richard Holt & Company requested Crown approval of a tin coinage for the American colonies, then referred to as plantations. The colonial coins would join tin farthings struck earlier for Charles II and halfpence for James II, bolstering depressed prices of Cornish tin.

Holt proposed that the new coins be of "Spanish style" and denomination to facilitate colonial use. They actually bore a very Un-Spanish equestrian portrait of James II and the four shields of England, Scotland, Ireland and France. Their denomination was 1/24 of a silver real or 1/192 of the silver 8 reales.

The issue was authorized, but there is no record as to when or where it was distributed. Circulation of the coins may have been attempted in 1698, when a group of Philadelphia merchants appealed to the Crown to suppress the "leaden and pewter farthings" that were about to be sent over. The usurpation of James II's throne by William of Orange in the 1688 revolution may have made the coins highly impolitic.

Restrikes were made from rusted original dies around 1828 by English coin dealer Matthew Young for distribution by W.S. Lincoln & Son. Restrike dies show the king's head only slightly left of BRI in legend, many with a bold die crack at FRAN.

1/24 real token (Stack's)

C.38. **1/24 Real:** Original, five varieties without heavy die rust. Roper EF, die break over N in HISPAN, $577.50; die crack A in FRA to I in HIB, $506.50.

1/24 real token restrike (Stack's)

C.39. **1/24 Real:** Restrike, three varieties with die rust and crack at obv. right. Garrett Choice BU, $2,600; Norweb Unc., $467.50.
C.40. **1/24 Real:** Original, bizarre 4 punched sideways in date. High R-6. Conn. Hist Soc. EF-AU, $1,980; Archbishop John Sharp coin, ST 9/93, AU, $3,200.
C.41. **1/24 Real:** Obv. legend ET HB REX in place of correct HIB, very rare. ST 9/93, EF, $6,000.

1/24 real token, transposed arms (Stack's)

C.42. **1/24 Real:** Transposed arms rev., Irish at right, Scots at left.

1694 Elephant Tokens

At one time, numismatists attributed these interesting pieces and the London elephant tokens to the Royal African Company and copper allegedly obtained in West Africa. This company was highly favored by Charles II, whose brother James, Duke of York, was a prominent stockholder, but it had no provable connection with these copper pieces.

Modern research suggests that the Carolina and New England tokens may have been only two of a series dedicated to all North American plantations, struck 1672-1684. They may have been lottery tokens which publicized the colonies. The Carolina and New England pieces are known on thick and thin flans. The London tokens have a solely emblematic association with America and are listed with Associated and Quasi-Colonial Coins.

1694 Carolina halfpenny token,
"PROPRIETERS" (Bowers & Merena)

C.43. **1694 Carolina Halfpenny:** Misspelling PROPRIETERS, eight known. Garrett prooflike Choice Unc., $30,000; Norweb prooflike AU-55, $35,200.

1694 Carolina halfpenny token,
"Corrected die" (Stack's)

C.44. **1694 Carolina Halfpenny:** Corrected die, O punched over E. Thick flan examples are very rare; medium flan rare; thin flan very rare. Thick, Stack's 1976 ANA EF, $9,500. Thin, Garrett Choice Unc., $9,500. Medium, Garrett EF-40, $17,600.

1694 New England halfpenny token
(Bowers & Merena)

C.45. **1694 New England Halfpenny:** Both thick and thinner flans are extremely rare; do not confuse with Joseph Merriam's 19th century struck copies. Thin, Garrett VG, $16,000. Thick, Norweb VF-30, $25,300.

French Colonies

There has been much confusion over just what French coins may have been intended for colonial circulation, compounded by dealer determination to "adopt" many strictly homeland types as American. Although coins were struck for Canada under Louis XIV, it was not until 1716 that France authorized an issue also intended for Louisiana. During the following year 12 and six denier coppers were struck at the

Perpignan Mint (Mint mark Q), but due to the poor quality of the copper the issue was soon discontinued.

In June 1721 a new edict authorized the issue of three different denominations to be struck at four Mints. Ultimately, only nine-denier pieces or sous were struck at La Rochelle (H Mint mark) and Rouen (B) using copper planchets obtained in Sweden.

The sous were poorly received at New Orleans, and even the edict of May 2, 1724, reducing their value to six deniers failed to increase their circulation. On Oct. 31, 1726, the Council of State issued a severe penal edict to force their circulation. The 1767 French Colonies issue, though traditionally included, has no rightful place in the American series. Louisiana west of the Mississippi had been ceded to Spain in 1762, and the area east of the river to Britain in 1763.

LOUIS XIV SILVER COINAGE FOR CANADA

These two silver coins were struck by the Paris Mint for the colony of Canada. They were eagerly sought by pioneer American numismatists, although their tie to this country is tenuous at best. The late Wayte Raymond always referred to the 15 sols with something approaching awe as "the famous Gloriam Regni."

C.46. **1670-A 15 Sols:** Obv. Mature bust of Louis XIV r. Rev. crowned shield, Latin GLORIAM REGNI TUI DICENTI, They shall speak of the Glory of your Kingdom, radiant sun privy mark. Similar bust for size and denomination. Garrett VF, 104.1 grains, $29,000; Roper Fine, 103.2 grains, $15,400.

C.47. **1670-A 5 Sols:** Similar bust for size and denomination. ST Roper Choice AU, 35.4 grains, $3,520; ST 9/93 Ch. EF, $1,500.

ISSUES INTENDED FOR LOUISIANA

C.48. **1717-Q Sol of 12 Deniers:** Perpignan Mint, copper or brass, very rare.
C.49. **1717-Q 6 Deniers:** Similar to preceding but for denomination.

1721-H sou of 9 deniers (Bowers & Merena)

C.50. **1721-H Sou of 9 Deniers:** Obv. Crowned double L's, BENEDICTUM SIT NOMEN DOMINI, May the Name of the Lord be Blessed. Rev. COLONIES FRANCOISES, date, Mint mark H, La Rochelle Mint. Roper Fine, $99.
C.51. **1721-B Sou of 9 Deniers:** As preceding, Rouen Mint. Roper VF, $253.
C.52. **1722/1-H Sou of 9 Deniers:** As preceding, La Rochelle overdate, scarce. Roper EF, $374.
C.53. **1722-H Sou of 9 Deniers:** As preceding, Normal date. Roper VF, $105.

Wood's Rosa Americana Coinage

Through the influence of the duchess of Kendall and Munster, mistress of the German elector of Hanover who had mounted the British throne as King George I, English metal manufacturer William Wood obtained a royal patent authorizing him to strike 300 tons of copper alloy coins for the American colonies.

Wood was the inventor of Bath metal, an alloy containing 75 percent copper, 24.7 percent double-refined zinc and .3 percent silver. Although quite attractive when new, Wood's brass coins were less than half the Tower Mint standard for British copper coins of the same denominations. This low weight and the debased metallic content brought Wood a maximum profit but caused the series to be rejected in America.

Modern research suggests that many of Wood's coins were struck at the Tower under the supervision of Sir Isaac Newton; the dies may have been cut by the Mint's talented engraver John Croker and finished by the private firm of Lammas, Harold and Standbroke. Many coins were struck on heated, cast planchets, whose edges needed hand filing before they could be released.

Sylvester S. Crosby included a variety of somewhat similar patterns in his listing of these coins, but only those demonstrably part of the American series are included here. The distinctive Latin motto *Utile Dulci*, the useful with the sweet, is derived from the writings of the Roman poet Horace.

Inclusion of Wood's Hibernia coins in the American series has been questioned by some numismatists. Researchers such as Eric P. Newman deny that these coins circulated in the 13 colonies. The late Walter Breen pointed to finds of these pieces in "non-collector accumulations" found in many of the same Colonies. Both coinages have long been collected as part of the American Colonial series.

1722 Rosa Americana Patterns:

Twopence pattern of 1722, "Iron Rosa"
(Bowers & Merena)

C.54. **(1722) Twopence:** Trial piece struck in copper without collar, famous as the "Iron Rosa," 270 grains (17.49 grams), three known. Garrett copper, slightly off-center, 269.3 grains, VF, $4,250; Norweb Bath metal 194.4 grains, off-center, AU-50, $2,750.

C.55. **(1722) Twopence:** Similar to preceding, double-struck brass piefort. Brand coll., Unique.

C.56. **(1722) Twopence:** Struck on copper penny planchet. Unique. Norweb VF-20, 153.2 grains, $1,870.

C.57. **(1722) Twopence:** "Finer Dies," legend .UTILE.DULCI. in plain field, two known, F.C.C. Boyd, Norweb EF-45, 214.8 grains, $1,155.

1722 penny pattern (Bowers & Merena)

C.58. **1722 Penny:** Legend *VTILE.DVLCI. Garrett copper Proof, 145.8 grains, $5,500. Norweb Bath metal, AU-50, 150.7 grains, $1,210.

C.59. **1722 Penny:** Legend .UTILE.DULCI., edge oblique reeding. Norweb Proof, 111.7 grains, $3,520.

Wood's Rosa Americana Patterns continued

1722 halfpenny pattern (Bowers & Merena)

C.60. **1722 Halfpenny:** Legends GEORGIUS. DEI. GRATIA. REX., reverse .ROSA AMERI: VTILE. DVLCI., Bath metal, 4-6 known. Garrett Fine, 57.2 grains, $2,500. Norweb Bath metal patterns with punctuation .ROSA: AMERI: VTILE. DVLCI., Fine-12, 67.7 grains, $302; rev. with ROSA. corrected from ROSA:, EF-40, 73.8 grains, $577.50.

C.61. **1722 Halfpenny:** Obv. legend GEORGIUS .D: G: REX. Bath metal, Garrett AU, 61.8 grains, $2,000; Norweb wide planchet AU-55, $825.

1722 Rosa Americana Regular Issues:

Undated twopence of 1722

C.62. **(1722) Twopence:** Regular issue without date, GEORGIVS, motto on scroll. Bath metal, Garrett AU, 211.7 grains, $3,750; Eliasberg 5/96 AU-50 $1,100.

1722 twopence

C.63. **1722 Twopence:** Regular issue with date, GEORGIUS, motto on scroll. Garrett AU, 261.9 grains, $3,250.

C.64. **1722 Penny:** Regular U and short hair ribbons on obv., *VTILE. DVLCI. rev. Garrett VF-EF, 118.1 grains, $1,000.

C.65. **1722 Penny:** U's on both sides, uncrowned rose and rev. UTILE. DULCI, Garrett AU, 130.7 grains, $2,500. Rev. *UTILE. DULCI., Norweb AU-50, 140.1 grains, $495.

1722 halfpenny

C.66. **1722 Halfpenny:** ROSA AMERICANA spelled out in full. .UTILE.DULCI., Garrett EF, 72.7 grains, $1,300. Rev. *UTILE.DULCI., Garrett EF, 67.9 grains, $3,000.

1723 Rosa Americana Patterns:

C.67. **1723 Twopence:** Pattern exists with different device punches and cross between ROSA and AMERICANA, two Proofs known.

1723 penny trial (Bowers & Merena)

C.68. **1723 Penny:** Struck on oversize 198.2-grain copper planchet as a trial piece. Unique, Garrett Fine, $1,100.

C.69. **1723 Halfpenny:** Uncrowned rose, very rare in Bath metal, silver and copper.

1723 Rosa Americana Regular Issues:

1723 twopence

C.70. **1723 Twopence:** Crowned rose reverse, period after REX., none after date. Garrett Choice AU, 212.6 grains, $3,750.

C.71. **1723 Twopence:** No period after REX or date. The H.P. Smith collection contained a German silver Proof without pellets. Norweb Bath metal, 230.4 grains, AU-55, $660.

C.72. **1723 Twopence:** Unique error reverse UTILE DULI, Newcomer collection.

1723 penny

C.73. **1723 Penny:** Crowned rose, several varieties. Period after REX, none after date. Garrett EF, 108.3 grains, $800; high period like apostrophe after REX', Norweb VF-30, 101.3 grains, $143.

C.74. **1723 Halfpenny:** Rev. uncrowned rose. Garrett EF, 67.9 grains, $3,000.

C.75. **1723 Halfpenny:** Regular issue, Crowned rose, at least two known in silver. Garrett Bath metal, Choice prooflike Unc., $4,500; Norweb Bath metal, MS-60, 63.4 grains, $550.

1724 Rosa Americana Patterns:

1724 twopence pattern (Bowers & Merena)

C.76. **1724 Twopence:** "Goiter Head" with exaggerated swelling at truncation, MA . B in royal titles. Bath metal (4 known), Brand AU, $3,520. The Unique copper-silverplate example engraved WW, VIII JUNE on rev. is believed to be Wood's personal pocket piece, Norweb VF-30, 245.8 grains, $1,540.

C.77. **1724 Twopence:** "Goiter Head," M.B in royal titles, three known in Bath metal, copper extremely rare, unique in silver. Garrett EF, Bath metal 198.9 grains, $6,000.

C.78. **1724/3 Penny:** Crowned rose, no period after REX, known in Bath metal and copper. Garrett copper, Fine-VF, 125.4 grains, $2,800.

1724/3 penny pattern (Bowers & Merena)

C.79. **1724/3 Penny:** Copper, Titles GEORGIUS.D. GRATIA. REX., Bath metal, Brand Unc., $5.060; Norweb Bath metal 86.6 grains without specific grade, $4,400; silverplate, Brand without specific grade, $2,310.

C.80. **1724/3:** Silver, "Goiter Head," period after REX, mortuary legend engr. in obv. field, unique, Norweb VF-20, $3,740.

1733 twopence

C.81. **1733 Twopence:** George II head left, rev. naturalistic rose with seven leaves and bud. Copper, four known. Garrett Choice Proof, $22,500; Norweb Proof-60-63, 275.6 grains, $19,800.

C.82. **1733 Twopence:** Similar, uniface strike in malleable steel, six known. ST 3/93, AU, $1,150. Another uniface in Bath metal is known, pierced through date, opposite side engraved MR. JACKSON.

Virginia

Virginia's 1606 charter empowered the colony to issue its own coins, but no attempt was made to exercise that right until 1773. On May 20 of that year, the Virginia Assembly passed an act to authorize coinage of distinctive copper halfpence by the Tower Mint in London. Engraver Richard Yeo prepared the dies and five tons of coins arrived in Virginia in February 1774.

Cautious colonial treasurer Richard Nicholas insisted on a royal proclamation before releasing the new coins to circulation. This arrived after nine months delay, just 50 days before the Revolutionary War began, and most of the new coins were hoarded until after the war.

The coins that reached circulation were well used and exist today in all grades. Many of the red Uncirculated coins now known originate in an original keg found before the Civil War at Richmond and owned by pioneer Baltimore numismatist Col. Mendes I. Cohen. He and his heirs slowly fed the halfpence into the market until the last 2,200 went to New York numismatist Wayte Raymond in 1929. It is these coins that make it possible for collectors to buy strictly Uncirculated Virginia halfpence today at reasonable cost.

Varieties are defined by presence or absence of a pellet after GEORGIVS, the number of harp strings, position of letters and heraldic elements to each other and the shield. Presentation pieces often called the "penny" and "shilling" are described below.

1773 "penny" (Bowers & Merena)

C.83. **1773 "Penny":** Copper pattern struck on 131-135 grain (8.48-8.74 gram) similar to the Irish halfpenny planchet weight with meticulously beaded rims and small 7's in date. Perhaps 20 known. Six harp strings, ST 5/93, Proof, $3,200; BM 3/92 Proof-63, $5,500.

1773 halfpenny (Stack's)

C.84. **1773 Halfpenny:** Period after GEORGIVS. Seven strings, Garrett Choice BU, 113.9 grains, $1,400. Eight harp strings, Garrett prooflike Choice BU, 119.3 grains, $1,100.

1773 halfpenny (Stack's)

C.85. **1773 Halfpenny:** No period after GEORGIVS. The Garrett collection sale included the following: Six harp strings, Choice BU, 114.9 grains, $1,300. Seven harp strings, Choice Unc., 115.6 grains, $1,000. Eight harp strings, unique, ST 9/93, prooflike Unc., $2,600.

Virginia coinage continued

1774 "shilling"

C.86. **1774 "Shilling":** Silver Proof muling of Thomas Pingo's obv. for George III gold guinea die and Virginia reverse, six known. Garrett Proof, 83.3 grains, $23,000.

Colonial Tokens

THE HIGLEY THREEPENCE

Among the first copper tokens struck in America were those made by Dr. Samuel Higley of Granby, Conn., in 1737. Yale graduate, surgeon and metallurgist, Higley was first in the colonies to make his own steel. He opened his copper mine in 1727, and soon exported much metal to England.

Higley used his copper to strike tokens inscribed threepence, a high value for the time. Increasing supply, light weight and perhaps local questioning of the value led him to inscribe later issues "value me as you please." After his death at sea in 1737, coinage continued under his brother John, and the mine later confined British prisoners of war in the Revolution.

Colonial jewelers melted many of these tokens, using the pure copper for alloying gold. All Higley coppers are very rare today; beware of counterfeits and electrotypes.

1737 threepence (Bowers & Merena)

C.87. **1737 Threepence:** Obv. Deer, hand below, THE. VALVE. OF. THREE. PENCE. Rev. three crowned hammers, CONNECTICVT, star & date below. Picker VF, $12,650; Roper Fine, 119.8 grains, $5,280.

C.88. **1737 Threepence:** Obv. similar, THE. VALVE. OF. THREE. PENCE. Rev. Similar, but I AM GOOD COPPER. ST 12/93, Good, $5,000.

1737 threepence

C.89. **1737 Threepence:** VALVE. ME. AS. YOU. PLEASE, deer, hand, star and III below. Rev. three crowned hammers, I. AM. GOOD. COPPER., three known. Roper Fine. 155.1 grains, $2,420.

C.90. **1737 Threepence:** Similar, but VALVE, eight known. Garrett Good-VG, 144.1 grains, $8,000.

Colonial tokens continued

Undated threepence ca. 1737 (Bowers & Merena)

C.91. **(1737?) Threepence:** Deer, star, hand and III below, VALUE. ME. AS. YOU. PLEASE. Rev. axe, J. CUT. MY. WAY. THROUGH., 7-9 known. Garrett EF, 162.2 grains, $45,000; ST 5/91, Good, $5,000; Eliasberg 5/96 Fine $12,650.

Undated threepence ca. 1737 (Stack's)

C.92. **(1737?) Threepence:** Wheel, hand below, THE. WHEELE. GOES. ROUND. Rev. axe, J. CUT. MY. WAY. THROUGH., Unique. Garrett VF/F, 151.9 grains, $75,000.

1739 threepence (Bowers & Merena)

C.93. **1739 Threepence:** Similar, VALUE. ME. AS. YOU. PLEASE. Rev. axe, date 1739, J. CUT. MY. WAY. THROUGH., five known. Roper Fine/VF, 132 grains, $7,700.

GLOUCESTER SHILLING

Little is known of these rare tokens, now believed to have been struck for Christopher Righault and Samuel Dawson of Gloucester County, Va. The legend identifies the county courthouse as the building on the obverse, the names of the issuers and date appear on the reverse.

1714 shilling

C.94. **1714 Shilling:** Brass, two crudely struck specimens known, neither with complete legends. Garrett Fine, 61.1 grains, $36,000.

NEW YORKE TOKEN

A lead trial of the NEW YORKE IN AMERICA token was discovered in a museum in The Hague in 1850. Since then brass and additional lead pieces have turned up, some among accumulations of Civil War tokens of the 1860s. American Numismatic Society Curator Dr. John Kleeberg has identified the eagle on ragged staff as the heraldic badge of the family of New York Colonial Governor Lovelace. Venus and Cupid under fanciful palms recall the 1562 illustrations of America by Jacques le Moyne.

"Farthing" token

C.95. **"Farthing":** Brass, possibly nine exist. Garrett F-VF, 44.6 grains, $5,250; Roper VF, 46.3 grains, $3,740; BM 1/91, Fine/VG, $2,090.

C.96. **"Farthing":** Lead, sometimes called pewter, four known. Roper VF, 72.2 grains, $3,960.

Associated & Quasi-Colonial Coins and Tokens

Listed here are coins, tokens and circulating medalets not originally struck for circulation in the American plantations. Some were introduced to the colonies after rejection elsewhere; others are related by design to strictly American issues. All have traditionally been collected with more obviously American items. The status of each will be examined with their descriptions.

SOMMER ISLANDS (BERMUDA)

Spanish navigator Juan de Bermudez discovered the islands that now bear his name in 1515. Sir George Sommers explored the stormy Bermudas in the *Sea Venture* in 1609. His ship was damaged in a hurricane, and he left some of his shipwrecked sailors behind which inspired William Shakespeare's play *The Tempest*. The island was overrun with pigs released there by the Spanish, and provided food for the stranded Englishmen.

After the English settlement was established, Virginia planter and Bermuda Governor Daniel Tucker arranged coinage of four denominations of "Hogge Money," whose inferior weight assured that they would remain in circulation only in Bermuda. Most existing specimens of these crude silverwashed brass coins are in low grade with varying degrees of corrosion. These are among the earliest British colonial coins.

Undated shilling of 1616

C.97. **(1616) Shilling:** Large sails. Roper VF, $11,000; thin planchet, ST Starr 1/93, Good/Fine, $6,500.

Quasi-Colonial issues continued

Undated shilling of 1616, "Small Sails" (Stack's)

C.98. **(1616) Shilling:** Small sails, rare but a number found in recent years on Bermuda. Thick planchet ex Sylvester S. Crosby, Norweb EF-40, $39,600; ST 9/94, Fine/VF, $5,000.

Undated sixpence of 1616, "Large portals" (Bowers & Merena)

C.99. **(1616) Sixpence:** Large portholes, Garrett EF, $20,000; BM 3/90, VF-20, $9,460.
C.100. **(1616) Sixpence:** Small portholes. Roper EF+, $8,800.

Undated threepence of 1616 (Bowers & Merena)

C.101. **(1616) Threepence:** Norweb VF-20, $70,400.

Undated twopence of 1616 (Bowers & Merena)

C.102. **(1616) Twopence:** Large star between hog's legs, Garrett Fine, $8,500.
C.103. **(1616) Twopence:** Small star, Roper Fine, $3,520; ST Sutcliffe, 9/94, VG/Poor, $3,600.

LONDON ELEPHANT TOKENS (1672-1684)

Although collected as part of the same series as the Carolina and New England elephant tokens, these pieces have only a stylistic association with the colonies. No specific reason is known for their striking, as their probable date is later than the terrible plague (1665) and subsequent fire (1666) that ravaged London.

Quasi-Colonial issues continued

Halfpenny token (Bowers & Merena)

C.104. Halfpenny: GOD PRESERVE LONDON, first obverse with tusks far from rim. Engraver's error placed sword in second quarter of shield (on observer's right). Diagonal lines at center of cross. About 172 grains (11.14 grams). Roper Choice Unc., 180 grains, $4,840.

Halfpenny token, "Corrected arms"
(Bowers & Merena)

C.105. Halfpenny: Same obv., corrected arms with diagonals, star below shield point, weight similar to preceding. Thin, 144.7 grains, Norweb EF-40, $2,200.

Halfpenny token, no diagonals (Stack's)

C.106. Halfpenny: Second obv. with tusks at rim, GOD PRESERVE LONDON, thick planchet, about 229 grains (14.83 grams), no diagonal lines at center of cross. Norweb AU-55, 243 grains, $1,320; BM 5/93, EF-45, $1,045; Eliasberg 5/96 Gem Unc. $9,240.

C.107. Halfpenny: Same dies, thin planchet, about 116 grains (7.51 grams). Rare. Overstruck on Carolus a Carolo Charles II halfpenny, Robison I, Choice Unc., $3,400. Normal planchet, Norweb MS-60, 134.1 grains, $2,310.

Halfpenny token, "LON DON" (Stack's)

C.108. Halfpenny: Second obv., arms without diagonals divide LON DON. Roper Choice Unc., 154.6 grains, $5,280.

SAINT PATRICK'S COINAGE

These enigmatic copper pieces are the subject of spirited numismatic debate. Some British writers and the late Walter Breen asserted that they were struck in the reign of embattled King Charles I, from dies by Tower Mint Engraver Nicholas Briot. His role was supposedly proven by the appearance of his privy mark, the martlet, the mythical legless bird of medieval heraldry and by letter punches from his Scottish coins. The head of kneeling King David resembles a radiate-crowned Charles I on Briot's pattern halfpenny (Peck 362, plate 4).

FLOREAT REX, May the King Flourish, appears on all obverses. The larger coins, called halfpence by later numismatists, show Saint Patrick with the Arms of the city of Dublin and motto Behold the Flock. The copper planchets included a brass "splasher" as an anti-counterfeiting device. The smaller coins, later called farthings, bear the plea, May the People be Quiet. Recent research suggests striking under the auspices of the Lord Lieutenant of Ireland around 1675.

In November 1681 some 14,000 of these coins were brought to New Jersey by Quaker immigrant Mark Newby (or Newbie). After this enterprising banker became a member of the provincial legislature, the larger coins were declared legal tender. They remained in circulation for decades and have been found in archeological digs in New Jersey, though no "farthings" have been so recovered.

The smaller coins show snakes, toads, winged bird and griffin (heraldic half lion, half eagle), presumably the "reptiles" driven from Ireland by the saint. There is no evidence that they actually circulated as farthings or anything else in the New Jersey of Newby's day. Most survivors are well worn from circulation somewhere, though not in New Jersey.

Halfpenny (Bowers & Merena)

C.109. Halfpenny: Legend spacing FLORE AT REX, large (very rare) and medium-letter varieties. Roper small letters ...FLORE A. T .REX., Choice VF, $1,155; large letters VG, $286. .FLOREAT .*. .REX., Garrett Unc., $17,000.

Halfpenny (Stack's)

C.110. Halfpenny: Legend FLOREAT. * .REX, several lettering varieties, one known in silver from Dr. Aquilla Smith collection. Roper AU, ex Dr. Edward Maris, 131.2 grains, $13,200 ST 5/91 Ch. VF, $3,200..

Farthing (Bowers & Merena)

C.111. Farthing: Nothing beneath King David, more than 70 varieties in lettering, spacing, pellet or colon punctuation. Most show bird with swept-back wings, serpent, griffin, one or more toads or "pigs" beneath standing St. Patrick. One toad, Norweb AU-50, 92 grains, $550; two toads Fine-15, 85.6 grains, $302.50.; One toad, silver 98 grains, ST 12/93, VF, $1,700.

Saint Patrick's coinage continued

Farthing, "Guinea" (Bowers & Merena)

C.112. Farthing: Unique gold "Guinea," FLOREAT :REX:, T of QUIESCAT just left of peak of mitre, 125.1 grains, authenticity debated. Norweb #2386, EF-45, unsold.

Farthing, "Shilling" (Bowers & Merena)

C.113. Farthing: Silver, sometimes called a "Shilling," Norweb coll. had four pieces. Legend FLOREAT :REX:, nothing under king, T in QUIESCAT atop mitre, 103.8 grains, AU-50, $4,180. FLOREAT :REX, T left of mitre, Garrett Unc., 116.3 grains, $13,000; Norweb EF-45, 99.5 grains, $3,250.

Farthing (Bowers & Merena)

C.114. Farthing: Straight ground lines beneath king, Roper Unc., $2,310. Broken ground beneath king, sometimes called dolphins, many punctuation varieties including colons, pellets or three-dot groups. Four toads or "pigs" under St. Patrick, Roper VF, $209.

Farthing (Bowers & Merena)

C.115. Farthing: Martlet (legless heraldic bird and Briot's privy mark) beneath king. Roper Fine, $198.

Farthing (Bowers & Merena)

C.116. Farthing: Double annulet (two rings forming figure 8) beneath king. Norweb VF-30, 88.4 grains, $176.

Saint Patrick's coinage continued

Farthing (Bowers & Merena)

C.117. Farthing: Double annulet and martlet beneath king. Norweb VF-20, 101.9 grains, $110.

Farthing (Bowers & Merena)

C.118. Farthing: Halo or nimbus around saint's head, three varieties in copper, Garrett EF, 105 grains, $1,700. Two known in silver, Roper 89.8 grains VF, $2,090; Garrett 108.1 grains, VF, $7,250.

WILLIAM WOOD'S HIBERNIA COINAGE

Wolverhampton entrepreneur William Wood received a second royal patent to provide halfpence and farthings for Ireland on July 12, 1722. Because of their supposedly inferior alloy, the stealthy preparation of the whole project without the consent of the Irish parliament and the violent propaganda campaign spearheaded by Jonathan Swift's polemic *The Drapier Letters*, the coins were resolutely rejected in Ireland.

Hibernia coins bear the same head of the "wee German lairdie," King George I, as the Rosa Americana pieces. Only halfpence and farthings were struck under the Irish patent. Major types are listed here with such patterns as clearly belong to this coinage.

1722 Hibernia Patterns:

1722 halfpenny pattern (Bowers & Merena)

C.119. 1722 Halfpenny: Old head r., GEORGIVS D;G. REX. Seated Hibernia holding harp at left, gazing at mass of rock on right. Often found well circulated. Norweb copper VF-35, 144.2 grains, $2,310; silver Fine-12, 112.2 grains, $1,540.

1722 farthing pattern (Bowers & Merena)

C.120. 1722 Farthing: Head r., GEORGIUS D: G :REX. Rev seated Hibernia with harp thrust left, possibly 10 known. Norweb copper Proof-60, 60.2 grains, $2,200.

1722 Hibernia Regular Issues:

1722 halfpenny (Stack's)

C.121. 1722 Halfpenny: Harp at left of seated Hibernia, 14 varieties known. Garrett prooflike Unc., 117.2 grains, $3,600; prooflike Norweb MS-60-63, $612.50.

C.122. 1722 Halfpenny: Obverse legend shows spelling blunder DEII, very rare.

1722 halfpenny (Bowers & Merena)

C.123. 1722 Halfpenny: Rev. Harp at right, under Hibernia's arm. A directly over Hibernia's head, Garrett AU, 135.4 grains, $1,000; Norweb MS-60-63, $467.50

1723 Hibernia Patterns:

C.124. 1723 Halfpenny: Star before date, three known.

1723 halfpenny pattern (Bowers & Merena)

C.125. 1723 Halfpenny: Large head, period before HIBERNIA. Extremely rare in silver. Norweb copper Proof-64, presentation strike, $2,860.

1723 farthing pattern (Bowers & Merena)

C.126. 1723 Farthing: Legend GEORGIUS .D:G .REX., often with reverse die crack through NIA. Very rare, four to six known. Garrett Choice Unc., 57.2 grains, $3,500.

1723 farthing (Stack's)

C.127. 1723 Farthing: Regular design, but silver. A is directly over Hibernia's head, Rarcoa Auction '89 Choice Proof, $3,300; ST 5/90, Proof, $3,750. A is just left of head, Norweb AU-50, 71.5 grains, $1,870.

1723 Hibernia Regular Issues:

1723/2 halfpenny (Bowers & Merena)

C.128. 1723/2 Halfpenny: Varieties exist with large or small 3 in date. Roper VF, 112.2 grains, $192.50.

C.129. 1723 Halfpenny: Period before H, small 3 in date, about 20 varieties. Norweb MS-63, 114.6 grains, $467.50.

C.130. 1723 Halfpenny: No period before H, large 3 in date, more than 20 varieties. Norweb MS-63-64, 103.2 grains, $715.

C.131. 1723 Halfpenny: No pellet before H, small 3. Most common type with more than 100 varieties. Norweb included these rev. vars.: A directly over head, MS-64-65, 123.2 grains, $660; IA over head, MS-63, 118.6 grains, $742.50; A over forehead, MS-60, 118.2 grains, $247.50.

C.132. 1723 Halfpenny: Engraver's blunder: R's corrected from B's, very rare.

C.133. 1723 Halfpenny: Beaded cincture appears before nose of harp's bust. Very rare, especially if clearly struck.

1723 farthing (Bowers & Merena)

C.134. 1723 Farthing: Regular issue, many varieties. A high over head, Garrett AU, 52.8 grains, $900; IA over head, Garrett AU, 61.7 grains, $850.

C.135. 1723 Farthing: Regular design, GEORGIUS punched over engraver's error GEORAIUS. Extremely rare.

1724 Hibernia Patterns:

C.136. 1724 Halfpenny: Pattern, DEI directly over king's head, HIBERNIA far left, A over her palm frond. Excessively rare.

1724 halfpenny pattern, "Goiter Head"
(Bowers & Merena)

C.137. 1724 Halfpenny: Pattern, "Goiter Head" with exaggerated swelling at truncation, title spaced GEORGIUS.DEI. GRATIA . REX., R in HIBERNIA almost touches over top of head. Taylor Proof-63, 128 grains, $3,740; BM 5/92, Proof-63, $4,400. Title spaced GEORGIUS . DEI, R high. Garrett EF, 118.1 grains, $4,500; Superior Auction '84, silver holed $3,300.

1724 halfpenny pattern (Bowers & Merena)

C.138. 1724 Halfpenny: Wood's patterns with scepter and trident reverse cannot be linked with certainty to this Irish series. Their Latin legend "One shall rule both (land and sea)" suggests an overseas or American connection. Norweb Proof-63, 129.2 grains, $6,160; Garrett Unc., 134.1 grains, $5,000.

Hibernia coinage continued

C.139. 1724 Halfpenny: "Goiter Head," rev. seated figure holding orb, sometimes called Britannia, but has no English insignia on her shield. Brass, Garrett VF-EF, 77.3 grains, $2,250; Norweb VG-8/F-12, 76.3 grains, $1,045.

1724 Hibernia Regular Issues:

1724 halfpenny (Bowers & Merena)

C.140. 1724 Halfpenny: Pellet after date, six varieties. Garrett EF, 112.4 grains, $550.
C.141. 1724 Halfpenny: No pellet after date, five varieties. date close to HIBERNIA, Norweb MS-63, 124 grains, $1,320; date distant from HIBERNIA, MS-63, 105.5 grains, $1,430.

1724 farthing (Bowers & Merena)

C.142. 1724 Farthing: Pellet after date, Garrett Choice BU, 59.1 grains, $3,000.
C.143. 1724 Farthing: No pellet after date. Roper EF, 57.4 grains, $176.

VOCE POPULI TOKENS

Irish military button manufacturer Roche of South King Street, Dublin, struck a variety of copper tokens bearing an unidentified laureate bust with Latin legend *VOCE POPULI*, By the Will of the People. Dated 1760, the halfpence have nine basic portrait types, and two for the scarcer farthings. Identification of the busts as Jacobite Pretender James III, his son Prince Charles Edward Stuart, or Irish parliamentarian John Hely-Hutchinson are discredited guesses. It is now thought that the broad, 129-154 grain pieces bearing the 'P' may have had official sanction, while the smaller squat bust types may be contemporary circulating counterfeits. These coppers have been found in association with other Irish pieces circulating in the colonies.

1760 halfpenny token, "Youthful Head"
(Bowers & Merena)

C.144. 1760 Halfpenny: Youthful head, rare. BM 3/90, AU-58 to MS-60, $1,320.

Voce Populi tokens continued

1760 halfpenny token, "Mature Bust"
(Bowers & Merena)

C.145. 1760 Halfpenny: Mature or "Stern" bust, deeply struck, giving feeling of an ancient Roman coin. Garrett Choice AU, 126.7 grains, $2,200; Roper Choice EF, 136 grains, $352.

1760 halfpenny token, "1700" error
(Bowers & Merena)

C.146. 1760 Halfpenny: Square head, four varieties including error date "1700." Norweb VF-30, 113.8 grains, $577.50; Roper Fine, 103.8 grains, $632.

1760 halfpenny token, "VOOE"
(Bowers & Merena)

C.147. 1760 Halfpenny: Sharp features, "fox face," rare variety shows engraver's blunder at C gives spelling VOOE. Roper Choice EF, 103.2 grains, $253; Norweb AU-50, 111.5 grains, $440.

1760 halfpenny token, "Long Head"
(Bowers & Merena)

C.148. 1760 Halfpenny: Long head, so-called "James III." Roper EF, 160 grains, $396.

1760 halfpenny token, "P before nose"
(Bowers & Merena)

C.149. 1760 Halfpenny: P in field before nose. Roper EF, 131.8 grains, $275; Garrett EF, 126.1 grains, $850.

Voce Populi tokens continued

1760 halfpenny token, "P under truncation" (Bowers & Merena)

C.150. 1760 Halfpenny: P under truncation. Roper Choice VF, 145.8 grains, $220; Norweb AU-50, 126.8 grains, $385.

1760 farthing (Bowers & Merena)

C.151. 1760 Farthing: large letters with loop on truncation. Roper AU, 64.6 grains, $1,430; ST Starr 1/93, AU, $1,500; BM 3/90, MS-60, $1,760.

1760 farthing (Bowers & Merena)

C.152. 1760 Farthing: Small letters, no loop. Norweb MS-60, 67.3 grains, $5,940.

Issues of the Revolutionary Era

PITT TOKENS OR MEDALETS

These pieces were struck from dies engraved by English gunsmith and engraver James Smithers to honor William Pitt, first Earl of Chatham, British statesman who successfully opposed implementation of the 1765 Stamp Act. The act had been conceived by the British government as a fund-raising measure to expedite defense of a British colonial empire enlarged by the annexation of New France (Canada).

The colonists saw the measure as an illegal extension of royal taxing authority and a dangerous encroachment on their rights as Englishmen. Increasingly violent resistance to the hated stamps and the government which issued them led in a direct line to the American Revolution. Although Pitt's eloquence in Parliament led to abolition of the stamps in 1766, the now established colonial anti-stamp leadership soon led the agitation for American independence.

The pieces often called halfpence and farthings were issued by the New York anti-stamp committee, the Friends of Liberty and Trade. Both sizes are found well circulated, but there is no evidence that either token passed as anything but a halfpenny.

Pitt tokens continued

1766 halfpenny (Stack's)

C.153. 1766 Halfpenny: Copper, Betts 519, some show traces of tin plating. Garrett Choice Unc., 85.1 grains, $4,750; Norweb AU-55, 85 grains, $2,640; 'Red Book' plate coin, ST 12/94, Ch. EF, $1,800.

C.154. 1766 Halfpenny: Brass, similar.

C.155. 1766 Halfpenny: White metal, possibly two exist

1766 farthing (Stack's)

C.156. 1766 Farthing: Brass, cast planchets, plain edge or crudely reeded, some may have been tin-plated. Perhaps as many as eight known. Roper EF, 64.2 grains, $6,600.

C.157. 1766 Farthing: Copper. Norweb F-15, 47.6 grains, $1,320.

CONTINENTAL CURRENCY COINAGE

In recent years, many facts and more theories have emerged about the coins known to numismatists as " Continental Dollars," These coins bear a sundial under a radiant sun with warning FUGIO, "I (time) Fly," with the corollary " Mind your Business" below. The reverse bore a continuous chain of 13 links, each bearing a state's name to symbolize the unity of the new nation, AMERICAN CONGRESS, WE ARE ONE at center.

The sundial and mottoes were long associated with Benjamin Franklin, but these elements graced the Feb. 17, 1776, Continental paper currency before appearing on these enigmatic coins. These notes are the work of New Jersey engraver Elisha Gallaudet, strongly suggesting that the signature on some varieties, "E.G. FECIT" should be read as "E(lisha) G(allaudet) Made It."

Researchers now believe that the silver Continental coins were struck in New York City and were intended to replace the one-dollar note just eliminated from the denomination roster. John J. Ford Jr. argues convincingly that the brass examples were actually pennies, intended to replace the jumble of lightweight coppers then in use.

The tin or pewter coins, most numerous of all, may have been emergency pieces struck after the plans for silver dollars and brass pennies collapsed for lack of bullion and the deteriorating military situation. None can now be called patterns with absolute certainty.

Spellings vary for the word Currency on coins, CURENCY, CURRENCY and CURRENCEY all made their appearance. Edges bear a twin-leaf pattern similar to that of the Spanish 8 reales.

Newman numbers refer to Eric P. Newman's 1952 study, *The 1776 Continental Currency Coinage.*

Continental Currency coinage continued

1776 CURENCY (Bowers & Merena)

C.158. 1776: CURENCY, brass, reverse chain made of dotted links. Two known: Newman 1-A, Brand AU, $26,400; Norweb VF-20, 314.1 grains, $11,000.

1776 CURENCY (Stack's)

C.159. 1776: CURENCY, brass, dotted lines now partly cut into lines. N 1-B, BM 5/92, AU-50, $13,750.
C.160. 1776: CURENCY, pewter. Large comma under small N in AMERICAN. N 1-B, dots into lines as preceding, Picker AU, $7,700.
C.161. 1776: CURENCY, pewter. N 1-C, Norweb MS-60-63, 260.8 grains, $13,200; BM 5/92, AU-50, $6,600; Eliasberg 4/97 MS-60 $16,500.

1776 CURENCY

C.162. 1776: CURENCY, copper, links now formed entirely by lines, seven-nine known. N 1-B, Garrett EF, 222.9 grains, $11,000.
C.163. 1776: CURENCY, silver, Unique. N 1-C, Garrett VG, 375 grains, $95,000.
C.164. 1776: CURRENCY, tin or pewter. N 2-C, ST 9/93, Ch. Unc. $6,400.
C.165. 1776: CURRENCY, copper, Unique.

Continental Currency coinage continued

1776 CURRENCY, E.G. FECIT
(Stack's)

C.166. **1776:** CURRENCY, E.G. FECIT, silver, two known.
C.167. **1776:** CURRENCY, E.G. FECIT, brass, Unique.
C.168. **1776:** CURRENCY, E.G. FECIT, pewter. N 3-D.; BM 3/90, MS-63, $11,000; Eliasberg 5/96 MS-63 $23,100.

1776 CURRENCEY

C.169. **1776:** CURRENCEY, pewter. N 4-D, Roper Choice EF, 277.5 grains, $6,050.
C.170. **1776:** CURRENCY*, tin or pewter, last two letters of CURRENCEY corrected on die to Y and quatrefoil. N 5-D, Norweb AU-50, 302 grains, $50,600.

RHODE ISLAND SHIP MEDAL

These medals bearing Dutch legends are now believed to have been struck in England for distribution in the Netherlands, then vocally supporting the American bid for independence. The pieces depict the flagship of Richard, Earl Howe under full sail, and Continental troops fleeing from a stylized Rhode Island in August 1778.

The medals were to convince the Dutch that the Americans would lose the war as they had Rhode Island. Confusion over this purpose is traced to the word *vlugtende*, fleeing, which was on the die below the ship. Since the Americans were fleeing, not the admiral, the offending word was filed off some finished medals; others have it obliterated in the die by a floral pattern.

1776, "vlugtende" below ship (Bowers & Merena)

C.171. 1778: Brass.*vlugtende* below ship, Garrett EF-50, 151.1 grains, $16,000.

1776, "vlugtende" removed (Stack's)

C.172. 1778: Brass, *vlugtende* removed from medal. Norweb MS-60, 147.7 grains, $6,600.
C.173. 1778: Pewter, similar. Roper AU, 169.1 grains, $3,520.

1776, "vlugtende" obliterated (Stack's)

C.174. 1778: Brass, floral pattern obliterates word *vlugtende*. Roper Unc., 153.4 grains, $2,750.
C.175. 1778: Pewter, similar, six known. Garrett EF-40, 129 grains, $5,000; ST 10/91, Unc., $4,800.

Confederation Period

Plans were made for a Federal coinage in 1776 and again in 1783, but due to the insolvency of the old government, its plans for establishing a Mint never materialized. Instead, Congress contracted in 1787 with New York entrepreneur James Jarvis for the manufacturer of copper coins. These are dealt with in the section on federal issues.

Under authority of Vermont, Connecticut, New Jersey and Massachusetts, private Mints struck great quantities of copper coins. In New York, coppers were issued without such authority. Minting coppers was a profitable business since the current value of the coins far exceeded the cost of their manufacture. It is incorrect to refer to Connecticut, Vermont, New Jersey or New York coinage as "cents," since these coins had no specific denomination. Like the English halfpence and French sous, all were known simply as "coppers." On the other hand, the Fugio cents struck under the authority of Congress and the state of Massachusetts cents and half cents bore the new decimal cent denominations.

There was virtually no coordination between Federal and State activities in coinage. For instance, the Federal ordinance of Oct. 16, 1786, permitted the state-franchised coppers to pass current at 175 ½ grains to the cent. But, with the exception of Massachusetts, no state even attempted to conform to this provision, nor did any state change or suspend mint operations after September 1, 1787, as required by the ordinance.

During all this time, foreign coins of various kinds continued to pour into the country, and numerous coppers were struck in Birmingham, England, expressly for U.S. consumption. Since private coinage was not prohibited under federal law, the greatest value a State franchise held was in the monopoly it conferred on the private coiners.

New Hampshire

Although the state of New Hampshire authorized a copper coinage on June 28, 1776, the project does not seem to have materialized. A number of pieces, presumably patterns, exist, and are cast rather than struck; and since these have turned up in accumulations as well as in collections, there seems to be no reason to doubt their authenticity. However, we have grave doubts concerning the authenticity of the struck and engraved "patterns," and have omitted them from the present listing.

New Hampshire coinage continued

1776 copper

C.176. 1776 Copper: Pine tree and harp, all cast. Seven-nine known. Garrett VG, ex Stickney, 154.9 grains, $13,000.

Massachusetts

Traditional assignment of the Massachusetts patterns to Paul Revere is buttressed by the similarity of the pieces to Revere's known engraving. Moreover, Revere is the only engraver who, at the time, expressed an interest in the seated Liberty device shown on all of these coins. But whether the patterns were struck in an official capacity, or a personal whim, is unknown. The I C L M on the penny probably stands for 1 CENT LAWFUL MONEY, if we understand CENT to mean 1/100th part of a Spanish dollar. Such a decimalized copper coinage was then under consideration by the Continental Congress.

On Oct. 17, 1786, after examining various bids from persons wishing to obtain a private coinage franchise, the Commonwealth of Massachusetts decided to establish its own Mint. Accordingly, in May 1787, Capt. Joshua Wetherle, a Boston goldsmith, was appointed Mint master and authorized to build all the necessary works.

An act of June 27, 1787, designated the devices for the coins. Unlike the "coppers" struck in Connecticut, Vermont and New Jersey, the Massachusetts coins were specified as cents and half cents, and are the first U.S. coins bearing these denominations.

Dies for the coinage were initially engraved by Joseph Calender, who learned his craft under Paul Revere, then by Jacob Perkins who worked for more reasonable pay. The Perkins' dies can be easily distinguished by his peculiar "S" punch which was closed like an "8".

PATTERNS

C.177. 1776 Penny: Pine Tree, seated Liberty, LIBERTY AND VIRTUE. Unique, Massachusetts Historical Society coll.

C.178. 1776 Penny.: Standing Indian, seated Liberty. ANS coll., worn and holed.

1776 halfpenny pattern, "Janus"
(Bowers & Merena)

C.179. 1776 Halfpenny: Janus design of three heads, Goddess Liberty. Unique. Garrett Fine-12, ex Matthew Stickney, $40,000.

DIES BY CALLENDER
1787 Massachusetts Issues:

1787 cent, "Transposed Arrows"
(Bowers & Merena)

C.180. 1787 Cent: Transposed Arrows in eagle's right talon (viewer's left), four leaves. Perhaps six known. (Ryder 2a-F) Roper ex Essex Institute VF, $7,700.

1787 cent

C.181. 1787 Cent: Rev. arrows on viewer's right, four leaves, die break at eagle's head gives name the "Horned Eagle." (Ryder 2b-A). ST 3/94, Ch. Unc., $1,300; Eliasberg 5/96 MS-64 $6,600.

1787 cent (Stack's)

C.182. 1787 Cent: Arrows in left talon, die defect places small pellet before COMMON, olive branch with five leaves. Taylor (R 3-G) AU-55, $1,320; ST Starr 1/93, Unc., $2,800; Eliasberg 5/96 (R 4-D) MS-64 $6,710.

1787 cent (Stack's)

C.183. 1787 Cent: No pellet, five leaves. Single or double exergue line, nine vars. Garrett (R 6-G) EF-45, $1,000.

1787 half cent (Stack's)

C.184. 1787 Half Cent: Varieties with close, heavy date; no period after MASSACHUSETTS. Taylor (R 4-B) VF-20, 72.6 grains, $330; (R 4-C) BM 1/90, MS-64, $3,740; Eliasberg 5/96 MS-64 $5,610.

Massachusetts coinage continued

C.185. 1787 Half Cent: Date spaced 17 87, pellet after MASSACHUSETTS. ST 3/94, (R 2-A) Ch. Unc., $1,700; Taylor (R 3-A) VF-30/EF-40, $577.50.

1788 Massachusetts Issues

1788 cent, normal S's (Stack's)

C.186. 1788 Cent: Normal "S's" period after MASSACHUSETTS, many varieties. ST 1/93 (R 7-M) Ch. AU, $1,800.

C.187. 1788 Cent: No pellet after MASSACHUSETTS. Roper (R 13-N) Unc., $2,420; ST 3/94 (R 6-N) Ch. AU, $1,800.

DIES BY PERKINS

1788 cent, closed S's (Stack's)

C.188. 1788 Cent: Tightly closed "S's" resemble "8's". Many vars. Roper (R 1-D) Choice AU, $1,540; Taylor (R 11-F) MS-60, $2,860; Roper (R 13-N) Unc., $2,420.

1788 half cent (Stack's)

C.189. 1788 Half Cent: Two vars., one with small leaves and divided date 1 78 8. Taylor (R 1-A) VF-30, $440; Garrett (R 1-B) MS-65, $4,500.

UNIDENTIFIED DIE SINKER

1787 cent (Bowers & Merena)

C.190. 1787 Cent: As preceding, open "S's" but distinctly fat, dumpy Indian, six leaves.;Taylor (R 5-I) VF-30, $3,740.

Vermont

Although Vermont is considered the first state to have issued its own copper coinage, it was not then a state under the Articles of Confederation. On June 15, 1785, the Vermont Assembly granted to Reuben Harmon Jr. of Rupert the exclusive right of coinage for two years beginning July 1, 1785. The act directed that each of the coins contain 160 grains pure copper, but fixed no limit to the amount that could be struck, nor even required Harmon to pay any royalty to the state. Moreover, on Oct. 27, the act was amended to reduce the weight of the copper to only 111 grains.

Harmon, who probably had little knowledge of coinage, is believed to have formed a partnership with William Coley and Daniel Van Vorhis, New York City goldsmiths, and Elias Jackson of Connecticut. On October 24, 1786, the state renewed their franchise for a period of eight years.

The first designs the Assembly ordered bore a radiant sun rising over the Green Mountains, with all-seeing eye in glory of rays closely copied from the Nova Constellatio, but proclaiming Vermont the "Fourteenth Star." The second issue was copied from a Connecticut copper with AUCTORI. VERMON and seated Liberty with legend INDE: ET: LIB. The change made the coins more closely resemble English halfpence, which formed the bulk of coppers in circulation.

In order to avoid loss of time (and thus profit), the Vermont group soon afterward obtained the use of a pair of worn-out Connecticut device punches from William Buel, son of Abel Buel, who was then the principal die sinker for a similar Connecticut coining company. Nevertheless, the Vermont coiners seemed to have been unable to continue making their own dies, with the result that on June 7, 1787, they entered into a desperate contract with a private New York Mint at Machin's Mill, to whom they relinquished the majority of their franchise.

James Atlee, who was associated with the latter group, is believed by some numismatists to have provided the remaining dies for the Vermont coinage. Evidence for Atlee's involvement in this and various other independence-era coinage is punch-linkage through the famous broken 'A' punch. This evidence is not wholly conclusive, since commercial punches were produced in some quantity, and a defective 'A' master punch would have produced similarly defective copies. RR numbers refer to the catalog of Hillyer Ryder, Br. numbers are those assigned in the modern study of the series by Kenneth Bressett.

LANDSCAPE OR GREEN MOUNTAINS COPPERS

1785 copper, "VERMONTS" (Stack's)

C.191. 1785 Copper: "Landscape," Sun over Green Mountains, All-seeing eye. VERMONTS, two vars. Roper (Ryder 2, Bressett 1-A) EF, $4,400; Garrett (RR-3, Br.2-B) MS-60, $6,800; Taylor (RR-3, Br.2-B) AU-50, $5,720; Eliasberg 5/96 EF-40 $7,480.

Vermont coinage continued

1785 copper, "VERMONTIS" (Stack's)

C.192. 1785 Copper: Similar to last, VERMONTIS legend. (RR-4, Br.3-C) Norweb VF-20, $1,540; Taylor EF-45, $1,760.

C.193. 1785 Copper: Sun rises to viewers left, VERMONTIS. Probably a circulating counterfeit. (RR-5) struck copper, Norweb VG-10, 122.6 grains, $37,500; cast copper, VG-8, 76.2 grains, $7,040; ST Starr 1/93, AG, $3,400; Eliasberg 5/96 EF-40 $4,020.

1786 copper, "VERMONTENSIUM" (Stack's)

C.194. 1786 Copper: VERMONTENSIUM, three vars. Taylor (RR-6, Br.4-D) VF-30, $1,320; Norweb (RR-7) AU-50, $3,960; Eliasberg 5/96 MS-60 $9,680.

1786 copper, "Baby Head"

C.195. 1786 Copper: Baby head right, Liberty seated with wheat on shield. Taylor (RR-9, Br.7-F) VF-30, grains $3,300; ST 9/93, EF, $3,300.

All of the above are generally found struck on defective flans.

VERMONT DIES FROM PUNCHES BY ABEL BUEL

1786 copper

C.196. 1786 Copper: Mailed bust left in Connecticut style. Roper (RR-10, Br.8-G) VF, $687; BM 11/92 ex 1914 ANS exhibition, VF-35, $1,100.

Vermont coinage continued

1787 copper (Bowers & Merena)

C.197. 1787 Copper: Mailed bust left, always shows immense die break at date. BR 7/81 (RR-15, Br.9-I) $6,995.; BM 11/91, F-15/VF-20, $8,525,

VERMONT DIES ATTRIBUTED TO JAMES ATLEE

1787 copper (Stack's)

C.198. 1787 Copper: Mailed bust resembling George III right, seated Britannia with legend INDE ET LIB. Many overstruck on Nova Constellatio coppers. (RR-12, Br.11-K) BM 11/91, VF-35, $1,980; Eliasberg 5/96 MS-60 $7,920.

1788 copper (Stack's)

C.199. 1788 Copper: Similar bust, INDE ET LIB. Many varieties; scarce with double exergue line, rare with both stars and crosses in legends (RR-28, Br.21-U) Taylor (RR-29) VF-30, $2,240; ST 12/94, Fine, $3,000.

VERMONT DIES ATTRIBUTED TO MACHIN'S MILL

1787 copper (Stack's)

C.200. 1787 Copper: Obv. George III-style "bastard head" right, VERMON AUCTORI. Rev. Seated Britannia. Researcher Gary Trudgen notes that this crude reverse is the product of a very worn die rather than any attempt at artificial aging as sometimes seen in evasion coppers. Two vars. Taylor (RR-13, Br.17-V) AU-50, $1,320. Norweb (RR-27) EF-40, $1,100.

C.201. 1787 Copper: Very crude George III-style "standard head" right. Rev. Crudely like preceding, but Reversed C in AUCTORI, Norweb (RR-30, Br.23-S) F-20, $13,200; BM 11/91, Fine-15/VF-20, $6,325.

Vermont coinage continued

1788 copper (Stack's)

C.202. 1788 Copper: Mailed bust r., ET LIB INDE. extremely rare without bisecting break. Most struck over counterfeit Irish halfpence; over Nova Constellatio copper, Norweb (RR-18, Br.19-X) EF-40, 122 grains, $9,350.

C.203. 1787 Copper: Obv. George III bust right, GEORGIVS. III. REX. Rev. Seated Britannia. (RR-1. Br.26-Z) Rev. of RR-29, rare, always crude planchet and strike. ST 9/93, AG, $1,150.

1787 copper (Bowers & Merena)

C.204. 1787 Copper: Obv. Crude "standard" bust, AUCTORI VERMON. Rev. IMMUNE COLUMBIA. Always crude, weakly struck and defective. (RR-, Br.-) Garrett VG-8, $3,400; Roper Fine, $1,540.

Connecticut

With more than 300 major varieties, the state coinage of Connecticut is unrivaled for its sheer bulk. The original contractors for the coinage were Samuel Bishop, James Hillhouse, John Goodrich, and Joseph Hopkins, who received their franchise on Oct. 20, 1785. According to the agreement, the coins were to weigh 144 grains each, and five percent of the emission was to be paid into the state treasury.

On Nov. 12, 1785, the contractors, together with four new partners, formed the Company for Coining Coppers. This company reorganized more than once, and in the end of the majority stockholder emerged as James Jarvis, whose father-in-law, Jeremiah Platt, superintended the coinage at a Mint in New Haven. According to an official report, the Mint ceased operations in mid-1787, but this was only a temporary shut-down due to lack of copper. It is clear from extant coins that the operations continued well into 1788.

The principal die sinkers for the Connecticut coinage was probably Abel Buel. James Atlee was long believed to have cut the dies for this series identified by the oft-cited defective 'A' punch discussed under Vermont above. As stated earlier, this evidence is regarded today as less than conclusive. The identity of the engravers of the 1785 mailed bust right and African Head dies has not been determined. Abel Buel can be assigned the 1785 and 1786 dies with mailed bust left and all those with draped bust left. James Atlee has traditionally been assigned all the mailed busts right, the 1787-8 mailed bust left, and the 1788 mailed busts right.

The Hercules Head die was made from the regular 1786 mailed bust left hub, but afterward heavily recut. The Muttonhead, or large mailed bust right of 1787, is stylistically unique, and is undoubtedly a contemporary counterfeit. The 1787 Horned Bust and Laughing Head varieties were long assigned to the Morristown, New Jersey,

Mint of Walter Mould on somewhat shaky punch-linkage.

There are hundreds of varieties and sub-varieties of Connecticut coppers. Only the major types are listed here. M numbers refer to Henry C. Miller's definitive catalog of this remarkable state copper coinage. Collectors should note that pieces found bearing white ink numbers in obverse fields are not defaced, but were so inscribed by Miller himself and perhaps one other contemporary during early research into this complex series.

1785 Connecticut Issues

1785 copper

C.205. 1785 Copper: Mailed bust right, vars. show colons or pellets between words, struck by Company for Coining Coppers, as all regular issues of this date. M 4.1-F.4, Garrett EF-AU, $2,250. M.4.4-D countermarked 'DCP' ST 3/94, Fine, $2,100. M 6.2-F.1, Taylor EF-45, $1,045.

1785 copper (Bowers & Merena)

C.206. 1785 Copper: Mailed Bust right, rev. INDE: ET LIR:. M.3.1-L, Miller plate coin, ST 6/94, Fine, $1,100. M 3.4-F.2, Steinberg EF, $2,970. M.6.5-M, ST 9/93, VF, $1,700.

1785 copper (Bowers & Merena)

C.207. 1785 Copper: Mailed bust left, several vars. in M-7 series. M 7.1-D, Garrett AU, $2,400. M 7.2-D, Taylor VF-20, $1,100; BM 5/92, Fine-15, $1,870.

1785 copper, "African Head" (Stack's)

C.208. 1785 Copper: African Head, maker unknown, two vars., TM.4.1-F.4, BM 11/91, EF-45/AU-50, $935; Taylor (M 4.2-4) AU-50, $1,870. 4.2-F-6.

1786 Connecticut Issues

C.209. 1786 Copper: Mailed bust right, INDE ET LIB. Taylor (M 1-A) VF-30 to EF-40, $330.

1786 copper (Bowers & Merena)

C.210. 1786 Copper: Mailed bust right ETLIB INDE, same maker. M 2.1-A, ST 9/93, EF, $2,000.

1786 copper (Bowers & Merena)

C.211. 1786 Copper: Large mailed bust right, same maker. M 3-D.1, Garrett VF-EF, $1,900.

1786 copper (Bowers & Merena)

C.212. 1786 Copper: Mailed bust left, several vars., all following of this type were struck by Company for Coining Coppers. M 5.2-I, Garrett AU-Unc, $1,500; M.5.7-O.2, ST 9/93, VF, $1,100.

1786 copper (Bowers & Merena)

C.213. 1786 Copper: Hercules Head, M 5.3-B.2, Garrett AU, $3,700. M.5.3-N, BM 11/94, VF-30, $467.

1786 copper, "Hercules Head" (Bowers & Merena)

1786 copper (Bowers & Merena)

C.214. 1786 Copper: Draped bust left. M 5.6-M, Garrett Unc., $2,200. M 5.9-Q, Norweb AU-50, $1,760. M 5.10-L, Norweb EF-45, $1,320. M.5.11-R, ST 9/13, VF, $2,100; ST 6/94, VF, $1,100.

1787 Connecticut Issues

1787 copper (Bowers & Merena)

C.215. **1787 Copper:** Small mailed bust right, INDE ETLIB. M 1.1-VV, Norweb without grade, $330.

C.216. **1787 Copper:** Similar obv., ET LIB INDE, same remarks. M 1.1-A, Taylor VF-30 to EF-40, $302.50.

C.217. **1787 Copper:** Medium mailed bust right. Rev. Liberty seated to right, ET LIB INDE. M 1.1.4-WW, two known, Norweb VF, $30,800.

1787 copper (Bowers & Merena)

C.218. **1787 Copper:** Muttonhead, large mailed bust right, INDE ET LIB, uncertain Mint, possibly in New York. M 1.2-C, Garrett VF, $1,100; ST 9/94, VF, $950.

1787 copper (Bowers & Merena)

C.219. **1787 Copper:** Similar obv., later var. with bare-breasted Liberty, reground die state of M 1.2-C, Taylor VF-20/30, $275.

C.220. **1787 Copper:** "Bradford" var. of Muttonhead, INDE ET.LIB. M 1.2-mm, four known. Taylor VF-20, $4,400; BM 11/90, VG-8, $3,520..

C.221. **1787/1887 Copper:** Similar obv., CONNECT, IND ET LIB. M 15-F, Taylor EF-40, $275.

1787/1887 copper (Bowers & Merena)

C.222. **1787/1887 Copper:** Mailed bust l., CONNEC, dot inside C; IND DE ET LIB. This and similar coins are attributed to Benjamin Buell, most show cinquefoils as stops. M 12-Q, Taylor AU-50, $1,760.

Connecticut coinage continued

1787 copper (Bowers & Merena)

C.223. 1787/1877 Copper: Similar obv., IN DE ET LIB. M 5-P, Norweb Fine-12, $935.
C.224. 1787 Copper: Similar obv., INDE ET LIB, pheons or broadarrows as stops. M 14-H, Garrett AU, $2,700.
C.225. 1787 Copper: Similar obv., CONNECT, INDE ET LIB. M 15-F, Taylor EF-40, $275.
C.226. 1787 Copper: Similar obv., INDL ET LIB, the "Fatal Break," heavy die break obscures LIB. M 15-S, Taylor VG-8, $352.50.
C.227. 1787 Copper: Similar obv., CONNEC, IN DE ET LIB. M 5-P, Garrett EF, $300.

1787 copper, "Laughing Head"
(Stack's)

C.228. 1787 Copper: Laughing Head left. Distinctive round laureate features with pointed nose, pursed mouth. Traditionally attributed to Walter Mould. Two vars. M 6.1-M, Garrett Choice Unc., $8,000.
C.229. 1787 Copper: Smiling or Simple Head left. M 6.2-M, Garrett Choice AU, $2,500.

1787 copper, "Horned Bust" (Stack's)

C.230. 1787 Copper: Mailed Bust left, Horned Bust var., late state of M 4-L with massive die break from shoulder, same Mint. Roper Choice AU, $660; ST/94, Ch. EF, $500.

1787 copper, "Hercules Head"
(Bowers & Merena)

C.231. 1787 Copper: Hercules Head, Company for Coining Coppers. M 7-I, Roper VF, $1,100.
C.232. 1787 Copper: Draped bust l., AUCTORI CONNEC., INDE ET LIB. Struck with numerous similar vars. by Company for Coining Coppers, dozens of varieties.
C.233. 1787 Copper: Similar, * AUCTORI:x x CONNEC: x INDE: x x X ETLIB: M 25-b, Norweb AU-Unc., $3,520.

Connecticut coinage continued

1787 copper (Stack's)

C.234. 1787 Copper: Similar, AUCTORI: * *CONNEC:, * INDE * * * ET.LIB* M 28-M, ST Starr 1/93, AU, $1,250.

C.235. 1787 Copper: Similar, * AUCTORI.* * CONNEC.*, Rev. *INDE. *** * ET LIB. M.32.2-X.1, ST 9/94, EF, $1,000. M 32.2-X.4, Taylor EF-45 to AU-50, $1,045.

C.236. 1787 Copper: Similar, rev. INDE ETLIR. M 33.17-gg.2, Taylor Fine-15, $110.

C.237. 1787 Copper: Similar obv., AUCTORI, INDE ETIIB, same maker. M 26-kk, Norweb VF-30, $302.

1787 copper (Bowers & Merena)

C.238. 1787 Copper: Draped bust l., FNDE ET LIB. This Jarvis and Co. engraver's blunder records the embezzling of the Federal copper intended for Fugio coinage: The engraver started a Connecticut die, absent-mindedly starting to punch FUGIO and getting as far as the letters FU before discovering his error. This coin is from the Federal copper stolen by Jarvis' father-in-law Samuel Broome to strike more profitable, light weight Connecticut coppers. M 32.5-aa, Taylor VF-30, $302.

C.239. 1787 Copper: Similar, Snipe Nose var., horizontal die break through nose. M 33.28-Z.16, Roper AU, $550.

C.240. 1787 Copper: Similar obv., CONNFC, same maker. M 33.37-Z.9, Garrett AU, $1,900.

C.241. 1787 Copper: Similar obv., AUCIORI, same maker. M 38-GG, Roper Choice EF, $330.

C.242. 1787 Copper: Similar obv., AUCTOBI, same maker. M 39-h.l, Taylor VF-20, $247; M.39.1-h.1, ST 6/94, AU, $3,400.

C.243. 1787 Copper: Similar obv., AUCTOPI, ETLIB, same maker. M 42-o, Taylor VG-8, four known, $330.

C.244. 1787 Copper: Similar., AUCTOPI, INDE ETIIB, same maker. M 41-ii, ST 9/94, Unc., $4,400.

C.245. 1787 Copper: Mailed Bust right. M 52-G.1, Taylor Fine-12/VF-20, $1,320.

1788 Connecticut Issues

1788 copper (Bowers & Merena)

C.246. 1788 Copper: Small Mailed bust right, Britannia std. with Union shield, struck at Machin's Mills. M 1-l, ST 3/94, AG, $1,400; ST 6/94, Fine, $1,700.

C.247. 1788 Copper: Mailed bust right with heavy features, five-pointed star stops, INDE ET LIB. M 2-D, Garrett EF-AU, $650; Eliasberg 5/96 6-pointed star stops, Miller 3-B.1 Eliasberg 5/96 MS-63 $9,020.

C.248. 1788 Copper: Mailed bust right, quatrefoil stops. M 4.1-B.1, Garrett EF, $1,900; M.4.1-K, ST 6/94, EF, $900.

Connecticut coinage continued

1788 copper, "Boxer Head"
(Bowers & Merena)

C.249. 1788 Copper: Boxer Head, six-pointed star stops, B's from R and L punches, attributed to Machin's Mills. M 6-H, Taylor EF-40, $715.

1788 copper (Bowers & Merena)

C.250. 1788 Copper: Mailed bust left, CONNLC, INDE * ET LIB *, 8's in date are S's, style of Benjamin Buell. M-13-A.1, Garrett AU, $1,000.

1788 copper (Stack's)

C.251. 1788 Copper: Draped bust left, struck by Jarvis & Co., * INDE. ET* * LIB. M 15.1-L.1, Taylor MS-60, $2,420. Rev. IN DE ETLIB. M 16.3-N, ST 6/94, EF, $1,300.

C.252. 1788 Copper: Draped bust left, CONNLC, INDE ET LIB, Struck by Jarvis & Co. M 17-Q, Roper Fine, $198.

New Jersey

Through the influence of Revolutionary War Gen. Matthias Ogden, the State of New Jersey on June 1, 1786, granted the exclusive right to strike copper coins to Walter Mould, Thomas Goadsby and Albion Cox. This act obligated the contractors to coin 3 million coppers (each weighing 150 grains) within two years, and for this privilege to pay 10 percent of the coins into the state treasury.

The coiners leased the mill of New Jersey Assemblyman Daniel Marsh for use as their Mint. This mill stood on the east side of what is now St. George's Ave. in Rahway, then part of Elizabeth Town. Gen. Ogden, another member of the New Jersey legislature, stood surety for Mould and Cox. Mould was initially a key member of the team, apparently claiming prior experience in British private Mints. His associates did not know that the prominent British *Gentleman's Magazine* had reported the 1776 arrest of Mould and his wife for counterfeiting.

On Nov. 17, 1786, Goadsby and Cox petitioned the legislature to permit them to coin independently of the uncooperative Mould who, they said, took no part in erecting the necessary works, and refused to post a bond with them. The severance was granted on the 22nd, and Mould was permitted to coin one-third of the original authorization separately. He moved to Morristown, in March 1787, and soon began operations on the property of John Clive Symmes, Chief Justice of the state of New Jersey. The agile Mould had convinced prominent local gentry that there was a fortune to be made coining coppers.

Legal troubles continued in January, 1788, when Cox sued Goadsby for return of Mint machinery which he claimed Goadsby had removed. As of June, all of the machinery was in the custody of the long-suffering Ogden, now appointed trustee pending the report of referees in the Cox-Goadsby quarrel. Directed by Governor Livingston to "perfect the contract" by finishing the coinage of two million pieces, the hardworking Ogden took the machinery to his home in Elizabeth Town, where he boosted production by overstriking quantities of lightweight, worn coppers with New Jersey dies.

To meet his need for operating capital, Mould resorted to striking unauthorized "Connecticut" coppers, including the distinctive Laughing Head and Horned Bust varieties. He finally defaulted on his New Jersey coinage contract and fled to the remote Ohio frontier in mid-1788, dying there in the following year. His widow pursued a young army officer to the frontier post of Losantiville, soon to be renamed Cincinnati by Gen. Arthur St. Clair.

Identification of die sinkers and assigning specific issues to specific Mints has been hampered by earlier researchers' often careless attempts to tie pieces to well-known names who may have had no New Jersey involvement. Such work by Don Taxay and the late Walter Breen has added materially to this confusion. At present, more scientific, in-depth research is under way by such researchers as P. Scott Rubin, Michael J. Hodder and others to correct many widely accepted but dubious interpretations.

There are hundreds of varieties and sub-varieties of the three dates of New Jersey copper coinage. Only major types are listed here. M numbers refer to the definitive catalog by Dr. Edward Maris.

1786 copper (Bowers & Merena)

C.253. 1786 Copper: Small horse's head; date below plow beam. Maris 7-C, Unique; M 7-E, Norweb VF-30, 150 grains, $41,800. M 8-F, four known, Garrett EF, 16.7 grains, $52,000.

C.254. 1786 Copper: Larger horse's head; date in exergue. No coulter (plow blade), curved beam, bold saw tooth borders. M 9-G, Taylor VF-30, $7.260. M 12-I, 22-P.

1786 copper (Stack's)

C.255. 1786 Copper: Horse with erect head, short snout; coulter and curved beam; slanting 1 in date, the "Drunken Die-Cutter's obv.," M 19-M, Garrett EF, $1,200. 20-N, Garrett EF, $2,500.

New Jersey coinage continued

The following show horse's head more erect than previously, and with longer snout than last, mane more neatly combed. All have coulter.

1786 copper (Stack's)

C.256. 1786 Copper: Curved beam. M 21-N, Garrett Unc., $13,000. M.21.R, BM 11/91, VG-6/8, $2,200; M 23.R, BM 3/92, MS-62, $5,820; M 24-P, Garrett AU, $4,000; M.24-R, VF-30, $1,265.

1786 copper, "Bridle" (Stack's)

C.257. 1786 Copper: Curved beam, "bridle" obv. with horizontal die crack below snout, actually die state of Maris obv. 18. M 18-J, Garrett AU, $4,400; M 18-M, Taylor MS-60-63, $6,380.

1786 copper (Stack's)

C.258. 1786 Copper: Straight beam, no knobs to plow handles. Maris obvs. 13-16, 25-26. M 15-L, Garrett Choice AU, $3,500. M 15-u, BM 3/92, VF-35/EF-40, $6,050. M 16-L, Garrett Unc., $8,500; Miller 15-T Eliasberg 5/96 MS-63 $36,300.

C.259. 1787 Copper: Straight beam, no knobs to plow handles. M 28-S, Garrett Choice Unc., $22,000. M 31-L, Garrett AU, $1,200.

1787 copper (Stack's)

C.260. 1787 Copper: Straight beam, knobs to plow handles. Maris obvs. 27, 29, 30, 32, 55. M 29-L. Norweb AU-50, $7,480. Includes two blundered dies: M 55-m, BUS over BSS, Garrett AU, $2,800. M.55-n, BM 3/92, AU-50, $2,009; M 27-S, CAESA over CAESR, Garrett EF, $2,500, same piece BM 3/92, EF-45, $4,840.

New Jersey coinage continued

1787 copper (Stack's)

C.261. 1787 Copper: Curved beam, no knobs to plow handles. M 37-Y, Garrett EF, $1,000. 39, 41-48, 68. M 43-d, Garrett Unc. $9,500. M 48-g, Norweb MS-60, $24,200; Miller 52.i Eliasberg 5/96 MS-62 $13,740.

C.262. 1787 Copper: Goiter Head, Maris' "Goiter" obv. Actually a die defect var., M 37-f, j, x. M 37-f, Garrett EF, $2,100; Taylor EF-45, $1,320. ST Starr M.37-X, Ch. Fine, $3,400; BM 3/92, Fine-15/VF-20, $3,080.

1786 copper (Bowers & Merena)

C.263. 1786 Copper: Coulter, curved beam, sprigs under shield. M 53-j, Garrett AU, $1,800.

1787 copper

C.264. 1787 Copper: Sprigs under head and shield. M 62-q, Garrett Choice Unc., $9,500. M.62.r, BM 3/92, Fine-12, $1,760. M 63-s, Norweb MS-60, $5,720.

Closely related to this 'family' of Maris numbers is the newly discovered Maris 62-1/2-r, a presently unique coin with bold raised-letter signature 'WM' of Walter Mould in place of the ordinary sprigs below the horse's head. This dramatic discovery, which had been publicized by Boston dealer John Higgins, measures 31.3mm, weighing 162 grains and is in slightly granular Fine with sharpness of VF. It was described in a *Coin World* article of 5/2/94 by Michael J. Hodder, who reported its finding in an old New England collection.

1787 copper (Stack's)

C.265. 1787 Copper: Without sprigs on either side. M 6-C, Garrett AU, $2,800. M 6-D, 59-o, 64-t. M 64-u. M.59.0, BM 11/91, VF-20, $3,080.

New Jersey coinage continued

1787 copper, "PLURIBS" (Stack's)

C.266. 1787 Copper: Sprigs under head and shield. Misspelling PLURIBS. M 60-P, Garrett AU, $3,600. M 61-p, BM 3/92, AU-55, $5,280.

1788 copper (Bowers & Merena)

C.267. 1788 Copper: Without sprigs on either side. M.65-u, Taylor EF, $660, Norweb VF-30, $742.50.

1788 copper (Bowers & Merena)

C.268. 1788 Copper: Horse with braided or plaited mane, unusually fine style. Six pointed stars as obv. stops. M 66-u, three known, Garrett VF-EF, $3,400.

1788 copper (Bowers & Merena)

C.269. 1788 Copper: Same obv., rev. with sprigs below shield. M 66-v, Taylor EF-45 to AU-50, $5280.

1788 copper (Bowers & Merena)

C.270. 1788 Copper: Obv. similar to last, but horse with neatly curled mane. Same rev. M 67-v, ST Starr , 1/93, AU, $2,500; Norweb AU-55, $1,800.

HORSE'S HEAD LEFT NEW JERSEY COINAGE

1788 copper, "Head Left" (Stack's)

C.271. 1788 Copper: Horse's head left, complex open-work plow, small shield. M 49-f, Garrett VF, $1,100.

C.272. 1788 Copper: Similar head left, tall open-work plow, large shield. M 50-f, BM 3/92 ex Ellsworth, MS63, $39,600; M 51-g, Garrett EF, $5,100.

"RUNNING FOX" OR "RUNNING HORSE" PRIVY MARK

1788 copper, "Running Fox or Horse"
(Bowers & Merena)

C.273. 1788 Copper: Drooping head right, straight beam, quatrefoil stops, ornate sprigs below shield. Tiny running fox or horse appears at lower left border, probably the privy mark of a still-unidentified die cutter. M 75-bb, Taylor EF-45-AU-50, $7,700. M 77-dd, Garrett AU, $6,250; Eliasberg 5/96 EF-45 $7,040.

C.274. 1788 Copper: Coulter and swingletree weak, invisible on most. M 74-bb appears to be coulterless due to a die defect, TBM 11/91, VF-35/EF-40, $3,960.

C.275. 1788 Copper: Similar to last, but small, running fox is at lower right border. M 76-cc, four known, Garrett VF, $15,000.; BM 3/92, VF-30, $14,400.

ELIZABETH TOWN MINT NEW JERSEY COINAGE

Virtually all Elizabeth Town coins were overstruck on lightweight coppers purchased at heavy discount by Gen. Ogden.

1786 copper (Bowers & Merena)

C.276. 1786 Copper: Straight beam, knobs to handles, rarely struck on normal planchet, commoner as overstrike. M 17-K, BM 11/93, EF-40, $1,430.

C.277. 1787 Copper: Small, delicate Filly Head with huge upright ears. M 36-J. Garrett EF-AU, $9,000; Taylor Fine-12, $2,090.

C.278. 1787 Copper: Smallest horse head, sprigs under small shield. M 38-b., BM 3/92 AU-50/55, $7,150.

C.279. 1787 Copper: Back-dated, unusually upright horse with erect posture, straight beam. M 17-J, Norweb VF-20, $154. Dies brought over from Rahway as in the case of the following.

C.280. 1786 Copper: Same obv., back-dated and probably struck with preceding, sprig below shield. M 17-b, BM 11/91, AU-55/58, $2,090.

PLAITED MANES NEW JERSEY COINAGE

1787 copper, "Deer Head" (Bowers & Merena)

C.281. **1787 Copper:** "Deer Head," horse with plaited mane, thick jowl and chest, sprig below. No obv. punctuation, no sprig below shield. M 34-J, Garrett AU, $2,388. M 35-J, BM 3/92, VG-8, $1,760.

C.282. **1787 Copper:** No obv. punctuation, sprig below shield. M 34-V, Taylor Fine-12/VG-08, $550. M 35-W, 40-b are extremely rare. M40-b, BM 11/91, VF-20/25, $2,860..

C.283. **1787 Copper:** Crude planchets and strike, quatrefoil before obv. legend. M 70-x, Garrett About Fine, $4,300; Taylor overstruck on Machin's Mills imitation British halfpenny, Fine-12, $3,080.

C.284. **1787 Copper:** Quatrefoil after obv. legend. M 71-y. Garrett About Fine, $3,000; Taylor overstruck on 1787 Draped Bust Connecticut copper, no grade assignable, $522.50. M.72.z, BM 3/92, EF-40, $3,300.

1787 copper (Bowers & Merena)

C.285. **1787 Copper:** Five-pointed stars after CAESAREA and UNUM. M 73-aa, Taylor overstrike on unidentified Connecticut copper, VF-20, $357.50; BM 3/92, EF-40, $2,420..

1787 copper, "Camel Head" (Stack's)

C.286. **1787 Copper:** Camel Head issues with sharply curved neck. M 56-n, Norweb AU-55, $2,530; another Norweb, overstruck on 1787 Connecticut copper with apparent date "178787," Fine-12, $577.50. M 58-n, BM 3/92, AU-50, $1,980.

C.287. **(1787) Copper:** NOVA CESEREA, crude strike and planchet show only partial design. M 69-w, two known. Garrett Good-VG, $2,700.

1787 copper, "Serpent Head" (Stack's)

C.288. **1787 Copper:** Serpent Head, horse with long serpentine neck and drooping head.. M 54-k, tBM 9/92, AU-55/MS-60, $4,840.

New York

BRASHER AND BAILEY

Although this state never authorized any coinage, private coiners were active nonetheless. John Bailey and his influential goldsmith partner Ephraim Brasher petitioned the legislature for a copper coinage contract on Feb. 11, 1787, but their proposal was rejected. Legislators showed hostility to state and imported coppers, passing an Act of April 20, 1787, to prohibit circulation of light weight pieces.

It is now believed that the EXCELSIOR coppers were engraved by Bailey at the same time as the famous Brasher doubloons. The EXCELSIOR pieces are regarded as patterns, but the NOVA EBORAC pieces were a purely private issue designed to resemble authorized coppers of other states and were struck in large quantities.

In a class all their own are the gold doubloons made by Brasher in 1787, bearing New York and Lima style designs. The New York type shows the sun rising over mountains from the state Arms, with the Federal spread eagle on the reverse. The Lima style coins are an adaptation of the crude cob-type Spanish-colonial design of 1747-50.

All of the doubloons bear Brasher's hallmark, EB in a recessed rectangle, intended for his silver ware. This EB punch was later used as a countermark and is known on a small number of surviving British, Portuguese, and French gold coins and a very few silver coins including a 1799 Draped Bust dollar.

Six New York style doubloons are known with EB on wing, one with this mark on the eagle's breast. A single half doubloon exists in the Josiah K. Lilly collection of the Smithsonian. Two Lima style doubloons are known, the first from J.W. Scott's 1894 Paris collection sale, the second from the Waldo C. Newcomer collection.

Groundless controversy removed these Lima style pieces from a popular guide book in the 1960s, although they were regarded by qualified numismatists as genuine products of Brasher's hand since the 1890s. Before the Garrett sale, numismatist Q. David Bowers and Vice President Richard Zdanis of The Johns Hopkins University took an undoubted New York style doubloon and a Lima style piece to the Bureau of Standards and Applied Physics Laboratory for exhaustive testing.

Tests including X-ray spectrography proved the alloy of both coins and surface characteristics to be identical. Through exacting photo overlay analysis, numismatist John J. Ford Jr. showed that the Lima coin's EB punch was identical to that of the New York pieces, but in an earlier state of wear, proving the Lima style pieces to have been struck before the New York issues.

Although the weight of both types of doubloon approximates the Spanish standard, numismatist Carl W.A. Carlson argued that they were gold strikes of a pattern for copper coinage, possibly presented to legislators considering the Brasher-Bailey contract coinage proposal. No pieces have ever been reported in copper and the weight of the gold coins confirms the intent to circulate as doubloons.

In relatively recent years, cheap cast or pot metal replicas of the Brasher doubloons have been churned out by the thousands. Many of these have a small T to the left of the date, indicating provenance of the Tatham Coin Company of Massachusetts, but absence of the T should not be taken as proof of genuineness. None of these replicas, which in some cases are part of a series of replicas of early coinage, has any collector value.

EXCELSIOR NEW YORK COPPERS

1787 copper (Bowers & Merena)

C.289. 1787 Copper: Obv. New York state arms, eagle on crest facing heraldic left, (viewer's right), state motto EXCELSIOR, ever higher, below. Rev. Federal eagle facing in same direction, arrows in its right claw, on viewer's left, "Transposed Arrows." Legend E PLURIBUS UNUM. Norweb VF-20, $18,700; BM 3/90, EF-40, $5,060.

1787 copper (Bowers & Merena)

C.290. 1787 Copper: As preceding, but eagle on state shield faces viewer's right, olive branch in eagle's right claw, on viewer's left. Garrett VF-20, $5,250; Norweb Fine-15, $2,860.

1787 copper (Stack's)

C.291. 1787 Copper: As preceding, but eagle in state crest now faces heraldic right, viewer's left. Garrett AU-50, $17.500; Norweb VF-35, $8,250; Eliasberg 5/96 VF-35 $9,900.

BRASHER DOUBLOONS

1787 doubloon

C.292. 1787 Doubloon: Obv. Sun over mountains, NOVA EBORACA (New York), COLUMBIA, EXCELSIOR. Rev. Federal eagle facing heraldic right (viewer's left), E PLURIBUS UNUM and date around. EB punch on left wing, six known. Garrett ex Stickney, MS-63, $725,000.

Thousands of cheap replicas of this and the following exist, from a variety of sources. No genuine Brasher doubloons are known in any metal but gold.

C.293. 1787 Doubloon: As preceding, punch on eagle's breast, Unique. Garrett VF, $625,000.

C.294. 1787 Half Doubloon: Discovered by David Proskey, 1928. Eventually to Josiah K. Lilly and Smithsonian, Unique.

New York coinage continued

1787 doubloon

C.295. 1787 Doubloon: Obv. Pillars of Hercules, L.8.V/P.V.A./7.4.2 in three lines at center, tiny BRASHER N.Y. under waves. Rev Cross divides lions of Leon, castles of Castile. The legends are halfway off the flan on both sides, but approximate the Latin coinage titles of King Philip V.; Two known.

NOVA EBORAC

1787 copper (Bowers & Merena)

C.296. 1787 Copper: Small Head, quatrefoil after NOVA. Rev Liberty seated right with New York arms on shield, legend VIRT ET LIB, Virtue and Liberty. Possibly 10 known. Garrett EF-45, $2,400; Eliasberg 5/96 EF-45 $2,090.

1787 copper (Stack's)

C.297. 1787 Copper: Similar obv., medium head, Liberty seated left on rev. Norweb AU-55, $6,160; Eliasberg 5/96 MS-63 $6,600.

1787 copper (Bowers & Merena)

C.298. 1787 Copper: Larger head, no quatrefoil after NOVA, Liberty seated left rev. Possibly 15-18 known. Garrett AU-55, $8,750; Norweb AU-55 to MS-60, $5,720, ST 9/93, VF, $1,300.

1787 copper (Bowers & Merena)

C.299. 1787 Copper: Small head with six-pointed star above, VIRT.ET above seated Liberty left, Dutch free hat on pole in place of normal cap. Possibly 10 known. Norweb Fine-15 to VF-20, $3,960.

OTHER NEW YORK ISSUES — WASHINGTON, NON VI VIRTUTE VICI

1786 copper (Stack's)

C.300. 1786 Copper: Obv. Large Washington bust right, NON VI VIRTUTE VICI. Rev. Seated Justice holding flag on capped pole. Two known. Baker 13a; Eliasberg 5/96 MS-63 $66,000.

C.301. 1786 Copper: Obv. Small Washington head. Rev. similar to preceding, no flag. Baker 13. Garrett EF, $12,000; BM 5/92, VF-35, $7,705.

MACHIN'S MILL

Competing with Brasher and Bailey for a New York state coinage contract was Captain Thomas Machin, whose "Hard Ware Manufactory" near Newburgh employed James Atlee to make high quality patterns for State Assembly consideration. This proposal was no more successful than that of Bailey and Brasher, and most of Machin's output consisted of unauthorized, light weight counterfeit British halfpence.

GEORGE CLINTON, LIBER NATUS COPPERS

1787 copper pattern

C.302. 1787 Copper: Obv. George Clinton bust right. Rev. state arms. Possibly 10 known, Stack's Mass. Hist. Soc. sale, Unc. $34,000, March 1973.

1787 copper pattern (Stack's)

C.303. 1787 Copper: Obv. Standing Indian, LIBER NATUS, LIBERTATEM DEFENDO, Born Free, I defend Liberty. Rev. State arms as preceding. Fewer than 12 known, Garrett EF, $21,000; Stack's Auction '89, Choice VF, $27,500; Eliasberg 5/96 $143,000. An idea of the popularity of this type can be gained from the $3,301 realized on a John A. Bolen struck copy overstruck on an 1821 quarter in BM 5/92.

1787 copper pattern, "Eagle on Globe" (Stack's)

C.304. 1787 Copper: Similar obv. Rev. eagle on globe NEO-EBORACUS, date, EXCELSIOR. Possibly eight known, Garrett AU, $37,000; Brand Unc., $24,200.

MACHIN'S MILL IMITATION HALFPENCE

Many varieties of counterfeit, lightweight halfpence were made at Machin's Mill. Most were struck from shallow dies to look worn as they fell from the press. From a George II piece dated 1747 to George III pieces dated 1771-1788, Machin's products were familiar to thousands of contemporary Americans. Weight and lack of outlines around the crosses on Britannia's shield identify most of Machin's counterfeits.

Nova Constellatio

PATTERNS

One of the major problems facing the new Confederation was the diversity of currencies and rates of exchange among the 13 former colonies. Assistant Superintendent of Finance Gouverneur Morris conceived a coinage that would unify at least 12 of these contending systems. He projected a Unit (with no other name) equal to 1/1440 Spanish milled dollar, equal to a quarter-grain of pure silver as the basis of a new national coinage. A gold coin of 10,000 Units would circulate with silver 1,000, 500 and 100 Units, with copper 8 and 5 Units bringing up the rear.

Benjamin Dudley cut the dies for the five denominations known today. These were the silver 1,000 Units or Mark; two types of 500 Units or Quint; 100 Units or Bit; and the copper five Units which had been presented to the exiled Loyalist Samuel Curwen, rediscovered only in 1977. Another denomination may yet be discovered.

Some numismatists have derided Morris' concept, but it was really a brilliant solution to a complex problem facing the new nation. The symbolism and mottos of this issue included a "new constellation" of 13 stars around the All-Seeing Eye, both a Christian and a Masonic emblem. The reverse motto promised Liberty and Justice, for which the Revolution had been fought.

Charles Thomson, Secretary to Congress, at one time held all of the silver patterns. The mark and the quint were discovered almost a century later by flamboyant Philadelphia coin dealer, Captain John W. Haseltine in a secret compartment of Thomson's desk. Haseltine sold them to Henry S. Adams of Boston. They were later part of the collection of the great bean baker-numismatist Lorin G. Parmelee. These historic rarities were later handled by Samuel Hudson and Henry Chapman, and were ultimately acquired by John Work Garrett. These two coins remained in the Garrett Collection until it was auctioned by Bowers and Ruddy Galleries in 1979.

The finest of the three known bits surfaced in a London pawn shop in the 1880's. It ultimately found its way to Parmelee and Colonel James Ellsworth before rejoining its fellows in the great Garrett Collection. A third example appeared in 1991 in Stack's auction which included Richard Picker colonials. The unique copper five Unit was owned by New Hampshire patriot and Declaration of Independence signer Josiah Bartlett. He gave it to the exiled Loyalist Samuel Curwen, once of Salem, in May 1784. The coin then vanished until it was rediscovered in Paris in 1977. The entire group resides in a famous American collection today.

Nova Constellatio continued

1783 1,000 Units or Mark (Bowers & Merena)

C.305. 1783 1,000 Units or Mark: Obv. NOVA CONSTELLATIO legend, Eye in rays with prominent eyebrow. Rev. Slanted U.S/1000 in circle wreath, LIBERTAS . JUSTITIA legend, Unique. Leaf pattern edge. Garrett prooflike MS-60, $190,000.

1783 500 Units or Quint (Bowers & Merena)

C.306. 1783 500 Units or Quint: Somewhat similar, but different in detail, trefoil at bottom. Rev. Upright U.S and 500 in circle wreath, Unique, edge as preceding. Garrett prooflike MS-65, $165,000.

1783 500 Units or Quint, "Stars at Border" (Bowers & Merena)

C.307. 1783 500 Units or Quint: Obv. Stars at border, rays fill field, no legend. Rev. as preceding. Edge shows faint leaf pattern. Unique, Garrett prooflike AU-55, $55,000.

1783 100 Units or Bit (Bowers & Merena)

C.308. 1783 100 Units or Bit: Obv. Generally similar to first Quint, with legend. Rev. slanted U.S, 100, twin-leaf edge. Garrett prooflike MS-65, $97,599; Stack's 5/91 Picker sale VF, $72,500 .

C.309. 1783 100 Units or Bit: As preceding, plain edge, Unique. Newman coll.

1783 Five Units

C.310. 1783 Five Units: Similar to first Quint, including trefoil. Rev. Upright U.S, slanting ...5. Unique, found by British dealer in Paris, 1977.

(An eight Unit coin may exist, yet to be discovered.)

NOVA CONSTELLATIO COPPERS AND RELATED PIECES

Much confusion characterized the first British newspaper report of the Nova Constellatio coppers, reported in the *London Morning Chronicle* of March 16, 1786, as struck in vast quantities by a Birmingham coiner for a "merchant in New York." The impossibly large numbers supposedly struck from the few dies reported made the story questionable. The merchant was long believed to be New York's Gouverneur Morris, who had worked closely with the silver Nova Constellatio patterns, but his involvement with the coppers is considered unlikely by modern researchers. The 1786 specimens are contemporary imitations, as is one variety dated 1785.

The Nova Constellatio coppers closely follow designs suggested by the Continental Congress and may well been struck with the machinery known to have been built for Robert Morris' proposed Mint described above. If they can be proven to have been struck in Philadelphia, then one shadowy era of American coinage will have been illuminated.

The several New Jersey-type Confederation patterns that follow are probably the work of Gen. Matthias Ogden's Elizabeth Town-Rahway Mint, struck in an attempt to find additional profitable work for his coining press. Ogden is known to have been an unsuccessful bidder for a Federal copper contract coinage in 1786.

1783 copper (Stack's)

C.311. 1783 Copper: Pointed rays. CONSTELLATIO, small U.S. Crosby 2-B, Garrett MS-60, $2,800; Roper Unc., $1,960.
C.312. 1783 Copper: Pointed rays. CONSTELLATIO, large U.S. C 3-B, Roper EF, $577.

1783 copper (Stack's)

C.313. 1783 Copper: Blunt rays. CONSTELATIO. C 3-C, Garrett MS-60, $2,800; Roper EF, $770

1785 copper (Stack's)

C.314. 1785 Copper: Pointed rays. CONSTELLATIO, elegant script US. C 3-B, Garrett MS-60, $2,700. C 5-E, Garrett AU-50, $1,700. C 4-C, Garrett EF-40, $550. C 4-D, Garrett EF-40, $1,400.

Nova Constellatio continued

1785 copper (Stack's)

C.315. 1785 Copper: Blunt rays, CONSTELATIO, die break engulfs several lower leaves in wreath. C 1-B, Roper VF, $210.

C.316. 1785 Copper: Unique contemporary counterfeit, crudely made with only 12 stars and rays. Newman coll.

1786 copper

C.317. 1786 Copper: Contemporary counterfeit. C 1-A, Garrett Fine, $6,500; Norweb Fine-12, $1,760.

CONFEDERATION ERA PATTERNS

1785 copper (Stack's)

C.318. 1785 Copper: Obv. Standing Diana at altar, foot on crown, INIMICA TYRANNIS AMERICA legend. Rev. CONFEDERATIO, large circle of 13 stars in rays. Possibly eight known. Roper Fine, $18,700.

1785 copper (Bowers & Merena)

C.319. 1785 Copper: Similar obv., different die, INIMICA TYRANNIS AMERICANA. Rev. CONFEDERATIO, small circle of stars. This slogan is believed part of a longer version beginning HAEC MANUS... This American Hand is Hostile to the Tyrant, suggested for one of the 13 battle standards suggested for the Continental Army. Garrett VF-EF, $21,000; Roper EF, $17,600. Note: Bolen's struck copies of this coin have a dot in the Y.

Nova Constellatio continued

1785 copper (Bowers & Merena)

C.320. 1785 Copper: Obv. IMMUNE COLUMBIA, seated Justice with scales, liberty cap on pole. Rev. NOVA CONSTELLATIO without extra star and period at border. Garrett Choice EF, $18,500.

C.321. 1785 Silver.: Same, R.E., extremely rare, Garrett VF, $25,000.

C.322. 1785 Silver: Same, P.E., two known, Roper VF, 4,400.

C.323. 1785 Copper: Obv. IMMUNE COLUMBIA. Rev. NOVA CONSTELLATIO, blunt rays. Norweb VF-20, $22,000.

1786 copper

C.324. 1786 Copper: Obv. IMMUNIS COLUMBIA. New Jersey-style shield, E PLURIBUS UNUM. Norweb VF-30, $11,000.

C.325. 1786 Copper: Obv. Washington bust. Rev. Heraldic eagle. Two known. Baker 10.

Copper mule (Stack's)

C.326. Copper: Bust of Washington, 1785 CONFEDERATIO, large stars. Baker 9. Seven known, Steinberg VF, $13,750; ST 5/93, VF, $12,000.

Undated copper mule (Bowers & Merena)

C.327. Copper: Bust of Washington, New Jersey-style shield. Baker 11, Maris 4-C, three known, Garrett EF, $50,000; ST 5/93, holed EF, $10,500.

C.328. Copper: 1785 CONFEDERATIO, large stars/LIBERTAS ET JUSTITIA (unused Nova Constellatio rev.), Boyd coll.

C.329. Copper: 1785 CONFEDERATIO, large stars/1787 Excelsior Heraldic eagle. Two reported, Norweb Fine, $7,480.

C.330. Copper: 1785 CONFEDERATIO, large stars/1786 IMMUNIS COLUMBIA (Wyon's die). Unique, Newman coll.

Nova Constellatio continued

1786 copper mule (Bowers & Merena)

C.331. Copper: 1786 Heraldic eagle/Shield. Maris 5-C, Unique, Garrett Unc., $37,500.

C.332. Silver uniface: Shield rev., struck on square planchet, die in very advanced state. Unique, possibly a much later strike.

IMMUNIS COLUMBIA

C.333. 1786 Copper: Obv. Seated Justice extending scales, capped flag pole in hand, IMMUNIS COLUMBIA. Rev. Spread eagle with pointed crest behind head, arrows in its right talon (viewer's left), E PLURIBUS UNUM. Roper EF, $23,000.

1787 copper pattern (Bowers & Merena)

C.334. 1787 Copper: Obv. Similar to preceding, Rev. Non-crested spread eagle, arrows in left talons (viewer's right). Broad, thick planchet, often shows die crack from beak to wing. Very rare, BM 11/94, EF-40, $1,705.

C.335. 1787 Copper: As preceding, thin, narrow planchet. Eliasberg 5/96 MS-63 $8,580.

Undated copper pattern of 1786 (Bowers & Merena)

C.336. (1786) Copper: Obv. Washington bust, NON VI VIRTUTE VICI. Rev. Shield, E PLURIBUS UNUM, an unused New Jersey -type reverse die. Baker 12. Garrett G-VG, $16,500.

Early Independence Period tokens

JOHN CHALMERS' COINAGE

The first privately issued silver coins in America of which we have any definitive information were made in 1783 by Captain John Chalmers, an Annapolis, Md., gold and silversmith. Chalmers' mint was located at Fleet and Cornhill Streets, and the original building is still standing.

Chalmers' first coin is the rare 1783 shilling, whose 13 linked rings recalls the Continental currency vignette and perhaps the 1776 coinage. His design of two doves fighting for the same worm may refer to interstate wrangling under the Confederation while foreign or domestic enemies symbolized by a serpent wait above.

1783 shilling, "Rings"

C.337. 1783 Shilling: Obv. Clasped hands, "Equal to ONE Shi." Rev. 13 rings, single unifying ring with cap on pole at base, small All-Seeing eye above. Five known, Garrett EF, $75,000; Roper Fine/VF, $24,200.

1783 shilling, "Short Worm"

C.338. 1783 Shilling: Short worm variety. Edge coarsely reeded with a file as on those to follow. ST 9/94, VF, $3,200; BM 1/92, VF-35, $2,090; Eliasberg 5/96 EF-45, $5,720.

1783 shilling, "Long Worm" (Stack's)

C.339. 1783 Shilling: Long worm var, Garrett EF, $2,900; Roper EF, $1,760; ST 9/93, AU, $1,500.

1783 sixpence

C.340. 1783 Sixpence: Small date and legend. ST 12/93, VG/Fine, $1,500.
C.341. 1783 Sixpence: Large date and legend. Robison EF, $3,000; Roper Choice VF, $1,870.

Early Independence Period tokens continued

1783 threepence

C.342. 1783 Threepence: Obv. Clasped hands. Rev. Olive spray in wreath. Garrett AU, $7,500, Oct. 1980; Roper Unc., $5,500; Eliasberg 5/96 MS-60 $9,460.

BAR COPPER

The appearance of this copper in circulation in New York was noted by the *New Jersey Gazette* during December 1785. Although the designs were copied from Continental army buttons, the workmanship of the bar cent would indicate an English origin. Genuine examples show the A passing over the S and a spine at bottom of the second raised bar; many display a tiny die crack near center of reverse.

Undated Bar copper of 1785 (Stack's)

C.343. (1785) Bar Copper: Obv. USA monogram. Rev. 13 raised bars. Beware of John A. Bolen's struck copies in silver purporting to be patterns. More forgeries, struck, cast, and electrotyped, exist of this issue than of any other American coin. Roper Unc., $2,530, BM 5/93 MS-60, $3,080; ST 9/93, broad ovoid planchet, EF, $3,200; Eliasberg 4/97 MS-65 $18,700.

AUCTORI PLEBIS TOKEN

This token was struck by Kempson of Birmingham, England, in imitation of the Draped Bust left Connecticut coppers. "By Authority of the People" is a strangely republican sentiment for Britain, where coinage has always been "By Authority of the King." Some of these may have been imported to America as a speculative venture.

1787 copper (Stack's)

C.344. 1787 Copper: Obv Draped bust left, copied from Jarvis & Co. Connecticut copper, legend AUCTORI. .PLEBIS., By Authority of the People. Rev. Hope seated with anchor, globe and reclining crowned British lion. (Design of Emsworth halfpenny (Dalton & Hammer Hampshire 9-011e). Garrett EF, $900.

STANDISH BARRY THREEPENCE

Struck by 27 year-old Baltimore silversmith Barry and carefully dated July 4, 1790. The portrait might be that of Washington or of Barry himself. The reverse die broke after 12 or more pieces were struck. As a rule, the planchets were too narrow to display the full design. Edges are crudely reeded.

Early Independence Period tokens continued

1790 threepence

C.345. 1790 Threepence: Obv. Clothed male bust left in circle, BALTIMORE TOWN, date around. Rev. STANDISH BARRY in ornate geometric border. ST 12/93, Fine, $4,200; BM 11/90, VF-25/30, $3,960; Eliasberg 5/96 AU $19,800.

ALBANY CHURCH PENNY

On Jan. 9, 1790, an issue of 1,000 coppers was authorized by the trustees of the First Presbyterian Church of Albany. These uniface tokens were to pass at 12 to a shilling, and to be paid out for a shilling to stop the contribution or severely worn, often counterfeit coppers. A script D was added to the die after release of the first tokens, perhaps more clearly symbolizing Penny than the written word for illiterates in the congregation.

C.346. (1790) Penny: CHURCH/(script) Penny. Uniface. Garrett holed VF, $10,000; Roper Fine, $2,530; ST Picker 5/91, VF, $2,600. Unique Canadian token of Montreal jeweler-watchmaker A. Mongeau struck over a Church penny, Unique, Picker VF, $3,300.

Undated penny of 1790, "D" (Stack's)

C.347. (1790) Penny: (Script) D/CHURCH/(Script)Penny. ST 1/92, Fine, $3,000; Picker VF, $4,400.

TRIANGLE (KENTUCKY) TOKEN

This token was probably struck in Birmingham by Westwood from dies by John Gregory Hancock. The plain edge pieces were imported by Eastern merchants and saw heavy circulation. The various lettered-edge tokens were probably struck for the eager British collectors or "virtuosos" of this era. The pyramid was a Masonic symbol; the pieces were once called "Kentucky tokens" because of the incised K on the top star.

Undated halfpenny token of 1792
(Stack's)

C.348. (1792) Halfpenny: P.E. Obv. Hand holds scroll inscribed OUR CAUSE IS JUST, legend UNANIMITY IS THE STRENGTH OF SOCIETY. Rev. E PLURIBUS UNUM surrounds triangle of 15 stars marked with state initials, all in sunburst. Garrett Unc., $1,400; Norweb MS-60, $605.

C.349. (1792) Halfpenny: As preceding but diagonally reeded edge, very rare. Garrett Choice prooflike Unc, $2,300; Norweb MS-60, $1,210.

C.350. (1792) Halfpenny: Edge: PAYABLE IN LANCASTER LONDON OR BRISTOL. Often shows die crack near scroll. Garrett AU, $1,000. Rare with blundered edge LANCASTERNDON.

C.351. (1792) Halfpenny: Edge: PAYABLE AT NUNEATON BEDWORTH OR HINKLEY. Extremely rare, Norweb AU 50, $1,760.

Early Independence Period tokens continued

C.352. (1792) Halfpenny: Edge: PAYABLE AT I. FIELDINGS MANCHESTER. Possibly Unique. Picker AU,
$1,595. Edge PAYABLE AT W. PAKERS OLD BIRMINGHAM WAREHOUSE. Unique., discovery
piece in ST 5/93, VF, $1,800.

C.353. (1792) Halfpenny: Edge: branch with two leaves, Unique, Newman coll.

FRANKLIN PRESS TOKEN

Produced at the height of Britain's token craze, this piece depicts the press at which
young Benjamin Franklin worked while in Lincoln's Fields, London, in 1726. They
were advertising pieces for Watt's Printing Works, but never circulated in America.
The obverse motto SIC ORITUR DOCTRINA SURGETQUE LIBERTAS, (From
the Press) Springs Learning and Liberty, a Franklin-like aphorism.

1794 halfpenny token (Stack's)

C.354. 1794 Halfpenny: P.E. Obv. Printing press (now in Smithsonian), Latin legend. Rev. PAYABLE AT THE
FRANKLIN PRESS LONDON. Garrett Unc., $1,100.

C.355. 1794 Halfpenny: Edge: AN ASYLUM FOR THE OPPRES'D OF ALL NATIONS, Unique.

C.356. 1794 Halfpenny: Edge diagonally reeded, Unique.

TALBOT, ALLUM & LEE TOKENS

Talbot, Allum & Lee, a leader in New York's East India trade, issued these tokens
of good weight and fine design in 1794-95. The pieces were struck by Peter Kempson
of Birmingham, England, and bore the decimal denomination ONE CENT. The rare
first design omitted the name New York, added above the ship on other 1794 varieties. The 1795 pieces were inscribed AT THE STORE OF TALBOT, ALLUM &
LEE NEW YORK on the reverse. In 1795 and 1796, the Philadelphia Mint bought
tens of thousands of these tokens to cut down for use as half cent planchets.

1794 cent token (Stack's)

C.357. 1794 Cent: Obv. Standing Liberty with cap on pole, LIBERTY & COMMERCE legend. Rev. Three-
masted ship right, company name and date. No NEW YORK, very rare. Edge: PAYABLE AT THE
STORE OF. ST 12/93, EF, $3,400.

1794 cent token, "NEW YORK"
(Bowers & Merena)

C.358. 1794 Cent: As preceding, NEW YORK over ship. Garrett Unc., $2,100.

Early Independence Period tokens continued

C.359. 1794 Cent: Plain edge, heavy and light planchets, possibly three each of thick and thin vars. Picker thick, VF, 157.3 grains, $632.

1795 cent token (Bowers & Merena)

C.360. 1795 Cent: Edge: WE PROMISE TO PAY THE BEARER ONE CENT. Rev. legend continues this message, AT THE STORE OF TALBOT ALLUM & LEE NEW YORK. Thick and thin planchets. Norweb MS-60, 145.8 grains, $577.50.
C.361. 1795 Cent: Edge: CURRENT EVERYWHERE, F.C.C. Boyd coll., Unique.
C.362. 1795 Cent: Olive leaf edge, Unique. Norweb, ex T.J. Clarke, VF-30, $4,400.
C.363. 1795 Cent: P.E., excessively rare. Norweb thin, EF-40, ex T.J. Clarke, 137.4 grains, $2,310; Picker EF, 148.3 grains, $632; ST Picker 5/91, AU, $2,100.
C.364. 1795 Cent: Edge: CAMBRIDGE BEDFORD HUNTINGDON. X. X., Unique. Norweb MS-60, $3,960.

Talbot, Allum & Lee Mules were struck for contemporary token collectors with a variety of unrelated reverses. These include Birmingham Halfpenny, cherub with coining press; Promissory Halfpenny, heron, BM 9/90, MS-64, $781; Earl Howe and the Glorious First of June; John Howard, Philanthropist, ST 3/94, EF, $500; Blofield Cavalry and York Minster. All are scarce to extremely rare, and edge varieties exist.

THEATRE AT NEW YORK PENNY

This handsome token was engraved by B. Jacobs and struck by token dealer Skidmore of London as part of his series on major public buildings sold during the British token craze. It is unlikely that this token was ever seen in America until after the birth of numismatics in the U.S. decades later.

1796 penny token (Stack's)

C.365. 1796 Penny: Obv. Elegant theater facade, THE THEATRE AT NEW YORK legend. Rev. Generic MAY COMMERCE FLOURISH design of cornucopia on wharf, sailing ships in background. Edge: WE PROMISE TO PAY THE BEARER ONE PENNY. Possibly 12 known. Garrett Choice Proof, $8,000; Norweb MS-60, $5,500; BM 11/90, prooflike MS-63, $4,840.

MYDDLETON TOKEN

This beautiful pattern was designed by Matthew Boulton's chief engraver Conrad Heinrich Kuechler and struck by Boulton & Watt for British entrepreneur Philip Parry Price Myddleton. They were intended as small change for the hundreds of English farmers and artisans preparing to settle on Myddleton's extensive lands in Kentucky.

Succeeding only too well in his recruitment, Myddleton was charged with "enticing artificers to emigrate to the United States" and jailed. His design was also dangerous, the reverse recalling British defeat in the Revolutionary War by a dejected Britannia holding spear point downward, fasces, scales and sword cast on the ground.

These tokens never got beyond the pattern stage and all are exceptionally rare today. Silver Proofs were offered in tight-fitting metal cases, a Boulton specialty. Recent identification of these collectors' Proofs as florins has no justification, as this silver denomination was not created until 1848. Copper Company of Upper Canada mules are collectors' pieces struck in 1806-10.

1796 halfpenny token

C.366. 1796 Halfpenny.: Obv. Hope presents two children to welcoming Liberty, legend BRITISH SETTLEMENTS KENTUCKY. Rev. Seated Britannia contemplates liberty cap springing from earth at her feet, legend PAYABLE BY P.P.P. MYDDLETON. Copper, possibly 10 known, Garrett Choice Proof, $9,900; Roper Proof, $5,720; Norweb Proof-63, $5,280.

C.367. 1796 Halfpenny: As preceding but silver, possibly as many as 20 known. Garrett Choice Proof, $6,750; Roper Proof, $5,500; ST Starr 1/93 Proof, $5,100; Eliasberg 5/96 Proof $5,280.

C.368. 1796 Halfpenny: Same obv., new rev. with ONE HALF PENNY legend, COPPER COMPANY OF UPPER CANADA at center. Roper Choice Proof, $3,960. This rev. with obv. of reclining river god and "cartwheel" rim inscribed FERTILITATEM DIVITAS QUE CIRCUMFERREMUS, Garrett Choice Proof, $3,600.

CASTORLAND MEDAL

This piece recalls the 1792 French settlement of Castorville ("Beaver town") near present-day Carthage, N.Y. The colony was a refuge for upper-class French families endangered by the revolutionary Terror, but was at first supposed to be directed from Paris. The colony's constitution stipulated that "the Commissioners in Paris shall receive no salary; but in recognition of the care they shall bestow upon the common concerns, there shall be given them an attendance fee for each general or special assembly when they meet on the affairs of the Company."

The late Walter Breen called these pieces half ecus, which in New York could have passed current as five-ninths of a dollar. The original silver pieces bear reeded edges, and the circulated examples known today testify to long use as money. They were almost certainly *jetons de presence,* serving as honorariums for the commissioners for attending meetings. A few pieces may later have circulated as coins in the colony itself.

They were struck by the Paris Mint from dies by Benjamin Duvivier. Following Mint practice, copy dies were made during the 19th century and restrikes in several metals are offered even today. The original dies can be identified by their cramped, hand-punched 18th century lettering. The UG in FRUGUM touch, the first A in AMERICANA is low, the date is low with 1 touching a denticle. These dies ultimately buckled at PARENS. Pieces struck from copy dies show regular, modern-style lettering and thinner planchets; plain edges bear an incuse privy mark and the name of the metal.

An approximate date for restrikes can be gained by noting that the *Antique Lamp* mark was used on gold and silver medals struck March 1832-October 1841; C *Anchor and C,* October 1841-September 1842 for all metals; *Antique Prow,* September 1842-June 1845; *Pointing Hand,* June 1845-October 1860; *Bee,* November 1860-December 1879; *Cornucopia,* January 1880 to present. Metals are stated as *OR,* gold; *ARGENT,* silver; *CUIVRE,* copper; and more recently *BRONZE.*

Early Independence tokens continued

1796 restrike

C.369. 1796 Silver: R.E. Obv. Mural-crowned city goddess left, legend FRANCO-AMERICANA COLONIA, CASTORLAND 1796 in exergue. Rev. Standing goddess Ceres with cornucopia and Maple-tapping drill watching tree yielding Maple sap, SALVE MAGNA PARENS FRUGUM, Hail Great Mother of Fruits. Thick planchet, 223-238 grains (14.45-15.45 grams). Garrett Proof, 238.5 grains, $4,250; ST 9/93, Ch. VF, $4,000; Norweb AU-50, 222.8 grains, $4,400;

C.370. 1796 Copper: R.E. As preceding, thick planchet. Garrett EF, 249.2 grains, $2,100; Norweb MS-63, thin planchet, P.E. but original dies, MS-63, 175 grains, $467.

C.371. 1796 Brass: R.E. As preceding, brass. Unique, Garrett Choice Unc., 220.7 grains, $5,750.

C.372. 1796: Thinner planchet restrikes exist with both plain and reeded edges, privy marks and metal designations described above. Only those struck from the original dies, which show breaks and buckling as they disintegrated, have significant numismatic value. Garret P.E. gold restrike from later copy dies, Proof, 305.2 grains, $1,100; Norweb Unc. P.E. but Cornucopia OR edgemark of post-1880 strike, 363.8 grains, $1,760.

TEXAS JOLAS

The only known tokens from the Spanish-Mexican territories later annexed by the U.S. were the 1817-18 copper Jolas struck in San Antonio, now Texas, a settlement then called San Fernando de Bexar. Governor Martinez authorized an issue of 8,000 pieces valued at a half real each, to be struck by local jeweler Manuel Barrera. None are known today as they were withdrawn the next year. An additional 8,000 were struck for Postmaster Jose Antonio de la Garza.

His initials J A G, date 1818 and value 1/2 comprise the obverse; a single star appears on the reverse, asserted by Texas patriots to be the first appearance of the Lone Star. Known specimens were discovered on the San Antonio river banks in 1959. Two varieties exist, all are rare.

1818 jola (Harmer Rooke)

C.373. 1818 Jola: 1 positioned between 1 and J. Harmer Rooke Dec. '84 EF $4,800.
C.374. 1818 Jola: 1 positioned between G and 8. Est. $2,500.

Back-dated & Associated Tokens

Here are presented tokens long associated with the early Independence era, sometimes believed to have been struck much later. Since they are still collected by many as part of this series, they are included here.

NORTH AMERICAN TOKEN

These pieces were struck by Irish token maker and medalist William S. Mossop Sr. around 1792. They were back-dated to pass in both Canada and the U.S. in the first quarter of the 19th century.

Backdated and Associated tokens continued

1781 token (Stack's)

C.375. 1781 Brass or copper: Obv. Seated Hibernia with harp, legend NORTH AMERICAN TOKEN, 1781 in exergue. Rev. Two-masted sailing ship, COMMERCE. Breton 1013. Also known in copper. Garrett copper, VF, $300; ST 9/93, Unc., $700.

MOTT TOKEN

Issued by a well-known New York importer of clocks, *objets d'art* and European fancy goods, this token bears the bold date 1789. A few years ago a Mott token struck over a large cent of far later date was discovered, leading some numismatists to believe that the Mott issue actually dated from the Hard Times era of the 1830s. Later research has cast doubt on the authenticity of the overstruck coin, suggesting that it was merely the impression of an already struck token hammered onto a large cent. Since this piece was the sole evidence for the later date, it is now probable that the original time of issue for the Mott pieces was in fact correct.

Copper token of 1839 (Stack's)

C.376. 1789 Copper: Obv. Ornate eagle-finial clock, company legend. Rev. Federal eagle, large 1789 above, legend describing company wares. Thick planchet. Later die states show prominent break at top left of clock. Roper EF, extra thick, 233.4 grains, $550; ST 9/94, AU, $850.

C.377. 1789 Copper: As preceding, P.E. thin planchet. ST 12/93, Ch. AU, $1,900.

C.378. 1789 Copper: As preceding, thin planchet with crudely engrailed edge. Roper Unc. 108.1 grains, $1,265; Norweb EF-45, thin planchet, 107.3 grains, $715.

C.379. 1789 White Metal: As preceding, Unique, Ford Coll.

Washington pieces

Coins, tokens and medals portraying George Washington were the favorites of early American numismatists. For patriotic and historic reasons, Washington pieces were the center of collecting life through the Civil War era. After date and Mint mark collecting came to the fore, Washingtonia went into a long decline, from which it has begun to emerge only in recent years.

Listed here are patterns, tokens and circulating medalets portraying the Revolution's commander in chief and the country's first president. Dates are given as they appear on each piece, but an idea of the actual date of striking will be provided whenever possible. Baker numbers refer to the revised edition of William S. Baker's 1885 classic catalog of Washington material.

GEORGIVS TRIUMPHO COPPER

It is not known where this curious token was struck, but that it circulated in the 1780s is shown by its use as ready-made planchets for Ogden's New Jersey coppers, Maris 73-aa, struck in 1789 at the Elizabeth Town, N.J., Mint. Since Ogden used only well-worn coppers for this purpose, it is presumed that the "Georgivs Triumpho" coins had enjoyed circulation for at least a few years. Examination of the design shows that George Washington is the victor whose triumph is honored. Similarity to George III results from the lack of authentic portraits of the American leader in the late 1780s. The message of this piece is revealed by the motto VOCE POPOLI (By Voice of the People, odd Italian spelling; proper Latin is POPULI), 13 stripes and fleurs de lis, all of which hail the victorious leader, the colonies and their French ally.

1783 copper (Bowers & Merena)

C.380. 1783 Copper: Obv. Laureate head right, GEORGIVS TRIUMPHO, I, George, triumph. Rev. Liberty behind 13-stripe frame with fleur de lis at corners, VOCE POPOLI. Always found softly struck. Picker EF, $357; ST 5/93, Ch. EF, $625.

WASHINGTON THE GREAT TOKEN

Also called the Ugly Head, this token may be the work of die-hard Loyalists who still opposed independence in the 1780s. The head is a hostile caricature, missing wig and false teeth, surrounded by the pseudo-royal title WASHINGTON THE GREAT D:G: The reverse recalls the 13 links of the Continental notes and the 1776 coins.

1784 copper (Stack's)

C.381. 1784 Copper: Obv. Caricature head right. Rev Linked chain. Excessively rare, four known, one countermarked with British navy broad arrow. Baker 8. Roper crude Good, 93 grains, $14,850.
C.382. 1784 White Metal: As preceding, possibly two known. Baker 8E. Garrett Poor, 125.5 grains, $3,600.

MILITARY BUST CENTS

1783 copper (Stack's)

C.383. 1783 Copper: Obv. Small laureate uniformed bust left, legend WASHINGTON & INDEPENDENCE. Rev. Liberty seated left, UNITED STATES; TWI, ES in exergue. P.E., struck ca. 1820. Baker 4A. Roper EF, $187.

Washington pieces continued

C.384. 1783 Copper: As preceding but center-grained edge. Baker 4B. Picker AU, $209.
C.385. 1783 Copper: As preceding but large military bust. Baker 4. Roper EF, $550.

DOUBLE HEAD CENT

Undated copper ca. 1820 (Stack's)

C.386. (Ca. 1820) Copper: Obv. Small military bust somewhat like preceding, WASHINGTON above. Rev. Same bust, ONE CENT above. Plain Edge, one known with center-grained edge. Struck 1815-20. Baker 6, 6A. Picker EF, $176; Garrett AU, $550.

UNITY STATES CENT

1783 copper (Stack's)

C.387. 1783 Copper: Obv Laureate draped bust left, legend WASHINGTON & INDEPENDENCE. Rev. Copy of 1797 cent, wreath around ONE CENT, UNITY STATES OF AMERICA legend, 1/100 under tie. Known with two or three leaves under OF. Evasion issue struck to look worn at issue. Roper EF, $660.

MANTLED BUST COPPER

1783 copper

C.388. 1783 Copper: Obv. Laureate draped bust without button left, legend WASHINGTON & INDEPEN-DENCE. Rev. Liberty seated left UNITED STATES above. Struck ca. 1820. Baker 2. Garrett AU, $475;
C.389. 1783 Copper: As preceding, but TWI, ES under exergue line on rev., Thomas W. Ingram, Edward Savage, maker and designer. Plain or center- grain edge. Struck about 1820. Baker 4, 4-A.
C.390. 1783 Copper: Similar but reworked dies, struck by London coin dealer William S. Lincoln in 1860. Center-grained or engrailed edge. Baker 3. Garrett Choice Proof, 146.4 grains, $750.
C.391. 1783 Silver: As preceding but for metal. Center-grained edge. Roper Choice Proof, $550.
C.392. 1783 Gold: As preceding, three struck.
C.393. 1783 Copper: As preceding but struck by Joseph W. Taylor in Birmingham, 1851 and scarcer than the Lincoln restrikes. P.E. Baker 3C. Roper Choice Proof, 105.7 grains $198.
C.394. 1783 Copper: As preceding but toga has button, with or without dot in D of UNITED. P.E. Baker 5A. Struck about 1820. Garrett VF-EF, $240.

ROMAN HEAD CENT

Struck by British token maker Obadiah Westwood from designs of the talented engraver John Gregory Hancock, this token supposedly lampooned Washington's refusal to allow his portrait to appear on coinage. The laureate, undraped bust is executed in the style of a Roman emperor.

Roman Head cent token (Stack's)

C.395. 1792 Copper: Obv. Undraped Roman style bust right, legend WASHINGTON PRESIDENT. Rev. Spread eagle with small wings, huge head and 13-stripe shield, six stars at neck, CENT above. Edge UNITED STATES OF AMERICA .X.X.X. Possibly 15 known. Baker 19. Garrett Proof, $13,000; ST 5/95, Proof, $10,000; ST James A. Stack, blundered edge, 11/89, Proof, $11,000.

C.396. 1792 White Metal: Similar, error PRESEDENT in legend, uniface, Unique, stolen in 1971 from Richard Picker, never recovered. Baker 19C

C.397. 1792 Copper: Somewhat similar J.G. HANCOCK under truncation, uniface, probably Unique, stolen at same time as preceding. Baker 19A.

WASHINGTON - EAGLE CENTS

This series of related pieces was again the work of John Gregory Hancock, struck by Westwood. Their obverses present a large uniformed Washington bust left; their reverses, early versions of the American eagle.

1791 copper (Stack's)

C.398. 1791 Copper: Obv. Large uniformed bust left, WASHINGTON PRESIDENT, date below. Rev. Large dropped-wing eagle with 13-stripe shield, ONE CENT above. Baker 15. Edge: UNITED STATES OF AMERICA .X. ST 5/93, Gem Unc., $3,400.
Several unfinished copper reverse die trials are known, Garrett #1701-03, $1,550-1,900; an obverse die trial brought $2,900. An incongruous muling exists of this reverse with a George III obv., Rulau 15AA.

1791 copper (Stack's)

C.399. 1791 Copper: Similar obv. without date. Rev. Small raised-wing eagle, clouds and stars at head, shield with "blue" chief above stripes, ONE CENT above, 1791 below. Edge: UNITED STATES OF AMERICA .X. ST 5/93 Very Ch. Unc., $3,400.

C.400. 1791 Brass: As preceding , possibly two known. Garrett VF-EF, $1,600; Roper EF, $2,200.

AMERICAN ARMIES COPPERS

A Hancock-Westwood project, these pieces present a large uniformed bust left, with a 10-line precis of Washington's career on the reverse. Obverses present titles WASHINGTON PRESIDENT or GEO. WASHINGTON BORN VIRGINIA.

1792 copper (Stack's)

C.401. 1792 Copper: Obv. Uniformed bust left, legend WASHINGTON PRESIDENT. Rev. 10-line career ending PRESIDENT OF THE UNITED STATES 1789. P.E. Baker 59. Garrett EF, $15,500.

C.402. 1792 Copper: As preceding, edge UNITED STATES OF AMERICA .X., four known. Baker 59A. Garrett VF, $6,000.

1792 copper (Stack's)

C.403. 1792 Copper: Obv. Similar bust, legend GEO. WASHINGTON BORN VIRGINIA, FEB. 11, 1732. (Old Style date, New Style is Feb. 22). Rev. As preceding. P.E. Baker 60. Garrett Choice prooflike Unc., $22,500; Roper VF, $3,190.

C.404. 1792 Silver: As preceding, P.E. Baker 60A. Two known unholed: Roper EF, $16,500; Steinberg ex Robison, VF, $3,960.

C.405. 1792 Restrikes: As preceding but uniface obverse impressions platinum, gold, silver and copper by Albert Collis in 1959. Die is currently in American Numismatic Association museum.

LIVERPOOL - SHIP HALFPENNY

These tokens gave Hancock's Washington portrait its widest use. The 1791 pieces are very rare; all Ship halfpence are actually overdates, 1793/2.

1791 copper (Stack's)

C.406. 1791 Copper: Obv. Uniformed bust left, WASHINGTON PRESIDENT. Rev. 3-masted sailing ship right, LIVERPOOL HALFPENNY above, laurel spray below. Edge: PAYABLE IN ANGLESEY LONDON OR LIVERPOOL .X. Baker 17. Garrett EF, $2,600; blundered edge NDON OR LIVERPOOL;BU*BU, inverted OR LIVERPOOL, Steinberg EF, $1,760. (A unique white metal strike is reported.)

C.407. 1793/2 Copper: Obv. Uniformed bust left, legend WASHINGTON PRESIDENT. REV Three-masted ship right, HALFPENNY above, date in frame below. Most known from buckled dies. Edge: PAYABLE IN ANGLESEY LONDON OR LIVERPOOL .X. Baker 18. Roper Choice EF, $880.

C.408. 1793/2 Copper: As preceding, P.E., three known. "Baker 18aa." ST 5/93, VF, $1,600; ST 9/94, VF, $1,300.

C.409. 1793/2 Brass: As preceding, two known: Garrett EF, $3,300, Roper VF, $990. Baker 18A.

LIBERTY AND SECURITY, GRATE TOKENS

Peter Kempson and Son of Birmingham struck handsome pennies bearing a high relief military bust of Washington designed by Thomas Wyon. The innovative reverse bore a shield half-stripes, half-stars, topped by a small eagle and reassuring legend LIBERTY AND SECURITY. The same designer created the Grate Halfpence hailing Washington as THE FIRM FRIEND OF PEACE AND HUMANITY on tokens of London stove dealers Clark and Harris.

The success of these tokens led William Lutwyche to create close copies by designers Arnold, Dixon and Mainwaring which combined the uniformed bust of the Grate tokens with a low relief imitation of the Liberty and Security reverse on widely used halfpence. All listed are copper unless otherwise indicated.

Undated penny token of 1795 (Stack's)

C.410. (1795) Penny: Obv. Uniformed bust left, legend GEORGE WASHINGTON. Rev. Shield, small eagle, legend LIBERTY AND SECURITY. Edge: AN ASYLUM FOR THE OPPRES'D OF ALL NATIONS :: Baker 30. Garrett Choice Unc., $2,000; Roper Choice Unc., $1,540; ST 9/94, Ch. Unc., $1,200.

C.411. (1795) Penny: As preceding, P.E., possibly 2-3 known. Baker 30A. Stack's Laird Park, AU, $1,150, Sept. 1976.

C.412. (1795) Penny: As preceding, brass, believed Unique. Baker 30C.

C.413. (1795) Penny: As preceding but fire-gilt. Possibly nine known. Baker 30D.

C.414. (1795) Penny: As preceding, Corded or engine-turned rims. 5-6 known. Baker 30E. Roper Choice AU, $3,300; ST 11/89, Ch. AU, $2,420; ST 5/93, prooflike Unc., $2,900.

1795 halfpenny token (Stack's)

C.415. 1795 Halfpenny: Obv Uniformed bust with large buttons right, legend G. WASHINGTON THE FIRM FRIEND OF PEACE & HUMANITY. Rev. Grate, legend PAYABLE BY CLARK & HARRIS 13 WORMWOOD ST. BISHOPSGATE. Edge: PAYABLE AT LONDON LIVERPOOL OR BRISTOL. Baker 29. Garrett Choice prooflike Unc., $1,050; ST 5/93, Unc., $1,000.

C.416. 1795 Halfpenny: As preceding, brass. Unique, Garrett VF, 2,600; Roper VF, $880.

C.417. 1795 Halfpenny: As preceding, edge diagonally reeded. Baker 29B. Roper AU, $286.50.

C.418. 1795 Halfpenny: As preceding but small buttons on coat. Baker 29D. Picker Choice AU, $605.

Washington pieces continued

1795 penny (Stack's)

C.419. 1795 Penny: Obv. Uniformed bust right, legend GEORGE WASHINGTON. Rev. Low relief copy of Kempson penny, date divided by shield point as 17 95. Edge: AN ASYLUM FOR THE OPPRESS'D OF ALL NATIONS. Baker 32. ST 5/93, obverse 13 digs, plate coin of Rulau-Fuld revision of Baker, VF, $1,700. A Unique P.E. example is known.

C.420. 1795 Halfpenny: Similar design to preceding. Edge: PAYABLE AT LONDON LIVERPOOL OR BRISTOL. Baker 31. Roper AU., $605.

C.421. 1795 Halfpenny: As preceding. Edge: AN ASYLUM FOR THE OPPRESS'D OF ALL NATIONS. Baker 31A. Steinberg EF-AU, $605.

C.422. 1795 Halfpenny: As preceding. Edge: BIRMINGHAM REDRUTH OR SWANSEA, rare. Baker 31B. Roper AU, $577.50.

Other Unique edge varieties exist, as do mules with IRISH HALFPENNY Garrett VF, $175) and FOR THE CONVENIENCE OF THE PUBLIC obverses.

NORTH WALES TOKENS

These British-made evasion pieces were probably struck by Lutwyche from shallow, deliberately damaged dies to look circulated when struck. The crowned Irish harp was a familiar symbol on lightweight coppers of this era throughout the former colonies.

Undated halfpenny token ca. 1792
(Stack's)

C.423. (Ca. 1792) Halfpenny: Obv. Uniformed bust left, misspelled legend GEORGEIVS WASHINGTON. Rev. Crowned harp, legend NORTH WALES. Brass. P.E. Baker 34. Roper VF, $467.50.

C.424. (Ca. 1792) Halfpenny: As preceding. Copper, edge PAYABLE AT LANCASTER LONDON OR BRISTOL. Possibly seven known. Baker 34A. Roper Fine, $990; blundered edge PAYABLE IN LANCADON OR BRISTOL, STER, LON, ST 5/93, Fine-VF, $1,025.

C.425. (Ca. 1792) Halfpenny: As preceding, but fleur de lis atop crown, four stars at bottom reverse. Copper. P.E. Baker 35. Steinberg Fine, $1,485.

REPUB. AMERI. PENNIES

Considered medals by some numismatists, these productions of Kempson and Wyon are the size and weight of British penny tokens and are therefore included here.

C.426. 1796 Penny: Obv. Civil bust right, legend GEORGE WASHINGTON, date below. Rev. Three-line concentric legend, career from 1775 military command to 1796 resignation of presidency. Copper. P.E. Baker 68. ST 5/93, Proof, $400; NASCA Kessler-Spangenberger Sale, Unc., $450; PCAC Paul Magriel Coll. AU, $130.

C.427. 1796 Penny: As preceding, white metal, rare. Baker 68A.

C.428. 1796 Penny: As preceding. Copper. Edge: PAYABLE IN LONDON LIVERPOOL OR ANGLESEY. Very rare. Baker 68B.

C.429. 1799 Penny: As preceding, but mortuary legend BORN FEB. 11. 1732. DIED DC. 21. 1799 below bust. Bronze. P.E. Baker 69. Garrett Proof, $450

C.430. 1799 Penny: As preceding, white metal. P.E. Baker 69A. Bowers & Ruddy Scott Coll, June '75 #450, Proof, $260.

C.431. 1799 Penny: As bronze but struck over British 1797 Cartwheel penny. P.E. Baker 69B. Extremely rare.

SUCCESS TOKENS

These enigmatic pieces have long been collected as part of this early token series, although their fabric strongly suggests the game counters or *Spielmarke* of the mid-19th century. The date 1793 was assigned long ago in an attempt to link them with Washington's second Inauguration.

"1793" Success token (Stack's)

C.432. "1793" Success Token: Obv. Uniformed bust right with straight nose, often with bold die crack nose to N, legend GEORGE WASHINGTON. Rev. 15 stars in sunburst, All-Seeing eye at center, (never sharply struck), SUCCESS TO THE UNITED STATES around. Large Size. R.E. Baker 265. Garrett Choice BU, $2,900; Roper brass, Choice AU, (die crack at nose) $605; Garrett brass gilt, Proof, $3,800.; BM 11/92, MS-60, $1,430.

C.433. "1793" Success Token: As preceding but engrailed edge. Roper Unc., no die crack, fully silvered, $880.

C.434. "1793" Success Token: Similar but different portrait with heavy curved nose. Brass. P.E. Baker 266. Roper VF, $242.

C.435. "1793" Success Token: Same portrait as preceding. Brass. R.E. Garrett VF, $325.

"1793" Success token (Stack's)

C.436. "1793" Success Token: Similar but small size brass, sometimes silvered. R.E. Baker 267. Roper silvered brass, Unc., $770.

C.437. "1793" Success Token: Similar, brass. P.E. Baker 267. Roper EF, $242.

GETZ HALF DOLLAR PATTERNS

Among the rarest and most fascinating patterns struck at the birth of our national coinage are the half dollars designed by Peter Getz of Lancaster, Pa. Their obverse design was prescribed by the Mint Act of April 2, 1792, "Upon one side there shall be an impression or representation of the head of the president of the United States of the time being, with an inscription which shall express the initial or first letter of his Christian or first name, and his surname at length, succession of the presidency numerically, and the year of the coinage..."

Around the uniformed bust facing left is the legend G. WASHINGTON. PRESIDENT. I. As many as 30 pieces were struck in silver, and 100 in copper for lobbying members of Congress. Fewer than 20 survive today in all metals.

C.438. 1792 Half Dollar: Obv. Uniformed bust left, G. WASHINGTON. PRESIDENT. I., date below. Rev. Large eagle with dropped wings legend UNITED STATES OF AMERICA, diagonal die-cancellation mark across breast. Silver. P.E. Baker 23. Unique, Garrett EF, $16,500.

Washington pieces continued

1792 half dollar pattern

C.439. 1792 Half Dollar: Similar obv. Rev. Smaller eagle with upraised wings, 15 stars around head. Silver, 35 mm. P.E. Baker 24. Struck over Louis XV half ecu aux lauriers, ST 5/93, VF, $12,500; Eliasberg 5/96 EF-40 $39,400.

C.440. 1792 Half Dollar: As preceding, silver, edge ornamented with circles and squares. Possibly five known. Baker 24A.

C.441. 1792 Half Dollar: As preceding, twin-leaf edge. Unique, Zabriskie, Wayte Raymond; Ford Coll. Baker 24B.

C.442. 1792 Half Dollar: As preceding, 15 star rev., copper P.E. Baker 24AA. Superior Auction '83, EF-40, $3,300.

C.443. 1792 Half Dollar: As preceding, 15 stars. Brass, unique. Witham Coll. Baker 24AB.

Smaller Diameter Pieces

C.444. 1792 Half Dollar: Similar to preceding but for diameter of 32 mm. Copper. P.E. Baker 25. Garrett prooflike Unc., $32,000. Stack's Auction '83, VF, $2,860.; ST 3/93, Ch. EF, $5,000.

C.445. 1792 Half Dollar: Similar, but die rust at star, A in STATES. Copper, thin planchet. Edge ornamented with circles and squares. Baker 25. Garrett Unc., $34,000.

C.446. 1792 Half Dollar: At least three strikings from these dies are known on 1794 or 1795 U.S. large cent planchets, including 1794 cent with edge ONE HUNDRED FOR A DOLLAR (leaf) in Kagin Coll., Unique.

First Federal Copper Coinage

James Jarvis' Fugio cents

Despite Robert Morris' advanced plans for a Federal Mint, none was established under the Confederation. A contract copper coinage was a different matter since the cost of manufacture was low enough to yield a substantial profit. Unfortunately, only speculators who understood the need for political influence could hope to obtain such a contract.

New York entrepreneur James Jarvis edged out such substantial contenders as Gen. Matthias Ogden, John Bailey and Ephraim Brasher to obtain the coveted contract by paying a $10,000 bribe to high-living Treasury Superintendent William Duer in May 1787. Jarvis contracted to furnish more than 32 million coins from nearly 32 long tons of Federal copper supplied him at preferential rates, expecting to strike them through the Company for Coining Coppers in New Haven, Connecticut.

Jarvis soon controlled this company, which he placed under the supervision of his father-in-law Samuel Broome. His bribe had exhausted his ready cash supply, and Jarvis went to England in a futile attempt to convince Matthew Boulton to supply dies and planchets. Boulton demanded cold cash, and Jarvis was unable to raise the necessary funds.

The contract specified the designs, obviously inspired by the 1776 Continental coins and notes. The obverse would bear a sundial under a radiant sun with Latin FUGIO, I (time) Fly, Mind Your Business. The reverse would bear a chain of 13 links, UNITED STATES, WE ARE ONE at center. Principal die sinker for the Fugios was the skillful Abel Buel.

The new heavy copper coins were to be called Cents, struck to a new Federal standard of 157.5 grains each, and were supposed to drive out of circulation the depreciated, light weight coppers of state and private issue.

While Jarvis was pleading with Boulton, Broome simply stole the Federal copper, striking fewer than 400,000 underweight Fugios, then shipping these to Philadelphia to distract an increasingly suspicious government. Broome used the rest of the embezzled copper to make more profitable lightweight Connecticut coppers. Unable to fulfill his contract, Jarvis defaulted and fled to Europe, followed soon after by Broome and Buell.

An ill-advised attempt was made to feed the supply of finished Fugios into commerce as "coppers," not cents, but New York merchant Royal Flint dumped the whole mass at once, causing a copper coin panic that devastated commerce. Some thousands of Uncirculated Fugios were locked away in an original keg in the vaults of the Bank of New York from 1788 until 1856, after which date they slowly trickled onto the market.

The N numbers refer to Eric P. Newman's definitive catalog of these first coppers struck under the authority of the fledgling United States.

PATTERN

1787 cent pattern (Bowers & Merena)

C.447. 1787 Cent: Obv. Radiant sun over sundial, FUGIO left, date right, MIND YOUR BUSINESS in exergue. As adopted but one quatrefoil in legend, rather than four. Rev. 13 links, each inscribed with the name of a state, AMERICAN CONGRESS, WE ARE ONE at center in sunburst. Perhaps three known. N 1-CC, Garrett EF, 144.6 grains, $17,500; Norweb AU-50, $63,800.

REGULAR ISSUES, POINTED RAYS

1787 Fugio cent (Stack's)

C.448. 1787 Cent: Obv. No cinquefoils, cross after date. Rev. UNITED STATES. Newman 1-B. Rare, Steinberg Choice AU, $2,750.

C.449. 1787 Cent : Obv. Cross after date Rev. STATES UNITED N 1-L Very rare. ST 12/93, VF, $1,250.

C.450. 1787 Cent: Obv. Close date. Rev. STATES UNITED, WE ARE ONE on label with raised rims. N 1-Z, Norweb AU-55, $23,100; ST 12/94, VF, $7,500.

Fugio cents continued

1787 cent (Stack's)

C.451. 1787 Cent: Obv. Widest date. Rev. WE ARE ONE on label with raised rims. N 19-Z. Extremely rare. BM 11/94, EF-45, $3,300.

1787 cent

C.452. 1787 Cent: Rev. UNITED above, STATES below. N 11-A. Very rare. Norweb MS-60-63, $5,060; ST 12/93, Unc., $5,500; Eliasberg 5/96 MS-65 $12,650.

1787 cent (Stack's)

C.453. 1787 Cent: UNITED STATES at sides of label. Cinquefoils on label, several vars. N 8-B, ST 12/93, Unc., $1,100. N 15-H, ST 12/94, Unc. $3,400.

1787 cent (Stack's)

C.454. 1787 Cent: Rev. UNITED STATES, WE ARE ONE corrected from WE ONE ONE. N 8-B, twice-cut planchet, ST 12/94, Ch. Unc., $1,400; triple struck, ST 12/94, Ch. Unc., $1,300.
C.455. 1787 Cent: Obv. 1 in date over horizontal 1. Rev. UNITED STATES. N 10-G. Extremely rare. ST 12/94, VF, $2,100.

1787 cent (Bowers & Merena)

C.456. 1787 Cent: Obv. 1 in date over horizontal 1. Rev. STATES UNITED. N 10-T, rare. Roper VF $484. N 10-oo discovered in 1988, Bowers & Merena Mann-Smedley Sept. '88 , VF-30 $5,720.

Fugio cents continued

C.457. 1787 Cent: Obv. Normal date. Rev. Cinquefoils on label, STATES UNITED, many vars. N 6-W, Norweb AU-50, $1,320.

1787 cent (Stack's)

C.458. 1787 Cent: Rev. STATES UNITED, two 8-pointed stars on label, only one shows on poorly struck pieces. N 15-Y, BM 3/92, EF-40, $1,210.

CLUB RAYS

C.459. 1787 Cent: Obv. Rays with concave ends, error legend FUCIO. Rev. UNITED STATES. N 2-C, ST 12/93, Choice Fine, $4,000; ST 3/94, VG/Fine, $1,700; Norweb VF-30, $3,190. 23-ZZ. Extremely rare.

1787 Fugio cent (Stack's)

C.460. 1787 Cent: Obv. 15 Club Rays with rounded ends. Rev. UNITED STATES. N 3-D. Rarely found above Fine, BM 11/94, AU-55, $2,090.

1787 cent (Stack's)

C.461. 1787 Cent: Obv. 10 Club Rays with rounded ends. Rev. UNITED STATES. N 4-E, Rarely found above Fine. ST 3/94, AU $950.

1787 cent (Bowers & Merena)

C.462. 1787 Cent: Obv. Rays with concave ends, normal FUGIO, cross-hatching on sundial. Rev. UNITED STATES. N 5-F, 5-HH. Extremely rare, Norweb VF-30, $4,860; ST 12/94, VG, $3,000.

"NEW HAVEN RESTRIKES"

"New Haven Restrike" (Stack's)

A number of pieces resembling the 1787 Fugio cents exist with incomplete obverse designs, thin-link reverses, straight rays at reverse center, All-Seeing Eye in such rays, five-pointed stars within thin links. These are mid-19th century fantasies made for Major Horatio N. Rust (after their supposed finding by young C. Wylls Betts on the site of the old Broome & Platt store) and later for Charles Ira Bushnell.

The largest selection of these pieces to see public auction in recent times comprised lots 3561-3569 in Bowers & Merena's Norweb Sale, Part III, Nov. 1988.; Stack's December 1993, March 1994 and December 1994 sales. N.98-XX, gold, BM 5/92, EF-40, $2,200; N.104-FF, Copper. BM 3/92, MS-64, $495; N.104-FF, Silver, ST 12/93, Unc., $1,000; ST 12/94, Silver, Unc., $1,100.

Copper Coinage

The first cents and half cents were thick and heavy with incuse-lettered edges. The original weight of the cent prescribed by the Mint Act of April 2, 1792, was 264 grains (17.11 grams), reduced to 208 grains (13.48 grams) by the amendatory act of Jan. 14, 1793. Copper prices continued to rise, however, and further reduction to 168 grains (10.89 grams) was proclaimed by President Washington on Dec. 27, 1795, to prevent profitable melting of new cents as scrap metal.

The first half cents were 104 grains (6.74 grams), reduced to 84 grains (5.44 grams) for the plain edge coins of 1796 and later issues. One purpose for half cent coinage was making change for the Spanish silver real or bit, valued at 12 ½ cents. The half cent never achieved widespread popularity.

The new Federal copper coins joined a miscellany of foreign, state and private coppers already in circulation. The act of May 8, 1792, provided for their withdrawal six months after the new U.S. Mint issued $50,000 worth of cents and half cents.

This proclamation was never issued, and tokens remained a part of America's coinage scene for decades. The new Federal copper coins had no legal tender status, and could be rejected by banks, merchants or private individuals with impunity. Wide-spread rejection of half cents in 1811 contributed to a 14-year suspension of this unpopular denomination.

During these early years, the Mint was crippled by an acute shortage of copper, and cheerfully received the needed metal in the form of utensils, nails and other scrap.

Quantities of early half cents were struck from cut down tokens of New York merchants Talbot, Allum & Lee and from defective large cents. After 1797, a steady supply of quality planchets was purchased from the great private Mint of the era, Boulton & Watt of Birmingham, England. Crocker Brothers of Taunton, Mass., became one of the few American suppliers decades later.

From the 1840s there was increasing agitation to replace the large cents with a more convenient coinage and to discontinue the half cent. The coins were clumsy and heavy, their soft metal quickly darkened and picked up contaminants.

By 1850, copper prices again rose, making the copper coinage unprofitable to the Mint. Many experiments were made, including reduced size and holed planchets, German silver, bronze and nickel-alloy patterns.

Half cent coinage was discontinued in February 1857, and many of the coins were redeemed with thousands of the large cents in the new small diameter copper-nickel Flying Eagle cents.

It was not until 1794 that the fledgling Mint employed a permanent engraver. A number of Mint employees cut dies for the early coppers, including Chief Coiner Henry Voigt, whose 1793 linked Chain reverse attracted much poorly reasoned criticism.

The Chain symbolized the union of states, but was soon replaced by a wreath, and wreaths in varied forms became standard on both cents and half cents. The 1793 Wreath cents and half cents are attributable to Adam Eckfeldt, who later succeeded Voigt as chief coiner.

Joseph Wright adapted the obverse of French medalist Augustin Dupre's Libertas Americana medal to the 1793 Liberty cap cent only weeks before his death in one of Philadelphia's devastating yellow fever epidemics. His basic concept was carried on by Assistant Engraver John Smith Gardner for the 1795-97 half cents and 1795-96 cents; Chief Engraver Robert Scot is responsible for most other 1794-1807 coppers.

German immigrant and former indentured servant, John Reich redesigned the copper coinage in 1808-09. One-time bank note plate engraver Christian Gobrecht was second engraver of the Mint from 1835-40 and chief engraver 1840-44. He redesigned the large cent several times between 1835 and 1839, adapting the final version to the half cent in 1840.

If they were unloved by their contemporaries, the early coppers have attracted the devoted interest of American numismatists. No other area of U.S. coinage has received the intense and enthusiastic study of the large cent and, to a lesser extent, the half cent.

Numismatists Sylvester S. Crosby, Dr. Edward Maris, W.W. Hays, Francis Doughty, Edouard Frossard, Ebenezer Gilbert, David Proskey, Thomas L. Elder, Frank Andrews and Howard R. Newcomb were among the early workers in this vineyard.

In later years Dr. William H. Sheldon, Dorothy Pascal, Roger S. Cohen, Paul Munson, John W. Adams, Robert Grellman, Jack H. Robinson, William C. Noyes, John D. Wright, Jules Reiver and Walter Breen have enriched numismatic literature with an entire specialized library devoted exclusively to these fascinating coins. In a numismatic age devoted largely to profit, the early coppers offer an oasis of study, and additional literature is continually added.

A note about photographs

Photographs of general types appear at the beginning of the listings for each general type, regardless of date; specific varieties, when illustrated, are placed with their individual listings.

A note about pricing

It is not the intention of the editors to present a comprehensive price guide for all pieces listed. Prices in the federal issues section are adapted from Coin World Trends.

Half cents

LIBERTY CAP, HEAD LEFT

Liberty Cap, Head Left

	G-4	VG-8	F-12	VF-20	EF-40
1793 .... (35,334)	1425.	2100.	3600.	5200.	10750.

Lettered Edge with two leaves after TWO HUNDRED FOR A DOLLAR. 4 vars, beware of electrotypes.
BR-3 Elisaberg 5/96 MS-62 $38,500

LIBERTY CAP, HEAD RIGHT

Liberty Cap, Head Right

	G-4	VG-8	F-12	VF-20	EF-40
1794 .... (81,600)	305.	625.	900.	1350.	3600.

Rev. with crowded leaves, type of 1794. Vars. include pointed or knob 9 in date. Large or small letters
on edge, single leaf after DOLLAR.
1794
Rev. with more open leaves, similar to large cent, type of 1795.

SMALL HEAD RIGHT

Small Head Right

	G-4	VG-8	F-12	VF-20	EF-40
1795 .... (25,600)	300.	600.	875.	1300.	3350.
Lettered Edge. 1 in date made with I punch in LIBERTY.					
1795	350.	700.	1000.	1600.	4500.
Lettered Edge. Punctuated Date, comma-like die break between 1 and 7.					
1795 .... (114,090)	275.	550.	750.	1150.	3250.
Plain Edge, Punctuated Date. Plain Edge coins were actually struck in 1796.					
1795	225.	375.	625.	1100.	3050.

Plain Edge. No Pole, many struck on newly rolled copper, but more than half on cut-down Talbot,
Allum & Lee tokens, plus a few on cut- down cents.

Half cents continued

With Pole (Bowers & Merena)

	G-4	VG-8	F-12	VF-20	EF-40
1796 With Pole .... (1,390)	9000.	13500.	16500.	20500.	30000.

Plain Edge. Beware of electrotypes and alterations. The Edwards Copy, a famous struck counterfeit, shows a crude head, toothed borders and larger letters.

1796 No Pole	19000.	27500.	38500.	65000.	—

Plain Edge. Mintage included above, beware of electrotypes, altered 1795s. BR-1 Elisaberg 5/96 MS-65 $506,000.

1797 .... (119,215)	225.	350.	675.	1100.	2900.

Plain Edge. 1 above 1, die cutter's blunder with first 1 too high, definitive 1 punched directly below it. BR-1 Elisaberg 5/96 MS-63 $19,800.

1797	275.	400.	800.	1250.	4500.

Plain Edge. Head properly centered, many struck like the preceding on cut-down Talbot, Allum & Lee tokens, rarely on spoiled large cents.

1797

Plain Edge. Low Head, placed so low that it crowds the date. Very rare.

1797	685.	1300.	2500.	5350.	26000.

Lettered Edge. Struck on cut-down cents, edge letters generally without tops or bottoms, struck in 1800. Very rare above VF. BR-3a Elisaberg 5/96 VF-30 $22,000.

1797	9500.	19000.	—	—	—

Gripped Edge, raised and indented lines suggesting seizure by pliers. Always found in lowest grades.

1797

Plain Edge. Struck on cut-down cents, usually found in low grade, generally shows obv. die crack from chin to rim.

DRAPED BUST

1804 Plain 4

	G-4	F-12	VF-20	EF-40	AU-50
1800 .... (202,908)	30.00	120.	200.	415.	650.

Very rarely struck over cut-down cents. Rev. similar to 1795-1797 type. Scarce in red Unc. BR-1 Elisaberg 5/96 MS-64 $13,750.

1802/0 .... (20,266)	13500.	45000.	—	—	—

Rev. of 1800, wreath ends in single leaves. All struck over cut-down cents. Very rare, 15-18 known.

1802/0	475.	2400.	8000.	—	—

Rev. of 1803, wreath ends in three leaves, two at r. Also struck on cut-down cent stock.

1803 .... (92,000)	35.00	130.	240.	675.	1500.

Vars. include wide or close fraction, 5 or (scarce) 6 berries on left side of wreath.

1804 .... (1,055,312)	35.00	75.00	110.	300.	650.

Crosslet 4, stems in wreath.

1804	40.00	90.00	160.	375.	625.

One obverse almost always displays a bold die gouge creating the popular Spiked Chin varieties.

1804	37.50	80.00	135.	500.	685.

Crosslet 4, No Stems, most struck in 1805.

1804	50.00	175.	300.	2000.	4000.

Plain 4, Stems, many struck during 1805.

1804	30.00	55.00	105.	265.	500.

Plain 4, No Stems, many struck 1805-06.

1805 .... (814,464)	585.	3500.	—	—	—

Small 5, Stems, excessively rare in VF or above.

1805	26.75	60.00	125.	340.	585.

Small 5, No Stems.

1805	30.00	80.00	135.	390.	675.

Large 5, Stems.

Half cents continued

	G-4	F-12	VF-20	EF-40	AU-50
1806 .... (356,000)	200.	675.	1250.	2650.	——
Small 6, Stems.					
1806	26.00	50.00	80.00	180.	385.
Small 6, No Stems.					
1806					
Large 6, Stems, most common of date.					
1807 .... (476,000)	30.00	80.00	130.	325.	650.
Mintage figure includes many pieces dated 1806.					
1808/7 .... (400,000)	175.	675.	1950.	4000.	——
Rare in Unc., normally found only in low grades.					
1808	28.00	90.00	195.	475.	1200.
Normal date.					

CLASSIC HEAD

Classic Head

	G-4	F-12	VF-20	EF-40	AU-50
1809 .... (1,154,572)	24.00	47.50	60.00	150.	325.
1809/6	26.00	45.00	85.00	175.	550.
Actually 9 over an inverted 9.					
1809	27.00	72.50	100.	375.	800.
0 over smaller 0, rare in higher grades.					
1810 .... (215,000)	29.00	80.00	190.	575.	1100.
Mintage figure includes many pieces dated 1809.					
1811 .... (63,140)	115.	600.	1050.	4800.	12000.
2 date position vars. BR-2 Elisaberg 5/96 MS-63 $28,600.					
1811					
Rev. of 1802. Private restrike of Joseph J. Mickley, 11 known.					
1825 .... (63,000)	27.00	55.00	77.50	140.	350.
Almost unobtainable in brilliant Unc.					
1826 .... (234,000)	23.00	37.00	57.50	115.	215.
1828 .... (606,000)	23.00	36.00	55.00	90.00	175.
Obv. 13 stars, many spotty red Unc. from hoard.					
1828	23.50	42.50	85.00	205.	390.
Blundered obv. 12 stars, very rare in evenly struck Unc.					
1829 .... (487,000)	23.00	35.00	52.00	88.00	155.
1831 .... (2,200)					
Rare in Unc., rarer in Proof. Originals have large berries, highest leaf point under right side of last S in STATES; early restrikes with rev. of 1836 show leaf tip under left side of S; later restrikes show broad rim, small berries of post-1840 coinage. Beware of alterations; stars larger than on 1832-36.					
1832 .... (154,000)	23.00	35.00	45.00	70.00	150.
3 rev. varieties, leaf under S or E, recut D in UNITED.					
1833 .... (120,000)	23.00	34.00	45.00	70.00	145.
Brown and red Uncs. exist from hoards; at least 30 original Proofs exist as well.					
1834 .... (141,000)	23.00	34.00	45.00	70.00	145.
1835 .... (398,000)	23.00	34.00	45.00	70.00	145.
Many spotty red Unc. coins from hoards.					
1836					

Proof only; originals show striking characteristics of 1830s; restrikes have buckled obverse, squared rims of later coinage. Norweb original Proof-63, $6,600; restrike Proof-63, $7,700.
Proof half cents of 1831, 1836, 1840-49 were struck to sell or trade to favored collectors and for presentation to dignitaries.
Originals of the 1840s generally have large berry reverses; restrikes, small berries. A tiny number of restrikes exist with large berries, for which see specialized literature.

CORONET HEAD

Proof Only Dates (Beware of Mint-made electrotypes of these dates)

Coronet, Proof-only dates (Bowers & Merena)

	Prf-60	Prf-63	Prf-64	Prf-65
1840 Original	3400.	5500.	8250.	15000.

Proof only, originals with large berries, wire rims less pronounced than on restrikes. Perhaps 20 known. Norweb Proof-63, $7,480.

1840 Restrike
Proof only, small berries, six known. Norweb first restrike Proof-63, $3,740; second restrike, $5,940.

1841 Original
Same rev. and comments as 1840.

1841 Restrike

1842 Original
Same rev. and comments as 1840.

1842 Restrike

1843 Original
Same rev. and comments as 1840.

1843 Restrike

1844 Original
Same rev. and comments as 1840.

1844 Restrike

1845 Original
Same rev. and comments as 1840.

1845 Restrike

1846 Original
Same rev. and comments as 1840.

1846 Restrike

1847 Original
Same rev. and comments as 1840.

1847 Restrike

1848 Original
Same rev. and comments as 1840. Top of extra 8 in denticles below date.

1848 Restrike

1849 Original
Small date; same rev. and comments as 1840.

1849 Restrike

CORONET HEAD

Circulation Coins

Coronet, circulation (restrike)

	F-12	VF-20	EF-40	AU-50	MS-60
1849 .... (39,864)	47.00	62.00	105.	185.	350.

Large date, rare in brilliant red Uncirculated.

1850 .... (39,812)	50.00	67.00	125.	225.	500.
1851 .... (147,672)	40.00	50.00	73.00	135.	210.

Always found with base of extra 1 to right of second 1.

Half cents continued

	F-12	VF-20	EF-40	AU-50	MS-60
1852 .... (—)					

Mint records show that some original Proof 1852-dated half cents were struck with Small Berry rev., no doubling of the word CENT, but none are known today. Perhaps as many as 50 restrikes exist with Small Berries, doubling around CENT; about five Large Berry restrikes from dies of the 1840-49 era are also known. Large Berries Elisaberg 5/96 Prf-63 $78,100.

	F-12	VF-20	EF-40	AU-50	MS-60
1853 .... (129,694)	45.00	55.00	75.00	125.	180.
1854 .... (55,358)	42.00	50.00	73.00	125.	180.
1855 .... (56,500)	42.00	50.00	73.00	130.	180.
1856 .... (40,430)	43.00	60.00	82.00	145.	225.
1857 .... (35,180)	52.00	80.00	125.	200.	350.

Large cents

FLOWING HAIR, CHAIN REVERSE

Flowing Hair, Chain AMERI.

	G-4	VG-8	F-12	VF-20	EF-40
1793 .... (36,103)	2750.	4150.	6500.	11500.	20500.

AMERI. abbreviated on rev., vine and bars edge, obv. always weak. Sheldon-1 plain borders, beware of electrotypes of all Chain cents.

Flowing Hair, Chain AMERICA

	G-4	VG-8	F-12	VF-20	EF-40
1793	2450.	3850.	6000.	8500.	19000.
AMERICA spelled out on rev.					
1793	2550.	4000.	6100.	9750.	20000.
Periods after date and LIBERTY.					

FLOWING HAIR, WREATH REVERSE

Flowing Hair, Wreath (Bowers & Merena)

	G-4	VG-8	F-12	VF-20	EF-40
1793 .... (63,353)	125000.	250000.	—	—	—

So-called Strawberry Leaf above date, ONE CENT centered in wreath.

Large cents continued	**G-4**	**VG-8**	**F-12**	**VF-20**	**EF-40**
1793					

So-called Strawberry Leaf, ONE CENT high in wreath, 1) ANS; 2) later Starr, $51,700; 3) Parmelee-Steigerwalt-Brand.

1793	850.	1250.	2400.	3300.	7500.

Three leaves above date, six vars. Vine and bars edge, beaded borders. Rare plain edge examples are Mint errors. S-8 Elisaberg 5/96 MS-63 $27,500.

1793	1050.	1400.	2800.	4250.	9250.

Lettered Edge. Double leaf after ONE HUNDRED FOR A DOLLAR.

1793

Lettered Edge. as preceding, single leaf after DOLLAR.

LIBERTY HEAD WITH CAP

Joseph Wright Design

Liberty Head with Cap, Wright design

	G-4	**VG-8**	**F-12**	**VF-20**	**EF-40**
1793 .... (11,056)	2100.	3750.	6750.	15000.	30000.

Beaded borders. S-13 Elisaberg 5/96 MS-64 $314,000.

1794 .... (11,000)	1050.	2150.	3250.	7750.	16500.

Head of 1793, S-17-20. Denticled borders, as on following.

Robert Scot Design

Liberty Head with Cap, Scot design
(Superior Galleries)

	G-4	**VG-8**	**F-12**	**VF-20**	**EF-40**
1794 .... (806,500)	155.	325.	475.	1000.	2350.

Heads of 1794, not so finely styled as preceding. Rev. shows three leaves under O of OF, those with only one berry just left of ribbon are very rare. S-24 Elisaberg 5/96 <S-65 $27,500; S-26 Elisaberg 5/96 MS-65 $34,100.

1794

No fraction bar, very rare above VF.

1794

Two leaves under O in OF.

1794	8750.	17000.	35000.	57500.	95000.

Starred Reverse, S-48, always found in low grades, finest known EF-40 in Bowers & Merena March 1986 Stuart C. Levine coll., $45,100.

John Smith Gardner Design

Liberty Head with Cap, Gardner design
(Superior Galleries)

	G-4	VG-8	F-12	VF-20	EF-40
1794 .... (80,000)	155.	325.	490.	1025.	2800.

Type of 1795, heads in flat relief with hair ending in five thick curls. S-67-71, NC-3.

1794 .... (20,021)

Exact head of 1795. S-72.

| 1795 .... (37,000) .... | 225. | 465. | 900. | 1750. | 4500. |

Lettered Edge. Wreath ends in three leaves, two at r. One leaf under O in OF.

1795

Lettered Edge. Wreath ends in single leaves; two leaves under O in OF. Very rare S-73 always shows hyphen-like die break between RT of LIBERTY; this break missing from S-74.

1795

Lettered Edge. Wreath ends in single leaves, one leaf under O, ONE CENT high, S-76a, Very rare above VG.

| 1795 .... (501,500) .... | 135. | 235. | 450. | 700. | 1850. |

Plain Edge. ONE CENT high, wide date, S-76b.

1795

Reeded Edge, six known, all in low grades. S-79.

John Harper Design

Liberty Head with Cap, Harper design

	G-4	VG-8	F-12	VF-20	EF-40
1795	7250.	12500.	20500.	40000.	—

Plain Edge. S-80, so-called Jefferson Head cents, now believed to be private patterns struck by John Harper to demonstrate his fitness for a private coinage contract if the Mint were abolished. Note mannish profile, lobster claw leaves in wreath.

1795

Lettered Edge. S NC-1, three known.

Scot Design Revised

Liberty Head with Cap, revised Scot design (Bowers & Merena)

	G-4	VG-8	F-12	VF-20	EF-40
1796 .... (109,825)	175.	335.	675.	1400.	3450.

S-83-91. S-84 Elisaberg 5/96 MS-65 $20,900.

DRAPED BUST

Draped Bust

	G-4	VG-8	F-12	VF-20	EF-40
1796 .... (363,375)	195.	575.	1150.	2000.	3400.

Rev. Type of 1794, wreath ends in three leaves, two at r. Single leaf under C of CENT. S-101-2, 106-112 and NC-5, very rare above Fine.

1796	250.	550.	1150.	2250.	7000.

LIHERTY obv., blundered die, B punched upside down, then corrected, S-103, rare above VG.

1796	130.	230.	475.	925.	2150.

Rev. Type of 1795, some also minted 1797-99. Wreath ends in single leaves, S-92-93, 95-99, 116, NC-2 and NC-4.

1796	120.	225.	460.	850.	2000.

Rev. Type of 1797, Large Fraction. Wreath ends in three leaves, two at r. which are nearly parallel; two leaves under C of CENT. S-105, 113-115, 117-119 and NC-6. The least rare is S-119, with many red Uncs. from the Nichols Find.

1796

Type of 1797, LIHERTY obv., rev. as preceding. S-104, very rare above VF.

1796

Type of 1797, Small Fraction. S-94, 100. NC-1 and NC-3. Extremely rare above Fine.

1797 .... (897,510)	85.00	235.	425.	850.	2500.

Rev. Type of 1795, wreath ends in single leaves. Some struck in 1798-99. S NC-1, 120a and 121a. Very rare above VF.

1797	80.00	180.	350.	800.	2250.

Same but gripped edge shows irregular ridges suggesting the grip of a pair of pliers. S-120b, 121b.

1797	60.00	140.	275.	525.	1400.

Rev. Type of 1797, regular rev., plus two blundered dies exist: E over M in AMERICA, S-124; M over E, S-128 and 129. Many varieties, S-123, 135 are frequently seen in red Unc. from Nichols find.

1797	150.	310.	575.	1300.	3750.

Rev. Type of 1797, regular rev., stemless wreath, 4 vars.

1797

Rev. Type of 1797, very small fraction, S-134.

1798 .... (1,841,745)	50.00	150.	335.	775.	2050.

This figure includes some 1796-97 cents, and several hundred thousand 1798s struck in 1799, after the 1799-dated coinage.

1798/7	145.	315.	525.	1050.	3500.

Head of 1797, no curl on Liberty's shoulder. Rev. of 1797. Extremely rare above VF.

1798

Head of 1797, wide date, rev. of 1795. S-155, very rare above VF.

1798

Obv. head of 1797, narrow date, small 8, rev. of 1795. S-156, excessively rare above VG.

1798

Head of 1797, large 8, rev. of 1797.

1798

Same obv., small 8, rev. of 1797.

1798	100.	290.	550.	1450.	6600.

Head of 1799, extra curl on shoulder, narrow date, small 8. Rev. of 1795. S-178, extremely rare above VG.

1798	40.00	90.00	225.	475.	2250.

Head of 1799, large 8, rev. of 1797.

1798

Same Obv., small 8, rev. of 1797.

Large cents continued

1799 Draped Bust

	G-4	VG-8	F-12	VF-20	EF-40
1799/8 ....(42,540)............	2050.	4250.	8000.	17000.	——
Excessively rare in full EF, as is the next.					
1799	1750.	3500.	7000.	13750.	57500.
Always found on rough, dark, narrow planchets from American supplier, Coltman Brothers. A classic rarity, many alterations and electrotypes exist. Elisaberg 5/96 VF-35 $46,200.					
1800/1798 ....(2,822,175)............	57.50	175.	550.	1250.	4000.
Head of 1797, very rare above VF.					
1800/179	45.00	120.	310.	600.	2000.
Head of 1799, five vars.					
1800	40.00	92.50	240.	550.	1250.
Normal date, many vars.					
1801 ....(1,362,837)............	29.00	75.00	160.	400.	750.
Normal dies, pointed first 1 in date. Very rare in full EF.					
1801					
Blunt 1's in date.					
1801					
Pointed 1's in date, error fraction 1/000. Very rare above Fine.					

Draped Bust, Error Fraction 1/000

	G-4	VG-8	F-12	VF-20	EF-40
1801	42.50	90.00	200.	450.	2000.
Blunt 1's in date, error fraction 1/000					
1801	85.00	165.	235.	560.	1900.
Corrected fraction 1/100 over 1/000.					
1801	140.	385.	750.	1550.	6000.
Three Errors rev.: one stem to wreath, fraction 1/000, IINITED caused by correcting upside down U. Pointed first 1 in date.					
1801					
Three Errors rev., blunt 1's in date. Very rare.					
1802 ....(3,435,100)............	28.50	72.50	185.	315.	700.
Normal dies, many of this date were also struck in 1803.					
1802	32.50	90.00	165.	325.	725.
Stemless wreath.					
1802					
Three Error rev.: stemless wreath, double fraction bar, last S of STATES boldly double-punched.					
1802	45.00	115.	250.	415.	975.
Error fraction 1/000					
1802					
T punched over Y in LIBERTY, occurs with two different revs.					
1803 ....(3,131,691)............	26.50	57.50	115.	255.	725.
Small date, blunt 1, small fraction. Many of this date were struck in 1804.					
1803					
Small date, large fraction.					

Large cents continued

	G-4	VG-8	F-12	VF-20	EF-40
1803	37.00	80.00	225.	540.	1200.

Stemless wreath, actually Three Error reverse of 1802 with double fraction bar, last S of STATES boldly repunched.

	G-4	VG-8	F-12	VF-20	EF-40
1803	40.00	105.	215.	635.	1500

Corrected fraction 1/100 over 1/000. Mumps variety caused by die chip under chin. Very rare in full EF.

	G-4	VG-8	F-12	VF-20	EF-40
1803	5500.	10250.	17500.	37500.	—

Large Date, pointed 1, small fraction, extremely rare above VG.

	G-4	VG-8	F-12	VF-20	EF-40
1803	92.50	225.	400.	875.	2850.

Large date, large fraction, always shows extensive rev. die failure. Very Rare in full EF.

1804 Draped Bust (Stack's)

	G-4	VG-8	F-12	VF-20	EF-40
1804 .... (96,500)	600.	1350.	2500.	3250.	8000.

Rarity of this date spawned many alterations and electrotypes. On genuine pieces, 0 of date lines up with O in OF.

	G-4	VG-8	F-12	VF-20	EF-40
1804	—	—	240.	285.	350.

Private restrike using altered S-261 1803 obv., 1820 rev.
Copper and white metal strikes exist, including uniface obv. and rev. Probably the work of Edward Cogan and Joseph J. Mickley using dies sold as scrap steel.

	G-4	VG-8	F-12	VF-20	EF-40
1805 .... (941,116)	30.00	70.00	165.	295.	800.

Blunt 1 in date.

	G-4	VG-8	F-12	VF-20	EF-40
1805	30.00	70.00	175.	375.	925.

Pointed 1 in date.

	G-4	VG-8	F-12	VF-20	EF-40
1806 .... (348,000)	40.00	110.	245.	425.	1300.

Mintage figure may include some dated 1805.

Draped Bust, 7 punched over 6

	G-4	VG-8	F-12	VF-20	EF-40
1807/6 .... (829,221)	30.00	75.00	195.	400.	925.

Large 7, pointed 1 in date.

	G-4	VG-8	F-12	VF-20	EF-40
1807/6	2750.	4400.	9000.	17500.	—

Small 7, blunt 1, very rare above VG

	G-4	VG-8	F-12	VF-20	EF-40
1807	28.50	57.50	160.	345.	865.

Large 7, large fraction.

1807

Small 7, large fraction. Very rare in full EF.

	G-4	VG-8	F-12	VF-20	EF-40
1807	34.00	90.00	250.	525.	2750.

Small 7, small fraction.

	G-4	VG-8	F-12	VF-20	EF-40
1807	36.00	80.00	225.	500.	2850.

Small 7, small fraction, Comet variety caused by heavy die failure behind head, S-271.

CLASSIC HEAD

Classic Head, 1 punched over 0

	G-4	VG-8	F-12	VF-20	EF-40
1808 ....(1,007,000)	40.00	120.	325.	525.	1750.

Mintage figure probably includes some dated 1807. On S-277, the 12 Star var., star 1 becomes progressively fainter due to rev. die failure and on late strikes is missing altogether.

	G-4	VG-8	F-12	VF-20	EF-40
1809 ....(222,867)	110.	225.	440.	825.	2400.

The 9 is cut over a smaller 9, probably from the half cent or half eagle punch.

	G-4	VG-8	F-12	VF-20	EF-40
1810/09 ....(1,458,500)	45.00	110.	250.	540.	1300.

Coarse obv. denticles.

	G-4	VG-8	F-12	VF-20	EF-40
1810	36.00	80.00	190.	425.	825.

Normal date, coarse obv. denticles, S-285; fine denticles, S-282- 284. Most are unevenly struck.

1810

Private restrike in white metal with reverse of 1820, two known plus uniface obv. strike. In all probability the work of Joseph J. Mickley.

	G-4	VG-8	F-12	VF-20	EF-40
1811/0 ....(218,025)	115.	210.	465.	1075.	4250.

Very rare above VF and on top quality planchets.

	G-4	VG-8	F-12	VF-20	EF-40
1811	110.	160.	400.	775.	2250.

Normal date, beware of alterations from 1814.

	G-4	VG-8	F-12	VF-20	EF-40
1812 ....(1,075,500)	34.00	72.50	200.	435.	875.

Large date. Elisaberg 5/96 MS-64 $15,400.

1812

Small date.

	G-4	VG-8	F-12	VF-20	EF-40
1813/12 ....(418,000)					

S-293, this overdate is discernible only in the earliest die state.

	G-4	VG-8	F-12	VF-20	EF-40
1813	60.00	115.	240.	525.	1350.

Normal date, wide and close date vars.

	G-4	VG-8	F-12	VF-20	EF-40
1814 ....(357,830)	40.00	80.00	225.	500.	1000.

Plain 4 in date, unavailable in perfect red Unc. because all were paid out to Mint workmen in Dec. 1814 for back wages.

	G-4	VG-8	F-12	VF-20	EF-40
1814	40.00	80.00	225.	500.	1000.

Crosslet 4, similarly unavailable in full Mint red.

MATRON HEAD

Matron Head (Stack's)

	F-12	VF-20	EF-40	AU-50	MS-60
1816 ....(2,820,982)	37.50	90.00	185.	345.	500.

Wide and close dates. Available in spotty or dull red Unc. from the Randall Hoard, discovered in 1868 with other dates through 1820.

	F-12	VF-20	EF-40	AU-50	MS-60
1817 ....(3,948,400)	30.00	67.50	175.	290.	425.

Wide date.

1817

Divided date 18 17.

1817

Close date, Randall Hoard as 1816.

	F-12	VF-20	EF-40	AU-50	MS-60
1817	45.00	145.	450.	900.	3150.

15 Stars, outstanding die cutter's blunder.

Large cents continued

	F-12	VF-20	EF-40	AU-50	MS-60
1818 .... (3,167,000)	29.00	55.00	145.	240.	320.
Wide date, circular die crack called connected stars, Randall Hoard.					
1818					
Close date.					
1819/8 .... (2,671,000)	45.00	100.	220.	360.	950.
Large date, tall 1 away from bust.					
1819/8					
Large Date, tall 1 nearly touches bust, overdate less clear.					
1819	30.00	55.00	150.	250.	400.
Small date, Randall Hoard as 1816, old or new style rev. lettering.					
1820/181 .... (4,407,550)					
Large date, use of preceding year's die with incomplete date 181-.					
1820/19	45.00	120.	400.	900.	1750.
Small date, part of 9 visible unlike preceding.					
1820					
Large date, Randall Hoard as 1816.					
1820	30.00	55.00	190.	290.	500.
Small date, vars. with curled or plain tail on R in AMERICA.					
1821 .... (389,000)	150.	525.	1325.	2750.	8000.
Two vars., close date shows last 1 low and is scarcer.					
1822 .... (2,072,339)	45.00	105.	350.	660.	1600.
Wide date.					
1822					
Close date.					
1823/22 .... (68,061)	290.	775.	2100.	5000.	12250.
All of this date were struck in 1824 and delivered the following year. All 1823s are very rare in Unc.					
1823	350.	875.	2400.	5500.	12500.
Normal date.					
1823	——	——	450.	650.	875.
Private restrike by Joseph J. Mickley from cracked and broken obv. die combined with a rev. die of 1813. Later strikes were made, including at least one in silver.					
1824/22 .... (1,193,939)	80.00	280.	1100.	2500.	6250.
All varieties of this date are very rare in Unc., the overdate especially so.					
1824	57.50	150.	575.	1250.	3650.
Wide date.					
1824					
Divided date.					
1824					
Close date.					
1825 .... (1,461,100)	50.00	140.	375.	925.	2400.
Vars. with large and small A's in rev. legend, many rare in Unc.					
1826/5 .... (1,517,425)	190.	400.	850.	1600.	3500.
1826	45.00	105.	285.	500.	1000.
Wide date.					
1826					
Close date.					
1827 .... (2,357,732)	40.00	100.	265.	475.	850.
1828 .... (2,260,624)	29.00	75.00	225.	400.	675.
Large date.					
1828/88					
Blundered die, large date.					
1828	65.00	135.	350.	650.	1050.
Small date.					
1829 .... (1,414,500)	37.00	80.00	230.	625.	875.
Large letters. Elisaberg 5/96 Bronzed Proof 64 $12,100.					
1829	145.	475.	1250.	3000.	——
Small letters, usually poorly struck on rev., extremely rare in Unc.					
1830 .... (1,711,500)	28.00	60.00	185.	305.	550.
Large letters, both wide and close dates.					
1830	125.	385.	950.	2400.	——
Small letters, usually weakly struck. Very rare in EF, excessively rare in Unc.					
1831 .... (3,539,260)	28.00	55.00	165.	300.	600.
Large letters, straight or curled tail on R in AMERICA.					
1831					
Small letters.					
1832 .... (2,362,000)	27.00	55.00	155.	295.	565.
Large letters.					
1832					
Small letters.					

Large cents continued

	F-12	VF-20	EF-40	AU-50	MS-60
1833/2 .... (2,739,000)					
1833	26.00	54.00	140.	285.	475.
Normal date.					
1834 .... (1,855,100)	32.50	57.50	140.	275.	445.
Large date, large stars, large letters rev.					
1834	315.	575.	2050.	4350.	—
Large date, large stars, small letter rev. Excessively rare in Unc.					
1834	27.00	55.00	205.	425.	800.
Large date, small stars, small letters rev.					
1834	27.00	55.00	205.	425.	800.
Small date, large stars, small letters rev., close and wide date vars.					
1835 .... (3,878,400)	34.00	70.00	365.	725.	1500.
Large date, large stars.					
1835	27.50	55.00	250.	450.	850.
Small date, small stars.					
1835	27.50	55.00	135.	275.	390.
Small letters rev. of 1836.					

CORONET HEADS

Smaller heads remodeled by Christian Gobrecht, several distinct head punches used 1835 to 1857

Coronet Head

	F-12	VF-20	EF-40	AU-50	MS-60
1835	24.50	57.50	150.	265.	500.
Type of 1836, narrower, pointed bust, Newcomb 7-8, 14-16.					
1836 .... (2,111,000)	24.00	52.00	95.00	240.	445.
1837 .... (5,558,300)	20.00	51.00	90.00	180.	450.
Type of 1836, plain hair cord, medium letters rev.					
1837	25.00	57.00	130.	275.	700.
Type of 1836, plain hair cord, small letters rev.					
1837	15.00	50.00	87.00	190.	460.
Type of 1837, new head, larger rounded bust.					

Coronet, Head of 1838

	F-12	VF-20	EF-40	AU-50	MS-60
1837					
Head of 1838, beaded hair cord, small letters.					
1838 .... (6,370,200)	16.00	50.00	85.00	185.	350.
Scarce with perfect E in LIBERTY, left top is usually weak or missing.					
1839/6 .... (3,128,661)	1250.	2500.	6000.	13000.	—
Head of 1836 with plain hair cord. Very rare in EF, excessively so in Unc.					
1839	23.00	58.00	130.	330.	750.
Head of 1838, beaded hair cords, line under CENT.					

Large cents continued

Silly Head

	F-12	VF-20	EF-40	AU-50	MS-60
1839	26.00	67.50	210.	525.	1250.

Silly Head, longer than preceding, extra long lock curls along brow. This name and the following were coined by 19th century Philadelphia dealer Ebenezer Locke Mason.

Booby Head (Bowers & Merena)

	F-12	VF-20	EF-40	AU-50	MS-60
1839	28.00	70.00	185.	510.	1075.

Booby Head, similar to preceding but curl goes under bust, leaving the end of shoulder bare. No line under CENT.

Petite Head (Bowers & Merena)

	F-12	VF-20	EF-40	AU-50	MS-60
1839	19.00	50.00	100.	185.	425.

Head of 1840, often called the Petite Head to distinguish it from the so-called Mature Head of 1843-1857. Both are actually the same head punch positioned differently.

	F-12	VF-20	EF-40	AU-50	MS-60
1840 .... (2,462,700)	17.00	32.00	70.00	175.	350.
Large date.					
1840	17.00	32.00	70.00	170.	245.
Small date.					
1840	25.00	52.50	150.	275.	450.
Small 18 over large 18, Newcomb 2.					
1840/39					
Small date, traces of 839 below; Newcomb 4, Grellman-Reiver attribute this to hub defects.					
1841 .... (1,597,367)	24.00	50.00	145.	265.	385.
1842 .... (2,383,390)	15.00	25.00	75.00	170.	250.
Small date.					
1842					
Large date.					
1843 .... (2,425,342)	15.00	35.00	105.	200.	335.
Obv. Type of 1842, point of bust over 8, small letters rev.					
1843	42.50	120.	295.	525.	1050.
Obv. Type of 1842, rev. of 1844, large letters.					

Large cents continued

Coronet, 1843-1857

	F-12	VF-20	EF-40	AU-50	MS-60
1843	19.00	42.50	87.50	180.	280.
Obv. Type of 1844, so-called Mature Head, point of bust over 1.					
1844 .... (2,398,752)	13.50	30.00	85.00	185.	300.

1844/81 Coronet

	F-12	VF-20	EF-40	AU-50	MS-60
1844/81	45.00	130.	425.	725.	1450.
Blundered die, date over upside down 184, Newcomb 2.					
1845 .... (3,894,804)	12.50	21.00	62.50	115.	230.
1846 .... (4,120,800)	16.00	30.00	100.	210.	425.
Tall date.					
1846	12.50	19.00	60.00	130.	255.
Medium date.					
1846	14.00	27.50	92.00	215.	375.
Small date, vars. show open or closed 6; various recut dates also exist.					
1846					
Boldly doubled small date, Newcomb 4, first punched too high and too far left.					
1847 .... (6,183,669)	13.25	21.00	67.50	125.	265.
1847/small 7	35.00	65.00	250.	500.	1000.
Smaller and narrower 7 first punched too high, its top appears like a crown on final digit.					
1847					
Doubled dates, several vars., notably Newcomb 1, first date punched too far left.					
1848 .... (6,415,799)	12.50	20.00	42.00	100.	215.
Open or closed 4 in date. The so-called Small Date is a contemporary counterfeit.					
1848					
Double date, first punched too high, too far left, Newcomb 4.					
1849/8 .... (4,178,500)					
Overdate visible in early die states.					
1849	12.75	21.00	55.00	110.	220.
Normal date.					
1850 .... (4,426,844)	12.50	18.00	42.00	90.00	195.
Open and closed 5 vars., latter caused by die crack joining knob to upright of 5.					
1851 .... (9,889,707)	12.50	18.00	42.00	90.00	195.
1851/81	26.00	55.00	125.	250.	450.
Blundered die, Newcomb 3, date punching started upside down.					
1852 .... (5,063,094)	12.50	18.00	42.00	90.00	195.
1852					
Double date, first punched too low, Newcomb 7 early state only.					
1853 .... (6,641,131)	12.50	18.00	42.00	90.00	195.
Several vars. show degrees of date repunching.					
1854 .... (4,236,156)	12.50	18.00	42.00	90.00	195.

Large cents continued

	F-12	VF-20	EF-40	AU-50	MS-60
1855 ....(1,574,829)	13.25	20.00	43.00	100.	225.

Upright 5's believed the work of a Mint apprentice.

Slanting 5 (Stack's)

	F-12	VF-20	EF-40	AU-50	MS-60
1855	17.00	32.50	75.00	210.	425.

Slanting or italic 5's, 13 stars and normal ear. This type 5 is believed the work of James B. Longacre.

	F-12	VF-20	EF-40	AU-50	MS-60
1855	17.00	37.50	75.00	200.	400.

Slanting 5's, Newcomb 9, knob on ear from progressive die break.

1855

Slanting 5's, 12 stars, die state of Newcomb 10 with star 6 filled. Almost always seen EF-Unc.

	F-12	VF-20	EF-40	AU-50	MS-60
1856 ....(2,690,463)	12.75	19.00	42.00	90.00	210.

Upright 5.

1856

Slanting or italic 5

	F-12	VF-20	EF-40	AU-50	MS-60
1857 ....(333,456)	50.00	55.00	95.00	175.	250.

Small date.

	F-12	VF-20	EF-40	AU-50	MS-60
1857	40.00	50.00	95.00	180.	310.

Large date, half dollar logotype.

Minor Coinage

Since 1850, The U.S. Mint had experimented with replacements for the increasingly unpopular pure copper large cent and half cent. Although it had rejected Dr. Lewis Feuchtwanger's insistent offers of his American Silver copper-nickel-zinc alloy in 1837, the Mint was exploring its own nickel-bearing alloys by 1854. Mint Director James Ross Snowden finally resolved upon a new 19.1 millimeter (³/₄-inch) cent struck in an alloy of 88 percent copper, 12 percent nickel, weighing 72 grains (4.66 grams). There were several reasons for the addition of the nickel.

The white metal presented a cleaner, harder coin than did pure copper, especially after long circulation. Nickel increased the intrinsic value of the issue, which was believed necessary to insure its acceptance by the public. Finally, the relatively high intrinsic value and difficulties involved in extracting nickel were thought to lessen the chance of counterfeiting.

The new cents were struck in unprecedented quantities in order to redeem the old coppers and, while Snowden was at it, Spanish and Mexican fractional silver demonetized by the same Act. The "nickels" were first hailed as a blessing, then roundly cursed as a non-legal tender nuisance which clogged the arteries of commerce.

Nevertheless, with the outbreak of the Civil War, the copper-nickel cents (along with all other coins) vanished from circulation and were replaced by a series of money substitutes including encased postage stamps and a flood of copper merchants' and patriotic tokens.

This fact, and the dangers of dependence entirely on Joseph Wharton's Pennsylvania nickel mine, led anti-nickel Mint Director James Pollock to urge the adoption of "French bronze" for the cent and new 2-cent piece. Despite opposition from Wharton, who exerted powerful political influence, Congress authorized the new coinage on April 22, 1864.

The bronze cent weighed 48 grains (3.11 grams), and contained 95 percent copper, 5 percent tin and zinc, an alloy of a durability vastly greater than that of soft, corrodible pure copper. The intrinsic value was now so small that the coins circulated freely. For the first time in history, the cent was made a legal tender, if only up to 10 cents.

The 96-grain (6.22 gram) 2-cent piece was useful in expediting the replacement of various coin substitutes in circulation, and was the first to bear the new motto, IN GOD WE TRUST. It soon became redundant, however, and was discontinued in 1873.

On March 3, 1865, at the insistence of the nickel interests, and after a wonderfully sudden turn-about by the agile Pollock, Congress authorized a copper-nickel 3-cent piece as a temporary replacement for the vanished silver 3 cents. The 17.9 mm coin weighed 30 grains (1.94 grams) and was struck in a more modern alloy of 75 percent copper, 25 percent nickel.

A five-cent piece of the same composition was authorized on May 16, 1866, weighing a disproportionate 77.6 grains (5 grams). There was some hope that this 5-cent nickel would be replaced with a silver coin after the resumption of specie payments.

Instead, the half dime was discontinued along with the silver 3-cent piece in 1873, and the 5-cent "nickel" has been coined to the present day. The copper-nickel 3-cent piece was struck until 1889, then discontinued largely because it was the same size as the dime and indistinguishable from it by the public and the earliest coin-operated machines.

No minor coins were struck for circulation at any Branch Mint before 1908, so great was the distaste for base metal coins felt in the West and South. In size and alloy, the bronze cent and "nickel," as the 5-cent piece came to be known, were remarkably stable since their introduction.

During World War II, tin immediately became a strategic material, followed quickly by copper and nickel. Military demand for large quantities of these metals led the Mint to experiment with iron, zinc, early plastics and even glass for cent coinage in 1942. Appearing in 1943 were zinc-coated steel cents weighing 41.5 to 42.5 grains (approximately 2.7 grams). These rapidly-oxidized coins proved highly unpopular.

The familiar "nickel" was struck in a composition of 56 percent copper, 35 percent silver and 9 percent manganese in 1942-45. The large Mint mark was placed above Monticello, including for the first time a P for Philadelphia.

Tin was omitted from cents struck 1944-1946 from recycled shell cases. A similar copper-zinc alloy was resumed by authority of Congress on Sept, 6, 1962. Metalurgically, this tin-less alloy is brass rather than bronze, but the coins struck from it do not show the characteristic yellow color of brass and are not considered a separate type.

In Late 1973, trial strikes of a 1974-dated aluminum cent were prepared in anticipation of a change in alloy planned for 1974. This change was defeated in Congress by lobbyists for the copper-mining states, and all of the trial strikes, including those given to Congressmen as samples of the would-be coin, were ordered recalled and destroyed.

Approximately 12 pieces were not recovered and surviving specimens exist in the National Collection at the Smithsonian Institution and undoubtedly elsewhere. Their legal status makes seizure by the Treasury probable if they should appear on the numismatic market.

During 1982, rising prices of copper finally forced the Mint to begin striking cents on zinc planchets "barrel-plated" with a thin layer of copper, an economy move bitterly fought by the copper-mining interests. At one point the Treasury was even sued to prevent the change, on the grounds that to do so would cause economic hardship for the copper producers.

The future of the cent, in any composition, remains uncertain, as it is widely perceived as a worthless coin useful only for making small change necessitated by sales taxes. The main reason it has not been discontinued is that no politician has been willing to be held responsible for the inevitable "rounding-up" of odd amounts to the next 5-cent increment.

Our 19th century minor coins, except for the coppers and the Liberty Head 5-cent piece, were designed by chief engraver James B. Longacre. However, the eagle on the 1856 cent was copied from the Gobrecht 1836-39 patterns for a silver dollar. In 1909, when the Indian head cent was exactly 50 years old, it was supplanted by the Lincoln head cent of Victor D. Brenner. Another, less fortunate change occurred in 1959 when the original Brenner wheat-ears reverse was abandoned in favor of the ungainly

Lincoln Memorial design.

The Liberty Head 5-cent piece is the work of Chief Engraver Charles Barber. On the first date, the denomination appeared only as a Roman V, or 5, with the result that the coins were gilded, given a reeded edge and passed off as half eagles. The word CENTS appears on all subsequent issues.

In 1913, the celebrated sculptor James E. Fraser designed the Indian Head-Buffalo (technically Bison) 5-cent piece which was issued until 1938. In that year it was replaced by a Jefferson head 5-cent piece, the work of Felix Schlag.

The artist's competition-winning, imaginative three-quarters perspective of Jefferson's home Monticello was too much for Mint officials, who replaced it with a lifeless head-on view of the facade. Beginning in 1966 Schlag's FS initials appear below the bust on the obverse.

Cents

FLYING EAGLE

FINE - Eagle eye sharp, beak line sharp, feather tips distinct
VF - All feather outlines must show.
EF - Only slight wear evident on highest points.
AU - Barely detectable wear on the highest points. Must have some Mint luster
UNC - No wear evident anyplace. Must have full Mint luster.

		Flying Eagle			
		F-12	VF-20	EF-40	AU-50	MS-60

1856 .... (?) .... 4850. 5250. 5750. 6150. 7050.
  Actually a pattern but a quantity of non-Proofs were placed in circulation, probably during the following year. It is estimated that nearly 1,400 pieces were struck in all, including proofs and restrikes. The John A. Beck hoard in Pittsburgh contained more than 500 pieces. Beware of alterations. On all genuine specimens the upright of the 5 connects with the center of the knob, and, on the great majority of these, the E's in the reverse legend are closed by large connecting serifs. Eliasberg 5/96 Prf-64/66 $15,400.
1857 .... (17,450,000) .... (485)   24.00   33.00   85.00   135.   220.
  Double dates exist. Rev. vars. with high and low leaves at CT.
1858/7 .... (24,600,000) ....   175.   350.   500.   950.   1750.
  Large letters, overdate most obvious in early die state pieces, rare.

Large Letters (left), Small Letters (right)

	F-12	VF-20	EF-40	AU-50	MS-60

1858 .... (80)   24.00   34.00   97.50   165.   245.
  Large letters . A and M of AMERICA are joined at their bases. Vars. with high and low leaves at CT, the former much commoner.
1858 .... (200)   24.00   32.50   92.50   155.   220.
  Small letters A and M are separated. High and low leaves at CT, latter very scarce.

INDIAN HEAD

FINE - Liberty fully legible, but worn.
VF - Liberty shows slight wear, hairlines distinct.
EF - All details sharp, wear only on highest points
AU - Barely discernible wear on highest points. Must show some Mint luster.
UNC - No wear any place. Full Mint luster. All diamonds in hair ribbon show.
PROOF - High rim all about, mirror-like fields. Surface of letters flat instead of rounded and show some doubling, reliefs frosted.

LAUREL WREATH REVERSE

Indian, Laurel Wreath

	F-12	VF-20	EF-40	AU-50	MS-60
1858 .... (?)					

Actually a pattern, several minor vars., a quantity of non-proofs were placed in circulation, probably the same year.

1859 .... (36,400,000) .... (800)	12.00	31.00	75.00	130.	200.
1859					

Doubled date, one date over another, excessively rare.

OAK WREATH AND SHIELD REVERSE

COPPER-NICKEL

Indian, Oak Wreath and Shield

	F-12	VF-20	EF-40	AU-50	MS-60
1859 .... (?)					

Actually a pattern, but a quantity of non-proofs were placed in circulation, probably the following year, rare.

1860 .... (20,566,000) .... (1,000)	15.00	40.00	75.00	130.	235.
Type I: pointed bust as in 1859, very rare.					
1860	8.50	13.50	42.00	75.00	130.
Type II: rounded bust as in 1861-64.					
1861 .... (10,100,000) .... (1,000)	24.00	36.00	72.00	145.	180.
1862 .... (28,075,000) .... (550)	7.50	11.00	23.00	54.00	95.00
1863 .... (49,840,000) .... (460)	7.00	10.00	21.00	40.00	65.00
Excessively rare reeded edge pieces of this date are patterns, see pattern #E.112.					
1864 .... (13,740,000) .... (300)	21.00	24.00	44.00	72.00	135.

BRONZE COMPOSITION

Indian, Rounded Bust, No L on Ribbon

	F-12	VF-20	EF-40	AU-50	MS-60
1864 .... (39,233,714) .... (150)	11.00	22.00	36.00	48.00	80.00

Rounded bust, no L on ribbon.

Indian Head cents continued

	F-12	VF-20	EF-40	AU-50	MS-60
1864 .... (20)	85.00	110.	175.	225.	300.

Pointed bust, L on ribbon, as on all to follow. On very worn specimens, L may be difficult or impossible to see. Various recut dates exist.

	F-12	VF-20	EF-40	AU-50	MS-60
1865 .... (35,429,286) .... (500)	10.00	17.00	30.00	45.00	77.50

Knob of 6 is distinctly round.

1865

Fancy-top 5, extremely rare.

1865

Plain-top 5.

1865/4

Supposed top of 4 appears over fancy top 5, extremely rare. Status as overdate controversial.

	F-12	VF-20	EF-40	AU-50	MS-60
1866 .... (9,826,500) .... (725)	48.00	82.50	150.	180.	220.

One variety has boldly double-punched second 6.

	F-12	VF-20	EF-40	AU-50	MS-60
1867 .... (9,821,000) .... (625)	50.00	90.00	150.	180.	225.
1867/small 67	75.00	150.	250.	350.	450.

67 punched high and too softly, then corrected, scarce.

	F-12	VF-20	EF-40	AU-50	MS-60
1868 .... (10,266,500) .... (600)	45.00	67.00	115.	160.	235.
1869 .... (6,420,000) .... (600)	170.	215.	260.	350.	450.

1869/69

Four vars, the usual with a die crack from the 9 to the curl. The pieces offered as over-dates are mere recut dates. The most common shows a trace of the original 9 above the figure, so-called 1869/8.

	F-12	VF-20	EF-40	AU-50	MS-60
1870 .... (5,275,000) .... (1,000)	150.	210.	260.	340.	435.
1871 .... (3,929,500) .... (960)	195.	250.	310.	390.	450.
1872 .... (4,042,000) .... (950)	210.	275.	350.	425.	550.
1873 .... (11,676,500) .... (1,100)	37.50	60.00	90.00	260.	325.

Closed 3.

	F-12	VF-20	EF-40	AU-50	MS-60
1873	600.	1100.	2250.	3400.	5850.

Closed 3, doubled LIBERTY, actually a doubled die. A lesser variety shows doubling only on the ERTY.

	F-12	VF-20	EF-40	AU-50	MS-60
1873	26.00	42.00	85.00	120.	175.

Open 3.

	F-12	VF-20	EF-40	AU-50	MS-60
1874 .... (14,187,500) .... (700)	25.00	35.00	78.00	110.	135.
1875 .... (13,528,000) .... (700)	29.00	34.50	77.00	110.	140.

Many Indian head dates from now on include double-punched date vars., many scarce to rare. Only boldest types will be listed here.

	F-12	VF-20	EF-40	AU-50	MS-60
1876 .... (7,944,000) .... (1,150)	40.00	48.00	95.00	130.	205.
1877 .... (852,500) .... (510)	750.	925.	1375.	1700.	2150.

Rarity of series, beware of counterfeits and alterations.

	F-12	VF-20	EF-40	AU-50	MS-60
1878 .... (5,797,500) .... (2,350)	44.00	63.00	105.	160.	190.
1879 .... (16,228,000) .... (3,200)	8.50	19.00	39.00	47.50	62.50
1880 .... (38,961,000) .... (3,955)	4.50	7.50	22.00	35.00	57.50
1881 .... (39,208,000) .... (3,575)	4.00	6.50	15.00	23.50	37.50
1882 .... (38,578,000) .... (3,100)	4.00	6.00	14.25	22.00	35.00
1883 .... (45,591,500) .... (6,609)	3.75	6.00	14.00	21.50	35.00
1884 .... (23,257,800) .... (3,942)	5.00	9.00	16.00	28.00	52.50
1885 .... (11,761,594) .... (3,790)	9.75	19.00	45.00	60.00	90.00
1886 .... (17,650,000) .... (4,290)	11.00	35.00	65.00	85.00	135.

Type I: last feather points between I and C.

	F-12	VF-20	EF-40	AU-50	MS-60
1886	15.00	50.00	85.00	140.	250.

Type II: last feather points between C and A, as on all that follow.

	F-12	VF-20	EF-40	AU-50	MS-60
1887 .... (45,223,523) .... (2,960)	3.00	5.50	11.50	18.50	32.00
1888/7 .... (37,489,832) .... (4,582)	1100.	1400.	1750.	2500.	—

Break in denticles over TED of UNITED, usually in low grade, extremely rare in Unc.

	F-12	VF-20	EF-40	AU-50	MS-60
1888	2.90	5.50	12.00	20.00	36.00
1889 .... (48,866,025) .... (3,336)	2.90	4.75	9.75	18.00	30.50
1890 .... (57,180,114) .... (2,740)	2.45	3.75	9.50	16.50	29.50
1891 .... (47,070,000) .... (2,350)	2.40	3.75	9.50	17.00	30.00
1892 .... (37,647,087) .... (2,745)	2.40	3.75	9.50	16.50	29.50
1893 .... (46,640,000) .... (2,195)	2.40	3.75	9.50	17.00	28.75
1894 .... (16,749,500) .... (2,632)	5.50	8.75	15.00	25.00	45.00

1894

Boldly doubled date, very scarce, regular prices plus 50 percent.

	F-12	VF-20	EF-40	AU-50	MS-60
1895 .... (38,341,574) .... (2,062)	2.40	3.50	9.00	16.00	28.00
1896 .... (39,055,431) .... (1,862)	2.40	3.50	8.75	15.00	27.50
1897 .... (50,464,392) .... (1,938)	2.15	3.25	8.50	15.00	27.50
1898 .... (49,821,284) .... (1,795)	2.15	3.25	8.00	14.00	26.00
1899 .... (53,598,000) .... (2,031)	2.15	3.25	8.00	14.00	26.00
1900 .... (66,831,502) .... (2,262)	1.90	2.25	6.50	12.75	21.00
1901 .... (79,609,158) .... (1,985)	1.90	2.25	6.00	12.50	20.00
1902 .... (87,374,704) .... (2,018)	1.90	2.25	6.00	12.50	20.00
1903 .... (85,092,703) .... (1,790)	1.90	2.25	6.00	12.50	20.00

Indian Head cents continued

			F-12	VF-20	EF-40	AU-50	MS-60
1904	(61,326,198)	(1,817)	1.90	2.25	6.00	12.50	20.00
1905	(80,717,011)	(2,152)	1.90	2.25	6.00	12.50	20.00
1906	(96,020,530)	(1,725)	1.90	2.25	6.50	12.75	20.50
1907	(108,137,143)	(1,475)	1.90	2.25	6.00	12.50	20.00
1908	(32,326,367)	(1,620)	1.90	2.25	6.50	13.00	21.00
1908-S	(1,115,000)		50.00	53.00	75.00	125.	180.
1909	(14,368,470)	(2,175)	2.50	3.50	8.50	13.50	26.00

1909-S

			F-12	VF-20	EF-40	AU-50	MS-60
1909-S	(309,000)		325.	375.	410.	435.	500.

LINCOLN HEAD

VF - Jaw and cheek separated. Wheat ears show all lines.
EF - Slight wear on high points only.
AU - Just the slightest wear on highest points. Must show some Mint luster.
UNC - No wear at all. Full Mint luster.
LATE PROOFS. See condition guide for Indian cents.
MATTE PROOFS. Planchets sandblasted or acid treated before strike, resulting in extremely granular surfaces but sharp strike, high rims. Check published die characteristics as many deceptive business strikes exist.

WHEAT EAR REVERSE

Lincoln, Wheat Ear

			F-12	EF-40	AU-50	MS-60	MS-65
1909 V.D.B.	(27,994,580)	(420)	2.00	2.90	4.45	9.50	39.00
Designer's initials on rev. between wheat stems.							
1909 V.D.B.							
Doubled obverse die., most visible on numbers.							
1909-S V.D.B.	(484,000)		435.	590.	650.	715.	1800.
Genuine specimens almost always have bold dots after initials V.D.B. but, on the whole, are somewhat softly struck. Beware of counterfeits or alterations.							
1909	(72,700,420)	(2,198)	0.95	2.75	5.75	12.50	60.00
Without designer's initials on the rev. as are those that follow.							
1909-S	(1,825,000)		50.00	80.00	105.	125.	325.
1909-S/Horizontal S			60.00	95.00	135.	190.	450.
Scarce.							
1910	(146,798,813)	(2,405)	0.30	2.00	4.50	14.00	67.50
Most Proofs are Satin.							
1910-S	(6,045,000)		8.00	19.00	47.50	55.00	275.
1911	(101,176,054)	(1,733)	0.50	4.00	8.00	19.00	190.
Satin, fewer Matte Proofs.							
1911-D	(12,672,000)		6.00	30.00	52.50	70.00	730.
1911-S	(4,026,000)		16.00	32.00	65.00	125.	975.
1912	(68,150,915)	(2,145)	1.50	6.75	13.00	23.50	125.
Matte Proofs.							
1912-D	(10,411,000)		7.00	35.00	58.00	115.	875.
1912-S	(4,431,000)		11.50	29.00	55.00	95.00	1300.
1913	(76,529,504)	(2,848)	1.00	8.00	15.00	22.00	225.
Matte Proofs.							
1913-D	(15,804,000)		4.00	20.00	42.00	65.00	950.
1913-S	(6,101,000)		7.00	24.00	50.00	110.	1450.
1914	(75,237,067)	(1,365)	1.50	8.50	17.50	35.00	200.
Matte Proofs.							

Lincoln cents continued

1914-D

	F-12	EF-40	AU-50	MS-60	MS-65
1914-D .... (1,193,000)	130.	410.	625.	1075.	5500.

Beware of altered dates and false mint marks, plus die struck counterfeits.

| 1914-S .... (4,137,000) .... | 11.00 | 35.00 | 75.00 | 190. | 5600. |

Only found brilliant when cleaned.

| 1915 .... (29,090,970) .... (1,150) | 4.50 | 31.00 | 55.00 | 80.00 | 360. |

Matte Proofs.

1915-D .... (22,050,000)	1.75	10.00	20.50	50.00	290.
1915-S .... (4,833,000)	7.50	27.00	45.00	92.50	2575.
1916 .... (131,832,627) .... (1,050)	0.40	2.50	5.50	12.00	100.

Modified obverse design used this year and following, Matte Proofs.

1916-D .... (35,956,000)	1.25	7.75	19.50	48.00	1350.
1916-S .... (22,510,000)	1.60	8.00	20.00	62.50	4750.
1917 .... (196,429,785)	0.30	2.25	4.75	12.00	125.

A very few clandestine Matte Proofs reported to exist.

| 1917 .... | 240. | 900. | 1100. | 1500. | 12000. |

Doubled die obverse, notably at date, very rare.

1917-D .... (55,120,000)	1.75	9.00	19.00	60.00	600.
1917-S .... (32,620,000)	0.75	6.75	16.00	62.50	2250.
1918 .... (288,104,634)	0.30	2.00	4.75	10.00	120.

Designer's initials VDB restored below shoulder as on those that follow.

1918-D .... (47,830,000)	1.50	8.00	19.50	47.50	900.
1918-S .... (34,680,000)	1.00	6.00	21.00	57.50	3800.
1919 .... (392,021,000)	0.30	2.00	4.50	9.00	65.00
1919-D .... (57,154,000)	0.60	4.50	16.50	45.00	610.
1919-S .... (139,760,000)	0.40	2.00	12.50	35.00	2650.
1920 .... (310,165,000)	0.35	2.00	4.50	10.50	70.00
1920-D .... (49,280,000)	0.65	5.75	18.50	55.00	675.
1920-S .... (46,220,000)	0.60	3.75	20.00	90.00	4900.
1921 .... (39,157,000)	0.50	4.50	14.00	35.00	160.
1921-S .... (15,274,000)	1.50	11.50	40.00	85.00	2750.
1922-D .... (7,160,000)	7.50	17.50	42.50	60.00	565.

1922 Missing D

	F-12	EF-40	AU-50	MS-60	MS-65
1922 (D)	385.	1350.	2600.	6000.	—

Plain, genuine, certifiable "No Mint Mark" coins were struck from obverse die ground down to remove clash marks; always found paired with an approximately normal reverse. Two other pairs of dies became heavily worn and/or filled with dirt, sometimes producing coins without Mint marks, but more often producing "weak D," aka "Broken D" pieces worth substantially less. These latter two die pairs are characterized by well worn or "mushy" reverse designs. Beware of removed D's.

| 1923 .... (74,723,000) .... | 0.30 | 2.75 | 5.00 | 14.50 | 185. |
| 1923-S .... (8,700,000) .... | 2.75 | 17.00 | 57.50 | 175. | 4000. |

Almost never found brilliant.

| 1924 .... (75,178,000) .... | 0.30 | 3.00 | 8.50 | 21.00 | 135. |
| 1924-D .... (2,520,000) .... | 11.50 | 50.00 | 115. | 230. | 2900. |

Branch mint coins of all denominations from this date through 1926 are usually weakly struck due to improper hardening of working dies. This issue is almost never found bright.

1924-S .... (11,696,000)	1.30	9.50	35.00	95.00	4500.
1925 .... (139,949,000)	0.20	1.75	4.25	9.25	60.00
1925-D .... (22,580,000)	0.60	7.00	16.50	45.00	900.
1925-S .... (26,380,000)	0.50	4.50	18.00	55.00	3750.
1926 .... (157,088,000)	0.20	1.75	3.75	8.00	37.50
1926-D .... (28,020,000)	0.60	5.50	14.00	35.00	900.
1926-S .... (4,550,000)	2.75	10.00	49.00	110.	—
1927 .... (144,440,000)	0.20	1.75	3.85	9.00	75.00

Lincoln cents continued

	F-12	EF-40	AU-50	MS-60	MS-65
1927-D ....(27,170,000)	0.50	3.50	11.00	32.50	800.
1927-S ....(14,276,000)	1.10	7.00	21.50	60.00	2850.
1928 ....(134,116,000)	0.20	1.45	3.00	8.50	55.00
1928-D ....(31,170,000)	0.40	2.50	9.50	24.00	475.
1928-S ....(17,266,000)	0.60	3.50	14.50	44.00	425.
1929 ....(185,262,000)	0.20	1.25	2.85	6.50	55.00
1929-D ....(41,730,000)	0.35	1.75	4.75	17.00	145.
1929-S ....(50,148,000)	0.35	1.40	3.00	9.00	110.
1930 ....(157,415,000)	0.20	1.00	2.25	4.75	29.00
1930-D ....(40,100,000)	0.35	1.75	4.50	13.00	70.00
1930-S ....(24,286,000)	0.35	1.15	2.50	6.50	45.00
1931 ....(19,396,000)	0.65	1.85	6.75	15.00	80.00
1931-D ....(4,480,000)	3.25	8.00	26.00	45.00	550.
1931-S ....(866,000)	33.00	40.00	47.00	57.50	195.

Genuine pieces have small, tight 3; hoarded in immense quantities, easily found in red Unc., frequently spotty.

	F-12	EF-40	AU-50	MS-60	MS-65
1932 ....(9,062,000)	1.75	3.50	9.00	16.50	57.50
1932-D ....(10,500,000)	1.25	2.00	7.00	14.00	49.00
1933 ....(14,360,000)	1.35	2.50	8.50	15.00	52.50
1933-D ....(6,200,000)	2.50	3.75	10.50	16.00	55.00

	EF-40	AU-50	MS-60	MS-65	PF-65
1934 ....(219,080,000)	0.75	1.50	3.00	13.75	*
1934-D ....(28,446,000)	5.00	8.75	11.50	30.00	*
1935 ....(245,388,000)	0.65	0.90	1.25	6.00	*
1935-D ....(47,000,000)	0.85	1.65	3.25	18.50	*
1935-S ....(38,702,000)	2.50	4.25	6.50	45.00	*
1936 ....(309,632,000) ....(5,569)	0.70	0.90	1.25	6.00	850.

1936
Proofs coinage resumed, found with Satin and Brilliant Proof finishes. Beware polished business strikes.

1936
Doubled die obv., Two vars.

	EF-40	AU-50	MS-60	MS-65	PF-65
1936-D ....(40,620,000)	0.85	1.00	1.85	10.00	*
1936-S ....(29,130,000)	1.00	1.60	2.65	10.75	*
1937 ....(309,170,000) ....(9,320)	0.50	0.60	0.80	6.00	110.
1937-D ....(50,430,000)	0.65	1.00	2.25	6.50	*
1937-S ....(34,500,000)	0.65	1.00	2.00	8.00	*
1938 ....(156,682,000) ....(14,734)	0.60	1.00	1.25	6.00	100.
1938-D ....(20,010,000)	0.85	1.00	1.85	6.50	*
1938-S ....(15,180,000)	0.80	1.00	2.50	9.50	*
1939 ....(316,466,000) ....(13,520)	0.30	0.40	0.50	6.00	95.00
1939-D ....(15,160,000)	1.00	1.30	1.75	13.00	*
1939-S ....(52,070,000)	0.75	1.00	1.30	12.50	*
1940 ....(586,810,000) ....(15,872)	0.40	0.45	0.60	3.00	90.00
1940-D ....(81,390,000)	0.60	0.70	0.90	3.75	*
1940-S ....(112,940,000)	0.60	0.90	1.25	5.75	*

Varieties with small S as in 1939 and large S as in 1942.

	EF-40	AU-50	MS-60	MS-65	PF-65
1941 ....(887,018,000) ....(21,100)	0.50	0.55	0.80	4.00	85.00
1941-D ....(128,700,000)	0.90	1.45	1.65	6.00	*
1941-S ....(92,360,000)	0.80	1.00	1.75	9.50	*

Varieties with small S as in 1939 and large S as in 1942.

	EF-40	AU-50	MS-60	MS-65	PF-65
1942 ....(657,796,000) ....(32,600)	0.40	0.45	0.65	2.75	87.00
1942-D ....(206,698,000)	0.40	0.45	0.60	3.75	*
1942-S ....(85,590,000)	1.00	1.50	2.50	20.00	*

1943
Very rare Mint error, struck on leftover bronze planchets, ANACS believes about 40 genuine pieces known, plus hundreds of copper-plated steel pieces fraudulently created. These are magnetic; authentication is strongly recommended.

1943-D
Same remarks as preceding, believed unique.

1943-S
Same remarks as preceding, perhaps seven known.

ZINC-COATED STEEL CENTS

	Zinc-coated steel				
	EF-40	AU-50	MS-60	MS-65	PF-65
1943 .... (684,628,670)	0.40	0.65	0.80	4.00	*
1943-D .... (217,660,000)	0.60	0.75	0.90	6.50	*
1943-S .... (191,550,000)	0.75	1.00	1.40	10.00	*

1944
Struck on steel blanks originally planned for U.S. cents, used for Belgian 2 francs 1944 (Y-56, KM-133). Another very rare Mint error, greatly overshadowed by the 1943 bronze cents.

1944-D
No Belgian coins were struck at branch Mints in 1944, making steel cents from either true transitional errors. Very rare but underappreciated.

1944-S
Same remarks as preceding.

SHELL-CASE BRASS CENTS

	Shell-case brass				
	EF-40	AU-50	MS-60	MS-65	PF-65
1944 .... (1,435,400,000)	0.20	0.35	0.42	1.75	*
1944-D .... (430,578,000)	0.30	0.35	0.40	2.50	*
1944-D/S	195.	245.	325.	1700.	*
Var. I with top half of S visible above the D is the more valuable.					
1944-D/S	90.00	100.	145.	875.	*
Var. II shows central portion of S inside and to left of D.					
1944-S .... (282,760,000)	0.25	0.35	0.40	2.50	*
1945 .... (1,040,515,000)	0.24	0.40	0.55	1.70	*
1945-D .... (226,268,000)	0.25	0.40	0.45	1.60	*
1945-S .... (181,770,000)	0.25	0.30	0.40	2.00	*
1946 .... (991,655,000)	0.20	0.25	0.30	1.25	*
1946-D .... (315,690,000)	0.20	0.25	0.30	1.50	*
1946-S .... (198,100,000)	0.30	0.35	0.40	2.00	*

BRONZE ALLOY RESUMED

	EF-40	AU-50	MS-60	MS-65	PF-65
1947 .... (190,555,000)	0.40	0.75	1.15	3.00	*
1947-D .... (194,750,000)	0.20	0.25	0.30	1.75	*
1947-S .... (99,000,000)	0.26	0.35	0.50	2.00	*
1948 .... (317,570,000)	0.30	0.35	0.40	2.25	*
1948-D .... (172,637,500)	0.35	0.40	0.45	2.50	*
1948-S .... (81,735,000)	0.50	0.85	0.90	3.00	*
1949 .... (217,775,000)	0.40	0.50	0.55	3.00	*
1949-D .... (153,132,500)	0.45	0.50	0.55	3.50	*
1949-S .... (64,290,000)	0.60	0.75	1.00	7.00	*
1950 .... (272,635,000) .... (51,386)	0.25	0.40	0.55	2.00	40.00
Proofs found with Satin and Brilliant finishes.					
1950-D .... (334,950,000)	0.20	0.25	0.45	1.50	*
1950-S .... (118,505,000)	0.25	0.55	0.65	2.65	*
1951 .... (294,576,000) .... (57,500)	0.25	0.40	0.55	2.00	30.00
1951-D .... (625,355,000)	0.20	0.25	0.30	1.65	*
1951-S .... (136,010,000)	0.35	0.40	0.45	3.00	*
1952 .... (186,765,000) .... (81,980)	0.25	0.35	0.50	2.75	25.00
1952-D .... (746,130,000)	0.15	0.20	0.23	1.60	*
1952-S .... (137,800,004)	0.25	0.50	0.75	3.30	*
1953 .... (256,755,000) .... (128,800)	0.15	0.16	0.18	1.20	22.00

Lincoln cents continued

	EF-40	AU-50	MS-60	MS-65	PF-65
1953-D ....(700,515,000)	0.15	0.16	0.18	1.25	*
1953-S ....(181,835,000)	0.16	0.26	0.35	1.75	*
1954.......................(71,640,050) ....(233,300)	0.20	0.30	0.35	1.50	12.00
1954-D ....(251,552,500)	0.10	0.20	0.25	0.50	*
1954-S ....(96,190,000)	0.08	0.10	0.12	0.60	*
1955.....................(330,580,000) ....(378,200)	0.09	0.10	0.12	0.75	11.50

Doubled obverse die

	EF-40	AU-50	MS-60	MS-65	PF-65
1955	480.	540.	675.	16500.	*

Doubled obv. die. Estimated 20,000 struck as part of above total. Date and legend must be clearly and fully doubled. Many counterfeits exist. Other pieces from genuine die, worn at last 5 worth little or no premium.

1955-D ....(563,257,500)	0.09	0.10	0.12	0.80	*
1955-S ....(44,610,000)	0.20	0.22	0.25	1.25	*

Widely hoarded in Unc. as last year of San Francisco Mint.

1956 ....(420,745,000) ....(669,384)	0.05	0.10	0.12	0.60	3.50
1956-D ....(1,098,201,100)	0.05	0.10	0.12	0.60	*
1957 ....(282,540,000) ....(1,247,952)	0.05	0.10	0.12	0.60	2.50

Peak year of Proof coin boom, this huge number was struck to break the market.

1957-D ....(1,051,342,000)	0.05	0.10	0.12	0.60	*
1958 ....(252,525,000) ....(875,652)	0.05	0.10	0.12	0.50	2.00
1958					

Doubled die obv., presently very rare.

1958-D ....(800,953,300)	0.05	0.10	0.12	0.50	*

Some 1958 P and D cents show hub flaws that may be remnants of a 7 under the 8, but which more likely are stray tool marks left by the engraver.

LINCOLN MEMORIAL REVERSE

Lincoln, Memorial

	EF-40	AU-50	MS-60	MS-65	PF-65
1959 ....(609,715,000) ....(1,149,291)	FV	FV	FV	0.50	1.50
1959-D ....(1,279,760,000)	FV	FV	FV	0.50	*

Small Date (left), Large Date (right)

	EF-40	AU-50	MS-60	MS-65	PF-65
1960 ....(586,405,000) ....(1,691,602)	0.85	1.00	1.25	6.00	19.00

Small date, top serif of 6 is short of an imaginary perpendicular line drawn straight up from ball of 6.

1960	FV	FV	FV	0.50	1.25

Large date, incl. in total above, top serif extends over imaginary line.

1960

Large over small date. Proof only, scarce.

1960-D ....(1,580,884,000)	0.10	0.12	0.15	1.65	*

Small date.

1960-D	FV	FV	FV	0.50	*

Large date, incl. in total above.

1960-D/D

Small date over large date, D over D, scarce.

1961 ....(753,345,000) ....(3,028,244)	FV	FV	FV	0.50	0.75
1961-D ....(1,753,266,700)	FV	FV	FV	0.50	*
1961-D					

Over horizontal D.

Lincoln cents continued

		EF-40	AU-50	MS-60	MS-65	PF-65
1962 .... (606,045,000) .... (3,218,019)		FV	FV	FV	0.50	0.75

During this year tin was dropped from the alloy used for cents, making it technically brass rather than bronze.

		EF-40	AU-50	MS-60	MS-65	PF-65
1962-D .... (1,793,148,400)		FV	FV	FV	0.50	*
1963 .... (754,110,000) .... (3,075,645)		FV	FV	FV	0.50	0.75
1963-D .... (1,774,020,400)		FV	FV	FV	0.50	*
1964 .... (2,648,575,000) .... (3,950,762)		FV	FV	FV	0.50	0.75

Frozen date, many struck in 1965. Counterfeit multi- strike coins exist.

		EF-40	AU-50	MS-60	MS-65	PF-65
1964-D .... (3,799,071,500)		FV	FV	FV	0.50	*
1965 .... (1,497,224,900)		FV	FV	FV	0.55	*

Struck at Philadelphia, Denver and San Francisco without Mint marks as Treasury response to so-called "coin shortage," then loudly blamed on collectors. 2,360,000 cents were included in Special Mint Sets (SMS) cobbled up as an inferior substitute for traditional Proof sets.

		EF-40	AU-50	MS-60	MS-65	PF-65
1966 .... (2,188,147,783)		FV	FV	FV	0.60	*

Struck at Philadelphia, Denver and San Francisco without Mint marks, 2,261,583 were included in SMS.

		EF-40	AU-50	MS-60	MS-65	PF-65
1967 .... (3,048,667,100)		FV	FV	FV	0.55	*

Struck at Philadelphia, Denver and San Francisco without Mint marks. 1,863,344 incl. in SMS.

		EF-40	AU-50	MS-60	MS-65	PF-65
1968 .... (1,707,880,970)		FV	FV	FV	0.50	*
1968-D .... (2,886,269,600)		FV	FV	FV	0.50	*
1968-S .... (258,270,001) .... (3,041,506)		FV	FV	FV	0.85	0.90

Proof coinage resumed.

		EF-40	AU-50	MS-60	MS-65	PF-65
1969 .... (1,136,910,000)		FV	FV	FV	1.35	*

Revised portrait introduced to restore obv. to Brenner's original proportions. Counterfeit doubled die pieces exist.

		EF-40	AU-50	MS-60	MS-65	PF-65
1969-D .... (4,002,832,200)		FV	FV	FV	0.50	*
1969-S .... (544,375,000) .... (2,934,631)		FV	FV	FV	0.50	0.90
1969-S		6500.	7750.	—	20000.	

Doubled die obverse, rare. A few were seized by zealous Secret Service agents as counterfeit; most were returned to owners over next few years.

		EF-40	AU-50	MS-60	MS-65	PF-65
1970 .... (1,898,315,000)		FV	FV	FV	1.00	*
1970-D .... (2,891,438,900)		FV	FV	FV	0.50	*
1970-S .... (690,560,004) .... (2,632,810)		9.50	11.00	19.00	62.50	55.00

High 7, so-called small date.

		EF-40	AU-50	MS-60	MS-65	PF-65
1970-S		FV	FV	FV	0.50	0.90

Low 7, so-called large date.

		EF-40	AU-50	MS-60	MS-65	PF-65
1971 .... (1,919,490,000)		FV	FV	FV	1.35	*
1971-D .... (2,911,045,600)		FV	FV	FV	1.10	*
1971-S .... (525,133,459) .... (3,220,733)		FV	FV	FV	1.00	0.90
1972 .... (2,933,255,000)		FV	FV	FV	0.50	*

1972 Doubled Die

		EF-40	AU-50	MS-60	MS-65	PF-65
1972		—	145.	160.	315.	*

Double die, Var. 1, date and motto clearly doubled. Counterfeits exist. Several lesser varieties with minor doubling worth only small premiums.

		EF-40	AU-50	MS-60	MS-65	PF-65
1972-D .... (2,665,071,400)		FV	FV	FV	0.50	*
1972-S .... (377,019,108) .... (3,260,996)		FV	FV	FV	0.50	0.90
1973 .... (3,728,245,000)		FV	FV	FV	0.50	*

Modified reverse this year only, large FG.

		EF-40	AU-50	MS-60	MS-65	PF-65
1973-D .... (3,549,576,588)		FV	FV	FV	0.50	*
1973-S .... (317,177,295) .... (2,760,339)		FV	FV	FV	0.50	0.90
1974 .... (4,232,140,523)		FV	FV	FV	0.50	*

Modified reverse introduced this year, medium FG. Aluminum and bronze-clad steel trial strikes, see introduction and pattern section.

		EF-40	AU-50	MS-60	MS-65	PF-65
1974-D .... (4,235,098,000)		FV	FV	FV	0.50	*
1974-S .... (409,426,660) .... (2,612,568)		FV	FV	FV	0.85	0.90
1975 .... (5,451,476,142)		FV	FV	FV	0.50	*
1975-D .... (4,505,275,300)		FV	FV	FV	0.50	*
1975-S .... (2,845,450)		*	*	*	*	3.00

Proof only.

		EF-40	AU-50	MS-60	MS-65	PF-65
1976 .... (4,674,292,426)		FV	FV	FV	0.50	*
1976-D .... (4,221,592,455)		FV	FV	FV	0.50	*
1976-S .... (4,123,056)		*	*	*	*	2.50

Proof only.

Lincoln cents continued

	EF-40	AU-50	MS-60	MS-65	PF-65
1977 .... (4,469,930,000)	FV	FV	FV	0.50	*

A 1977/6 cent was authenticated by the U.S. Mint Laboratory as genuine, but later condemned after other, altered coins of wholly different fabric were found and seized. The owner of the coin, an immigrant, allegedly confessed to altering some coins, but was not prosecuted. No duplicate of the specimen originally authenticated has been reported.

	EF-40	AU-50	MS-60	MS-65	PF-65
1977-D .... (4,194,062,300)	FV	FV	FV	0.50	*
1977-S .... (3,236,798)	*	*	*	*	1.50
Proof only.					
1978 .... (5,558,605,000)	FV	FV	FV	0.50	*
1978-D .... (4,280,233,400)	FV	FV	FV	0.50	*
1978-S .... (3,120,285)	*	*	*	*	1.60
Proof only.					
1979 .... (6,018,515,000)	FV	FV	FV	0.50	*
1979-D .... (4,139,357,254)	FV	FV	FV	0.50	*
1979-S .... (3,677,175)	*	*	*	*	2.00
Proof only. Type I S, blurry, same as 1978.					
1979-S	*	*	*	*	2.50

Type II S, clear, same as 1980. Found on approximately two coins out of nine overall, though original shipping boxes usually contain one or the other.

	EF-40	AU-50	MS-60	MS-65	PF-65
1980 .... (7,414,705,000)	FV	FV	FV	0.50	*
1980-D .... (5,140,098,660)	FV	FV	FV	0.50	*
1980-S .... (3,554,806)	*	*	*	*	1.00
Proof only.					
1981 .... (7,491,750,000)	FV	FV	FV	0.50	*
1981-D .... (5,373,235,677)	FV	FV	FV	0.50	*
1981-S .... (4,063,083)	*	*	*	*	1.50
Proof only, minor varieties in Mint mark style exist.					
1982 .... (10,712,525,000)	FV	FV	0.12	0.50	*
Brass, large date.					
1982	FV	FV	0.17	1.00	*
Brass, small date.					
1982-D .... (6,012,979,368)	FV	FV	0.12	0.70	*
Brass, large date only.					
1982-S .... (3,857,479)	*	*	*	*	2.00
Brass, Proof only.					

COPPER PLATED ZINC

1982 copper-plated zinc

	EF-40	AU-50	MS-60	MS-65	PF-65
1982 .... (incl. above)	FV	FV	0.22	0.95	*
Zinc, large date.					
1982 .... (incl. above)	FV	FV	0.67	1.75	*
Zinc, small date.					
1982-D .... (incl. above)	FV	FV	0.17	1.20	*
Zinc, large date					
1982-D .... (incl. above)	FV	FV	0.14	0.85	*
Zinc, small date.					
1983 .... (7,752,355,000)	FV	FV	FV	0.50	*
1983	—	130.	145.	250.	*
Doubled die rev., lettering boldly doubled.					
1983-D .... (6,467,199,428)	FV	FV	FV	0.50	*
1983-S .... (3,279,126)	*	*	*	*	2.75
Proof only.					
1984 .... (8,151,079,000)	FV	FV	FV	0.50	*
1984	—	90.00	135.	190.	*
Doubled die obverse.					
1984-D .... (5,569,238,906)	FV	FV	0.17	0.75	*
1984-S .... (3,065,110)	*	*	*	*	2.00
Proof only.					
1985 .... (5,648,489,887)	FV	FV	FV	0.50	*
1985-D .... (5,287,399,926)	FV	FV	FV	0.50	*
1985-S .... (3,362,821)	*	*	*	*	2.00
Proof only.					

Lincoln cents continued

		EF-40	AU-50	MS-60	MS-65	PF-65
1986	(4,491,395,493)	FV	FV	0.15	0.90	*
1986-D	(4,442,866,698)	FV	FV	FV	0.50	*
1986-S	(3,010,497)	*	*	*	*	5.50
Proof only.						
1987	(4,682,466,931)	FV	FV	FV	0.50	*
1987-D	(4,879,389,514)	FV	FV	FV	0.50	*
1987-S	(3,792,233)	*	*	*	*	1.75
Proof only.						
1988	(6,092,810,000)	FV	FV	FV	0.50	*
1988-D	(5,253,740,443)	FV	FV	FV	0.50	*
1988-S	(2,600,618)	*	*	*	*	2.00
Proof only.						
1989	(7,261,535,000)	FV	FV	FV	0.50	*
1989-D	(5,345,467,711)	FV	FV	FV	0.50	*
1989-S	(3,220,914)	*	*	*	*	2.50
Proof only.						
1990	(6,851,765,000)	FV	FV	FV	0.50	*
1990-D	(4,922,894,553)	FV	FV	FV	0.50	*
1990-S	(3,299,559)	*	*	*	*	4.50
Proof only. Some Proofs missing Mint mark, Prf-65 $1,200.						
1991	(5,165,940,000)	FV	FV	FV	0.50	*
1991-D	(4,158,442,076)	FV	FV	FV	0.50	*
1991-S	(2,867,787)	*	*	*	*	5.50
Proof only.						
1992	(4,648,905,000)	FV	FV	FV	0.50	*
1992-D	(4,448,673,300)	FV	FV	FV	0.50	*
1992-S	(4,176,544)	*	*	*	*	3.50
Proof only.						
1993	(5,684,705,000)	FV	FV	FV	0.50	*
1993-D	(6,426,650,571)	FV	FV	FV	0.50	*
1993-S	(2,569,882)	*	*	*	*	5.00
Proof only.						
1994	(6,500,850,000)	FV	FV	FV	0.50	*
1994-D	(7,131,765,000)	FV	FV	FV	0.50	*
1994-S	(3,222,140)	*	*	*	*	4.00
Proof only.						
1995	(6,411,440,000)	FV	FV	FV	0.50	*

1995 doubled obverse die

		EF-40	AU-50	MS-60	MS-65	PF-65
1995		—	14.00	19.00	25.00	*

Doubled Die obv. Strong doubling at LIBERTY and in IN GOD. Apparent rotation pivot at 4 o'clock. Early die states bring the premium. Later die states show severe polishing to correct die clashing, a die chip in the date, and a die crack at the back of Lincoln's head. Latest die states show mushy doubling, barely visible. At least two reverse dies were used, the first probably replaced after clashing.

		EF-40	AU-50	MS-60	MS-65	PF-65
1995-D	(7,128,560,000)	FV	FV	FV	0.50	*
1995-S	(2,791,067)	*	*	*	*	5.50
Proof only.						
1996	(6,612,465,000)	FV	FV	FV	0.50	*
1996-D	(6,510,795,000)	FV	FV	FV	0.50	*
1996-S	(2,920,158)	*	*	*	*	4.50
Proof only.						
1997	(NR)	FV	FV	FV	0.50	*
1997-D	(NR)	FV	FV	FV	0.50	*
1997-S	(NR)	*	*	*	*	6.00
Proof only.						

Two cents

FINE - Motto complete. WE visible but thickened.
VF - All shield lines visible.
EF - All details sharp.
AU - Barely detectable wear on highest points. Must show some Mint luster.
UNC - No wear discernible anywhere. Full Mint luster.
PROOF - As in Indian Cents

*Small Motto obverse and reverse, and
Large Motto obverse*

	VF-20	AU-50	MS-60	MS-65	PF-65
1864 .... (19,847,500) .... (100)	200.	415.	515.	3300.	65000.

Small motto, O of GOD is almost round and is higher than D which is distant, S in TRUST has no serifs.

| 1864 .... | 24.00 | 50.00 | 97.50 | 900. | 4250. |

Large motto, O of GOD is oval, and is lower than D, which almost touches, S in TRUST has marked serifs.

1864
Doubled date, Vars. exist.
1864
Tripled date, very rare.

| 1865 .... (13,640,000) .... (500) | 24.00 | 52.50 | 100. | 1025. | 3250. |

1865
Fancy-top 5.
1865
Plain-top 5.
1865
Doubled date, several vars. exist.
1865/4
Fancy-top 5 shows supposed corner of 4 between knob and upright; status as true overdate uncertain, very rare.

| 1866 .... (3,177,000) .... (725) | 25.00 | 56.00 | 110. | 1600. | 1850. |

1866
Doubled date. Original figures slant upwards boldly.

| 1867 .... (2,938,750) .... (625) | 24.00 | 65.00 | 115. | 1550. | 2050. |

1867
Doubled die obv., date and motto vars.

| 1868 .... (2,803,750) .... (600) | 24.00 | 75.00 | 120. | 1650. | 1825. |
| 1869 .... (1,546,500) .... (600) | 26.00 | 85.00 | 120. | 1700. | 1900. |

1869/69
So-called 1869/8, usually with die break to left from base of 1.

| 1870 .... (861,250) .... (1,000) | 35.00 | 95.00 | 160. | 1950. | 2025. |
| 1871 .... (721,250) .... (960) | 40.00 | 125. | 215. | 2400. | 2050. |

1871
New hubs used 1871-73.
1871
Doubled die obverse.

| 1872 .... (65,000) .... (950) | 285. | 585. | 750. | 2850. | 2150. |

Many times rarer in Unc. than as a Proof.

| 1873 .... (600) | | 1100. | 1250. | —— | 2800. |

Closed 3, Proof only

| 1873 .... (500?) | | —— | 1450. | —— | 6000. |

Open 3, restrike proof only, rare.

Three cents

FINE - All hair curls well defined.
VF - Details sharp, but easily seen wear on high points.
EF - Wear visible only on close examination.
AU - As EF, but with some Mint luster.
UNC - Full Mint luster. No wear evident anywhere.
PROOF - As in Indian Cents.

		Copper-nickel 3 cents			
	VF-20	**AU-50**	**MS-60**	**MS-65**	**PF-65**
1865 .... (11,382,000) .... (400)	15.00	35.00	80.00	675.	5500.
1865					
Doubled date. Vars. exist.					
1866 .... (4,801,000) .... (725)	15.00	35.00	80.00	685.	1950.
1867 .... (3,915,000) .... (625)	15.00	36.00	82.00	700.	1100.
1867					
Doubled date, first date punched too high.					
1868 .... (3,252,000) .... (600)	15.00	37.00	83.00	685.	1225.
1868					
Doubled date.					
1869 .... (1,604,000) .... (600)	15.00	38.00	85.00	775.	975.
1869					
Doubled date, first date punched too low, scarce.					
1870 .... (1,335,000) .... (1,000)	15.00	40.00	88.00	750.	1100.
1870					
Doubled date, first date punched too far to the left, and too low.					
1871 .... (604,000) .... (960)	15.00	50.00	105.	750.	1000.
1872 .... (862,000) .... (950)	15.00	48.00	93.00	1200.	950.
1873 .... (1,100)	22.00	65.00	140.	2100.	925.
Closed 3, all Proof this var.					
1873 .... (1,173,000)	18.00	40.00	88.00	2050.	—
Open 3, business strikes only.					
1874 .... (790,000) .... (700)	15.00	48.00	105.	2000.	950.
1875 .... (228,000) .... (700)	21.00	70.00	115.	690.	1050.
1876 .... (162,000) .... (1,150)	23.00	80.00	165.	1750.	800.
1877 .... (510)	1050.	1100.	1125.	*	2250.
Normal date, late state of overdate die with underdate polished away. Proof-only issue.					
1877/6					
Scarce early die state of Proof-only issue.					
1878 .... (2,350)	400.	450.	475.	*	625.
Proof only.					
1879 .... (38,000) .... (3,200)	65.00	135.	220.	715.	560.
1880 .... (21,000) .... (3,955)	90.00	180.	230.	690.	530.
1881 .... (1,077,000) .... (3,575)	9.50	36.00	80.00	690.	520.
1882 .... (22,200) .... (3,100)	82.00	165.	245.	950.	525.
1883 .... (4,000) .... (6,609)	200.	280.	375.	2350.	520.
Beware low quality Proofs offered as rarer business strikes.					
1884 .... (1,700) .... (3,942)	365.	430.	485.	3500.	535.
Scarce and underrated as a non-Proof, rarer in Unc.					
1885 .... (1,000) .... (3,790)	475.	600.	700.	2000.	545.
Same remarks as 1883.					
1886 .... (4,290)	425.	475.	350.	*	535.
Proof only, varying quality.					
1887 .... (5,001) .... (2,960)	285.	325.	365.	1000.	1100.
1887/886	385.	500.	400.	*	725.
Proof and (rarely) business strikes.					
1888 .... (36,501) .... (4,582)	47.00	95.00	180.	650.	515.
1889 .... (18,125) .... (3,436)	89.00	115.	220.	665.	505.

Five cents

SHIELD AND RAYS

FINE - Half of each obverse leaf is worn smooth.
VF - Shield lines virtually complete.
EF - Only slight wear on all high points
AU - Barely visible on highest points only. Must show some Mint luster.
UNC - No wear evident anyplace. Full Mint luster.
PROOF - High rims, mirror-like fields, letter surfaces, flat instead of rounded. Letters show some doubling, devices frosted.

Shield and Rays

		F-12	EF-40	AU-50	MS-60	MS-65
1866 .... (14,742,500) .... (125)		22.00	100.	145.	200.	2300.

Comes with and without center dots.

1866
Doubled date, first date punched too high and to right, rare in Unc.
1866
Doubled date, first date punched far to right, 18666. Prohibitively rare Unc.
1866
Doubled date, first date punched too low.

		F-12	EF-40	AU-50	MS-60	MS-65
1867 .... (2,019,000) .... (25)		27.00	130.	190.	265.	3400.

Eliasberg 5/96 Prf-65 $57,200.

WITHOUT RAYS ON REVERSE

Rays removed from reverse

		F-12	EF-40	AU-50	MS-60	MS-65
1867 .... (28,890,500) .... (625)		15.00	32.00	57.00	90.00	615.
1867						

Doubled date, first date punched too high, vars.

1867
Tripled date, first date punched far too high and to right, very rare.

| 1868 .... (28,817,000) .... (600) | | 15.00 | 32.00 | 59.00 | 90.00 | 600. |

Type I, rev. of 1867: stars distant from 5, high S's in STATES. Type II, rev. of 1868, stars close to 5, normal S's in STATES.

1868
Doubled date, several vars. including date at ball below shield and sloping date.

| 1869 .... (16,395,000) .... (600) | | 15.00 | 35.00 | 62.00 | 95.00 | 590. |

Rare with Type I rev.; found with narrow and wide numerals. Type II rev. found with wide numerals only, and with several vars. of recut dates, one of which is often confused with the overdate.

1869/8
Narrow numerals. Type I Status as overdate controversial..

| 1870 .... (4,806,000) .... (1,000) | | 17.00 | 37.00 | 70.00 | 115. | 1000. |

Usual doubled dates exist, beware of struck copper-nickel counterfeits of the period. Those dating 1870-76 are especially prevalent.

1871 .... (561,000) .... (960)		55.00	125.	175.	275.	1250.
1872 .... (6,036,000) .... (950)		15.00	37.00	70.00	125.	1000.
1872						

Doubled date. Original figures very far to l.

1872
Doubled obv. Doubling marked on cross, shield, extra vertical stripes far into horizontal, scarce.

Shield 5 cents continued

	F-12	EF-40	AU-50	MS-60	MS-65
1873 .... (1,100)	37.50	115.	155.	225.	1100.
Closed 3.					
1873 .... (4,550,000)	16.00	40.00	72.50	115.	635.
Open 3, different degrees of openness.					
1873					
Open 3, doubled die obv.					
1873/72					
Open 3 over possible fragments of a 2, not among the boldest overdates, if one at all; rare.					
1874 .... (3,538,000) .... (700)	24.00	55.00	80.00	130.	1150.
1875 .... (2,097,000) .... (700)	30.00	62.50	95.00	145.	1450.
One var. shows jumbled overdate of uncertain identity.					
1876 .... (2,530,000) .... (1,150)	26.00	60.00	82.50	130.	1200.
Usually weakly struck up at borders, some show double-punched dates.					
1876					
Tripled die obv. most visible at top of shield and cross.					
1877 .... (510)	1050.	1150.	1200.	1250.	2200.
Proof only, varying quality, some dull and lifeless.					
1878 .... (2,350)	525.	575.	600.	650.	950.
Proof only, same remarks as preceding.					
1879 .... (25,900) .... (3,200)	350.	450.	500.	585.	1500.
Business strikes of all 1879-81 nickels are far more elusive than Proofs; they are fully as rare as their mintages indicate.					
1879/8					
Seen on some Proofs, far fewer business strikes.					
1880 .... (16,000) .... (3,955)	390.	550.	640.	1050.	3200.
1881 .... (68,800) .... (3,575)	225.	360.	400.	560.	1150.
1882 .... (11,473,500) .... (3,100)	15.00	35.00	57.00	92.50	585.
Very often found with a filled 2, sometimes erroneously offered as an 1882/1 overdate.					
1883 .... (1,451,500) .... (5,419)	15.00	38.00	57.00	92.50	575.
Often found with double-cut or recut dates, which are confused with overdates.					
1883/82	120.	210.	260.	350.	1850.
2 to left of 3. Most struck from a lapped die, and only show top and bottom of 2. Specimens in which the whole 2 is visible are very rare. Valuations are for specimens in which large portion of underdate is visible.					
1883/82					
2 within 3, vars. exist.					

LIBERTY HEAD

FINE - LIBERTY is complete
VF - Corn grains at bottom of rev. wreath faintly visible.
EF - All details sharp. Corn grains are strongly visible.
AU - Barely discernible wear. Must show some Mint luster.
UNC - No wear visible anywhere. Full Mint luster.
PROOF - As in Shield Nickels.

Liberty Head, without CENTS below V

	F-12	EF-40	AU-50	MS-60	MS-65
1883 .... (5,474,300) .... (5,219)	5.00	8.00	11.00	23.00	265.
Without CENTS below wreath. Contemporary gilt and reeded racketeer pieces have been joined by numerous latter-day pieces so altered for sale to beginning or non-collectors; these are of no numismatic value.					

Liberty Head 5 cents continued

Liberty Head, CENTS added

		F-12	EF-40	AU-50	MS-60	MS-65
1883 .... (16,026,200) .... (6,783)		13.50	36.00	60.00	72.50	445.

With CENTS; minor double-punched date vars. exist of this and many other dates of this series.

		F-12	EF-40	AU-50	MS-60	MS-65
1884 .... (11,270,000) .... (3,942)		15.00	42.00	77.50	125.	750.
1885 .... (1,472,700) .... (3,790)		360.	590.	685.	800.	1950.
1886 .... (3,326,000) .... (4,290)		160.	270.	365.	500.	1700.
1887 .... (15,260,692) .... (2,960)		17.00	40.00	62.50	75.00	650.
1888 .... (10,715,901) .... (4,582)		19.50	55.00	100.	125.	640.
1889 .... (15,878,025) .... (3,336)		15.00	35.00	60.00	75.00	625.
1890 .... (16,256,532) .... (2,740)		15.00	38.00	61.00	80.00	675.
1891 .... (16,832,000) .... (2,350)		11.00	37.00	60.00	70.00	700.
1892 .... (11,696,897) .... (2,745)		11.50	37.50	62.50	80.00	635.
1893 .... (13,368,000) .... (2,195)		11.00	35.00	60.00	70.00	625.
1894 .... (5,410,500) .... (2,632)		36.00	135.	155.	190.	775.
1895 .... (9,977,822) .... (2,062)		10.50	36.00	55.00	75.00	800.
1896 .... (8,841,058) .... (1,862)		12.50	41.00	65.00	77.50	975.
1897 .... (20,426,797) .... (1,938)		5.50	21.00	49.00	67.50	1000.
1898 .... (12,530,292) .... (1,795)		5.85	25.00	55.00	70.00	700.
1899 .... (26,027,000) .... (2,031)		4.35	18.50	46.00	57.50	420.

Exists with wide, filled second 9, possibly an overdate. Two die vars., rare and usually found in lower grade.

		F-12	EF-40	AU-50	MS-60	MS-65
1900 .... (27,253,733) .... (2,262)		4.35	17.00	38.00	57.50	390.
1901 .... (26,478,228) .... (1,985)		4.50	18.00	35.00	55.00	395.
1902 .... (31,487,561) .... (2,018)		4.25	17.00	35.00	55.00	405.
1903 .... (28,004,935) .... (1,790)		4.50	17.00	35.00	57.50	395.
1904 .... (21,401,350) .... (1,817)		4.75	17.50	36.00	57.50	395.
1905 .... (29,825,124) .... (2,152)		4.25	16.50	35.00	52.50	400.
1906 .... (38,612,000) .... (1,725)		4.25	17.00	35.00	55.00	400.
1907 .... (39,213,325) .... (1,475)		4.25	16.50	35.00	52.50	400.
1908 .... (22,684,557) .... (1,620)		4.25	16.50	35.00	55.00	465.
1909 .... (11,585,763) .... (4,763)		4.35	21.00	50.00	62.50	415.
1910 .... (30,166,948) .... (2,405)		4.00	16.50	35.00	50.00	400.
1911 .... (39,557,639) .... (1,733)		4.00	16.00	35.00	50.00	395.
1912 .... (26,234,569) .... (2,145)		4.00	16.00	35.00	50.00	405.
1912-D .... (8,474,000)		5.00	41.00	88.00	140.	1050.

Almost always weakly struck up on curls and forelock, as is the next.

		F-12	EF-40	AU-50	MS-60	MS-65
1912-S .... (238,000)		95.00	475.	600.	700.	2350.

Beware of alterations from 1912-D.

1913 Liberty Head 5 cents
(Thomas K. DeLorey)

1913

5 reported at one time, 4 traceable today. Not a regular issue, apparently struck for or by Samuel W. Brown, one-time clerk and storekeeper of the Philadelphia Mint, who went public in December 1919 by advertising to buy specimens in Proof at $500 each. Heavily publicized by B. Max Mehl through his self-promoting offers to buy when all known pieces were accounted for during the 1930s. Superior Galleries Jerry Buss sale, Unc., $385,000, Jan. 1985 to Reed Hawn. Stack's Oct. 1993 Reed Hawn Sale, $962,500, including 10% buyer's fee. Eliasberg 5/96 Prf-66 $1,485,000.

INDIAN HEAD OR BUFFALO 5 CENTS

FINE - Most of buffalo's horn shows. Full obverse rim.
VF - Full horn shows.
EF - Full horn, Indian's hair ribbon intact but slightly worn.
AU - Barely discernible wear on highest points only. Must have some Mint luster.
UNC - Absolutely no wear anyplace. Full Mint luster.
MATTE PROOF - Planchets sandblasted or acid treated before striking resulting in extremely granular surfaces but sharp
    strikes, high rims.

Indian Head, Bison on Mound

	F-12	EF-40	AU-50	MS-60	MS-65
1913 ....(30,992,000) ....(1,520)	6.00	12.00	20.00	30.00	90.00
Type I: FIVE CENTS on raised mound filling the exergue.					
1913-D ....(5,337,000)	10.00	19.00	36.00	48.00	180.
Type I.					
1913-S ....(2,105,000)	20.00	42.00	50.00	65.00	650.
Type I.					

Bison on Plain reverse

	F-12	EF-40	AU-50	MS-60	MS-65
1913 ....(29,857,186) ....(1,514)	7.00	12.00	22.00	32.00	285.
Type II: FIVE CENTS centered in hollowed-out exergue. Thick line above.					
1913-D ....(4,156,000)	58.00	75.00	110.	160.	750.
Type II.					
1913-S ....(1,209,000)	155.	200.	265.	335.	3650.
Type II. Often found weakly struck or from clashed dies.					
1914/3	700.	1500.	6950.	—	—
1914 ....(20,664,463) ....(1,275)	10.00	15.00	26.00	41.00	295.
1914-D ....(3,912,000)	58.00	105.	135.	205.	1200.
1914-S ....(3,470,000)	14.00	35.00	55.00	180.	1750.
Often weakly struck on the reverse.					
1915 ....(20,986,220) ....(1,050)	5.50	11.00	21.00	42.00	200.
Proofs often show curved die crack across bison.					
1915-D ....(7,569,500)	21.00	46.50	70.00	145.	1650.
1915-S ....(1,505,000)	40.00	135.	200.	460.	2400.
1916 ....(63,497,466) ....(600)	3.00	6.00	14.00	40.00	260.
New obv. type: Indian with longer nose, LIBERTY in higher relief.					
1916	4900.	11000.	17000.	24500.	—
Doubled die obv., elusive in high grade, very rare.					
1916-D ....(13,333,000)	13.00	50.00	67.00	135.	2400.
Denver and San Francisco coins of this date are seldom well struck.					
1916-S ....(11,860,000)	11.00	49.00	68.00	145.	2100.
1917 ....(51,424,029)	2.75	10.00	26.00	43.00	385.
Controversial Matte Proofs reported to exist.					
1917-D ....(9,910,800)	16.50	82.50	140.	315.	2400.
1917-S ....(4,193,000)	20.00	145.	215.	390.	2700.
1918 ....(32,086,314)	3.50	16.50	30.00	45.00	1600.

Indian Head 5 cents continued

1918/7-D

	F-12	EF-40	AU-50	MS-60	MS-65
1918/7-D .... (8,362,000)	1075.	4400.	7500.	16000.	175000.

Most strikes show die crack at left end of jaw, excessively rare in Unc.

	F-12	EF-40	AU-50	MS-60	MS-65
1918-D	20.00	165.	200.	385.	3150.
1918-S .... (4,882,000)	19.00	135.	240.	650.	20000.
1919 .... (60,868,000)	2.00	8.00	21.00	40.00	375.
1919-D .... (8,006,000)	22.00	175.	240.	445.	4400.
1919-S .... (7,521,000)	15.00	165.	250.	535.	11500.
1920 .... (63,093,000)	2.00	9.00	23.00	40.00	530.
1920-D .... (9,418,000)	21.00	200.	315.	490.	4750.
1920-S .... (9,689,000)	11.00	135.	215.	365.	19500.
1921 .... (10,663,000)	3.00	19.00	40.00	80.00	525.

Distinctive shape to 1's appearing only this year.

	F-12	EF-40	AU-50	MS-60	MS-65
1921-S .... (1,557,000)	55.00	675.	875.	1350.	4650.

Beware added mint mark embossed from below through opening made in the coin's edge.

	F-12	EF-40	AU-50	MS-60	MS-65
1923 .... (35,715,000)	2.00	8.00	18.00	35.00	450.
1923-S .... (6,142,000)	10.00	160.	245.	435.	9250.
1924 .... (21,620,000)	2.00	9.50	27.00	45.00	500.
1924-D .... (5,258,000)	8.00	125.	185.	375.	3250.
1924-S .... (1,437,000)	40.00	1100.	1375.	1750.	8500.

Beware added mint mark embossed from below through opening made in the coin's edge.

	F-12	EF-40	AU-50	MS-60	MS-65
1925 .... (35,565,100)	2.00	9.00	20.00	31.00	325.
1925-D .... (4,450,000)	24.00	160.	235.	425.	3450.
1925-S .... (6,256,000)	10.00	140.	220.	435.	32500.
1926 .... (44,693,000)	1.50	6.00	17.00	28.00	140.
1926-D .... (5,638,000)	17.00	120.	165.	260.	2900.
1926-S .... (970,000)	23.00	725.	1250.	2400.	24000.

Beware added mint mark embossed from below through opening made in the coin's edge.

	F-12	EF-40	AU-50	MS-60	MS-65
1927 .... (37,981,000)	1.25	5.00	17.50	28.00	185.
1927-D .... (5,730,000)	5.00	42.50	70.00	115.	2350.

Generally not well struck.

	F-12	EF-40	AU-50	MS-60	MS-65
1927-S .... (3,430,000)	2.00	57.50	115.	400.	14500.
1928 .... (23,411,000)	1.25	6.00	16.00	25.00	225.
1928-D .... (6,436,000)	4.00	17.00	30.00	38.00	600.
1928-S .... (6,936,000)	1.30	11.00	30.00	130.	4950.
1929 .... (36,446,000)	0.80	5.00	14.00	21.00	250.
1929-D .... (8,370,000)	2.00	13.00	28.00	43.00	1350.
1929-S .... (7,754,000)	1.05	8.00	17.50	40.00	325.
1930 .... (22,849,000)	0.85	4.50	14.00	23.00	90.00

1930

Tripled obverse die., very rare.

	F-12	EF-40	AU-50	MS-60	MS-65
1930-S .... (5,435,000)	1.05	6.50	20.00	32.00	375.
1931-S .... (1,200,000)	4.00	10.00	28.00	43.00	165.
1934 .... (20,213,003)	0.65	4.50	12.00	23.00	270.
1934-D .... (7,480,000)	1.30	10.00	21.00	40.00	1100.

Mint mark varieties Medium D of 1917-1934 and Large D of 1934-1938.

	F-12	EF-40	AU-50	MS-60	MS-65
1935 .... (58,264,000)	0.65	2.10	7.75	16.00	75.00

Poorly detailed, two-legged coins are contemporary counterfeits, as are similar 1936 coins.

	F-12	EF-40	AU-50	MS-60	MS-65
1935-D .... (12,092,000)	1.55	9.00	25.00	32.00	360.
1935-S .... (10,300,000)	0.75	3.50	11.00	23.00	125.
1936 .... (118,997,000) .... (4,420)	0.70	2.35	6.75	13.00	65.00

Proof coinage resumed, Proofs found with Satin and Brilliant finishes.

	F-12	EF-40	AU-50	MS-60	MS-65
1936-D .... (24,814,000)	0.75	5.00	13.00	17.00	100.
1936-S .... (14,930,000)	0.75	3.50	11.00	15.00	70.00
1937 .... (79,480,000) .... (5,769)	0.70	2.25	6.50	11.00	30.00

Reeded edge pieces are privately made alterations offered for sale at the 1941 Philadelphia ANA Convention.

	F-12	EF-40	AU-50	MS-60	MS-65
1937-D .... (17,826,000)	0.75	2.75	7.75	14.50	34.00

Indian Head 5 cents continued

Three-legged bison

	F-12	EF-40	AU-50	MS-60	MS-65
1937-D	250.	410.	575.	1350.	17000.

Three-legged Buffalo. The first leg was polished off above the hoof while removing clash marks from the die during a busy time at the Depression-era Denver Mint. Beware of alterations. On genuine pieces 1) E PLURIBUS UNUM is smaller, and the P and first U do not touch animal; 2) the beard, tip from belly and last leg are all thinner as is the mound between the third and fourth legs; 3) There is a row of raised dots almost vertically below belly; 4) Obverse die is severely eroded at back of Indian's neck. A so-called 2-1/2 Legged Buffalo variety was claimed in late 1994.

1937-S ....(5,635,000)	0.75	3.00	8.50	13.00	40.00
1938-D ....(7,020,000)	0.70	2.10	7.50	11.50	29.00
1938-D/D	4.00	7.00	11.00	19.00	50.00
1938-D/S	9.00	20.00	26.00	35.00	110.

Varieties exist.

JEFFERSON

VF - Rev. second pillar from right strong.
EF - All details strong.
AU - Trace of wear only on highest points. Must have some Mint luster.
UNC - No wear at all. Full Mint luster.
PROOF - High rims, mirror-like finish. Letter surfaces flat instead of rounded and show double striking.

Jefferson 5 cents

	EF-40	AU-50	MS-60	MS-65	PF-65
1938 ....(19,496,000) ....(19,365)	0.65	0.90	2.25	4.50	80.00
1938-D ....(5,376,000)	1.75	2.25	3.50	14.00	*
1938-S ....(4,105,000)	2.25	2.75	3.75	19.00	*
1939 ....(120,615,000) ....(12,535)	0.45	0.75	1.35	4.00	60.00
Normal rev. of 1938.					
1939					
Rev. of 1940, rare on Proofs; common on business strikes. Compare steps and handrails with 1938 or 1941 specimens.					
1939	70.00	125.	165.	575.	*
Doubled rev. die. Doubled MONTICELLO, FIVE CENTS					
1939-D ....(3,514,000)	7.50	16.50	25.00	70.00	*
Found with both revs., newer type scarcer.					
1939-S ....(6,630,000)	3.25	7.75	14.00	39.50	*
Found with both revs., newer type scarcer.					
1940 ....(176,485,000) ....(14,158)	0.25	0.60	0.75	2.85	60.00
Normal rev. of 1941.					
1940					
Rev. of 1938, Proof only, rare.					
1940-D ....(43,540,000)	0.50	1.45	2.25	5.50	*
1940-S ....(39,690,000)	0.55	1.00	1.90	5.00	*
1941 ....(203,265,000) ....(18,720)	0.30	0.40	0.65	2.10	55.00
1941-D ....(53,432,000)	0.55	1.40	2.15	4.85	*
1941-S ....(43,445,000)	0.60	1.75	2.75	6.00	*
Found with small S of earlier dates, large S is scarce.					
1942 ....(49,789,000) ....(29,600)	0.45	0.70	1.25	6.25	50.00
1942-D ....(13,938,000)	2.75	7.00	14.00	35.00	*
1942-D	—	—	475.	2850.	*
Over horizontal D. Rare.					

COPPER-SILVER-MANGANESE ALLOY, MINT MARK ABOVE MONTICELLO

Large Mint mark above Monticello

	EF-40	AU-50	MS-60	MS-65	PF-65
1942-P .... (57,873,000) .... (27,600)	1.10	3.00	5.25	11.50	80.00
1942-S .... (32,900,000)	2.00	2.75	5.00	25.00	*

1942-S
   S to right of building as on 1941-S. Struck in silver alloy, but exact composition uncertain. Believed Unique, reason for striking unknown, if indeed struck by the U.S. Mint.

	EF-40	AU-50	MS-60	MS-65	PF-65
1943-P .... (271,165,000)	1.10	1.75	2.75	15.00	*
1943/42-P	90.00	135.	200.	625.	*
1943-P	49.00	87.50	115.	400.	*

   Doubled die obv., strongly doubled eye.

	EF-40	AU-50	MS-60	MS-65	PF-65
1943-D .... (15,294,000)	1.50	2.10	2.50	13.00	*
1943-S .... (104,060,000)	1.10	1.75	2.90	13.25	*
1944-P .... (119,150,000)	1.15	2.00	2.75	17.00	*

   Copper-nickel pieces without Mint mark are counterfeits.

	EF-40	AU-50	MS-60	MS-65	PF-65
1944-D .... (32,309,000)	1.80	3.00	6.50	13.50	*
1944-S .... (21,640,000)	1.90	3.00	3.75	13.00	*
1945-P .... (119,408,100)	1.50	2.00	2.65	12.00	*
1945-P	30.00	47.50	75.00	440.	*

   Doubled die rev., scarce.

	EF-40	AU-50	MS-60	MS-65	PF-65
1945-D .... (37,158,000)	1.75	2.35	2.65	7.50	*
1945-S .... (58,939,000)	1.25	1.50	2.15	7.25	*

1946
   Struck in apparent error on Wartime composition planchet. Breen reports four authenticated specimens. A VG-8 specimen authenticated and encapsulated by ANACS in Feb. 1995 is the same coin photocertified by ANACS in 1978, and identified by Ed Fleischman for Coin World's "Collectors' Clearinghouse" column in 1970.

COPPER-NICKEL RESUMED

	EF-40	AU-50	MS-60	MS-65	PF-65
1946 .... (161,116,000)	0.20	0.30	0.50	1.85	*
1946-D .... (45,292,200)	0.30	0.45	0.55	5.50	*
1946-D/Horizontal D	140.	225.	275.	1350.	*
1946-S .... (13,560,000)	0.35	0.40	0.50	5.00	*
1947 .... (95,000,000)	0.20	0.30	0.55	2.00	*
1947-D .... (37,822,000)	0.40	0.60	0.70	2.25	*
1947-S .... (24,720,000)	0.25	0.30	0.35	2.00	*
1948 .... (89,348,000)	0.20	0.32	0.40	1.80	*
1948-D .... (44,734,000)	0.45	0.60	0.85	2.65	*
1948-S .... (11,300,000)	0.40	0.45	0.50	2.25	*

   Minor vars. of S.

	EF-40	AU-50	MS-60	MS-65	PF-65
1949 .... (60,652,000)	0.30	0.45	0.65	3.25	*
1949-D .... (36,498,000)	0.45	0.55	0.75	4.00	*
1949-D/S	70.00	95.00	145.	425.	*

   Scarce post-war over-Mint mark.

	EF-40	AU-50	MS-60	MS-65	PF-65
1949-S .... (9,716,000)	0.75	0.90	1.15	5.00	*
1950 .... (9,796,000) .... (51,386)	0.45	0.70	0.80	3.65	42.50
1950-D .... (2,630,030)	5.25	5.35	6.00	18.00	*

   Hoarded in wholesale quantities, a speculator's favorite; for this date, circulated pieces are scarce.

	EF-40	AU-50	MS-60	MS-65	PF-65
1951 .... (28,552,000) .... (57,500)	0.30	0.35	0.75	2.75	37.50
1951-D .... (20,460,000)	0.45	0.55	0.65	2.65	*
1951-S .... (7,776,000)	0.70	1.00	1.50	5.00	*
1952 .... (63,988,000) .... (81,980)	0.10	0.50	0.70	2.25	27.00
1952-D .... (30,638,000)	0.25	0.75	1.00	3.35	*
1952-S .... (20,572,000)	0.25	0.35	0.60	2.50	*
1953 .... (46,644,000) .... (128,800)	0.10	0.20	0.22	1.10	26.50
1953-D .... (59,878,600)	0.15	0.18	0.21	1.25	*
1953-S .... (19,210,900)	0.25	0.30	0.38	3.50	*

			EF-40	AU-50	MS-60	MS-65	PF-65
1954	(47,684,050)	(233,300)	0.10	0.15	0.19	1.25	20.00
1954-D	(117,136,560)		0.10	0.15	0.19	1.35	*
1954-S	(29,384,000)		0.10	0.20	0.23	1.75	*
1954-S/D			16.00	22.00	30.00	130.	*

Presently rare.

Jefferson 5 cents continued			**EF-40**	**AU-50**	**MS-60**	**MS-65**	**PF-65**
1955	(7,888,000)	(378,200)	0.30	0.35	0.40	6.00	10.00
1955-D	(74,464,100)		0.10	0.15	0.19	2.00	*
1955-D/S			17.00	26.00	32.50	165.	*

Ten different varieties, only the one showing strong S valuable.

1956	(35,216,000)	(669,384)	FV	FV	0.16	0.75	4.00
1956-D	(67,222,940)		FV	FV	0.16	0.75	*
1957	(38,408,000)	(1,247,952)	FV	FV	0.17	0.85	1.75

New obv. with larger star.

1957-D	(136,828,900)		FV	FV	0.16	0.75	*

Same remarks as preceding.

1958	(17,088,000)	(875,652)	0.17	0.20	0.25	1.65	2.50
1958-D	(168,249,120)		FV	FV	0.16	0.75	*
1959	(27,248,000)	(1,149,291)	FV	FV	0.16	0.75	1.75

New obv., smaller star as before 1957.

1959-D	(160,738,240)		FV	FV	0.16	0.75	*

Same remarks as preceding.

1960	(55,416,000)	(1,691,602)	FV	FV	0.16	0.75	0.65
1960-D	(192,582,180)		FV	FV	0.16	0.75	*
1961	(73,640,000)	(3,028,144)	FV	FV	0.16	0.75	0.50
1961-D	(229,342,760)		FV	FV	0.16	0.75	*
1962	(97,384,000)	(3,218,019)	FV	FV	0.16	0.75	0.50
1962-D	(280,195,720)		FV	FV	0.16	0.75	*
1963	(175,776,000)	(3,075,645)	FV	FV	0.16	0.75	0.50
1963-D	(276,829,460)		FV	FV	0.16	0.75	*
1964	(1,024,672,000)	(3,950,762)	FV	FV	0.16	0.75	0.50

Frozen date year.

1964-D	(1,787,297,160)		FV	FV	0.16	0.75	*
1965	(136,131,380)		FV	FV	0.13	0.85	

Designer's initials FS added below truncation

			EF-40	AU-50	MS-60	MS-65	PF-65
1966	(156,208,283)		FV	FV	0.13	0.85	*

Designer's initials FS added to obv. below truncation.

1967	(107,325,800)		FV	FV	0.13	0.85	*

New rev. hub.

1968-D	(91,227,800)		FV	FV	0.13	0.35	*
1968-S	(100,396,004)	(3,041,506)	FV	FV	0.13	0.35	0.40
1969-D	(202,807,500)		FV	FV	0.13	0.35	*
1969-S	(120,075,000)	(2,934,631)	FV	FV	0.13	0.35	0.40
1970-D	(515,485,380)		FV	FV	0.13	0.35	*
1970-S	(238,832,004)	(2,632,810)	FV	FV	0.13	0.35	0.40
1971	(106,884,000)		FV	FV	0.45	2.00	*

New obv. and rev. hubs.

1971-D	(316,144,800)		FV	FV	0.20	1.50	*

Same remarks as preceding.

1971-S		(3,220,733)	*	*	*	*	1.25

Proof Only.

1971 (S)		(est. 1,655, incl. above)	*	*	*	*	500.

No Mint mark Proof error struck at San Francisco Assay Office.

1972	(202,036,000)		FV	FV	0.13	0.35	*
1972-D	(351,694,600)		FV	FV	0.13	0.35	*
1972-S		(3,260,996)	*	*	*	*	1.25

Proof only.

1973	(384,396,000)		FV	FV	0.13	0.35	*
1973-D	(261,405,400)		FV	FV	0.13	0.35	*
1973-S		(2,760,339)	*	*	*	*	0.80

Proof Only.

1974	(601,752,000)		FV	FV	0.13	0.35	*
1974-D	(277,373,000)		FV	FV	0.15	0.45	*

Jefferson 5 cents continued

	EF-40	AU-50	MS-60	MS-65	PF-65
1974-S .... (2,612,568)	*	*	*	*	0.85
Proof only.					
1975 .... (181,772,000)	FV	FV	0.25	0.75	*
1975-D .... (401,875,300)	FV	FV	0.20	0.60	*
1975-S .... (2,845,450)	*	*	*	*	1.00
Proof only.					
1976 .... (367,124,000)	0.12	0.14	0.25	0.85	*
1976-D .... (563,964,147)	FV	FV	0.30	1.50	*
1976-S .... (4,123,056)	*	*	*	*	0.75
Proof only.					
1977 .... (585,376,000)	FV	FV	0.13	0.35	*
New obv. and rev. hubs, sharp details from latter.					
1977-D .... (297,313,422)	FV	FV	0.28	1.25	*
Same remarks as preceding.					
1977-S .... (3,236,798)	*	*	*	*	0.65
Proof only. Same remarks as preceding.					
1978 .... (391,308,000)	FV	FV	0.13	0.35	*
1978-D .... (313,092,780)	FV	FV	0.15	1.00	*
1978-S .... (3,120,285)	*	*	*	*	0.45
Proof only.					
1979 .... (463,188,000)	FV	FV	0.13	0.35	*
1979-D .... (325,867,672)	FV	FV	0.13	0.35	*
1979-S .... (3,677,175)	*	*	*	*	0.60
Proof only. Type I S, blurry, same as 1978.					
1979-S .... (included above)	*	*	*	*	1.25
Proof only. Type II S, clear, same as 1980, found on approximately two coins out of eleven.					
1980-P .... (593,004,000)	FV	FV	0.13	0.35	*
1980-D .... (502,323,448)	FV	FV	0.13	0.35	*
1980-S .... (3,554,806)	*	*	*	*	0.75
Proof only.					
1981-P .... (657,504,000)	FV	FV	0.13	0.35	*
1981-D .... (364,801,843)	FV	FV	0.13	0.35	*
1981-S .... (4,063,083)	*	*	*	*	0.75
Proof only, Filled S					
1981-S	*	*	*	*	1.75
Proof only, Clear S					
1982-P .... (292,355,000)	FV	FV	0.14	2.00	*
1982-D .... (373,726,544)	FV	FV	0.25	3.00	*
1982-S .... (3,857,479)	*	*	*	*	1.10
Proof only.					
1983-P .... (561,615,000)	FV	FV	0.87	1.50	*
1983-D .... (536,726,276)	FV	FV	0.80	1.75	*
1983-S .... (3,279,126)	*	*	*	*	1.50
Proof only.					
1984-P .... (746,769,000)	FV	FV	0.10	0.85	*
1984-D .... (517,675,146)	FV	FV	0.15	1.25	*
1984-S .... (3,065,110)	*	*	*	*	2.00
Proof only.					
1985-P .... (647,114,962)	FV	FV	0.13	0.85	*
1985-D .... (459,747,446)	FV	FV	0.15	1.25	*
1985-S .... (3,362,821)	*	*	*	*	1.50
Proof only.					
1986-P .... (536,883,493)	FV	FV	0.10	0.85	*
1986-D .... (361,819,144)	FV	FV	0.15	1.65	*
1986-S .... (3,010,497)	*	*	*	*	4.50
Proof only.					

		MS-63	MS-64	MS-65	PF-65
1987-P .... (371,499,481)		0.25	0.30	0.35	*
1987-D .... (410,590,604)		0.25	0.30	0.35	*
1987-S .... (3,792,233)		*	*	*	2.00
Proof only.					
1988-P .... (771,360,000)		0.25	0.30	0.35	*
1988-D .... (663,771,652)		0.25	0.30	0.35	*
1988-S .... (2,600,618)		*	*	*	2.50
Proof only.					
1989-P .... (898,812,000)		0.25	0.30	0.35	*
1989-D .... (570,842,474)		0.25	0.30	0.35	*
1989-S .... (3,220,914)		*	*	*	2.00
Proof only.					

Jefferson 5 cents continued

			MS-63	MS-64	MS-65	PF-65
1990-P	(661,636,000)		0.25	0.30	0.35	*
1990-D	(663,938,503)		0.25	0.30	0.35	*
1990-S		(3,299,559)	*	*	*	3.50
Proof only.						
1991-P	(614,104,000)		0.25	0.30	0.35	*
1991-D	(436,496,678)		0.25	0.30	0.35	*
Jefferson 5 cents continued						
1991-S		(2,867,787)	*	*	*	4.00
Proof only.						
1992-P	(399,552,000)		0.25	0.30	0.35	*
1992-D	(450,565,113)		0.25	0.30	0.35	*
1992-S		(4,176,544)	*	*	*	3.50
Proof only.						
1993-P	(412,076,000)		0.25	0.30	0.35	*
1993-D	(406,084,135)		0.25	0.30	0.35	*
1993-S		(2,569,882)				3.50
Proof only.						
1994-P	(722,160,000)		0.25	0.30	0.35	——

1994-P Matte Finish

			MS-63	MS-64	MS-65	PF-65
1994-P	(167,703)		40.00	60.00	75.00	

An unusual packaging option for the 1994 Thomas Jefferson commemorative silver dollar included a $2 Federal Reserve note and a 5–cent piece double-struck from sandblast dies, essentially a Matte Proof. Original plans had been for a limit of 50,000 of these sets, but a failure to state such in the pre-issue literature forced the Mint's hand to strike to demand, until the limited mintage of the Jefferson commem dollar reached its maximum.

			MS-63	MS-64	MS-65	PF-65
1994-D	(715,762,110)		0.25	0.30	0.35	*
1994-S		(3,222,140)	*	*	*	3.50
Proof only.						
1995-P	(774,156,000)		0.25	0.30	0.35	——
1995-D	(888,112,000)		0.25	0.30	0.35	*
1995-S		(2,791,067)	*	*	*	3.00
Proof only.						
1996-P	(829,332,000)		0.25	0.30	0.35	——
1996-D	(817,736,000)		0.25	0.30	0.35	*
1996-S		(2,920,158)	*	*	*	3.00
Proof only.						
1997-P	(NR)		0.25	0.30	0.35	——
1997-P	(25,000)					
Matte Finish from Botanic Garden Coinage & Currency set:						
1997-D	(NR)		0.25	0.30	0.35	*
1997-S		(NR)	*	*	*	2.00
Proof only.						

Silver & Clad Coinage

The Act of April 2, 1792, provided for silver coins of the denominations of a dollar, half dollar, quarter dollar, disme, and half disme. The dollar was to weigh 416 grains and have a fineness of .8924, believed to be that of the Spanish milled dollar or piece of eight. This coin actually weighed 420 grains when new, which left a sufficient disparity to attract bullion dealers.

U.S silver dollars were thus shipped to the West Indies where they could be exchanged for the heavier Spanish pieces, and the latter sent to the Philadelphia Mint for recoining into dollars. This "perpetual chain" practice resulted in the suspension of the dollar denomination from 1805 to 1835. (The 19,570 dollars issued in 1804 were struck from leftover 1803 dies. The only 1804-dated dollars known were made from 1834-35 or later.)

Because of the vast number of Spanish and Mexican fractional coins in circulation, the Mint used the bulk of its silver to strike half dollars for more than 50 years. Half dime coinage was suspended from 1806 to 1828 and dimes were issued for only one year between 1812 and 1819. The Act of Jan. 18, 1837, reduced the weight of the silver dollar to 412 ½ grains, and fixed its fineness at .900. This had been suggested as early as 1795 by Mint Director David Rittenhouse, to facilitate the operation of refining.

Reflecting the great California gold discoveries of 1849, the relative value of silver began to steadily increase. After 1850, silver coins were no longer seen in circulation and, on Feb. 21, 1853, Congress reduced the intrinsic value of all but the dollar by some 7 percent. The weight of the half dollar was accordingly changed to 192 grains, and that of the smaller coins proportionately.

Arrows were added to the date on all coins from half dime to half dollar; rays appeared on the reverse of the 1853 quarter and half dollar to identify new weight coins and facilitate withdrawal of the older, heavier coins for melting. Arrows were again added to the dies in 1873 when the weight of the half dollar was revised to 192.9 grains (12.5 grams) in an abortive effort to encourage metric reckoning, the quarter and dime being raised proportionately.

The Seated Liberty silver dollar continued to be exported and was virtually never seen in domestic circulation. Due to incredible bungling by Treasury Department officials, the subsidiary coins were distributed in an illegal manner and struck in such excessive quantities that they soon clogged the channels of trade. Nevertheless, with the Civil War, they disappeared from circulation along with all other coins, and were not seen again until the resumption of specie payments in 1876.

The discontinuation of the silver dollar by Act of Feb. 12, 1873, aroused little interest at the time. True, it had been profitable to melt down silver dollars for their bullion value, but, by the same token, it was unprofitable to bring silver to the Mint for coinage into dollars. However, from 1871 on the price of silver steadily declined, and within a few years silver producers were backing a powerful lobby to increase their market by vastly expanding silver dollar coinage

Thus, the coinage of silver dollars was resumed under the Bland-Allison Act of 1878 and the Sherman Act of 1890. Tied to mandatory purchase of 187 tons of newly mined silver each month, this dollar coinage continued out of all proportion to any real public needs until 1904. It was then suspended for sixteen years and was resumed for the last time 1921-1935.

By Executive Order of President Lyndon B. Johnson, more than 300,000 1964-dated Peace dollars struck at the Denver Mint in May 1965 to meet the needs of Nevada casino owners. Denver Mint employees were allowed to purchase the new dollars at face value before the President rescinded his own order authorizing the coinage.

Mint authorities confessed that no clear records were kept on how many of the new coins were purchased, but insist that as many pieces as were sold were melted. It seems almost certain that some 1964-D dollars escaped the melting pot, but their legal status would make them liable to seizure by Treasury agents.

The history of our ephemeral silver issues is no less interesting than that of mainstream coinage. The silver 3-cent piece, or trime as it was sometimes called, was authorized by Act of March 3, 1851. This denomination was intended to facilitate purchase of postage stamps under the new 3-cent rate.

These tiny coins would also replace some of the well worn, Spanish and Spanish-colonial fractional silver coins still in use. A fineness of .750 was adopted to offset the pecuniary advantage of the depositor of such worn silver. This odd fineness persisted until the Act of March 3, 1853, which raised it to .900, bringing the 3 cents into conformity with the other silver coins. Adoption of a copper-nickel 3-cent piece in 1865 made the silver coin redundant, and it was discontinued in 1873.

Twenty-cent pieces were issued for a period of only four years, from 1875 to 1878. This coin was proposed for West Coast use because of Westerners' refusal to accept base metal minor coins of 1 to 5 cents. Half dime coinage had ceased in 1873, making it a challenge to make change for a quarter.

Thus, if a customer purchased a 10-cent article with a quarter, he was often forced to accept a dime or Spanish "bit" for the whole of his change. Showing extremely poor judgment, Treasury Department officials rejected several distinctive pattern designs for the 20-cent piece.

An obverse almost identical to the quarter was adopted, with the ungainly eagle from the Trade dollar for the reverse. The smooth edge was supposed to distinguish the new coin from the quarter, but confusion was inevitable and the 20 cents became a major public nuisance.

The Trade dollar is the only U.S. coin that has ever been repudiated by the government. It was originally projected as a "commercial dollar," to compete with the Mexican peso in Chinese trade. Because of Chinese merchants' strong preference for the familiar Mexican coins, regular U.S. dollars were received in China, or exchanged for Mexican pesos, at a substantial discount. Unfortunately, through error or (as it seems more likely) by the connivance of the silver interests, the Trade dollar was listed alongside our subsidiary coins in the Mint Act of Feb. 12, 1873, and made a legal tender for domestic use.

As the value of silver continued to decline, it became profitable to have it coined into "Trades." On June 22, 1876, Congress unwisely revoked the legal tender status of the coins, causing them to be manipulated by brokers to the disadvantage of the poorer classes. Finally, in February 1878, Trade dollar coinage was suspended. Only Proofs were struck after that year, and, in February 1887, Congress passed a law to redeem all but those pieces chop-marked in Chinese trade.

As early as 1795, the Mint resorted to outside artists to improve the appearance of the silver coinage. In that year, a new bust was sketched by Gilbert Stuart, to replace the Flowing Hair Liberty and "render her a steady matron." Philadelphia artist John Eckstein took the sketches and prepared a pair of hubs for the silver dollar. Mint engraver Robert Scot copied this dowdy design in making dies for the other silver coins as well as for the cent and half cent.

In 1836, Philadelphia artist Thomas Sully designed an elegant seated Liberty for Mint Director Robert M. Patterson. Titian Peale sketched a majestic flying eagle, and both were modeled by Mint engraver Christian Gobrecht for the new silver dollar. Gobrecht placed his signature C. GOBRECHT F. above the date, but criticism caused it to be moved to the base on which Liberty was seated.

A variety of beautiful patterns were struck from 1836 to 1839 using variations of this design. 1836 dies struck 1,000 circulating dollars with eagle flying upward on the starry field, struck to the pre-1804 standard. In 1837 at least 600 more dated 1836 were released with the new 412 1/2-grain weight and .900 fineness.

The inspired flying eagle was dropped on the post-1840 coinage in favor of the same lifeless spread eagle with shield used in the smaller denominations. The seated Liberty had been remodeled by another local artist, Robert Ball Hughes, for the definitive design. For unknown reasons, the Hughes version of Liberty was never adopted on the half dollar, though it appeared on the dollar, quarter dollar, dime and half-dime.

In 1891, mounting criticism of the coinage resulted in an unsuccessful public competition for new designs, and the adoption in 1892 of the Liberty head and eagle models by Mint engraver Charles Barber. The Barber designs were used on the subsidiary coinage until 1916, when they were supplanted by the beautiful designs of Adolph A. Weinman on the dime and half dollar, and of Hermon MacNeil on the quarter.

In 1921, Anthony de Francisci's splendid Peace dollar replaced the long-lived Morgan design. Although a design competition for a quarter marking the Bicentennial of George Washington's birth was won by sculptress Laura Gardin Fraser, Treasury Secretary William Woodin decreed that John Flanagan's design was the winner. After World War II, Mint Engraver John R. Sinnock created the Roosevelt dime and Franklin half dollar. The Kennedy half dollar bore an obverse by Gilroy Roberts and reverse by Frank Gasparro.

As a poor solution to the silver shortage, Congress, on July 23, 1965, replaced .900 silver coinage with laminated base metal issues. The half dollar was reduced to an overall fineness of .400 while the quarter dollar and dime became mere tokens, with layers of copper-nickel (75:25%) bonded to a core of pure copper. After much unnecessary delay, the clad alloy was adopted for half dollars starting with the issues of 1971. Removed from public consciousness for some seven years, the half never regained the wide circulation it had enjoyed until 1964. The Eisenhower dollar was struck in the normal clad alloy from 1971 to until 1978. From 1971 to 1974, Proof and Uncirculated dollars were struck for collectors in .400 silver. Numismatists' agitation for coins commemorating the Bicentennial of the American Revolution resulted in a public design competition for new reverses for the dollar, half dollar and quarter. Dennis R. Williams created a moon and Liberty Bell reverse for the Eisenhower dollar; Seth G. Huntington placed the facade of Independence Hall on the Kennedy half; Jack L. Ahr's Colonial drummer graced the new quarter.

Criticisms were many, beginning with the retention of existing obverses with only the dual dates 1776-1976 to distinguish them from the familiar coinage. Huntington's Independence Hall was compared to Sinnock's 1926 Sesquicentennial gold quarter eagle, while Ahr's highly successful quarter was compared to a 1973 postage stamp.

Of course, any two detailed views of a public building must be similar, and the Drummer can easily be traced back to the famous Archibald Willard painting, "The Spirit of '76." Proof sets were struck in 40 percent silver, without Mint marks, for public display. All were allegedly destroyed, although a strong probability exists of one or two sets remaining in private hands after the rest were melted.

Proof sets were struck for public sale in both copper-nickel clad and 40 percent silver with the S Mint mark of San Francisco. Circulating copper-nickel clad pieces in all denominations were struck at Philadelphia and Denver. The Proof sets sold poorly, with many of the 40 percent silver sets ultimately returning to the smelter in the early 1980s after years of profitless storage.

Ranking with the 20-cent piece as a coinage failure was the 25.5mm Susan B. Anthony dollar, struck in clad metal 1979-81. Lack of foresight resulted in a dollar coin dangerously similar in color, size and weight to the quarter, and public rejection of the SBA was almost absolute. Some 100 million of the unwanted coins remain in Treasury storage as a monument to this expensive fiasco. As this edition was going to press, Treasury had publically stated support for a small-sized dollar coin to replace the Anthony dollar. Authorizing legislation was pending.

Silver 3-cent pieces

VG - Shield outline, date and legend all clear.
F - All clear but star points worn smooth.
VF - Partial wear on star.
EF - Wear on high points only.
AU - Barest traces of wear on highest points; must have some Mint luster.
UNC- Absolutely no wear. Must have full Mint luster.
PROOF-High rims, mirror like surfaces. Letter surfaces flat instead of rounded, some evidence of double striking. Star, shield, etc., frosted.

TYPE I: SINGLE OUTLINE TO STAR

Single outline to star

	F-12	EF-40	AU-50	MS-60	MS-65
1851 .... (5,447,400)	23.00	58.00	115.	145.	1100.
Found with light and heavy dates.					
1851-O .... (720,000)	33.00	110.	210.	300.	2350.
1852 .... (18,663,500)	23.00	58.00	115.	145.	1100.
1852					
Double Date					
1852 1 Over Inverted 2					
1853 .... (11,400,000)	23.00	58.00	115.	145.	1200.

TYPE II: THREE OUTLINES TO STAR

		Three outlines to star			
	F-12	EF-40	AU-50	MS-60	MS-65

1853
Trial strike. Present location unknown, see Pattern listing E.511.

1854 .... (671,000)	24.00	90.00	215.	325.	4100.

Usually found with trace of a 5 between 8 and 5.

1855 .... (139,000)	45.00	150.	230.	525.	10500.

Majority have recut 855.

1855
Four outlines to star, blundered die. Extremely rare.

1856 ....(1,458,000)	23.00	85.00	165.	310.	4450.

Often with weak date; numismatist Q. David Bowers believes this to be the rarest silver three cents in Mint State.

1857 ....(1,042,000)	25.00	85.00	220.	290.	4150.

Usually found with heavy obverse die striae.

1858 ....(1,604,000) .... (80)	23.00	85.00	165.	260.	4100.

Often with weak date.

TYPE III: TWO OUTLINES TO STAR
SMALLER LEGENDS AND DATES

		Two outlines to star			
	F-12	EF-40	AU-50	MS-60	MS-65

1859 .... (365,000) .... (800)	23.00	60.00	115.	160.	1050.
1860 .... (286,000) .... (1,000)	24.00	65.00	115.	160.	1075.

Beware of struck German silver counterfeits of this date and the Civil War years.

1860
Doubled Date

1861 .... (497,000) .... (1,000)	24.00	60.00	115.	160.	1050.
1862/1	30.00	75.00	125.	210.	1050.

Usually with die break through first 1.

1862 .... (343,000) .... (550)	24.00	62.00	115.	160.	1000.

Found with light and heavy dates.

1862
Doubled date. Varieties exist.

	AU-50	MS-60	MS-63	MS-65	PF-65
1863 .... (21,000) .... (460)	400.	525.	775.	1450.	1250.
1863	425.	*	*	*	4500.

So-called 1863/2 the result of a die gouge within the 3. Proofs only.
From this point on, choice Mint State business strikes are scarcer than Proofs and always sell for higher prices.

1864 .... (12,000) .... (470)	410.	525.	965.	1500.	1300.

Modern struck counterfeits exist.

1865 .... (8,000) .... (500)	410.	535.	825.	1700.	1300.

Top of D in UNITED beginning to wear thin. Usually a die crack left of date.

1866 .... (22,000) .... (725)	410.	535.	825.	1550.	1300.

D in UNITED open at top as on all that follow.

1867 .... (4,000) .... (625)	415.	550.	1150.	2900.	1275.
1868 .... (3,500) .... (600)	420.	560.	1200.	5750.	1275.
1869 .... (4,500) .... (600)	425.	575.	890.	3000.	1350.
1869/8	625.	*	*	*	4900.

Reported, not confirmed.

1870 .... (3,000) .... (1,000)	430.	585.	935.	2500.	1350.
1871 .... (3,400) .... (960)	425.	565.	835.	1500.	1300.
1872 .... (1,000) .... (950)	575.	700.	1350.	6000.	1250.
1873 .... (600)	575.	*	*	*	1700.

Closed 3, Proof only.

Half dimes

FLOWING HAIR

G - Main features outlined but without details. Date must be legible.
VG - Some details in face, all legends legible.
F - Hair ends, ear show.
VF - Hairlines clear at top, around ear, in body of hair.
EF - All details clear and sharp. No blurring of hairlines.
AU - Barest amount of wear on highest points only. Some Mint luster.
UNC - No wear evident anyplace. Full Mint luster, as it should look in a coin of this age.

		Flowing Hair			
	G-4	**F-12**	**VF-20**	**EF-40**	**AU-50**

The 1792 Half Disme is a pattern, E.540.
1794 .... (7,756) .... 675. 1250. 1800. 3000. 4750.
All struck the following year.
1795 .... (78,660) .... 515. 900. 1325. 2100. 2850.

Year	G-4	F-12	VF-20	EF-40	AU-50
1794	675.	1250.	1800.	3000.	4750.
1795	515.	900.	1325.	2100.	2850.

DRAPED BUST, SMALL EAGLE

		Draped Bust, Small Eagle			
	G-4	**F-12**	**VF-20**	**EF-40**	**AU-50**

1796/5 .... (10,230) .... 625. 1400. 2450. 4350. 10500.
On authentic overdate, berry is under E of UNITED, 5 touches bust, 6 is free of drapery. Valentine 2. Extremely rare, almost all known are in EF or above. Eliasberg 5/96 V-8 MS-67 $50,600.
1796 .... 550. 1200. 1800. 3400. 5000.
Normal date
1796 .... 550. 1300. 1900. 3600. 6750.
Recut 6, late die state appears to read LIKERTY. Popular and collected as a type coin in the mistaken belief that it is from a blundered die. V-1, very rare in full Unc.
1797 .... (18,144) .... 525. 1200. 1775. 3000. 3900.
15 Stars on obverse, all 1797s are very rare in Unc. Eliasberg 5/96 V-2 MS-65 $59,400.
1797 .... (16,620) .... 540. 1250. 1800. 3150. 4150.
16 Stars.
1797 .... (9,763) .... 650. 1500. 2550. 4000. 6100.
13 Stars. The Newlin coin is thought the only Unc., very rare in all grades, 10 or 11 known in EF or AU.

DRAPED BUST, HERALDIC EAGLE

		Draped Bust, Heraldic Eagle			
	G-4	**F-12**	**VF-20**	**EF-40**	**AU-50**

1800 .... (40,000) .... 425. 780. 1175. 2300. 3300.
1800 .... 435. 795. 1225. 2350. 3500.
Common LIBEKTY variety is the result of a broken R punch, not a blundered die.

Half dimes continued

	G-4	F-12	VF-20	EF-40	AU-50
1801 .... (27,760)	475.	805.	1250.	2400.	3800.

Always weakly struck, extremely rare in Unc., very rare in EF.

1802 .... (3,060)	7750.	18500.	32500.	67500.	——

Unknown in Unc., excessively rare in EF, extremely rare in all lower grades. Eliasberg 5/96 EF-40 $42,900.

1803 .... (37,850)	450.	790.	1200.	2325.	3450.

Large date, crude 8 made from joining two circles, very scarce. Norweb MS-63, $25,300. Eliasberg 5/96 V-2 MS-67 $53,900.

1803

Small date, 8 smaller than 1, extremely rare in Unc.

1805 .... (15,600)	595.	900.	1600.	3000.	5500.

Single var., one of the scarcest half dimes with perhaps 100 known, nearly all in lower grades, possibly one in full Unc.

CAPPED BUST LEFT

VG - Letters, date complete. At least 3 letters show in LIBERTY.
F - Full LIBERTY.
VF - Full rims, ear and clasp full
EF - All details, rim sharp and full.
AU - Barely visible wear only on highest points. Must show some Mint luster.
UNC - No wear visible anywhere. Full Mint luster.

Capped Bust Left

	F-12	VF-20	EF-40	AU-50	MS-60
1829 .... (1,230,000)	29.00	55.00	120.	185.	290.

Stripes in shield are made up of two or three raised lines, the latter a little scarcer. 1829 obverse die continued in use in later years.

1830 .... (1,240,000)	29.00	55.00	115.	180.	285.

Many made in subsequent years.

1830

C in AMERICA over horizontal C. V-1, very rare.

1831 .... (1,242,700)	29.00	55.00	115.	180.	280.

Many made in subsequent years.

1832 .... (965,000)	29.00	55.00	115.	185.	285.

Many made in subsequent years.

1833 .... (1,370,000)	29.00	55.00	115.	180.	280.

Mintage probably includes many dated 1829-1832.

1834 .... (1,480,000)	29.00	55.00	115.	185.	280.

1834

3 over inverted 3, V-5, scarce.

1835 .... (2,760,000)	29.00	55.00	115.	180.	280.

Four major varieties, none scarce. 1) Large date and 5 C.; 2) Large date and small 5 C.; 3) Small date and large 5 C; 4) Small date and 5 C. Small dates are slightly less tall than stars; small 5 C. much shorter than other letters. Mintage probably includes many dated 1829-1834.

1836 .... (1,900,000)	29.00	55.00	115.	190.	285.

Small and large 5 C. varieties, both about equally rare. Mintage includes many dated 1835.

1836

3 over inverted 3, V-4.

1837 .... (871,000)	29.00	55.00	115.	185.	280.

Large 5 C.

1837	40.00	97.50	240.	425.	825.

Small 5 C., V-2, scarce and underrated.

SEATED LIBERTY, NO STARS

VG - 3 letters visible in LIBERTY
F - LIBERTY complete but weak
VF - LIBERTY strong
EF - All details sharp
AU - Wear only on highest points. Must have some Mint luster.
5UNC - No wear evident anyplace. Full Mint luster.
PROOF- High rims, mirror-like fields. Letter surfaces are flat, not rounded, and show evidence of double striking. Liberty devices are frosted.

Seated Liberty, No Stars (Stack's)

	F-12	VF-20	EF-40	AU-50	MS-60
1837 .... (1,405,000) .... (20)	48.00	90.00	180.	340.	525.
Large Date, curved along top, pointed-top 1 as on bust coins.					
1837	45.00	77.00	150.	255.	490.
Small Date in straight line, flat-top 1.					
1838-O .... (70,000)	200.	375.	600.	1375.	2550.
Virtually unknown in Unc., two date position varieties.					

STARS, NO DRAPERY AT ELBOW

	F-12	VF-20	EF-40	AU-50	MS-60
1838 .... (2,255,000)	11.00	25.00	60.00	115.	240.
1838	45.00	85.00	145.	265.	575.
Small stars, not from smaller punches as on the dime, but from a ground-down die. Usually shows die rust around drapery.					
1839 .... (1,069,150)	10.25	22.00	55.00	105.	240.
1839-O .... (1,034,039)	1100.	—	—	3750.	—
Large O, virtually unknown in Unc. very rare in all grades.					
1839-O	19.00	32.00	65.00	190.	425.
Medium O.					
1839-O					
Small O, sometimes shows repunched 19.					
1840 .... (1,034,000)	10.25	22.00	60.00	125.	310.
1840-O .... (695,000)	21.00	35.00	67.50	235.	445.
Large O, very rare in Unc.					
1840-O					
Medium O, very rare, most in low grades.					
1840-O					
Small O.					
1840-O					
No drapery, but new reverse hub intended for drapery obverse shows split berries, extremely rare.					

DRAPERY AT ELBOW

Drapery at Elbow

	F-12	VF-20	EF-40	AU-50	MS-60
1840 .... (310,085)	45.00	85.00	160.	275.	525.
1840-O .... (240,000)	80.00	165.	265.	800.	—
Excessively rare in Unc.					
1841 .... (1,150,000)	10.25	20.00	45.00	100.	155.
1841-O .... (815,000)	26.00	37.50	120.	300.	600.
Large, medium and small O varieties, the former rare.					
1842 .... (815,000)	10.25	20.00	45.00	100.	165.
1842-O .... (350,000)	62.00	175.	675.	1500.	2600.
No Drapery pieces are the result of an over-polished die.					
1843 .... (1,165,000)	10.25	20.00	44.00	100.	145.
1843					
Doubled date, very scarce early die state of V-6.					

Half dimes continued

	F-12	VF-20	EF-40	AU-50	MS-60
1844 .... (430,000)	10.25	22.00	50.00	110.	170.
Several varieties of recut dates exist.					
1844-O .... (220,000)	175.	350.	700.	——	4000.
Large O, rare, usually found in low grade.					
1844-O	250.	515.	850.	1700.	4900.
Small O, unique in full Unc. (Atwater), seldom seen EF or above.					
1845 .... (1,564,000)	10.25	21.00	45.00	92.00	145.
1845					
Doubled date, first punched too far left, often mistaken for 1845/3.					
1846 .... (27,000)	400.	650.	1500.	3100.	——
Excessively rare in Unc.					
1847 .... (1,274,000)	10.25	20.00	43.00	92.00	145.
1848 .... (668,000)	28.00	40.00	75.00	190.	475.
Large date with each digit overlapping base. Most are in low grades, rare in Unc.					
1848	10.25	20.00	43.00	92.00	145.
Medium date, only 1 touches rock.					
1848-O .... (600,000)	27.50	42.50	100.	225.	425.
Large, medium and small O varieties, the small is extremely rare.					
1849/46 .... (1,309,000)	26.00	45.00	77.00	145.	375.
At least three distinct varieties, some in significantly different die states. Sometimes interpreted as 1849/8, 1849/8/6, or 1849/horizontal 9. All are probably descended from five unused 1846 obv. dies returned from the New Orleans Mint.					
1849	10.25	19.50	42.00	95.00	145.
Variety with recut 9 should not be confused with the above.					
1849-O .... (140,000)	80.00	185.	450.	950.	2200.
Nearly always found in low grade, excessively rare in Unc.					
1850 .... (955,000)	10.25	19.50	42.00	95.00	150.
1850-O .... (690,000)	25.00	50.00	110.	245.	650.
Large O.					
1850-O					
Medium O, V-3.					
1850-O					
Small thin O, rare, struck from rusted dies, V-4.					
1851 .... (781,000)	10.25	19.50	42.00	95.00	155.
1851-O .... (860,000)	24.00	35.00	72.00	175.	350.
Very rare in Unc., generally in lower grades.					
1852 .... (1,000,500)	10.25	19.50	42.00	95.00	155.
1852-O .... (260,000)	65.00	100.	235.	450.	1150.
Almost always flatly struck, excessively rare in Unc.					
1853 .... (135,000)	55.00	90.00	195.	350.	500.
Most were melted for recoinage as lighter, With Arrows type.					
1853-O .... (160,000)	300.	585.	1350.	2950.	6800.
Same remarks as last, date weakly struck, prooflike Uncs. are excessively rare, EF-AU rare.					

SEATED LIBERTY, ARROWS AT DATE

Arrows at Date

	F-12	VF-20	EF-40	AU-50	MS-60
1853 .... (13,210,020)	9.50	15.00	45.00	80.00	155.
Highest mintage of this series. A very rare variety with die crack through 3 was once heavily promoted as an overdate, V-4a.					
1853-O .... (2,200,000)	13.00	20.00	52.00	135.	275.
1854 .... (5,740,000)	9.75	15.00	45.00	82.00	175.
1854-O .... (1,560,000)	13.00	20.00	55.00	145.	325.
1855 .... (1,750,000)	9.50	17.00	45.00	85.00	175.
1855-O .... (600,000)	27.50	55.00	120.	235.	425.

ARROWS REMOVED

No arrows

	F-12	VF-20	EF-40	AU-50	MS-60
1856 ....(4,880,000)	10.00	18.00	40.00	80.00	130.
Denticles almost always flatly struck, a rare variety shows boldly doubled date.					
1856-O ....(1,100,000)	19.00	35.00	70.00	185.	385.
1857 ....(7,280,000)	10.00	18.00	40.00	77.00	120.
1857-O ....(1,380,000)	15.00	29.00	55.00	130.	250.
High oval O and low round O varieties.					
1858 ....(3,500,000) ....(80)	10.00	18.00	40.00	77.00	120.
1858/ inverted 1858.	55.00	115.	200.	300.	475.
Spectacularly blundered die, rare.					
1858	75.00	155.	245.	325.	675.
Double date, first date cut too high, very rare.					
1858-O ....(1,660,000)	12.00	32.00	57.50	150.	260.
1859 ....(340,000) ....(800)	18.00	31.00	53.00	105.	155.
New obv. hub: hollow-center stars, reworked seated figure with larger head and modified LIBERTY.					
1859-O ....(560,000)	23.00	45.00	95.00	175.	255.
All from pre-1859 obv. hub.					
1859 ....(12-15 known)					
Hollow-center stars obv. of 1859 muled with wreath rev. of 1860. See the following.					
1860 ....(100)	—	—	—	—	1800.

Same obverse as last but for date; neither of these "stateless" half dimes bear the nation's name. These are fantasies made by Mint Director James Ross Snowden for private distribution, often incorrectly called "transitional patterns." See pattern section.

LEGEND OBVERSE, CEREAL WREATH REVERSE

Legend Obverse, Cereal Wreath Reverse

	F-12	VF-20	EF-40	AU-50	MS-60
1860 ....(798,000) ....(1,000)	10.25	17.50	31.00	67.00	115.
Variety with boldly repunched 1 and 0 in date is rare.					
1860-O ....(1,060,000)	17.00	23.00	45.00	87.00	135.
1861 ....(3,360,000) ....(1,000)	10.50	18.00	31.00	67.00	115.
1861	52.50	85.00	175.	325.	515.
Some show a blob atop the lower-left serif of the second 1, the result of a defective punch, the so-called 1861/O.					
1862 ....(1,492,000) ....(550)	10.25	18.00	31.00	67.00	110.
Most common half dime in mint state, although the doubled or slanting date varieties are rare and extremely rare respectively.					
1863 ....(18,000) ....(460)	225.	290.	340.	450.	500.
Non-proofs from 1863 to 1867 are R6, and very much rarer than proofs; Proof restrikes exist.					
1863-S ....(100,000)	35.00	60.00	105.	285.	450.
Very rare in Unc. Many S Mint half dimes from 1863-71 show traces of mounting from use on stickpins or buttons.					
1864 ....(48,000) ....(470)	405.	525.	665.	800.	925.
Originals with closed-top D are rare; open-top D in UNITED Proof restrikes are extremely rare.					
1864-S ....(90,000)	62.50	100.	200.	375.	660.
Rare in Unc.					
1865 ....(13,000) ....(500)	345.	390.	475.	550.	750.
Rare in Unc., some Proofs exhibit double-base 1.					

Half dimes continued

		F-12	VF-20	EF-40	AU-50	MS-60
1865-S	(120,000)	28.50	40.00	90.00	370.	700.
1865/5-S						

So-called 1865/3, it is actually 5/5.

		F-12	VF-20	EF-40	AU-50	MS-60
1866	(10,000) (725)	335.	425.	540.	600.	725.
1866-S	(120,000)	28.50	55.00	95.00	290.	550.

Rare in Unc.

1867	(8,000) (625)	415.	505.	575.	665.	765.
1867-S	(120,000)	34.00	57.00	75.00	225.	350.

Scarce in Unc.

1868	(88,600) (600)	90.00	160.	235.	310.	425.
1868-S	(280,000)	18.00	27.00	60.00	145.	275.
1869	(208,000) (600)	17.50	26.50	52.00	95.00	225.

Doubled date variety is rare.

1869-S	(230,000)	16.50	25.00	60.00	130.	255.
1870	(535,600) (1,000)	11.25	13.50	30.50	65.00	115.
1870-S						

Unique. Presumably struck for cornerstone of second San Francisco Mint, unknown until 1978.

1871	(1,873,000) (960)	10.25	14.50	29.00	62.50	110.
1871-S	(161,000)	32.00	42.50	65.00	135.	245.
1872	(2,947,000) (950)	9.00	13.50	29.00	60.00	105.
1872						

Doubled die obverse, extremely rare.

1872-S	(837,000)	11.25	14.50	30.00	60.00	105.

Mint mark within wreath.

1872-S		11.25	14.50	30.00	60.00	105.

Mint mark below wreath.

1873	(712,000) (600)	9.00	13.50	29.00	60.00	105.

Closed 3 only.

1873-S	(324,000)	16.00	25.00	42.00	80.00	115.

Closed 3 only.

Dimes

DRAPED BUST, SMALL EAGLE

G - Bust, eagle outlined, date legible, no details.
VG - Only deepest drapery fold visible. Suggestion of hairlines, some curls.
F - Hair is partly worn but drapery lines are intact.
VF - Everything visible, though worn.
EF - Everything visible and sharp.
AU - Wear only on highest points. Must have some Mint luster.
UNC - No wear at all. Full Mint luster.
PROOF- High rims, mirror-like fields. Letter surfaces are flat, not rounded, and show evidence of double striking. Liberty devices are frosted.

Draped Bust, Small Eagle

		F-12	VF-20	EF-40	AU-50	MS-60
1796	(22,135)	1700.	2850.	4400.	5650.	7750.

Four and five berry varieties exist. Norweb John Reich-1 MS-63, $23,100. Eliasberg 5/96 JR-6 Four Berries MS-65 $83,600.

1797	(10,244)	1500.	2800.	4500.	6900.	12500.

16 stars, excessively rare in Unc. Mintage figure may include some 1796.

1797	(15,017)	1525.	2900.	4750.	7100.	13000.

13 stars, excessively rare in Unc. Mintage figure may include some 16 stars.

DRAPED BUST, HERALDIC EAGLE

Draped Bust, Heraldic Eagle

	F-12	VF-20	EF-40	AU-50	MS-60
1798/7 .... (27,550)	900.	1550.	2900.	4500.	6800.

Small 8, 16 stars on rev., very rare in Unc. Struck with reverse die of 1797 quarter eagles. Most 1798s are weakly struck at center.

1798/7	4300.	6500.	—	—	30000.

Small 8, 13 stars on rev. Excessively rare in Unc., very rare in EF and AU, rare in lesser grades.

1798	1000.	1750.	2500.	4750.	9500.

Small 8, excessively rare in Unc., rare in lower grades.

1798	650.	1000.	1650.	2200.	4000.

Medium 8, extremely rare in Unc., reverse of 1798 quarter eagles.

1800 .... (21,760)	625.	875.	1650.	2400.	4800.

Large A's in rev. legend, JR-2, excessively rare in Unc., Norweb MS-63, $18,700.

1800					

Medium A's in rev. legend, JR-1, excessively rare in Unc. Some with reverse of 1798 quarter eagles.

1801 .... (34,640)	650.	975.	2200.	4350.	9000.

Excessively rare in Unc., Norweb MS-60 to 63, $20,900.

1802 .... (10,975)	1550.	2700.	4950.	8750.	27500.

Excessively rare in Unc., very rare EF, thin beak JR-4 extremely rare.

1803 .... (33,040)	635.	1000.	1950.	3100.	8250.

Close 03 in date is very scarce; distant 03 rare. Excessively rare in Unc., very rare in EF.

1804 .... (8,265)	2400.	4500.	10000.	20000.	—

13 stars on reverse, extremely rare above VF, excessively rare in Unc., JR-1.

1804	2750.	5000.	—	22500.	—

14 stars on reverse. Rev. die also used to strike quarter eagles. Unknown in Unc., Norweb AU-50 $32,000.

1805 .... (120,780)	750.	1250.	2150.	4250.	—

Reverse shows large stars, 5 berries and wide A's in legend, JR-1. Very rare in Unc., scarce in higher grades as is the following.

1805	600.	775.	1450.	1900.	3800.

Normal stars on rev., 4 berries, JR-2. Often found with weak borders. Norweb MS-65, $30,800.

1807 .... (165,000)	610.	800.	1450.	1850.	3750.

Generally struck from injured dies. Weak at stars and letters, very rare with full denticulation, edge is found almost plain on many examples.

CAPPED BUST LEFT, OPEN COLLAR 1809-27

G - Date, letters, stars, bust legible.
VG - At least 3 letters in LIBERTY.
F - LIBERTY complete, ear, clasp and part of rim visible.
VF - Full LIBERTY, ear, clasp, rim, etc.
EF - All details sharp and clear.
AU - Wear only on highest points. Must have some Mint luster.
UNC - No wear on any part of coin. Full Mint luster.
PROOF- High rims, mirror-like fields. Letter surfaces are flat, not rounded, and show evidence of double striking. Liberty devices are frosted.

Capped Bust, Open Collar

	F-12	VF-20	EF-40	AU-50	MS-60
1809 .... (51,065)	325.	500.	1000.	1650.	4250.

Mintage figure includes the 6,355 struck in 1810. Very rare in Unc., elusive with full denticulation.

1811/09 .... (65,180)	285.	450.	950.	1500.	2400.

Underdate fades on later strikes, very rare in Unc.

1814 .... (34,500)	105.	225.	400.	675.	1850.

Small date, JR-1, extremely rare in Unc., underrated in all grades.

Dimes continued

	F-12	VF-20	EF-40	AU-50	MS-60
1814 .... (387,000)	58.00	140.	345.	535.	975.

Large date, JR-2-4, varieties with and without period after 10 C.

1814	72.00	175.	375.	640.	1150.

Rev. legend STATESOFAMERICA, JR-5, extremely rare in Unc.

1820 .... (942,587)					

Found with various combinations of large or small O in date, large or small C in 10 C., and old-style (as on 1809-1820) or modern (as on 1820-1837) rev. lettering. Many were struck in 1821.

1820	60.00	165.	425.	825.	1650.

STATESOFAMERICA rev. of 1814, JR-1, extremely rare in Unc.

1820	45.00	110.	325.	575.	925.

STATESOFAMERICA rev. of 1814, JR-1, extremely rare in Unc.

1820

Large O, old-style rev. lettering normally spaced, JR-8.

1820

Large O, large C., modern rev. lettering as on all that follow. Several vars.

1820

Large O, small C., JR-10, 11.

1820	50.00	130.	345.	550.	950.

Small O, (same height as 1), large C., JR-2 is popular Office Boy rev. with many die cutter's blunders.

1821 .... (1,186,512)	41.00	88.00	270.	500.	900.

Large date.

1821	55.00	115.	335.	650.	1200.

Small date.

1822 .... (100,000)	775.	1375.	2250.	4250.	9750.

Most of the mintage probably dated 1821. Excessively rare in Unc.

1823/22 .... (440,000)	40.00	85.00	275.	505.	925.

Small E's in legend, JR-1, scarce.

1823/22	40.00	85.00	275.	505.	900.

Legend shows E's larger than S in STATES. Two vars., rarest shows star 7 pointing to upper curl.

1824/22 .... (100,000)	88.00	260.	475.	1050.	1800.

Very rare earliest die state shows as 1824/3/2. Mintage figure of the Aug. 22, 1825, delivery and may include some also dated 1823 and 1825.

1825 .... (410,000)	32.50	83.00	260.	490.	850.
1827 .... (1,305,000)	32.50	83.00	260.	490.	850.

Several vars., repunched 7 is JR-1. Includes 90,000 delivered in Jan. 1828.

CAPPED BUST LEFT, CLOSED COLLAR 1828-1837

Capped Bust, Closed Collar

	F-12	VF-20	EF-40	AU-50	MS-60
1828 .... (35,000)	60.00	150.	335.	600.	1000.

Small date. Square based 2. Extremely rare in Unc. though quite a few cleaned EF-AU pieces exist and are sometimes offered as Mint State.

1828	165.	275.	575.	925.	2400.

Large date. Curled base 2, extra large 10 C. Excessively rare in Unc. Apparently struck in 1829 or later. Eliasberg 5/96 MS-66 $40,700.

1829 .... (770,000)					

Curved neck, square base 2, Extra large 10 C, entirely filling up space between border and eagle, JR-1, excessively rare in Unc., most known are in lower grades.

1829	95.00	175.	400.	585.	1800.

Large 10 C, JR-2.

1829	40.00	80.00	180.	300.	875.

Medium 10 C, square base 2, several vars., stripes in shield made up of three lines each. One scarce var., JR-12, shows two lines each and narrow oval O, actually coined in 1831.

1829	40.00	80.00	180.	300.	875.

Small 10 C, square base 2, round O, smaller than 1, four vars.

1829

Small 10 C over large 10 C, square base 2, JR-9, very scarce.

1830/29 .... (510,000)	85.00	135.	350.	575.	1200.

Overdate fades in later die states, authentication recommended.

1830	25.00	55.00	175.	265.	615.

Medium 10 C, one rare late die state has no period after C.

1830

Small 10 C. The O is round as in 1829, JR-1, 2. Mintage includes many dated 1829.

Dimes continued

	F-12	VF-20	EF-40	AU-50	MS-60
1831 .... (771,350)	25.00	52.50	175.	250.	600.

Two-line stripes. Mintage includes many dated 1829 and 1830.

1831

Three-line stripes.

	F-12	VF-20	EF-40	AU-50	MS-60
1832 .... (522,500)	25.00	52.50	175.	260.	615.

Mintage includes many dated 1831.

	F-12	VF-20	EF-40	AU-50	MS-60
1833 .... (485,000)	25.00	52.50	175.	250.	610.

Last 3 high, two vars., coin with progressively higher TED in UNITED is very rare. Mintage includes many dated 1832.

	F-12	VF-20	EF-40	AU-50	MS-60
1834 .... (635,000)	25.00	52.50	175.	250.	610.

Large 4 perfect or with broken crossbar.

1834

Small 4, one var.

	F-12	VF-20	EF-40	AU-50	MS-60
1835 .... (1,410,000)	25.00	52.50	175.	250.	600.

Several vars. with large 0 in 10 C. Rare small O is almost as tall as 1, JR-6.

	F-12	VF-20	EF-40	AU-50	MS-60
1836 .... (1,190,000)	25.00	52.50	175.	250.	625.

Vars. with 0 in 10 C smaller, larger and same height as 1.

	F-12	VF-20	EF-40	AU-50	MS-60
1837 .... (359,500)	25.00	52.50	175.	250.	625.

Fancy 8 in date, JR-4; block 8 vars. include rare JR-2 with double period after 10 C.

SEATED LIBERTY, NO STARS

Seated Liberty, No Stars

	F-12	VF-20	EF-40	AU-50	MS-60
1837 .... (682,500) .... (30)	70.00	250.	475.	565.	950.

Large curved date, flat-top 3.

1837

Small date, round-top 3

	F-12	VF-20	EF-40	AU-50	MS-60
1838-O .... (406,034)	95.00	290.	625.	1175.	2600.

First emission May 7-8, 1838, consisted of 30 pieces which were distributed as souvenirs, 10 going into the cornerstone of the New American Theatre in New Orleans. Extant mint state pieces are probably from the remaining 20. Mintage figure includes some pieces struck in Jan. 1839. Extremely rare in Unc. without die rust.

STARS, NO DRAPERY AT ELBOW

	Seated Liberty, Stars, No Drapery at Elbow (Bowers & Merena)				
	F-12	VF-20	EF-40	AU-50	MS-60
1838 .... (30,000)	47.50	72.50	155.	290.	650.

Small stars, initial delivery of March 31, 1838.

	F-12	VF-20	EF-40	AU-50	MS-60
1838 .... (1,962,500)	15.00	25.00	60.00	150.	285.

Large stars.

	F-12	VF-20	EF-40	AU-50	MS-60
1838	50.00	90.00	175.	275.	425.

The so-called partial drapery coins are from a clashed die.

	F-12	VF-20	EF-40	AU-50	MS-60
1839 .... (1,053,115)	15.50	26.00	55.00	145.	270.

Repunched 39 or 9 vars. known.

	F-12	VF-20	EF-40	AU-50	MS-60
1839-O .... (1,323,000)	350.	475.	750.	—	—

Large O, rev. of 1838-O. The O Mint marks on this series are found in three sizes: 1) Large, same height as letters in legend; 2) Medium, 2/3 height of letters; 3) Small, half or less height of letters and round.

	F-12	VF-20	EF-40	AU-50	MS-60
1839-O	23.00	44.00	90.00	265.	600.

Medium O.

1839-O

Small O

	F-12	VF-20	EF-40	AU-50	MS-60
1840 .... (981,000)	14.00	26.00	52.50	135.	270.

Whiskers var. shows die file marks under chin.

	F-12	VF-20	EF-40	AU-50	MS-60
1840-O .... (1,175,000)	24.00	50.00	100.	285.	950.

Known with Small and Tall O, latter very rare.

DRAPERY AT ELBOW, NEW REVERSE HUB

			Drapery at Elbow		
	F-12	**VF-20**	**EF-40**	**AU-50**	**MS-60**
1840 .... (377,500)	75.00	135.	265.	650.	1750.

Excessively rare in Unc.

| 1841 .... (1,622,500) .... | 14.00 | 25.00 | 55.00 | 130. | 270. |

Proofs of this year struck from over-polished obv. die with drapery removed, not from the No Drapery hub, two known.

| 1841-O .... (2,007,500) | 1400. | 2350. | — | — | — |

Large O, from leftover die made from 1837-40 rev. hub, with smaller letters in legend. extremely rare, unknown in Unc.

| 1841-O .... | 17.00 | 37.50 | 85.00 | 215. | 900. |

Medium O, very rare in Unc.

| 1841-O .... | 3000. | — | — | — | — |

Small O, usually found in lower grades.

| 1842 .... (1,887,500) .... | 13.00 | 18.00 | 37.00 | 120. | 265. |
| 1842-O .... (2,020,000) .... | 22.50 | 45.00 | 200. | 1200. | 2750. |

Medium O, scarce and generally found in low grade.

1842-O

Small O, excessively rare in Unc.

| 1843 .... (1,370,000) .... | 13.00 | 18.00 | 37.00 | 125. | 275. |
| 1843 .... | 27.00 | 60.00 | 115. | 185. | 375. |

Double date, first date punched too high, very rare.

| 1843-O .... (150,000) .... | 130. | 215. | 500. | 1550. | 2700. |

Usually weakly struck, virtually unknown in Unc.

| 1844 .... (72,500) .... | 350. | 600. | 975. | 1900. | — |

Above and beyond its low mintage, the rarity of this date has been greatly exaggerated. It is actually far commoner in used conditions than the 1846, but very rare in Unc. Eliasberg 5/96 Prf-65 $88,000.

| 1845 .... (1,755,000) .... | 12.50 | 19.00 | 37.00 | 110. | 225. |

Rare Proofs are known with repunched 45.

| 1845-O .... (230,000) .... | 62.50 | 190. | 600. | 1300. | — |

Excessively rare in Unc., scarce in all grades. Eliasberg 5/96 MS-67 $90,200.

| 1846 .... (31,300) .... | 165. | 285. | 775. | 1750. | — |

Scarce in lower grades, rare AU, Norweb AU-55 to MS-60 $1,320.

| 1847 .... (245,000) .... | 35.00 | 60.00 | 120. | 340. | 575. |

1847

All digits overlap base heavily, rare.

| 1848 .... (451,500) .... | 16.00 | 37.00 | 75.00 | 175. | 600. |
| 1849 .... (839,000) .... | 15.00 | 25.00 | 52.00 | 140. | 300. |

1849/849

Rare variety, do nor confuse with merely repunched 9.

| 1849-O .... (300,000) .... | 45.00 | 90.00 | 300. | 775. | 3000. |

Large and rare small O varieties, both excessively rare in Unc.

| 1850 .... (1,931,500) .... | 12.00 | 18.00 | 37.00 | 115. | 225. |
| 1850-O .... (510,000) .... | 37.00 | 75.00 | 175. | 350. | 1350. |

Large O.

1850-O

Medium O, very rare.

1850-O

Small O, rare, extremely rare in Unc.

| 1851 .... (1,026,500) .... | 12.00 | 17.00 | 37.00 | 110. | 290. |

Closed 5 and rare open 5 vars.

| 1851-O .... (400,000) .... | 27.00 | 75.00 | 200. | 500. | 1750. |

Large O, rare above Fine.

1851-O

Small O, extremely rare.

| 1852 .... (1,535,500) .... | 12.00 | 18.00 | 37.00 | 105. | 230. |
| 1852-O .... (430,000) .... | 40.00 | 77.00 | 210. | 550. | 1700. |

Rare in low grades, very rare in Unc.

Dimes continued	**F-12**	**VF-20**	**EF-40**	**AU-50**	**MS-60**
1853 .... (95,000)	110.	160.	290.	450.	775.

Many melted at the Mint as worth more than face value at prevailing silver prices, rare above VF.

ARROWS AT DATE

PROOF - Coins show a high, sharp rim, mirror-like fields, frosted figure of Liberty. Letter surfaces should be flat instead of rounded and should show some signs of doubling.

		Arrows at Date			
	F-12	**VF-20**	**EF-40**	**AU-50**	**MS-60**
1853 .... (12,078,010) .... (5)	10.50	16.00	38.00	110.	275.
1853-O .... (1,100,000)	24.00	35.00	90.00	345.	850.
1854 .... (4,470,000)	10.75	16.00	38.00	115.	285.
1854-O .... (1,770,000)	10.50	21.00	65.00	190.	585.
Vars. with incomplete O, 54 touching are rare.					
1855 .... (2,075,000)	11.25	16.50	50.00	120.	430.

ARROWS REMOVED

1856 .... (150,000)	14.00	19.00	50.00	160.	275.
Large date.					
1856 .... (5,630,000)	10.25	16.00	37.00	115.	225.
Small Date, Longacre's slanting 5.					
1856-O .... (1,180,000)	14.00	25.00	75.00	210.	600.
Large O, often weakly struck.					
1856-O					
Large O, double date, two varieties.					
1856-O					
Medium O, round Mint mark, rare.					
1856-O					
Small O, Unique? Federal Coin 1964 ANA sale, #618, possibly only a garbled description.					
1856-S .... (70,000)	225.	425.	750.	1750.	3500.
Double-punched S extremely rare; most Seated Liberty S dimes are extremely rare in Unc.					
1857 .... (5,580,000)	9.00	13.00	37.00	90.00	230.
1857-O .... (1,540,000)	12.00	24.00	65.00	175.	315.
Large O, repunched date in very rare.					
1857-O					
Medium O, open 5 rare.					
1858 .... (1,540,000) .... (80)	9.00	13.00	37.00	90.00	225.
1858-O .... (290,000)	35.00	70.00	125.	350.	675.
Extremely rare in Unc.					
1858-S .... (60,000)	225.	375.	675.	1300.	2750.
Extremely rare in Unc.					
1859 .... (430,000) .... (800)	10.50	21.00	55.00	145.	300.
1859 .... (12)					
Obv. without nation's name, Proof only. Muled with cereal wreath rev. of 1860, fantasy coin made by Mint Director James Ross Snowden for private distribution. See Pattern section.					
1859-O .... (480,000)	23.50	37.00	80.00	185.	315.
Large O, var. with heavy O is rare.					
1859-O					
Medium O, placed low in the die, rare in Unc.					
1859-S .... (60,000)	230.	425.	900.	1750.	——
Excessively rare in Unc.					
1860-S .... (140,000)	47.00	115.	275.	700.	2250.
Excessively rare in Unc.					

LEGEND OBVERSE, CEREAL WREATH REVERSE

		Legend obverse, Cereal Wreath reverse			
	F-12	**VF-20**	**EF-40**	**AU-50**	**MS-60**
1860 .... (606,000) .... (1,000)	14.00	20.00	37.00	69.00	150.

Two hubs used this year and following year. Type I shows 2 1/2 double stripes or five individual lines above LIBERTY on shield. Type II (used 1860-91) shows 3 double stripes above LIBERTY on Proofs of this date, extremely rare.

Seated Liberty dimes continued

	F-12	VF-20	EF-40	AU-50	MS-60
1860-O .... (40,000)	625.	1000.	2650.	5250.	10250.
Excessively rare in Unc., Type I shield only.					
1861 .... (1,883,000) .... (1,000)	13.00	18.00	36.00	65.00	140.
1861-S .... (172,500)	120.	225.	390.	700.	1800.
All Type I shield, extremely rare in Unc.					
1862 .... (847,000) .... (550)	13.00	18.00	36.00	65.00	165.
1862-S .... (180,750)	77.50	165.	365.	685.	1600.
Excessively rare in Unc.					
1863 .... (14,000) .... (460)	415.	565.	700.	775.	1175.
In this and later dates. non-Proof or business strikes are rarer than Proofs, strictly more rare than 1870-S and 1872-CC. Their market value still lags behind that of the popular Proofs.					
1863-S .... (157,500)	45.00	85.00	165.	550.	1550.
Extremely rare in Unc.					
1864 .... (11,000) .... (470)	375.	475.	675.	750.	925.
Non-Proofs, same remarks as 1863.					
1864-S .... (230,000)	40.00	80.00	160.	375.	875.
Extremely rare in Unc.					
1865 .... (10,000) .... (500)	460.	560.	685.	800.	925.
Non-Proofs, same remarks as 1863.					
1865-S .... (175,000)	50.00	95.00	260.	675.	2300.
Thin S rare, thick S more rare, all excessively rare in Unc.					
1866 .... (8,000) .... (725)	535.	685.	800.	950.	1175.
Non-Proofs, same remarks as 1863.					
1866-S .... (135,000)	47.50	100.	250.	475.	1900.
Same remarks as 1865-S.					
1867 .... (6,000) .... (625)	575.	675.	750.	1050.	1350.
Non-Proofs, same remarks as 1863.					
1867-S .... (140,000)	60.00	125.	225.	490.	2200.
Extremely rare in Unc.					
1868 .... (464,000) .... (600)	20.00	32.50	60.00	135.	350.
Some Proofs show base of misplaced 1 below gown.					
1868-S .... (260,000)	32.00	65.00	115.	210.	665.
1869 .... (256,000) .... (600)	28.00	50.00	105.	205.	585.
1869-S .... (450,000)	30.00	45.00	75.00	145.	450.
1870 .... (470,500) .... (1,000)	11.50	23.00	50.00	125.	225.
1870-S .... (50,000)	340.	435.	585.	950.	1900.
Rare in any grade, extremely rare in Unc.					
1871 .... (752,650) .... (960)	11.00	20.00	37.00	130.	310.
Rare Proofs show doubled date.					
1871-S .... (320,000)	32.00	67.50	155.	350.	685.
Rare in Unc., doubled date var. extremely rare in all grades.					
1871-CC .... (20,100)	1550.	2900.	5000.	7250.	14500.
First Carson City dime, very rare in low grades, excessively rare in Unc.					
1872 .... (2,395,500) .... (950)	10.75	18.00	34.00	90.00	150.
Proofs found with extra 2 in base.					
1872-S .... (190,000)	72.50	125.	225.	425.	1050.
Rare in Unc.					
1872-CC .... (35,480)	800.	1800.	3400.	7000.	26000.
A classic of the dime series, excessively rare EF and above.					
1873 .... (1,508,000) .... (600)	20.00	30.00	40.00	85.00	170.
Closed 3 in date.					
1873 .... (60,000)	40.00	60.00	105.	210.	550.
Open 3 in date, very rare in all grades, excessively rare in Unc.					
1873-CC .... (12,400)					
Unique Unc. ex Eliasberg collection. Probably a coin saved for the annual Assay Commission and rescued from the melting pot. Eliasberg 5/96 MS-65 $550,000.					

ARROWS AT DATE

Arrows at Date

	F-12	VF-20	EF-40	AU-50	MS-60
1873 .... (2,377,700) .... (800)	21.75	40.00	150.	235.	425.
1873	500.	775.	1000.	—	—
Doubled die obv., excessively rare.					

Seated Liberty dimes continued

	F-12	VF-20	EF-40	AU-50	MS-60
1873-S .... (455,000)	30.00	60.00	165.	300.	700.
1873-CC .... (18,791)	1800.	3500.	4850.	8250.	22500.

Excessively rare above Fine, unique Unc. ex F.C.C. Boyd coll. Usually struck on rough planchets.

1874 .... (2,940,000) .... (700)	22.00	40.00	150.	260.	440.
1874-S .... (240,000)	50.00	115.	275.	500.	925.

Usually in low grade, tiniest S variety is rare.

1874-CC .... (10,817)	6500.	10750.	18500.	24500.	37500.

Extremely rare in any grade, beware added mint marks, genuine show die crack through CC. Norweb MS-63/65 $15,730.

ARROWS REMOVED

1875 .... (10,350,000) .... (700)	10.25	12.00	25.00	60.00	120.
1875-S .... (9,070,000)	10.25	12.00	20.25	60.00	130.

Mint mark in wreath.

1875-S	10.25	12.50	20.00	60.00	130.

Mint mark below wreath, Medium S, about 3/4 height of letters in legend; var. with S taller than bow's thickness is rare.

1875-S
Mint mark below wreath, Small S, about 1/2 height of letters in legend.

1875-CC .... (4,645,000)	24.00	35.00	60.00	125.	265.

Two varieties: wide or very rare close CC in wreath.

1875-CC	14.00	24.00	39.00	70.00	200.

Mint mark below wreath, scarce.

1876 .... (11,460,000) .... (1,150)	10.25	12.00	20.00	57.50	120.

Two types, using old (1860-78) and new reverse hubs. 1) E in ONE almost touches wreath. Obv. varieties with large and small knobs on 6. 2) E is farther from wreath, which also shows many minor differences. Both types used 1876-78.

1876-S .... (10,420,000)	10.50	16.00	34.00	60.00	130.

Both hubs used, Type II reverses are very rare.

1876-CC .... (8,270,000)	12.00	16.00	32.50	67.50	200.

Both hubs, Type II reverse extremely rare.

1876-CC	50.00	85.00	225.	315.	475.

Doubled obverse die, crude enough for a counterfeit due to poor die quality; authentication suggested.

1876-CC
Doubled reverse die, rare.

1877 .... (7,310,000) .... (510)	10.25	12.00	20.00	57.50	115.

Type I very rare, Type II scarce in Unc.

1877-S .... (2,340,000)	14.00	19.00	28.00	57.50	120.

Type I extremely rare; tall S Type II very rare, small S most common.

1877-CC .... (7,700,000)	11.50	15.00	30.00	65.00	155.

Coins from Type I hub rare.

1878 .... (1,678,000) .... (800)	12.25	16.00	24.50	57.50	185.

Coins with Type I rev. very rare.

1878-CC .... (200,000)	100.	160.	240.	465.	725.

Coins with Type II rev. very rare.

1879 .... (14,000) .... (1,100)	235.	280.	330.	400.	500.

Non-Proofs, same remarks as 1863, very underrated.

1880 .... (36,000) .... (1,355)	210.	240.	275.	350.	455.

Same remarks as preceding.

1881 .... (24,000) .... (975)	215.	275.	340.	375.	460.

Same remarks as preceding.

1882 .... (3,910,000) .... (1,100)	10.50	12.00	20.00	55.00	115.
1883 .... (7,674,673) .... (1,039)	10.50	12.00	20.00	55.00	115.
1884 .... (3,365,505) .... (875)	10.50	12.00	20.00	55.00	115.
1884-S .... (564,969)	24.00	35.00	85.00	225.	635.

Large S.

1884-S
Small S.

1885 .... (2,532,497) .... (930)	10.50	12.00	20.00	55.00	115.
1885-S .... (43,690)	750.	1400.	2250.	3400.	5750.

Extremely rare in Unc.

1886 .... (6,376,684) .... (886)	9.50	11.75	20.00	55.00	115.
1886-S .... (206,524)	55.00	85.00	115.	225.	525.
1887 .... (11,283,229) .... (710)	9.50	11.75	20.00	55.00	115.
1887-S .... (4,454,450)	10.50	13.50	24.00	57.00	120.

Large over small S var. is very rare.

1888 .... (5,495,655) .... (832)	10.00	11.75	20.00	55.00	115.
1888-S .... (1,720,000)	10.50	13.00	32.00	85.00	235.
1889 .... (7,380,000) .... (711)	10.00	11.75	20.00	55.00	115.
1889-S .... (972,678)	22.00	35.00	65.00	210.	465.

Large S, not rare, but extensively hoarded.

Seated Liberty dimes continued

	F-12	VF-20	EF-40	AU-50	MS-60
1889-S					
Small S, two minor vars., both rare.					
1890 .... (9,910,951) .... (590)	10.25	12.00	20.00	55.00	115.
1890-S .... (1,423,076)	25.00	39.00	60.00	150.	325.
Large S.					
1890-S					
Large S over small S, very rare.					
1890-S					
Small S, rare.					
1891 .... (15,310,000) .... (600)	10.00	11.75	20.00	55.00	115.
Double date and repunched 9 vars. are rare.					
1891-O .... (4,540,000)	11.50	13.00	25.00	60.00	135.
One variety has O over O or an S but identification impossible.					
1891-O/horizontal O	115.	165.	225.	425.	—
Extremely rare					
1891-S .... (3,196,116)	11.25	14.00	30.00	70.00	155.

BARBER

F - All letters in LIBERTY show.
VF - LIBERTY strong, all hairlines show.
EF - All details sharp although some wear is evident.
AU - Wear only on highest points. Must have some Mint luster.
UNC - No wear at all evident. Full Mint luster.
PROOF- High rims, mirror-like fields. Frosted head. Letter surfaces are flat, not rounded and show some double striking

Barber, Cereal Wreath reverse

	F-12	VF-20	EF-40	AU-50	MS-60
1892 .... (12,120,000) .... (1,245)	14.00	19.00	25.00	50.00	92.50
1892-O .... (3,841,700)	27.00	38.00	50.00	70.00	140.
1892-S .... (990,710)	150.	180.	220.	250.	375.
Double-punched S rare.					
1893/92	—	130.	275.	400.	550.
Reported as Proof and business strikes; attribution as true overdates is questionable.					
1893 .... (3,340,000) .... (792)	18.00	25.00	37.00	57.50	105.
1893-O .... (1,760,000)	100.	110.	140.	170.	265.
1893-S .... (2,491,401)	25.00	39.00	55.00	125.	250.
Found with double and triple-punched Mint mark, the former with a recut 3.					
1894 .... (1,330,000) .... (972)	90.00	105.	125.	175.	275.
1894-O .... (720,000)	165.	225.	325.	625.	1500.
1894-S .... (24)					
Private striking for friends of Mint Superintendent J. Daggett. Top auction prices include James A. Stack sale, ST 1/90, Ch. Proof $275,000; Eliasberg 5/96 Prf-64 $451,000.					
1895 .... (690,000) .... (880)	290.	400.	475.	525.	650.
1895-O .... (440,000)	700.	975.	1850.	2600.	3250.
1895-S .... (1,120,000)	95.00	140.	200.	285.	475.
Double-punched 95 and S rare.					
1896 .... (2,000,000) .... (762)	40.00	62.50	75.00	110.	175.
1896-O .... (610,000)	235.	300.	390.	575.	1050.
1896-S .... (575,056)	200.	275.	350.	450.	675.
1897 .... (10,868,533) .... (731)	6.50	10.00	25.00	55.00	100.
1897-O .... (666,000)	245.	315.	390.	505.	775.
1897-S .... (1,342,844)	65.00	87.00	125.	225.	400.
1898 .... (16,320,000) .... (735)	6.50	10.00	23.00	50.00	90.00
1898-O .... (2,130,000)	75.00	95.00	145.	230.	450.
1898-S .... (1,702,507)	25.00	35.00	58.00	115.	285.
1899 .... (19,580,000) .... (846)	6.50	9.00	22.50	50.00	85.00
1899-O .... (2,650,000)	63.00	80.00	140.	235.	465.
1899-S .... (1,867,493)	17.00	25.00	39.00	105.	290.
1900 .... (17,600,000) .... (912)	6.50	9.00	21.00	50.00	85.00
Doubled final 0 var. is rare					
1900-O .... (2,010,000)	80.00	100.	225.	425.	750.

Barber dimes continued

	F-12	VF-20	EF-40	AU-50	MS-60
1900-S .... (5,168,270)	9.75	13.00	24.00	72.50	190.
Doubled final 0 var. is rare.					
1901 .... (18,859,665) .... (813)	5.00	8.50	20.50	48.00	85.00
New hubs this year and all following.					
1901-O .... (5,620,000)	12.00	19.00	45.00	125.	370.
Double-punched O very rare.					
1901-S .... (593,022)	275.	345.	435.	650.	1025.
1902 .... (21,380,000) .... (777)	5.00	7.50	20.50	48.00	85.00
1902-O .... (4,500,000)	14.00	25.00	46.00	140.	425.
1902-S .... (2,070,000)	45.00	60.00	100.	160.	350.
1903 .... (19,500,000) .... (755)	5.00	7.50	20.50	48.00	85.00
1903-O .... (8,180,000)	9.50	17.00	30.00	100.	250.
1903-S .... (613,300)	290.	450.	750.	850.	1250.
1904 .... (14,600,357) .... (670)	5.50	10.00	20.50	20.00	85.00
1904-S .... (800,000)	150.	185.	275.	440.	785.
1905 .... (14,551,623) .... (727)	5.00	7.50	20.00	48.00	85.00
1905-O .... (3,400,000)	32.00	45.00	65.00	120.	225.
Large O.					
1905-O	65.00	92.00	150.	300.	850.
Small O, excessively rare above VF.					
1905-S .... (6,855,199)	8.00	13.00	32.00	80.00	165.
1906 .... (19,957,731) .... (675)	4.50	7.50	20.00	48.00	85.00
1906-D .... (4,060,000)	10.00	15.50	31.00	75.00	160.
1906-O .... (2,610,000)	45.00	60.00	90.00	125.	210.
1906-S .... (3,136,640)	11.00	19.00	40.00	90.00	240.
1907 .... (22,220,000) .... (575)	4.25	7.50	20.00	48.00	85.00
1907-D .... (4,080,000)	9.00	16.00	40.00	95.00	235.
1907-O .... (5,058,000)	32.00	45.00	55.00	77.00	190.
1907-S .... (3,178,470)	9.50	19.00	43.00	100.	300.
1908 .... (10,600,000) .... (545)	4.00	7.50	20.00	48.00	85.00
1908-D .... (7,490,000)	7.50	12.00	32.00	57.00	100.
1908-O .... (1,789,000)	45.00	60.00	80.00	160.	290.
1908-S .... (3,220,000)	9.00	16.00	35.00	140.	265.
1909 .... (10,240,000) .... (650)	4.00	7.50	20.00	48.00	85.00
1909-D .... (954,000)	60.00	90.00	120.	235.	475.
1909-O .... (2,287,000)	9.00	18.00	30.00	85.00	170.
1909-O/inverted D					
Reported but not confirmed.					
1909-S .... (1,000,000)	80.00	110.	155.	285.	575.
1910 .... (11,520,000) .... (551)	7.00	10.00	20.00	50.00	85.00
1910-D .... (3,490,000)	8.00	17.00	42.00	95.00	185.
1910-S .... (1,240,000)	52.00	70.00	105.	175.	275.
1911 .... (18,870,000) .... (543)	4.00	7.50	20.00	47.00	85.00
1911-D .... (11,209,000)	4.50	8.00	21.00	55.00	95.00
1911-S .... (3,520,000)	9.00	16.00	35.00	83.00	135.
1912 .... (19,350,000) .... (700)	4.00	7.75	21.00	50.00	85.00
1912-D .... (11,760,000)	4.25	8.00	20.50	50.00	87.50
1912-S .... (3,420,000)	8.00	13.00	33.00	85.00	175.
1913 .... (19,760,000) .... (622)	4.00	7.50	20.00	47.00	85.00
1913-S .... (510,000)	80.00	115.	190.	275.	400.
1914 .... (17,360,230) .... (425)	4.00	7.50	20.00	47.00	85.00
1914-D .... (11,908,000)	4.00	7.75	21.00	50.00	90.00
1914-S .... (2,100,000)	9.00	15.00	34.00	70.00	125.
1915 .... (5,620,000) .... (450)	4.00	8.25	20.00	45.00	85.00
1915-S .... (960,000)	28.00	40.00	60.00	130.	250.
1916 .... (18,490,000)	4.00	7.75	20.00	50.00	85.00
1916-S .... (5,820,000)	5.75	8.00	21.00	51.00	87.50

WINGED LIBERTY HEAD OR MERCURY DIMES

F - All rods in rev. fasces defined but diagonal binding is smooth at center.
VF - Band is defined but worn.
EF - All details complete but show slight wear.
AU - Wear only on highest points. Must have some Mint luster.
UNC - No wear visible anywhere. Full Mint luster.
PROOF- High rims, mirror-like fields. Letter surfaces are flat,not rounded and show some double striking

Winged Liberty Head

	VF-20	EF-40	AU-50	MS-60	MS-65
1916 ....(22,180,080)	6.00	9.00	20.00	26.00	85.00
Struck in broad collar causing wide rim and dished appearance. Alterations of 1916-D can be distinguished by these characteristics, but authentication is recommended.					
1916-D .... (264,000)	1500.	2450.	3750.	4500.	10750.
Beware of added Mint marks.					
1916-S .... (10,450,000)	8.00	15.00	20.00	35.00	275.
Usually weakly struck at lower half of fasces.					
1917 ....(55,230,000)	4.50	6.00	13.00	23.00	140.
1917-D .... (9,402,000)	16.00	37.00	70.00	135.	1350.
Comes with small D of 1916-17 and medium D of 1917-34.					
1917-S .... (27,330,000)	5.00	9.00	26.00	55.00	465.
1918 ....(26,680,000)	9.50	26.00	38.00	67.50	350.
1918-D .... (22,674,800)	9.00	18.00	39.00	95.00	725.
Striking quality is generally poor.					
1918-S ....(19,300,000)	7.00	13.00	30.00	80.00	600.
1919 ....(35,740,000)	5.00	9.00	21.00	29.00	350.
1919-D .... (9,939,000)	15.00	30.00	68.00	190.	1900.
1919-S ....(8,850,000)	12.00	28.00	65.00	170.	850.
1920 ....(59,030,000)	4.00	7.00	14.00	24.00	225.
1920-D ....(19,171,000)	6.75	15.00	40.00	100.	750.
1920-S ....(13,820,000)	7.00	14.75	34.00	95.00	1350.
1921 ....(1,230,000)	210.	440.	685.	900.	3000.
Genuine coins show distinctive concave-sided 1's with tiny serifs. Altered 1941's have straight-sided 1's.					
1921-D .... (1,080,000)	230.	460.	750.	1000.	3050.
Same remarks as preceding.					
1923 ....(50,130,000)	3.75	6.00	13.00	27.00	100.
1923-D					
Exists only as a contemporary counterfeit.					
1923-S ....(6,440,000)	11.00	47.00	85.00	160.	1600.
1924 ....(24,010,000)	5.00	9.00	23.00	30.00	185.
1924-D ....(6,810,000)	11.00	42.00	90.00	140.	1250.
1924-S ....(7,120,000)	9.00	37.00	88.00	140.	1200.
1925 ....(25,610,000)	5.00	7.00	18.00	31.00	200.
1925-D ....(5,117,000)	30.00	95.00	180.	375.	1600.
1925-S ....(5,850,000)	9.00	43.00	85.00	165.	1900.
1926 ....(32,160,000)	3.50	4.75	12.50	24.00	265.
1926-D ....(6,828,000)	7.00	18.00	39.00	95.00	550.
1926-S ....(1,520,000)	37.00	170.	400.	775.	2950.
1927 ....(28,080,000)	3.50	5.00	11.00	20.00	165.
1927-D ....(4,812,000)	18.00	43.00	95.00	200.	1375.
1927-S ....(4,770,000)	6.00	21.00	48.00	235.	1750.
1928 ....(19,480,000)	3.50	5.00	15.00	24.00	140.
1928-D ....(4,161,000)	18.00	40.00	80.00	125.	800.
1928-S ....(7,400,000)	4.25	13.00	35.00	85.00	475.
Comes with small S of 1916-28 and scarce medium S of 1928-42.					
1929 ....(25,970,000)	3.30	4.25	10.00	19.00	60.00
1929-D ....(5,034,000)	7.00	11.50	21.00	28.00	80.00
1929-S ....(4,730,000)	3.50	6.50	20.00	37.50	130.
1930 ....(6,770,000)	3.50	5.50	13.00	25.00	145.
1930-D					
Exists only as a contemporary counterfeit.					
1930-S ....(1,843,000)	5.75	12.00	38.00	67.00	155.
1931 ....(3,150,000)	4.00	9.00	20.00	35.00	140.

Winged Liberty Head dimes continued

	VF-20	EF-40	AU-50	MS-60	MS-65
1931-D .... (1,260,000)	16.00	30.00	45.00	80.00	210.
1931-S .... (1,800,000)	6.00	12.00	33.00	65.00	210.
1934 ....(24,080,000)	2.25	4.00	7.00	14.00	38.00
1934-D ....(6,772,000)	6.00	11.00	21.00	33.00	75.00

Comes with medium D of 1917-34 and large D of 1934-45.

	VF-20	EF-40	AU-50	MS-60	MS-65
1935 ....(58,830,000)	1.35	2.50	5.00	8.00	37.00
1935-D ....(10,477,000)	5.00	10.00	19.50	29.00	65.00
1935-S ....(15,840,000)	1.85	3.25	9.00	19.00	36.00
1936 ....(87,500,000) .... (4,130)	1.35	2.00	3.25	8.00	25.00

Satin Finish Proofs are extremely rare, most Brilliant.

	VF-20	EF-40	AU-50	MS-60	MS-65
1936-D ....(16,132,000)	3.00	6.00	12.00	20.00	42.00
1936-S ....(9,210,000)	1.80	3.50	9.00	15.00	27.50
1937 ....(56,860,000) .... (5,756)	1.35	1.95	4.00	8.00	23.00
1937-D ....(14,146,000)	2.00	4.00	8.00	18.00	45.00
1937-S ....(9,740,000)	2.25	3.00	7.00	16.00	35.00
1938 ....(22,190,000) .... (8,728)	1.30	2.50	6.00	10.00	21.00
1938-D ....(5,537,000)	2.25	4.50	9.00	12.50	30.00
1938-S ....(8,090,000)	1.75	3.00	6.00	13.50	33.00
1939 ....(67,740,000) .... (9,321)	1.30	1.95	3.00	8.00	25.00
1939-D ....(24,394,000)	1.50	2.00	4.00	7.00	22.50
1939-S ....(10,540,000)	2.00	4.00	9.00	19.00	40.00
1940 ....(65,350,000) .... (11,827)	1.00	1.95	2.75	5.00	25.00
1940-D ....(21,198,000)	1.25	2.50	5.00	6.75	25.00
1940-S ....(21,560,000)	1.25	1.75	3.00	7.00	24.00
1941 ....(175,090,000) .... (16,557)	1.00	1.50	2.00	5.50	18.00
1941-D ....(45,634,000)	1.25	1.85	4.00	7.00	22.50
1941-S ....(43,090,000)	1.25	1.85	2.50	9.00	23.00

Comes with medium S of 1928-42 and large S of 1941-45.

	VF-20	EF-40	AU-50	MS-60	MS-65
1942 ....(205,410,000) .... (22,329)	1.00	1.50	2.00	5.00	17.00

1942/41

	VF-20	EF-40	AU-50	MS-60	MS-65
1942/41	350.	385.	500.	1450.	6850.

Always weakly struck on forelock. Counterfeits and alterations abound, authentication recommended.

	VF-20	EF-40	AU-50	MS-60	MS-65
1942-D ....(60,740,000)	1.25	1.85	2.75	7.00	23.00

Doubled D Mint mark is believed rare.

	VF-20	EF-40	AU-50	MS-60	MS-65
1942/41-D	365.	475.	1050.	1750.	5750.

Overdate weaker than that of the P mint, authentication recommended.

	VF-20	EF-40	AU-50	MS-60	MS-65
1942-S ....(49,300,000)	1.35	2.00	2.50	9.00	25.00

Known with medium S of 1928-42 (scarce) and large S of 1941-45.

	VF-20	EF-40	AU-50	MS-60	MS-65
1943 ....(191,710,000)	1.00	1.50	2.25	5.50	17.00
1943-D ....(71,949,000)	1.25	1.85	2.50	7.00	22.50
1943-S ....(60,400,000)	1.25	1.85	2.75	9.00	22.00
1944 ....(231,410,000)	1.00	1.25	2.00	5.00	17.00
1944-D ....(62,224,000)	1.25	1.85	2.50	7.00	22.00
1944-S ....(49,490,000)	1.25	1.75	2.25	7.50	23.00
1945 ....(159,130,000)	1.00	1.25	2.25	5.50	22.00
1945-D ....(40,245,000)	1.25	2.00	3.50	7.00	22.00
1945-S ....(41,920,000)	1.25	1.90	2.50	7.00	25.00
1945-S	2.50	5.00	15.00	19.50	57.00

Microscopic S, formerly heavily promoted; of little current interest.

ROOSEVELT DIMES

EF - All details sharp.
AU - All details sharp and must have some Mint luster.
UNC - No wear visible anywhere. Full Mint luster.
PROOF- High rims, mirror-like fields. Letter surfaces are flat, not rounded and show some double striking

Franklin Roosevelt

	EF-40	AU-50	MS-60	MS-65	PF-65
1946 .... (255,250,000)	0.63	0.65	0.70	4.75	*

Two obv. hubs were used this year. Type I: Y distant from forelock; JS small, thin and slightly misshapen. Type II: Y closer to forelock. JS larger and perfect.

	EF-40	AU-50	MS-60	MS-65	PF-65
1946-D .... (61,043,500)	0.60	0.65	0.85	7.00	*
1946-S .... (27,900,000)	1.15	1.25	1.50	10.50	*

Two different styles of S were used 1946-55: Type I, bell-shaped tail on S or Type II, knob-end S.

	EF-40	AU-50	MS-60	MS-65	PF-65
1947 .... (121,520,000)	0.70	0.90	1.40	4.50	*
1947-D .... (46,835,000)	1.35	1.75	2.20	11.00	*
1947-S .... (34,840,000)	0.90	1.25	1.75	13.00	*

Type III, sans-serif style S used this year only.

	EF-40	AU-50	MS-60	MS-65	PF-65
1948 .... (74,950,000)	0.90	1.55	4.00	14.00	*
1948-D .... (52,841,000)	1.35	2.00	2.50	10.00	*
1948-S .... (35,520,000)	0.95	1.25	1.90	12.00	*
1949 .... (30,940,000)	2.25	4.00	9.00	18.00	*
1949-D .... (26,034,000)	1.65	3.25	3.75	13.00	*
1949-S .... (13,510,000)	3.50	6.25	15.00	37.50	*
1950 .... (50,130,114) .... (51,386)	1.25	1.40	1.90	8.00	37.50
1950-D .... (46,803,000)	0.85	1.00	3.00	8.00	*
1950-S .... (20,440,000)	2.85	6.00	9.50	22.50	*
1951 .... (102,880,102) .... (57,500)	0.70	0.75	1.30	3.75	29.00
1951-D .... (56,529,000)	0.75	0.85	1.40	4.00	*
1951-S .... (31,630,000)	1.75	3.50	5.25	10.00	*
1952 .... (99,040,093) .... (81,980)	0.80	0.85	1.75	4.00	20.00
1952-D .... (122,100,000)	0.75	0.80	1.00	4.25	*
1952-S .... (44,419,500)	1.25	1.50	3.75	9.50	*
1953 .... (53,490,120) .... (128,800)	0.85	0.95	1.10	4.25	18.50
1953-D .... (136,433,000)	0.60	0.65	0.90	3.75	*

A rare var. shows D over horizontal D.

	EF-40	AU-50	MS-60	MS-65	PF-65
1953-S .... (39,180,000)	0.50	0.55	0.70	3.30	*
1954 .... (114,010,203) .... (233,300)	0.52	0.53	0.55	3.35	9.00
1954-D .... (106,397,000)	0.52	0.53	0.55	3.20	*
1954-S .... (22,860,000)	0.55	0.60	0.65	3.20	*
1955 .... (12,450,181) .... (378,200)	0.65	0.70	0.75	5.00	8.50
1955-D .... (13,959,000)	0.62	0.63	0.65	3.40	*
1955-S .... (18,510,000)	0.62	0.63	0.65	4.75	*
1956 .... (108,640,000) .... (669,384)	0.53	0.55	0.58	2.90	3.50
1956-D .... (108,015,100)	0.55	0.57	0.60	2.80	*
1957 .... (160,160,000) .... (1,247,952)	0.53	0.55	0.58	2.90	3.00

Peak year of Proof set boom, broken by huge mintage.

	EF-40	AU-50	MS-60	MS-65	PF-65
1957-D .... (113,354,330)	0.55	0.60	0.65	3.85	*
1958 .... (31,910,000) .... (875,652)	0.55	0.57	0.60	4.00	3.50
1958-D .... (136,564,600)	0.52	0.53	0.55	3.75	*
1959 .... (85,780,000) .... (1,149,291)	0.52	0.53	0.55	2.60	2.00
1959-D .... (164,919,790)	0.55	0.57	0.60	3.00	*
1960 .... (70,390,000) .... (1,691,602)	0.50	0.53	0.55	2.55	1.00

1960

Doubled die obv., Proofs only.

	EF-40	AU-50	MS-60	MS-65	PF-65
1960-D .... (200,160,400)	0.50	0.53	0.55	2.55	*
1961 .... (93,730,000) .... (3,028,244)	0.50	0.53	0.55	2.30	0.95
1961-D .... (209,146,550)	0.50	0.53	0.55	2.30	*
1962 .... (72,450,000) .... (3,218,019)	0.50	0.53	0.55	2.30	0.95
1962-D .... (334,948,380)	0.50	0.53	0.55	2.75	*
1963 .... (123,650,000) .... (3,075,645)	0.50	0.53	0.55	2.25	0.95
1963-D .... (421,476,530)	0.50	0.53	0.55	2.25	*
1964 .... (929,360,000) .... (3,950,762)	0.50	0.53	0.55	2.25	0.95

Roosevelt dimes continued

	EF-40	AU-50	MS-60	MS-65	PF-65
1964-D .... (1,357,517,180)	0.70	0.75	0.78	2.25	*

New hub with blunt 9 is introduced during 1964. Earlier hub with pointed 9 is scarce. Frozen-date 1964-dated silver dimes were struck through late 1965.

1965

Silver error striking, extremely rare.

CLAD COINAGE

1964

Copper-nickel clad error striking, extremely rare.

	MS-60	MS-63	MS-65	PF-65
1965 .... (1,652,140,570)	0.23	0.40	0.70	*
1966 .... (1,382,734,540)	0.25	0.40	0.70	*
1967 .... (2,244,007,320)	0.23	0.40	0.70	*
1968 .... (424,470,400)	0.23	0.40	0.70	*
1968-D .... (480,748,280)	0.23	0.40	0.70	*
1968-S .... (3,041,506)	*	*	*	0.60
Proof only.				
1968 (No S)	*	*	*	4850.
Proof error, very rare.				
1969 .... (145,790,000)	0.35	0.75	1.00	*
1969-D .... (563,323,870)	0.25	0.40	0.65	*
1969-S .... (2,934,631)	*	*	*	0.60
Proof only.				
1970 .... (345,570,000)	0.23	0.40	0.65	*
1970-D .... (754,942,100)	0.23	0.40	0.65	*
1970-S .... (2,632,810)	*	*	*	0.60
Proof only.				
1970 (No S)	*	*	*	350.
Proof error, rare.				
1971 .... (162,690,000)	0.27	0.45	0.75	*
1971-D .... (377,914,240)	0.23	0.40	0.65	*
1971-S .... (3,220,733)	*	*	*	0.95
Proof only.				
1972 .... (431,540,000)	0.27	0.40	0.70	*
1972-D .... (330,290,000)	0.25	0.40	0.65	*
1972-S .... (3,260,996)	*	*	*	0.95
Proof only.				
1973 .... (315,670,000)	0.23	0.40	0.65	*
1973-D .... (455,032,426)	0.23	0.40	0.65	*
1973-S .... (2,760,339)	*	*	*	0.50
Proof only.				
1974 .... (470,248,000)	0.23	0.40	0.65	*
1974-D .... (571,083,000)	0.23	0.40	0.65	*
1974-S .... (2,612,568)	*	*	*	0.50
Proof only.				
1975 .... (585,673,900)	0.25	0.45	0.70	*
1975-D .... (313,705,300)	0.25	0.40	0.65	*
1975-S .... (2,845,450)	*	*	*	0.75
Proof only.				
1975 (No S)	*	*	*	28000.
Proof error, exceedingly rare.				
1976 .... (568,760,000)	0.25	0.55	0.80	*
1976-D .... (695,222,774)	0.25	0.55	0.80	*
1976-S .... (4,123,056)	*	*	*	0.75
Proof only.				
1977 .... (796,930,000)	0.20	0.35	0.65	*
1977-D .... (376,607,228)	0.21	0.35	0.70	*
1977-S .... (3,236,798)	*	*	*	0.75
Proof only.				
1978 .... (663,980,000)	0.20	0.35	0.65	*
1978-D .... (282,847,540)	0.21	0.35	0.70	*
1978-S .... (3,120,285)	*	*	*	0.60
Proof only.				
1979 .... (315,440,000)	0.20	0.35	0.65	*
1979-D .... (390,921,184)	0.20	0.35	0.65	*
1979-S .... (3,677,175)	*	*	*	0.60

Proof only, Type I S is blurry, same as 1978;

1979-S

Type II S is clear, same as 1980, appearing on about 20 percent of this coinage.

Roosevelt dimes continued

	MS-60	MS-63	MS-65	PF-65
1980-P .... (735,170,000)	0.20	0.35	0.50	*
1980-D .... (719,354,321)	0.20	0.35	0.50	*
1980-S .... (3,554,806)	*	*	*	0.60
Proof only.				
1981-P .... (676,650,000)	0.20	0.35	0.50	*
1981-D .... (712,284,143)	0.20	0.35	0.50	*
1981-S .... (4,063,083)	*	*	*	0.60
Proof only, minor varieties of mint mark style exist.				
1982-P .... (519,475,000)	0.85	1.45	—	*
1982 (P)	85.00	90.00	125.	*
No Mint mark error, found sharply or weakly struck, the latter less valuable.				
1982-D .... (542,713,584)	0.30	0.55	—	*
1982-S .... (3,857,479)	*	*	*	0.60
Proof only.				
1983-P .... (647,025,000)	0.30	0.95	—	*
1983-D .... (730,129,224)	0.28	0.95	—	*
1983-S .... (3,279,126)	*	*	*	0.60
Proof only.				
1983 (No S)	*	*	*	250.
Proof error, rare.				
1984-P .... (856,669,000)	0.20	0.50	—	*
1984-D .... (704,803,976)	0.20	0.55	—	*
1984-S .... (3,065,110)	*	*	*	0.60
Proof only.				
1985-P .... (705,200,962)	0.21	0.60	—	*
1985-D .... (587,979,970)	0.20	0.50	—	*
1985-S .... (3,362,821)	*	*	*	0.60
Proof only.				
1986-P .... (682,649,693)	0.20	0.75	—	*
New hubs now show sharper detail and letter definition.				
1986-D .... (473,326,970)	0.20	0.75	—	*
1986-S .... (3,010,497)	*	*	*	0.95
Proof only.				
1987-P .... (762,709,481)	0.20	0.35	—	*
1987-D .... (653,203,402)	0.20	0.35	—	*
1987-S .... (3,792,233)	*	*	*	0.85
Proof only.				
1988-P .... (1,030,550,000)	0.20	0.40	—	*
1988-D .... (962,385,498)	0.20	0.35	—	*
1988-S .... (2,600,618)	*	*	*	0.85
Proof only.				
1989-P .... (1,298,400,000)	0.20	0.35	—	*
1989-D .... (896,535,597)	0.20	0.35	—	*
1989-S .... (3,220,914)	*	*	*	0.85
Proof only.				
1990-P .... (1,034,340,000)	0.20	0.35	—	*
1990-D .... (839,995,824)	0.20	0.35	—	*
1990-S .... (3,299,559)	*	*	*	1.60
Proof only.				
1991-P .... (927,220,000)	0.20	0.35	—	*
1991-D .... (601,241,114)	0.20	0.35	—	*
1991-S .... (2,867,787)	*	*	*	3.00
Proof only.				
1992-P .... (593,500,000)	0.20	0.35	—	*
1992-D .... (616,273,932)	0.20	0.35	—	*
1992-S .... (2,858,903)	*	*	*	3.00
Proof only.				
1992-S .... (1,317,641)	*	*	*	4.00
90% silver, struck for inclusion in special Proof sets.				
1993-P .... (766,180,000)	0.20	0.35	—	*
1993-D .... (750,110,166)	0.20	0.35	—	*
1993-S .... (2,569,882)	*	*	*	4.50
Proof only.				
1993-S .... (790,994)	*	*	*	6.00
90% silver, struck for inclusion in special Proof sets.				
1994-P .... (1,189,000,000)	0.20	0.35	—	*
1994-D .... (1,303,268,110)	0.20	0.35	—	*
1994-S .... (2,443,590)	*	*	*	4.00
Proof only.				
1994-S .... (778,550)	*	*	*	6.00
90% silver, struck for inclusion in special Proof sets.				

Roosevelt dimes continued

			MS-60	MS-63	MS-65	PF-65
1995-P	(1,125,500,000)		0.20	0.35	——	*
1995-D	(1,274,890,000)		0.20	0.35	——	*
1995-S		(2,124,790)	*	*	*	3.00
Proof only.						
1995-S		(666,277)	*	*	*	4.25
90% silver, struck for inclusion in special Proof sets.						
1996-P	(1,421,630,000)		0.20	0.35	——	*
1996-D	(1,400,300,000)		0.20	0.35	——	*
1996-S		(2,145,077)	*	*	*	2.50
Proof only.						
1996-S		(775,081)	*	*	*	3.75
90% silver, struck for inclusion in special Proof sets.						
1996-W	(1,450,440)		7.00	7.25	12.00	*
Struck to celebrate the 50th anniversary of the type, for inclusion in Uncirculated Mint sets only.						
1997-P	(NR)		0.20	0.35	——	*
1997-D	(NR)		0.20	0.35	——	*
1997-S		(NR)	*	*	*	2.50
Proof only.						
1997-S		(NR)	*	*	*	4.25
90% silver, struck for inclusion in special Proof sets.						

20-cent pieces

G - All letters and date legible except LIBERTY on shield.
VG - Details sharp, but no LIBERTY.
F - Half of LIBERTY shows.
VF - LIBERTY full but weak.
EF - All details sharp.
AU - All details sharp and must have some Mint luster.
UNC - No wear visible anywhere. Full Mint luster.
PROOF- Rim high and sharp, fields mirror-like. Letters flat on surfaces instead of rounded, and should show some signs of doubling. Figure of liberty should be frosted.

					Seated Liberty		
			VF-20	AU-50	MS-60	MS-65	PF-65
1875	(38,500)	(2,790)	100.	325.	540.	5350.	6600.
1875-S	(1,155,000)	(12)	100.	275.	460.	5150.	45000.
Twelve proofs struck from polished dies later used for business strikes. Many deceptive early strikes exist. Authentication recommended.							
1875-S							
Double-punched Mint mark resembles dollar sign $, scarce.							
1875-CC	(133,290)		155.	425.	725.	7500.	——
1876	(14,750)	(1,260)	200.	450.	640.	6000.	6600.
One rev. shows doubling, and hollows in the wings due to die polishing.							
1876-CC	(10,000)						
Only 16-18 pieces are known, most in Mint State. Beware of altered dates; all genuine pieces have LIBERTY doubled. The Norweb MS-64 to 65 brought $69,300, Nov. 1987; James A. Stack sale, ST 3/95 $99,000; Eliasberg 4/97 MS-65 $148,500.							
1877		(350)	1600.	1900.	1950.	7500.	7500.
Proof only							
1878		(600)	1300.	1550.	1550.	7200.	7200.
Proof only							

Quarter dollars

DRAPED BUST, SMALL EAGLE

G - Legible date, outlined bust, no details.
VG - Only deepest drapery fold, hairlines, curls visible.
F - Drapery lines complete.
VF - Left side of drapery indistinct, all details show.
EF - All details sharp.
AU - Wear only on highest points. Must show some Mint luster
UNC - No wear visible anywhere. Full Mint luster.

Draped Bust, Small Eagle

	G-4	F-12	VF-20	AU-50	MS-60
1796 .... (6,146)	3450.	7750.	9750.	16500.	24500.

Mintage includes 252 struck in 1797. Comes with low 6 and high 6 (Browning 1 and 2) but usually collected by type rather than variety. Many prooflike specimens were saved as examples of the new denomination. Counterfeits in G-VG condition exist, possibly in higher grades as well. Eliasberg 5/96 B-1 MS-65 $176,000.

DRAPED BUST, HERALDIC EAGLE

Draped Bust, Heraldic Eagle

	G-4	F-12	VF-20	AU-50	MS-60
1804 .... (6,738)	885.	2250.	3250.	16000.	—

Extremely rare in Unc., very rare in EF.

	G-4	F-12	VF-20	AU-50	MS-60
1805 .... (121,394)	180.	390.	725.	2350.	7500.

Five berries on reverse, four vars. Private restrikes made from discarded 1805 obverse are known.

1805

Four berries on reverse, B-4, excessively rare in Unc., very rare above Fine.

	G-4	F-12	VF-20	AU-50	MS-60
1806 over 5 .... (286,424)	180.	385.	785.	3100.	7750.

4 berries, excessively rare in Unc. One of the few examples of an overdated die used in both years shown, as the initial use of a die normally renders it too brittle to be redated.

	G-4	F-12	VF-20	AU-50	MS-60
1806	175.	365.	710.	2150.	3800.

Mintage figure includes 80,300 quarters delivered Jan. 24, 1807. Eliasberg 4/97 B-9 MS-64 $35,200.

	G-4	F-12	VF-20	AU-50	MS-60
1807 .... (140,343)	175.	360.	700.	2100.	3750.

Large date, five berries, scarce; small date, four berries varieties. Eliasberg 4/97 B-1 MS-65 $165,000.

CAPPED BUST LEFT, LARGE DIAMETER, OPEN COLLAR

G - Stars, letters, date legible. Cap lines, hair under band smooth. Wear rims.
VG - Full LIBERTY, rims defined, main details visible.
F - Shoulder clasp, hairlines show, drapery partially visible.
VF - All details distinct, but visibly worn on high spots.
EF - All details sharp.
AU - Wear only on highest points. Must show some Mint luster.
UNC - No wear visible anywhere. Full Mint luster.

Capped Bust, Open Collar

	G-4	F-12	VF-20	AU-50	MS-60
1815 .... (89,235)	45.00	120.	310.	1050.	2100.

Mintage figure include 20,003 quarters delivered in January 1816.
1815 and 1825 quarters exist with countermarks E, L and possibly R applied while the coin rested in the lower die. Letters do not indicate weight variation, since weights of coins examined are normal. The late Walter Breen's idea of use as academic awards is merely amusing; Mark B. Hotz' theory that letters record experimental die cantings, right, left or even (level) to eliminate uneven striking is the most plausible, but unproven.

	G-4	F-12	VF-20	AU-50	MS-60
1818/5 .... (361,174)	48.00	125.	315.	1125.	2250.

Overdates with large and small 5 exist.

1818	45.00	95.00	280.	1000.	1950.

Five vars. A patchwork private restrike exists from discarded 1818 quarter obverse muled with 1818 cent reverse, struck over 1860 quarter. Eliasberg 4/97 B-2 MS-65 $42,900.

1819 .... (144,000)	45.00	87.00	265.	1000.	1950.

Large 9.

1819
Small 9.

1820 .... (127,444)	45.00	87.00	275.	975.	1950.

Large 0.

1820	45.00	95.00	280.	1050.	2200.

Small 0.

1821 .... (216,851)	45.00	87.00	265.	975.	1950.

Eliasberg 4/97 Prf-66 $121,000.

1822 .... (64,080)	55.00	140.	325.	1600.	2550.
1822	1650.	3950.	5250.	15000.	25000.

25 over 50 on rev., B-2, a classic engraver's blunder and early American rarity. This reverse used again in 1828. A number known in Mint State from Col. E.H.R. Green hoard. Eliasberg 4/97 Prf-65 $192,500.

1823/2 .... (17,800)	8500.	18000.	22500.	50000.	——

Perhaps 13 known, long recognized as extremely rare, most of mintage evidently coined from 1822 dies. Defective top and middle arrows identify genuine pieces. Norweb prooflike AU-50, $28,600.

1824/2 .... (24,000)	75.00	190.	525.	2150.	6000.

Scarce.

1825/4/3 .... (144,000)	45.00	87.00	250.	950.	1950.

B-1, wide 25 C. with large 5, rare.

1825/2	145.	300.	650.	1900.	3750.

B-2, small 5 in 25 C. Actually 25/24/23, 4 not plain.

1827/3 .... (4,000)
Original, Curled Base 2 in date and 25 C., about 12 Proofs known, Norweb Proof-64, $61,600 3/88. Most, if not all of the 4,000 reported were probably dated 1825. Eliasberg 4/97 VF-20/30 $39,600.

1827/3
Restrike, Square Base 2 in 25 C., die rust. Perhaps 12 known, Norweb Gem Proof-65, $39,600, 3/88. Eliasberg 4/97 Prf-65 $77,000.

1828 .... (102,000)	45.00	87.00	250.	950.	2150.
1828	140.	400.	850.	3600.	8500.

1822 rev. 25 over 50, B-3, very rare in Unc.

CAPPED BUST LEFT, SMALL DIAMETER, CLOSED COLLAR

		Capped Bust, Closed Collar			
	G-4	**F-12**	**VF-20**	**AU-50**	**MS-60**
1831 .... (398,000)	36.00	50.00	80.00	480.	850.
Small date, small letters, curve base 2, berries on branch, B-1.					
1831					
Small date, small letters, square base 2, no berries, short arrowheads, B-2.					
1831					
Small date, small letters, square base 2, no berries, long arrowheads, B-3 extremely rare, B-4.					
1831					
Small date, large letters, curve base 2, long arrowheads, B-6.					
1831					
Large over small 1's, large letters, curve base 2, long arrowheads, B-5.					
1831					
Large date, large letters, short arrowheads. ANS coll., Unique?					
1832 .... (320,000)	36.00	50.00	80.00	500.	940.
Long and short arrowhead vars.					
1833 .... (156,000)	40.00	60.00	115.	725.	1350.
Period after 25 C., most from rusty dies.					
1833					
No period after 25 C. Dies always rusty, B-2 shows re-engraved OF on rev.					
1834 .... (286,000)	36.00	50.00	80.00	480.	875.
Period after 25 C.					
1834					
No period after 25 C., three vars., B-1 shows two lines in stripes.					
1835 .... (1,952,000)	36.00	50.00	80.00	480.	850.
Period after 25 C.					
1835					
No period after 25 C., B-7.					
1836 .... (472,000)	36.00	50.00	80.00	525.	1200.
Eliasberg 4/97 Prf-64 $71,500.					
1837 .... (252,400)	36.00	50.00	80.00	525.	900.
Struck in old and new weights and finenesses.					
1838 .... (366,000)	36.00	50.00	80.00	480.	925.
Eliasberg 4/97 MS-66 $35,200.					

SEATED LIBERTY, NO DRAPERY AT ELBOW

VG - At least 3 letters in LIBERTY, rim mostly complete.
F - LIBERTY weak but complete.
VF - All details evident but may show considerable wear
EF - All details sharp.
AU - Wear only on highest points. Must show some Mint luster
UNC - No wear visible anywhere. Full Mint luster.
PROOF- High rims, mirror-like fields, frosted LIBERTY, eagle, etc. Letter surfaces flat, not rounded.

		Seated Liberty, No Drapery at Elbow			
	G-4	**F-12**	**VF-20**	**AU-50**	**MS-60**
1838 .... (466,000)	13.25	30.00	72.50	525.	875.
Eliasberg 4/97 MS-65 $25,300.					
1839 .... (491,146)	13.50	29.50	60.00	495.	700.
Rev. of 1838, eagle has tongue, relatively straight claws.					

Quarter dollars continued

	G-4	F-12	VF-20	AU-50	MS-60

1839
Rev. of 1839, eagle has tongue, sharply curved claws. Eliasberg 4/97 MS-66 $37,400.

		G-4	F-12	VF-20	AU-50	MS-60
1840-O .... (317,200)		14.25	31.00	85.00	550.	1200.

Scarce in Unc. New reverse hub, has curved claws, no tongue.

SEATED LIBERTY WITH DRAPERY AT ELBOW

Drapery at Elbow (Stack's)

	G-4	F-12	VF-20	AU-50	MS-60
1840 .... (188,127)	19.00	45.00	80.00	340.	800.

Scarce in Unc. New reverse hub with thicker rim and denticles, as on those that follow.

	G-4	F-12	VF-20	AU-50	MS-60
1840-O .... (108,000)	300.	600.	1100.	—	—

Large O very rare in Unc., vars. show medium, small O.

	G-4	F-12	VF-20	AU-50	MS-60
1840-O	23.00	57.50	125.	525.	1175.

Small O

	G-4	F-12	VF-20	AU-50	MS-60
1841 .... (120,000)	44.50	87.50	140.	435.	1050.

Now known in Unc. due to a hoard.

1841
Doubled die reverse. Very rare.

	G-4	F-12	VF-20	AU-50	MS-60
1841-O .... (452,000)	18.00	40.00	70.00	310.	650.

Rare in Unc.

	G-4	F-12	VF-20	AU-50	MS-60
1842 .... (88,000)	70.00	175.	250.	875.	2800.

Large date, extremely rare in Unc.

	G-4	F-12	VF-20	AU-50	MS-60
1842	—	—	—	—	25000.

Small date, Proof only and extremely rare, Norweb Proof-63 to 64, $46,200, 3/88; Eliasberg 4/97 Prf-63 $66,000.

	G-4	F-12	VF-20	AU-50	MS-60
1842-O .... (769,000)	16.25	36.00	70.00	585.	2050.

Large date, very rare in Unc.

	G-4	F-12	VF-20	AU-50	MS-60
1842-O	400.	1150.	2000.	7500.	16500.

Small date, excessively rare in Unc.

	G-4	F-12	VF-20	AU-50	MS-60
1843 .... (645,600)	14.00	23.00	35.00	190.	475.

Rare in Unc.

	G-4	F-12	VF-20	AU-50	MS-60
1843-O .... (968,000)	75.00	200.	400.	—	—

Large O, virtually unknown in Unc.

	G-4	F-12	VF-20	AU-50	MS-60
1843-O	18.50	50.00	100.	800.	—

Small O, excessively rare in Unc., Norweb MS-60 $5,280, 3/88.

	G-4	F-12	VF-20	AU-50	MS-60
1844 .... (421,200)	13.00	23.00	35.00	185.	475.

Doubled date, very rare.

	G-4	F-12	VF-20	AU-50	MS-60
1844-O .... (740,000)	15.75	35.00	60.00	390.	1950.

Rare in Unc.

	G-4	F-12	VF-20	AU-50	MS-60
1845 .... (922,000)	13.00	22.50	35.00	200.	490.
1846 .... (510,000)	14.50	27.00	35.00	190.	480.

Doubled or partly repunched dates rare.

	G-4	F-12	VF-20	AU-50	MS-60
1847 .... (734,000)	13.00	22.50	32.50	185.	450.
1847	16.00	50.00	62.50	285.	—

Doubled die reverse, rare.

	G-4	F-12	VF-20	AU-50	MS-60
1847-O .... (368,000)	19.50	57.50	97.50	685.	3200.

Very rare in Unc.

	G-4	F-12	VF-20	AU-50	MS-60
1848 .... (146,000)	25.00	82.50	140.	400.	1050.

Excessively rare in Unc., one rev. has hole at top of first vertical stripe, in exact center of reverse.

	G-4	F-12	VF-20	AU-50	MS-60
1848	40.00	87.50	170.	590.	—

Doubled date, rare.

	G-4	F-12	VF-20	AU-50	MS-60
1849 .... (340,000)	18.00	37.50	67.50	300.	950.

Very rare in Unc., one reverse has center hole as last.

	G-4	F-12	VF-20	AU-50	MS-60
1849-O .... (16,000)	385.	1025.	1600.	6250.	—

Very rare in lower grades, excessively rare in Unc., included in mint report for 1850-O.

	G-4	F-12	VF-20	AU-50	MS-60
1850 .... (190,800)	22.50	60.00	82.50	330.	875.

One var. has base of extra 1 atop rim, missing on lower grades. Rare in Unc., many 1850-52 quarters of both mints were melted at Philadelphia after July 1853 because bullion value exceeded face.

	G-4	F-12	VF-20	AU-50	MS-60
1850-O .... (396,000)	17.75	55.00	85.00	490.	1400.

Very rare in Unc.

	G-4	F-12	VF-20	AU-50	MS-60
1851 .... (160,000)	32.50	80.00	125.	315.	800.

Very rare in Unc.

Quarter dollars continued

	G-4	F-12	VF-20	AU-50	MS-60
1851-O .... (88,000)	150.	390.	625.	2650.	5050.
Virtually unknown in Unc.					
1852 .... (177,060)	31.50	80.00	135.	360.	875.
Rare in Unc.					
1852-O .... (96,000)	175.	400.	725.	3500.	6000.
Very rare in all grades and apparently Unique (Miles) in Unc.					
1853/53 .... (44,200)	195.	375.	600.	1900.	3150.
Doubled 3 rather than overdate, often mistaken for 1853/2.					

SEATED LIBERTY, ARROWS AT DATE, RAYS AROUND EAGLE

Arrows and Rays (Stack's)

	G-4	F-12	VF-20	AU-50	MS-60
1853 .... (15,210,000) .... (5)	12.50	23.50	37.00	300.	775.
Eliasberg 4/97 probable Prf-64 $71,500.					
1853/1854	35.00	145.	200.	800.	2350.
Probably a blunder made in late 1853 as dies for 1854 were being prepared. Possibly a backdated die made up in 1854 to mate with a usable but obsolete With Rays reverse die.					
1853-O .... (1,332,000)	14.75	28.50	57.50	1500.	2650.
1853-O/Horizontal O	27.50	75.00	150.	1800.	——

SEATED LIBERTY, ARROWS AT DATE, NO RAYS

No Rays

	G-4	F-12	VF-20	AU-50	MS-60
1854 .... (12,380,000)	12.75	22.00	29.00	235.	475.
One reverse has center hole like 1848.					
1854-O .... (1,484,000)	13.50	30.00	50.00	305.	1050.
Large O.					
1854-O					
Small O, excessively rare.					
1854-O.	90.00	190.	350.	——	——
Huge O, very rare, excessively rare in Unc. Exceptionally crude Mint mark applied at New Orleans Mint, crushing R. D of QUAR. DOL.					
1855 .... (2,857,000)	12.50	21.50	28.00	235.	550.
1855-O .... (176,000)	32.50	100.	250.	1550.	3250.
Excessively rare in Unc. Eliasberg 4/97 MS-66 $88,000.					
1855-S .... (396,400)	30.00	65.00	140.	1100.	1950.
Very rare in Unc.					

SEATED LIBERTY, NO ARROWS

	No Arrows				
	G-4	**F-12**	**VF-20**	**AU-50**	**MS-60**
1856 .... (7,264,000)	13.00	21.50	27.00	130.	290.

One rev. has center hole like 1848.

1856-O .... (968,000)	14.00	24.00	45.00	450.	1200.

Very rare in Unc.

1856-S .... (286,000)	35.00	85.00	185.	1025.	3250.

Normal Mint mark.

1856-S	42.50	135.	275.	1600.	——

Large S over small S, very rare.

1857 .... (9,644,000)	13.00	21.50	27.00	120.	280.

One rev. has center hole like 1848. Very rarely found with clash marks on reverse from reverse die of a Flying Eagle cent!

1857-O .... (1,180,000)	13.25	27.00	45.00	325.	1100.
1857-S .... (82,000)	60.00	205.	335.	1150.	2900.

Very rare in Unc.

1858 .... (7,368,000) .... (80)	13.00	21.50	27.00	120.	285.

One reverse has center hole like 1848.

1858-O .... (520,000)	16.75	32.00	52.50	445.	1500.
1858-S .... (121,000)	50.00	165.	250.	1900.	——

Unknown in Unc.

1859 .... (1,344,000) .... (800)	13.25	22.00	29.00	145.	395.

Type I (1840-59) and Type II (1859-65) obverse hubs and Type I (1840-65) and Type II (1859-65) reverse hubs used this year.

1859-O .... (260,000)	17.50	33.50	52.50	375.	1450.

Type I obv. and rev. only.

1859-S .... (80,000)	85.00	210.	320.	3100.	——

Unknown in Unc. Type I obv. and rev. only.

1860 .... (804,400) .... (1,000)	13.00	21.50	29.00	135.	385.

Type I (rare) and II reverses.

1860-O .... (388,000)	16.25	36.00	47.50	300.	1050.

Type I rev. only.

1860-S .... (56,000)	170.	425.	900.	10000.	——

Unknown in Unc, Type I rev. only.

1861 .... (4,853,600) .... (1,000)	13.00	21.50	28.50	120.	290.

Type I (rare) and II reverses.

1861-S .... (96,000)	55.00	190.	285.	3250.	——

Excessively rare in Unc., Type I rev. only.

1862 .... (932,000) .... (550)	13.75	24.00	31.00	140.	375.

Type II rev. only.

1862-S .... (67,000)	50.00	175.	250.	1350.	2750.

Extremely rare in Unc., Type I rev. only.

1863 .... (191,600) .... (460)	28.50	52.50	72.50	300.	750.

Type II rev. only

1864 .... (93,600) .... (470)	47.50	105.	160.	430.	850.

Type II rev. only.

1864-S .... (20,000)	290.	650.	1050.	3500.	——

Possibly unique in Unc. if the Miles Coin is ex. Harlan P. Smith. Eliasberg 4/97 MS-66 $104,500. Type I rev. only.

1865 .... (58,800) .... (500)	55.00	145.	200.	365.	775.

Type II rev. only.

1865-S .... (41,000)	70.00	200.	240.	1200.	2000.

Possibly unique in Unc. if the Miles Coin is ex. H. P. Smith.
Type I rev. only.
Note: Type I reverses used on Branch Mint coins 1860-65 were produced in or before 1859 but only slowly used up due to the small size of the mintages.

1866

No motto. Fantasy coin produced for a friend of the Mint. Unique, stolen in 1967 and never recovered.

SEATED LIBERTY WITH MOTTO

			With Motto IN GOD WE TRUST			
		G-4	F-12	VF-20	AU-50	MS-60
1866 .... (16,800) .... (725)		275.	465.	575.	1050.	1600.
Very rare in Unc.						
1866-S .... (28,000)		195.	500.	800.	1900.	3850.
Extremely rare in Unc., Norweb MS-64 $3,080, 3/88.						
1867 .... (20,000) .... (625)		155.	245.	315.	575.	975.
1867-S .... (48,000)		155.	350.	490.	1750.	4500.
Extremely rare in Unc.						
1868 .... (29,400) .... (600)		87.50	200.	260.	415.	675.
1868-S .... (96,000)		55.00	130.	215.	1300.	2800.
Very rare in Unc.						
1869 .... (16,000) .... (600)		240.	430.	485.	950.	1750.
Extremely rare as a non-Proof.						
1869-S .... (76,000)		70.00	175.	265.	1350.	2550.
Extremely rare in Unc.						
1870 .... (86,400) .... (1,000)		47.50	95.00	145.	375.	800.
Business strikes are far rarer than Proofs.						
1870-CC .... (8,340)		1850.	4500.	9750.	37500.	—
The Miles coll. Unc. is believed Unique, very rare above Fine. Eliasberg 4/97 MS-64 $187,000.						
1871 .... (118,200) .... (960)		32.50	52.50	87.50	300.	750.
1871-S .... (30,900)		285.	465.	575.	1650.	3750.
1871-CC .... (10,890)		1150.	3500.	4500.	27500.	—
Only two Unc. pieces known, very rare above Fine. Eliasberg 4/97 MS-65 $165,000.						
1872 .... (182,000) .... (950)		30.00	52.50	82.50	280.	875.
1872-S .... (83,000)		350.	1200.	1900.	5650.	7500.
1872-CC .... (22,850)		375.	1300.	2250.	—	—
Virtually unknown in Unc., very rare in EF. Eliasberg 4/97 MS-66 $99,000.						
1873 .... (40,000) .... (600)		160.	350.	460.	1125.	2900.
Closed 3.						
1873 .... (172,000)		30.00	52.50	95.00	275.	550.
Open 3.						
1873-CC .... (4,000)						
Excessively rare, three to five known, Norweb MS-63 to 64, $88,000 3/88; Eliasberg 4/97 MS-62/ 63 $187,000.						

SEATED LIBERTY, ARROWS AT DATE

			Arrows at Date			
		G-4	F-12	VF-20	AU-50	MS-60
1873 .... (1,271,160) .... (540)		14.50	29.00	55.00	350.	650.
1873-S .... (156,000)		25.00	80.00	160.	600.	1200.
1873-CC .... (12,462)		1300.	4350.	8250.	—	—
Very rare in all grades, excessively rare in Unc., Norweb MS-65, $44,000 3/88; Eliasberg 4/97 MS-63/65 $88,000.						
1874 .... (471,200) .... (700)		16.75	32.50	60.00	325.	750.
1874-S .... (392,000)		20.00	60.00	130.	500.	825.
Hoard of two Unc. rolls may still exist.						

Quarter dollars continued	G-4	F-12	VF-20	AU-50	MS-60

SEATED LIBERTY, NO ARROWS

1875 ....(4,292,800) ....(700)	13.00	21.25	27.00	100.	230.

New reverse hub this year. Leftover reverse working dies used this year and next at all Mints except 1875-CC. A single Type I Proof reverse die was used on Proof quarters 1872-80.

1875-S ....(680,000)	39.00	72.50	110.	285.	550.

Large S, Type II rev.

1875-S

Medium S, Type II rev.

1875-S

Small S, both Type I (rare) and Type II revs.

1875-CC ....(140,000)	50.00	140.	250.	660.	1200.

Type 2 rev., scarce.

1876 ....(17,816,000) ....(1,150)	13.00	21.25	27.00	100.	225.
1876-S ....(8,596,000)	13.25	21.25	27.00	130.	230.

Large S, Type II rev.

1876-S

Medium S, Type I (rare), Type II revs.

1876-CC ....(4,944,000)	13.35	22.00	31.00	145.	350.

Small and Large CC, Types I and II revs.

1876-CC

Fine reeding, 153 reeds instead of the usual 119. Dozens of times rarer than preceding and not found on any other issue. Found with both large and small CC.

1877 ....(10,911,200) ....(510)	13.00	21.25	27.00	100.	225.
1877-S ....(8,996,000)	25.00	75.00	175.	275.	750.

Medium S over horizontal S, rare.

1877-S	13.00	22.00	28.00	105.	235.

Small S, highly placed, nearly over space.

1877-S

Microscopic S, placed above the R.

1877-CC ....(4,192,000)	13.25	22.50	32.00	140.	275.

1877-CC

Repunched 77.

1878 ....(2,260,000) ....(800)	13.00	21.25	27.00	100.	240.
1878-S ....(140,000)	75.00	190.	265.	750.	1275.

Scarce in all conditions, rare in AU and Unc.

1878-CC ....(996,000)	18.00	40.00	60.00	225.	375.
1879 ....(13,600) ....(1,100)	140.	205.	250.	350.	420.

Proof figure controversial, may be 250.

1880 ....(13,600) ....(1,355)	140.	210.	250.	355.	415.

Many Philadelphia Mint quarters of 1880-1889 exist as prooflike Unc. Many first strikes have been offered by error as Proofs.

1881 ....(12,000) ....(975)	145.	215.	265.	350.	445.
1882 ....(15,200) ....(1,100)	150.	215.	265.	365.	500.
1883 ....(14,400) ....(1,039)	145.	215.	265.	360.	495.
1884 ....(8,000) ....(875)	175.	260.	320.	370.	575.
1885 ....(13,600) ....(930)	145.	215.	260.	355.	415.
1886 ....(5,000) ....(886)	190.	275.	325.	700.	850.
1887 ....(10,000) ....(710)	160.	245.	285.	375.	500.
1888 ....(10,000) ....(832)	160.	245.	285.	375.	500.
1888-S ....(1,216,000)	13.35	22.00	28.00	140.	390.
1889 ....(12,000) ....(711)	145.	245.	280.	385.	525.
1890 ....(80,000) ....(590)	50.00	85.00	110.	200.	425.
1891 ....(3,920,000) ....(600)	13.00	21.50	27.00	100.	235.
1891-O ....(68,000)	135.	300.	475.	1550.	2950.

Very rare in Unc., two Branch Mint Proofs known. Eliasberg 4/97 MS-66 $61,600.

1891-S ....(2,216,000)	13.50	23.00	32.50	145.	275.

BARBER

G - LIBERTY invisible, all else legible.
VG - At least 3 letters in LIBERTY visible.
F - LIBERTY weak but complete.
VF - All details legible but not sharp.
EF - All details sharp.
AU - Wear only on highest points. Must show some Mint luster
UNC - No wear visible anywhere. Full Mint luster.
PROOF- High rims, mirror-like fields, frosted head, eagle, etc. Letter surfaces flat, not rounded.

	F-12	EF-40	AU-50	MS-60	MS-63
1892 .... (8,236,000) .... (1,245)	20.00	72.50	125.	145.	250.
Type I: eagle's wing covers only half of E in UNITED.					
1892					
Type II: eagle's wing covers most of the E.					
1892-O .... (2,640,000)	24.00	80.00	150.	250.	400.
Type I: eagle's wing covers only half of E in UNITED.					
1892-O					
Type II: eagle's wing covers most of the E.					
1892-S .... (964,079)	55.00	125.	275.	400.	750.
Type I: eagle's wing covers only half of E in UNITED.					
1892-S					
Type II: eagle's wing covers most of the E.					
1892-S/S	65.00	195.	375.	600.	1400.
1893 .... (5,444,023) .... (792)	23.00	72.50	125.	205.	300.
1893-O .... (3,396,000)	25.00	77.50	155.	265.	550.
1893-S .... (1,454,535)	37.50	130.	275.	420.	950.
Double-punched S var. rare. Many dates in Barber series show minor Mint mark repunching.					
1894 .... (3,432,000) .... (972)	24.00	75.00	135.	210.	355.
1894-O .... (2,852,000)	30.00	85.00	195.	345.	750.
1894-S .... (2,648,821)	28.00	80.00	175.	325.	700.
1895 .... (4,440,000) .... (880)	24.00	72.50	135.	225.	475.
1895-O .... (2,816,000)	35.00	95.00	220.	400.	900.
1895-S .... (1,764,681)	38.00	100.	220.	375.	925.
1895-S/S	50.00	150.	300.	525.	1550.
1896 .... (3,874,000) .... (762)	24.00	72.50	135.	230.	400.
1896-O .... (1,484,000)	65.00	335.	625.	875.	1850.
1896-S .... (188,039)	625.	1600.	3000.	4400.	7500.
1897 .... (8,140,000) .... (731)	20.00	72.50	125.	150.	225.
1897-O .... (1,414,800)	75.00	350.	625.	850.	1700.
1897-S .... (542,229)	110.	325.	650.	950.	1750.
1898 .... (11,100,000) .... (735)	20.00	70.00	125.	150.	225.
1898-O .... (1,868,000)	55.00	205.	415.	625.	1500.
1898-S .... (1,020,592)	32.00	75.00	180.	400.	1200.
1899 .... (12,624,000) .... (846)	20.00	65.00	125.	150.	225.
1899-O .... (2,644,000)	28.00	92.50	260.	385.	800.
1899-S .... (708,000)	40.00	105.	230.	415.	1200.
1900 .... (10,016,000) .... (912)	18.50	65.00	125.	150.	225.
1900-O .... (3,416,000)	48.00	125.	325.	550.	950.
1900-S .... (1,858,585)	35.00	65.00	125.	360.	950.

Barber

Quarter dollars continued

			New hubs		
	F-12	**EF-40**	**AU-50**	**MS-60**	**MS-63**
1901 .... (8,892,000) .... (813)	20.00	65.00	125.	150.	225.
New obv. & rev. hubs as on following.					
1901-O .... (1,612,000)	85.00	350.	615.	775.	2000.
1901-S .... (72,664)	4500.	8000.	10000.	14000.	19500.
Eliasberg 4/97 MS-67 $52,800.					
1902 .... (12,196,967) .... (777)	19.00	65.00	125.	150.	225.
1902-O .... (4,748,000)	35.00	100.	200.	385.	1150.
1902-S .... (1,524,612)	35.00	85.00	200.	385.	825.
1903 .... (9,669,309) .... (755)	19.00	65.00	125.	150.	475.
1903-O .... (3,500,000)	33.00	85.00	225.	400.	1000.
1903-S .... (1,036,000)	38.00	110.	250.	430.	850.
1904 .... (9,588,143) .... (670)	19.00	65.00	125.	150.	265.
1904-O .... (2,456,000)	45.00	175.	375.	765.	1350.
1905 .... (4,967,523) .... (727)	23.00	65.00	125.	150.	375.
1905-O .... (1,230,000)	60.00	200.	345.	475.	1100.
1905-S .... (1,884,000)	35.00	90.00	210.	325.	1000.
1906 .... (3,655,760) .... (675)	19.50	65.00	125.	150.	225.
1906-D .... (3,280,000)	23.00	65.00	145.	220.	465.
1906-O .... (2,056,000)	29.00	85.00	200.	290.	500.
1907 .... (7,192,000) .... (575)	19.00	65.00	125.	150.	225.
1907-D .... (2,484,000)	25.00	80.00	175.	235.	775.
1907-O .... (4,560,000)	19.00	65.00	135.	185.	400.
1907-S .... (1,360,000)	38.00	110.	250.	445.	1000.
1908 .... (4,232,000) .... (545)	19.00	65.00	125.	190.	300.
1908-D .... (5,788,000)	19.00	65.00	125.	215.	400.
1908-O .... (6,244,000)	19.00	65.00	125.	185.	275.
1908-S .... (784,000)	63.00	250.	425.	700.	1400.
1909 .... (9,268,000) .... (650)	19.00	65.00	110.	150.	225.
1909-D .... (5,114,000)	19.00	65.00	150.	180.	335.
1909-O .... (712,000)	72.00	285.	465.	750.	1475.
1909-S .... (1,348,000)	28.00	65.00	180.	275.	750.
1910 .... (2,244,000) .... (551)	22.00	65.00	140.	180.	290.
1910-D .... (1,500,000)	36.00	100.	225.	335.	1025.
1911 .... (3,720,000) .... (543)	19.00	72.00	130.	165.	250.
1911-D .... (933,600)	65.00	285.	450.	625.	1250.
1911-S .... (988,000)	45.00	135.	285.	375.	725.
1912 .... (4,400,000) .... (700)	19.00	65.00	125.	150.	225.
1912-S .... (708,000)	38.00	100.	220.	375.	1050.
1913 .... (484,000) .... (613)	58.00	375.	550.	950.	1150.
1913-D .... (1,450,800)	30.00	80.00	160.	265.	400.
1913-S .... (40,000)	1750.	3500.	4250.	5000.	7300.
Eliasberg 4/97 MS-67 $39,600.					
1914 .... (6,244,230) .... (380)	16.00	60.00	110.	150.	225.
1914-D .... (3,046,000)	16.00	65.00	110.	150.	225.
1914-S .... (264,000)	145.	385.	575.	900.	1350.
1915 .... (3,480,000) .... (450)	16.00	65.00	110.	150.	225.
1915-D .... (3,694,000)	16.00	65.00	110.	150.	225.
1915-S .... (704,000)	27.00	75.00	185.	240.	440.
1916 .... (1,788,000)	17.00	60.00	125.	150.	225.
1916-D .... (6,540,800)	16.00	60.00	110.	150.	325.
1916-D	40.00	110.	185.	400.	950.
Large D over small D intended for cents, five cents and new silver designs.					

STANDING LIBERTY

G - Date barely legible. Right leg and toes flat.
VG - Date clear, toes faint.
F - Left leg shows slight wear, right leg flat. Right drapery lines visible at sides of leg.
VF - Garment line faint across right leg. All other details clear.
EF - All details sharp.
AU - Wear only on highest points. Must show some Mint luster.
UNC - No wear visible anywhere. Full Mint luster.
NOTE: Coins exhibiting Full Head on Liberty usually bring far higher prices than Uncs. without this feature.

TYPE I: BARE BREAST, NO STARS BELOW EAGLE

		Standing Liberty, Bare Breast, No Stars under Eagle			
	F-12	EF-40	AU-50	MS-60	MS-65
1916 ....(52,000)	1900.	3050.	4100.	5250.	14000.

Specimens with date worn off can be identified as follows: drapery does not touch base; big toe slightly overlaps base. On subsequent issue, drapery is embedded in base and big toe is on top.

1917 ....(8,740,000)	27.00	60.00	115.	150.	775.

New obv. hub. Die-struck counterfeits exist.

1917-D ....(1,509,200)	28.00	85.00	135.	225.	950.
1917-S ....(1,952,000)	28.00	130.	180.	280.	1650.

Eliasberg 4/97 MS-67 Full Head $37,400.

TYPE II: MAIL-CLAD LIBERTY, STARS UNDER EAGLE

		Mailed Breast, Stars under Eagle			
	F-12	EF-40	AU-50	MS-60	MS-65
1917 ....(13,880,000)	20.00	47.50	72.00	120.	550.
1917-D ....(6,224,400)	50.00	90.00	125.	150.	1400.
Rare with well struck Full Head.					
1917-S ....(5,552,000)	37.00	75.00	105.	160.	925.
Full Head scarce.					
1918 ....(14,240,000)	22.00	45.00	80.00	135.	600.
Full Head rare.					
1918-D ....(7,380,000)	43.00	82.50	140.	215.	1350.
Often found weakly struck, including head.					
1918-S ....(11,072,000)	27.00	45.00	80.00	170.	1450.
Full Head rare.					

		1918/7-S			
	F-12	EF-40	AU-50	MS-60	MS-65
1918/7-S	1925.	4500.	7800.	14500.	85000.
Many alterations exist; authentication recommended.					
1919 ....(11,324,000)	42.00	67.50	92.50	140.	575.
1919-D ....(1,944,000)	115.	280.	485.	625.	2250.
Often found weakly struck up. Full Heads almost unknown.					
1919-S ....(1,836,000)	115.	375.	525.	875.	3000.
Often weakly struck, Full Heads excessively rare.					

Quarter dollars continued

	F-12	EF-40	AU-50	MS-60	MS-65
1920 .... (27,860,000)	21.00	35.00	65.00	125.	410.
1920-D .... (3,586,400)	60.00	105.	165.	210.	1750.
Often found weakly struck, Full Heads rare.					
1920-S .... (6,380,000)	27.00	55.00	94.00	225.	2250.
Often found weakly struck, Full Heads rare.					
1921 .... (1,916,000)	145.	275.	335.	440.	1550.
Beware of alterations, this date has distinctive style 1's.					
1923 .... (9,716,000)	25.00	37.00	65.00	120.	445.
1923-S .... (1,360,000)	260.	435.	500.	600.	1750.
Full Head rare.					
1924 .... (10,920,000)	20.00	32.00	63.00	115.	400.
1924-D .... (3,112,000)	46.00	90.00	120.	145.	420.
Top of date always weak. Full Head extremely rare.					
1924-S .... (2,860,000)	27.50	85.00	175.	350.	1950.
Full Head excessively rare.					
1925 .... (12,280,000)	5.00	26.50	57.00	105.	440.
Full Head rare.					

New type with recessed date beginning 1925. The front of the pedestal on which Liberty stands was depressed in the hub and appears thus on all the following issues. The change was made because of the tendency of the date to wear off quickly.

	F-12	EF-40	AU-50	MS-60	MS-65
1926 .... (11,316,000)	5.00	25.00	55.00	105.	390.
Full Head rare.					
1926-D .... (1,716,000)	14.00	45.00	80.00	110.	435.
Full Head very rare.					
1926-S .... (2,700,000)	10.00	95.00	215.	345.	2050.
Full Head very rare.					
1927 .... (11,912,000)	5.00	26.00	50.00	100.	380.
1927-D .... (976,400)	14.00	80.00	132.	155.	400.
Full head rare.					
1927-S .... (396,000)	52.50	1000.	3200.	3800.	10000.
Full head excessively rare.					
1928 .... (6,336,000)	5.00	26.00	52.00	100.	360.
1928-D .... (1,627,600)	7.00	37.50	77.50	135.	410.
Full head scarce.					
1928-S .... (2,644,000)	6.00	30.00	67.00	130.	370.
Small S of 1917-28 (scarce) and large S of 1928-30 known.					
1929 .... (11,140,000)	5.00	25.00	52.00	100.	375.
1929-D .... (1,358,000)	8.00	31.50	65.00	135.	445.
1929-S .... (1,764,000)	5.50	29.00	60.00	115.	350.
Full head scarce.					
1930 .... (5,632,000)	4.50	25.00	52.00	95.00	350.
1930-S .... (1,556,000)	4.50	25.00	58.00	115.	500.
Almost never found with Full Head, strikes are weak overall.					

WASHINGTON

VG - Eagles wings outlined. Full rims but letter tops are flat.
F - Hairlines visible at ear, breast feathers show.
VF - All details clear, but show wear.
EF - All details sharp.
AU - Wear only on highest points. Must show some Mint luster
UNC - No wear visible anywhere. Full Mint luster.
PROOF- High rims, mirror-like surfaces. Letter surfaces flat, not round and show some double striking.

George Washington

	VF-20	AU-50	MS-60	MS-65	PF-65
1932 .... (5,404,000)	5.50	12.50	19.00	175.	*
1932-D .... (436,800)	60.00	240.	465.	4400.	*
1932-S .... (408,000)	46.00	130.	260.	2350.	*
1934 .... (31,912,052)	7.00	11.00	26.00	175.	*
Type of 1932: light motto, low relief, not clearly outlined, middle stroke of W below outer ones.					

Quarter dollars continued	VF-20	AU-50	MS-60	MS-65	PF-65
1934	3.00	7.50	17.00	60.00	*

Type of 1935: medium motto, middle stroke of W is below outer ones.

| 1934 | 75.00 | 230. | 565. | 2850. | * |

Doubled die, Type of 1935: doubled motto; numerals of date, LIBERTY are also heavier than usual.

1934

Type of 1936: heavy motto; middle stroke of W is above outer ones.

| 1934-D .... (3,527,200) | 7.50 | 47.50 | 90.00 | 1050. | |

Medium and heavy (rare) motto varieties, the former sometimes with doubled Mint mark.

| 1935 .... (32,484,000) | 3.00 | 8.00 | 17.00 | 55.00 | * |

Medium motto only.

| 1935-D .... (5,780,000) | 7.25 | 40.00 | 90.00 | 625. | * |

Medium motto only.

| 1935-S .... (5,660,000) | 5.00 | 25.00 | 40.00 | 180. | * |

Medium motto only.

| 1936 .... (41,300,000) .... (3,837) | 3.00 | 7.75 | 15.00 | 45.00 | 1000. |

Heavy motto only, as on following. Proofs found only with brilliant finish.

1936

Doubled die obv. Very rare.

| 1936-D .... (5,374,000) | 14.00 | 120. | 285. | 650. | * |

Varieties exist with doubled and tripled D. D over horizontal D reported, not confirmed.

| 1936-S .... (3,828,000) | 6.25 | 26.00 | 37.50 | 100. | * |
| 1937 .... (19,696,000) .... (5,542) | 3.25 | 15.00 | 20.00 | 68.00 | 335. |

New reverse hub used for Proofs only 1937-42 and 1950-55. Used on all Proofs 1956-64 and 1968-72, with worn or unacceptable proof reverses used on relatively few business strikes during same periods.

1937-D .... (7,189,600)	6.00	19.00	30.00	70.00	*
1937-S .... (1,652,000)	10.00	55.00	77.50	160.	*
1938 .... (9,472,000) .... (8,045)	8.00	22.50	32.50	125.	220.

From this date on, the profile is more sharply defined than previously.

1938-S .... (2,832,000)	8.25	28.00	42.00	100.	*
1939 .... (33,540,000) .... (8,795)	2.50	7.00	12.50	37.50	167.
1939-D .... (7,092,000)	6.00	13.00	24.00	36.00	*
1939-D/S					

Very rare.

1939-S .... (2,628,000)	6.00	32.50	47.50	115.	*
1940 .... (35,704,000) .... (11,246)	2.15	6.00	9.00	37.50	145.
1940-D .... (2,797,600)	8.50	30.00	45.00	110.	*
1940-S .... (8,244,000)	3.00	9.00	13.00	60.00	*
1941 .... (79,032,000) .... (15,287)	2.15	3.50	5.00	23.00	138.
1941-D .... (16,714,800)	2.85	6.00	13.25	37.50	*
1941-D	2.60	6.00	13.50	57.50	*

Doubled die obv., scarce.

| 1941-S .... (16,080,000) | | | | | |

Small S of 1932-41 and large S of 1941-44 varieties known.

1942 .... (102,096,000) .... (21,123)	2.50	3.50	4.00	22.00	105.
1942-D .... (17,487,200)	2.85	5.25	8.00	37.00	*
1942-D					

Doubled die obv., rare.

1942-S .... (19,384,000)	3.00	15.00	37.00	85.00	*
1943 .... (99,700,000)	2.60	3.00	3.75	21.00	*
1943-D .... (16,095,600)	2.50	6.00	11.50	26.00	*
1943-S .... (21,700,000)	2.60	11.00	13.75	38.00	*
1943-S	125.	225.	375.	1550.	*

Doubled die obv., rare.

| 1944 .... (104,956,000) | 2.15 | 3.00 | 3.50 | 14.00 | * |

New hub: profile much more sharply outlined than previously, especially in hair at back of neck. Initials JF are large and distorted.

1944-D .... (14,600,800)	2.15	4.75	6.75	21.00	*
1944-S .... (12,560,000)	2.15	4.50	7.25	25.00	*
1945 .... (74,372,000)	2.15	2.40	2.50	13.00	*

Hub retouched, JF corrected.

| 1945-D .... (12,341,600) | 2.75 | 4.25 | 5.75 | 22.50 | * |
| 1945-S .... (17,004,001) | 2.35 | 3.75 | 4.25 | 21.00 | * |

Two styles of mint mark used simultaneously over next several years.

1946 .... (53,436,000)	2.15	2.75	3.75	12.00	*
1946-D .... (9,072,800)	2.35	2.90	3.25	12.00	*
1946-D					

Doubled die; plainest on eagle's neck and QUARTER.

| 1946-S .... (4,204,000) | 2.50 | 2.85 | 3.00 | 17.00 | * |

Two styles of Mint mark known.

| 1947 .... (22,556,000) | 2.15 | 3.75 | 5.25 | 12.00 | * |

Quarter dollars continued

	VF-20	AU-50	MS-60	MS-65	PF-65
1947-D .... (15,338,400)	2.35	3.00	3.75	18.50	*
1947-S .... (5,532,000)	2.35	3.00	3.25	15.00	*
Two styles of Mint mark known					
1948 .... (35,196,000)	2.15	3.00	3.25	11.00	*
1948-D .... (16,766,800)	2.35	3.15	3.50	13.00	*
1948-S .... (15,960,000)	2.35	3.15	4.00	18.50	*
1949 .... (9,312,000)	2.85	7.00	15.00	20.00	*
1949-D .... (10,068,400)	2.35	4.00	5.50	19.00	*
1950 .... (24,920,126) .... (51,386)	2.15	2.85	3.00	9.00	60.00
1950-D .... (21,075,600)	2.15	2.90	3.25	10.50	*
1950-D/S	70.00	175.	225.	875.	*
Scarce.					
1950-S .... (10,284,004)	2.15	4.00	5.50	14.00	*
1950-S/S/D	77.50	200.	235.	650.	*
Double-punched S over D, rare.					
1951 .... (43,448,102) .... (57,500)	2.15	2.75	3.00	9.50	45.00
1951-D .... (35,354,800)	2.15	2.75	2.90	8.00	*
D/S reported, not confirmed.					
1951-S .... (9,048,000)	2.15	6.50	8.50	28.00	*
1952 .... (38,780,093) .... (81,980)	2.15	2.55	2.65	7.00	37.50
1952 Doubled die rev, Proof only, rare.					
1952-D .... (49,795,200)	2.15	2.65	2.75	8.00	*
1952-S .... (13,707,800)	2.15	4.50	6.75	25.00	*
1953 .... (18,536,120) .... (128,800)	2.45	2.55	2.65	8.00	24.00
1953-D .... (56,112,400)	1.90	2.00	2.05	8.00	*
1953-S .... (14,016,000)	2.35	2.50	2.75	20.00	*
1954 .... (54,412,203) .... (233,300)	1.45	1.65	1.75	5.00	12.50
1954-D .... (42,305,500)	1.25	1.35	1.40	4.75	*
1954-S .... (11,834,722)	1.85	1.95	2.00	8.00	*
1955 .... (18,180,181) .... (378,200)	1.75	1.85	1.90	5.00	10.50
1955-D .... (3,182,400)	1.90	2.05	2.15	10.00	*
1956 .... (44,144,000) .... (669,384)	1.50	1.65	1.70	4.75	8.50
Dies from Proof reverse hub occasionally used for business strikes 1956-64, and again 1968-72.					
1956-D .... (32,334,500)	1.75	1.95	2.15	6.50	*
D over horizontal D reported, not confirmed.					
1957 .... (46,532,000) .... (1,247,952)	1.50	1.65	1.70	5.00	4.00
1957-D .... (77,924,160)	1.50	1.65	1.70	4.50	*
1958 .... (6,360,000) .... (875,652)	1.60	1.70	1.75	4.75	7.00
1958-D .... (78,124,900)	1.35	1.45	1.65	4.15	*
1959 .... (24,384,000) .... (1,149,291)	1.50	1.60	1.55	5.00	5.00
1959-D .... (62,054,232)	1.35	1.45	1.55	4.15	*
1960 .... (29,164,000) .... (1,691,602)	1.30	1.40	1.60	4.75	2.25
1960-D .... (63,000,324)	1.30	1.40	1.60	3.65	*
1961 .... (37,036,000) .... (3,028,244)	1.35	1.45	1.60	5.50	1.75
1961-D .... (83,656,928)	1.30	1.40	1.55	3.65	*
1962 .... (36,156,000) .... (3,218,019)	1.30	1.40	1.55	3.65	1.75
1962-D .... (127,554,756)	1.30	1.40	1.60	3.65	*
1963 .... (74,316,000) .... (3,075,645)	1.25	1.35	1.45	3.50	1.75
1963-D .... (135,288,184)	1.25	1.35	1.45	3.50	*
1964 .... (560,390,585) .... (3,950,762)	1.25	1.35	1.45	3.50	1.75
Some struck from new rev. hub intended for clad coinage.					
1964-D .... (704,135,528)	1.25	1.35	1.45	3.50	*
Some struck from new rev. hub intended for clad coinage.					
1965					
.900 fine silver, error striking, extremely rare.					

CLAD COINAGE

	VF-20	AU-50	MS-60	MS-65	PF-65
1964					
Error striking in clad alloy, extremely rare.					
1965 .... (1,819,717,540)	FV	FV	0.50	1.50	*
1966 .... (821,101,500)	FV	FV	0.50	1.50	*
1967 .... (1,524,031,848)	FV	FV	0.50	1.75	*
1968 .... (220,731,500)	FV	FV	0.40	1.25	*
1968-D .... (101,534,000)	FV	FV	0.42	1.30	*
1968-S .... (3,041,506)	*	*	*	*	0.85
Proof only.					
1969 .... (176,212,000)	FV	FV	0.40	1.25	*
1969-D .... (114,372,000)	FV	FV	0.50	1.30	*
1969-S .... (2,934,631)	*	*	*	*	0.85
Proof only.					

Quarter dollars continued

	VF-20	AU-50	MS-60	MS-65	PF-65
1970 .... (136,420,000)	FV	FV	0.35	0.95	*
1970-D .... (417,341,364)	FV	FV	0.35	0.95	*
1970-S .... (2,632,810)	*	*	*	*	0.85
Proof only.					
1971 .... (109,284,000)	FV	0.35	0.50	1.10	*
1971-D .... (258,634,428)	FV	0.35	0.40	1.05	*
1971-S .... (3,220,733)	*	*	*	*	1.00
Proof only.					
1972 .... (215,048,000)	FV	FV	0.35	1.00	*
1972-D .... (311,067,732)	FV	FV	0.35	1.00	*
1972-S .... (3,260,996)	*	*	*	*	1.00
Proof only.					
1973 .... (346,924,000)	FV	FV	0.30	1.00	*
1973-D .... (232,977,400)	FV	FV	0.30	1.00	*
1973-S .... (2,760,339)	*	*	*	*	0.75
Proof only.					
1974 .... (801,456,000)	FV	FV	0.30	1.00	*
Struck in 1974 and first half 1975.					
1974-D .... (353,160,300)	FV	FV	0.30	1.00	*
Struck in 1974 and first half 1975.					
1974-S .... (2,612,568)	*	*	*	*	0.65
Proof only.					

Note: No 1975-dated quarters struck.

WASHINGTON, DUAL DATE, BICENTENNIAL REVERSE

Commemorative date, Bicentennial reverse

	VF-20	AU-50	MS-60	MS-65	PF-65
1776-1976 .... (809,784,016)	0.30	0.32	0.41	1.00	*
Included in 1975 and 1976 Mint sets.					
1776-1976-D .... (860,118,839)	0.30	0.32	0.41	1.00	*
Included in 1975 and 1976 Mint sets.					
1776-1976-S .... (6,968,506)	*	*	*	*	0.75
Copper-nickel Clad, Proof only, included in 1975 and 1976 standard Proof sets.					
1776-1976-S .... (4,908,319) .... (3,998,621)	—	—	1.50	3.75	2.00
40 percent silver.					

Net mintages represent official sales figures for three piece Uncirculated and Proof sets. Original mintages were 11 and 4 million respectively, unsold balance melted.

1776-1976
No Mint mark. 40 percent silver, Proof only, struck 8-12-74 for display at the ANA convention that month. Several three-piece sets distributed, said to have been recalled later and melted. Current existence uncertain.

WASHINGTON, EAGLE REVERSE RESUMED, MODIFIED HUBS

	VF-20	AU-50	MS-60	MS-65	PF-65
1977 .... (468,556,000)	FV	FV	0.30	1.00	*
1977-D .... (256,524,978)	FV	FV	0.30	1.00	*
1977-D					
40 percent silver error striking, excessively rare.					
1977-S .... (3,236,798)	*	*	*	*	0.85
Proof only.					
1978 .... (521,452,000)	FV	FV	——	——	*
1978-D .... (287,373,152)	FV	FV	——	——	*
1978-S .... (3,120,285)	*	*	*	*	0.85
Proof only.					
1979 .... (515,708,000)	FV	FV	0.40	——	*
1979-D .... (489,789,780)	FV	FV	0.40	——	*
1979-S .... (3,677,175)	*	*	*	*	0.85
Proof only, Type I S blurry, same as 1978.					

Quarter dollars continued

	VF-20	AU-50	MS-60	MS-65	PF-65
1979-S	*	*	*	*	1.25

Type II S clear, same as 1980, found on approximately one coin in six.

	VF-20	AU-50	MS-60	MS-65	PF-65
1980-P .... (635,832,000)	FV	FV	—	—	*
1980-D .... (518,327,487)	FV	FV	—	—	*
1980-S .... (3,554,806)	*	*	*	*	0.85

Proof only.

1981-P .... (601,716,000)	FV	FV	—	—	*
1981-D .... (575,722,833)	FV	FV	—	—	*
1981-S .... (4,063,083)	*	*	*	*	0.85

Proof only, minor varieties of Mint mark style exist.

1982-P .... (500,931,000)	FV	1.50	2.25	—	*
1982-D .... (480,042,788)	FV	FV	—	—	*
1982-S .... (3,857,479)	*	*	*	*	1.00

Proof only.

1983-P .... (673,535,000)	FV	2.50	3.35	—	*

Modified obverse, as on following.

1983-D .... (617,806,446)	FV	1.10	2.00	—	*
1983-S .... (3,279,126)	*	*	*	*	1.65

Proof only.

1984-P .... (676,545,000)	FV	FV	—	—	*
1984-D .... (546,483,064)	FV	1.10	1.25	—	*
1984-S .... (3,065,110)	*	*	*	*	1.00

Proof only.

1985-P .... (775,818,962)	FV	1.10	1.25	—	*
1985-D .... (519,962,888)	FV	1.75	2.25	—	*
1985-S .... (3,362,821)	*	*	*	*	0.65

Proof only.

1986-P .... (551,199,333)	FV	1.75	2.50	—	*
1986-D .... (504,298,660)	FV	1.50	2.00	—	*
1986-S .... (3,010,497)	*	*	*	*	1.50

Proof only.

	MS-63	MS-65	PF-64	PF-65
1987-P .... (582,499,481)	0.55	—	*	*
1987-D .... (655,594,696)	0.55	—	*	*
1987-S .... (3,792,233)	*	*	0.65	0.85

Proof only.

	MS-63	MS-65	PF-64	PF-65
1988-P .... (562,052,000)	1.65	—	*	*
1988-D .... (596,810,688)	0.60	—	*	*
1988-S .... (2,600,618)	*	*	0.65	0.85

Proof only.

	MS-63	MS-65	PF-64	PF-65
1989-P .... (512,868,000)	0.85	—	*	*

1989 (P)

So-called No Mint Mark quarter, struck from grease-filled die. Received national publicity in May-June 1989.

	MS-63	MS-65	PF-64	PF-65
1989-D .... (896,733,858)	0.85	—	*	*
1989-S .... (3,220,914)	*	*	0.65	0.85

Proof only.

	MS-63	MS-65	PF-64	PF-65
1990-P .... (613,792,000)	0.55	—	*	*
1990-D .... (927,638,181)	0.55	—	*	*
1990-S .... (3,299,559)	*	*	1.50	2.00

Proof only.

	MS-63	MS-65	PF-64	PF-65
1991-P .... (570,960,000)	0.55	—	*	*
1991-D .... (630,966,693)	0.55	—	*	*
1991-S .... (2,867,787)	*	*	2.00	2.75

Proof only.

	MS-63	MS-65	PF-64	PF-65
1992-P .... (384,764,000)	0.55	—	*	*
1992-D .... (389,777,107)	0.55	—	*	*
1992-S .... (2,858,903)	*	*	2.70	3.75

Proof only.

	MS-63	MS-65	PF-64	PF-65
1992-S .... (1,317,641)	*	*	3.50	4.50

90% silver, struck for inclusion in special Proof sets.

	MS-63	MS-65	PF-64	PF-65
1993-P .... (639,276,000)	0.55	—	*	*
1993-D .... (645,476,128)	0.55	—	*	*
1993-S .... (2,569,882)	*	*	4.00	5.00

Proof only.

	MS-63	MS-65	PF-64	PF-65
1993-S .... (790,994)	*	*	6.00	7.00

90% silver, struck for inclusion in special Proof sets.

	MS-63	MS-65	PF-64	PF-65
1994-P .... (825,600,000)	0.55	—	*	*
1994-D .... (880,034,110)	0.55	—	*	*

Quarter dollars continued

	MS-63	MS-65	PF-64	PF-65
1994-S .... (2,443,590)	*	*	3.00	4.00
Proof only.				
1994-S .... (778,550)	*	*	5.50	6.25
90% silver, struck for inclusion in special Proof sets.				
1995-P .... (1,004,336,000)	0.55	——	*	*
1995-D .... (1,103,216,000)	0.55	——	*	*
1995-S .... (2,124,790)	*	*	2.75	3.50
Proof only.				
1995-S .... (666,277)	*	*	4.00	5.00
90% silver, struck for inclusion in special Proof sets.				
1996-P .... (925,040,000)	0.55	——	*	*
1996-D .... (906,868,000)	0.55	——	*	*
1996-S Clad .... (2,145,077)	*	*	1.50	3.00
Proof only.				
1996-S Silver .... (775,081)	*	*	3.75	4.75
90% silver, struck for inclusion in special Proof sets.				
1997-P .... (NR)	0.55	——	*	*
1997-D .... (NR)	0.55	——	*	*
1997-S Clad .... (NR)	*	*	1.50	2.00
Proof only.				

1997-S 90% silver

	MS-63	MS-65	PF-64	PF-65
1997-S Silver .... (NR)	*	*	3.75	4.25
90% silver, struck for inclusion in special Proof sets.				

Half dollars

FLOWING HAIR

G- Date letters legible. Bust, eagle outlined.
VG - Lettering clear but worn. Wreath, eagle, etc., clear.
F- Some shape and lines to hair. Ends show.
VF - Most details, hairlines clear.
EF - All details bold.
AU - Wear on highest points only. Must have some Mint luster.
UNC - No wear discernible anyplace. Full Mint luster.

Flowing Hair (Stack's)

	G-4	F-12	EF-40	AU-50	MS-60
1794 .... (23,464)	1100.	2550.	13000.	28500.	——

Eight major vars., mintage includes 18,164 pieces delivered Feb. 4, 1795. Obverses show first star piercing lowest curl, Overton-101-103; joined to first curl, O-105-106; or curl free of first stars, O-108. Reverses are classified by number of berries at left and right: 10 left, 11 right; 9-8, 9-9, 9-10. All are scarce to extremely rare, all but one are excessively rare in Unc. Eliasberg 4/97 O-101 AU-58 $77,000; Eliasberg 4/97 O-105 AU-55 $66,000.

	G-4	F-12	EF-40	AU-50	MS-60
1795 .... (299,680)	385.	815.	4350.	8250.	23000.

32 vars., rev. types with 10-8, 9-8, 10-7, 9-10, 8-8, 7-9 8-9, 7-10 berries. Most show two leaves on wreath under wings. Only the most distinctive varieties are listed separately.

Double-punched date; three-leaves inside wreath under wings

	G-4	F-12	EF-40	AU-50	MS-60
1795	975.	3250.	14000.	31500.	——

Boldly double-punched date, first cut much too low, then corrected, BE in LIBERTY recut. Rev. three leaves inside wreath under each wing, O-111, rare.

1795

STATES punched over STETES, O-113, scarce. Eliasberg 4/97 MS-63 $68,750.

1795

Y of LIBERTY is punched over a star, O-121, rare. Eliasberg 4/97 MS-64 $82,500.

1795

Small head, only such obverse, O-126, berries 9-8, rare; recut T in LIBERTY, berries 9-9, O-128 very rare. Slightly larger Narrow Head, berries 9-8, O-127, very rare.

1795

STATES punched over STATED, O-129, scarce.

DRAPED BUST, SMALL EAGLE

Draped Bust, Small Eagle 15 Stars

	G-4	F-12	EF-40	AU-50	MS-60
1796 .... (934)	10000.	18750.	33000.	65000.	—

15 Stars, O-101, struck in 1797, this is the rarest date in the early half dollar series. Norweb prooflike MS-60, $99,000 11/88. Eliasberg 4/97 MS-63 $110,000.

| 1796 .... | 11000. | 20000. | 41000. | — | — |

16 Stars, O-102, struck in 1797, extremely rare in all grades, excessively rare in Unc. Eliasberg 4/97 MS-63 $143,000.

| 1797 .... (2,984) .... | 10500. | 19250. | 36000. | 63500. | 125000. |

Second rarest early half dollar date. The 1796-97 Small Eagle half dollars comprise the rarest regular issue silver Type coin in the U.S. series. Norweb prooflike MS-63 to 65, $220,000 11/88. Eliasberg 4/97 O-101a MS-60 $104,500.

DRAPED BUST, HERALDIC EAGLE

Draped Bust, Heraldic Eagle

	G-4	F-12	EF-40	AU-50	MS-60
1801 .... (30,289)	190.	500.	3250.	10500.	—

13 arrows in eagle's claw, O-101, excessively rare in Unc. Eliasberg 4/97 MS-62 $31,900.

1801

12 arrows, O-102, unverified in Unc., very rare in EF.

| 1802 .... (29,890) .... | 180. | 450. | 3200. | 8800. | 26500. |

Extremely rare in Unc.

| 1803 .... (188,234) .... | 135. | 230. | 825. | 2350. | 5400. |

Mintage includes 156,519 pieces struck in 1804. Large 3, 12 arrows rev., O-101.

1803

Large 3, small rev. stars, 13 arrows, O-102.

1803

Large 3, large rev. stars, O-103.

| 1803 .... | 150. | 315. | 1175. | 3250. | 7150. |

Small 3, O-104.

| 1805/4 .... (211,722) .... | 205. | 480. | 1900. | 7000. | 30000. |

Close overdate. Two rev. varieties with 12 and 13 arrows, O-101-102, scarce, unverified in Unc. Eliasberg 4/97 MS-63 $82,500.

1805/4

Wide overdate, the die breaks badly at first two stars. O-103, virtually unknown in Unc., extremely rare above Fine.

| 1805 .... | 135. | 235. | 850. | 2450. | 5650. |

13 vars., including 4 and 5 berry revs., 13 and arrows, all are rare to extremely rare in Unc.

| 1806/5 .... (839,576) .... | 135. | 225. | 700. | 2050. | 5150. |

Knobbed 6., four berries, O-104, rare.

1806/5

Knobbed 6, 0 over horizontal 0, rev. five berries, O-101, 103.

1806/5

Knobbed 6, 0 over horizontal 0, rev. six berries, O-102.

Half dollars continued

	G-4	F-12	EF-40	AU-50	MS-60
1806	135.	215.	685.	1700.	4250.

Knobbed 6, small stars. Stem through eagle's claw. O-105-107.

1806

Knobbed 6, small stars. Stem not through eagle's claw, O-108, excessively rare in all grades.

1806/Inverted 6	190.	450.	1800.	3850.	9500.

Sometimes improperly called 6 over inverted 9, O-110-111. Pointed 6, stem through claw. Rim break develops over TED in UNITED. Very rare in all grades, extremely rare in Unc.

1806	125.	210.	650.	1650.	4100.

Pointed 6. Small stars. Stem through eagle's claw, several vars.

1806	125.	210.	650.	1650.	4100.

Pointed 6. Small stars. Stem not through eagle's claw, O-109. Eliasberg 4/97 MS-65 $126,500.

1807 .... (301,076)	125.	210.	650.	1650.	4100.

10 vars., new edge device without stars or other ornaments between the words. O-107, die line joining olive stem to denticles right of tail is very rare.

CAPPED BUST LEFT, LETTERED EDGE

G- Date, letters legible, Bust outlined.
VG - LIBERTY, legends, clasp at shoulder visible.
F- Clasp and curl above it clear.
VF - Clasp, curl strong. Hair over brow visible.
EF - All details strong.
AU - Wear only on highest points. Must have some Mint luster.
UNC - No wear visible any place. Full Mint luster.

	Capped Bust				
	F-12	VF-20	EF-40	AU-50	MS-60
1807 .... (750,500)	180.	290.	825.	2350.	4500.

Large stars, normal rev. O-114.

1807	155.	250.	475.	1400.	3500.

Large stars, rev. shows 50 cut over "20," actually an inverted 5 in denomination, O-111-112. Most early date examples are weakly struck.

1807	775.	1250.	2500.	7250.	——

"Bearded Goddess" var. shows bold die crack from chin to breast, O-111b.

1807	190.	345.	800.	2200.	3800.

Small stars. Always weakly struck at centers, O-113, (rare in Unc.), O-114.

1808/7 .... (1,368,600)	80.00	160.	435.	825.	2250.
1808	60.00	100.	210.	545.	1450.

REMODELED PORTRAIT AND EAGLE

The liberty head has a shorter neck, larger ear, shorter curls. The eagle has differently shaped wings, spread talons. The period after UNUM is deleted. The regular FIFTY CENTS OR HALF A DOLLAR device appears on about 80 percent of 1809 halves. Two experimental edges were also used 1809 only. Some 15 percent of those struck display vertical lines between the words; the rarer five percent show crisscrossing between the words.

Remodeled portrait and eagle

	F-12	VF-20	EF-40	AU-50	MS-60
1809 .... (1,405,810)	58.00	95.00	200.	585.	1500.
Normal lettered edge.					
1809	65.00	115.	245.	675.	2000.
Vertical lines between the words on edge.					
1809	60.00	110.	230.	650.	1800.
Crisscrossing between the words on edge.					
1810 .... (1,276,276)	50.00	75.00	165.	400.	1300.
A notch on one point of star 13 on some varieties is believed the "signature" of John Reich, engraver of the Capped Bust design.					
1811/0 .... (1,203,644)	77.00	145.	300.	585.	1250.
"Punctuated Date" shows as 18.1'1, O-101; reworked die with fainter overdate is rare O-102.					
1811	57.00	80.00	170.	500.	1000.
Large date, O-103-104.					
1811	57.00	80.00	160.	385.	775.
Small 8, normal date, several vars.					
1812/1 .... (1,628,059)	3750.	6750.	11000.	—	—
Large 8, O-101, very rare.					
1812/1	80.00	165.	365.	675.	1700.
Small 8, O-102.					
1812	50.00	65.00	135.	375.	685.
Normal date, several vars.					
1813 .... (1,241,903)	52.00	73.00	160.	380.	925.
1813	70.00	135.	270.	550.	1900.
Inverted UNI beneath 50 C., scarce blundered die var., O-101; reworked die shows UNI, talons and stem less clearly, O-101a.	52.00	75.00	185.	410.	
1050.					
1814/3 .... (1,039,075)	92.00	150.	375.	635.	2050.
O-101.					
1814	80.00	120.	325.	750.	2000.
Normal date. Beginning this year, a star is added on the edge of the half dollars, several vars.					
1814					
E in STATES punched over an earlier A, O-108.					
1815/2 .... (47,150)	1275.	1550.	2650.	3650.	8750.
Entire mintage recorded the following year. Extremely rare in full Mint State.					
1817/3 .... (1,215,567)	175.	350.	675.	1600.	4500.
Scarce without die cracks above EF.					
1817/4	52500.	110000.	—	—	—
Discovered in 1930 by E.T. Wallis of California and first listed in 1953 in Wayte Raymond's Standard Discovered in 1930 by E.T. Wallis of California and first listed in 1953 in Wayte Raymond's *Standard Catalogue of United States Coins* through efforts of half dollar researcher Al C. Overton. Perhaps eight known, excessively rare in any grade. Eliasberg 4/97 EF-45 $209,000 ex Wallis.					
1817	44.00	63.00	170.	340.	950.
New, low-relief head punch used this year on some vars., including "Punctuated Date" 181.7, O-103.					
1817	80.00	120.	240.	750.	2150.
"Comet" variety. O-106, Beistle 9 L, heavy die break from back of head creates comet-like effect, a popular dealer designation of 1930s.					
1818/7 .... (1,960,322)	45.00	75.00	180.	550.	1250.
First 8 large, head of 1812-17, O-101, 103.					
1818/7					
Small 8's, very wide date, head of 1817-18, O-102.					

Half dollars continued

	F-12	VF-20	EF-40	AU-50	MS-60
1818	38.00	55.00	130.	280.	675.

Head of 1818-24, var. with broken-top 8's called pincer or lobster-claw 8's, O-108. Many 1818-26 halves, and all 1824-25 coins show Liberty's mouth open to varying degrees. Eliasberg 4/97)-113 Prf-65 $103,400.

	F-12	VF-20	EF-40	AU-50	MS-60
1819/8 ...... (2,208,000)	50.00	72.00	150.	425.	900.

Small, narrow 9, O-101.

1819/8	50.00	72.00	150.	425.	900.

Large, broad 9, five vars., O-102-106.

1819	38.00	53.00	135.	275.	775.

Normal date, several vars.

1820/19 Overdate

	F-12	VF-20	EF-40	AU-50	MS-60
1820/19 ...... (751,122)	70.00	150.	300.	700.	1600.

Small square base 2, O-101.

1820/19	65.00	140.	275.	625.	1400.

Small curl base 2, O-102.

1820	65.00	125.	275.	585.	1250.

Small date, curl base 2, O-103.

1820	60.00	115.	250.	525.	1100.

Large date, knobbed square base 2. Wide and close date vars.

1821 ...... (1,305,797)	45.00	62.00	145.	450.	800.

Seven vars.

1822/1 ...... (1,559,573)	70.00	135.	275.	635.	1275.

Two vars., O-101-102, latter with base of second 2 heavier than first, rare.

1822	40.00	60.00	135.	265.	675.

Button appears in fold of Liberty cap, not seen in any other date or var., O-107.

1822

Extra-large E's, defective A's in reverse legend, O-114, scarce.

1823 ...... (1,694,200)	72.00	125.	415.	800.	1650.

Broken 3 leaning right, O-101.

1823	60.00	80.00	150.	500.	1400.

Patched 3, punch at center strengthens spindly digit, O-101a, scarce; missing inside serifs of A's on reverse, O-102, rare.

1823	65.00	90.00	165.	575.	1450.

Ugly 3, another repunched-center 3 with flattened curves, die crack links denticles, 3 and curl, O-110a, scarce.

1823	37.00	58.00	125.	255.	600.

Normal date.

1824/1 ...... (3,504,954)	44.00	95.00	210.	315.	885.

Small 1, as on 1821 coinage, O-2101-102, latter with wide 50 C. rev. is rare.

1824	38.00	52.00	150.	550.	1100.

Overton's "jumble of recuttings," often called "over various dates". Apparently an 1820 die that was altered to read 1822, and then not used until 1824 when it was again overpunched. Other explanations are possible, and additional research is needed.

1824/4	40.00	52.00	145.	325.	825.

Top of first 4 visible left of final 4, two varieties with different 2's, O-109-110. Not a 4/1, but the remains of the diagonal are often mistaken for the peak of a 1. Unlike the true overdates, these have a large 1 in the date.

1824	36.00	46.00	105.	265.	575.

Normal date.

1825 ...... (2,943,166)	35.00	45.00	100.	205.	525.

Large 1. Plain and fancy 2 varieties. The plain 2 ends in a slant; the fancy 2 has a more extended curl, and points upward almost vertically. Frequent changes of head punch from here to end of series.

1825

Rev. UNITEDSTATES placed so close as to appear one word, O-101.

1826 ...... (4,004,180)	35.00	44.00	90.00	190.	505.

Plain and fancy 2 vars., OFAMERICA as one word, O-112.

1827/6 ...... (5,493,400)	38.00	85.00	200.	375.	950.

Three minor vars., O-101-103.

Half dollars continued

	F-12	VF-20	EF-40	AU-50	MS-60
1827	36.00	48.00	87.00	190.	600.

Square base 2, plain and fancy 2 varieties. Eliasberg 4/97 O-121 Prf-65 $110,000.

	F-12	VF-20	EF-40	AU-50	MS-60
1827	43.00	70.00	110.	225.	525.

Curl base 2, O-146 scarce, O-147, very rare.

	F-12	VF-20	EF-40	AU-50	MS-60
1828 .... (3,075,200)	35.00	44.00	75.00	175.	500.

Large, curl base 2, no knob, O-101-105.

1828

Large, curl base 2 with knob, O-106-107, scarce.

	F-12	VF-20	EF-40	AU-50	MS-60
1828	36.00	48.00	85.00	235.	525.

Square base 2 with knob, large 8's; rev. large letters, large C in 50 C., O-108-109.

	F-12	VF-20	EF-40	AU-50	MS-60
1828	35.00	43.00	77.00	230.	520.

Square-base 2, small 8's/large letters, large C in 50 C., several vars., O-118 shows UNITEDSTATES as one word; die reused in 1829.

	F-12	VF-20	EF-40	AU-50	MS-60
1828	75.00	100.	195.	625.	1300.

Square-base 2, small 8's/small letters, small C in 50 C, partly filled A's in rev. legend, STA boldly repunched in STATES, O-119, rare.

	F-12	VF-20	EF-40	AU-50	MS-60
1829/27 .... (3,712,156)	48.00	60.00	125.	350.	950.

Curved-base 2 punched over square-base 2. O-101-102. In early die states the curved top of the 7 is visible; rev. 50 C.

	F-12	VF-20	EF-40	AU-50	MS-60
1829	35.00	43.00	75.00	175.	500.

Small letters rev., several vars., O-110 shows UNITEDSTATES as one word.

1829

Large letters rev., O-110 and 116, scarce.

	F-12	VF-20	EF-40	AU-50	MS-60
1830 .... (4,764,800)					

New obv. punch; outline of neck is very straight. Base of chin is less angular and has a cleft.

	F-12	VF-20	EF-40	AU-50	MS-60
1830	35.00	43.00	75.00	170.	485.

Small 0 in date, O-101-118. O-114 shows UNITEDSTATES as one word, very rare. Some vars. found with the 1814-30 edge which is plain between words; or rare 1830-31 edge with plaques with diagonal reeding between the words.

1830

Medium 0 in date, O-119.

	F-12	VF-20	EF-40	AU-50	MS-60
1830	35.00	43.00	75.00	175.	490.

Large 0 in date, O-120-123.

	F-12	VF-20	EF-40	AU-50	MS-60
1831 .... (5,873,660)	35.00	43.00	75.00	170.	475.

Short-serif 1's in date, O-101-102. Most halves of this date show shallow reeding between the words, typical of 1831-37 strikes.

1831

Long-serif 1's in date, several vars.

1831

Blunt 1's, several vars.

	F-12	VF-20	EF-40	AU-50	MS-60
1832 .... (4,797,000)	41.00	85.00	135.	225.	540.

Large letter rev., heavy curving die break begins above leaves and crosses left wing, O-101, scarce.

	F-12	VF-20	EF-40	AU-50	MS-60
1832	35.00	43.00	75.00	170.	475.

Many vars. O-112 shows raised "dash" left of base of 1, rare. Eliasberg 4/97 O-123 Prf-65 $225,500.

	F-12	VF-20	EF-40	AU-50	MS-60
1833 .... (5,206,000)	35.00	43.00	75.00	170.	485.

Small 50 C., several vars.

1833

Large 50, small C., O-103-104.

1833

Mint restrike with rev. and flat rims of 1836 (engraver's scratch at end of olive stem). Struck by steam-powered coining press, lettered edge crushed by plain restraining collar, four known. Norweb Proof-64/65, $30,800.

1834 half dollar

	F-12	VF-20	EF-40	AU-50	MS-60
1834 .... (6,412,004)	35.00	43.00	75.00	170.	485.

Large date, letters and 50C., O-101-103.

Half dollars continued

	F-12	VF-20	EF-40	AU-50	MS-60

1834
Large date, small letters and small 50, large C., O-104-108.

1834
Small date, small letters and 50 C. Liberty head remodeled with more slender and graceful neck. O-118 displays many blunders and recuttings of rev. legend, very rare.

1834
Mint restrike resembling that of 1833, Overton unlisted. Stack's Dec. 1994, Choice Brilliant Proof, $34,500.

1834
"Child's head," O-111 similar to last, but Liberty has a pug nose and even more youthful appearance.

1835/4? .... (5,352,006)
Status as overdate is debatable, raised mark at right of curve of 5 is held by some to be crosspiece of a 4, O-105.

1835 .... 35.00 43.00 75.00 170. 475.
Curved-top 5's, large C. in denomination, O-101-102, 105 and 107.

1835
Straight-top 5's, large C., O106, 108-110. Eliasberg 4/97)-111 Prf-66 $121,000.

1835
Straight-top 5's, small C., O-103; 1 recut in date, virtually no rev. denticles, very rare.

1836/34? .... (6,545,000)
Overton's "Bar-dot Varieties" are believed by some to be vestigial overdates, but this is unproven, O-118, 120-121.

1836/1336 .... 35.00 43.00 75.00 210. 525.
3 plain under 8 in date, O-108, scarce.

1836 .... 75.00 165. 250. 685. 1600.
50 over 00, curve-top 5, large C., O-116, rare.

1836 .... 35.00 43.00 75.00 170. 475.
Normal denomination. Curved-top 5, large C., several vars.

1836
Curved-top 5, small C. O-105, 114, 123.

1836
Straight-top 5, large C.

1836
Straight-top 5, small C., O-104, 109, latter scarce.

CAPPED BUST LEFT, REEDED EDGE

50 CENTS

G- LIBERTY faint but visible.
VG - LIBERTY partially clear.
F- LIBERTY clear and complete.
VF - Strong LIBERTY, shoulder clasp.
EF - All details sharp.
AU - Wear on highest points only. Must have partial Mint luster.
UNC - No wear at all, full Mint luster.

Capped Bust, Reeded Edge, 50 CENTS

	F-12	VF-20	EF-40	AU-50	MS-60

1836 .... (1,200) .... 900. 1250. 1800. 3400. 9000.
First steam coinage of halves, called a pattern by Judd despite the quantity of non-Proofs that were placed in circulation. A short diagnostic die crack descends from denticle just right of final S in STATES. Jules Reiver's John Reich 1 and 2. Eliasberg 4/97 Prf-64 $23,100.

1837 .... (3,629,820) .... 45.00 75.00 120. 250. 600.
Struck within four collars of four different sizes, resulting in four different diameters, from 29.5 up to 31.6 mm; 27 JR vars. codified by Reiver.

1837
"Hole" at left end of three lowest crossbars in shield, perhaps a compass point on hub, JR-12, rare.

Half dollars continued

	F-12	VF-20	EF-40	AU-50	MS-60

1837

"Inverted G," often called "inverted G instead of C in AMERICA". Actually caused by slip of the graver, since the "G" would have been upside down and backwards. JR-16, rare.

HALF DOL. REVERSE

Capped Bust, Reeded Edge, HALF DOL.

	F-12	VF-20	EF-40	AU-50	MS-60
1838 ....(3,546,000)	45.00	75.00	120.	255.	625.

17 vars.

1838-O	—	—	42500.	80000.	115000.

Mint mark O above date on obverse, Branch mint proof and classic American rarity; 20 believed struck to test New Orleans press, 11 traced today. Kagin's 1983 San Diego ANA sale, AU-50, $27,000; the James B. Wilson, R. Coulton Davis, W. Elliot Woodward, J.N.T. Levick, Norweb Proof-64 to 65 realized $93,500 Nov. 1988; Eliasberg 4/97 Prf-60 $121,000.

1839 ....(1,362,160)	45.00	85.00	160.	350.	950.

Normal large reverse letters near denticles, 9 vars.

1839

Small letters distant from denticles, reverse intended for new Liberty Seated obverse, possibly three known.

1839-O ....(178,976)	240.	310.	585.	1125.	2800.

O Mint mark double-punched at bottom and lower left, very rare, JR-1; O doubled under right bottom, JR-2, very rare, the five Proofs known of this var. are rarer than more famous 1838-O.

SEATED LIBERTY, NO DRAPERY AT ELBOW

SMALL LETTERS REVERSE 1839-42

G- Rim worn, no LIBERTY.
VG - Rim defined, LIBERTY has 3 letters.
F- LIBERTY weak, but complete.
VF - All details visible.
EF - All details sharp.
AU - Wear only on highest points. Must have some Mint luster.
UNC - No wear at all, full Mint luster.
PROOF - High rims, mirror-like fields, Liberty, eagle, etc., frosted. Surfaces of letters flat, rather than rounded.

Seated Liberty, No Drapery at Elbow

	F-12	VF-20	EF-40	AU-50	MS-60
1839 ....(1,972,400)	115.	265.	615.	1400.	4000.

Closed 9 and rare open 9 vars., all rare in full Unc.

SEATED LIBERTY, DRAPERY AT ELBOW, SMALL LETTERS REVERSE

1839 ....(incl. above)	48.00	85.00	135.	275.	550.
1840 ....(1,435,008)	53.00	75.00	110.	250.	585.

Rev. type of '39; small letters.

Half dollars continued

	F-12	VF-20	EF-40	AU-50	MS-60
1840 (O)	225.	295.	525.	1100.	2750.

Without Mint mark. Rev. type of '38: medium letters, struck in New Orleans Mint combining Seated Liberty obv. with no-Mint mark rev. originally intended for use with Mint-marked Capped Bust obv. Very rare in Unc.

1840-O

	F-12	VF-20	EF-40	AU-50	MS-60
1840-O .... (855,100)	50.00	70.00	105.	230.	600.

Large O. Mint mark on reverse below eagle as on all following.

1840-O
Medium O, very rare.

1840-O
Small O, rare.

	F-12	VF-20	EF-40	AU-50	MS-60
1841 .... (310,000)	85.00	150.	250.	425.	1200.
1841-O .... (401,000)	48.00	88.00	125.	235.	800.

Some also struck in 1842, after following.

	F-12	VF-20	EF-40	AU-50	MS-60
1842-O	1350.	2000.	4150.	8500.	——

Small date, rare above EF and unknown in Unc.

LARGE LETTERS REVERSE 1842-1891

Drapery at Elbow, Large Letters reverse

	F-12	VF-20	EF-40	AU-50	MS-60
1842 .... (191,000)	55.00	70.00	175.	400.	875.

Small date, extremely rare in Unc., four Proofs known, Norweb Proof-63/65, $14,300, Nov. 1988.

	F-12	VF-20	EF-40	AU-50	MS-60
1842 .... (1,821,764)	49.00	62.00	90.00	185.	400.

Large date

1842
Double and rare triple-punched date vars.

	F-12	VF-20	EF-40	AU-50	MS-60
1842-O .... (754,000)	39.00	57.00	120.	300.	725.

Large date. Eliasberg 4/97 MS-62 $33,000.

	F-12	VF-20	EF-40	AU-50	MS-60
1843 .... (3,844,000)	43.00	53.00	73.00	180.	395.
1843-O .... (2,268,000)	47.00	60.00	90.00	195.	700.
1844 .... (1,766,000)	38.00	47.00	70.00	175.	390.

Varieties exist with recut dates.

	F-12	VF-20	EF-40	AU-50	MS-60
1844-O .... (2,005,000)	35.00	48.00	82.00	225.	735.

Large O.

1844-O
Medium O.

	F-12	VF-20	EF-40	AU-50	MS-60
1844-O	1100.	1550.	2100.	6500.	12000.

Doubled date, first date punched much too high and deep into base of liberty. Small O, excessively rare in Unc.

	F-12	VF-20	EF-40	AU-50	MS-60
1845 .... (589,000)	55.00	87.50	180.	340.	900.

Very scarce in all grades, minor positional vars.

	F-12	VF-20	EF-40	AU-50	MS-60
1845-O .... (2,094,000)	40.00	58.00	125.	255.	725.

Found with large and small Mint marks. Rarely found without drapery, the result of over-polished dies. This problem of over-polishing removing drapery recurs throughout the series, but is of interest primarily to the specialist.

Half dollars continued

	F-12	VF-20	EF-40	AU-50	MS-60

1845-O
: Doubled date recut to the right, very rare.

1845-O
: Tripled date, three cuttings, one above the other, very rare.

1846/5 .... (2,210,000)
: Small date, difficult to see as only knob and very tip of 5 show plainly in known vars., very rare.

	F-12	VF-20	EF-40	AU-50	MS-60
1846	38.00	52.00	88.00	200.	400.

Small date.

	F-12	VF-20	EF-40	AU-50	MS-60
1846	43.00	60.00	120.	250.	535.

Tall date, same punches as on 1846 large date cent.

	F-12	VF-20	EF-40	AU-50	MS-60
1846/horizontal 6.	275.	340.	500.	1200.	3500.

Small date, rare in all grades, unknown in Choice Unc.

1846/5-O .... (2,304,000) ....
: Small date, very rare.

	F-12	VF-20	EF-40	AU-50	MS-60
1846-O	35.00	53.00	95.00	250.	750.

Small date, "No Drapery" and recut dates exist, and should not be confused with the preceding or following.

1846-O
: Doubled small date, second date punched higher than first, Drapery at elbow.

1846-O
: Doubled small date, second date punched lower than first.

	F-12	VF-20	EF-40	AU-50	MS-60
1846-O	360.	475.	1100.	2000.	3950.

Tall date, unknown in Choice Unc.

	F-12	VF-20	EF-40	AU-50	MS-60
1847/46 .... (1,156,000)	2850.	3600.	6750.	—	—

Very rare.

	F-12	VF-20	EF-40	AU-50	MS-60
1847	33.00	43.00	80.00	155.	400.

Normal date, some repunched vars. known.

	F-12	VF-20	EF-40	AU-50	MS-60
1847-O .... (2,584,000)	38.00	55.00	125.	290.	800.
1848 .... (580,000)	75.00	125.	215.	475.	775.

Very scarce in all grades, excessively rare AU-Unc.

	F-12	VF-20	EF-40	AU-50	MS-60
1848-O .... (3,180,000)	36.00	45.00	130.	325.	810.

Small O reported, unconfirmed.

	F-12	VF-20	EF-40	AU-50	MS-60
1849 .... (1,252,000)	48.00	68.00	140.	350.	805.
1849	2750.	3750.	5150.	8500.	—

Doubled date, second date punched far to right, very rare. Excessively rare in Unc.

1849
: Doubled date, second date punched to left, extremely rare, excessively rare in Unc.

	F-12	VF-20	EF-40	AU-50	MS-60
1849-O .... (2,310,000)	43.00	59.00	115.	245.	650.
1850 .... (227,000)	335.	415.	550.	825.	1650.

Eliasberg 4/97 Prf-65 $46,200.

	F-12	VF-20	EF-40	AU-50	MS-60
1850-O .... (2,456,000)	42.00	57.00	115.	235.	550.

Closed 5, var. with medium instead of small O was listed in Ten Eyck sale catalog, but is unverified.

	F-12	VF-20	EF-40	AU-50	MS-60
1851 .... (200,750)	415.	500.	600.	775.	1200.

Rare in all grades, very rare in Unc. Many of this year and the next were melted at the Mint after July 1853 as bullion value exceeded face value.

	F-12	VF-20	EF-40	AU-50	MS-60
1851-O .... (402,000)	53.00	85.00	185.	385.	675.
1852 .... (77,130)	500.	600.	825.	1025.	1200.
1852-O .... (144,000)	175.	350.	515.	1150.	3750.

Very rare in Unc.

1853-O
: Excessively rare, three positively known: 1) H.O. Granberg-Louis Eliasberg; 2) Col. E.H.R. Green- C.A. Cass, "Empire" sale; 3) J.W. Haseltine-Garrett, VF-20, $40,000, Nov. 1979. Beware of alterations from 1858. In the genuine, the date logotype is the same as the Arrows variety; in alterations from 1858-O, the 5 is of much different style. Weight should be pre-reduction standard of 13.36 grams. Eliasberg 4/97 VG-8 $154,000.

SEATED LIBERTY, ARROWS AT DATE, RAYS AROUND EAGLE

Arrows and Rays

	F-12	VF-20	EF-40	AU-50	MS-60
1853 ....(3,532,708)	40.00	80.00	225.	400.	1275.

Found with recut date varieties. Greatly hoarded because of its type coin potential; actually no rarer than its mintage would suggest, although elusive in full Unc. Eliasberg 4/97 Prf-63 $63,800.

| 1853-O ....(1,328,000) .... | 55.00 | 150. | 250. | 850. | 2750. |

Found with recut date varieties and die-polish "No Drapery" discussed under 1845-O.

RAYS REMOVED

No Rays

	F-12	VF-20	EF-40	AU-50	MS-60
1854 ....(2,982,000)	34.00	42.00	100.	255.	585.

Found with recut date vars., triple-punched date is very rare.

| 1854-O ....(5,240,000) .... | 33.00 | 41.00 | 90.00 | 250. | 475. |

1854-O
Doubled date and arrows.
1854-O
Tripled date and arrows, rare.

| 1855 ....(759,500) .... | 41.00 | 60.00 | 110. | 280. | 850. |
| 1855/854. .... | 125. | 170. | 375. | 750. | 1750. |

Repunched slightly higher and to right of final date.

| 1855-O ....(3,688,000) .... | 35.00 | 45.00 | 100. | 270. | 790. |

Found with recut date varieties.
1855-O
Doubled date and arrows, rare.
1855-O
Over horizontal O, extremely rare.

| 1855-S ....(129,950) .... | 850. | 1250. | 3100. | 6700. | 14500. |

Extremely rare in Unc., also die-polish "No Drapery" as 1845-O.

ARROWS REMOVED

1856 ....(938,000)	35.00	45.00	71.00	145.	375.
1856-O ....(2,658,000)	36.00	43.00	75.00	165.	405.

Found with recut date varieties.

| 1856-S ....(211,000) .... | 100. | 205. | 375. | 1300. | 3500. |

Rare in Unc., excessively rare Choice.

| 1857 ....(1,988,000) .... | 33.00 | 40.00 | 71.00 | 145. | 380. |

One rare var. has bottom of extra 857 in base of rock.

| 1857-O ....(818,000) .... | 43.00 | 58.00 | 125. | 275. | 725. |
| 1857-S ....(158,000) .... | 140. | 250. | 525. | 900. | 3350. |

Large S, 1.6 mm. high as in 1855-56, rare.
1857-S
Medium S, 1.4 mm. high, scarce.

| 1858 ....(4,226,000) ....(80) | 32.00 | 40.00 | 71.00 | 145. | 375. |

Type I reverse of 1842-64, normal.

Half dollars continued

	F-12	VF-20	EF-40	AU-50	MS-60
1858					

Type II reverse of 1858-66. Very rare, possibly struck in 1859.

1858-O .... (7,294,000)	35.00	45.00	73.00	195.	400.

Type I rev. only. One rare obv. has traces of numerals on base over 18, another has base of 1 on border below date.

1858-S .... (476,000)	55.00	90.00	140.	340.	1050.

Large S. Type I rev. only.

1858-S

Medium S.

1858-S

Small S. Mint mark about 1.1mm. high. Reported, not confirmed.

NOTE: Philadelphia Mint half dollars ca. 1859-65 and "S" Mint ca. 1861-65 are now relatively common in scrubbed Unc. due to a large Guatemala find.

1859 .... (748,000) .... (800)	49.00	68.00	100.	210.	395.

Type I rev.

1859

New Type II rev. hub with more delicate letters, shorter thinner claws, and more widely separated arrowheads. Not regularly used at branch Mints until 1865 because of supply of leftover dies. Following coins are from Type II hub unless specified.

1859-O .... (2,834,000)	38.00	45.00	75.00	190.	390.

Type I rev. only.

1859-S .... (566,000)	50.00	85.00	165.	290.	925.

Large S, Type I rev. only, very rare in Choice Unc. Eliasberg 4/97 MS-66 $52,800.

1859-S

Medium S, Type I rev. only, rare in Choice Unc. Eliasberg 4/97 MS-66 $50,600.

1860 .... (302,700) .... (1,000)	45.00	60.00	110.	235.	600.

Type I and II rev. known.

1860-O .... (1,290,000)	43.00	56.00	72.00	180.	380.

Type I (rare) and Type II rev. known.

1860-S .... (472,000)	44.00	58.00	110.	240.	650.

Varieties with large and medium "S", the latter with a shorter upward curve. Type I rev. only.

1861 .... (2,887,400) .... (1,000)	31.00	38.00	71.00	145.	375.
1861-O .... (2,532,633)	42.00	55.00	78.00	215.	400.

Coins struck by the U.S. during Jan. (330,000). Struck by Louisiana Feb.-Mar. (1,240,000). Struck by the Confederacy, Apr. (962,633). The above cannot be distinguished. Type I and II rev., the former rare. A Type II die-polish "No Drapery" var. exists, as discussed above.

1861-O	125.	175.	250.	385.	925.

"Confederate obverse," later die state of obv. previously used to strike four Confederate States pattern half dollars. Advanced die break from bridge of nose to edge, passing close to star seven. Very rare in AU, extremely rare in Unc. This is the only Union-type coin that can be positively identified as having been struck solely for the Confederacy.

1861-S .... (939,500)	39.00	58.00	130.	265.	900.

Large S, Type I rev. only.

1861-S

Medium S, Type I rev. only.

1862 .... (253,000) .... (550)	58.00	90.00	185.	310.	525.
1862-S .... (1,352,000)	38.00	49.00	83.00	250.	475.

Large S, Type I rev.

1862-S

Medium S, Type I rev. scarce.

1862-S

Small S, Type II rev. Mint mark broken at top, rare.

1863 .... (503,200) .... (460)	47.00	63.00	135.	265.	460.
1863-S .... (916,000)	43.00	50.00	82.00	245.	510.

All with small S, usually broken at top.

1864 .... (379,100) .... (470)	51.00	75.00	150.	275.	500.
1864-S .... (658,000)	42.00	53.00	85.00	255.	550.

Large S, Type I rev.

1864-S

Small S, Type II rev., Mint mark broken at top.

1864-S

Small thin S. Type II rev., standard for all following.

1865 .... (511,400) .... (500)	48.00	70.00	140.	285.	515.
1865-S .... (675,000)	42.00	58.00	105.	365.	835.

Small S, broken at top.

1865-S

Small thin S.

1866

No motto, fantasy struck for private distribution, Unique. See similar 1866 quarter and dollar.

1866-S .... (60,000)	215.	415.	825.	1850.	4650.

No Motto, extremely rare in Unc. Small, thin S of 1864-66, different than that on With Motto rev.

SEATED LIBERTY WITH MOTTO ABOVE EAGLE

		Motto Above Eagle			
	F-12	VF-20	EF-40	AU-50	MS-60
1866 .... (744,900) .... (725)	43.00	65.00	95.00	175.	385.
1866-S .... (994,000)	40.00	63.00	100.	265.	475.
1867 .... (449,300) .... (625)	57.00	95.00	145.	255.	435.
1867-S .... (1,196,000)	37.00	48.00	80.00	170.	500.
Small S and leaning S vars.					
1868 .... (417,600) .... (600)	80.00	145.	265.	375.	525.
1868-S .... (1,160,000)	40.00	52.00	110.	235.	700.
1869 .... (795,300) .... (600)	38.00	51.00	90.00	175.	365.
1869-S .... (656,000)	42.00	54.00	115.	400.	975.
1870 .... (633,900) .... (1,000)	40.00	58.00	105.	190.	345.
1870-S .... (1,004,000)	43.00	63.00	120.	265.	650.
1870-CC .... (54,617)	1500.	2650.	4500.	9500.	——
Rare above Fine, excessively rare in Unc.					
1871 .... (1,203,600) .... (960)	38.00	58.00	73.00	165.	340.
1871-S .... (2,178,000)	35.00	45.00	80.00	225.	575.
Small wide (rare), small thin S varieties, sometimes very weak.					
1871-CC .... (153,950)	325.	550.	1000.	1900.	5000.
Excessively rare in Unc., very rare in EF. Large CC.					
1872 .... (880,600) .... (950)	37.00	48.00	70.00	180.	335.
1872					
Doubled die rev. Rare.					
1872-S .... (580,000)	60.00	90.00	190.	350.	1275.
Small and medium S varieties.					
1872-CC .... (257,000)	225.	300.	675.	1500.	3250.
Large CC.					
1873 .... (587,000) .... (600)	66.00	88.00	140.	300.	410.
Closed 3.					
1873 .... (214,200)	4200.	5900.	7750.	11500.	25000.
Open 3. Two die varieties, both rare.					
1873-S .... (5,000)	290.	550.	1150.	2850.	6000.
Listed in Beistle, but no specimen currently known. Beware removed arrows.					
1873-CC .... (122,500)	290.	450.	1300.	2650.	6000.
Small CC, scarce in lower grades, rare in Unc.					

SEATED LIBERTY WITH ARROWS AT DATE

		Arrows at Date			
	F-12	VF-20	EF-40	AU-50	MS-60
1873 .... (1,815,150) .... (550)	40.00	73.00	190.	350.	875.
Long arrowheads.					
1873					
Short arrowheads, quadruple stripes in obv. shield (doubled die), rare.					
1873					
Short arrowheads, triple stripes, rare.					

Half dollars continued

	F-12	VF-20	EF-40	AU-50	MS-60
1873-S .... (228,000)	115.	190.	390.	850.	2000.
Small wide and small thin S varieties.					
1873-CC .... (214,560)	285.	525.	1500.	2650.	5850.
Large (rare) and small CC vars.					
1874 .... (2,359,600) .... (700)	40.00	70.00	180.	350.	875.
Varieties with long and short arrowheads.					
1874-S .... (394,000)	73.00	145.	290.	650.	1600.
Medium, very small, (both rare), and small S varieties. All rare in Unc. Eliasberg 4/97 MS-66 $55,000.					
1874-CC .... (59,000)	565.	1000.	1700.	3500.	7000.
Very rare in Unc. Small CC; large CC reported, not confirmed. Eliasberg 4/97 MS-63/64 $60,500.					

ARROWS REMOVED

		No Arrows (Stack's)			
	F-12	VF-20	EF-40	AU-50	MS-60
1875 .... (6,026,800) .... (700)	32.00	40.00	68.00	160.	335.
1875-S .... (3,200,000)	47.00	60.00	90.00	165.	345.
Small and very small S varieties.					
1875-S					
Medium S, tilting to left, very scarce.					
1875-CC .... (1,008,000)	60.00	80.00	170.	300.	600.
Small CC (scarce) and medium CC.					
1875-CC					
Tall CC reported, untraced.					
1876 .... (8,418,000) .... (1,150)	30.00	38.00	65.00	160.	335.
Type I (rev. hub of 1866-81); lower berry on branch split.					
1876					
Type II, (rev. hub of 1876-91); lower berry on branch pointed.					
1876-S .... (4,528,000)	30.00	38.00	65.00	190.	400.
Type I and Type II, as above. Very small and micro S vars.					
1876-CC .... (1,956,000)	60.00	75.00	135.	285.	650.
Small, medium and tall CC vars., Type I rev. only.					
1877 .... (8,304,000) .... (510)	30.00	38.00	65.00	160.	335.
Type I (rare except Proofs) and Type II rev. vars.					
1877/6					
Very Rare. Top of 6 shows atop crossbar of 7. Visible only in high grades.					
1877-S .... (5,356,000)	31.00	40.00	65.00	170.	350.
Very small and micro S varieties, Type I and Type II (rare) rev. vars.					
1877-S/S					
Dramatically doubled Mint mark appears as "SS," first S almost full width to left of second S, Type I rev, rare.					
1877-CC .... (1,420,000)	52.00	65.00	130.	260.	600.
Small and medium CC vars., Type I and Type II rev.					
1878 .... (1,377,600) .... (800)	50.00	60.00	90.00	235.	435.
Type II only.					
1878-S .... (12,000)	10500.	13500.	18500.	23000.	35000.
Type II only, very small S. Very rare in all grades, Robison Gem Unc., $16,000, Feb. 1982; Norweb AU-50, $22,000, Nov. 1988; Eliasberg 4/97 MS-61 $39,600.					
1878 CC .... (62,000)	550.	1050.	2000.	3050.	5750.
Type II only, medium CC, extremely rare in Choice Unc. Eliasberg 4/97 MS-65 $77,000.					
1879 .... (4,800) .... (1,100)	260.	290.	380.	465.	535.
Non-Proofs from this date through 1890 are rarer than Proofs, but their values have been overshadowed by the latter. Type I (Proof only) and Type II rev. vars.					
1880 .... (8,400) .... (1,355)	250.	285.	360.	460.	550.
Type I (Proof only) and type II rev. vars.					
1881 .... (10,000) .... (975)	245.	280.	355.	455.	555.
Type I (Proof only) and Type II rev. vars.					
1882 .... (4,400) .... (1,100)	285.	330.	405.	490.	565.
Type II only as on following					

Half dollars continued

			F-12	VF-20	EF-40	AU-50	MS-60
1883	(8,000)	(1,039)	250.	310.	395.	475.	565.
1884	(4,400)	(875)	290.	330.	425.	515.	570.

Proofs and business strikes from same dies, making attribution unusually difficult.

			F-12	VF-20	EF-40	AU-50	MS-60
1885	(5,200)	(930)	280.	325.	420.	505.	725.

Proofs and business strikes from same dies, same problem as preceding.

1886	(5,000)	(886)	415.	440.	475.	575.	765.

Same remarks as preceding.

1887	(5,000)	(710)	475.	525.	600.	700.	850.

Same remarks as preceding.

1888	(12,000)	(832)	245.	270.	390.	455.	540.
1889	(12,000)	(711)	245.	280.	400.	460.	545.
1890	(12,000)	(590)	250.	300.	410.	470.	560.
1891	(200,000)	(600)	83.00	100.	140.	250.	400.

BARBER

G- Legible but no LIBERTY visible.
VG - 3 letters visible in LIBERTY.
F- LIBERTY complete but fuzzy.
VF - LIBERTY even and clear.
EF - All details sharp.
AU - Wear on highest points only. Must show some Mint luster.
UNC - No wear visible anywhere, full Mint luster.
PROOF - High rims, mirror-like fields, frosted head, eagle, etc. Letter surfaces flat and show some evidence of double-striking.

Barber

			F-12	EF-40	AU-50	MS-60	MS-63
1892	(934,000)	(1,245)	47.00	175.	280.	380.	775.
1892-O	(390,000)		270.	425.	450.	875.	1250.

Medium O.

		F-12	EF-40	AU-50	MS-60	MS-63
1892-O		2500.	3500.	4500.	7500.	17500.

Small O Mint mark made in error from punch used for quarter dollar, extremely rare. Eliasberg 4/97 MS-67 $59,400.

		F-12	EF-40	AU-50	MS-60	MS-63
1892-S	(1,029,028)	225.	400.	600.	900.	1850.

Medium S.

1892-S
Small S, punch used for quarter dollars; unverified.

			F-12	EF-40	AU-50	MS-60	MS-63
1893	(1,826,000)	(792)	45.00	160.	320.	515.	1000.
1893-O	(1,389,000)		70.00	275.	375.	565.	900.
1893-S	(740,000)		165.	425.	550.	1175.	2550.
1894	(1,148,000)	(972)	65.00	225.	350.	465.	925.
1894-O	(2,138,000)		60.00	235.	300.	535.	925.
1894-S	(4,048,690)		48.00	200.	350.	475.	1150.
1895	(1,834,338)	(880)	50.00	175.	310.	570.	925.
1895-O	(1,766,000)		55.00	235.	375.	600.	1350.
1895-S	(1,108,086)		65.00	265.	400.	535.	1200.
1896	(950,000)	(762)	55.00	210.	325.	550.	950.
1896-O	(924,000)		90.00	360.	665.	1300.	3000.

Eliasberg 4/97 MS-65/66 $44,000.

			F-12	EF-40	AU-50	MS-60	MS-63
1896-S	(1,140,948)		120.	375.	575.	1250.	2550.
1897	(2,480,000)	(731)	32.00	135.	310.	445.	780.
1897-O	(632,000)		345.	875.	1200.	1600.	2975.
1897-S	(933,900)		275.	700.	1025.	1350.	3000.
1893	(2,956,000)	(735)	28.00	140.	315.	410.	780.
1898-O	(874,000)		95.00	400.	500.	975.	2500.
1898-S	(2,358,550)		42.00	205.	365.	850.	2300.

Half dollars continued

		F-12	VF-20	EF-40	AU-50	MS-60
1899	(5,538,000) .... (846)	27.00	135.	305.	410.	780.
1899-O	(1,724,000)	45.00	225.	355.	550.	1050.
1899-S	(1,686,411)	49.00	220.	350.	635.	1600.
1900	(4,762,000) .... (912)	28.00	135.	315.	410.	775.
1900-O	(2,744,000)	39.00	250.	315.	800.	2650.
1900-S	(2,560,322)	40.00	195.	320.	625.	1900.
1901	(4,268,000) .... (813)	28.00	135.	315.	410.	750.

New obv. and rev. hubs on this and following, most visible in position of letters in motto.

		F-12	VF-20	EF-40	AU-50	MS-60
1901-O	(1,124,000)	52.00	290.	475.	1350.	3200.
1901-S	(847,044)	110.	550.	900.	1600.	4100.

Eliasberg 4/97 MS-66 $35,200.

		F-12	VF-20	EF-40	AU-50	MS-60
1902	(4,922,000) .... (777)	28.00	135.	265.	385.	725.
1902-O	(2,526,000)	38.00	195.	360.	725.	2350.
1902-S	(1,460,670)	48.00	200.	375.	635.	1800.
1903	(2,278,000) .... (755)	38.00	170.	325.	460.	1375.
1903-O	(2,100,000)	44.00	185.	325.	700.	1350.
1903-S	(1,920,772)	44.00	215.	365.	600.	1625.
1904	(2,992,000) .... (670)	30.00	130.	300.	410.	1100.
1904-O	(1,117,600)	52.00	310.	500.	1100.	2800.
1904-S	(553,038)	135.	675.	1000.	1950.	4250.
1905	(662,000) .... (727)	52.00	225.	325.	550.	1200.
1905-O	(505,000)	75.00	260.	425.	725.	1700.

Eliasberg 4/97 MS-66 $33,000.

		F-12	VF-20	EF-40	AU-50	MS-60
1905-S	(2,494,000)	38.00	200.	350.	625.	1900.
1906	(2,638,000) .... (675)	28.00	130.	310.	410.	775.
1906-D	(4,028,000)	29.00	130.	300.	410.	775.
1906-O	(2,446,000)	35.00	165.	325.	600.	1100.
1906-S	(1,740,154)	43.00	192.	325.	600.	1100.
1907	(2,598,000) .... (575)	27.00	192.	325.	410.	725.
1907-D	(3,856,000)	28.00	140.	310.	425.	750.
1907-O	(3,946,600)	28.00	150.	310.	510.	825.

Usually found softly struck, rarely with swellings at neck and lower cheek of Liberty from worn die, the "mumps" variety.

		F-12	VF-20	EF-40	AU-50	MS-60
1907-S	(1,250,000)	75.00	325.	525.	925.	3100.
1908	(1,354,000) .... (545)	30.00	155.	310.	425.	725.

New obv. and rev. hubs on this and following.

		F-12	VF-20	EF-40	AU-50	MS-60
1908-D	(3,280,000)	30.00	145.	310.	425.	725.
1908-O	(5,360,000)	29.00	145.	310.	500.	850.
1908-S	(1,644,828)	45.00	195.	340.	765.	2100.
1909	(2,368,000) .... (650)	28.00	130.	265.	390.	725.
1909-O	(925,400)	42.50	265.	500.	750.	1550.
1909-S	(1,764,000)	30.00	180.	340.	575.	1200.
1910	(418,000) .... (551)	65.00	280.	425.	600.	1150.
1910-S	(1,948,000)	30.00	180.	340.	625.	1800.
1911	(1,406,000) .... (543)	30.00	135.	310.	425.	750.
1911-D	(695,080)	40.00	195.	265.	550.	850.
1911-S	(1,272,000)	33.00	165.	340.	560.	1275.
1912	(1,550,000) .... (700)	28.00	145.	310.	410.	725.

New hubs on this and following.

		F-12	VF-20	EF-40	AU-50	MS-60
1912-D	(2,300,800)	28.00	130.	310.	435.	750.
1912-S	(1,370,000)	30.00	165.	325.	525.	1000.

1913

		F-12	EF-40	AU-50	MS-60	MS-63
1913	(188,000) .... (627)	105.	360.	700.	950.	1650.

Scarce and popular, beware of removed Mint mark alterations.

		F-12	EF-40	AU-50	MS-60	MS-63
1913-D	(534,000)	36.00	180.	300.	455.	875.
1913-S	(604,000)	45.00	195.	350.	600.	1175.

Half dollars continued	F-12	VF-20	EF-40	AU-50	MS-60
1914 .... (124,230) .... (380)	165.	495.	750.	975.	1500.
Beware of removed Mint mark alterations.					
1914-S .... (992,000)	35.00	180.	350.	560.	1050.
1915 .... (138,000) .... (450)	87.50	375.	725.	1025.	1850.
Beware of removed Mint mark alterations.					
1915-D .... (1,170,400)	27.00	130.	265.	390.	725.
1915-S .... (1,604,000)	29.00	145.	265.	425.	725.

WALKING LIBERTY

VG- Motto complete.
F - All skirt lines and sandal details clear.
VF- All details clear but worn.
EF- All details sharp.
AU- Wear only on highest points. Must have partial Mint luster.
UNC - No wear apparent anyplace, full Mint luster.
PROOF - High rims, mirror-like fields and devices. Letter surfaces flat and show some evidence of double striking.

Walking Liberty

	F-12	EF-40	AU-50	MS-60	MS-65
1916 .... (608,000)	57.00	150.	200.	270.	1400.
Circulated patterns of various designs known. Controversial Satin Proofs reported to exist.					
1916-D .... (1,014,400)	35.00	132.	175.	255.	1950.
1916-S .... (508,000)	145.	500.	625.	925.	4600.
1917 .... (12,292,000)	9.75	28.00	60.00	105.	900.
Usually softly struck. Controversial Satin Proofs reported to exist.					

Mint mark locations

	F-12	EF-40	AU-50	MS-60	MS-65
1917-D .... (765,400)	39.00	130.	250.	475.	6600.
Mint mark on obv. below TRUST.					
1917-S .... (952,000)	46.00	650.	1075.	1950.	14750.
Mint mark on obv.					
1917-D .... (1,940,000)	29.00	185.	400.	700.	17500.
Mint mark on rev. at left rim under pine.					
1917-S .... (5,554,000)	15.00	45.00	135.	300.	10500.
Mint mark on rev., as on following.					
1918 .... (6,634,000)	16.00	125.	240.	450.	3000.
New obv. hub used thru 1936.					
1918-D .... (3,853,040)	21.00	145.	350.	825.	20000.
Rarely found with designer's initials polished off reverse die. Even more rarely collected as such. Eliasberg 4/97 MS-65 $33,000					
1918-S .... (10,282,000)	14.00	55.00	132.	365.	16500.
1919 .... (962,000)	39.00	400.	600.	1050.	4800.
1919-D .... (1,165,000)	45.00	575.	900.	2650.	85000.
Eliasberg 4/97 MS-65 $71,500.					
1919-S .... (1,552,000)	33.00	725.	1500.	2300.	11500.
Eliasberg 4/97 MS-65 $13,200.					
1920 .... (6,372,000)	12.00	60.00	115.	275.	6400.
1920-D .... (1,551,000)	29.00	360.	675.	1100.	9350.
1920-S .... (4,624,000)	13.00	225.	385.	675.	9425.

Half dollars continued

1921

		F-12	EF-40	AU-50	MS-60	MS-65
1921	(246,000)	195.	1400.	2200.	3000.	11000.

Crude alterations from 1941 occasionally encountered, as are removed Mint mark alterations.

		F-12	EF-40	AU-50	MS-60	MS-65
1921-D	(208,000)	250.	2000.	2600.	3250.	13250.
1921-S	(548,000)	65.00	5000.	6500.	8700.	55000.

Eliasberg 4/97 MS-66 $37,400.

		F-12	EF-40	AU-50	MS-60	MS-65
1923-S	(2,178,000)	21.00	205.	575.	1150.	12000.
1927-S	(2,392,000)	11.00	85.00	285.	675.	8225.
1928-S	(1,940,000)	12.00	105.	300.	675.	8000.

Large and small S varieties.

		F-12	EF-40	AU-50	MS-60	MS-65
1929-D	(1,001,200)	11.00	75.00	165.	280.	2150.
1929-S	(1,902,000)	9.00	77.50	175.	325.	2350.

Rarely found with designer's initials polished off reverse die. Even more rarely collected as such.

		F-12	EF-40	AU-50	MS-60	MS-65
1933-S	(1,786,000)	8.00	42.00	175.	500.	3000.
1934	(6,964,000)	3.50	10.00	25.00	50.00	400.
1934-D	(2,361,400)	5.50	25.00	60.00	125.	900.

Small (as on 1916-34) and Large (as on 1934-47) D varieties.

		F-12	EF-40	AU-50	MS-60	MS-65
1934-S	(3,652,000)	4.00	25.00	87.00	240.	2900.
1935	(9,162,000)	3.50	7.50	22.00	44.00	310.

From this date on, the heads are generally a little more sharply struck.

		F-12	EF-40	AU-50	MS-60	MS-65
1935-D	(3,003,800)	4.00	22.00	55.00	120.	1175.
1935-S	(3,854,000)	3.50	23.00	87.00	170.	1925.
1936	(12,614,000) ... (3,901)	2.75	6.50	22.00	36.00	145.

Proofs were again offered to the public with this issue, struck with brilliant finish only.

		F-12	EF-40	AU-50	MS-60	MS-65
1936-D	(4,252,400)	3.50	16.00	45.00	72.00	325.
1936-S	(3,884,000)	3.50	20.00	55.00	120.	400.
1937	(9,522,000) ... (5,728)	2.75	7.00	22.00	37.00	175.

New obv. hub used 1937 only, all Mints.

		F-12	EF-40	AU-50	MS-60	MS-65
1937-D	(1,676,000)	8.00	27.00	80.00	145.	365.
1937-S	(2,090,000)	6.00	17.00	60.00	120.	350.
1938	(4,110,000) ... (8,152)	4.00	9.75	40.00	65.00	265.

New obv. hub used through 1947. Proofs rarely found with designer's initials polished off die.

		F-12	EF-40	AU-50	MS-60	MS-65
1938-D	(491,600)	25.00	100.	250.	400.	800.

Scarce in lower grades, rare in Unc.

		F-12	EF-40	AU-50	MS-60	MS-65
1939	(6,812,000) ... (8,808)	2.75	7.50	22.00	40.00	120.

Proofs rarely found with designer's initials polished off of die.

		F-12	EF-40	AU-50	MS-60	MS-65
1939-D	(4,267,800)	3.50	9.00	23.00	38.00	105.
1939-S	(2,552,000)	6.50	12.50	50.00	100.	160.
1940	(9,156,000) ... (11,279)	2.65	6.00	12.00	28.00	115.

Proofs and business strikes are rarely found with designer's initials polished off die. Even more rarely collected as such.

		F-12	EF-40	AU-50	MS-60	MS-65
1940-S	(4,550,000)	3.00	8.00	19.We	30.00	300.

Always found weakly struck.

		F-12	EF-40	AU-50	MS-60	MS-65
1941	(24,192,000) ... (15,412)	2.65	5.75	8.75	23.00	105.

Proofs commonly found with designer's initials polished off of the die.

		F-12	EF-40	AU-50	MS-60	MS-65
1941-D	(11,248,400)	3.00	6.00	15.00	36.00	120.

Variety exists from doubled obv. die, the doubling plainest on rays and D UST in motto.

		F-12	EF-40	AU-50	MS-60	MS-65
1941-S	(8,098,000)	3.00	7.00	27.00	72.00	1250.

Small S only, usually found weakly struck.

		F-12	EF-40	AU-50	MS-60	MS-65
1942	(47,818,000) ... (21,120)	2.65	5.75	8.75	23.00	85.00
1942						

Doubled rev. die, rare.

		F-12	EF-40	AU-50	MS-60	MS-65
1942-D	(10,973,800)	3.00	6.00	17.00	36.00	150.
1942-D/S		—	80.00	200.	475.	3500.

Excessively rare.

		F-12	EF-40	AU-50	MS-60	MS-65
1942-S	(12,708,000)	3.00	7.00	16.00	35.00	400.

Large and Small S varieties exist. Rarely found with designer's initials polished off reverse die; even more rarely collected as such.

Half dollars continued

	F-12	EF-40	AU-50	MS-60	MS-65
1943 .... (53,190,000)	2.65	5.75	8.75	23.00	85.00

The so-called 1943/2-PDS overdates appear to be the result of a doubled master die with 3/3 rather than 3/2.

	F-12	EF-40	AU-50	MS-60	MS-65
1943-D .... (11,346,000)	3.00	6.00	19.00	40.00	135.
1943-S .... (13,450,000)	3.00	6.00	18.00	33.00	360.

Rarely found with designer's initials polished off reverse die. Even more rarely collected as such.

	F-12	EF-40	AU-50	MS-60	MS-65
1944 .... (28,206,000)	2.65	5.75	8.75	24.00	120.

Same remarks as preceding.

	F-12	EF-40	AU-50	MS-60	MS-65
1944-D .... (9,769,000)	3.00	6.00	16.00	31.00	110.
1944-S .... (8,904,000)	3.00	6.00	16.00	31.00	435.
1945 .... (31,502,000)	2.65	5.75	8.75	23.00	90.00

Same remarks as 1943-S.

	F-12	EF-40	AU-50	MS-60	MS-65
1945-D .... (9,966,800)	3.00	6.00	15.00	29.00	95.00
1945-S .... (10,156,000)	3.00	6.00	15.00	28.00	120.
1946 .... (12,118,000)	2.65	6.00	11.00	25.00	120.
1946					

Doubled die rev., rare.

	F-12	EF-40	AU-50	MS-60	MS-65
1946-D .... (2,151,000)	5.75	10.00	19.00	20.00	90.00
1946-S .... (3,724,000)	3.00	6.00	17.00	24.50	100.
1947 .... (4,094,000)	3.25	8.00	18.00	25.50	120.
1947-D .... (3,900,600)	3.25	8.00	18.00	26.00	100.

FRANKLIN

EF - All details sharp
AU - Slight wear on highest points only. Must have some Mint luster.
UNC - No wear at all. Full Mint luster.
PROOF - High rims, mirror-like fields and devices. Letter surfaces flat and show some evidence of double striking.

Benjamin Franklin, Liberty Bell

	EF-40	AU-50	MS-60	MS-65	PF-65
1948 .... (3,006,814)	4.25	5.50	14.00	75.00	*
1948-D .... (4,028,600)	4.75	5.50	9.00	160.	*
1949 .... (5,614,000)	5.25	11.00	29.00	120.	*
1949-D .... (4,120,600)	7.00	13.00	30.00	1000.	*
1949-S .... (3,744,000)	11.00	23.00	45.00	145.	*
1950 .... (7,742,123) .... (51,386)	4.00	7.00	21.00	125.	250.

Proofs with satin or brilliant finishes.

	EF-40	AU-50	MS-60	MS-65	PF-65
1950-D .... (8,031,600)	3.75	8.00	18.00	550.	*
1951 .... (16,802,102) .... (57,500)	3.25	4.25	14.00	75.00	180.
1951-D .... (9,475,200)	4.25	13.00	18.00	275.	*
1951-S .... (13,696,000)	4.50	11.00	19.00	110.	*
1952 .... (21,192,093) .... (81,980)	3.00	4.75	7.00	70.00	88.00
1952-D .... (25,395,600)	2.90	4.50	7.00	225.	*
1952-S .... (5,526,000)	4.75	19.00	28.00	105.	*
1953 .... (2,668,120) .... (128,800)	4.75	10.00	12.00	250.	55.00
1953-D .... (20,900,400)	2.90	4.50	6.00	160.	*
1953-S .... (4,148,000)	3.75	9.00	9.50	70.00	*
1954 .... (13,188,203) .... (233,300)	2.90	3.50	5.00	72.00	35.00
1954-D .... (25,445,580)	2.90	3.50	5.00	145.	*
1954-S .... (4,993,400)	3.75	5.00	5.75	60.00	*
1955 .... (2,498,181) .... (378,200)	5.50	6.50	7.00	50.00	21.00

Miami dealer William Fox Steinberg dubbed a clashed-die var. the "Bugs Bunny" half, promoting it widely.

	EF-40	AU-50	MS-60	MS-65	PF-65
1956 .... (4,032,000) .... (669,384)	4.00	4.75	5.25	40.00	18.50

All business strikes and a small percentage (perhaps 5%) of Proofs are from Type I reverse hub of 1948-63. The great majority of Proofs are from Type II reverse hub of 1956-63, which was used on all proofs 1957-63. Worn or otherwise defective Type II Proof reverses were also used on some business strikes of 1958 and 1959 (q.v.).

Half dollars continued

	EF-40	AU-50	MS-60	MS-65	PF-65
1957 .... (5,114,000) .... (1,247,952)	3.15	3.50	5.00	40.00	14.00

All business strikes are from old rev. hub. All proofs are from new rev. hub, as are all subsequent Proofs through 1963.

	EF-40	AU-50	MS-60	MS-65	PF-65
1957-D .... (19,966,850)	2.75	3.25	4.75	40.00	*

Type I rev. only.

1958 .... (4,042,000) .... (875,652)	4.00	3.50	5.50	45.00	14.00

Perhaps 20% of business strikes and all of Proofs are from Type II reverse hub.

1958-D .... (23,962,412)	2.50	3.00	3.50	40.00	*

Type I rev. only.

1959 .... (6,200,000) .... (1,149,291)	2.50	3.00	3.75	125.	9.00

1959

Doubled die reverse, Type II hub over Type I hub. Eagle in low relief, three feathers to left of perch.

1959-D .... (13,053,750)	2.50	3.00	4.00	140.	*

Type I rev.; Type I rev. used exclusively on all following business strikes.

1960 .... (6,024,000) .... (1,691,602)	2.50	3.00	3.50	160.	9.00
1960-D .... (18,215,812)	2.50	3.00	4.00	775.	*
1961 .... (8,290,000) .... (3,028,244)	2.35	2.50	3.50	240.	9.00
1961-D .... (20,276,442)	2.35	2.50	4.00	425.	*
1962 .... (9,714,000) .... (3,218,019)	2.35	2.50	3.50	320.	9.00
1962-D .... (35,473,281)	2.35	2.50	3.50	400.	*
1963 .... (22,164,000) .... (3,075,645)	2.35	2.50	3.00	95.00	9.00
1963-D .... (67,069,292)	2.35	2.50	3.00	80.00	*

KENNEDY, PRESIDENTIAL SEAL/EAGLE REVERSE

John F. Kennedy, Presidential Eagle

	MS-60	MS-63	MS-65	PF-63	PF-65
1964 .... (273,304,004) .... (3,950,762)	2.50	3.00	9.00	5.00	7.00

Some scarce Proofs show bolder detail in hair.

1964

Doubled die obv. or rev. Several varieties, including Proofs.

1964-D .... (156,205,446)	2.50	3.00	12.00	*	*

1964-D

Doubled die obv. or rev. Several varieties.

1965 (D)

90 percent silver; all 1965 halves were struck in Denver, without Mint marks. This transitional silver error is extremely rare.

A 1964-dated 40 percent silver striking is reported but is unlikely as no 40 percent coins were ever struck in Philadelphia.

CLAD COINAGE, 40 PERCENT SILVER

	MS-60	MS-63	MS-65	PF-63	PF-65
1965 .... (65,879,366)	1.20	1.25	9.50	*	*

Mintage includes 2,360,000 for Special Mint Sets. Business strikes produced in Denver, Special Mint Sets in San Francisco Assay Office. SMS substituted for discontinued Proof sets that fell victim to the so-called "coin shortage."

1966 .... (108,984,932)	1.25	1.40	11.00	*	*

Mintage includes 2,261,583 for SMS. A widely publicized over-polished die var. lacks engraver's initials FG on rev.

1967 .... (295,046,978)	1.25	1.50	9.50	*	*

Mintage includes 1,863,344 double-struck coins for Special Mint Sets.

1968-D .... (246,951,930)	1.25	1.50	9.00	*	*
1968-S .... (3,041,506)	*	*	*	2.25	3.00

Proof only.

1969-D .... (129,881,800)	1.20	1.25	7.50	*	*
1969-S .... (2,934,631)	*	*	*	2.25	2.50

Proof only.

Half dollars continued	MS-60	MS-63	MS-65	PF-63	PF-65
1970-D .... (2,150,000)	9.50	10.50	32.00	*	*

Issued only in Mint sets; 2,038,134 sets sold with the remainder believed melted.

1970-S .... (2,632,810)	*	*	*	5.50	8.00

Proof only.

Because of the rising price of silver, vast quantities of common date coins were melted in 1965-80. Other huge amounts were taken off the coin market in $1,000 bags of "junk silver," some to fill silver contracts on the commodities markets. Millions of pieces were melted as silver approached $50 per ounce in January 1980, peak of the silver frenzy. Before silver plunged to $10.80 on March 27, 1980, many coin dealers and collectors had joined the bullion speculators to hoard millions of common date pieces in Uncirculated and Proof conditions. While they will probably never be scarce, it is possible that future numismatists will know these coins only in top grades.

The value of silver coins may be computed by multiplying the daily spot price per ounce of silver by 60 percent. Thus if silver is $5 per ounce, coins should bring about three times face ($5 X .60 = $3.00). Prices will vary somewhat according to locale, quantity and market conditions.

COPPER-NICKEL CLAD COPPER

	MS-60	MS-63	MS-65	PF-63	PF-65
1971 .... (155,164,000)	0.95	1.50	12.00	*	*

New obv. and rev. hubs.

1971-D .... (302,097,424)	0.95	1.25	5.00	*	*
1971-S .... (3,220,733)	*	*	*	1.25	2.00

Proof only.

1972 .... (153,180,000)	1.00	1.50	9.00	*	*
1972-D .... (141,890,000)	1.00	1.50	6.00	*	*
1972-S .... (3,260,996)	*	*	*	1.00	1.50

Proof only.

1973 .... (64,964,000)	1.00	1.50	6.00	*	*
1973-D .... (83,171,400)	0.95	1.25	5.50	*	*
1973-S .... (2,760,339)	*	*	*	1.00	1.25

Proof only.

1974 .... (201,596,000)	0.90	1.00	4.75	*	*
1974-D .... (79,066,300)	0.90	1.00	6.00	*	*
1974-S .... (2,612,568)	*	*	*	0.90	1.10

Proof only.
No 1975-dated half dollars were struck.

KENNEDY, DUAL DATES, BICENTENNIAL REVERSE

Commemorative date, Bicentennial reverse

	MS-60	MS-63	MS-65	PF-63	PF-65
1776-1976 .... (234,308,000)	0.90	1.00	10.00	*	*

Included in 1975 and 1976 Mint sets.

1776-1976-D .... (287,565,248)	0.90	1.00	4.75	*	*

Included in 1975 and 1976 Mint sets.

1776-1976-S .... (6,968,506)	*	*	*	0.80	1.00

Copper-nickel clad, Proof only, included in 1975 and 1976 standard Proof sets.

1776-1976-S .... (4,908,319) .... (3,998,621)	2.75	3.50	6.50	3.00	4.00

40 Percent silver Unc., included in three-piece Uncirculated or Proof sets.

Net mintages represent official sales figures for three-piece Uncirculated and Proof sets. Original mintages 11 and 4 million respectively, balance melted.

1776-1976
No mint mark, 40 percent silver, Proof only; see quarters.

KENNEDY, PRESIDENTIAL SEAL/EAGLE REVERSE RESUMED

	MS-60	MS-63	MS-65	PF-63	PF-65
1977 .... (43,598,000)	1.10	1.40	6.75	*	*
1977-D .... (31,449,106)	1.10	1.40	6.00	*	*
1977-S .... (3,236,798)	*	*	*	0.90	1.35

Proof only.

1978 .... (14,350,000)	1.05	1.40	6.50	*	*

Half dollars continued

	MS-60	MS-63	MS-65	PF-63	PF-65
1978-D .... (13,765,799)	1.00	1.25	6.50	*	*
1978-S .... (3,120,285)	*	*	*	0.90	1.00
Proof only, Type I S, blurry and often filled.					
1979 .... (68,312,000)	0.95	1.00	5.50	*	*
1979-D .... (15,815,422)	0.95	1.15	6.00	*	*
1979-S .... (3,677,175)	*	*	*	0.75	1.00
Proof only, Type I S, blurry, same as 1978.					
1979-S					
Proof only, Type II S, clear and sharp, same as 1980. Found on approximately one coin out of nine					
1980-P .... (44,134,000)	0.90	1.00	5.00	*	*
1980-D .... (33,456,449)	0.90	0.95	4.75	*	*
1980-S .... (3,554,806)	*	*	*	1.00	1.50
Proof only.					
1981-P .... (29,544,000)	1.00	1.40	5.00	*	*
1981-D .... (27,839,533)	0.95	1.40	4.50	*	*
1981-S .... (4,063,083)	*	*	*	1.00	1.50
Proof only, minor vars. of Mint mark style exist.					
1982-P .... (10,819,000)	1.10	1.65	5.00	*	*
1982-P	7.00	10.00	——		*
Missing designer's initials FG.					
1982-D .... (13,140,102)	1.25	1.65	5.00	*	*
1982-S .... (3,857,479)	*	*	*	0.90	1.10
Proof only.					
1983-P .... (34,139,000)	1.05	1.35	——	*	*
1983-D .... (32,472,244)	1.05	1.35	5.00	*	*
1983-S .... (3,279,126)	*	*	*	1.50	2.50
Proof only.					
1984-P .... (26,029,000)	1.25	1.45	5.00	*	*
1984-D .... (26,262,158)	1.25	1.45	——	*	*
1984-S .... (3,065,110)	*	*	*	2.50	4.00
Proof only.					
1985-P .... (18,706,962)	1.25	1.50	5.00	*	*
1985-D .... (19,814,034)	1.25	1.50	5.00	*	*
1985-S .... (3,362,821)	*	*	*	1.65	2.20
Proof only.					
1986-P .... (13,107,633)	2.75	3.00	9.00	*	*
1986-D .... (15,366,145)	3.25	3.35	7.00	*	*
1986-S .... (3,010,497)	*	*	*	8.00	12.00
Proof only.					
1987-P .... (2,890,758)	2.15	3.00	9.00	*	*
Issued only in Mint sets and Uncirculated souvenir sets sold at the Mint.					
1987-D .... (2,890,758)	2.15	3.00	9.00	*	*
Issued only in Mint sets and Uncirculated souvenir sets sold at the Mint.					
1987-S .... (3,792,233)	*	*	*	1.75	2.25
Proof only.					
1988-P .... (13,626,000)	0.90	1.00	9.00	*	*
1988-D .... (12,000,096)	1.00	1.35	6.00	*	*
1988-S .... (2,600,618)	*	*	*	2.50	3.50
Proof only.					
1989-P .... (24,542,000)	1.00	1.25	9.00	*	*
1989-D .... (23,000,216)	0.90	1.10	9.50	*	*
1989-S .... (3,220,914)	*	*	*	2.00	3.75
Proof only.					
1990-P .... (22,278,000)	0.90	1.10	15.00	*	*
1990-D .... (20,096,242)	0.90	1.10	——	*	*
1990-S .... (3,299,559)	*	*	*	5.00	8.00
Proof only.					
1991-P .... (14,874,000)	0.90	1.10	7.00	*	*
1991-D .... (15,054,678)	0.90	1.10	11.00	*	*
1991-S .... (2,867,787)	*	*	*	7.00	12.50
Proof only.					
1992-P .... (17,628,000)	0.90	1.10	6.00	*	*
1992-D .... (17,000,106)	0.90	1.10	6.00	*	*
1992-S .... (2,858,903)	*	*	*	6.00	13.50
Proof only.					
1992-S .... (1,317,641)	*	*	*	5.50	13.00
90% silver, struck for inclusion in special Proof sets.					
1993-P .... (15,510,000)	0.90	1.10	10.00	*	*
1993-D .... (15,000,006)	0.90	1.10	9.00	*	*
1993-S .... (2,569,882)	*	*	*	5.50	13.00
Proof only.					

Half dollars continued

	MS-60	MS-63	MS-65	PF-63	PF-65
1993-S .... (790,994)	*	*	*	7.00	18.50
90% silver, struck for inclusion in special Proof sets.					
1994-P .... (NR)	0.90	1.10	6.00	*	*
1994-D .... (NR)	0.90	1.10	6.00	*	*
1994-S .... (NR)	*	*	*	4.75	10.00
Proof only.					
1994-S .... (NR)	*	*	*	5.75	14.50
90% silver, struck for inclusion in special Proof sets.					
1995-P .... (NR)	0.90	1.10	8.00	*	*
1995-D .... (NR)	0.90	1.10	6.00	*	*
1995-S .... (NR)	*	*	*	4.75	11.00
Proof only.					
1995-S .... (NR)	*	*	*	5.00	11.50
90% silver, struck for inclusion in special Proof sets.					
1996-P	0.90	1.10	9.00	*	*
1996-D	0.90	1.10	6.00	*	*
1996-S Clad	*	*	*	4.75	10.00
Proof only.					
1996-S silver	*	*	*	5.25	11.50
90% silver, struck for inclusion in special Proof sets.					
1997-P	0.90	1.10	9.00	*	*
1997-D	0.90	1.10	6.00	*	*
1997-S Clad	*	*	*	4.50	7.00
Proof only.					
1997-S silver	*	*	*	5.25	11.00
90% silver, struck for inclusion in special Proof sets.					

Silver dollars

FLOWING HAIR

FAIR - Identifiable
G- No details: date, letters legible.
VG - Main details legible, deeply worn.
F- Hair ends and top hairlines visible.
VF - Most details, hairlines, etc., clear.
EF - All details sharp.
AU - Slight wear on highest points only. Must have partial Mint luster.

Flowing Hair; Small Eagle

	G-4	F-12	VF-20	EF-40	AU-50
1794 .... (1,758)	7500.	24000.	36500.	62500.	105000.

Single die var., Bolender-1, always weakly struck at left on both sides. One of the Lord St. Oswald Unc. pieces sold by Superior in 1972 at $110,000; its companion, Norweb MS-60/63, $242,000, Nov. 1988.

	G-4	F-12	VF-20	EF-40	AU-50
1795 .... (160,295)	675.	1475.	2000.	4450.	7250.

Rev. shows two leaves below each wing, B-1, 2, 4, 13. B-1 obv. shows 7 punched over an earlier 1, first blundered die in the silver dollar series. This date is sometimes found with central plug as made by the Mint, apparently the result of an attempt to raise the weight of otherwise useless lightweight planchets. Eliasberg 4/97: B-18 EF-45 $52,800; B-2 MS-65 $93,500.

1795
Wide dates, six vars.

1795
Close dates, four vars.

Three Leaves below wing

	G-4	F-12	VF-20	EF-40	AU-50
1795	650.	1350.	1800.	4350.	7000.

Three leaves below each wing, several vars. Eliasberg 4/97: B-7 MS-63 $61,600; B-5 MS-62 $77,000.

DRAPED BUST, SMALL EAGLE

Draped Bust, Small Eagle

		G-4	F-12	VF-20	EF-40	AU-50
1795	(42,738)	590.	1050.	1550.	3300.	6900.

Mintage figure probably includes some of earlier type. Major obv. vars. show Bust placed too far left (B-14) and properly centered (B-15). Eliasberg 4/97 B-14 MS-67 $308,000.

1796	(72,920)	675.	1150.	1600.	3400.	7300.

Small date, small letters, B-1-3.

1796		625.	1075.	1575.	3350.	6950.

Large date, small letters, B-5, excessively rare in Unc.

1796		590.	1000.	1500.	3300.	6900.

Small date, large letters, B-4, 6, excessively rare in Unc.

1797	(7,776)	485.	950.	1450.	3250.	6350.

15 stars: 9 left, rev. large letters, B-1. Rare, very rare in Unc. Eliasberg 4/97 B-1 MS-60 $52,800.

1797		1150.	2350.	3250.	7500.	17500.

Similar obv., small letters rev., B-2. Rare, very rare in Unc.

1797		485.	950.	1450.	3200.	6250.

16 stars, 10 left, 6 right, B-3, large letters. Rare in Unc. Eliasberg 4/97 B-3 MS-63 $176,000.

1798	(327,536)	675.	1200.	1900.	4000.	11000.

13 stars, B-1, 1797 rev. die. Extremely rare in Unc. Mintage includes Heraldic Eagle revs.

1798		825.	1800.	2350.	4500.	13500.

15 stars, obv. is an uncompleted 1796-97 die with last digit omitted. This rev. die used in 1795, 1796 and 1797. B2, excessively rare in Unc.

DRAPED BUST, HERALDIC EAGLE

G - Letters, date legible. Motto worn off.
VG - Partial motto, few deep details.
F - Drapery lines visible, some hairlines show.
VF - Most details show but left side of drapery is smooth.
EF - All details sharp.
AU - Slight wear on highest points only. Must have some Mint luster.
UNC - No wear visible anywhere, full Mint luster.

Heraldic Eagle

		G-4	F-12	VF-20	EF-40	AU-50
1798		370.	530.	775.	1200.	3200.

13 stars, Knob 9, several vars., five berries, arrows vary from 10 to 13, the bundles often include headless sticks. The first two Heraldic Eagle reverse used, BB-91 and BB-92, have five lines in vertical stripes; later ones have four.

Silver dollars continued

	G-4	F-12	VF-20	EF-40	AU-50

1798
  13 stars, pointed 9, several vars., five berries, arrows vary from 10 to 13, the bundles often include headless sticks. Rev. of B-8 is the only one with four berries. Eliasberg 4/97 B-27 MS-61 $33,000.

1799/8 .... (423,515) .... 395. 545. 785. 1350. 3500.
  13 stars on reverse, B-1-2. Extremely rare in Unc. Eliasberg 4/97 MS-63 $77,000.

1799/8
  15 stars on rev., B-3. Only the points of two extra stars protrude from enlarged first and last clouds, blundered die.

1799 .... 370. 530. 775. 1200. 3150.
  Obv. 7 + 6 stars. Rev. 13 stars. Several vars., usually with large berries. However, B-11, 12 have no berries; B-15 has small berries (rare) and B-17 has extra large berries. Eliasberg 4/97 B-10 MS-64 $77,000.

1799
  Obv. 7 + 6 stars, rev. 15 stars, B-4. Extremely rare in Unc.

1799 .... 415. 615. 825. 1500. 3650.
  Obv. 8 + 5 stars, B-23, excessively rare in Unc.

1800 .... (220,920) .... 380. 530. 780. 1225. 3200.
  Most show 13 arrows except B-17 which has 10. B.12 has smaller berries than usual. Eliasberg 4/97 B-8 MS-63 $46,200.

1800 .... 395. 540. 785. 1250. 3250.
  AMERICAI reverse shows bold upright raised line suggesting letter I after AMERICA, possibly a fragment of another letter punched by mistake. Eliasberg 4/97 MS-62 $33,000.

1800 .... 395. 540. 800. 1275. 3500.
  The famous "dotted date," B-14, is from a rusted obv. die. Eliasberg 4/97 MS-63 $77,000.

1801 .... (54,454) .... 420. 590. 800. 1800. 3600.
  Mintage figure probably includes many dated 1800. Very rare in Unc. Eliasberg 4/97 MS-62 $55,000.

1802/1 .... (41,650) .... 380. 540. 785. 1500. 3650.
  Narrow and wide overdate varieties.

1802 .... 395. 540. 780. 1250. 3200.
  Narrow and wide Normal date vars.

1803 .... (85,634) .... 380. 535. 780. 1275. 3550.
  Mintage figure includes 19,570 recorded struck in 1804. Six vars., incl. large and small 3. Very rare in Unc. Eliasberg 4/97 B-6 MS-62 $35,200.

1804 DOLLARS AND ASSOCIATED RESTRIKES

No silver dollars bearing the date 1804 were actually struck in that year. High quality die steel was scarce, and as was standard procedure, serviceable older obverse dies dated 1803 or perhaps earlier were used to strike the dollars produced early in 1804. If production had continued and these dies had worn out, it is probable that new dies actually dated 1804 might eventually have been engraved.

The new American silver dollars failed to circulate in this country. Instead they were exported in quantity by bullion dealers and exchanged in the West Indies for heavier Spanish colonial 8 reales for shipment to the Philadelphia Mint for recoinage into silver dollars. This profitable "perpetual chain" led to suspension of silver dollar coinage in mid-1804, a situation continued by order of President Thomas Jefferson in 1806. Such dollars already struck were duly recorded in the Mint Report for 1804, and the silver dollar disappeared from the American monetary scene for 32 years. The gold $10 eagle was also discontinued at this time for the same reasons, although a number of 1804-dated eagles had actually been struck in that year.

Then in 1834, the Department of State requested of the Mint several Proof sets containing "specimens of each kind now in use, whether of gold, silver or copper" to be presented as gifts by diplomatic missions then being sent to governments in the Near and Far East.

Interpreting this request literally, Mint Director Samuel Moore included specimens of the silver dollar and eagle bearing the last date in which they had been reported struck, 1804. The sets, containing nine 1834-dated and two 1804-dated coins, were then taken abroad for the Sultan of Muscat, the King of Siam and the Emperors of Vietnam and Japan.

Four additional dollars were kept by the Mint, and one was used by Jacob R. Eckfeldt and William E. DuBois to illustrate their controversial *Manual of Gold and Silver Coins of All Nations, Struck within the Past Century*. This triggered Matthew Stickney's interest in the coin, inducing the wealthy New England numismatist to trade a number of exotic rarities for a specimen of the coveted dollar in 1843.

By the late 1850s this coin was recognized by the growing collector community as a major American rarity. The Mint had long sold its extras, and now prepared to strike some more. The 1804 obverse made in 1834 was still available, but the reverse was now missing and a new one was produced.

Before the Mint could proceed with its plans, however, its young night watchman Theodore Eckfeldt struck several pieces and sold them to Philadelphia area coin dealers including Dr. Montroville W. Dickeson. Son of the chief coiner and member of a family long associated with the Mint, young Eckfeldt had been hawking other clandestine strikes for some time.

Lacking the skill to letter the edges of his planchets, Eckfeldt made do with plain edges on his "second restrikes." These edges excited suspicion and one buyer reported the situation to Mint officials. Anxious to conceal their own plans to restrike 1804 dollars, these officials quietly repurchased all the extant plain edge pieces and reported them destroyed.

In fact, the coins thus recovered remained in a Mint vault for nearly 20 years, after all but one of the recovered dollars were disguised by having edge lettering added. This single piece, having been obviously struck over a cut-down 1857 Swiss shooting taler of Canton Bern, was left undisturbed as the sole surviving "Class II" 1804 dollar.

The altered-edge "Class III" pieces were sold by Mint officials at $1,000 or more each, often with false attestations of their "original" status. The full story of the 1804 dollar and other related restrikes appears in *The Fantastic 1804 Dollar* by Eric P. Newman and Kenneth E. Bressett, and in an update published in the American Numismatic Society's *America's Silver Coinage, 1794-1891*, 1987.

Proof restrikes of dollars dated 1801, 1802 and 1803 were made after the 1804 dollars revealed the possibilities of such a restrike program. With widely varying weights, mixtures of modern and old-style numerals and striking characteristics, they entered the numismatic market only in 1876 through a leading Mint "insider," coin dealer William Idler.

1801 .... (4 to 6 known)
    Proof restrike, die crack links base of digits to first two stars, B-6.
1802 .... (6 to 10 known)
    Proof restrike with old-style 180, 1820s style 2 in date.
1803 .... (6 to 10 known)
    Proof restrike with old-style digits.

U.S. Mint specimen (Smithsonian)

1804 .... (8 known)
    "Class I," beware of altered 1800 and 1801 coins, cast copies and electrotypes. A VF specimen, stolen from Willis H. DuPont in 1967, was recovered and subsequently donated to the American Numismatic Association Museum in Colorado Springs in 1995. Eliasberg 4/97 Prf-63 $1,815,000.

Silver dollars continued

1804 ....(1 known)
"Class II," plain edge Theodore Eckfeldt specimen, struck over a cut-down 1857 Bern shooting taler. Electrotypes exist; Dr. Charles Spiers obtained his directly from William E. DuBois at the Mint; it was long exhibited by the Society of California Pioneers museum as genuine, despite the word COPY under the right claw.

Class III, Adams-French specimen
(Stack's)

1804 ....(6 known)
"Class III" with lettered edge applied long after their clandestine striking. The Linderman/James Ten Eyck specimen, stolen from Willis H. DuPont in 1967, was recovered in 1981 after it was identified by ANACS Senior Authenticator Thomas K. DeLorey, when presented for authentication at ANA headquarters. This coin was donated to the Smithsonian in January 1995.

SEATED LIBERTY, FLYING EAGLE

For more than a century, confusion surrounded the Seated Liberty-Flying Eagle dollars dated 1836-1839. Several plain and reeded edge varieties are known in silver and copper, as are pieces with the artist's signature in different locations.

Known to be either patterns or restrikes are 1836 dollars with relief letters C. GOBRECHT F., "Christian Gobrecht made it," in the field between the base of Liberty and the date. These are known with the eagle flying against a background of 26 stars or against a plain background.

Plain edge, 1836-dated coins with C. GOBRECHT F. incised on the base and the starry reverse have been shown by R.W. Julian to have been circulation strikes, released through the Bank of the United States. A tiny 1839-dated issue of 300 Proofs without reverse stars is now also recognized as having been released to normal circulation.

Listed here are only those Seated Liberty dollars struck in silver that research has indicated were placed in circulation. Similar coins of 1836-39 in various metals and design variations will be found under patterns.

It is believed that original strikes will show the eagle flying upward into the sky if the coin is carefully rotated on its horizontal axis (Julian's Die Alignment I) or if the coin is rotated along its vertical axis (Die Alignment II). Restrikes will show the eagle flying horizontally if similarly rotated (Die Alignments III (horizontal axis) and IV (vertical axis). For an alternate view on this theory, see the section on Patterns.

To numismatists, the Mint's decision to discard the bold Flying Eagle in favor of the hackneyed spread eagle that was a dreary feature of the minor coinage represents one of the real tragedies of the 19th century silver coinage.

C. GOBRECHT F. on Base, Die
Alignment I, Stars, plain edge

	AU-50	PF-60	PF-63	PF-64	PF-65
1836 ....(1,000)	6350.	7500.	15000.	20000.	50000.

C. GOBRECHT F. incised on base, rev. eagle flying upward into a starry sky, plain edge, weight 416 grains (26.96 grams). Proofs without evidence of handling are very rare. Die Alignment I.

Silver dollars continued	AU-50	PF-60	PF-63	PF-64	PF-65
1836 .... (600)	7250.	9000.	18500.	30000.	65000.

As preceding, but Die Alignment II, weight 412.5 grains (26.73 grams), rarer than preceding in unimpaired Proof.

| 1839 .... (300) | — | 9500. | 20000. | 39500. | — |

Reeded edge, weight of last, generally in worn condition. Die Alignment I.

SEATED LIBERTY, SPREAD EAGLE

VG - Most of 3 letters of LIBERTY visible.
F - LIBERTY full but weak.
VF - All details visible but worn.
EF - All details sharp.
AU - Slight wear on highest points only. Must show some Mint luster.
UNC - No wear anyplace, full Mint luster.
PROOF- High rims, mirror-like fields, frosted devices. Letter surfaces flat, not rounded, and show some double striking.

Seated Liberty, Spread Eagle

	G-4	F-12	EF-40	AU-50	MS-60
1840 .... (61,005)	175.	225.	425.	675.	2400.

Proof restrikes exist for all dates 1840-53.

| 1841 .... (173,000) .... | 90.00 | 170. | 300. | 525. | 2000. |

Some Proofs exhibit smaller stars from over-polished obverse die.

1842 .... (184,618)	87.50	160.	265.	450.	1000.
1843 .... (165,100)	87.50	160.	285.	550.	2050.
1844 .... (20,000)	180.	290.	475.	800.	3100.

Business strikes from doubled obv. die with quadruple stripes, very rare in Unc.

| 1845 .... (24,500) .... | 175. | 260. | 450. | 785. | 15000. |

Proofs have 84 strongly repunched. Eliasberg 4/97 Prf-65/66 $99,000.

| 1846 .... (110,600) .... | 88.00 | 165. | 320. | 475. | 1450. |

Some Proofs have date strongly repunched at bottom, often mistaken for 1846/1845. Eliasberg 4/97 Ms-65 $46,200.

1846-O .... (59,000)	135.	255.	475.	1200.	5000.
1847 .... (140,750)	87.50	155.	280.	435.	1400.
1848 .... (15,000)	275.	425.	650.	1175.	4650.

Very rare in Unc. Eliasberg 4/97 Prf-64/65 $30,800.

| 1849 .... (62,600) .... | 120. | 200. | 375. | 575. | 2100. |

Early die state "Whiskers" pieces show die file marks under chin. Eliasberg 4/97 Prf-64 $44,000.

| 1850 .... (7,500) .... | 325. | 575. | 1100. | 1900. | 5500. |

Open or closed 5 vars., rare in any grade. Seated Liberty dollar researcher Weimar White believes no MS-65 may exist. Eliasberg 4/97 Prf-64 $33,000.

| 1850-O .... (40,000) .... | 175. | 300. | 1300. | 3250. | 13000. |
| 1851 .... (1,300) .... | | | | | |

High date original is very rare in Unc. Centered date Proof restrike extremely rare, 10-30 known, Norweb Proof-63, $17,600. Original MS-60 $17500. MS-63 $31000. MS-65 $80000. Restrike Proof 63 $29000. One restrike from a third die pair on a previously struck dollar shows a ghost of an O Mint mark from the host coin.

| 1852 .... (1,100) | | | | | |

Very rare in any grade; 10 to 40 restrike Proofs may exist. AU-55 $13000. MS-60 $18000. MS-63 $32500. MS-65 $70000.

| 1853 .... (46,110) .... | 140. | 275. | 510. | 750. | 2450. |
| 1854 .... (33,140) .... | 725. | 1250. | 3550. | 4500. | 6150. |

Dollars 1854-57 always found softly struck on head and parts of eagle, rare in Unc. Eliasberg 4/97 Prf-64 $33,000.

| 1855 .... (26,000) .... | 625. | 1025. | 2950. | 3700. | 8000. |

Proofs less rare than full Unc.

Silver dollars continued

	G-4	F-12	EF-40	AU-50	MS-60
1856 .... (63,500)	250.	400.	1275.	1700.	3950.

Another die-file "whiskers" var. is known; so-called 1856/4 shows a line across loop of 6, extremely rare.

1857 .... (94,000)	245.	385.	1150.	1450.	2300.
1858 .... (80)	*	2900.	4250.	5000.	5500.

Proof only

1859 .... (256,500) .... (800)	225.	325.	525.	1175.	3150.

Same remarks as 1855.

1859-O .... (360,000)	85.00	140.	265.	390.	925.

Comparatively common in Unc. due to three original bags released from Treasury Department hoards ca. 1963.

1859-S .... (20,000)	240.	385.	1075.	3400.	8000.

Very rare in Unc., repunched S var. extremely rare.

1860 .... (217,600) .... (1,330)	165.	285.	435.	540.	1400.
1860-O .... (515,000)	85.00	140.	265.	385.	900.

Comparatively common in Unc. due to six original bags released from Treasury Department hoards ca. 1963.

1861 .... (77,500) .... (1,000)	500.	725.	1250.	1800.	2850.

New rev. hub, as on following.

1862 .... (11,540) .... (550)	475.	675.	1000.	1700.	3100.
1863 .... (27,200) .... (460)	200.	350.	750.	1300.	2550.
1864 .... (30,700) .... (470)	190.	325.	625.	1400.	2800.
1865 .... (46,500) .... (500)	175.	300.	565.	1100.	2650.
1866 .... (two known)	—	—	*	*	*

Fantasy coin struck by Mint for private purpose. See comments under quarters, one piece stolen from Willis H. DuPont, never recovered.

SEATED LIBERTY WITH MOTTO ABOVE EAGLE

	Motto Above Eagle				
	G-4	F-12	EF-40	AU-50	MS-60
1866 .... (48,900) .... (725)	155.	265.	485.	900.	1750.
1867 .... (46,900) .... (625)	160.	280.	510.	950.	2150.

Some proofs have large date over small date.

1868 .... (162,600) .... (600)	150.	240.	450.	925.	2000.
1869 .... (423,700) .... (600)	120.	220.	355.	850.	1550.
1870 .... (415,000) .... (1,000)	100.	165.	325.	510.	1225.

1870-S

No official record exists of this coinage, which was not issued for normal circulation. Apparently struck as souvenirs of the laying of the cornerstone of the second San Francisco Mint. Approximately 12 pieces are known, Norweb AU-50, $126,500, Nov. 1988. James A. Stack, ST 3/95 prooflike Unc. $420,000 +10%; Eliasberg 4/97 EF-45/AU-50 $264,000.
See also 1870-S half dime and $3.

1870-CC .... (12,462)	260.	445.	1450.	2750.	9000.

Lower grade pieces are scarce, excessively rare in MS-65. Numismatist John Kroon identified four rev. Mint mark vars. in *Gobrecht Journal* 1982; a fifth has surfaced since.

1871 .... (1,073,800) .... (960)	95.00	155.	270.	500.	1150.

Comparatively common Unc. due to two bags in Treasury Department hoards released ca. 1963.

1871-CC .... (1,376)	1650.	3650.	7500.	17500.	—

Very rare in any grade, beware added CC. Eliasberg 4/97 AU-58 $25,850.

1872 .... (1,105,500) .... (950)	92.50	155.	275.	500.	1175.

Comparatively common Unc. due to Treasury Department hoards released ca. 1963.

1872-S .... (9,000)	225.	380.	1300.	2700.	9750.

Only really collectible With Motto S-Mint dollar, rare in Unc., excessively rare in MS-65.

1872-CC .... (3,150)	750.	2050.	4400.	8500.	30000.

Rare in any grade, very rare Unc. and excessively rare in MS-65. Beware added CC.

Silver dollars continued

	G-4	F-12	EF-40	AU-50	MS-60
1873 .... (293,000) .... (600)	115.	225.	300.	575.	1200.
1873-S .... (700)					

No example is known in any grade; all are believed melted, if indeed ever struck.

| 1873-CC .... (2,300) .... | 3250. | 6750. | 18000. | 33500. | — |

Most elusive CC dollar, very rare in any grade. Beware added CC. AU-58 $39,600.

MORGAN

VF - Well defined ear, most hairlines show. Eagles breast feathers worn.

EF - All details sharp.

AU - Slight wear on highest points only; must show some Mint luster.

UNC - No wear at all anywhere; full Mint luster.

PROOF - High rims, mirror-like fields, frosted devices. Letter surfaces flat, not rounded, and show some evidence of double striking.

Prooflike Morgan dollars, a prized category of the Morgan series, must not be confused with true Proofs. The result of "basining" of the slightly convex dies with a zinc lap, they exhibit a deep mirror surface and relief frosting, but not the squared rims or lettering of a true Proof.

Morgan's Liberty

	VF-20	EF-40	AU-50	MS-60	MS-65
1878 .... (749,500) .... (500)	20.00	24.00	32.00	65.00	900.
Type I: 8 feathers in eagle's tail. Eliasberg 4/97 Prf-67 $35,200.					
1878 .... (9,759,050)	21.00	28.00	45.00	75.00	1850.
7 over 8 feathers. Several vars. showing differing amounts of the original feathers behind the seven. Numismatist Bill Fivaz has suggested the description "7 over various feathers".					
1878 .... (500)	16.00	17.00	20.00	34.00	925.
7 feathers. Type II: Rev. of 1878, with parallel feathers on the arrows.					
1878	14.00	15.00	23.00	45.00	1900.
Type III: Rev. of 1879 on, with slanting feathers on the arrows. Proofs exist of both types, the latter rare.					
1878-S .... (9,774,000)	13.00	14.00	16.00	24.00	170.
All Type II rev.					
1878-CC .... (2,212,000)	39.00	48.00	56.00	85.00	850.
All Type II rev., small CC.					
1879 .... (14,806,000) .... (1,100)	11.00	12.00	14.00	19.00	625.
1879-O .... (2,887,000) .... (12)	12.50	14.00	20.00	70.00	2450.
Large and medium O varieties. Large O Proofs were struck to commemorate the reopening of the New Orleans Mint.					
1879-S .... (9,110,000)	15.00	17.00	35.00	95.00	4650.
Small S, Type II rev. of 1878.					
1879-S	11.00	12.00	15.00	18.00	105.
Medium S, Type III rev. (normal)					
1879-CC .... (756,000)	120.	325.	750.	1350.	12500.
Large CC.					
1879-CC	120.	300.	600.	1275.	14000.
Large CC over Small CC, very unappreciated variety, usually discounted due to engraver's marks meant to obliterate smaller CC.					
1880/79 .... (12,600,000) .... (1,355)					
Several varieties, some rare.					
1880	10.50	11.00	13.00	18.00	700.
Normal date, represents most of year's mintage.					
1880-O 80/79					
Several varieties some rare.					
1880-O .... (5,305,000)	10.00	12.50	18.00	62.50	13500.
Small O.					

Silver dollars continued

	VF-20	EF-40	AU-50	MS-60	MS-65

1880
    Medium O.
1880 8/7-S
    Several varieties, none rare. A reported 1880/1-S is apparently a misattributed 1880/9-S, VAM-11.

	VF-20	EF-40	AU-50	MS-60	MS-65
1880-S .... (8,900,000)	10.00	13.00	15.00	19.00	105.

    Large S as on Trade dollars.
1880-S
    Medium S.
1880/79-CC .... (591,000)
    Small CC, Rev. of 1878, eagle's breast flat, VAM-4.
1880 8/7-CC
    Varieties exist, VAM 5 and 6 strongest. Small CC. Rev. of 1879. Underdate less plain on VAM 8 and 10.

	VF-20	EF-40	AU-50	MS-60	MS-65
1880-CC	72.00	95.00	135.	180.	1550.

    Small CC, Rev. of 1878, traces of underdate 8/7 VAM-7.

	VF-20	EF-40	AU-50	MS-60	MS-65
1880-CC	72.00	95.00	125.	155.	500.

    Large CC, Rev. of 1879. VAM 3 and 9.

	VF-20	EF-40	AU-50	MS-60	MS-65
1881 .... (9,163,000) .... (975)	10.00	12.00	14.00	20.00	625.
1881-O .... (5,708,000)	10.00	12.00	14.00	17.00	1150.
1881-S .... (12,760,000)	10.00	11.00	14.00	17.00	105.

    Medium S only, used until 1900.

	VF-20	EF-40	AU-50	MS-60	MS-65
1881-CC .... (296,000)	125.	130.	145.	170.	375.

    A variety with second 8/7 is reported, not confirmed.

	VF-20	EF-40	AU-50	MS-60	MS-65
1882 .... (11,100,000) .... (1,100)	10.00	11.00	14.00	17.00	550.

    Several varieties with 2/1 reported, not confirmed.

	VF-20	EF-40	AU-50	MS-60	MS-65
1882-O .... (6,090,000)	10.00	11.00	14.00	17.00	550.

    Several varieties with 2/1 reported, not confirmed.

	VF-20	EF-40	AU-50	MS-60	MS-65
1882-O/S	20.00	23.00	55.00	150.	—

    Varieties exist.

	VF-20	EF-40	AU-50	MS-60	MS-65
1882-S .... (9,250,000)	10.00	12.00	15.00	18.00	110.
1882-CC .... (1,133,000)	42.00	52.00	55.00	72.00	250.

    Very common in Unc. from GSA sale.

	VF-20	EF-40	AU-50	MS-60	MS-65
1883 .... (12,290,000) .... (1,039)	10.00	11.00	14.00	17.50	135.
1883-O .... (8,725,000) .... (12)	9.50	12.00	13.00	16.00	125.
1883-S .... (6,250,000)	14.00	23.00	100.	375.	23500.

    Eliasberg 4/97 MS-66 $137,500.

	VF-20	EF-40	AU-50	MS-60	MS-65
1883-CC .... (1,204,000)	42.00	46.00	50.00	72.00	195.

    Very common in Unc. from GSA sale.

	VF-20	EF-40	AU-50	MS-60	MS-65
1884 .... (14,070,000) .... (875)	10.00	11.00	14.00	17.00	210.

1884
    Raised dot just right of engraver's initial M on both sides. Vars. exist.

	VF-20	EF-40	AU-50	MS-60	MS-65
1884-O .... (9,730,000)	9.50	11.00	12.00	16.00	105.

    Oval and round O varieties.

	VF-20	EF-40	AU-50	MS-60	MS-65
1884-S .... (3,200,000)	16.00	34.00	195.	3200.	110000.

    Very rare in Unc., beware added Mint marks.

	VF-20	EF-40	AU-50	MS-60	MS-65
1884-CC .... (1,136,000)	42.00	48.00	50.00	72.00	195.

    Very common in Unc. from GSA sale.

	VF-20	EF-40	AU-50	MS-60	MS-65
1885 .... (17,786,837) .... (930)	9.50	11.00	12.00	16.00	120.
1885-O .... (9,185,000)	9.50	11.00	12.00	17.00	105.
1885-S .... (1,497,000)	15.00	19.00	50.00	100.	1450.
1885-CC .... (228,000)	165.	175.	185.	200.	435.
1886 .... (19,963,000) .... (886)	9.50	11.00	12.00	16.00	105.
1886-O .... (10,710,000)	13.00	16.00	65.00	325.	23000.

    Very rare in Unc. or prooflike. Eliasberg 4/97 MS-64 $143,000.

	VF-20	EF-40	AU-50	MS-60	MS-65
1886-S .... (750,000)	33.00	45.00	65.00	135.	1950.
1887 .... (20,290,000) .... (710)	9.50	11.00	12.00	16.00	105.
1887/6	25.00	42.00	90.00	175.	3900.

    Do not confuse with next.
1887
    Repunched 87, earlier digits visible below tops.

	VF-20	EF-40	AU-50	MS-60	MS-65
1887-O .... (11,550,000)	11.00	12.50	21.00	31.00	3850.
1887/6-O	27.00	48.00	120.	310.	16500.

    Do not confuse with next.
1887-O
    Repunched 1887, final digits punched to left.

	VF-20	EF-40	AU-50	MS-60	MS-65
1887-S .... (1,771,000)	15.00	18.00	32.00	67.50	2600.
1888 .... (19,183,000) .... (832)	9.50	12.50	13.00	17.00	140.
1888-O .... (12,150,000)	10.00	12.00	15.00	17.00	375.

    Oval and round O vars.
1888-O
    Doubled die obv., especially bold at lips, unknown in Unc.

Silver dollars continued

	VF-20	EF-40	AU-50	MS-60	MS-65
1888-S .... (657,000)	28.00	36.00	63.00	120.	3000.
1889 .... (21,726,000) .... (811)	10.00	11.50	12.00	17.00	275.
1889-O .... (11,875,000)	11.00	14.00	29.00	80.00	3900.
Oval and round O varieties.					
1889-S .... (700,000)	25.00	31.00	50.00	115.	1075.
1889-CC .... (350,000)	440.	950.	2550.	6850.	80000.
Beware added Mint marks. Eliasberg 4/97 MS-66 $462,000.					
1890 .... (16,802,000) .... (590)	10.00	12.00	14.00	17.00	2600.
1890-O .... (10,701,000)	10.00	12.50	21.00	30.00	1550.
1890-S .... (8,230,373)	11.00	12.00	21.00	34.00	700.
1890-CC .... (2,309,041)	40.00	55.00	90.00	200.	3850.
1891 .... (8,693,556) .... (650)	10.50	11.00	21.00	40.00	4900.
1891-O .... (7,954,529)	11.00	14.50	32.00	80.00	5100.
1891-S .... (5,296,000)	11.00	13.50	21.00	38.00	1150.
1891-CC .... (1,618,000)	40.00	55.00	85.00	145.	2100.
Eliasberg 4/97 MS-66 $121,000.					
1892 .... (1,036,000) .... (1,245)	13.50	19.00	60.00	120.	2700.
Extremely rare in Gem.					
1892-O .... (2,744,000)	12.00	17.00	48.00	85.00	5000.
1892-S .... (1,200,000)	42.00	185.	1300.	12000.	75000.
Eliasberg 4/97 MS-67 $132,000.					
1892-CC .... (1,352,000)	75.00	110.	210.	400.	3750.
1893 .... (389,000) .... (792)	85.00	115.	195.	325.	4500.
1893-O .... (300,000)	120.	195.	485.	1450.	87500.
Eliasberg 4/97 MS-66 $176,000.					
1893-S .... (100,000)	1675.	3550.	11500.	24500.	260000.
Classic rarity of the series, beware added Mint marks. Norweb MS-65, $357,500, Nov. 1988. Eliasberg 4/97 MS-65/67 $198,000					
1893-CC .... (677,000)	185.	450.	750.	1300.	35000.
1894 .... (110,000) .... (972)	300.	350.	550.	1025.	18000.
Beware removed Mint mark.					
1894-O .... (1,723,000)	38.00	50.00	150.	625.	32500.
1894-S .... (1,260,000)	48.00	105.	210.	400.	3600.
1895 .... (880)	13500.	14500.	16000.	17000.	30000.
Unknown except in Proof, sometimes circulated. Beware of altered dates and removed Mint marks. Norweb Proof-65, $33,000, Nov. 1988. Traditionally, 12,000 business strikes were reported issued, but none are known to exist, and indeed none may ever have been struck. Eliasberg 4/97 Prf-67 $71,500.					
1895-O .... (450,000)	170.	250.	965.	9250.	110000.
Eliasberg 4/97 MS-66/67 $253,000.					
1895-S .... (400,000)	215.	480.	700.	1450.	17500.
1896 .... (9,976,000) .... (762)	10.00	11.00	12.00	16.00	145.
Various repunched dates, sometimes misattributed as overdates.					
1896-O .... (4,900,000)	14.50	19.50	110.	850.	72500.
Medium O, oval (rare) or round.					
1896-O					
Small O, intended for fractional silver, rare.					
1896-S .... (5,000,000)	44.00	175.	385.	750.	7000.
1897 .... (2,822,000) .... (731)	11.00	13.00	14.00	21.00	250.
1897-O .... (4,004,000)	13.00	21.00	95.00	600.	31500.
1897-S .... (5,825,000)	10.50	12.50	21.00	35.00	425.
1898 .... (5,884,000) .... (735)	10.00	11.75	12.50	18.00	165.
1898-O .... (4,440,000)	14.00	15.00	16.00	19.00	115.
1898-S .... (4,102,000)	16.50	24.00	60.00	135.	1275.
1899 .... (330,000) .... (846)	35.00	43.00	60.00	70.00	500.
1899-O .... (12,290,000)	11.50	12.00	13.00	18.00	120.
Large O.					
1899-O					
Small O, as in 1896, scarce.					
1899-S .... (2,562,000)	18.00	30.00	65.00	140.	1100.
Medium S as in 1879-1900 and large, wide S as used 1899-1904.					
1900 .... (8,830,000) .... (912)	10.00	11.50	13.00	17.00	145.
Old hub and new reverse hub introduced late in year.					
1900					
Doubled die rev., rare.					
1900-O .... (12,590,000)	11.00	11.50	14.00	17.00	130.
Large O, old hub only.					
1900-O					
Small O as in 1896, old hub, rare.					
1900-O/CC	35.00	47.50	95.00	180.	1075.
Struck from rev. dies salvaged from Carson City, vars. exist.					

Silver dollars continued

	VF-20	EF-40	AU-50	MS-60	MS-65
1900-S .... (3,540,000)	19.00	29.00	48.00	95.00	1050.

Old hub with either S; new hub with large S only.

	VF-20	EF-40	AU-50	MS-60	MS-65
1901 .... (6,962,000) .... (813)	30.00	59.00	250.	1800.	130000.

Old and new hubs, very rare Choice or Gem.

1901
Doubled die rev. most obvious at tail feathers, rare.

	VF-20	EF-40	AU-50	MS-60	MS-65
1901-O .... (13,320,000)	10.00	11.00	14.00	17.00	200.

Old and new hubs.

	VF-20	EF-40	AU-50	MS-60	MS-65
1901-S .... (2,284,000)	27.50	47.50	125.	275.	2700.

Old and new hubs, large S.

	VF-20	EF-40	AU-50	MS-60	MS-65
1902 .... (7,994,000) .... (777)	11.00	12.50	21.00	37.50	445.

New hub only.

	VF-20	EF-40	AU-50	MS-60	MS-65
1902-O .... (8,636,000)	11.00	12.00	13.50	17.00	125.

Large O, new hub.

1902-O
Small O as in 1896, old hub, rare.

	VF-20	EF-40	AU-50	MS-60	MS-65
1902-S .... (1,530,000)	60.00	85.00	115.	160.	2500.

New hub only, large S.

	VF-20	EF-40	AU-50	MS-60	MS-65
1903 .... (4,652,000) .... (755)	15.00	18.00	20.00	29.00	170.
1903-O .... (4,450,000)	120.	130.	150.	155.	315.

A classic rarity destroyed by sudden release of bags of dollars from Treasury vaults, value fell in 1962 from $1,500 to around $15 per coin.

	VF-20	EF-40	AU-50	MS-60	MS-65
1903-S .... (1,241,000)	65.00	285.	900.	2450.	6000.

Large S, rare Unc.

1903-S
Small S intended for fractional silver, rare.

	VF-20	EF-40	AU-50	MS-60	MS-65
1904 .... (2,788,000) .... (650)	12.00	17.00	32.00	67.50	2150.
1904-O .... (3,720,000)	11.00	12.50	14.00	17.00	120.

Almost always softly struck.

	VF-20	EF-40	AU-50	MS-60	MS-65
1904-S .... (2,304,000)	40.00	185.	500.	900.	6250.

New hubs, lower relief, minute Mint marks

	VF-20	EF-40	AU-50	MS-60	MS-65
1921 .... (44,690,000)	8.50	8.75	9.00	10.50	125.

Completely new obv. and rev. hubs, in lower relief. Generally softly struck, especially around the eye. An unknown number of low quality Proofs exist, supposedly made for ANA spokesman Farran Zerbe, Norweb Proof-65, $8,250, Nov. 1988; 12 Proofs of far greater quality were supposedly struck for coin dealer Henry Chapman. Recently discovered evidence indicates that Mint Engraver George T. Morgan may have made these Proofs as a private business venture. Eliasberg 4/97 ex Zerbe Prf-66 $14,300.

	VF-20	EF-40	AU-50	MS-60	MS-65
1921-D .... (20,345,000)	8.50	8.75	10.00	22.00	225.

Always poorly struck.

	VF-20	EF-40	AU-50	MS-60	MS-65
1921-S .... (21,695,000)	8.50	8.75	10.00	22.50	1100.

Always poorly struck. Proof strikings reported; an ambiguously cataloged Proof-65 in Superior Galleries' sale of the "Wayne Miller Collection," realized $7,700 in Jan. 1986.

PEACE

VF - Hair lines strong over ear, worn over eye. Some eagle feathers show top and outside right wing.
EF - All details strong.
AU - Slight wear on highest point. Some Mint luster.
UNC - No wear at all, full Mint luster.

Peace, high relief

	VF-20	EF-40	AU-50	MS-60	MS-65
1921 .... (1,006,473)	40.00	48.00	82.00	130.	1700.

Concave fields, heavy letters, 3 berries on branch and 22 rays. Very rare in Matte or Satin finish Proof, authentication recommended. Norweb Matte Proof-65, $46,200, Nov. 1988; Stack's, Dec. 1994, Gem Matte Proof, $55,000.

1922

Type of 1921, Proof only, some circulated. Very rare, Norweb Matte Proof-65, $35,200, Nov. 1988.

	VF-20	EF-40	AU-50	MS-60	MS-65
1922 .... (51,737,000)	7.85	8.00	8.50	10.50	140.

Flat fields, light letters, 4 berries on branch, 25 rays as on all that follow. Three Satin finish Proofs reported.

	VF-20	EF-40	AU-50	MS-60	MS-65
1922-D .... (15,063,000)	8.25	8.75	10.00	17.50	500.
1922-S .... (17,475,000)	8.00	8.50	10.50	18.50	2000.
1923 .... (30,800,000)	7.85	8.00	9.00	10.75	135.
1923-D .... (6,811,000)	8.25	8.50	13.50	28.50	1500.
1923-S .... (19,020,000)	8.25	8.75	10.75	19.00	5000.
1924 .... (11,811,000)	7.85	8.00	8.50	11.00	145.
1924-S .... (1,728,000)	11.50	15.00	47.00	145.	5900.
1925 .... (10,198,000)	8.00	8.75	9.50	11.50	150.
1925-S .... (1,610,000)	10.00	11.50	25.00	48.00	9500.
1926 .... (1,939,000)	9.00	10.50	17.00	22.00	335.
1926-D .... (2,348,700)	9.25	12.50	26.00	48.00	550.
1926-S .... (6,980,000)	8.00	9.75	16.50	30.00	950.
1927 .... (848,000)	18.00	22.50	31.00	48.00	2500.
1927-D .... (1,268,900)	17.00	25.00	65.00	120.	4400.
1927-S .... (866,000)	17.00	22.00	55.00	95.00	6400.
1928 .... (360,649)	135.	145.	155.	180.	2850.

Beware removed Mint mark.

	VF-20	EF-40	AU-50	MS-60	MS-65
1928-S .... (1,632,000)	17.00	18.00	37.00	90.00	13000.

Large and small S varieties.

Modified obverse

	VF-20	EF-40	AU-50	MS-60	MS-65
1934 .... (954,057)	16.00	20.00	32.50	62.50	1150.

Modified obverse design, as on following.

Silver dollars continued

	VF-20	EF-40	AU-50	MS-60	MS-65
1934-D .... (1,569,500)	15.00	18.00	30.00	75.00	1650.
Large and small D varieties.					
1934-D					
Doubled die obv. Rare.					
1934-S .... (1,011,000)	45.00	130.	410.	1000.	6000.
Beware added Mint mark.					
1935 .... (1,576,000)	13.00	16.00	24.00	42.00	640.
1935-S .... (1,964,000)	14.00	19.00	65.00	120.	975.
1935-S					

New reverse hub. Four rays below ONE.

1964-D .... (316,076)
Conventional wisdom holds that these were struck at the Denver Mint in May 1965, and some sold to Mint employees but not otherwise released. At least one well-placed Mint employee denies the tale, and indicates there may be some confusion with the release of the then-new 1964 Kennedy half dollars. Nevertheless, most numismatists believe at least a few 1964 Peace dollars exist.

EISENHOWER, MOON LANDING REVERSE

Dwight D. Eisenhower, Moon Landing reverse

	MS-60	MS-63	MS-65	PF-63	PF-65
1971 .... (47,799,000)	2.75	3.00	95.00	*	*
Copper-Nickel clad.					
1971-D .... (68,587,424)	2.25	2.50	21.00	*	*
Copper-Nickel clad.					
1971-S .... (6,868,530) .... (4,265,234)	3.50	4.00	12.00	3.00	4.00
Silver-clad.					
1972 .... (75,890,000)	2.25	2.50	180.	*	*
Copper-Nickel clad.					
1972-D .... (92,548,511)	2.25	2.75	45.00	*	*
Copper-Nickel Clad.					
1972-S .... (2,193,056) .... (1,811,631)	3.50	4.00	9.00	3.25	4.00
Silver-Clad.					
1973 .... (2,000,056)	3.50	4.00	50.00	*	*
Copper-Nickel clad, issued only in Mint Sets. 1,769,258 sets sold, balance melted.					
1973-D .... (2,000,000)	3.50	4.00	42.00	*	*
Copper-Nickel clad, issued only in Mint Sets.					
1973-S .... (2,760,339)	*	*	*	3.50	4.00
Copper-Nickel clad, Proof only.					
1973-S .... (1,883,140) .... (1,013,646)	3.75	4.00	9.00	10.00	11.50
Silver-clad.					
1974 .... (27,366,000)	2.00	2.50	50.00	*	*
Copper-Nickel clad.					
1974-D .... (45,517,000)	2.00	2.50	18.00	*	*
Copper-Nickel clad.					
1974-D					
40 percent silver error striking, rare. Published in Coin World, Oct. 1974.					
1974-S .... (2,612,568)	*	*	*	3.50	4.00
Copper-Nickel clad, Proof only.					
1974-S .... (1,900,156) .... (1,306,579)	3.50	3.75	8.00	4.25	4.75
Silver-clad.					

No 1975-dated dollars were struck.

EISENHOWER, DUAL DATES, BICENTENNIAL REVERSE

Variety I: thick letters reverse, first U of UNUM almost under first U of PLURIBUS.
Variety II: Thin letters reverse, first U of UNUM centered under LU of PLURIBUS. Obverse changes not
as obvious.

		Commemorative date, Bicentennial reverse			
	MS-60	**MS-63**	**MS-65**	**PF-63**	**PF-65**
1776-1976 .... (4,019,000)	3.00	3.50	95.00	*	*
Var. I, included in 1975 Mint Sets.					
1776-1976 .... (113,318,000)	2.25	2.50	70.00	*	*
Var. II, included in 1976 Mint Sets.					
1776-1976-D .... (21,048,710)	2.50	2.75	39.00	*	*
Var. I, included in 1975 Mint Sets.					
1776-1976-D .... (82,179,564)	2.25	2.50	13.00	*	*
Var. II, included in 1976 Mint Sets.					
1776-1976-D					
40 percent silver striking, very rare. Authentication recommended.					
1776-1976-S .... (2,845,450)	*	*	*	3.50	5.50
Copper-nickel clad, Var. I, included in 1975 Proof sets.					
1776-1976-S .... (4,123,056)	*	*	*	3.50	4.25
Copper-nickel clad, Var. II, included in 1976 Proof sets.					
1776-1976-S .... (4,908,319) .... (3,998,621)	7.00	7.50	16.00	6.50	8.00
Var. I, 40 percent silver.					

Net mintages represent official sales figures for three-piece Uncirculated and Proof sets. Original
mintages 11 and 4 million respectively, balance melted. (Note: Three-piece Unc. sets packaged 1975-
76 were given special handling and have a broad, white coding stripe along one of the long edges.
Sets packaged in later years without the stripe were made up from coins struck at high speeds and
dumped in bags in the rush to meet the striking deadline for the 40 percent silver issues. Despite the
fact that these mass-produced pieces were officially condemned on the day they were made due to
indifferent strikes and excessive bag marks, they were used to make up sets in the early 1980s, once
the original production run was finally sold out.)

1776-1976
No Mint mark. Var. I, 40 percent silver, Proof only. Struck under the same circumstances as no Mint
mark quarter and half dollar, which see. Not to be confused with following.

1776-1976
No Mint mark. Var. II, 40 percent silver, Proof only. Unique? One lightly impaired Proof known,
reportedly discovered in a cash register at Woodward and Lothrup Department Store in Washington,
D.C. in mid-1977. Weight 383.25 grains, vs 350 grs. for copper-nickel clad. See *Coin World,* June 7,
1978, p. 21. Reason for and location of striking unknown, though presumably a "trial piece" like the
Var. I No Mint Mark Proof.

EISENHOWER, MOON LANDING REVERSE RESUMED

1977 .... (12,596,000)	2.25	2.50	29.00	*	*
1977-D .... (32,983,006)	2.25	2.50	18.00	*	*
1977-D					
40 percent silver error striking, very rare.					
1977-S .... (3,236,798)	*	*	*	3.25	3.75
Proof only.					
1978 .... (25,702,000)	2.25	2.50	30.00	*	*
1978-D .... (33,012,890)	2.25	2.50	18.00	*	*
1978-S .... (3,120,285)	*	*	*	3.25	4.00
Proof only.					

SUSAN B. ANTHONY

	MS-60	MS-63	MS-65	PF-63	PF-65
Susan B. Anthony					
1979-P .... (360,222,000)	1.15	1.75	9.00	*	*
Normal date.					
1979-P	3.50	7.00	25.00	*	*
So-called "Near Date" variety with date nearer the rim has commanded a premium in the recent past.					
1979-D .... (288,015,744)	1.15	1.75	9.00	*	*

	MS-60	MS-63	MS-65	PF-63	PF-65
Mint mark varieties					
1979-S .... (109,576,000) .... (3,677,175)	1.20	1.75	6.00	3.00	3.75
Proof, Type I S, blurry, same as 1978-S Eisenhower dollar.					
1979-S .... (included above)	*	*	*	45.00	53.00
Proof only, Type II S, clear, same as 1980. Found on approximately one coin out of nine.					
1980-P .... (27,610,000)	1.15	1.75	9.00	*	*
1980-D .... (41,628,708)	1.15	1.75	9.00	*	*
1980-S .... (20,422,000) .... (3,554,806)	1.20	1.75	6.00	3.00	3.50
1981-P .... (2,908,145)	3.00	4.00	75.00	*	*
Issued only in Mint Sets.					
1981-D .... (2,908,145)	2.50	2.75	30.00	*	*
Issued only in Mint Sets.					
1981-S .... (2,908,145) .... (4,063,083)	2.65	3.00	260.	3.00	4.00
Uncs. Issued only in Mint Sets.					
1981-S	*	*	*	40.00	50.00
Clear S, Proof only.					

TRADE DOLLARS

VG - Half of both mottoes show, rims well defined.
F- Full but worn mottoes.
VF - All details legible but show wear.
EF - All details sharp.
AU - Slight wear on highest points only; must show some Mint luster.
UNC - No wear at all, full Mint luster.
PROOF - See Morgan Dollars.

	VF-20	AU-50	MS-60	MS-65	PF-65
Trade dollars					
1873 .... (396,635) .... (863)	135.	210.	660.	7000.	6600.

Most 1873-4 issues, from all three Mints, went to China and were eventually chop-marked and/or melted. Eliasberg 4/97 Prf-66 $23,100.

1873-S .... (703,000) .... 140. 315. 750. 13000. *
1873-CC .... (124,500) .... 300. 900. 1500. 17500. *
Small CC only.
1874 .... (987,100) .... (700) 135. 215. 715. 12500. 6500.
1874-S .... (2,549,000) .... 115. 210. 400. 15000. *
Large (rare), medium and small (scarce) S vars.
1874-CC .... (1,373,200) .... 160. 375. 1150. 15500. *
Large and small CC vars.
1875 .... (218,200) .... (700) 350. 700. 1250. 13000. 6400.
Type I, rev. hub of 1873-76: berry under claw above 900, narrow berries, broad leaves. Type II, rev.
hub of 1875-1885: no berry under claw, larger, round berries, narrow leaves. Type I scarce on this
issue.
1875-S .... (4,487,000) .... 115. 195. 380. 6000. *
Small and large S vars, both on Type I and II revs.; Small S, Type II combination scarcest.
1875-S/CC .... 385. 1150. 2000. 16000. *
Always with rev. die breaks at right, very rare.
1875-CC .... (1,573,700) .... 135. 325. 785. 14500. *
Type II rev. hub rare, large CC only.
1876 .... (455,000) .... (1,150) 115. 205. 390. 6250. 6375.
Scarce from Type I rev. hub. Always seen with Type I obv.
1876-S .... (5,227,000) .... 115. 210. 400. 8250. *
Large S. Type I obv. and rev. only.
1876-S
Small S. Normally found with Type I obv. and Type II rev. Rarely found with Type I obv. and rev.
1876-S
Small S, Type II obv. (hub of 1876-85); LIBERTY repositioned on ribbon, RT apart at tops, lower ends of
ribbon extended downwards. Type II rev. only.
1876-S
Doubled die obv., extremely rare.
1876-CC .... (509,000) .... 155. 500. 2500. 20000. *
All from Type I obv. hub. Type I rev. with either large or small CC rare. Type II rev. with Large CC
normal. Eliasberg 4/97 MS-66 $63,800.
1876-CC
Doubled rev. die, Type I, large CC, rare.
1877 .... (3,039,200) .... (510) 115. 250. 425. 14500. 6300.
Type II obverse and reverse only, as on following.
1877-S .... (9,519,000) .... 115. 205. 395. 7000. *
Large and small (rare) S vars.
1877-CC .... (534,000) .... 240. 600. 1475. 19500. *
Large CC only.
1878 .... (900) 875. 1150. * * 6350.
Proof only.
1878-S .... (4,162,000) .... 115. 210. 415. 5900. *
Large and medium S vars.
1878-CC .... (97,000) .... 875. 3050. 6000. 67500. *
Large CC only.
1879 .... (1,541) 800. 1100. * * 6050.
Proof only.
1880 .... (1,987) 750. 1050. * * 6000.
Proof only.
1881 .... (960) 875. 1100. * * 6100.
Proof only.
1882 .... (1,097) 875. 1125. * * 6150.
Proof only.
1883 .... (979) * * * * 6200.
Proof only.
1884 .... (10) * * 45000. * 400000.
Numismatist Carl W.A. Carlson has demonstrated that the dies for proof 1884 Trade Dollars were
routinely produced and recorded in the *Die Record Book* kept by A.W. Straub of the U.S. Mint, since
donated by Stack's to the National Numismatic Collection at the Smithsonian. Stack's Floyd T. Starr,
Oct. 1992, Gem Proof $160,000; Eliasberg 4/97 Prf-66 $396,000.
1885 .... (5) * * 175000. * 900000.
Privately struck for distribution by Mint officials. Norweb Proof-60 to 63, $121,000, Mar. 1988;
Eliasberg 4/97 Prf-65 $907,500.

Gold Coinage

From 1795 to 1933, the United States Mint struck 353,545,358 gold coins with an approximate face value of $4.256 billion. Data today indicates that less than $300 million in face value gold coinage is still in existence.

This attrition can be laid to fluctuations of gold prices relative to silver from 1795 to 1804 and after 1849, as well as the hoarding and export of coins in wartime and business panics. By far the most massive destruction of this numismatic heritage followed President Franklin D. Roosevelt's Executive Order of April 5, 1933, ordering surrender of gold coin and notes by May 1 of that year.

While "gold coins having a recognized special value to collectors of rare and unusual coins" were exempted from the general surrender, millions of other coins were turned in to be melted en masse into featureless ingots of precious metal later immured in the Fort Knox Bullion Depository.

Mint reports reveal that by June 30, 1954, of 174,105,606 double eagles or $20 gold pieces minted, some 67,856,029 or 39 percent had been melted by the Mint; of 57,683,485 eagles, 21,423,342 pieces or 37 percent were melted; of 78,911,869 half eagles minted, 27,539,662 or 35 percent melted; of 20,426,833 quarter eagles minted, 3,123,311 or 15.4 percent melted.

Three dollar gold pieces totals show 539,792 minted, 6,441 or just a bit more than 1 percent melted. One-dollar gold coins show 19,874,754 minted, 29,343 or 1.46 percent melted. These totals, of course, record only official meltings, ignoring additional destruction by private bullion speculators over the years.

When gold coinage began in 1795, its basic unit was to be the .917 fine gold eagle or $10 piece, accompanied by the half eagle of $5 and the quarter eagle, $2.50. This system mirrored the silver progression of 25 cents, 50 cents and one dollar. Robert Scot's Liberty facing right in a tall, fez-like hat of the early Federal era appeared on the first gold pieces struck.

The first quarter eagles presented this Liberty without a circle of stars; the earliest half eagles and eagles added a varying number of stars on their obverses. As many as 16 stars were crowded onto these larger coins before the number 13 was fixed for both historic and practical reasons.

Although the 15:1 ratio between gold and silver was tolerably correct when formulated in 1790, the next decade brought a steady increase in the market price of gold. By 1800, gold coins had already begun to disappear from circulation. In 1805 eagle coinage was suspended. This was followed, in 1809, by a 12-year suspension of quarter eagles.

Capped Head, Capped Bust of the same fineness, and .8992 fine Classic head coinage followed at rather irregular intervals and usually in small quantities. The discovery of large gold deposits in Georgia and the Carolinas during the mid-1820s brought a great deal of gold to the Mint despite the adverse ratio, and resulted finally in a revaluation of the two metals under the act of June 8, 1834.

A minor adjustment was made under the Mint Act of Jan. 18, 1837, fixing the fineness of gold coinage at an even .900. Christian Gobrecht's long-lived Coronet Liberty coins with their spread eagle reverse began in 1838 for the eagle, 1839 for the half eagle and 1840 for the quarter eagle. The motto IN GOD WE TRUST was added to the larger coins in 1866 and coinage continued into the next century.

The tremendous gold finds in California made possible the authorization of gold dollars and double eagles under the act of March 3, 1849. A $3 gold piece was included in the Feb. 21, 1853, bill authorizing reduced weight, arrows at date silver coinage.

This new coin had no other use than in purchasing 100 3-cent pieces or 100 3-cent stamps, and did not fit in smoothly with the normal decimal progression. Despite its unpopularity, the $3 was issued in small quantities through 1889.

Like the silver issues, gold coins disappeared from circulation during the early days of the Civil War, and were not seen again until after the resumption of specie payments in 1876. The Coronet Head gold, even more than the Liberty Seated silver, seemed destined to continue on forever.

Until the early 1900s, all gold coin designs were the work of U.S. Mint engravers. In 1905, however, the energetic President Theodore Roosevelt intervened forcefully to seek an artistic standard comparable to that of the ancient Greeks for the nation's coinage.

World-renowned American sculptor Augustus Saint-Gaudens was commissioned to redesign the eagle and double eagle, but due to the petty jealousy of Chief Engraver Charles E. Barber, many obstacles were placed in the way of this program.

Saint-Gaudens' first double eagle models were in extremely high relief, and dies made from them required nine blows on a hydraulic press to fully strike up a single coin. Several pairs of modified dies had to be made before production could begin, and the beauty of the original double eagle models suffered drastic reworking, emerging tragically emasculated from this process.

The new Indian eagle bore an eagle in profile from the Theodore Roosevelt Inaugural medal by Adolph Alexander Weinman. A similar eagle would grace the new half and quarter eagles, the work of Boston sculptor Bela Lyon Pratt. Bearing a craggy, gaunt Indian in feathered headdress on their obverses, Pratt's imaginative coins featured devices in normal relief, but recessed below the level of the fields.

This return to an ancient Egyptian concept called incuse-relief was advanced by Dr. William Sturgis Bigelow, a close friend of President Roosevelt. A knowledgeable collector, Bigelow was influenced by the "1837" Bonomi pattern crown of Queen Victoria, actually struck in similar incuse-relief style for her 1887 Golden Jubilee for antiquarian J. Rochelle Thomas.

Pratt's new coins were savagely criticized by many, including the vindictive Samuel H. Chapman, Philadelphia coin dealer and narrow-minded traditionalist, whose allegations included the charge that the incuse areas would be "a great receptacle for dirt and a conveyor of disease, and the coin will be the most unhygienic ever issued." In fact, the new coins were a success and were issued until 1929 without decimating the population.

Gold coinage ceased in 1933 and strenuous efforts were made to relegate gold to the status of a "barbarous relic," a term beloved of Keynesian economists. Fortunately, large holdings of double eagles and other denominations in Swiss and other European banks preserved quantities of U.S. gold coins from the official vandalism under way on this side of the Atlantic.

Until December 31, 1974, gold ownership by American citizens was severely restricted. A separate bureaucracy was created to police gold, often expressing itself in seizures from museum and private collections. Since that date, gold returned to the headlines and to the investment portfolios of millions of Americans.

Gold commemorative coins returned in 1984, and since 1986 a series of gold bullion coins bearing the troy weights of one, one-half, one-quarter and one-tenth ounces has been struck bearing a variant of Saint-Gaudens' striding Liberty with a "family of eagles" reverse by Texas sculptor Miley Busiek. These bullion coins bore Roman numeral dates from MCMLXXXVI (1986) through MCMLXCI (1991), after which the more familiar (Arabic) dates began with 1992.

This series was patterned closely after the very successful South African Krugerrand and Canadian Maple Leaf bullion coins, but given nominal face values of $50, $25, $10 and $5. Numismatists have criticized these denominations as having no relationship to historic American coinage.

In 1997 the United States Mint began striking and selling platinum bullion coins, of the same sizes and weights as the gold American Eagles, but with denominations of $100, $50, $25 and $10.

Gold coin condition guide

Except for rarities, gold coins are usually collected in grades from Fine to Proof. When grading gold coins, be sure to inspect the edges for signs of loop removal, and the surfaces for the peculiar mottled effect that contact with the salts in human skin leaves, as well as other signs of restoration and repairs. A sizeable percentage of gold coins appearing on the market these days has been used as jewelry.

FINE - All details appear on the coin, with the exception of the most minute. Surfaces may be marked and edges slightly banged.

VF - Every detail is apparent on coin though the smallest will be blurred in spots. Field and edge damage will be less pronounced.

EF - All details will be sharp, though some signs of wear will be visible on the high points. Fields and edges will be mostly unmarred.

AU - Very slight wear will be detectable only on the highest points. Fields and edges should be virtually perfect, and the coin will show some Mint luster.

UNC - Full Mint luster will be present, and no wear at all will be detectable. Fields and edges will show nothing other than normal slight bag marks.

PROOF - Rim is high and sharp and letter surfaces are flat, not rounded. Fields are mirror-like and portrait and devices are frosted in some coins. Letters are usually slightly doubled.

MATTE PROOF - Has all the characteristics of above except that the entire coin surface is rough from either sand-blasting or chemical treatment of the planchet prior to striking.

Gold dollars

CORONET LIBERTY HEAD

TYPE I

Coronet, Open Wreath (Smithsonian)

	VF-20	EF-40	AU-50	MS-60	MS-65
1849 .... (1,000)	150.	215.	285.	750.	8000.

Variety 1: small head, coronet points midway between two stars, no L on truncation, open wreath.

Gold dollars continued

	VF-20	EF-40	AU-50	MS-60	MS-65
1849 .... (687,567)	140.	160.	205.	360.	7450.

Variety 2: small head, L on truncation, open wreath. Usually with concave obv. field, wire edge.

	VF-20	EF-40	AU-50	MS-60	MS-65
1849	140.	160.	200.	350.	6250.

Variety 3: large head, coronet points closer to star above it, open wreath. Varieties with heavy and thin dates.

	VF-20	EF-40	AU-50	MS-60	MS-65
1849	140.	155.	190.	335.	7250.

Variety 4: large head, closed wreath, branches end very close to numeral. Rare with thin date.

1849-C

	VF-20	EF-40	AU-50	MS-60	MS-65
1849-C .... (11,634)	225000.	—	—	—	—
Variety 3, open wreath, five known. Stack's June 1986, VF, $25,850.					
1849-C	525.	1100.	2750.	8400.	—
Variety 4: closed wreath, scarce. ST Jan. 1995 BU $15,500.					
1849-D .... (21,588)	500.	800.	1300.	4350.	41500.
Variety 3 only.					
1849-O .... (215,000)	165.	210.	325.	1050.	18000.
Variety 3 only.					
1850 .... (481,953)	150.	160.	180.	355.	8250.
1850-C .... (6,966)	650.	1300.	2500.	10000.	—
1850-D .... (8,382)	615.	1275.	2600.	11250.	—
1850-O .... (14,000)	290.	400.	800.	3750.	27500.
1851 .... (3,317,671)	140.	155.	175.	330.	5850.
1851-C .... (41,267)	490.	775.	975.	2300.	30000.
1851-D .... (9,882)	505.	950.	2000.	5350.	41000.
Among the rarest Dahlonega dollars. ST James A. Stack March 95, CH. AU $1,980.					
1851-O .... (290,000)	165.	225.	265.	675.	16500.
1852 .... (2,045,351)	140.	155.	175.	330.	5950.
1852-C .... (9,434)	500.	1050.	1950.	5000.	41000.
1852-D .... (6,360)	575.	1350.	2200.	8000.	—
1852-O .... (140,000)	170.	235.	430.	1500.	26500.
1853 .... (4,076,051)	140.	155.	175.	330.	5800.
1853-C .... (11,515)	535.	1025.	1900.	6000.	—
1853-D .... (6,583)	590.	1400.	2700.	9000.	70000.
1853-O .... (290,000)	160.	190.	275.	700.	14000.
1854 .... (855,502)	140.	155.	175.	330.	7000.
1854-D .... (2,935)	900.	2100.	4650.	15500.	—
1854-S .... (14,632)	350.	490.	650.	2300.	28000.

INDIAN HEAD

LARGE SIZE, TYPE II

Large planchet, Small Indian Head

	VF-20	EF-40	AU-50	MS-60	MS-65
1854 .... (783,943) .... (5)	325.	390.	600.	2500.	42500.

This and other dates of this type are usually weakly struck on the rev. at the 8 and LL. One variety (1854) has a triple row of beads above Liberty, the result of a hubbing error.

	VF-20	EF-40	AU-50	MS-60	MS-65
1855 .... (758,269)	325.	390.	590.	2500.	41000.
1855-C .... (9,803)	1300.	2600.	5750.	19000.	—

The Harold Bareford specimen was believed the only known Unc., but this date is now unknown in strict Mint State, excessively rare in AU. ST March 1995 AU $3,080.

Gold dollars continued

	VF-20	EF-40	AU-50	MS-60	MS-65
1855-D .... (1,811)	2400.	5250.	8750.	30000.	——
Excessively rare in Unc., extremely rare in EF and AU.					
1855-O .... (55,000)	385.	675.	1075.	5400.	——
1856-S .... (24,600)	675.	1050.	1750.	5900.	——
1856-S					
Repunched S, not as rare as sometimes asserted.					

LARGE INDIAN HEAD, TYPE III

Large Indian Head

	VF-20	EF-40	AU-50	MS-60	MS-65
1856 .... (33,660)	140.	165.	300.	650.	5750.
Upright 5.					
1856 .... (1,729,276)	130.	145.	170.	265.	2300.
Slanting 5.					
1856-D .... (1,460)	3750.	5000.	7150.	34000.	——
U of UNITED is always weak, O in DOLLAR filled.					
1857 .... (774,789)	130.	145.	170.	260.	2250.
1857-C .... (13,280)	525.	1350.	3950.	12250.	——
1857-D .... (3,533)	900.	1800.	4000.	11750.	——
Excessively rare in Unc.					
1857-S .... (10,000)	385.	575.	1100.	4500.	——
1858 .... (117,995)	130.	160.	185.	270.	3650.
The large letters var. is a pattern.					
1858-D .... (3,477)	650.	1250.	2400.	10000.	82500.
1858-S .... (10,000)	290.	425.	1150.	5250.	——
1859 .... (168,244) .... (80)	140.	160.	190.	270.	3800.
Proofs show repunched date, extremely rare.					
1859-C .... (5,235)	430.	1800.	4000.	19000.	125000.
1859-D .... (4,952)	675.	1250.	2700.	11000.	——
1859-S .... (15,000)	250.	425.	1350.	5850.	——
1860 .... (36,514) .... (154)	145.	165.	195.	435.	4050.
1860-D .... (1,566)	2400.	3850.	5800.	27500.	——
Characteristically weak at U of UNITED.					
1860-S .... (13,000)	250.	350.	550.	2350.	27500.
1860-S					
Inverted S, rare.					
1861 .... (527,150) .... (349)	130.	150.	180.	255.	3500.

1861-D "Confederate" (enlarged)

	VF-20	EF-40	AU-50	MS-60	MS-65
1861-D .... (?)	5750.	8000.	16500.	32000.	225000.
Mintage unknown, all struck for Confederate States of America. Rare in any grade, excessively rare in Unc. ST Nov. 1994 Ch. Unc. $35,000.					
1862 .... (1,361,365) .... (35)	130.	150.	175.	255.	3100.
1862					
Doubled die obv, rare.					
1863 .... (6,200) .... (50)	425.	1000.	2150.	4000.	19500.

Gold dollars continued

	VF-20	EF-40	AU-50	MS-60	MS-65
1864 .... (5,900) .... (50)	315.	335.	525.	1050.	7600.
1865 .... (3,700) .... (25)	375.	425.	575.	1550.	8750.
1866 .... (7,100) .... (30)	315.	375.	415.	800.	5500.
1867 .... (5,200) .... (50)	380.	400.	575.	875.	6000.
1868 .... (10,500) .... (25)	250.	300.	390.	775.	5950.

Doubled date coins are counterfeits.

	VF-20	EF-40	AU-50	MS-60	MS-65
1869 .... (5,900) .... (25)	325.	370.	525.	775.	6250.
1870 .... (6,300) .... (35)	240.	285.	375.	575.	4500.
1870-S .... (3,000)	400.	675.	1100.	2600.	32500.

An estimated 30 or fewer known; mintage figure may include 2,000 struck by error without S Mint mark punched into the dies. ST Oct. 1994 Ch. Unc. $4,700.

	VF-20	EF-40	AU-50	MS-60	MS-65
1871 .... (3,900) .... (30)	240.	280.	355.	550.	4050.
1872 .... (3,500) .... (30)	250.	325.	390.	900.	5750.

ST March 1995 Proof $8,800.

	VF-20	EF-40	AU-50	MS-60	MS-65
1873 .... (1,800) .... (25)	375.	700.	1000.	1950.	22500.

Closed 3, very rare.

	VF-20	EF-40	AU-50	MS-60	MS-65
1873 .... (123,300)	130.	150.	170.	265.	2350.

Open 3. Varieties show word LIBERTY illegible and then missing, the result of progressive wear on the hub. The latter is scarce.

	VF-20	EF-40	AU-50	MS-60	MS-65
1874 .... (198,800) .... (20)	130.	150.	175.	260.	2225.

Like preceding, this comes with LIBERTY visible, illegible and missing. The first is evidently from a new hub used on following.

	VF-20	EF-40	AU-50	MS-60	MS-65
1875 .... (400) .... (20)	2200.	3450.	4500.	5850.	28000.

Beware prooflike business strikes with spine down from chin offered as Proofs.

	VF-20	EF-40	AU-50	MS-60	MS-65
1876 .... (3,200) .... (45)	230.	275.	375.	525.	3650.
1877 .... (3,900) .... (20)	180.	250.	360.	450.	3500.
1878 .... (3,000) .... (20)	190.	270.	350.	500.	3600.
1879 .... (3,000) .... (30)	170.	215.	275.	485.	3550.

Apparently always weakly struck at BER.

	VF-20	EF-40	AU-50	MS-60	MS-65
1880 .... (1,600) .... (36)	140.	155.	175.	235.	2150.
1881 .... (7,620) .... (87)	140.	155.	175.	235.	2175.
1882 .... (5,000) .... (125)	145.	160.	190.	275.	2200.
1883 .... (10,800) .... (207)	140.	155.	175.	235.	2150.
1884 .... (5,230) .... (1,006)	140.	155.	175.	245.	2200.
1885 .... (11,156) .... (1,105)	140.	155.	175.	240.	2175.
1886 .... (5,000) .... (1,016)	140.	155.	185.	270.	3050.

One Var. has a recut 6 and is sometimes mistaken for an overdate.

	VF-20	EF-40	AU-50	MS-60	MS-65
1887 .... (7,500) .... (1,043)	140.	155.	175.	235.	2150.
1888 .... (15,501) .... (1,079)	140.	155.	175.	235.	2125.
1889 .... (28,950) .... (1,779)	140.	155.	175.	235.	2100.

Quarter eagles

CAPPED BUST RIGHT

	Capped Bust, No Obverse Stars			
	F-12	VF-20	EF-40	AU-50	MS-60
1796 .... (963)	10500.	18000.	29500.	51000.	165000.

No obv. stars on obv, 16 stars rev. ST Oct. 1994 AU $75,000.

Quarter eagles continued

16 Stars obverse and reverse

	F-12	VF-20	EF-40	AU-50	MS-60
1796 .... (432)	8750.	13500.	23500.	45000.	115000.
16 stars on obv. and rev.					
1797 .... (427)	8250.	10750.	13000.	27500.	125000.
13 stars obv. 16 stars rev., very rare.					
1798 .... (1,094)	3400.	5050.	9000.	22500.	45000.
13 stars obv. and rev. as on following, compact date and four berries, Mintage includes 480 recorded in the following year.					
1798					
Wide date, 5 berries.					
1804 .... (3,327)	3250.	4150.	5250.	7200.	22500.
14 stars rev.					
1804 .... extremely rare, unknown above EF-40.	16500.	27500.	57500.	115000.	—
13 star rev., extremely rare, unknown above EF-40.					
1805 .... (1,781)	2950.	4200.	5450.	7200.	23500.
1806/4 .... (1,136)	3150.	4100.	5150.	7150.	22500.
Stars 8 + 5.					
1806/5 .... (480)	7000.	14000.	—	—	—
Stars 7 + 6, obv. die previously used in 1805, unverified in strict Unc.					
1807 .... (6,812)	2750.	3900.	5050.	7100.	21000.

CAPPED DRAPED BUST LEFT

Capped Draped Bust

	F-12	VF-20	EF-40	AU-50	MS-60
1808 .... (2,710)	8250.	14000.	20000.	32500.	60000.
Excessively rare in Unc., Norweb EF-40, $39,600, Mar. 1988.					

CAPPED HEAD LEFT
DIAMETER REDUCED

Capped Head

	F-12	VF-20	EF-40	AU-50	MS-60
1821 .... (6,448)	3000.	3425.	4650.	6750.	18750.
Very rare in Unc., Proofs exist in tiny quantities of many dates from now until 1858.					
1824/1 .... (2,600)	2950.	3400.	4550.	5600.	16000.
Very rare in Unc.					
1825 .... (4,434)	2900.	3450.	4450.	5500.	14500.
1826 .... (760)	3650.	4500.	5500.	11000.	37500.
The one obverse known shows vague traces of a possible underdate.					
1827 .... (2,800)	3750.	4450.	5150.	10000.	22500.
Usually flatly struck.					

CAPPED HEAD LEFT, NARROW PLANCHETS, BEADED BORDERS

Narrow planchets, beaded borders

	F-12	VF-20	EF-40	AU-50	MS-60
1829 .... (3,403)	2700.	3250.	4325.	5300.	9500.
1830 .... (4,540)	2800.	3350.	4350.	5350.	9500.
1831 .... (4,520)	2850.	3375.	4400.	5400.	9750.
1832 .... (4,400)	2800.	3350.	4350.	5375.	12000.
1833 .... (4,160)	3050.	3500.	4500.	5600.	13000.
1834 .... (4,000)	6750.	10000.	16500.	26000.	35000.

Plain or crosslet 4 in date, perhaps 11 known, as nearly all were melted before release; perhaps two Proofs exist. The Eliasberg plain 4 was cataloged as MS-60, $16,500, Oct. 1982. ST Oct. 1994 AU $29,000.

CLASSIC HEAD LEFT

NO REVERSE MOTTO

Small Classic Head

	F-12	VF-20	EF-40	AU-50	MS-60
1834 .... (112,234)	200.	260.	400.	625.	1750.

Small Classic head, date distant from curl, roll of curls at back of head straight, continuous. Small and large arrowhead vars., former very rare.

1834

Large Booby head, 4 almost touches curl, two rolls of curls separated behind head.

1835 .... (131,402)	200.	260.	415.	690.	2100.

New hub, head taller than preceding. Mintage includes some 1834.

1836 .... (547,986)	200.	260.	400.	600.	1950.

Booby head of 1834, extended hair ribbon ends, rare. Mintage includes some 1835 coins.

1836

Head of 1835 with unbroken locks behind head, upper ribbon ends barely visible and small forelock close to star 6.

1836

Head of 1837 with slightly more of ribbon end visible, no forelock, hair above headband slopes back more than on preceding.

1837 .... (45,080)	200.	260.	415.	725.	2750.

Mintage includes some 1836.

1838 .... (47,030)	200.	260.	400.	700.	2150.

New head, similar to 1834 Booby head.

1838-C .... (7,880)	575.	1150.	2500.	7000.	30000.

All show repunched C.

1839/838 .... (27,021)	210.	270.	650.	1750.	4750.

Very rare in Unc.

1839/8-C .... (18,140)	475.	900.	1900.	2700.	22500.

Rare in Unc.

1839-C

Recut 39, sometimes confused with overdate.

1839/38-D .... (13,674)	550.	1150.	2150.	4750.	26000.

Excessively rare in Unc.

1839-O .... (17,781)	350.	450.	875.	1500.	5250.

Wide and narrow date vars.

CORONET HEAD, NO MOTTO ON REVERSE

Coronet

	F-12	VF-20	EF-40	AU-50	MS-60
1840 .... (18,859)	160.	350.	775.	3850.	7000.
Usually weakly struck, excessively rare above MS-60.					
1840-C .... (12,822)	355.	675.	1300.	4500.	16500.
1840-D .... (3,532)	800.	2050.	7750.	22500.	——
Unknown in strictly Unc.					
1840-O .... (33,580)	190.	330.	725.	1900.	8000.
Includes mintage recorded for 1841. Usually weakly struck, Large (rare) and small O vars.					

Little Princess

	F-12	VF-20	EF-40	AU-50	MS-60
1841	——	——	65000.	125000.	——
Proof only. Famed "Little Princess," Eliasberg Proof-63, $82,500; ST Oct. 1994 Ch. VF $60,000.					
1841-C .... (10,281)	280.	650.	1200.	3050.	21000.
1841-D .... (4,164)	550.	1200.	2750.	10750.	25500.
1842 .... (2,823)	330.	800.	3100.	——	——
Unknown in Unc., extremely rare in EF.					
1842-C .... (6,729)	575.	1150.	2150.	9500.	20000.
Unknown in Unc., excessively rare in EF.					
1842-D .... (4,643)	650.	1400.	2800.	14000.	——
Unknown in Unc.					
1842-O .... (19,800)	250.	585.	1500.	2950.	16000.
1843 .... (100,546)	145.	160.	230.	400.	1800.
1843-C .... (2,988)	1075.	2000.	4400.	8750.	——
Small date and Mint mark, crosslet 4, rare.					
1843-C .... (23,076)	500.	625.	1075.	3600.	8250.
Large date and Mint mark, plain 4.					
1843-D .... (32,672)	415.	575.	1100.	1950.	8500.
Small D.					
1843-D .... (3,537)					
Large D, very rare.					
1843-O .... (288,002)	155.	190.	265.	425.	1750.
Small date, crosslet 4.					
1843-O .... (76,000)	225.	325.	500.	2750.	9000.
Large date, plain 4, rarer than preceding.					
1844 .... (6,784)	275.	490.	900.	2250.	——
Rare in all higher grades.					
1844-C .... (11,622)	390.	875.	1550.	6500.	——
1844-D .... (17,332)	365.	600.	1175.	1900.	8000.
1845 .... (91,051)	150.	220.	290.	475.	1700.
1845-D .... (19,460)	400.	700.	1200.	2650.	11750.
1845-O .... (4,000)	550.	1150.	2300.	5750.	15000.
Struck in Jan. 1846, not included in Mint report, giving B. Max Mehl a discovery in the 1940s. Still unknown in Unc.					
1846 .... (21,598)	215.	365.	525.	1150.	6400.
1846-C .... (4,808)	575.	950.	2200.	8500.	20500.
Extremely rare in Unc.					
1846-D .... (19,303)	445.	675.	1025.	2600.	11000.
1846-O .... (62,000)	160.	280.	480.	1050.	5850.
1847 .... (29,814)	140.	235.	420.	975.	5500.
1847-C .... (23,226)	420.	590.	1075.	1950.	6500.
1847-D .... (15,784)	430.	650.	1050.	2075.	10750.
1847-O .... (124,000)	150.	275.	445.	1050.	4000.
1848 .... (7,497)	300.	525.	950.	1650.	6250.

Quarter eagles continued

CAL. countermarked above eagle

	F-12	VF-20	EF-40	AU-50	MS-60
1848 CAL .... (1,389)	7000.	9000.	15000.	19000.	32500.

Struck from the first 282 ounces of California gold sent east to Secretary of War William L. Marcy. Some of this metal was used for military medals for Generals Scott and Taylor, the balance coined into quarter eagles countermarked CAL. while each coin rested in the die. Few were handled with care and most existing specimens show signs of handling.

	F-12	VF-20	EF-40	AU-50	MS-60
1848-C .... (16,788)	400.	625.	1300.	2650.	14750.
1848-D .... (13,771)	425.	600.	1150.	2050.	8500.
1849 .... (23,294)	145.	255.	450.	1000.	3100.
1849-C .... (10,220)	410.	700.	1550.	4100.	23000.
1849-D .... (10,945)	430.	725.	1275.	3250.	14500.
1850 .... (252,923)	135.	160.	195.	305.	1250.
1850-C .... (9,148)	325.	775.	1400.	3500.	16500.
1850-D .... (12,148)	375.	700.	1300.	3100.	15000.
1850-O .... (84,000)	160.	250.	350.	1250.	5000.
1851 .... (1,372,748)	135.	150.	180.	215.	370.
1851-C .... (14,923)	350.	700.	1250.	3950.	17000.
1851-D .... (11,264)	400.	700.	1250.	3200.	13500.
1851-O .... (148,000)	145.	165.	325.	975.	5050.
1852 .... (1,159,681)	135.	160.	190.	240.	375.
1852-C .... (9,772)	400.	700.	1450.	4050.	—
1852-D .... (4,078)	485.	1050.	2800.	7500.	22000.
1852-O .... (140,000)	145.	185.	300.	800.	5250.
1852-O					

Heavy O, possibly added to the die at the New Orleans Mint, as the 1854 Huge O would be to the quarter dollar die, very rare.

	F-12	VF-20	EF-40	AU-50	MS-60
1853 .... (1,404,668)	135.	150.	170.	205.	365.
1853/2					

Reported, verification as true overdate unsettled.

	F-12	VF-20	EF-40	AU-50	MS-60
1853-D .... (3,178)	550.	1300.	2300.	4750.	17250.

Excessively rare in Unc.

	F-12	VF-20	EF-40	AU-50	MS-60
1854 .... (596,258)	135.	150.	170.	205.	380.
1854-C .... (7,295)	365.	825.	1800.	4100.	18500.

Always weakly struck.

	F-12	VF-20	EF-40	AU-50	MS-60
1854-D .... (1,760)	1900.	2850.	7000.	14750.	—

Rare in all grades, unknown in Unc.

	F-12	VF-20	EF-40	AU-50	MS-60
1854-O .... (153,000)	150.	200.	250.	425.	1650.
1854-S .... (246)	32500.	57500.	—	—	—

Perhaps a dozen known in low grades, unknown in Unc. Eliasberg VG-8, $7,150, Oct. 1982, Norweb VF-35, $17,600, Mar. 1988.

	F-12	VF-20	EF-40	AU-50	MS-60
1855 .... (235,480)	135.	150.	180.	215.	385.
1855-C .... (3,677)	620.	1350.	3250.	6000.	32500.

Very rare in all grades, unique in Unc.

	F-12	VF-20	EF-40	AU-50	MS-60
1855-D .... (1,123)	1900.	3900.	7750.	21000.	—

Rare in any grade. ST Oct. 1994 AU $21,000.

	F-12	VF-20	EF-40	AU-50	MS-60
1856 .... (384,240)	125.	150.	180.	205.	355.

Possibly two Proofs known.

	F-12	VF-20	EF-40	AU-50	MS-60
1856-C .... (7,913)	490.	900.	2200.	4550.	19000.

Unknown in Unc.

	F-12	VF-20	EF-40	AU-50	MS-60
1856-D .... (874)	3950.	5500.	9250.	19500.	37500.

Very rare in any grade, a very few Uncs. known.

	F-12	VF-20	EF-40	AU-50	MS-60
1856-O .... (21,100)	175.	425.	675.	1350.	7500.
1856-S .... (71,120)	150.	205.	415.	1300.	5850.
1857 .... (214,130)	135.	150.	185.	205.	360.
1857-D .... (2,364)	500.	1000.	2000.	3300.	13250.

Rare in strict Unc.

	F-12	VF-20	EF-40	AU-50	MS-60
1857-O .... (34,000)	155.	180.	350.	1175.	5400.
1857-S .... (69,200)	150.	180.	375.	950.	8250.

Mintage includes 1,200 struck in Jan. '58. Unverified in strictly Unc. Superior Jan. 1994 MS60 $5,638.

	F-12	VF-20	EF-40	AU-50	MS-60
1858 .... (47,377) .... (5?)	135.	155.	220.	350.	1400.

Scarce, 5-6 Proofs known.

	F-12	VF-20	EF-40	AU-50	MS-60
1858-C .... (9,056)	340.	600.	1250.	2950.	10250.

Extremely rare in Unc.

Quarter eagles continued

	F-12	VF-20	EF-40	AU-50	MS-60
1859 .... (39,444) .... (80)	135.	155.	270.	500.	1250.

Type I (large arrowheads) and Type II (small arrowheads) rev. hubs used at Philadelphia this year. After 1861, only Type II used at Philadelphia, although San Francisco Mint thriftily used its old reverses exclusively through 1876. The 80 proofs were all Type I.

	F-12	VF-20	EF-40	AU-50	MS-60
1859-D .... (2,244)	550.	1250.	2350.	4200.	25500.

Type I rev. only, extremely rare in Unc.

1859-S .... (15,200)	225.	500.	825.	2700.	9500.

Type I rev. only.

1860 .... (22,563) .... (112)	135.	155.	255.	475.	1100.

Type II rev. only.

1860-C .... (7,469)	375.	850.	1750.	3700.	26500.

Always weakly struck, Type I rev. only.

1860-S .... (35,600)	195.	300.	700.	1225.	4200.
1861 .... (1,272,428) .... (90)	135.	150.	185.	205.	345.

Type I (rare) and Type II rev.

1861-S .... (24,000)	210.	425.	950.	3750.	—

Type I rev. only.

1862 .... (112,318) .... (35)	140.	170.	255.	500.	1600.
1862/1	600.	1000.	2200.	3500.	12000.

Rare in any grade, very rare EF-AU.

1862-S .... (8,000)	485.	950.	2000.	4250.	20000.
1863 .... (30)					

Proof only. Prf 60 $19000 Prf 63 $37500 Prf 64 $50000.

1863-S .... (10,800)	400.	650.	1700.	4450.	19000.

Always weakly struck, very rare in Unc.

1864 .... (2,824) .... (50)	2750.	5500.	14000.	27500.	—

Unknown in Unc.

1865 .... (1,520) .... (25)	2200.	4250.	8500.	23000.	—
1865-S .... (23,376)	180.	285.	625.	1600.	5750.

Excessively rare in Unc.

1866 .... (3,080) .... (30)	650.	1350.	3500.	7000.	16500.

Unknown in Unc.

1866-S .... (38,960)	195.	325.	950.	1950.	9750.
1867 .... (3,200) .... (50)	200.	385.	575.	1400.	3600.
1867-S .... (28,000)	190.	270.	600.	1650.	—

Known struck from a doubled rev. die.

1868 .... (3,600) .... (25)	160.	205.	345.	615.	2800.
1868-S .... (34,000)	160.	190.	475.	1100.	5750.

Known struck from a doubled rev. die.

1869 .... (4,320) .... (25)	165.	185.	375.	650.	3500.
1869-S .... (29,500)	175.	235.	450.	1350.	5500.
1870 .... (4,520) .... (35)	155.	180.	350.	650.	3250.
1870-S .... (16,000)	160.	200.	425.	1000.	5150.

Extremely rare in Unc.

1871 .... (5,320) .... (30)	160.	180.	300.	500.	2250.
1871-S .... (22,000)	155.	175.	340.	510.	2350.
1872 .... (3,000) .... (30)	250.	425.	650.	1250.	6000.

ST March 1995 Ch. Proof $19,800.

1872-S .... (18,000)	165.	225.	490.	1225.	5000.
1873 .... (55,200) .... (25)	140.	155.	175.	250.	625.

Closed 3.

1873 .... (122,800)	135.	150.	165.	190.	345.

Open 3.

1873-S .... (27,000)	170.	220.	475.	1200.	2600.

Closed 3 only.

1874 .... (3,920) .... (20)	180.	230.	365.	725.	2650.
1875 .... (400) .... (20)	2500.	3500.	4650.	7500.	19000.

A single full Unc. is known, most survivors are Proofs. ST Oct. 1994 Ch. Proof $36,000. Beware removed Mint mark, check rev. hub.

1875-S .... (11,600)	145.	190.	350.	675.	4050.

Type I rev. only, usually weakly struck, very rare in Unc.

1876 .... (4,176) .... (45)	170.	320.	535.	1100.	3550.

Excessively rare above MS-60.

1876-S .... (5,000)	145.	215.	525.	1125.	3900.

Type I rev. only.

1877 .... (1,632) .... (20)	305.	385.	540.	875.	2750.
1877-S .... (35,400)	140.	155.	165.	220.	750.

Type II rev., as on following.

1878 .... (286,240) .... (20)	135.	150.	155.	180.	325.
1878-S .... (178,000)	135.	150.	160.	200.	385.

Varieties with narrow and wide S.

Quarter eagles continued

	F-12	VF-20	EF-40	AU-50	MS-60
1879 .... (88,960) .... (30)	135.	150.	155.	185.	345.
1879-S .... (43,500)	140.	170.	225.	850.	2200.
1880 .... (2,960) .... (36)	155.	225.	290.	475.	1300.
1881 .... (640) .... (51)	725.	1400.	2450.	4450.	10500.
1882 .... (4,000) .... (67)	180.	220.	255.	390.	725.
1883 .... (1,920) .... (82)	180.	245.	475.	800.	1900.
1884 .... (1,950) .... (73)	180.	230.	385.	525.	1700.
1885 .... (800) .... (87)	400.	750.	1500.	2250.	4200.
1886 .... (4,000) .... (88)	165.	210.	275.	450.	1275.
1887 .... (6,160) .... (122)	165.	190.	220.	350.	1050.
1888 .... (16,006) .... (92)	165.	180.	195.	255.	500.
1889 .... (17,600) .... (48)	165.	180.	195.	220.	435.
1890 .... (8,720) .... (93)	165.	180.	195.	230.	530.
1891 .... (10,960) .... (80)	165.	180.	190.	210.	425.
Business strikes all from doubled rev. die.					
1892 .... (2,440) .... (105)	165.	205.	275.	485.	950.
1893 .... (30,000) .... (106)	145.	160.	185.	205.	400.
1894 .... (4,000) .... (122)	155.	180.	270.	375.	635.
1895 .... (6,000) .... (119)	135.	145.	190.	230.	450.
1896 .... (19,070) .... (132)	135.	145.	155.	175.	325.
1897 .... (29,768) .... (136)	135.	150.	160.	185.	310.
1898 .... (24,000) .... (165)	135.	145.	155.	175.	300.
1899 .... (27,200) .... (150)	135.	145.	155.	190.	320.
1900 .... (67,000) .... (205)	135.	145.	155.	175.	300.
1901 .... (91,100) .... (223)	135.	145.	155.	175.	300.
1902 .... (133,540) .... (193)	135.	145.	155.	175.	300.
1903 .... (201,060) .... (197)	135.	145.	155.	175.	300.
1904 .... (160,790) .... (170)	135.	145.	155.	175.	300.
1905 .... (217,800) .... (144)	135.	145.	155.	175.	300.
1906 .... (176,330) .... (160)	135.	145.	155.	175.	300.
1907 .... (336,294) .... (154)	135.	145.	155.	175.	300.

INDIAN HEAD

Indian Head

	F-12	EF-40	AU-50	MS-60	MS-65
1908 .... (564,821) .... (236)	130.	155.	170.	260.	3850.
Matte Proofs.					
1909 .... (441,760) .... (139)	130.	155.	170.	290.	3900.
Satin (Roman) Finish Proofs with satiny finish.					
1910 .... (492,000) .... (682)	130.	155.	170.	265.	4750.
Proofs as preceding.					
1911 .... (704,000) .... (191)	130.	155.	170.	260.	4450.
Matte Proofs.					

1911-D

	F-12	EF-40	AU-50	MS-60	MS-65
1911-D .... (55,680)	400.	950.	1400.	3000.	45000.
Beware of counterfeits and altered Mint marks. On genuine coins the Mint mark is always very weakly struck, and there are usually high wire rims.					
1912 .... (616,000) .... (197)	130.	160.	180.	300.	6000.
Fine Matte Proofs.					
1913 .... (722,000) .... (165)	130.	155.	170.	270.	4350.
Proofs as preceding.					
1914 .... (240,000) .... (117)	135.	165.	185.	550.	10250.
Matte Proofs., Norweb Matte Proof-65, 24,200, Oct. 1987.					

Quarter eagles continued	F-12	EF-40	AU-50	MS-60	MS-65
1914-D .... (448,000)	130.	160.	175.	300.	24000.
1915 .... (606,000) .... (100)	130.	155.	170.	260.	4050.
Most Matte Proofs melted at Mint.					
1925-D .... (578,000)	130.	150.	165.	250.	3950.
1926 .... (446,000)	130.	150.	165.	250.	3950.
1927 .... (388,000)	130.	150.	165.	250.	4100.
1928 .... (416,000)	130.	150.	165.	250.	4000.
1929 .... (532,000)	130.	150.	165.	250.	4300.

Three dollars

INDIAN HEAD

Small Letters in DOLLARS

	F-12	EF-40	AU-50	MS-60	MS-65
1854 .... (138,618)	420.	630.	825.	2000.	15500.
Type I rev., small letters in DOLLARS, five or six Proofs known.					
1854-D .... (1,120)	4750.	13000.	23500.	80000.	—
Only Dahlonega $3, generally crudely struck, Unknown in Unc., very rare in EF. Eliasberg EF-45, $13,500, Oct. 1982; ST Sept. 1994 EF $21,000.					
1854-O .... (24,000)	470.	1250.	2500.	22500.	—
Extremely rare in Unc.					

Large Letters in DOLLARS

	F-12	EF-40	AU-50	MS-60	MS-65
1855 .... (50,555)	420.	640.	845.	2150.	17000.
Type II rev., large letters in DOLLARS, as on all to follow. Very rare in Unc., three or more Proofs known.					
1855-S .... (6,600)	650.	1700.	4900.	21000.	—
Unknown above MS-60.					
1856 .... (26,010)	420.	650.	850.	2150.	21500.
Proofs have large DOLLARS hubbed over small DOLLARS.					
1856-S .... (34,500)					
Large S, very rare.					
1856-S	525.	1050.	1900.	9000.	—
Medium S, extremely rare in Unc.					
1856-S					
Small S, excessively rare in Unc.					
1857 .... (20,891)	420.	650.	950.	2650.	28500.
Possibly five Proofs known. Some genuine pieces have missing upper left serif on I of UNITED and AMERICA. Counterfeit dies copied from these coins were used to strike fake 1857s and other years.					
1857-S .... (14,000)	675.	1850.	4100.	17000.	—
1858 .... (2,133)	625.	1300.	2300.	6750.	—
Rare in Unc., perhaps 12 Proofs known.					
1859 .... (15,638) .... (80)	420.	650.	875.	2200.	17250.
1860 .... (7,036) .... (119)	420.	665.	1050.	2250.	17750.
1860-S .... (4,408)	550.	1700.	4500.	—	—
Net mintage. 7,000 struck of which 2,592 were never released and melted in Dec. 1869 as under weight. Excessively rare Unc., Eliasberg MS-65, $20,900, Oct. 1982.					
1861 .... (5,959) .... (113)	535.	750.	1200.	2550.	22500.
1862 .... (5,750) .... (35)	535.	750.	1250.	2750.	24250.

Three dollars continued

	F-12	EF-40	AU-50	MS-60	MS-65
1863 .... (5,000) .... (39)	550.	750.	1275.	2775.	20000.
Extremely rare in Unc.					
1864 .... (2,630) .... (50)	560.	775.	1300.	2800.	23500.
1865 .... (1,140) .... (25)	700.	2200.	3350.	11000.	47500.
Excessively rare in Unc., Proof restrikes exist.					
1866 .... (4,000) .... (30)	600.	800.	1200.	2700.	23250.
Extremely rare above MS-60.					
1867 .... (2,600) .... (50)	580.	850.	1275.	2650.	22750.
Same remarks as preceding.					
1868 .... (4,850) .... (25)	565.	790.	1150.	2600.	23000.
Same remarks as preceding. Most proofs struck from rotated dies.					
1869 .... (2,500) .... (25)	585.	875.	1300.	4000.	26500.
Same remarks as preceding.					
1870 .... (3,500) .... (35)	585.	875.	1325.	4100.	37500.
Same remarks as preceding.					
1870-S .... (1)					

1870-S — Ex Eliasberg collection, Unique. This coin was supposed to have been placed in the cornerstone of the San Francisco Mint building, the "Granite Lady." Either was not so placed, was removed, or two were struck contrary to letter by San Francisco Mint Superintendent LaGrange to Mint Director Pollock on May 27, 1870. Eliasberg EF-40 with traces of jewelry use, $687,500, Oct. 1982. EF-40 $900,000.

	F-12	EF-40	AU-50	MS-60	MS-65
1871 .... (1,300) .... (30)	600.	900.	1350.	3300.	24500.
Same remarks as 1870.					
1872 .... (2,000) .... (30)	590.	875.	1325.	3400.	25500.
Same remarks as preceding. ST March 1995 Ch. Proof $18,700.					
1873 .... (25)			10750.	17000.	90000.
Open 3; Proof only, coins with die rust are restrikes.					
1873	1900.	4000.	5750.	21000.	——
Closed 3; Proofs extremely rare, most business strikes survive in low grade. Dished-die restrike Proofs exist.					
1874 .... (41,800) .... (20)	410.	625.	720.	1950.	14500.
1875 .... (20)	——	——	——	40000.	215000.
Proof only, Restrikes exist. Theodore Ullmer sale, $150,000 May 1974.					
1876 .... (45)	——	——	11000.	17500.	72500.
Proof only.					
1877 .... (1,468) .... (20)	745.	2650.	5750.	15500.	——
1878 .... (82,304) .... (20)	405.	620.	710.	1900.	14250.
1879 .... (3,000) .... (30)	460.	825.	1100.	2150.	15500.
1880 .... (1,000) .... (36)	470.	1250.	2000.	2300.	16250.
1881 .... (500) .... (54)	600.	2000.	3950.	6500.	40000.
Very rare above MS-60.					
1882 .... (1,500) .... (76)	500.	1075.	1600.	2300.	17000.
1883 .... (900) .... (89)	505.	1100.	1800.	3600.	18750.
Same remarks as 1881.					
1884 .... (1,000) .... (106)	700.	1300.	1850.	3400.	19250.
Same remarks as preceding.					
1885 .... (800) .... (110)	650.	1250.	1750.	3550.	19750.
Same remarks as preceding.					
1886 .... (1,000) .... (142)	575.	1200.	1800.	3650.	20000.
1887 .... (6,000) .... (160)	470.	725.	1050.	2150.	15000.
Business strikes from doubled obv. die. A few Proofs were struck from rotated dies, then overstruck from corrected dies!					

1888

	F-12	EF-40	AU-50	MS-60	MS-65
1888 .... (5,000) .... (291)	470.	725.	1050.	2150.	15100.
1889 .... (2,300) .... (129)	470.	725.	1050.	2150.	15100.

Half eagles

CAPPED BUST RIGHT, SMALL EAGLE

Capped Bust, Small Eagle

	F-12	VF-20	EF-40	AU-50	MS-60
1795 .... (8,707)	5850.	7500.	11000.	16000.	36500.
Wide date, 15 obv. stars, rev vars. include four or three berries; final S in STATES over D.					
1795					
Narrow date, rev. vars include four or three berries.					
1796/5 .... (6,196)	6750.	9000.	15500.	22000.	60000.
Extremely rare in Unc.					
1797 .... (3,609)	8750.	14500.	29000.	45000.	——
15 star obv. Mintage includes next, and probably some 1796 dated coins. Essentially unknown in full Unc.					
1797	7750.	11000.	25500.	39500.	105000.
16 star obv., excessively rare in Unc.					
1798	——	——	215000.	——	——
13 stars obv., 7 known. Mintage included below.					

CAPPED BUST RIGHT, HERALDIC EAGLE

Capped Bust, Heraldic Eagle, 15 Obverse Stars

	F-12	VF-20	EF-40	AU-50	MS-60
1795	6250.	7500.	18000.	38000.	100000.
15 stars obv., 16 rev., struck in late 1797 or early 1798 with usable old dies taken from storage after the yellow fever epidemic had passed. ST Oct. 1994 BU $95,000.					
1797/5	5000.	8000.	17500.	57500.	——
15 star obv., 16 rev. Unused die of 1795, updated and pressed into use as was preceding. Unknown in Unc. ST Oct. 1994 Ch. AU $65,000.					
1797	——	——	——	——	——
16 stars obv. and rev., unique, Smithsonian collection.					
1798 .... (24,867)	1550.	2250.	3050.	5750.	16500.
Large 8 in date. Mintage includes above four emergency issues. 13 stars obv. and rev. as on following, except as noted.					
1798	1850.	2950.	7250.	18500.	——
Large 8. Rev. with 14 stars, of which one is always weak. Excessively rare in Unc.					
1798	1700.	2650.	5250.	16500.	——
Small 8 in date.					

Half eagles continued

	F-12	VF-20	EF-40	AU-50	MS-60
1799 .... (7,451)					
Last 9 small, small stars. Some of this date struck in 1800.					
1799	1950.	2650.	5000.	——	——
Last 9 small, large stars, unknown in Unc.					
1799	1600.	1850.	3750.	——	——
Last 9 large, recut. Small stars.					
1799					
Last 9 large, recut, large stars. Extremely rare in Unc.					
1800 .... (37,628)	1325.	1600.	2000.	3400.	5800.
Includes mintage reported for 1801 and some for 1799.					
1802/1 .... (53,176)	1300.	1575.	1850.	2900.	5050.
No coins were struck from die before overdating.					
1803/2 .... (33,506)	1300.	1575.	1850.	2900.	5000.
1804 .... (30,475)	1400.	1635.	1875.	2950.	5500.
Small 8.					
1804	1425.	1650.	2200.	3450.	6250.
Small over large 8, very rare in Unc.					
1805 .... (33,183)	1350.	1625.	1850.	2900.	5150.
Vars. with wide date, blunt 1 (rare) and close date, perfect 1.					

8 Stars Left, 5 Right, Pointed 6

	F-12	VF-20	EF-40	AU-50	MS-60
1806 .... (9,676)	1550.	1725.	2025.	3900.	9000.
Obv. stars 8 left, 5 right, pointed-top 6. Very rare in Unc.					

7 Stars Left, 6 Right, Knobbed 6

	F-12	VF-20	EF-40	AU-50	MS-60
1806 .... (54,417)	1300.	1550.	1825.	2875.	5000.
Obv. stars 7 left, 6 right, knob-top 6. Always weakly struck in center of obv.					
1807 .... (32,488)	1350.	1575.	1900.	2900.	5050.
Small date, small obv. stars, small rev. stars.					
1807					
Small date, large obv. stars, large rev. stars, very rare.					
1807					
Large date, Large obv. and rev. stars.					

CAPPED DRAPED BUST LEFT

Capped Draped Bust

	F-12	VF-20	EF-40	AU-50	MS-60
1807 .... (51,605)	1375.	1625.	1850.	2950.	5150.

Half eagles continued

	F-12	VF-20	EF-40	AU-50	MS-60
1808/7 .... (55,578)	1575.	1800.	2100.	5500.	11500.
Two different dies, wide date rare, on later strikes the underdate fades.					
1808	1325.	1575.	1825.	2875.	5100.
Normal date.					
1809/8 .... (33,875)	1300.	1550.	1800.	2850.	5000.
On late strikes the underdate fades.					
1810 .... (100,287)	1375.	1600.	1875.	2875.	5000.
Large date, large 5 in denomination.					
1810	4000.	5000.	8000.	16000.	——
Large date, small 5, excessively rare, perhaps 6 known including 1 example with initials removed from field.					
1810	1700.	1900.	2050.	3350.	6350.
Small date, large 5, rare.					
1810	9500.	14000.	25000.	45000.	——
Small date, small 5, very rare. ST March 1995 Ch. EF $26,400.					
1811 .... (99,581)	1375.	1600.	1900.	3250.	6000.
Small date, large 5. Mintage figure includes quantity dated 1810.					
1811	1325.	1575.	1850.	2850.	4950.
Small 5.					
1812 .... (58,087)	1275.	1525.	1800.	2850.	5000.
Close and wide 5 D. vars.					

CAPPED HEAD LEFT

Capped Head

	F-12	VF-20	EF-40	AU-50	MS-60
1813 .... (95,428)	1500.	1575.	1825.	3100.	5900.
Most of mintage probably dated 1812.					
1814/3 .... (15,454)	1675.	2000.	2400.	3900.	8500.
On later strikes the underdate fades, very rare in Unc.					
1815 .... (635)	——	——	45000.	75000.	155000.
Almost all known are Unc. Very rare in any grade. Beware of alterations from 1813. Norweb AU-55, $82,500, Oct. 1987. ST March 1995 AU $55,000.					
1818 .... (48,588)	1650.	1950.	2350.	4000.	8250.
Very rare in Unc.					
1818	——	——	3750.	5900.	16500.
Rare with STATES OF very close together.					
1818	——	——	——	11500.	——
5D over 50, unknown in Unc.					
1819 .... (51,723)	——	——	25000.	55000.	——
1819	——	9250.	17000.	35000.	——
5D over 50. Only one known in Unc. Very rare in any grade. ST Oct. 1994 Ch. AU $50,000.					
1820 .... (263,806) 1775.	2150.	4600.	7000.	——	
Curved-base 2, small letters, very rare in Unc.					
1820	1800.	2175.	4650.	7250.	——
Curved-base 2, large letters, very rare in Unc. ST Oct. 1994 Gem Unc. $120,000.					
1820	1750.	2125.	2800.	5300.	9000.
Square-base 2, large letters, very rare in Unc.					
1821 .... (34,641)	2300.	3700.	8100.	16750.	32500.
Rare in all grades, unique Proof-63 to 64, Norweb $198,000, Oct. 1987.					
1822 .... (17,796)	——	——	——	——	——
Three known, two in Smithsonian. Eliasberg VF-30, $687,500, Oct. 1982.					
1823 .... (14,485)	1825.	2075.	4250.	6900.	——
1824 .... (17,340)	3750.	6100.	11000.	20500.	34000.
Most of 14 to 18 survivors are Unc.					
1825/1 .... (29,060)	3500.	4750.	7000.	16500.	31500.
Extremely rare in Unc.					
1825/4	——	——	265000.	——	——
Two known, Eliasberg Proof-60, $220,000, Oct. 1982.					

Half eagles continued

	F-12	VF-20	EF-40	AU-50	MS-60
1826 .... (18,069)	2900.	6000.	8050.	17000.	28000.
1827 .... (24,913)	—	—	—	—	—

Very rare. Most known are Unc., apparently none less than EF.

1828/7 .... (28,029)	—	—	—	37500.	115000.

All non-Proofs survivors are Unc., four or five known.

1828	—	—	—	32500.	75000.

Extremely rare in all grades.

1829

Large date, seven known, all Unc. except for one impaired specimen. Eliasberg MS-65/67, $82,500. Mintage included below.

CAPPED HEAD LEFT, NARROW PLANCHETS, BEADED BORDERS

Narrow planchets, beaded border (Bowers & Merena)

	F-12	VF-20	EF-40	AU-50	MS-60
1829 .... (57,442)	—	—	75000.	175000.	—

Small date, possibly six known, Norweb Proof-64 to 65, $352,000, Oct. 1987.

1830 .... (126,351)	3500.	5550.	6500.	8400.	17500.

Small 5 D., very rare in Unc., rare in any grade.

1830	3800.	5800.	7050.	9250.	19000.

Large 5 D., very rare in Unc., rare in any grade. ST Oct. 1994 Ch. Unc. $36,000.

1831 .... (140,594)	3950.	6000.	7900.	11750.	30000.

Small 5 D., very rare in Unc., rare in any grade.

1831	3600.	5650.	6600.	8400.	18500.

Large 5 D., very rare in Unc., rare in any grade.

1832	—	100000.	—	—	360000.

Curved-base 2, 12 stars, excessively rare. Eliasberg EF-45, $44,000, Oct. 1982.

1832 .... (157,487)	—	5900.	7150.	11500.	20000.

Square-base 2, 13 stars, perhaps 20 known. ST Oct. 1994 BU $22,000.

1833 .... (193,630)	3450.	5550.	6400.	8250.	16000.

Large wide date. Rare.

1833

Small close date. Very rare.

1834 .... (50,141)	4250.	6100.	8750.	16500.	40000.

Net mintage. 74,709 struck, 24,568 melted during June 1834. Plain 4. Excessively rare in strictly Unc.

1834	3500.	5600.	6450.	10500.	19500.

Plain 4. Excessively rare in strictly Unc.

CLASSIC HEAD

Classic Head

	F-12	VF-20	EF-40	AU-50	MS-60
1834 .... (658,028)	240.	300.	400.	750.	2700.

First head, large plain 4. ST Oct. 1994 Br. Proof $27,000.

1834

Second head, small plain 4.

1834	600.	1400.	2850.	5250.	16500.

Second head, small crosslet 4, rare.

1835 .... (371,534)	240.	295.	415.	675.	2650.

Three vars. head and date size.

1836 .... (553,147)	240.	295.	400.	675.	2600.

Same remarks as preceding, large and small 5 in 5 D.

Half eagles continued

	F-12	VF-20	EF-40	AU-50	MS-60
1837 .... (207,121)	260.	310.	470.	750.	3600.
Single forelock, large date, large 5. Rare.					
1837					
Double forelock, large date, small 5.					
1837					
Single forelock, small date, rev. shows small 5, no berry. Very rare.					
1838 .... (286,588)	250.	305.	435.	700.	3450.
Large 5, small arrows, rare.					
1838					
Small 5, large arrows.					
1838-C .... (17,179)	950.	1750.	3900.	14500.	37500.
May not exist in full Unc.					
1838-D .... (20,583)	910.	1600.	2850.	5650.	31000.
Extremely rare in Unc.					

CORONET HEAD, NO MOTTO ON REVERSE

Broad mill, Mint mark above date

	F-12	VF-20	EF-40	AU-50	MS-60
1839 .... (118,143)	210.	250.	425.	1100.	3150.
Type I obv. First head. Truncation of neck well curved as on 1838 eagle. ST Oct. 1994 Ch. Unc. $17,000.					
1839/8					
Probably only an early die state of an 1839/9; two or three Proofs known of this state.					
1839-C .... (17,205)	575.	1200.	2700.	6000.	23500.
Mint mark above date. ST Oct. 1994 Ch. AU $17,000.					
1839-D .... (18,939)	500.	1050.	2450.	5700.	17250.
Mint mark above date. ST Oct. 1994 Ch. AU $19,000.					
1840 .... (137,382)	215.	245.	850.	2300.	8250.
Type II obv., second head with truncation less curved. Broad mill, diameter of 1839 coins.					
1840	190.	210.	375.	1350.	3850.
Narrow mill, diameter of later coins.					
1840-C .... (18,992)	435.	850.	2850.	8900.	30500.
Broad or narrow mill known. Mint mark below eagle, as on following.					
1840-D .... (22,896)	440.	775.	1600.	4750.	17500.
Broad (rare) and narrow mill. ST Oct. 1994 Ch. AU $26,000.					
1840-O .... (40,120)	235.	425.	925.	1700.	6750.
Broad (rare) and narrow mill, the latter with small or medium O. Mint mark below eagle, as on following.					
1841 .... (15,833)	245.	415.	975.	1600.	6000.
A small hoard of Uncs. was dispersed in 1950s.					
1841-C .... (21,467)	380.	800.	1675.	2650.	21500.
Very rare in Unc.					
1841-D .... (29,392)	385.	725.	1550.	3250.	11000.
Medium (rare) and small O varieties. ST Oct. 1994 Ch. Unc. $80,000.Z					
1841-O .... (50)					
None known to exist today.					
1842 .... (27,578)	165.	350.	1050.	3750.	—
Type I rev., small letters, excessively rare in Unc.					
1842	400.	825.	2000.	4250.	—
Type II rev., large letters, unknown in Unc.					

Half eagles continued

Narrow mill, Small Date, Mint mark under eagle

	F-12	VF-20	EF-40	AU-50	MS-60
1842-C .... (27,432)	2750.	7500.	27500.	72500.	140000.
Small date, Type I rev. Rare in any grade, excessively rare in Unc.					
1842-C	390.	775.	1625.	3500.	24500.
Large Date. Type I rev., extremely rare in Unc.					
1842-D .... (59,608)	525.	800.	1050.	2750.	16000.
Small date, Type I rev., unverified in Unc.					
1842-D	1150.	2150.	4400.	15250.	47500.
Large date, Type II rev., unknown in Unc., rare in any grade.					
1842-O .... (16,400)	375.	900.	3500.	13750.	—
Type I rev. only. Extremely rare in Unc.					
1843 .... (611,205)	145.	170.	200.	270.	1600.
Type II rev.					
1843-C .... (44,277)	400.	760.	1350.	4650.	21000.
Type I rev., extremely rare in Unc.					
1843-D .... (98,452)	390.	650.	925.	2500.	7000.
Large D, Type II rev.					
1843-D					
Small D, Type II rev.					
1843-O .... (19,075)	365.	725.	1800.	3000.	30000.
Small O, Type I rev.					
1843-O .... (82,000)	180.	260.	1200.	2350.	14500.
Large O, Type II rev. Extremely rare in Unc. ST Oct. 1994 CH. UNC. $42,500.					
1844 .... (340,330)	155.	175.	200.	265.	1500.
Type II rev., as on following.					
1844-C .... (23,631)	675.	1100.	3650.	8750.	33000.
Excessively rare in Unc.					
1844-D .... (88,982)	500.	675.	1200.	2450.	13000.
Very rare in Unc.					
1844-O .... (364,600)	160.	200.	300.	925.	5000.
Very rare in Unc, sometimes found with small weak stars. 1 Proof and 1 polished UNC Proof.					
1845 .... (417,099)	155.	185.	220.	270.	1700.
Rare with heavily recut date.					
1845-D .... (90,629)	535.	685.	1200.	1850.	13250.
Sometimes the Mint mark is very weak on this and later years, very rare in Choice Unc.					
1845-O .... (41,000)	255.	400.	725.	3500.	14500.
Extremely rare in Unc.					
1846 .... (395,942)	145.	170.	215.	325.	1750.
Large date.					
1846	160.	180.	230.	700.	3250.
Small date, rare.					
1846-C .... (12,995)	550.	1150.	2800.	6000.	29000.
Excessively rare in Unc.					
1846-D .... (80,294)	445.	650.	1075.	3800.	8000.
Very rare in Unc. Sometimes seen with D/D, first D overlapping branch.					
1846-O .... (58,000)	235.	375.	1000.	4000.	10000.
1847 .... (915,981)	145.	170.	195.	325.	1400.
Several varieties of recut dates exist. One variety shows part of a 1 at Liberty's throat.					
1847-C .... (84,151)	450.	640.	1300.	3400.	17000.
Unknown in Unc.					
1847-D .... (64,405)	465.	625.	1200.	2100.	6650.
Extremely rare in Unc.					
1847-O .... (12,000)	600.	2500.	6600.	16000.	—
Unknown in Unc.					
1848 .... (260,775)	155.	185.	205.	425.	1400.
1848-C .... (64,472)	475.	700.	1050.	2500.	19500.
Excessively rare in Unc.					
1848-D .... (47,465)	440.	725.	1175.	2450.	13500.
Excessively rare in Unc.					
1849 .... (133,070)	145.	180.	225.	625.	2900.
An overdate is reported, not confirmed. Repunched dates common for this year.					

Half eagles continued

	F-12	VF-20	EF-40	AU-50	MS-60
1849-C .... (64,823)	410.	600.	1150.	2200.	15000.
Extremely rare in Unc.					
1849-D .... (39,036)	425.	655.	1200.	2850.	15500.
Excessively rare in Unc. ST Oct. 1994 Ch. AU $11,000.					
1850 .... (64,491)	210.	275.	675.	1050.	3750.
Very rare in Unc.					
1850-C .... (63,591)	415.	600.	925.	2450.	15000.
Extremely rare in Unc. Mint mark is usually very weak.					
1850-D .... (43,984)	425.	850.	1350.	4150.	24000.
Possibly unique in full Unc.					
1851 .... (377,505)	155.	175.	210.	280.	1800.
1851-C .... (49,176)	450.	660.	1200.	3000.	18000.
Excessively rare in Unc.					
1851-D .... (62,710)	400.	675.	1375.	3100.	14000.
Extremely rare in Unc.					
1851-O .... (41,000)	290.	575.	1250.	3800.	14000.
Excessively rare in Unc.					
1852 .... (573,901)	145.	160.	185.	260.	1350.
1852-C .... (72,574)	400.	625.	925.	2400.	6850.
Very rare in Unc.					
1852-D .... (91,452)	405.	625.	1050.	2750.	10500.
Very rare in Unc.					
1853 .... (305,770)	155.	165.	200.	265.	1300.
1853-C .... (65,571)	400.	600.	875.	1800.	7400.
Very rare in Unc.					
1853-D .... (89,678)	405.	610.	950.	1500.	5500.
Very rare in Unc.					
1854 .... (160,675)	165.	215.	255.	600.	1500.
1854-C .... (39,283)	435.	800.	1200.	3300.	20000.
Excessively rare in Unc.					
1854-D .... (56,413)	390.	615.	1000.	2250.	7300.
Very rare in Unc, Mint mark sometimes very faint.					
1854-O .... (46,000)	240.	300.	400.	1450.	8000.
Excessively rare in Choice Unc.					
1854-S .... (268)					
Three known: 1) Lilly, now in Smithsonian; 2) Wolfson, later Norweb, not in Oct. 1987 sale; Eliasberg, ex F.C.C. Boyd, AU-55, $187,000, Oct. 1982. AU-55 $210000.					
1855 .... (117,098)	155.	175.	230.	300.	1500.
1855-C .... (39,788)	475.	850.	1650.	2700.	18000.
Extremely rare in Unc.					
1855-D .... (22,432)	500.	800.	1200.	2750.	17500.
Perhaps six reported in Unc.					
1855-O .... (11,100)	380.	700.	1800.	4750.	21000.
Excessively rare in Unc.					
1855-S .... (61,000)	215.	325.	1200.	2900.	——
Excessively rare in Unc.					
1856 .... (197,990)	150.	165.	190.	265.	1550.
1856-C .... (28,457)	425.	725.	1650.	2900.	21500.
Excessively rare in Unc.					
1856-D .... (19,786)	415.	775.	1200.	2750.	13000.
1856-O .... (10,000)	400.	600.	1650.	5250.	19000.
Excessively rare in Unc.					
1856-S .... (105,100)	200.	285.	725.	1200.	——
Large (rare) and medium S vars.					
1857 .... (98,188)	155.	170.	190.	305.	1450.
1857-C .... (31,360)	370.	625.	1400.	2400.	10500.
Unknown in Unc.					
1857-D .... (17,046)	415.	650.	1200.	3050.	16000.
Excessively rare in Unc.					
1857-O .... (13,000)	355.	675.	1125.	4250.	——
Excessively rare in Unc.					
1857-S .... (87,000)	205.	290.	700.	1350.	7250.
Large and small S vars.					
1858 .... (15,136)	195.	240.	400.	700.	3750.
Excessively rare in Unc., perhaps four Proofs known.					
1858-C .... (38,856)	395.	700.	1050.	2750.	16500.
Excessively rare in Unc.					
1858-D .... (15,362)	425.	750.	1050.	2100.	11250.
Large and medium (rare) D vars., excessively rare in Unc.					
1858-S .... (18,600)	475.	875.	2500.	7500.	——
Excessively rare in Unc.					

Half eagles continued

	F-12	VF-20	EF-40	AU-50	MS-60
1859 .... (16,814) .... (80)	200.	260.	400.	775.	4750.

Type III rev., shorter claws, used on all Philadelphia strikes 1859-65. Never used on branch Mints. Excessively rare in Choice Unc.

	F-12	VF-20	EF-40	AU-50	MS-60
1859-C .... (31,847)	390.	825.	1650.	3850.	18500.

All branch Mint coins struck from leftover Type II revs. 1859 through the 1866-S No Motto.

	F-12	VF-20	EF-40	AU-50	MS-60
1859-D .... (10,366)	440.	785.	1200.	2350.	12500.
1859-S .... (13,220)	600.	1650.	5050.	7750.	——

Excessively rare in Unc.

	F-12	VF-20	EF-40	AU-50	MS-60
1860 .... (19,763) .... (62)	190.	250.	275.	800.	3750.

Very rare in Unc.

	F-12	VF-20	EF-40	AU-50	MS-60
1860-C .... (14,813)	425.	950.	1950.	3500.	14250.

Extremely rare in Unc.

	F-12	VF-20	EF-40	AU-50	MS-60
1860-D .... (14,635)	430.	925.	1700.	3450.	12500.

Very rare in Unc. ST Oct. 1994 Unc. $13,000.

	F-12	VF-20	EF-40	AU-50	MS-60
1860-S .... (21,200)	550.	1050.	1550.	9000.	——

Excessively rare in Unc.

	F-12	VF-20	EF-40	AU-50	MS-60
1861 .... (688,084) .... (66)	145.	160.	175.	275.	1400.
1861-C .... (6,879)	750.	2000.	4250.	8500.	37500.

Struck for U.S., 5,992; struck for Confederacy, 887 with die rust and crack across AMERI. One of the best struck Charlotte dates, unknown in strict Unc. ST Oct. 1994 AU $14,000.

	F-12	VF-20	EF-40	AU-50	MS-60
1861-D .... (1,597)	2750.	4000.	6900.	19500.	45000.

Additional unknown quantity struck for Confederacy. Excessively rare in AU and above. ST Oct. 1994 AU $14,500.

	F-12	VF-20	EF-40	AU-50	MS-60
1861-S .... (18,000)	525.	1200.	4000.	10000.	——

Unknown in Unc.

	F-12	VF-20	EF-40	AU-50	MS-60
1862 .... (4,430) .... (35)	455.	850.	1400.	3500.	——

Unknown in Unc.

	F-12	VF-20	EF-40	AU-50	MS-60
1862-S .... (9,500)	1300.	2950.	5400.	19000.	——

Unknown in Unc.

	F-12	VF-20	EF-40	AU-50	MS-60
1863 .... (2,442) .... (30)	450.	1175.	3500.	7750.	——

Excessively rare in Unc., perhaps a dozen Proofs known.

	F-12	VF-20	EF-40	AU-50	MS-60
1863-S .... (17,000)	625.	1450.	4250.	13500.	——

Unknown in Unc.

	F-12	VF-20	EF-40	AU-50	MS-60
1864 .... (4,170) .... (50)	360.	675.	1350.	3650.	15500.

Unknown in Choice Unc. ST Oct. 1994 Ch. Proof $17,000.

	F-12	VF-20	EF-40	AU-50	MS-60
1864-S .... (3,888)	2900.	8000.	18000.	45000.	——

Excessively rare in Unc.

	F-12	VF-20	EF-40	AU-50	MS-60
1865 .... (1,270) .... (25)	500.	1400.	3250.	12500.	——
1865-S .... (27,612)	525.	1475.	1950.	5500.	23500.

Large (always weak) and small (very rare) S vars. Unknown in Unc. ST Oct. 1994 Ch. AU $19,000.

	F-12	VF-20	EF-40	AU-50	MS-60
1866-S .... (9,000)	775.	1750.	4350.	14000.	——

Unknown in Unc.

CORONET HEAD WITH MOTTO ON REVERSE

Motto added to reverse (Bowers & Merena)

	F-12	VF-20	EF-40	AU-50	MS-60
1866 .... (6,700) .... (30)	375.	850.	1450.	3400.	——

Type IV rev. with motto In God We Trust. Extremely rare above EF, unknown in strict Unc.

	F-12	VF-20	EF-40	AU-50	MS-60
1866-S .... (34,920)	600.	900.	3000.	9250.	——

Excessively rare in Unc.

	F-12	VF-20	EF-40	AU-50	MS-60
1867 .... (6,870) .... (50)	275.	350.	1375.	3150.	——

Excessively rare in Unc.

	F-12	VF-20	EF-40	AU-50	MS-60
1867-S .... (29,000) 425	750.	1350.	2750.	14250.	——

Unknown in Unc., excessively rare in EF

	F-12	VF-20	EF-40	AU-50	MS-60
1868 .... (5,700) .... (25)	265.	345.	925.	3250.	12000.

Excessively rare in Unc. ST Oct. 1994 Unc. $9,500.

	F-12	VF-20	EF-40	AU-50	MS-60
1868-S .... (52,000)	280.	375.	1475.	3300.	18000.

Unknown in Unc.

	F-12	VF-20	EF-40	AU-50	MS-60
1869 .... (1,760) .... (25)	425.	900.	1450.	4150.	——

Unknown in Unc.

Half eagles continued

	F-12	VF-20	EF-40	AU-50	MS-60
1869-S .... (31,000)	365.	525.	1800.	9500.	—
Unknown in Unc., extremely rare EF-AU.					
1870 .... (4,000) .... (35)	350.	700.	1750.	3350.	—
Unknown strictly Unc., very rare EF-AU.					
1870-S .... (17,000)	500.	1050.	2500.	13000.	—
Unknown in Unc., excessively rare in EF-AU.					
1870-CC .... (7,675)	1850.	4250.	14500.	39000.	—
Unknown in Unc., excessively rare in EF-AU.					
1871 .... (3,200) .... (30)	385.	700.	1400.	2850.	13000.
Unknown in Unc., extremely rare in EF.					
1871-S .... (25,000)	270.	320.	1150.	4150.	17000.
Unknown in Unc., extremely rare in EF.					
1871-CC .... (20,770)	650.	1250.	3500.	—	—
Unknown in Unc., extremely rare in EF.					
1872 .... (1,660) .... (30)	400.	650.	1000.	2850.	12250.
Very rare in Unc. ST March 1995 Ch. Proof $35,200.					
1872-S .... (36,400)	275.	550.	800.	3250.	21000.
Extremely rare in Unc.					
1872-CC .... (16,980)	575.	1100.	5250.	22500.	—
Excessively rare in Unc.					
1873 .... (112,480) .... (25)	150.	165.	190.	500.	1200.
Closed 3, rare Choice Unc.					
1873	145.	160.	185.	300.	665.
Open 3, rare in Unc.					
1873-S .... (31,000)	340.	675.	800.	3150.	21000.
Closed 3, unknown in Unc., very rare EF-AU.					
1873-CC .... (7,416)	1250.	2750.	11500.	32500.	—
Closed 3, unknown in Unc., excessively rare EF-AU.					
1874 .... (3,488) .... (20)	315.	500.	950.	2500.	—
Only one known Unc., very rare EF. Business strikes all from doubled reverse die. Eliasberg Proof-65, $15,400, Oct. 1982.					
1874-S .... (16,000)	425.	800.	1500.	5000.	—
Unknown in Unc.					
1874-CC .... (21,198)	410.	675.	2600.	12000.	34000.
Excessively rare in above AU.					
1875 .... (200)					
Unknown in Unc., excessively rare in EF. Eliasberg Proof-65, $60,500. $50000 EF-45 $67500 AU-50 $115000 Prf 63 $60000 Prf 64 $110000.					
1875-S .... (9,000)	500.	775.	2400.	6250.	27500.
Virtually unknown in Unc., excessively rare in EF. ST Oct. 1994 BU $42,500.					
1875-CC .... (11,828)	700.	1600.	3500.	—	—
Extremely rare above AU.					
1876 .... (1,432) .... (45)	445.	825.	1950.	3550.	12500.
Rare in all grades.					
1876-S .... (4,000)	800.	1350.	3850.	—	—
Unknown in Unc.					
1876-CC .... (6,887)	550.	1350.	4350.	12500.	—
Unknown in Unc.					
1877 .... (1,132) .... (20)	420.	825.	1750.	3500.	—
Excessively rare in Choice Unc.					
1877-S .... (26,700)	175.	275.	575.	1850.	—
Excessively rare above AU.					
1877-CC .... (8,680)	465.	1000.	3600.	8250.	—
Unknown in Unc., excessively rare in EF.					
1878 .... (131,720) .... (20)	130.	155.	170.	230.	450.
1878-S .... (144,770)	130.	155.	175.	240.	1075.
1878-CC .... (9,054)	1400.	3000.	6750.	22000.	—
Unknown in Unc., excessively rare in EF.					
1879 .... (301,920) .... (30)	130.	145.	160.	185.	400.
New obv. hub this and following. Same design.					
1879-S .... (426,200)	140.	155.	170.	210.	1050.
1879-CC .... (17,281)	345.	475.	1500.	2950.	—
1880 .... (3,166,400) .... (36)	130.	145.	160.	180.	245.
1880-S .... (1,348,900)	130.	145.	160.	180.	260.
1880-CC .... (51,017)	270.	375.	725.	1450.	11500.
1881/80	250.	315.	600.	800.	1350.
Very rare. Several repunched dates also exist, authentication recommended.					
1881 .... (5,708,760) .... (42)	130.	145.	160.	180.	240.
1881-S .... (969,000)	130.	145.	160.	180.	255.
1881-CC .... (13,886)	330.	450.	1600.	6500.	20000.

Half eagles continued

	F-12	VF-20	EF-40	AU-50	MS-60
1882 .... (2,514,520) .... (48)	130.	145.	160.	180.	240.
1882-S .... (969,000)	130.	145.	160.	180.	265.
1882-CC .... (82,817)	235.	265.	450.	725.	6750.
1883 .... (233,400) .... (61)	130.	145.	160.	190.	300.
1883-S .... (83,200)	145.	165.	200.	235.	925.
1883-CC .... (12,958)	290.	385.	900.	3150.	18500.
Two or three known in full Unc.					
1884 .... (191,030) .... (48)	130.	160.	175.	220.	950.
1884-S .... (177,000)	150.	170.	180.	220.	325.
1884-CC .... (16,402)	315.	500.	950.	2750.	——
1885 .... (601,440) .... (66)	130.	145.	160.	180.	245.
1885-S .... (1,211,500)	130.	145.	160.	180.	230.
1886 .... (388,360) .... (72)	130.	155.	165.	185.	270.
1886-S .... (3,268,000)	130.	145.	160.	185.	230.
1887 .... (87)					
Proof only, ST Oct. 1994 Ch. Proof $57,500.					
1887-S .... (1,912,000)	130.	145.	160.	185.	230.
1888 .... (18,202) .... (94)	140.	165.	200.	280.	550.
1888-S .... (293,900)	155.	175.	230.	330.	1100.
1889 .... (7,520) .... (45)	150.	250.	330.	525.	950.
Rare in all grades, very rare in Unc. ST Oct. 1994 Ch. Proof $13,500.					
1890 .... (4,240) .... (88)	215.	325.	485.	675.	1600.
Very rare in Choice Unc. ST Oct. 1994 Ch. Proof $18,000.					
1890-CC .... (53,800)	185.	245.	320.	450.	1000.
1891 .... (61,360) .... (53)	130.	160.	190.	225.	500.
1891-CC .... (208,000)	175.	240.	290.	380.	700.
1892 .... (753,480) .... (92)	130.	145.	160.	170.	230.
1892-O .... (10,000)	360.	460.	750.	1200.	2700.
Very rare in Unc.					
1892-S .... (298,400)	130.	165.	180.	230.	675.
1892-CC .... (82,968)	180.	240.	315.	450.	1550.
1893 .... (1,528,120) .... (77)	130.	145.	160.	170.	230.
1893-O .... (110,000)	140.	185.	215.	275.	1075.
1893-S .... (224,000)	130.	165.	175.	200.	450.
1893-CC .... (60,000)	185.	245.	325.	550.	1575.
1894 .... (957,880) .... (75)	130.	145.	160.	170.	230.
1894-O .... (16,600)	140.	175.	260.	350.	1450.
1894-S .... (55,900)	150.	200.	325.	600.	2400.
1895 .... (1,345,855) .... (81)	130.	145.	160.	170.	215.
1895-S .... (112,000)	135.	195.	280.	500.	3000.
1896 .... (58,960) .... (103)	130.	155.	175.	200.	350.
1896-S .... (155,400)	145.	190.	285.	525.	1700.
1897 .... (867,800) .... (83)	130.	145.	160.	170.	215.
1897-S .... (354,000)	135.	165.	240.	290.	875.
1898 .... (633,420) .... (75)	130.	145.	160.	170.	225.
1898-S .... (1,397,400)	135.	150.	165.	190.	250.
1899 .... (1,710,630) .... (99)	130.	145.	160.	170.	220.
1899-S .... (1,545,000)	130.	150.	165.	180.	240.
Two Proofs known.					
1900 .... (1,405,500) .... (230)	130.	145.	160.	170.	215.
1900-S .... (329,000)	135.	160.	190.	230.	375.
1901 .... (615,900) .... (140)	130.	145.	160.	170.	215.
1901/0-S	140.	170.	210.	265.	360.
Scarce.					
1901-S .... (3,648,000)	130.	145.	160.	170.	215.
1902 .... (172,400) .... (162)	130.	145.	160.	180.	205.
1902-S .... (939,000)	130.	145.	160.	170.	215.
1903 .... (226,870) .... (154)	130.	145.	160.	180.	240.
1903-S .... (1,855,000)	130.	145.	160.	170.	215.
1904 .... (392,000) .... (136)	130.	145.	160.	170.	215.
1904-S .... (97,000)	135.	160.	185.	270.	1050.
Rare in Unc. Eliasberg MS-67, $12,100					
1905 .... (302,200) .... (108)	130.	145.	160.	180.	235.
1905-S .... (880,700)	135.	155.	170.	225.	600.
1906 .... (348,735) .... (85)	130.	145.	160.	170.	225.
1906-D .... (320,000)	130.	145.	160.	170.	220.
1906-S .... (598,000)	130.	155.	165.	175.	320.
1907 .... (626,100) .... (92)	130.	145.	160.	170.	215.
1907-D .... (888,000)	130.	145.	160.	170.	215.
1908 .... (421,874)	130.	145.	160.	170.	220.

INDIAN HEAD

Indian Head

	F-12	EF-40	AU-50	MS-60	MS-65
1908 .... (577,845) .... (167)	160.	200.	240.	345.	13500.
Matte Proofs. ST Oct. 1994 Very Ch. Matte Proof $20,000.					
1908-D .... (148,000)	160.	200.	240.	340.	25000.
1908-S .... (82,000)	180.	375.	475.	1150.	14250.
1909 .... (627,060) .... (78)	160.	200.	240.	365.	13500.
Satin (Roman) Finish or excessively rare Matte Proofs.					
1909-O .... (34,200)	350.	1000.	1850.	6500.	—
Rare in Unc., generally weakly struck, beware altered or added Mint mark. ST Oct. 1994 Ch. Unc. $90,000.					
1909-D .... (3,423,560)	160.	200.	240.	340.	13500.
Common in scruffy Unc. from a hoard.					
1909-S .... (297,200)	185.	225.	295.	1250.	41500.
1910 .... (604,000) .... (250)	160.	200.	240.	350.	20000.
Satin Finish Proofs. ST Oct. 1994 hybrid Matte/Satin Proof $8,500.					
1910-D .... (193,600)	165.	205.	265.	420.	——
1910-S .... (770,200)	180.	220.	300.	1100.	——
1911 .... (915,000) .... (139)	160.	200.	240.	340.	14000.
Matte Proofs.					
1911-D .... (72,500)	250.	450.	625.	2950.	——
Extremely rare in Unc.					
1911-S .... (1,416,000)	180.	210.	255.	485.	——
1912 .... (790,000) .... (144)	160.	200.	245.	340.	15000.
Matte Proofs.					
1912-S .... (392,000)	180.	210.	315.	1350.	——
1913 .... (916,000) .... (99)	160.	200.	250.	340.	13500.
Matte Proofs.					
1913-S .... (408,000)	185.	230.	385.	1400.	——
1914 .... (247,000) .... (125)	165.	200.	250.	365.	15000.
Matte Proofs.					
1914-D .... (247,000)	165.	205.	255.	365.	37500.
1914-S .... (263,000)	180.	210.	315.	1450.	—
1915 .... (588,000) .... (75)	165.	200.	250.	335.	13500.
Matte Proofs.					
1915-S .... (164,000)	185.	350.	465.	1850.	—
1916-S .... (240,000)	180.	250.	280.	675.	20000.
Two or three known without the S, apparently from a clogged die.					

1929

	F-12	EF-40	AU-50	MS-60	MS-65
1929 .... (662,000)	—	3800.	4300.	5750.	29500.
Most melted at Mint, 100-150 known, mostly Unc. from small hoard.					

Eagles

CAPPED BUST RIGHT, SMALL EAGLE

			Capped Bust, Small Eagle				
		F-12	**VF-20**	**EF-40**	**AU-50**	**MS-60**
1795 .... (5,583)	6250.	8500.	12500.	19000.	42500.
15 obv. stars, rev. 13 leaves in branch.					
1795	16500.	26500.	36000.	57500.	165000.
Rev. 9 leaves, extremely rare.					
1796 .... (4,146)	6850.	9500.	15000.	24000.	57500.
16 obv. stars, rev. 11 leaves.					
1797 .... (3,615)	8000.	13750.	26000.	44000.	——
16 obv. stars, very rare in Unc.					

CAPPED BUST RIGHT, HERALDIC EAGLE

			Capped Bust, Heraldic Eagle				
		F-12	**VF-20**	**EF-40**	**AU-50**	**MS-60**
1797 .... (10,940)	2550.	3500.	4800.	7750.	18000.
16 stars obv., 13 stars rev. (as on following).					
1798/7 .... (900)	6250.	12500.	25000.	37500.	72500.
13 stars obv., 9 + 4, extremely rare in any grade. ST March 1995 Ch. AU $46,200.					
1798/7 .... (842)	21500.	37500.	57500.	95000.	225000.
13 stars obv., 7 + 6, extremely rare in any grade. ST March 1995 Ch. AU $73,700.					
1799 .... (37,449)	2250.	2750.	4250.	5750.	10000.
Large obv. stars.					
1799					
Small obv. stars, wide and narrow date vars.					
1800 .... (5,999)	2600.	3550.	4600.	6250.	17500.
Very rare in Unc.					
1801 .... (44,344)	2275.	2775.	4275.	5800.	10100.
Includes mintage recorded for 1802.					
1803 .... (15,017)	2450.	3350.	4500.	6100.	12500.
Rev. Large stars and berries. Extremely rare in Unc.					
1803	2400.	3050.	4400.	6000.	12000.
Rev. Small stars and berries. Very rare in Unc.					

Eagles continued

Crosslet 4 (left) and Plain 4

	F-12	VF-20	EF-40	AU-50	MS-60
1804 .... (3,757)	3750.	4500.	5750.	8250.	28500.

Original impressions have a crosslet 4, extremely rare in Unc., Eliasberg MS-63 to 65/MS-65 to 67, $32,200, Oct. 1982.

1804

Plain 4 var. is a Proof restrike made in 1834 for diplomatic presentation sets, see 1804 Dollars. Eliasberg Proof-55, $33,000, Oct. 1982.

CORONET HEAD, NO MOTTO ON REVERSE

Coronet (Bowers & Merena)

	F-12	VF-20	EF-40	AU-50	MS-60
1838 .... (7,200)	600.	1150.	2900.	6250.	27500.

Type I obv. and rev. First head: Truncation of neck well curved, ending in sharp point. Large letters rev. Very rare in Unc. Perhaps 4 Unc and 3 Proofs are known. Eliasberg AU-55/MS-60, $30,800, Oct. 1982.

	F-12	VF-20	EF-40	AU-50	MS-60
1839 .... (25,801)	535.	900.	1650.	3850.	22500.

Type I, large Letters, very rare in Unc. An overdate, 1839/8 is reported, not confirmed.. Eliasberg Proof-65, $121,000, Oct. 1982; ST March 1995 Unc. $28,600.

1839 .... (12,447)	850.	1750.	3200.	6750.	—

Type II obv.and rev., truncation less curved; smaller letters rev. Excessively rare in Unc.

1840 .... (47,338)	305.	360.	575.	1600.	12000.

Very rare in Unc.

1841 .... (63,131)	300.	325.	550.	1500.	8500.

Extremely rare in Unc.

1841-O .... (2,500)	1250.	2200.	4500.	11500.	—

Unknown in Unc.

1842 .... (18,623)	270.	330.	400.	2050.	6500.

Small date.

1842 .... (62,884)	280.	340.	450.	1250.	7500.

Large date. Excessively rare in Unc.

1842-O .... (27,400)	285.	375.	625.	2550.	29000.

Large date. Unknown in Unc.

1843 .... (75,462)	280.	330.	400.	1700.	—

Very rare in Unc.

1843

Doubled date.

1843-O .... (175,162)	275.	320.	375.	1200.	16000.

Extremely rare in Unc.

1844 .... (6,361)	575.	1500.	2700.	6000.	18000.

Excessively rare in Unc.

1844-O .... (118,700)	265.	330.	440.	1650.	17000.

Very rare in Unc. Perhaps one Proof known, Parmelee & Woodin.

1845 .... (26,153)	400.	525.	750.	2000.	12500.

Very rare in Unc.

1845-O .... (47,500)	280.	360.	700.	1800.	19000.

Extremely rare in Unc.

1846 .... (20,095)	450.	575.	1075.	5500.	—

Unknown in Unc.

1846/5-O	320.	625.	1050.	3100.	—

Very Rare.

1846-O .... (81,780)	290.	425.	700.	5250.	—

Extremely rare in Unc.

1847 .... (862,258)	245.	260.	340.	525.	3500.
1847-O .... (571,500)	265.	300.	375.	650.	4500.

Eagles continued

1848

	F-12	VF-20	EF-40	AU-50	MS-60
1848 .... (145,484)	270.	320.	400.	700.	5300.

Type III obv., minor changes in outline of hair bun and truncation of neck, extremely rare in Unc.

	F-12	VF-20	EF-40	AU-50	MS-60
1848-O .... (35,850)	320.	500.	1100.	3750.	15000.

Excessively rare in full Unc.

1849 .... (653,618)	255.	275.	350.	600.	3550.

Rare in Unc.

1849/1849	450.	700.	975.	1800.	—

Date strongly repunched down and to left. Often mistaken for an overdate. Recut dates are common for this year, no doubt due to Longacre's preoccupation with the gold $1 and $20 designs.

1849-O .... (23,900)	385.	750.	1700.	5750.	—

Unknown in Unc.

1850 .... (291,451)	255.	275.	370.	650.	3950.

Large date, extremely rare in Unc.

1850	320.	375.	950.	2350.	9500.

Small date, from half eagle date punch, very rare.

1850-O .... (57,500)	295.	425.	1000.	2500.	

Extremely rare in Unc.

1851 .... (176,328)	255.	270.	395.	925.	4650.

Very rare in Unc.

1851-O .... (263,000)	250.	265.	500.	1075.	6000.

Extremely rare in Unc.

1852 .... (263,106)	255.	270.	335.	600.	4050.
1852-O .... (18,000)	370.	685.	1125.	3550.	—

One rare var. shows ring at top of stripe two in shield. No vars. known in Unc.

1853 .... (201,253)	255.	280.	335.	560.	3750.

Very rare in Unc.

1853/2	420.	600.	800.	1650.	—

Reported, status as true overdate uncertain.

1853-O .... (51,000)	290.	320.	425.	1000.	—

One ring var. as 1852-O, all extremely rare in Unc.

1854 .... (54,250)	295.	315.	385.	775.	5700.

Extremely rare in Unc.

1854-O .... (52,500)	270.	350.	675.	1400.	—

Small date. Unknown in Unc.

1854-O	365.	500.	800.	1800.	8500.

Large date from silver dollar date punch, rare. Unknown in Unc.

1854-S .... (123,826)	275.	305.	425.	1275.	10750.

Very rare in Unc.

1855 .... (121,701)	260.	280.	360.	575.	4750.

Very rare in Unc.

1855-O .... (18,000)	315.	575.	1300.	6750.	—

Excessively rare in Unc.

1855-S .... (9,000)	750.	1150.	2350.	5500.	—

Unknown in Unc.

1856 .... (60,490)	270.	285.	350.	575.	4650.

Extremely rare in Unc.

1856-O .... (14,500)	415.	625.	975.	3750.	—

Unknown in Unc.

1856-S .... (68,000)	250.	290.	525.	1100.	8750.

Rare large S, unknown in Unc.; Small S, excessively rare in Unc.

1857 .... (16,606)	290.	525.	875.	1950.	—

Unknown in Unc., Eliasberg Proof-65, $77,000, Oct. 1982.

1857-O .... (5,500)	600.	1100.	1850.	3200.	22500.

Unknown in Unc. ST Oct. 1994 Unc. $24,000.

1857-S .... (26,000)	315.	415.	1100.	2100.	—

Unknown in Unc.

Eagles continued

1858

	F-12	VF-20	EF-40	AU-50	MS-60
1858 .... (2,521)	——	4750.	7250.	14500.	——

Date widely promoted by B. Max Mehl. Business strikes from overpolished die, curls detached from back of neck and from each other, the lower curls well away from neckline. Extremely rare Proofs exhibit normal curls. Very rare in any condition, Unique in Unc.

	F-12	VF-20	EF-40	AU-50	MS-60
1858-O .... (20,000)	270.	330.	625.	1650.	9500.

Very rare in Unc.

1858-S .... (11,800)	800.	1600.	3000.	5500.	——

Excessively rare in Unc.

1859 .... (16,093) .... (80)	285.	365.	700.	1250.	——

Type III rev. with thinner claws, used on all Philadelphia strikes 1859-65, never used on branch Mints. Unknown in Unc. Eliasberg Proof-65, $41,800, Oct. 1982.

1859-O .... (2,300)	1800.	3750.	7700.	17000.	——

Very rare in any grade, unknown in Unc. All Branch Mint coins struck from leftover type II revs. 1859 thru 1866-S No Motto.

1859-S .... (7,000)	1100.	1650.	4000.	14750.	——

Unknown in Unc.

1860 .... (15,055) .... (50)	260.	415.	650.	1600.	5800.

Extremely rare in Unc.

1860-O .... (11,100)	375.	550.	950.	1750.	——

Extremely rare in Unc.

1860-S .... (5,000)	1850.	3400.	5500.	15500.	——

Unknown in Unc. Rare in any grade.

1861 .... (113,164) .... (69)	250.	300.	355.	525.	3900.
1861-S .... (15,500)	625.	1650.	2600.	7000.	——

Unknown in Unc., very rare EF.

1862 .... (10,960) .... (35)	255.	600.	975.	1900.	——

Excessively rare in Unc.

1862-S .... (12,500)	650.	1750.	2800.	6500.	——

Unknown in Unc.

1863 .... (1,218) .... (30)	——	3650.	7500.	17000.	52500.

Very rare in any grade.

1863-S .... (10,000)	675.	1725.	3000.	9750.	31500.

Excessively rare in Unc. Rare in any grade.

1864 .... (3,530) .... (50)	725.	1600.	2750.	6150.	19000.

The few known business strikes VF or lower, majority of Proofs melted at Mint. ST March 1995 V. Ch. Proof $39,600.

1864-S .... (2,500)	2750.	5250.	10500.	26000.	——

Unknown in Unc., excessively rare in EF. Very rare in any grade.

1865 .... (3,980) .... (25)	700.	1750.	3200.	6350.	——

Unknown today in Unc., business strikes from doubled rev. die. ST March 1995 V. Ch. Proof $52,800.

1865-S .... (16,700)	2250.	6750.	12000.	——	——

Unknown in Unc., rare in any grade.

1865/inverted 186-S	1100.	2300.	5750.	17000.	——

Outstanding die cutter's blunder, very rare in any grade.

1866-S .... (8,500)	1350.	2400.	3400.	9500.	——

Unknown in Unc., excessively rare in EF, very rare in any grade. Type 2 rev. of 1839-66.

CORONET HEAD WITH MOTTO ON REVERSE

Motto added to reverse

	F-12	VF-20	EF-40	AU-50	MS-60
1866 .... (3,750) .... (30)	515.	850.	1700.	3950.	——
Type IV rev. with motto In God We Trust, unknown in Unc.					
1866-S .... (11,500)	575.	1550.	3450.	7250.	——
Unknown in Unc.					
1867 .... (3,090) .... (50)	600.	1475.	2300.	5000.	——
Unknown in Unc.					
1867-S .... (9,000)	1100.	2150.	4750.	10250.	——
Unknown in Unc.					
1868 .... (10,630) .... (25)	440.	475.	725.	1900.	17500.
Excessively rare in Unc.					
1868-S .... (13,500)	600.	1300.	2250.	4250.	——
Unknown in Unc.					
1869 .... (1,830) .... (25)	750.	1200.	2600.	6750.	24500.
Rare, unknown in Unc., do not confuse with weak-S coins,					
1869-S .... (6,430)	825.	1800.	2650.	7000.	27500.
S always weak, excessively rare in Unc.					
1870 .... (3,990) .... (35)	435.	600.	1100.	2150.	——
Unknown in Unc.					
1870-S .... (8,000)	675.	1250.	2650.	7250.	——
Unknown in Unc.					
1870-CC .... (5,908)	4500.	10500.	28500.	——	——
Unknown in Unc., very rare in any grade.					
1871 .... (1,790) .... (30)	——	1050.	1775.	3800.	16500.
Very rare in any grade.					
1871-S .... (16,500)	625.	1100.	1800.	5500.	——
Unknown in Unc.					
1871-CC .... (8,085)	1350.	2100.	4950.	19000.	——
Unknown in Unc., very rare in any grade.					
1872 .... (1,620) .... (30)	1300.	1900.	3500.	12500.	27000.
Unknown in Unc., very rare in any grade. ST March 1995 Ch. Proof $29,700.					
1872-S .... (17,300)	400.	585.	950.	1750.	——
Unknown in Unc.					
1872-CC .... (4,600)	1600.	3450.	10750.	——	——
Unknown in Unc.					
1873 .... (800) .... (25)	——	4500.	9500.	——	——
Unknown in Unc. Excessively rare in any grade.					
1873-S .... (12,000)	585.	950.	2300.	4750.	——
Unknown in Unc.					
1873-CC .... (4,543)	2000.	6750.	13500.	——	——
Very rare in any grade.					
1874 .... (53,140) .... (20)	240.	265.	280.	350.	1850.
Very rare in Unc.					
1874-S .... (10,000)	600.	1200.	3500.	7750.	——
Unknown in Unc.					
1874-CC .... (16,767)	560.	875.	2300.	10000.	——
CC always weak. Eliasberg MS-60, $17,600.					
1875 .... (100) .... (20)					
Unknown above EF, extremely rare in any grade. Norweb Proof-60 to 63, $57,200.					
1875-CC .... (7,715)	1900.	3500.	9000.	——	——
CC always weak, excessively rare in Unc.					
1876 .... (687) .... (45)	——	3100.	6000.	17500.	——
Unknown in Unc., excessively rare in any grade.					
1876-S .... (5,000)	625.	1000.	1950.	5600.	——
Unknown in Unc., extremely rare in EF.					
1876-CC .... (4,696)	1650.	3150.	6850.	19500.	——
Unknown in Unc., very rare in any grade.					
1877 .... (797) .... (20)	——	1950.	3400.	9000.	——
Excessively rare in any grade.					

Eagles continued

	F-12	VF-20	EF-40	AU-50	MS-60
1877-S .... (17,000)	325.	475.	700.	2200.	—
Unknown in Unc.					
1877-CC .... (3,332)	1550.	2500.	5000.	—	—
Unknown in Unc., very rare in any grade.					
1878 .... (73,780) .... (20)	230.	250.	290.	355.	1300.
1878-S .... (26,100)	300.	400.	600.	2250.	—
1878-CC .... (3,244)	2700.	4300.	7750.	20000.	—
Unknown in Unc., extremely rare in EF.					
1879 .... (384,740) .... (30)	225.	250.	265.	340.	775.
1879-O .... (1,500)	2050.	2500.	3800.	9000.	—
Unknown in Unc., rare in any grade.					
1879-S .... (224,000)	225.	245.	255.	280.	1350.
1879-CC .... (1,762)	3100.	7500.	20000.	—	—
Unknown in Unc. Excessively rare in any grade. ST March 1995 Ch. AU $30,800.					
1880 .... (1,644,840) .... (36)	220.	235.	240.	260.	345.
1880-O .... (9,200)	265.	385.	750.	1000.	9000.
Unknown in Unc.					
1880-S .... (506,250)	225.	265.	285.	350.	465.
Vars. with tiny S of 1866-78 and medium S of 1879-1900, the latter scarcer.					
1880-CC .... (11,190)	340.	450.	725.	1500.	12500.
1881 .... (3,877,220) .... (42)	215.	225.	245.	265.	310.
1881-O .... (8,350)	250.	375.	650.	1225.	7750.
Excessively rare in Unc.					
1881-S .... (970,000)	215.	225.	245.	280.	400.
1881-CC .... (24,015)	315.	360.	475.	875.	6750.
1882 .... (2,324,440) .... (44)	215.	225.	245.	270.	315.
1882-O .... (10,820)	260.	300.	525.	1025.	8250.
1882-S .... (132,000)	225.	245.	270.	305.	450.
1882-CC .... (6,764)	475.	650.	1100.	2800.	—
Extremely rare in Unc.					
1883 .... (208,700) .... (49)	225.	240.	255.	285.	360.
1883-CC .... (12,000)	340.	400.	650.	2250.	11500.
Excessively rare in Choice Unc.					
1883-O .... (800)	1350.	3550.	7000.	10250.	—
Extremely rare in Unc. Very rare in any grade.					
1883-S .... (38,000)	235.	270.	350.	400.	1350.
Very rare in Unc.					
1884 .... (76,890) .... (45)	225.	245.	255.	275.	875.
1884-S .... (124,250)	225.	240.	270.	315.	650.
1884-CC .... (9,925)	395.	600.	900.	2100.	10000.
Raised diagonal die-cancellation marks seen on Liberty's neck, although this could represent damage in shipping, excessively rare in Unc.					
1885 .... (253,462) .... (67)	220.	235.	265.	285.	410.
1885-S .... (228,000)	220.	235.	255.	270.	375.
1886 .... (236,100) .... (60)	230.	240.	265.	290.	385.
1886-S .... (826,000)	215.	230.	245.	265.	345.
1887 .... (53,600) .... (80)	220.	240.	250.	330.	825.
1887-S .... (817,000)	225.	235.	245.	265.	355.
1888 .... (132,924) .... (72)	230.	245.	265.	325.	825.
1888-O .... (21,335)	215.	230.	260.	320.	550.
1888-S .... (648,700)	215.	230.	250.	275.	350.
1889 .... (4,440) .... (45)	275.	355.	500.	900.	3500.
1889-S .... (425,400)	215.	220.	250.	270.	315.
1890 .... (57,980) .... (63)	235.	250.	270.	330.	950.
1890-CC .... (17,500)	310.	350.	475.	725.	2200.
1891 .... (91,820) .... (48)	220.	250.	260.	280.	335.
1891-CC .... (103,732)	275.	335.	385.	475.	725.
1892 .... (797,480) .... (72)	225.	235.	245.	265.	310.
1892-O .... (28,688)	230.	255.	270.	300.	400.
1892-S .... (115,500)	235.	260.	265.	285.	385.
1892-CC .... (40,000)	295.	325.	400.	625.	3200.
1893 .... (1,840,840) .... (55)	215.	230.	245.	265.	305.
1893-O .... (17,000)	225.	250.	290.	325.	600.
1893-S .... (141,350)	235.	260.	265.	300.	575.
1893-CC .... (14,000)	325.	400.	600.	1450.	—
1894 .... (2,470,735) .... (43)	215.	230.	240.	260.	300.
1894-O .... (107,500)	215.	230.	285.	375.	1000.
1894-S .... (25,000)	250.	295.	440.	1025.	3250.
Very rare in Choice Unc.					
1895 .... (567,770) .... (56)	215.	230.	235.	250.	300.

Eagles continued

	F-12	VF-20	EF-40	AU-50	MS-60
1895-O .... (98,000)	220.	250.	275.	320.	450.
1895-S .... (49,000)	255.	305.	365.	825.	2500.
1896 .... (76,270) .... (78)	220.	240.	250.	270.	300.
1896-S .... (123,750)	235.	255.	325.	500.	2750.
1897 .... (1,000,090) .... (69)	215.	230.	240.	255.	295.
1897-O .... (42,500)	220.	240.	295.	355.	775.
1897-S .... (234,750)	235.	265.	300.	370.	850.
1898 .... (812,130) .... (67)	215.	230.	235.	250.	295.
1898-S .... (473,600)	225.	235.	265.	295.	400.
1899 .... (1,262,219) .... (86)	215.	230.	235.	250.	285.
1899-O .... (37,047)	235.	265.	285.	320.	500.
1899-S .... (841,000)	235.	245.	255.	280.	335.

Varieties with medium S as on 1879-1900, and with smaller, more open S as on 1899-1906.

	F-12	VF-20	EF-40	AU-50	MS-60
1900 .... (293,840) .... (120)	220.	235.	245.	255.	295.
1900-S .... (81,000)	230.	270.	295.	375.	975.

Vars. with medium S (rare) and small S.

	F-12	VF-20	EF-40	AU-50	MS-60
1901 .... (1,718,740) .... (85)	215.	230.	240.	260.	290.
1901-O .... (72,041)	220.	245.	265.	305.	410.
1901-S .... (2,812,750)	215.	230.	235.	250.	290.
1902 .... (82,400) .... (113)	220.	235.	250.	285.	345.
1902-S .... (469,500)	215.	230.	240.	255.	295.
1903 .... (125,830) .... (96)	220.	240.	255.	280.	330.
1903-O .... (112,771)	215.	230.	265.	300.	375.
1903-S .... (538,000)	230.	245.	260.	285.	335.
1904 .... (161,930) .... (108)	220.	235.	240.	255.	305.
1904-O .... (108,950)	230.	250.	260.	280.	385.
1905 .... (200,992) .... (86)	220.	240.	245.	260.	295.
1905-S .... (369,250)	230.	250.	270.	330.	1250.
1906 .... (165,420) .... (77)	220.	240.	245.	260.	310.

Fragmentary 5 under 6 visible on some specimens.

	F-12	VF-20	EF-40	AU-50	MS-60
1906-O .... (86,895)	235.	265.	280.	350.	575.
1906-D .... (981,000)	215.	230.	235.	250.	300.
1906-S .... (457,000)	230.	250.	260.	290.	485.
1907 .... (1,203,899) .... (74)	215.	230.	235.	250.	295.
1907-D .... (1,030,000)	230.	245.	255.	280.	345.
1907-S .... (210,500)	235.	250.	265.	300.	725.

Mint mark slightly smaller than previous. Scarcer than its mintage seems to indicate.

INDIAN HEAD, NO MOTTO ON REVERSE

Indian Head, Wire Edge, Periods

	F-12	VF-20	EF-40	AU-50	MS-60
1907 .... (500)	—	—	4500.	5850.	7400.

Wire rim, triangular periods before and after motto E Pluribus Unum. This coin is actually pattern #E.1808. ST March 1995 Unc. $8,250.

1907
Same, plain edge Satin Proof is Unique pattern, #E.1809.

1907 .... (42)	—	—	13500.	21000.	32500.

Rolled rim, triangular periods as preceding. Eliasberg Matte Proof-67/65, $38,500, Oct. 1982. Actually a pattern, #E.1810.

1907 .... (239,406)	350.	370.	385.	405.	575.

Rolled rim, no periods before and after legends, 46-star edge.

1908 .... (33,500)	360.	390.	415.	500.	725.

Without motto In God We Trust.

1908-D .... (210,000)	360.	390.	400.	440.	825.

Without motto In God We Trust; Mint mark above branch end, tilted to follow rim.

INDIAN HEAD WITH MOTTO ON REVERSE

Motto added to reverse

	F-12	VF-20	EF-40	AU-50	MS-60
1908 .... (341,370) .... (116)	355.	370.	380.	390.	500.
Type II rev. with additional motto. Matte Proofs, Norweb Proof-65, $82,500, Mar. 1988.					
1908-D .... (836,500)	370.	390.	405.	415.	725.
Mint mark below branch end, as on following.					
1908-S .... (59,850)	385.	395.	415.	440.	1950.
Very rare in Unc.					
1909 .... (184,789) .... (74)	350.	375.	380.	390.	510.
Matte Proofs, Norweb Satin Proof-64 to 65, $37,400, Mar. 1988.					
1909-D .... (121,540)	360.	380.	390.	400.	850.
Vars. with D before or just below arrow points.					
1909-S .... (292,350)	370.	385.	395.	405.	650.
Norweb MS-65, $37,400, Mar. 1988.					
1910 .... (318,500) .... (204)	355.	370.	375.	385.	485.
Satin Finish Proofs, Norweb Proof-65, $33,000.					
1910-D .... (2,356,640)	355.	365.	370.	380.	480.
1910-S .... (811,000)	355.	385.	395.	405.	775.
1911 .... (505,500) .... (95)	340.	355.	365.	375.	475.
Matte Proofs.					
1911-D .... (30,100)	400.	450.	650.	875.	4050.
Extremely rare in Unc., Norweb MS-65, 132,000, Mar. 1988.					
1911-S .... (51,000)	360.	390.	475.	600.	1000.
1912 .... (405,000) .... (83)	345.	360.	375.	385.	490.
New edge device has 48 stars.					
1912-S .... (300,000)	350.	365.	390.	425.	950.
1913 .... (442,000) .... (71)	335.	350.	365.	375.	475.
1913-S .... (66,000)	365.	405.	650.	900.	4150.
Very rare in Unc.					
1914 .... (151,000) .... (50)	340.	355.	370.	380.	495.
1914-D .... (343,500)	340.	355.	365.	375.	495.
1914-S .... (208,000)	350.	370.	385.	425.	725.
1915 .... (351,000) .... (75)	340.	360.	375.	385.	485.
1915-S .... (59,000)	370.	390.	550.	800.	2400.
Very rare in Unc.					
1916-S .... (138,500)	365.	385.	415.	430.	700.
1920-S .... (126,500)	4750.	5750.	7000.	9100.	15000.
Most of mintage melted at Mint, usually found in Unc., Norweb MS-64, $52,800, Mar. 1988.					
1926 .... (1,014,000)	340.	355.	365.	375.	460.
1930-S .... (96,000)	—	—	—	5500.	7500.
Rarely seen below Unc. ST March 1995 Ch. Unc. $12,100.					
1932 .... (4,463,000)	340.	350.	355.	365.	450.

1933

	F-12	VF-20	EF-40	AU-50	MS-60
1933 .... (312,500)	—	—	—	—	65000.

Only collectible coin of final date of circulating U.S. gold coinage, possibly 20 known. Extremely rare, Norweb MS-64, $95,700, Mar. 1988.

Double eagles

LIBERTY HEAD, NO MOTTO ON REVERSE

Liberty Head

	F-12	VF-20	EF-40	AU-50	MS-60
1849					

See section on Mint patterns, E.1811.

	F-12	VF-20	EF-40	AU-50	MS-60
1850 .... (1,170,261)	485.	535.	635.	1100.	3400.

Type I obv., LIBERTY misspelled LLBERTY, discovered by ANACS 1978. Vars. also known with open (rare) and closed 5; in latter, knob joins the vertical.

	F-12	VF-20	EF-40	AU-50	MS-60
1850-O .... (141,000)	565.	655.	1250.	3750.	—

Very rare in Unc.

	F-12	VF-20	EF-40	AU-50	MS-60
1851 .... (2,087,155)	470.	490.	530.	775.	2550.
1851-O .... (315,000)	510.	550.	710.	1450.	14750.

Very rare in Unc.

	F-12	VF-20	EF-40	AU-50	MS-60
1852 .... (2,053,026)	475.	495.	525.	750.	2700.
1852-O .... (190,000)	500.	540.	660.	1375.	15000.
1853/2	515.	585.	900.	3250.	35000.

Traces of some digit under 3, status as true overdate unclear.

	F-12	VF-20	EF-40	AU-50	MS-60
1853 .... (1,261,326)	470.	485.	530.	840.	4900.
1853-O .... (71,000)	580.	615.	775.	2350.	19000.

Excessively rare in Unc.

	F-12	VF-20	EF-40	AU-50	MS-60
1854 .... (757,899)	490.	515.	565.	900.	4750.

Small date, half dollar and cent punches.

1854

Large date, silver dollar punches. Rare.

	F-12	VF-20	EF-40	AU-50	MS-60
1854-O .... (3,250)	—	15000.	35000.	62500.	—

Excessively rare in any grade. Eliasberg AU-50, $44,000, Oct. 1982.

	F-12	VF-20	EF-40	AU-50	MS-60
1854-S .... (141,468)	495.	520.	635.	850.	2800.

Uncs. invariably show salt-water damage, shipwreck recovery.

	F-12	VF-20	EF-40	AU-50	MS-60
1855 .... (364,666)	490.	510.	625.	800.	5900.

Very rare in Unc.

	F-12	VF-20	EF-40	AU-50	MS-60
1855-O .... (8,000)	1900.	2750.	5000.	16500.	—

Unknown in Unc., very rare in any grade.

	F-12	VF-20	EF-40	AU-50	MS-60
1855-S .... (879,675)	475.	495.	635.	925.	7900.
1856 .... (329,878)	475.	485.	520.	685.	8000.

Very rare in Unc.

	F-12	VF-20	EF-40	AU-50	MS-60
1856-O .... (2,250)	—	15000.	31500.	65000.	—

Excessively rare in any grade, presently Unique in Unc.

	F-12	VF-20	EF-40	AU-50	MS-60
1856-S .... (1,189,750)	475.	490.	515.	700.	3850.
1857 .... (439,375)	485.	495.	505.	620.	3400.

An 1857 Flying Eagle cent is known with clash marks on its obv. die from a $20 obv. die. $20 pieces with corresponding cent clash marks may exist.

	F-12	VF-20	EF-40	AU-50	MS-60
1857-O .... (30,000)	685.	800.	1450.	3500.	—
1857-S .... (970,500)	475.	495.	535.	700.	3400.
1858 .... (211,714)	490.	535.	640.	1300.	4200.
1858-O .... (35,250)	825.	1050.	1500.	3900.	—

Excessively rare in Unc.

	F-12	VF-20	EF-40	AU-50	MS-60
1858-S .... (846,710)	475.	495.	585.	875.	7400.
1859 .... (43,597) .... (80)	685.	950.	1950.	3800.	25000.

Type II obv. LIBERTY corrected, J.B.L. moved, other minor changes.

	F-12	VF-20	EF-40	AU-50	MS-60
1859-O .... (9,100)	1800.	2850.	6050.	15500.	—
1859-S .... (636,445)	470.	500.	550.	1100.	3600.

Double eagles continued

	F-12	VF-20	EF-40	AU-50	MS-60
1860 .... (577,611) .... (59)	490.	505.	525.	625.	3300.
1860-O .... (6,600)	2500.	3500.	6500.	15000.	——
Excessively rare in Unc, very rare in any grade.					
1860-S .... (544,950)	505.	525.	610.	1200.	5250.
1861 .... (2,976,387) .... (66)	475.	485.	500.	620.	2000.

Paquet reverse

1861
   Type II or Anthony C. Paquet rev. with distinctive tall lettering. (See section on Mint Patterns). Norweb MS-67, $660,000, Nov. 1988.

1861-O .... (17,741)	750.	1450.	3100.	6200.	——

   Struck for U.S., 5,000; for state of Louisiana, 9,750; for the Confederacy, 2,991. The later strikes are from worn dies (date fades) and show atypical alloy.

1861-S .... (748,750)	500.	535.	575.	975.	7500.
1861-S .... (19,250)	——	5250.	11500.	23500.	——

   Type II or Paquet rev., one-year type, see 1861 Philadelphia. Rare, virtually unknown in full Unc.

1862 .... (92,098) .... (35)	535.	725.	1400.	2900.	10000.
1862-S .... (854,173)	495.	545.	725.	1500.	14000.
1863 .... (142,760) .... (30)	480.	600.	850.	1500.	13000.
Excessively rare in Unc.					
1863-S .... (966,570)	475.	520.	645.	1275.	5600.
1864 .... (204,235) .... (50)	465.	525.	680.	1400.	8250.
Excessively rare in Unc.					
1864-S .... (793,660)	515.	570.	800.	1475.	7100.
Excessively rare in Unc.					
1865 .... (351,175) .... (25)	475.	500.	640.	825.	5100.
1865-S .... (1,042,500)	465.	535.	675.	1150.	6500.
1866-S .... (120,000)	775.	1600.	2000.	8750.	——
Unknown in Unc.					

LIBERTY HEAD WITH MOTTO

Motto added to reverse, commonly called Type Two

	F-12	VF-20	EF-40	AU-50	MS-60
1866 .... (698,745) .... (30)	460.	490.	625.	1250.	5100.

   Type II obv., Type III rev. of 1866 with IN of motto low, as on following, except as noted. Very rare in Unc.

1866
   Business strikes with rev. of 1865 pattern, with IN high, tilted 1. Rare.
1866
   Doubled Die reverse with rev. of 1866 over rev. of 1865. IN strongly doubled.

1866-S .... (722,250)	470.	515.	640.	1850.	18000.

   Business strikes with doubled die rev., type of 1866 over type of 1865, IN strongly doubled. Rare.

1867 .... (251,015) .... (50)	435.	455.	585.	690.	1800.

   Proofs with reverse motto style of 1865 and 1866.

Double eagles continued

	F-12	VF-20	EF-40	AU-50	MS-60
1867-S .... (920,750)	455.	495.	650.	1200.	15500.
Excessively rare in Unc.					
1868 .... (98,575) .... (25)	530.	510.	950.	1350.	8000.
1868-S .... (837,500)	460.	495.	630.	1100.	11000.
1869 .... (175,130) .... (25)	460.	480.	625.	850.	4600.
1869-S .... (686,750)	445.	490.	545.	690.	4300.
1870 .... (155,150) .... (35)	465.	485.	740.	1450.	7500.
1870-S .... (982,000)	440.	485.	560.	725.	5200.
1870-CC .... (3,789)	19500.	40000.	80000.	—	—
Believed rarest of all circulation double eagles, excessively rare in any grade, Eliasberg VF-20/30, $22,000, Oct. 1982.					
1871 .... (80,120) .... (30)	475.	515.	675.	1250.	3600.
1871-S .... (928,000)	460.	475.	525.	660.	3550.
1871-CC .... (17,387)	1200.	2250.	4400.	9000.	—
Second rarest Carson City double eagle, unknown in Unc.					
1872 .... (251,850) .... (30)	435.	455.	500.	650.	2200.
ST March 1995 Ch. Proof $71,500.					
1872-S .... (780,000)	450.	465.	505.	615.	2300.
1872-CC .... (26,900)	750.	1000.	1400.	3500.	24500.
Rare in all grades, excessively rare in Unc.					
1873 .... (1,709,800) .... (25)	520.	560.	675.	800.	2550.
Closed 3, rarest var. of date					
1873	440.	445.	455.	525.	670.
Open 3.					
1873-S .... (1,040,600)	455.	490.	520.	565.	1600.
Closed 3.					
1873-S	525.	550.	600.	950.	4700.
Open 3, very rare.					
1873-CC .... (22,410)	640.	775.	1375.	3250.	22500.
Closed 3 only, excessively rare in Unc.					
1874 .... (366,780) .... (20)	455.	460.	480.	560.	1100.
1874-S .... (1,214,000)	455.	470.	485.	565.	1250.
1874-CC .... (115,085)	535.	560.	615.	1100.	6850.
1875 .... (295,720) .... (20)	450.	460.	490.	550.	825.
1875-S .... (1,230,000)	445.	465.	485.	550.	865.
ST March 1995 Superb Gem Unc. $82,500.					
1875-CC .... (111,151)	540.	560.	560.	775.	2100.
1876 .... (583,860) .... (45)	445.	465.	475.	535.	700.
Also see section on patterns. ST March 1995 Ch. Proof $20,900.					
1876-S .... (1,597,000)	440.	460.	480.	530.	665.
1876-CC .... (138,441)	530.	565.	585.	875.	4750.

LIBERTY HEAD, HEAD AND STARS REARRANGED, REV. TWENTY DOLLARS

Head and Stars rearranged, TWENTY DOLLARS reverse, known as Type Three

	F-12	VF-20	EF-40	AU-50	MS-60
1877 .... (397,650) .... (20)	445.	465.	485.	530.	560.
Type III obv., Type IV rev., as on following.					
1877-S .... (1,735,000)	435.	455.	470.	540.	580.
1877-CC .... (42,565)	575.	650.	775.	1275.	16000.
Very rare in Unc.					
1878 .... (543,625) .... (20)	450.	470.	480.	530.	620.
1878-S .... (1,739,000)	445.	470.	490.	555.	775.
1878-CC .... (13,180)	675.	800.	1200.	3200.	20000.
Excessively rare in Unc.					

Double eagles continued	F-12	VF-20	EF-40	AU-50	MS-60
1879 .... (207,600) .... (30)	455.	475.	495.	540.	875.
1879-O .... (2,325)	1850.	2900.	3900.	8850.	28500.
Extremely rare in Unc., very rare in any grade.					
1879-S .... (1,223,800)	450.	470.	490.	545.	1250.
1879-CC .... (10,708)	725.	1050.	1400.	3900.	22500.
1880 .... (51,420) .... (36)	460.	485.	530.	650.	2900.
1880-S .... (836,000)	455.	475.	500.	555.	950.
1881 .... (2,220) .... (61)	2250.	3600.	7000.	11500.	38500.
Unknown in Unc., excessively rare in any grade. Beware of removed Mint marks.					
1881-S .... (727,000)	455.	470.	490.	525.	850.
1882 .... (590) .... (59)	—	8500.	16000.	29500.	—
Extremely rare as non-Proof, beware removed Mint marks.					
1882-S .... (1,125,000)	450.	465.	480.	520.	625.
Large and small (rare) S varieties.					
1882-CC .... (39,140)	545.	570.	675.	1100.	6150.
1883 .... (92)					
Proof only. Norweb Proof-65, $88,000, Nov. 1988. Prf 60 $30000 Prf 63 $44000 Prf 64 $80000.					
1883-S .... (1,189,000)	450.	460.	470.	520.	560.
1883-CC .... (59,962)	560.	580.	660.	800.	4350.
1884 .... (71)					
Proof only. Prf 60 $35000 Prf 63 $48500 Prf 64 $85000. ST Marcyh 1995 Very Ch. Proof $57,750.					
1884-S .... (916,000)	440.	455.	460.	520.	555.
1884-CC .... (81,139)	520.	560.	605.	875.	2400.
1885 .... (751) .... (77)	—	—	6250.	9000.	34000.
Extremely rare as a non-Proof.					
1885-S .... (683,500)	445.	460.	470.	520.	545.
1885-CC .... (9,450)	750.	900.	1350.	3450.	10750.
1886 .... (1,000) .... (106)	—	5750.	11000.	18500.	40000.
Excessively rare in non-Proof. ST March 1995 Ch. AU $16,500.					
1887 .... (121)					
Proof only. Prf 60 $17500 Prf 63 $31000 Prf 64 $55000.					
1887-S .... (283,000)	445.	475.	485.	540.	560.
1888 .... (226,164) .... (105)	450.	470.	495.	535.	750.
1888-S .... (859,600)	445.	460.	475.	490.	545.
1889 .... (44,070) .... (41)	450.	465.	490.	560.	725.
Scarce as non-Proof.					
1889-S .... (774,700)	445.	465.	485.	515.	540.
1889-CC .... (30,945)	590.	655.	750.	1025.	3400.
1890 .... (75,940) .... (55)	455.	465.	490.	535.	610.
1890-S .... (802,750)	455.	465.	490.	520.	540.
1890-CC .... (91,209)	540.	590.	575.	850.	2750.
1891 .... (1,390) .... (52)	—	2950.	4000.	7750.	—
Excessively rare in non-Proof.					
1891-S .... (1,288,125)	425.	445.	460.	485.	530.
1891-CC .... (5,000)	1150.	1650.	2500.	4600.	12500.
Excessively rare in Unc.					
1892 .... (4,430) .... (93)	725.	900.	1350.	2000.	4900.
Excessively rare in Unc., rare as non-Proof, beware removed Mint marks.					
1892-S .... (930,150)	445.	455.	470.	505.	540.
1892-CC .... (27,265)	625.	650.	650.	1050.	2350.
1893 .... (344,280) .... (59)	435.	445.	460.	515.	550.
1893-S .... (996,175)	445.	455.	465.	495.	535.
1893-CC .... (18,402)	615.	650.	750.	1150.	2000.
1894 .... (1,368,940) .... (50)	425.	440.	460.	490.	525.
1894-S .... (1,048,550)	435.	450.	470.	510.	540.
1895 .... (1,114,605) .... (51)	415.	435.	460.	480.	510.
1895-S .... (1,143,500)	425.	445.	470.	495.	530.
1896 .... (792,535) .... (128)	425.	445.	460.	490.	510.
1896-S .... (1,403,925)	435.	450.	470.	495.	580.
1897 .... (1,383,175) .... (86)	425.	445.	460.	485.	510.
1897-S .... (1,470,250)	425.	445.	460.	495.	525.
1898 .... (170,395) .... (75)	445.	455.	475.	510.	615.
1898-S .... (2,575,175)	415.	435.	445.	470.	500.
1899 .... (1,669,300) .... (84)	415.	435.	445.	470.	500.
1899-S .... (2,010,300)	425.	440.	455.	490.	535.
1900 .... (1,874,460) .... (124)	415.	435.	445.	470.	500.
New rev. hub, as on following.					
1900-S .... (2,459,500)	415.	435.	445.	490.	550.
1901 .... (111,430) .... (96)	415.	435.	445.	475.	530.
1901-S .... (1,596,000)	445.	465.	470.	500.	535.

Double eagles continued

	F-12	VF-20	EF-40	AU-50	MS-60
1902 ....(31,140) ....(114)	445.	465.	490.	665.	1000.
1902-S ....(1,753,625)	440.	460.	475.	495.	515.
1903 ....(287,270) ....(158)	415.	435.	445.	470.	500.
ST March 1995 Ch. Proof $31,900.					
1903-S ....(954,000)	435.	455.	470.	495.	525.
1904 ....(6,256,699) ....(98)	415.	430.	440.	465.	495.
1904-S ....(5,134,175)	415.	435.	445.	470.	505.
1905 ....(58,919) ....(92)	450.	470.	520.	600.	1250.
1905-S ....(1,813,000)	445.	465.	485.	510.	545.
1906 ....(69,596) ....(94)	445.	470.	505.	545.	725.
1906-D ....(620,250)	435.	450.	460.	490.	605.
1906-S ....(2,065,750)	425.	445.	455.	480.	510.
1907 ....(1,451,786) ....(78)	415.	435.	445.	470.	500.
1907-D ....(842,250)	425.	445.	455.	485.	510.
1907-S ....(2,165,800)	420.	440.	445.	475.	515.

SAINT-GAUDENS, NO MOTTO ON REVERSE

Saint-Gaudens ultra high relief (Stack's)

	F-12	EF-40	AU-50	MS-60	MS-65
MCMVII ....(24)		*	*	*	350000.

Ultra high relief, lettered edge. Satin Proof only, this issue is the ultimate expression of the quality sought by Saint-Gaudens and President Theodore Roosevelt. Eliasberg brilliant Proof-67, $242,000, Oct. 1982; Bloomfield Collection Sale, Sotheby's 12/96, Proof 60 $825,000. This is actually pattern #E.1867.

MCMVII
Plain edge. Unique, see pattern #E.1869.

High relief

	F-12	EF-40	AU-50	MS-60	MS-65
MCMVII ....(11,250)	2400.	3400.	4750.	7400.	22000.

High relief, vars. with and without wire rim. Counterfeits exist; authentication recommended. Rumored to have been restruck at the Mint in the 1920s, though none seen match the striking characteristics of that decade. Eliasberg Proof-67, $50,600, Oct. 1982. ST March 1995 Flat Rim Very Ch. Unc. $44,000.

Double eagles continued

<table>
<tr><td></td><td colspan="5">Arabic numerals in date</td></tr>
<tr><td></td><td>F-12</td><td>EF-40</td><td>AU-50</td><td>MS-60</td><td>MS-65</td></tr>
</table>

	F-12	EF-40	AU-50	MS-60	MS-65
1907 .... (361,667)	440.	465.	500.	550.	2750.

Arabic numerals, Type II Obv. and rev., low relief as on all that follow. Proofs extremely rare; a unique Matte Proof exists with large edge lettering as on high relief coins.

1908 .... (4,271,551) .... (101)	440.	465.	485.	540.	1300.

Long and short rays behind Liberty vars., few of the reported Proof strikings were released to collectors. Norweb Matte Proof-64 to 65, $50,600, Nov. 1988.

1908-D .... (663,750)	465.	490.	515.	555.	14000.

Same remarks as preceding.

SAINT-GAUDENS WITH MOTTO

<table>
<tr><td></td><td colspan="5">Motto added to reverse</td></tr>
<tr><td></td><td>F-12</td><td>EF-40</td><td>AU-50</td><td>MS-60</td><td>MS-65</td></tr>
</table>

	F-12	EF-40	AU-50	MS-60	MS-65
1908 .... (156,258) .... (Incl. above)	450.	480.	505.	580.	9750.

Long rays Obv. Type III rev. with motto, as on following. Matte Proofs.

1908-D .... (349,500)	465.	500.	515.	565.	3200.
1908-S .... (22,000)	495.	800.	1350.	3700.	50000.
1909/8	470.	525.	640.	1500.	31500.

Rare in Unc.

1909 .... (161,215) .... (67)	465.	495.	530.	700.	75000.

Satin Finish Proofs.

1909-D .... (52,500)	475.	545.	685.	1375.	30000.

1909-D/small D
Norweb MS-65, $71,500, Nov. 1988.

1909-S .... (2,774,925)	440.	465.	490.	555.	5000.
1910 .... (482,000) .... (167)	440.	465.	490.	535.	6250.

Satin Finish Proofs, Norweb Proof-65, $71,500, Nov. 1988.

1910-D .... (429,000)	440.	465.	490.	530.	2400.
1910-S .... (2,128,250)	440.	465.	490.	560.	9500.
1911 .... (197,250) .... (100)	440.	475.	525.	555.	10500.

Matte Proofs. ST March 1995 Ch. Matte Proof $23,000.

1911-D .... (846,500)	440.	470.	490.	520.	1700.
1911-S .... (775,750)	440.	475.	500.	540.	3500.
1912 .... (149,750) .... (74)	440.	480.	530.	555.	12500.

Type III Obv. with 48 stars as on all that follow. Matte Proofs this year.

1913 .... (168,780) .... (58)	440.	470.	500.	610.	22500.

Matte Proofs.

1913-D .... (393,500)	440.	465.	485.	545.	4000.
1913-S .... (34,000)	460.	515.	565.	1100.	50000.
1914 .... (95,250) .... (70)	440.	495.	530.	580.	12000.

Matte Proofs.

1914-D .... (453,000)	440.	470.	495.	530.	2200.
1914-S .... (1,498,000)	440.	465.	485.	525.	2050.
1915 .... (152,000) .... (50)	450.	480.	535.	595.	11750.

Matte Proofs.

1915-S .... (567,500)	440.	475.	495.	555.	1800.
1916-S .... (796,000)	440.	470.	495.	540.	1700.
1920 .... (228,250)	440.	475.	500.	585.	—

Double eagles continued

	F-12	EF-40	AU-50	MS-60	MS-65
1920-S .... (558,000)	—	8000.	13000.	26500.	—
Excessively rare in any grade.					
1921 .... (528,500)	—	10000.	15500.	38000.	225000.
Excessively rare in any grade. Counterfeits exist.					
1922 .... (1,375,500)	440.	465.	485.	515.	3100.
1922-S .... (2,658,000)	460.	530.	610.	825.	32500.
1923 .... (566,000)	440.	465.	480.	510.	6500.
1923-D .... (1,702,250)	440.	465.	480.	520.	1100.
1924 .... (4,323,500)	440.	465.	480.	515.	1075.
1924-D .... (3,049,500)	—	850.	1200.	2200.	50000.
1924-S .... (2,927,500)	—	—	1050.	2050.	53500.
1925 .... (2,831,750)	440.	465.	480.	510.	1050.
1925-D .... (2,938,500)	—	—	1350.	2600.	52500.
1925-S .... (3,776,500)	750.	1050.	1650.	5500.	60000.
1926 .... (816,750)	440.	465.	480.	520.	1100.
1926-D .... (481,000)	—	—	2650.	7000.	—
1926-S .... (2,041,500)	—	825.	1150.	1750.	32500.
1927 .... (2,946,750)	440.	465.	480.	510.	1025.
1927-D .... (180,000)	—	—	—	—	650000.
Most melted at the Mint, extremely rare, beware of added Mint mark. Eliasberg MS-64, $176,000, Oct. 1982.					
1927-S .... (3,107,000)	—	3750.	6250.	12000.	105000.
1928 .... (8,816,000)	440.	465.	480.	510.	1025.
1929 .... (1,779,750)	—	—	7000.	8750.	46000.
Most melted at the Mint.					
1930-S .... (74,000)	—	—	14000.	19500.	80000.
Most melted at the Mint.					
1931 .... (2,938,250)	—	—	12750.	16000.	55000.
Most melted at the Mint.					
1931-D .... (106,500)	—	—	10500.	12500.	50000.
Most melted at the Mint. Norweb MS-64/65, $39,600, Nov. 1988.					
1932 .... (1,101,750)	—	—	—	11000.	45000.
1933 .... (445,500)					

Several examples were in collector hands without incident until 1944, when Treasury agents seized the Col. James W. Flanagan coin out of a New York auction. Others were seized despite court action by a Tennessee collector; the specimen in the King Farouk, alias "Palace Collection" of Egypt was withdrawn but not surrendered after vehement representations by the U.S. government and is untraced today. Others undoubtedly exist but are still liable to seizure.

American Eagle bullion

After Treasury non-cooperation effectively derailed the American Arts Gold Medallion program of troy ounce and half ounce medals which had been mandated by Congress in 1980, the South African Krugerrand gold bullion coin and its fractions dominated the American gold market. In 1986, anxious to supplant the South African bullion coins, Congress authorized the American Eagle series in the same sizes, weights and fineness (.9167 fine) as the South African issues.

A .999 fine one troy ounce silver coin was added to the developing program to assure the support of the silver producing states in enacting the entire program. Designs chosen included obverses adapted from earlier U.S. coin designs, the Saint-Gaudens $20 of 1907 for the gold coins and Adolph A. Weinman's Walking Liberty for the silver.

In another interesting political concession, the new reverse of the gold coins was designed by Texas artist Miley Busiek, a protege of the Treasury Secretary and House Banking Committee chairman. A heraldic eagle by Mint engraver John Mercanti was vaguely derived from earlier U.S. coins.

All of the pieces were assigned nominal face values to make them legal tender coins protected by anti-counterfeiting laws, but these values were made very low to prevent the coins from ever circulating normally. Indirectly confirming its intention, Treasury set the value of the quarter-ounce gold coin at $10, disproportionate to the $5 for the tenth ounce, the $25 for the half ounce and the $50 for the full ounce.

The new bullion silver piece was monetized as one dollar, giving the country a commemorative silver dollar at the pre-1936 standard and a bullion silver dollar of another standard altogether.

In 1986, only the 1-ounce silver and gold coins were struck in Proof; in 1987, the half-ounce gold was also struck in Proof and was made available individually or in a two-coin Proof set. Starting in 1988, all four gold coins were struck in Proof, to be offered individually or in a four-piece set.

In 1997, .999 fine platinum coins were added to the stable, in sizes and weights of the gold coins, but with denominations of $10, $25, $50 and $100. The obverse by John Mercanti features a close-up of the Statue of Liberty. Thomas D. Rogers Sr.'s reverse of an eagle in flight may prove to be a one-year type.

ONE OUNCE SILVER DOLLAR

		One-ounce silver	
	ISSUE PRICE	BU	PROOF
1986 .... (5,393,005)		9.50	*
1986-S .... (1,446,778)	21.00	*	17.00
Proof only.			
1987 .... (11,442,335)		6.80	*
1987-S .... (904,732)	23.00	*	17.00
Proof only.			
1988 .... (5,004,646)		7.20	*
1988-S .... (557,370)	23.00	*	37.50
Proof only.			
1989 .... (5,203,327)		7.10	*
1989-S .... (617,694)	23.00	*	17.00
Proof only.			
1990 .... (5,840,110)		7.10	*
1990-S .... (695,510)	23.00	*	17.50
Proof only.			
1991 .... (7,191,066)		6.90	*
1991-S .... (511,924)	23.00	*	17.50
Proof only.			
1992 .... (5,540,068)		6.90	*
1992-S .... (498,543)	23.00	*	18.00
Proof only.			

Bullion coins continued	ISSUE PRICE	BU	PROOF
1993 .... (6,763,762)		6.80	*
1993-P .... (403,625)	23.00	*	45.00
Proof only.			
American Eagle bullion continued			
1994 .... (4,227,319)		7.15	*
1994-P .... (372,168)	23.00	*	40.00
Proof only.			
1995 .... (4,672,051)		6.90	*
1995-P .... (438,511)	23.00	*	37.00
Proof only.			
1995-W .... (30,125)		*	650.
Proof only. West Point Mint mark issued only in 10th Anniversary sets, along with four gold Proofs, to the dismay of many collectors.			
1996 .... (3,603,386)		6.85	*
1996-P .... (500,000)	23.00	*	24.00
Proof only. Mintage limited to 500,000.			
1997 .... (NR)		6.80	*
1997-P .... (NR)	23.00	*	22.50
Proof only.			

TENTH-OUNCE GOLD $5

Tenth-ounce gold

	ISSUE PRICE	BU	PROOF
MCMLXXXVI (1986) .... (912,609)		46.00	
MCMLXXXVII (1987) .... (580,266)		46.00	
MCMLXXXVIII (1988) ...... (159,500)		50.00	
MCMLXXXVIII-P (1988) .... (143,881)	65.00	*	70.00
Proof only.			
MCMLXXXIX (1989) .... (264,790)		47.00	*
MCMLXXXIX-P (1989) .... (84,647)	65.00	*	67.50
Proof only.			
MCMXC (1990) .... (210,210)		47.00	*
MCMXC-P (1990) .... (99,349)	70.00	*	70.00
Proof only.			
MCMXCI (1991) .... (165,200)		48.00	*
MCMXCI-P (1991) .... (70,334)	70.00	*	70.00
Proof only.			
1992 .... (209,300)		47.00	*
Arabic numerals used in date hereafter.			
1992-P .... (64,874)	70.00	*	80.00
Proof only.			
1993 .... (210,709)		47.00	*
1993-P .... (58,649)	70.00	*	82.50
Proof only.			
1994 .... (206,380)		47.00	*
1994-P .... (62,849)	70.00	*	82.50
Proof only.			
1995 .... (223,025)		46.00	*
1995-W .... (62,673)	70.00	*	85.00
Proof only.			
1996 .... (401,964)		45.00	*
1996-W .... (56,700)	75.00	*	77.50
Proof only.			
1997 .... (NR)		45.00	*
1997-W .... (NR)	75.00	*	77.50
Proof only.			

QUARTER-OUNCE GOLD $10

Quarter-ounce gold

	ISSUE PRICE	BU	PROOF
MCMLXXXVI (1986) .... (726,031)		102.	*
MCMLXXXVII (1987) .... (269,255)		105.	*
MCMLXXXVIII (1988) .... (49,000)		107.	*
MCMLXXXVIII-P (1988) .... (98,028)	150.	*	128.
Proof only.			
MCMLXXXIX (1989) .... (81,789)		105.	*
MCMLXXXIX-P (1989) .... (54,170)	150.	*	138.
Proof only.			
American Eagle bullion continued			
MCMXC (1990) .... (41,000)		107.	*
MCMXC-P (1990) .... (62,674)	150.	*	148.
Proof only.			
MCMXCI (1991) .... (36,100)		107.	*
MCMXCI-P (1991) .... (50,839)	150.	*	148.
Proof only.			
1992 .... (59,546)		103.	*
Arabic numerals used in date hereafter.			
1992-P .... (46,269)	150.	*	158.
Proof only.			
1993 .... (71,864)		103.	*
1993-P .... (46,464)	150.	*	168.
Proof only.			
1994 .... (72,650)		103.	*
1994-P .... (48,172)	150.	*	168.
Proof only.			
1995 .... (83,752)		103.	*
1995-W .... (47,484)	150.	*	168.
Proof only.			
1996 .... (60,318)		103.	*
1996-W .... (37,900)	159.	*	150.
Proof only.			
1997 .... (NR)		103.	*
1997-W .... (NR)	159.	*	150.
Proof only.			

HALF-OUNCE GOLD $25

Half-ounce gold

	ISSUE PRICE	BU	PROOF
MCMLXXXVI (1986) .... (599,566)		205.	*
MCMLXXXVII (1987) .... (131,255)		201.	*
MCMLXXXVII-P (1987) .... (143,398)	295.	*	225.
Proof only.			
MCMLXXXVIII (1988) .... (45,000)		230.	*
MCMLXXXVIII-P (1988) .... (76,528)	295.	*	245.
Proof only.			
MCMLXXXIX (1989) .... (44,829)		270.	*

Bullion coins continued

	ISSUE PRICE	BU	PROOF
MCMLXXXIX-P (1989) .... (44,798)	295.	*	270.
Proof only.			
MCMXC (1990) .... (31,000)		350.	*
MCMXC-P (1990) .... (51,636)	285.	*	270.
Proof only.			
MCMXCI (1991) .... (24,100)		285.	*
MCMXCI-P (1991) .... (53,125)	285.	*	275.
Proof only.			
1992 .... (54,404)		210.	*
Arabic numerals used in date hereafter.			
1992-P .... (40,976)	285.	*	255.
Proof only.			
1993 .... (73,324)		205.	*
1993-P .... (43,319)	285.	*	265.
Proof only.			
1994 .... (62,400)		205.	*
1994-P .... (44,584)	285.	*	280.
Proof only.			
1995 .... (53,474)		205.	*
1995-W .... (45,442)	285.	*	280.
Proof only.			
1996 .... (39,287)		200.	*
1996-W .... (34,700)	299.	*	250.
Proof only.			
1997 .... (NR)		195.	*
1997-W .... (NR)	299.	*	250.
Proof only.			

ONE OUNCE GOLD $50

One-ounce gold

	ISSUE PRICE	BU	PROOF
MCMLXXXVI (1986) ..... (1,362,650)		390.	*
MCMLXXXVI-W (1986) .... (446,290)	550.	*	465.
Proof only.			
MCMLXXXVII (1987) .... (1,045,500)		390.	*
MCMLXXXVII-W (1987) .... (147,498)	585.	*	455.
Proof only.			
MCMLXXXVIII (1988) ...... (465,500)		390.	*
MCMLXXXVIII-W (1988) .... (87,133)	585.	*	455.
Proof only.			
MCMXXXIX (1989) .... (415,790)		390.	*
MCMLXXXIX-W (1989) .... (54,570)	585.	*	450.
Proof only.			
MCMXC (1990) .... (373,210)		390.	*
MCMXC-W (1990) .... (62,401)	570.	*	475.
Proof only.			
MCMXCI (1991) .... (243,100)		390.	*
MCMXCI-W (1991) .... (50,411)	570.	*	485.
Proof only.			

Bullion coins continued

Roman numerals (left) in 1988, Arabic numerals in date

	ISSUE PRICE	BU	PROOF
1992 .... (275,000)		390.	*
Arabic numerals used in date hereafter.			
1992-W .... (44,826)	570.	*	500.
Proof only.			
1993 .... (480,192)		390.	*
1993-W .... (34,389)	570.	*	525.
Proof only.			
1994 .... (221,633)		390.	*
1994-W .... (46,674)	570.	*	550.
Proof only.			
1995 .... (200,636)		390.	*
1995-W .... (46,484)	570.	*	550.
Proof only.			
1996 .... (189,148)		380.	*
1996-W .... (36,000)	589.	*	575.
Proof only.			
1997 .... (NR)		375.	*
1997-W .... (NR)	589.	*	575.
Proof only.			

TENTH-OUNCE PLATINUM $10

Tenth-ounce platinum

	ISSUE PRICE	BU	PROOF
1997 .... (NR)		—	
1997-W .... (NR)	99.00		—
Proof only.			

QUARTER-OUNCE PLATINUM $25

	ISSUE PRICE	BU	PROOF
1997 .... (NR)		—	
1997-W .... (NR)	199.		—
Proof only.			

HALF-OUNCE PLATINUM $50

	ISSUE PRICE	BU	PROOF
1997 .... (NR)		—	
1997-W .... (NR)	395.		—
Proof only.			

ONE-OUNCE PLATINUM $100

1-ounce platinum

	ISSUE PRICE	BU	PROOF
1997 ....(NR)		—	
1997-W .... (NR)	695.		—
Proof only.			

Commemorative Coinage

Use of coinage to commemorate military and naval victories, major civic events such as coronations and anniversaries is nearly as old as coinage itself. The ancients made effective use of commemoratives, perhaps the most famous of which (and long the record-holder as the world's most expensive coin) is the Athenian tetradrachm of 470 B.C., marking the great victory over the Persians at Marathon a few years earlier.

Much of Roman coinage was commemorative in nature, publicizing the emperor and his family, conquests, public games and distribution of largesse to the masses. With the downfall of the Western Empire commemoratives lapsed, to reappear with the Renaissance and become a regular feature of most countries' ongoing coinage.

Some numismatists insist that the 1848 CAL. quarter eagle was America's first coin with commemorative intent, but the 1892 half dollar for the World's Columbian Exposition is generally recognized as the first coin designed and struck solely for commemorative purposes.

Since that issue, "the coin everybody's grandfather brought home from the Chicago fair," coins have appeared hailing national, state and local anniversaries, major expositions and specific events such as the inauguration of bridges, historic trails and even a motion picture festival. One complete non-event, the supposed Cincinnati Music Center golden anniversary, was honored in 1936.

From a small beginning in 1892, commemorative coinage gathered momentum in the 1920s and enjoyed a full-scale speculative boom in the mid-1930s. The marketing techniques of special commissions set up to handle sales included favoritism toward major coin dealers, and open-ended issues struck by all three Mints year after year.

Accusations of over-charging and private profit-making helped kill this boom, and there was no return to plentiful commemoratives after World War II. The Iowa Centennial half dollar showed how successful a carefully administered program could be, but it was overshadowed by the scandals swirling around the Booker T. Washington and Washington-Carver half dollar issues struck from 1946 through 1954.

Citing a ritualized list of such past abuses, the U.S. Treasury and Mint displayed absolute opposition to further commemorative issues after 1955. After decades of battering against this official stone wall, collectors grudgingly recognized the seemingly permanent loss of this important area of national coinage.

Most commemoratives struck in the first period (1892-1954) exist only as business strikes, and many survivors show wear, marks from careless handling or harsh cleaning by non-numismatic owners. Many commemorative gold dollars were used as jewelry. Gem specimens of many silver and gold issues are rare today as a result.

Brilliant Proofs of the World's Columbian coins are known but are extremely scarce. Ultra-rare brilliant and matte Proofs have surfaced of some later issues, created specially for well-placed dignitaries such as U.S. Mint Engraver John R. Sinnock. Little is known of these exciting rarities and new discoveries continue to be made from time to time.

By 1982, most numismatists had written off further effort to break the Mint's commemorative blockade as futile. Then, out of the blue came silver half dollars hailing the 250th anniversary of George Washington's birth and virtually overnight commemoratives were once again a regular feature of U.S. coinage. In short order silver, gold and clad coins appeared for events ranging from the Olympics to the Constitution Bicentennial; from the Statue of Liberty to the Bicentennial of Congress, the Korean and Vietnam Wars.

In a dramatic break with the practice of the 1930s, the new wave commemoratives were now struck in both Proof and Uncirculated and sold directly by the Mint. The 1982 Washington coins appeared in plastic capsules in a gold-stamped cardboard box. Subsequent issues were offered in an increasingly complex array of packaging as sets, partial sets and singles, or were included in the new Prestige Proof Sets.

The proliferation of Mint-marked varieties of the Oregon Trail and Texas Centennial half dollars soon had its 1980s equivalent in the unexpected issue of low-mintage Mint-marked versions of the 1984 Olympic gold coinage. In short order, a wide variety of modern commemoratives would appear bearing the Mint marks of Philadelphia, Denver, San Francisco and the newest Mint of all, West Point, N.Y.

Criticism of designs began early, especially of the "headless torsos" 1984 Olympic, "bowling pins" reverse of the Constitution Bicentennial and cluttered Korean War silver dollars. The ouster of U.S. Mint Chief Engraver Elizabeth Jones did the program little good, and the too-public intrigues of her would-be successor did even less. Design competitions, as former Chief Engraver Frank Gasparro has pointed out, have increasingly favored graphic artists skilled at pen and ink sketches, rather than medallic sculptors.

Pricing has become a major concern for collectors on limited budget, with a complete set of one of the ambitious Olympic programs costing more than $2,000 for all Proof and Uncirculated coins issued. While commemorative programs raised millions of dollars for retirement of the national debt, concern has been expressed about the uses of profits by some private agencies which have shared in the proceeds.

Few modern commemoratives have performed well on the secondary market. Members of the general public without previous numismatic experience who have bought modern commemoratives from the Mint have found that their coins can only be sold at a significant loss. Purchases that have diverted millions from the numismatic market have brought infuriating losses blamed on the "coin market." The angry buyers were never actually part of this market, however, but owe their experiences wholly to a government agency, the U.S. Mint.

Tragically, the hope that these buyers' interest in commemoratives would lead to involvement in the wider world of numismatics has been disappointed. Anger and rejection of any wider exploration of numismatics has been the result.

No method of listing commemorative coins will please all collectors. This catalog offers an essentially chronological listing of all gold and silver commemoratives from the World's Columbian Exposition of 1892-93 to the final Washington-Carver half dollars of 1954. An alphabetical listing could be used, but only if the names of all issues were rigidly standardized.

Please note that mintages are net figures, coins remaining after official melting of unsold coins. In most cases the number authorized to be struck was far higher. Coins struck since the rebirth of commemoratives follow in chronological order, allowing the orderly (but no doubt rapid) expansion of this section of the catalog in the future.

Commemorative Coinage, 1892-1954

World's Columbian Exposition

Columbus half dollar

	EF-40	AU-50	MS-60	MS-63	MS-65
1892 Half Dollar .... (949,897) .... (103)	10.00	13.00	32.00	85.00	775.

Obv. Bust of Columbus, designed by Olin W. Warner and adapted without credit to this artist by Charles E. Barber. Rev. Columbus's flagship *Santa Maria* over two hemispheres, designed by George T. Morgan. Common in circulated condition, elusive in Gem.

	EF-40	AU-50	MS-60	MS-63	MS-65
1893 Half Dollar .... (1,548,300) .... (1)	10.00	13.00	32.00	80.00	800.

Same remarks as preceding.

Queen Isabel quarter dollar

	EF-40	AU-50	MS-60	MS-63	MS-65
1893 Quarter Dollar .... (24,088) .... (103)	200.	230.	300.	515.	2400.

Obv. Crowned bust of Queen Isabel (*Isabel la primera*, Anglicized to Isabella). Rev. Kneeling female with distaff in act of winding flax, symbolizing patient industry. Designed by Charles E. Barber after Caroline Peddle's designs were rejected. Most pieces were mishandled by non-numismatic buyers, rare Choice.

Lafayette Monument

Lafayette dollar

	EF-40	AU-50	MS-60	MS-63	MS-65
1900 Dollar .... (36,000) 225	240.	300.	550.	1450.	8800.

Obv. conjoined heads of Washington and an aged Lafayette, copied by Charles E. Barber from Peter L. Krider's 1881 Yorktown Centennial Medal. Rev. Paul Wayland Bartlett's equestrian statue of Lafayette at Paris. Four minor die varieties exist. All coins struck Dec. 14, 1899, centennial of Washington's death. Most mishandled by non-numismatic buyers, very rare Choice; one brilliant Proof known. Several types of counterfeits exist.

Louisiana Purchase Exposition

Louisiana-Jefferson gold dollar

	EF-40	AU-50	MS-60	MS-63	MS-65
1903 Gold Dollar .... (17,400) .... (100)	315.	360.	445.	750.	2000.

Obv. Bust of Thomas Jefferson after John Reich. Rev. Expo legend, date and denomination with olive branch, designed by Charles E. Barber.

Louisiana-McKinley gold dollar

	EF-40	AU-50	MS-60	MS-63	MS-65
1903 Gold Dollar .... (17,400) .... (100)	300.	330.	400.	675.	2250.

Obv. Bust of William McKinley, adapted by Charles E. Barber from his U.S. Mint McKinley medal. Rev. Same as last. Portrayed are the President who concluded the Louisiana Purchase and the President who authorized the exposition. Many of both mishandled as described above, rare Choice. Excessively rare Proofs exist in sealed frames with attestation by Chief Coiner Rhine R. Freed and Superintendent John Landis. Counterfeits of both dates exist.

Lewis & Clark Exposition

Lewis & Clark gold dollar
(Anthony Swiatek)

	EF-40	AU-50	MS-60	MS-63	MS-65
1904 Gold Dollar .... (9,997)	430.	525.	800.	1800.	5900.

Obv. Bust of Meriweather Lewis, date. Rev. Bust of William Clark, denomination. Coin honors explorers of the Northwest and their 1803-06 expedition across the Louisiana Purchase territory to the Pacific. Designed by Charles E. Barber.

	EF-40	AU-50	MS-60	MS-63	MS-65
1905 Gold Dollar .... (10,000)	430.	475.	975.	3000.	13500.

Rare Proofs exist of each date; many business strikes were mishandled as described above, rare Choice. Counterfeits exist.

Panama-Pacific Exposition

Panama-Pacific half dollar

	EF-40	AU-50	MS-60	MS-63	MS-65
1915-S Half Dollar .... (27,134)	160.	190.	335.	675.	2100.

Obv. Standing Columbia scattering flowers and child holding cornucopia, designed by Charles E. Barber. Rev. Eagle standing on U.S. shield, designed by George T. Morgan. Most pieces mishandled as last, very rare Choice. Counterfeits exist. Proofs known without Mint mark, one known in gold, Norweb MS-60, $66,000, Nov. 1988.

Panama-Pacific Exposition continued

Panama-Pacific gold dollar

	EF-40	AU-50	MS-60	MS-63	MS-65
1915-S Gold Dollar .... (15,000)	300.	360.	400.	550.	2000.

Obv. Head of Panama Canal Worker. Rev. Dolphins surrounding denomination, designed by Charles Keck. Many mishandled as described above, rare Choice. Silver trial strikes known without Mint mark. Counterfeits exist.

Panama-Pacific quarter eagle

	EF-40	AU-50	MS-60	MS-63	MS-65
1915-S Quarter Eagle .... (6,749)	1050.	1250.	1650.	3000.	4500.

Obv. Columbia on mythical seahorse. Rev. Defiant eagle on standard, designed by George T. Morgan. Many mishandled as above, very rare Choice. Counterfeits exist.

Panama-Pacific $50 round (Bowers & Merena)

	EF-40	AU-50	MS-60	MS-63	MS-65
1915-S Fifty Dollars .... (483)	22000.	24000.	28000.	41000.	120000.

Round Planchet. Obv. Armored and helmeted bust of Minerva, date MCMXV on shield. Rev. Owl on Ponderosa pine branch, designed by Robert Aitken.

Panama-Pacific $50 octagonal (Superior Galleries)

	EF-40	AU-50	MS-60	MS-63	MS-65
1915-S Fifty Dollars .... (645)	18500.	20000.	23000.	37500.	110000.

Similar, but on octagonal planchet recalling Augustus Humbert's "slugs" of Gold Rush era with designs reduced to fit new format, dolphins inserted in angles.

McKinley Memorial

McKinley Memorial gold dollar
(Anthony Swiatek)

	EF-40	AU-50	MS-60	MS-63	MS-65
1916 Gold Dollar .... (9,977)	265.	295.	360.	625.	1800.

Obv. Head of assassinated President William McKinley, designed by Charles E. Barber. Rev. Memorial in Niles, Ohio, designed by George T. Morgan.

	EF-40	AU-50	MS-60	MS-63	MS-65
1917 Gold Dollar .... (10,000)	305.	375.	525.	1075.	2750.

Proofs known of each. Rare choice. Counterfeits known for 1917, possible (or inevitable?) for 1916.

Illinois Centennial

Illinois Centennial half dollar

	EF-40	AU-50	MS-60	MS-63	MS-65
1918 Half Dollar .... (100,000)	58.00	72.00	85.00	95.00	600.

Obv. Beardless Lincoln bust, designed by George T. Morgan after sculpture of Andrew O'Connor. Rev. State seal, motto NATIONAL UNION, STATE SOVEREIGNTY on coin despite objections of Treasury Secretary William Gibbs McAdoo. Designed by John R. Sinnock. Elusive in Choice Unc., Proofs exist. Incorrectly called the Lincoln commemorative.

Maine Centennial

Maine Centennial half dollar

	EF-40	AU-50	MS-60	MS-63	MS-65
1920 Half Dollar .... (50,000)	60.00	72.00	90.00	160.	575.

Obv. Incuse-relief state Arms of Maine. Rev. Centennial inscription in wreath of pine cones and needles. Designed by Anthony de Francisci. Matte Proofs exist.

Pilgrim Tercentenary

Pilgrim Tercentenary half dollar

	EF-40	AU-50	MS-60	MS-63	MS-65
1920 Half Dollar .... (152,000)	46.00	52.50	65.00	85.00	500.

Obv. Half length bust of Governor William Bradford of Plimoth Plantation. Rev. Reconstruction of colonists' ship *Mayflower*. Designed by Cyrus E. Dallin. Two proofs known.

	EF-40	AU-50	MS-60	MS-63	MS-65
1921 Half Dollar .... (20,000)	85.00	100.	120.	150.	700.

Same, date 1921 added to obv. field.

Missouri Centennial

Missouri Centennial half dollar

	EF-40	AU-50	MS-60	MS-63	MS-65
1921 Half Dollar .... (15,400)	175.	220.	465.	640.	6300.

Obv. Bust of youthful Daniel Boone. Rev. Standing figures of Boone and Indian, designed by Robert Aitken. Counterfeits exist.

Missouri Centennial, 2★4 added

	EF-40	AU-50	MS-60	MS-63	MS-65
1921 Half Dollar .... (5,000)	285.	385.	490.	925.	6250.

Same, 2★4 added to obv. field, symbolizing the 24th state.

Alabama Centennial

Alabama Centennial half dollar

	EF-40	AU-50	MS-60	MS-63	MS-65
1921 Half Dollar .... (59,000)	65.00	88.00	210.	500.	2400.

Obv. Conjoined busts of Alabama Governors William Bibb and Thomas Kilby. Rev. Adaptation of Alabama State Seal, designed by Laura Gardin Fraser. It has long been the popular belief that the Kilby bust violated the laws prohibiting portraits of living persons on U.S. coins. Close reading of the statutes indicates that they prohibit such portraiture on paper currency only. (*Coin World*, Feb. 7, 1990). Actual centennial dates were 1819-1919, as indicated on rev.

Alabama Centennial, 2X2

	EF-40	AU-50	MS-60	MS-63	MS-65
1921 Half Dollar .... (5,000)	115.	165.	325.	525.	2800.

Same, 2X2 added to obv. field, symbolizing 22nd state.

Grant Memorial

Grant Memorial half dollar

	EF-40	AU-50	MS-60	MS-63	MS-65
1922 Half Dollar .... (67,350)	62.00	72.00	85.00	175.	775.

Obv. Uniformed bust of General Ulysses S. Grant, victorious Union commander in Civil War. Rev. Grant's Ohio birthplace in Point Pleasant, Ohio. Designed by Laura Gardin Fraser. Matte Proofs reported.

Grant Memorial half dollar, star added to obverse field

	EF-40	AU-50	MS-60	MS-63	MS-65
1922 Half Dollar .... (4,250)	465.	650.	1050.	1650.	7700.

Same, incuse star added to right obv. field. Proofs known. Beware added stars, genuine coins will show traces of die clash near chin and tie. Eliasberg 4/97 MS-65 $27,500.

Grant Memorial continued

Grant Memorial gold dollar (Anthony Swiatek)

	EF-40	AU-50	MS-60	MS-63	MS-65
1922 Gold Dollar .... (5,000)	1075.	1200.	1325.	1650.	2700.

Same but for size and metal.

	EF-40	AU-50	MS-60	MS-63	MS-65
1922 Gold Dollar .... (5,000)	1075.	1200.	1450.	1850.	2650.

Same, incuse star added to right obv. field. Both are often weakly struck above cabin. Rare choice. Counterfeits exist.

Monroe Doctrine Centennial

Monroe Doctrine half dollar

	EF-40	AU-50	MS-60	MS-63	MS-65
1923-S Half Dollar .... (274,000)	25.00	30.00	45.00	120.	2400.

Obv. Conjoined busts of Presidents James Monroe and John Quincy Adams. Rev. Draped female figures form map of North and South America, design feature appropriated by Chester Beach from Ralph Beck's 1901 Pan American Exposition Medal. Very common in circulated condition, rare Choice. Coin was actually struck for a Los Angeles Motion Picture Exposition.

Huguenot-Walloon Tercentenary

Huguenot-Walloon Tercentenary half dollar

	EF-40	AU-50	MS-60	MS-63	MS-65
1924 Half Dollar .... (142,000)	65.00	80.00	95.00	110.	550.

Obv. Conjoined busts of French Huguenot Admiral Gaspard de Coligny and Dutch leader William the Silent. Rev. Ship *Nieuw Nederlandt*, which brought the Walloon families from what is now Belgium to Dutch New Netherland, now New York. Designed by George T. Morgan. Promotion of this controversial issue had blatant sectarian overtones. Neither obv. figure was related to the settlement commemorated, but were rather historic leaders in the Wars of Religion. Common in circulated condition, rare Choice.

Lexington-Concord Sesquicentennial

Lexington-Concord Sesquicentennial half dollar

	EF-40	AU-50	MS-60	MS-63	MS-65
1925 Half Dollar .... (161,914)	52.00	60.00	72.00	105.	700.

Obv. "The Minute Man," statue by Daniel Chester French. Rev. Old Belfry at Lexington, designed by Chester Beach. Very common in circulated condition, rare choice. Coin marks the April 19, 1775 outbreak of battle between Massachusetts Patriots and British forces.

Stone Mountain Memorial

Stone Mountain Memorial half dollar

	EF-40	AU-50	MS-60	MS-63	MS-65
1925 Half Dollar .... (1,310,000)	30.00	33.00	42.00	55.00	200.

Obv. Equestrian figures of Generals Robert E. Lee and Thomas Jonathan "Stonewall" Jackson. Rev Eagle on crag, memorial to the valor of the soldier of the South. Confederate President Jefferson Davis was omitted from the obverse, and the name of disgraced President Warren G. Harding was deleted from the original reverse proposal. Designed by Gutzon Borglum, klansman who was carving monumental figures (finished by other hands decades later) on Georgia's Stone Mountain. Counterfeits exist. Common in circulated condition, scarce Choice. Sometimes found with doubled obv. die. Promotional pieces counterstamped with state abbreviations and/or numbers exist and are worth substantial premiums. Beware false counterstamps.

California Diamond Jubilee

California Diamond Jubilee half dollar

	EF-40	AU-50	MS-60	MS-63	MS-65
1925-S Half Dollar .... (86,394)	80.00	100.	115.	175.	775.

Obv. Forty-niner panning gold. Rev. Grizzly bear from the flag of the ephemeral Mexican War-era California Republic. Designed by California artist Jo Mora.

Fort Vancouver Centennial

Fort Vancouver Centennial half dollar

	EF-40	AU-50	MS-60	MS-63	MS-65
1925 (S) Half Dollar .... (14,966)	200.	235.	280.	375.	1050.

Obv. Dr. John McLoughlin, British-Canadian Father of Oregon and founder of Fort Vancouver. Rev. Frontiersman, fort and mountain in background. Designed by Laura Gardin Fraser and struck at San Francisco without S Mint mark. Counterfeits exist. Matte Proofs reported.

American Independence Sesquicentennial

American Independence Sesquicentennial half dollar

	EF-40	AU-50	MS-60	MS-63	MS-65
1926 Half Dollar .... (140,592)	45.00	55.00	75.00	150.	4750.

Obv. Conjoined busts of Presidents George Washington and Calvin Coolidge. Rev. Liberty Bell. Designed in exceptionally low relief by John Lewis, modeled by John R. Sinnock. Matte Proofs known.

American Independence Sesquicentennial quarter eagle (Anthony Swiatek)

	EF-40	AU-50	MS-60	MS-63	MS-65
1926 Quarter Eagle .... (45,793)	240.	265.	300.	575.	3600.

Obv. Liberty standing with torch and scroll. Rev. Independence Hall, Philadelphia, faint rays of rising sun behind. Designed by John R. Sinnock. Never found fully struck, many mishandled by non-numismatic buyers and scarce Choice. Rare Matte Proofs known. Counterfeits exist.

Oregon Trail Memorial

Oregon Trail Memorial half dollar

	EF-40	AU-50	MS-60	MS-63	MS-65
1926 Half Dollar .... (47,925)	80.00	90.00	100.	120.	195.

Obv. Ox-drawn covered wagon rolling westward toward setting sun, designed by James Earle Fraser. Rev. Indian standing, with arm outstretched, U.S. map behind, designed by Laura Gardin Fraser. Proofs known 1926-P only. Though one of the most powerful designs of the first series, the Oregon was the classic example of open-ended issues stretching on for years. Some dates officially dedicated to individual pioneers, such as Jason Lee and Ezra Meeker, but these are not recorded on the coins. The Oregon was finally terminated by Congressional Act of August 1939.

	EF-40	AU-50	MS-60	MS-63	MS-65
1926-S Half Dollar .... (83,000)	80.00	90.00	100.	120.	195.
1928 Half Dollar .... (6,000)	130.	150.	165.	180.	295.
1933-D Half Dollar .... (4,998)	220.	230.	245.	275.	425.
1934-D Half Dollar .... (7,000)	120.	135.	150.	165.	285.
1936 Half Dollar .... (10,000)	100.	110.	120.	130.	210.
1936-S Half Dollar .... (5,000)	100.	120.	130.	160.	275.
1937-D Half Dollar .... (12,000)	110.	125.	140.	150.	190.
1938 Half Dollar .... (6,000)					
1938-D Half Dollar .... (6,000)					
1938-S Half Dollar .... (6,000)					
1938 PDS set	—	—	575.	650.	800.
1939 Half Dollar .... (3,000)					
1939-D Half Dollar .... (3,000)					
1939-S Half Dollar .... (3,000)					
1939 PDS set	—	—	1175.	1325.	2000.

Vermont-Bennington Sesquicentennial

Vermont-Bennington Sesquicentennial half dollar

	EF-40	AU-50	MS-60	MS-63	MS-65
1927 Half Dollar .... (28,108)	125.	140.	155.	200.	875.

Obv. Bust right of Ira Allen, founder of the revolutionary Vermont Republic. Rev. Catamount or mountain lion, symbolizing Catamount Tavern in Bennington, patriot headquarters. This version of Charles Keck's design was adopted over violent objections of Vermont committee, who wanted the battle monument or a view of the tavern itself as depicted on one coin model and on the official medal also designed by Keck.

Hawaii Discovery Sesquicentennial

Hawaii Sesquicentennial half dollar

		EF-40	AU-50	MS-60	MS-63	MS-65
1928 Half Dollar .... (9,950) .... (50)		900.	1050.	1350.	1950.	4800.

Obv. Uniformed bust of British Pacific explorer Capt. James Cook, discoverer of Hawaii, who was ambushed and killed there in 1779. Rev. Native chief with spear and feather cloak overlooking Waikiki beach. Designed by Juliette May Frazer, modeled by Chester Beach. Matte Proofs made for dignitary distribution; the Bank of Hawaii hoard of 137 Uncirculated pieces dispersed at auction by Bowers & Merena, Jan. 1986. Several counterfeits exist.

Maryland Tercentenary

Maryland Tercentenary half dollar

	EF-40	AU-50	MS-60	MS-63	MS-65
1934 Half Dollar .... (25,000)	105.	115.	125.	140.	360.

Obv. Facing bust of English Catholic nobleman Cecil Calvert, second Lord Baltimore, proprietor of Maryland, first American colony to guarantee religious liberty. Rev. Arms of state, adapted from family arms of the Calverts. Designed by Hans Schuler, whose Tercentenary Medal depicted Governor Leonard Calvert and colonists' ships *Ark* and *Dove*. Excessively rare Matte Proofs known.

Texas Independence Centennial

Texas Independence Centennial half dollar

	EF-40	AU-50	MS-60	MS-63	MS-65
1934 Half Dollar .... (61,350)	78.00	85.00	90.00	95.00	145.

Obv. Kneeling winged Liberty with arm around the Alamo; small roundel busts of Sam Houston and Stephen A. Austin, six flags above. Rev. Eagle in profile superimposed on Lone Star. The busiest commemorative, designed by Pompeo Coppini.

		EF-40	AU-50	MS-60	MS-63	MS-65
1935 Half Dollar .... (9,988)						
1935-D Half Dollar .... (10,000)						
1935-S Half Dollar .... (10,000)						
1935 P-D-S set		—	—	300.	315.	435.

Texas Independence Centennial continued

			EF-40	AU-50	MS-60	MS-63	MS-65
1936 Half Dollar (8,903)							
1936-D Half Dollar (9,032)							
1936-S Half Dollar (9,057)							
1936 P-D-S set			—	—	300.	315.	435.
1937 Half Dollar (6,566)							
1937-D Half Dollar (6,599)							
1937-S Half Dollar (6,630)							
1937 P-D-S set			—	—	300.	315.	435.
1938 Half Dollar (3,775)							
1938-D Half Dollar (3,770)							
1938-S Half Dollar (3,808)							
1938 P-D-S set			—	—	600.	775.	1025.

Daniel Boone Bicentennial

Daniel Boone Bicentennial half dollar

	EF-40	AU-50	MS-60	MS-63	MS-65
1934 Half Dollar (10,000)	62.00	70.00	82.00	88.00	145.

Obv. Fictitious bust of frontiersman Daniel Boone. Rev. Standing figures of Boone and Shawnee chief Black Fish, Fort Boonesborough behind. Designed by Augustus Lukeman.

	EF-40	AU-50	MS-60	MS-63	MS-65
1935 Half Dollar (10,000)					
1935-D Half Dollar (5,000)					
1935-S Half Dollar (5,000)					
1935 P-D-S set	—	—	255.	300.	455.

1934 added above PIONEER YEAR

	EF-40	AU-50	MS-60	MS-63	MS-65
1935 Half Dollar (10,000)					

With small 1934 added above PIONEER YEAR on rev.

	EF-40	AU-50	MS-60	MS-63	MS-65
1935-D Half Dollar (2,000)					
1935-S Half Dollar (2,000)					
1935 Small 1934 P-D-S set	—	—	600.	800.	1800.
1936 Half Dollar (12,000)					
1936-D Half Dollar (5,000)					
1936-S Half Dollar (5,000)					
1936 P-D-S set	—	—	255.	285.	480.
1937 Half Dollar (9,800)					
1937-D Half Dollar (2,500)					
1937-S Half Dollar (2,500)					
1937 P-D-S set	—	—	625.	720.	1150.
1938 Half Dollar (2,100)					
1938-D Half Dollar (2,100)					
1938-S Half Dollar (2,100)					
1938 P-D-S set	—	—	800.	1025.	1500.

Counterfeits known for 1937-P, others possible. One 1937-P-D-S Matte Proof set reported, ex Sinnock estate.

Connecticut Tercentenary

Connecticut Tercentenary half dollar

	EF-40	AU-50	MS-60	MS-63	MS-65
1935 Half Dollar .... (25,000)	145.	165.	195.	205.	550.

Obv. Hartford's "Charter Oak," in which the colonists hid their charter to prevent its confiscation by Sir Edmund Andros, acting for King James II. Rev. Bold standing eagle. One of the most powerful designs in the U.S. series, designed by Henry Kreis. Perhaps six Matte Proofs exist.

Arkansas Centennial

Arkansas Centennial half dollar

	EF-40	AU-50	MS-60	MS-63	MS-65
1935 Half Dollar .... (13,000)					

Obv. Conjoined heads of modernistic Liberty and Indian. Rev. Eagle with outstretched wings, guarding symbol of Arkansas flag, itself derived from the Confederate battle flag. Designed by Edward Everett Burr and modeled by Emily Bates. Identification of obverse and reverse has been subject to debate.

	EF-40	AU-50	MS-60	MS-63	MS-65
1935-D Half Dollar .... (5,500)					
1935-S Half Dollar .... (5,500)					
1935 P-D-S set			230.	270.	720.
1936 Half Dollar .... (9,650)	55.00	62.00	65.00	72.00	230.
1936-D Half Dollar .... (9,650)					
1936-S Half Dollar .... (9,650)					
1936 P-D-S set			235.	270.	1000.
1937 Half Dollar .... (5,500)					
1937-D Half Dollar .... (5,500)					
1937-S Half Dollar .... (5,500)					
1937 P-D-S set			240.	300.	1050.
1938 Half Dollar .... (3,150)					
1938-D Half Dollar .... (3,150)					
1938-S Half Dollar .... (3,150)					
1938 P-D-S set.			360.	440.	2000.
1939 Half Dollar .... (2,100)					
1939-D Half Dollar .... (2,100)					
1939-S Half Dollar .... (2,100)					
1939 P-D-S set			660.	900.	2800.

A Unique 1935 Proof is reported; two 1938-P-D-S Proof sets known.

Arkansas-Robinson

Arkansas-Robinson half dollar

	EF-40	AU-50	MS-60	MS-63	MS-65
1936 Half Dollar .... (25,250)	63.00	72.00	80.00	85.00	260.

Obv. Bust of Democratic Senator Joseph T. Robinson, New Deal statesman and 1928 vice presidential candidate with New York Governor Al Smith. Designed by Henry Kreis. Rev. Same as on 1935 Arkansas Centennial. Extremely rare Satin Proofs known.

Hudson, N.Y., Sesquicentennial

Hudson, N.Y., Sesquicentennial
half dollar

	EF-40	AU-50	MS-60	MS-63	MS-65
1935 Half Dollar .... (10,000)	380.	450.	500.	515.	1325.

Obv. Henry Hudson's sailing ship, the *Halve Maene* (Half Moon). Rev. Adaptation of the city seal with Neptune riding spouting whale. Although English, Hudson explored the coasts for the United Provinces of the Netherlands. The whale is a compliment to the city's founders, seafaring families fron Nantucket and Martha's Vineyard. Designed by Chester Beach. Counterfeits exist. Matte Proofs reported.
"Capture" of 75 percent of the coins within days of issue by New York dealer Julius Guttag made the Hudson a byword for commemorative abuses in the 1930s.

California-Pacific Exposition

California-Pacific Exposition half dollar

	EF-40	AU-50	MS-60	MS-63	MS-65
1935-S Half Dollar .... (70,000)	48.00	55.00	60.00	63.00	90.00

Obv. Helmeted Minerva seated with spear and shield, Grizzly at her side. Rev. California Tower and dome of chapel of Saint Francis in geometric frame. Designed by Robert Aitken. Satin Proofs reported. Usually known as the San Diego commemorative.

	EF-40	AU-50	MS-60	MS-63	MS-65
1936-D Half Dollar .... (30,000)	56.00	60.00	65.00	70.00	100.

Upper tower always poorly detailed.

Old Spanish Trail

Old Spanish Trail half dollar

	EF-40	AU-50	MS-60	MS-63	MS-65
1935 Half Dollar .... (10,000)	735.	765.	800.	850.	1025.

Obv. Longhorn skull, punning on name of Alvar Nunez Cabeza de Vaca, "Head of a Cow." Rev. Map of explorer's route and later Camino Real from New Smyrna, Florida, to El Paso, Texas. Alvar Nunez' actual expedition was commanded by the ill-fated Panfilo de Narvaez in 1527-42 and was a seven and a half-year trail of disaster through the Gulf states. Designed by L. W. Hoffecker, modeled by Edmund J. Senn. Several counterfeits exist. Matte Proofs known, one ex Sinnock estate.

Providence, R.I., Tercentenary

Providence, R.I., Tercentenary half dollar

	EF-40	AU-50	MS-60	MS-63	MS-65
1936 Half Dollar .... (20,000)	60.00	65.00	72.00	80.00	200.
1936-D Half Dollar .... (15,000)					
1936-S Half Dollar .... (15,000)					
1936 P-D-S set	—	—	230.	260.	700.

Obv. Roger Williams, religious liberal refugee from Puritan Massachusetts, landing at site of Providence. Rev. State seal, anchor symbolizing hope, motto HOPE. Bold-letter *art naif* style by Arthur Graham Carey, who perfected his approach with the Harvard University Tercentenary Medal, and John Howard Benson. Usually known as the Rhode Island commemorative, as the designer neglected to include the word Providence.

Cleveland Centennial & Great Lakes Exposition

Cleveland Centennial & Great Lakes Exposition half dollar

	EF-40	AU-50	MS-60	MS-63	MS-65
1936 Half Dollar .... (50,000)	52.00	60.00	65.00	65.00	210.

Obv. Bust of Moses Cleaveland, revolutionary soldier and founder of the city. Rev. Stylized compass over a map of the Great Lakes, nine stars marking major lake ports, largest marking Cleveland. Designed by Brenda Putnam. First 200 pieces struck were issued in notarized holders, distributed by coin dealer Thomas G. Melish. The Western Reserve Numismatic Club countermarked 100 commemoratives with its emblem in 1941, and 20 pieces in 1971.

Wisconsin Territorial Centennial

Wisconsin Territorial Centennial
half dollar

	EF-40	AU-50	MS-60	MS-63	MS-65
1936 Half Dollar .... (25,000)	140.	150.	170.	180.	225.

Obv. Wisconsin Territorial seal, arm holds pickaxe over heap of galena ore (natural lead). Rev. Badger over arrows and olive branch. Designed by New York sculptor Benjamin Hawkins after Wisconsin art student David Parsons' amateurish models were rejected.

Cincinnati Music Center

Cincinnati Music Center half dollar

	EF-40	AU-50	MS-60	MS-63	MS-65
1936 Half Dollar .... (5,000)	190.	220.	235.	240.	480.
Obv. Bust of Stephen Foster, "America's Troubador."					
1936-D Half Dollar .... (5,000)					
1936-S Half Dollar .... (5,000)					
1936 P-D-S set	—	—	745.	785.	1775.

This issue was the acme of the 1930s commemorative boom. It commemorates nothing, since none of Cincinnati's great musical achievements took place in 1886, nor was Stephen Foster associated with the city except briefly as a bookkeeper. Coin dealer Thomas G. Melish cobbled up the issue solely for profit, charging an unheard-of $7.75 for a three-coin set, which climbed rapidly to $75 on the aftermarket. Compare this price with the $2,000- plus retail cost of a complete set of some recent gold and silver commemoratives and the Cincinnati's offenses seem trivial indeed.

Long Island Tercentenary

Long Island Tercentenary half dollar

	EF-40	AU-50	MS-60	MS-63	MS-65
1936 Half Dollar .... (81,773)	60.00	65.00	68.00	72.00	400.

Obv. Conjoined massive-jawed Dutch settler and Indian. Rev. Stylized three-masted Dutch sailing ship. Designed by Howard K. Weinman. Coin marks anniversary of Dutch settlement on Jamaica Bay called Breuckelin on the south coast of Lange Eylandt, now Brooklyn, Long Island. Sculptor was son of coin designer A.A. Weinman, brother of prominent medallic sculptor Robert A. Weinman.

York County, Maine, Tercentenary

York County, Maine, Tercentenary
half dollar

	EF-40	AU-50	MS-60	MS-63	MS-65
1936 Half Dollar .... (25,000)	130.	135.	145.	160.	200.

Obv. View of Brown's Garrison at Saco. Rev. York County seal, red St. Andrew's cross with pine tree in first quarter based on early Revolutionary flag. Designed by Walter H. Rich, modeled by G.S. Pacetti Co. This issue whose obverse resembles nothing more than a carnival throw is an example of the trivialization which contributed powerfully to the downfall of commemoratives.

Bridgeport Centennial

Bridgeport, Conn., Centennial half dollar

	EF-40	AU-50	MS-60	MS-63	MS-65
1936 Half Dollar .... (25,000)	90.00	100.	105.	115.	300.

Obv. Bust of Phineas T. Barnum, showman, Bridgeport mayor and long-time civic booster. Rev. Exceptionally modernistic profile eagle, designed by Henry Kreis. Counterfeits exist. Bridgeport was first settled as Pequonnock in 1639; 1836 date is that of incorporation as a city. Barnum was born in Bethel, Conn., and launched his uproarious career partly in reaction to his home town's aggressive Puritan dullness.

Lynchburg, Va., Sesquicentennial

Lynchburg, Va., Centennial half dollar

	EF-40	AU-50	MS-60	MS-63	MS-65
1936 Half Dollar .... (20,000)	135.	145.	155.	170.	315.

Obv. Bust of Senator Carter Glass, architect of national bank reform and the Federal Reserve System. The senator strongly opposed the use of his portrait but his objections did not sway the local committee. Rev. Liberty in welcoming posture, old Lynchburg Courthouse and Confederate monument behind. Designed by Charles Keck.

Albany, N.Y., Charter 250th Anniversary

Albany, N.Y., Charter 250th Anniversary
half dollar

	EF-40	AU-50	MS-60	MS-63	MS-65
1936 Half Dollar .... (17,658)	180.	195.	205.	215.	350.

Obv. Governor Thomas Dongan, later Earl of Limerick congratulates Secretary Robert Livingston and Mayor Peter Schuyler with new Charter. Rev. Beaver on maple branch, designed by Gertrude Lathrop, noted wildlife sculptor. This Irish Catholic nobleman was sent by James, Duke of York to the then-bankrupt colony in 1682. He convened the first representative assembly, which enacted a Charter of Liberties forbidding taxation without representation and made New York the second colony to guarantee religious freedom. Dongan's Albany Charter was in force until 1870; that of New York City was unchanged for 135 years.

Elgin, Ill., Pioneer Memorial

Elgin, Ill., half dollar

	EF-40	AU-50	MS-60	MS-63	MS-65
1936 Half Dollar .... (20,000)	150.	160.	165.	180.	230.

Obv. Pioneer head left in fur hat. Rev. Group of five pioneers that were to form a heroic monument never actually built. Both coin and proposed statuary were designed by Trygve Rovelstad. Never found fully detailed, especially on the face of the infant in the mother's arms. A single Satin Proof reported.

San Francisco-Oakland Bay Bridge

San Francisco-Oakland Bay Bridge
half dollar

	EF-40	AU-50	MS-60	MS-63	MS-65
1936-S Half Dollar .... (71,369)	80.00	90.00	110.	125.	300.

Obv. Monarch II, celebrated California grizzly bear in Golden Gate Park zoo. Rev. Perspective of Embarcadero, bridge with Yerba Buena Island and hills on mainland. Designed by Jacques Schnier. Usually known simply as the Bay Bridge commemorative.

Columbia, S.C., Sesquicentennial

*Columbia, S.C., Sesquicentennial
half dollar*

	EF-40	AU-50	MS-60	MS-63	MS-65
1936 Half Dollar .... (9,000)	135.	150.	155.	170.	210.

Obv. Justice without blindfold, standing between 1786 and 1936 state houses. Rev. State Palmetto tree in circle of stars, crossed arrows tied to trunk. Designed by A. Wolfe Davidson. Another disappointing, token-like design.

1936-D Half Dollar .... (8,000)					
1936-S Half Dollar .... (8,000)					
1936 P-D-S set	—	—	520.	550.	725.

Delaware Tercentenary

Delaware Tercentenary half dollar

	EF-40	AU-50	MS-60	MS-63	MS-65
1936 Half Dollar .... (20,978)	170.	200.	210.	220.	350.

Obv. Swedish ship *Kalmar Nyckel* under full sail. Rev. Old Swedes' Church at Wilmington. Designed by Carl L. Schmitz. Authorized and dated 1936, struck 1937, also bears Tercentenary dates 1638-1938. Sweden issued a 2-kronor coin for this event in 1938 and a 100 kronor in 1988 with more accurate views of the ship.

Battle of Gettysburg 75th Anniversary

Battle of Gettysburg half dollar

	EF-40	AU-50	MS-60	MS-63	MS-65
1936 Half Dollar .... (26,900)	225.	250.	270.	275.	560.

Obv. Conjoined busts of Union and Confederate soldiers. Rev. Union and Confederate shields joined by double edged fasces. Blue and Gray Reunion refers to actual meeting of Grand Army of the Republic and United Confederate Veterans members on the battlefield on July 1-3, 1936, a remarkable demonstration of reconciliation. Designed by Frank Vittor. Authorized and dated 1936, struck 1937, also bears 75th anniversary dates 1863-1938.

Norfolk, Va., Bicentennial and Tercentenary

Norfolk, Va., Bicentennial half dollar

	EF-40	AU-50	MS-60	MS-63	MS-65
1936 Half Dollar .... (16,923)	325.	340.	350.	360.	400.

Obv. Seal of Norfolk with ship, plow and wheat garbs. Rev. Norfolk Royal Mace, presented 1753, Land Grant date 1636 between dogwood sprays. Designed by William Marks Simpson and Marjorie Emory Simpson. This handsome coin is actually a dual commemorative, hailing the Bicentennial of the borough and Tercentenary of the original land grant.

Roanoke Colonization 350th Anniversary

Roanoke Colonization 350th Anniversary half dollar

	EF-40	AU-50	MS-60	MS-63	MS-65
1937 Half Dollar .... (29,000)	145.	155.	170.	185.	240.

Obv. Bust of Sir Walter Raleigh in Elizabethan costume with earring. Rev. Eleanor Dare holding infant daughter Virginia. Designed by William Marks Simpson. The Fine Arts Commission and authorizing act used spelling Raleigh, although the swashbuckling adventurer himself apparently signed his name Ralegh. A number of Satin Finish Proofs exist, authentication recommended.

Battle of Antietam 75th Anniversary

Battle of Antietam half dollar

	EF-40	AU-50	MS-60	MS-63	MS-65
1937 Half Dollar .... (18,000)	365.	400.	445.	450.	600.

Obv. Conjoined busts of Union General George B. McClellan and Confederate General Robert E. Lee. Rev. View of Burnside Bridge, pivot of battle. Antietam was one of the most sanguinary Civil War battles, technically a Union victory, but the McClellan's habitual timidity cheated the North of its chance to follow up with the destruction of Lee's Army of Northern Virginia. Designed by William Marks Simpson. Counterfeits exist.

New Rochelle, N.Y., 250th Anniversary

New Rochelle, N.Y., 250th Anniversary half dollar

	EF-40	AU-50	MS-60	MS-63	MS-65
1938 Half Dollar .... (15,251)	245.	265.	275.	295.	345.

Obv. "Fatt calfe" being delivered to John Pell, Lord of the Manor of Pelham. Rev. Stylized fleur-de-lis, recalling French Huguenot settlers from La Rochelle, France in 1688. Designed by Gertrude Lathrop. Authorized 1936, struck 1937, dated 1938. Fifty brilliant Proof-like presentation pieces were struck with one blow of polished dies on Proof planchets. Possibly 14 Matte Proofs were also struck, authentication recommended.

Iowa Statehood Centennial

Iowa Statehood Centennial half dollar

	EF-40	AU-50	MS-60	MS-63	MS-65
1946 Half Dollar .... (100,000)	60.00	72.00	77.00	80.00	105.

Obv. Iowa state seal, eagle and scrolls bearing motto Our Liberties We Prize And Our Rights We Shall Maintain. Rev. Old Stone Capitol in Iowa City, Iowa Capitol. Designed by U.S. Mint engraver Adam Pietz. Interestingly, 1,000 pieces were reserved for anniversaries to be celebrated in 1996 and 2046.

Booker T. Washington Memorial

Booker T. Washington Memorial half dollar

	EF-40	AU-50	MS-60	MS-63	MS-65
1946 Half Dollar .... (1,000,000)	10.00	10.50	12.00	16.00	35.00

Obv. Bust of Black educator and intellectual giant Booker T. Washington. Rev. Hall of Fame for Great Americans at New York University and Virginia slave cabin. Designed by Isaac Scott Hathaway, Black sculptor who owned a life mask of Washington, after Charles Keck's previously approved models were summarily discarded. The larger mintages are very common in circulated condition. Most issues are very scarce in well-struck condition, and are usually found heavily bagmarked.

	EF-40	AU-50	MS-60	MS-63	MS-65
1946-D Half Dollar .... (200,000)					
1946-S Half Dollar .... (500,000)					
1946 P-D-S set	—	—	38.00	50.00	130.

Booker T. Washington Memorial continued

1947 Half Dollar .... (100,000) ....
1947-D Half Dollar .... (100,000) ....
1947-S Half Dollar .... (100,000) ....

1947 P-D-S set..	—	—	50.00	80.00	275.

Note: Approximately half of each of the 1946 P-D-S and 1947 P-D-S mintages were melted at the Mint, exact figures unknown.

1948 Half Dollar .... (8,000) ....
1948-D Half Dollar .... (8,000) ....
1948-S Half Dollar .... (8,000) ....

1948 P-D-S set..	—	—	100.	115.	185.

1949 Half Dollar .... (6,000) ....
1949-D Half Dollar .... (6,000) ....
1949-S Half Dollar .... (6,000) ....

1949 P-D-S set..	—	—	180.	220.	290.

1950 Half Dollar .... (6,000) ....
1950-D Half Dollar .... (6,000) ....
1950-S Half Dollar .... (512,000) ....
    Slightly more than half melted at Mint.

1950 P-D-S set..	—	—	90.00	115.	165.

1951 Half Dollar .... (510,000) ....
    Slightly more than half melted at Mint.
1951-D Half Dollar .... (7,000) ....
1951-S Half Dollar .... (7,000) ....

1951 P-D-S set..	—	—	110.	140.	175.

Booker T. Washington - George Washington Carver

Booker T. Washington-George
Washington Carver half dollar

	EF-40	AU-50	MS-60	MS-63	MS-65
1951 Half Dollar .... (110,000)	10.00	11.50	12.50	18.00	50.00

Obv. Conjoined heads of Washington and botanist-agronomist Carver. Rev. Map rather unnecessarily inscribed U.S.A. Designed by Isaac Scott Hathaway. Like the preceding, the Washington-Carver coins were a project of S.J. Phillips. The second issue was to have borne the American Legion emblem and name of its National Americanism Commission until State Department protests led to substitution of the banal map. Proceeds were to "oppose the spread of Communism among Negroes in the interest of national defense." The sheer ugliness of the coin and financial defalcations of promoter Phillips helped sink commemoratives into undeserved oblivion for 28 years. The 1952 issue is very common in circulated condition; other large mintages also found circulated. All issues very rare in well-struck condition, and are usually found heavily bagmarked.

1951-D Half Dollar .... (10,000) ....
1951-S Half Dollar .... (10,000) ....

1951 P-D-S set..	—	—	80.00	100.	500.

1952 Half Dollar .... (2,006,000) ....
    Slightly less than half melted at Mint.
1952-D Half Dollar .... (8,000) ....
1952-S Half Dollar .... (8,000) ....

1952 P-D-S set..	—	—	56.00	125.	400.

1953 Half Dollar .... (8,000) ....
1953-D Half Dollar .... (8,000) ....
1953-S Half Dollar .... (108,000) ....
    Slightly more than half melted at Mint.

1953 P-D-S set..	—	—	57.50	120.	510.

1954 Half Dollar .... (12,000) ....
1954-D Half Dollar .... (12,000) ....
1954-S Half Dollar .... (122,000) ....
    Slightly more than half melted at Mint.

1954 P-D-S set..	—	—	72.00	90.00	475.

Commemorative coinage since 1982

Washington's Birth 250th Anniversary

George Washington's Birth 250th Anniversary half dollar

	MS-60	MS-63	MS-64	MS-65	PF-65
1982-D Half Dollar ...... (2,210,458)	4.00	4.50	5.00	5.75	*

Obv. Washington on horseback. Rev. 3/4 perspective of Mount Vernon. Designed by Mint Chief Engraver Elizabeth Jones and assistant Matthew Peloso, whose initials are concealed in shrubbery. 90 percent silver as pre-1965 coinage. Uncirculated only.

	MS-60	MS-63	MS-64	MS-65	PF-65
1982-S Half Dollar .... (4,894,044)	*	*	*	*	5.75

Proof only.

Games of XXIII Olympiad, Los Angeles

Discus Thrower dollar

	MS-60	MS-63	MS-64	MS-65	PF-65
1983-P Dollar .... (294,543)	8.00	8.50	8.75	10.00	*

Obv. Stylized reiteration of ancient sculptor Myron's discus thrower, Olympic Rings and logo. Rev Eagle's head. Designed by Elizabeth Jones and John Mercanti. .900 silver of earlier coinages. Uncirculated only.

	MS-60	MS-63	MS-64	MS-65	PF-65
1983-D Dollar .... (174,014)	9.00	10.00	11.00	13.00	*

As preceding, Uncirculated only.

	MS-60	MS-63	MS-64	MS-65	PF-65
1983-S Dollar .... (174,014) .... (1,577,025)	8.00	8.25	8.50	9.00	10.00

As preceding, Uncirculated and Proof versions, sold in Unc. sets and various Proof issues.

Los Angeles Olympics continued

Olympic Gateway dollar

	MS-60	MS-63	MS-64	MS-65	PF-65
1984-P Dollar .... (217,954)	13.00	13.50	14.00	14.50	*

Obv. "Olympic Gateway" sculpture in front of Los Angeles Colosseum, no Olympic Rings. Rev. Eagle on pedestal. Designed by Robert Graham, creator of sculpture on obverse. Uncirculated only.

| 1984-D Dollar .... (116,675) .... | 22.00 | 22.50 | 23.00 | 24.50 | * |

As preceding, Uncirculated only.

| 1984-S Dollar .... (116,675) .... (1,801,210) | 23.00 | 23.50 | 24.00 | 25.00 | 11.50 |

As preceding, Unc. and Proof versions.

Torchbearers eagle

	MS-60	MS-63	MS-64	MS-65	PF-65
1984-P Eagle .... (33,309)	*	*	*	*	275.

Obv. male and female runners carry Olympic torch, Rings to left. Rev. Spread eagle without national shield. Designed by Jim Peed and John Mercanti. Proof only, specifications of earlier gold eagle coinage.

| 1984-D Eagle .... (34,533) .... | * | * | * | * | 245. |

As preceding, Proof only.

| 1984-S Eagle .... (48,551) .... | * | * | * | * | 210. |

As preceding, Proof only.

| 1984-W Eagle .... (75,886) .... (381,085) | — | — | 200. | 205. | 225. |

As preceding, first commemorative to bear West Point Mint mark, Proofs outnumber Uncirculated pieces. Lazard Freres' ambitious proposal for 53 coins including a silver $10 and gold $50 and $100 was derailed by the opposition of Rep. Frank Annunzio. As issued, however, Olympic coins still appeared in a confusing assortment of singles and sets, alone or in conjunction with the 1983 and 1984 silver dollars. Figures given represent total sales for each date and Mint.

Statue of Liberty - Ellis Island Centennial

Immigrant half dollar

	MS-60	MS-63	MS-64	MS-65	PF-65
1986-D Half Dollar .... (928,008)	4.00	4.25	4.50	5.50	*

Copper-nickel clad. Obv. Statue of Liberty seen from its right side, by Edgar Z. Steever. Rev. Immigrants on Ellis Island looking toward Manhattan skyline, by Sherl J. Winter. Uncirculated only.

| 1986-S Half Dollar ...... (6,925,627) .... | * | * | * | * | 5.50 |

Copper-nickel clad. As preceding, Proof only.

Statue of Liberty — Ellis Island Centennial continued

Ellis Island dollar

	MS-60	MS-63	MS-64	MS-65	PF-65
1986-P Dollar .... (723,635)	9.00	9.50	10.50	12.00	*

Obv. Ellis Island immigrant reception building with Statue of Liberty right. Rev. Detail of torch, quote from Emma Lazarus' poem "The New Colossus." Designed by John Mercanti, poem inscription by Matthew Peloso. Specifications of earlier silver dollars, Uncirculated only.

	MS-60	MS-63	MS-64	MS-65	PF-65
1986-S Dollar .... (6,414,638)	*	*	*	*	11.00

As preceding, Proof only

Statue of Liberty half eagle

	MS-60	MS-63	MS-64	MS-65	PF-65
1986-W Half Eagle .... (95,248) .... (404,013)	—	—	108.	115.	107.

Obv. Upturned face of Statue of Liberty. Rev. Striking eagle. Designed by Elizabeth Jones. Proofs outnumber Uncs. once again. Standards of previous half eagles. Proceeds of coin sales aided restoration of the statue and the construction of the visitors' center and museum on Ellis Island.

Constitution Bicentennial

Constitution Bicentennial dollar

	MS-60	MS-63	MS-64	MS-65	PF-65
1987-P Dollar .... (451,629)	7.50	7.75	8.00	8.50	*

Obv. Parchment, quill pen, We the People...; Rev. Citizens in period costumes, denomination DOLLAR 1. Designed by Patricia Verani. Uncirculated only.

	MS-60	MS-63	MS-64	MS-65	PF-65
1987-S Dollar .... (2,747,116)	*	*	*	*	8.50

As preceding, Proof only.

Constitution Bicentennial continued

Constitution Bicentennial half eagle

	MS-60	MS-63	MS-64	MS-65	PF-65
1987-W Half Eagle .... (651,659) .... (214,225)	—	—	102.	104.	98.00

Obv. Eagle in profile holding quill pen. Rev. Upright quill, We the People... Designed by Marcel Jovine. Specifications of 1986 gold coin.

Games of XXIV Olympiad

Calgary, Alberta; Seoul, Korea

Games of XXIV Olympiad dollar

	MS-60	MS-63	MS-64	MS-65	PF-65
1988-D Dollar .... (191,368)	9.75	10.00	10.25	10.50	*

Obv. Statue of Liberty's torch lights Olympic torch, OLYMPIAD without number above. Rev. 1/DOLLAR, USA and Olympic Rings in laurel wreath. Designed by Patricia Lewis Verani (obv.), Sherl J. Winter (rev.). Such use of the word Olympiad is incorrect, as it represents a period of four years, not the actual games. These are properly called Games of the XXIV (or other number) Olympiad.

	MS-60	MS-63	MS-64	MS-65	PF-65
1988-S Dollar .... (1,359)	*	*	*	*	8.50

As preceding, Proof only.

Games of XXIV Olympiad half eagle

	MS-60	MS-63	MS-64	MS-65	PF-65
1988-W Half Eagle .... (62,913) .... (281,465)	—	—	107.	110.	104.

Obv. Facing head of Nike, goddess of Victory Rev. Stylized torch, Olympic Rings enclosing USA above. Designed by Elizabeth Jones (obv.), Marcel Jovine (rev.).

Bicentennial of Congress

Bicentennial of Congress half dollar

	MS-60	MS-63	MS-64	MS-65	PF-65
1989-D Half Dollar	9.00	9.50	9.75	10.00	*

Copper-nickel clad. Obv. Detail of statue, Goddess of Freedom Triumphant, from peak of Capitol dome. Rev. U.S. Capitol in circle of stars. Designed by Patricia Lewis Verani (obv.), William Woodward (rev.). Uncirculated only.

1989-S Half Dollar	*	*	*	*	6.00

As preceding, Proof only.

Bicentennial of Congress dollar

	MS-60	MS-63	MS-64	MS-65	PF-65
1989-D Dollar	14.00	14.50	14.75	15.00	*

Obv. Full length rendering of Goddess of Freedom Triumphant against clouds and sunburst. Rev. Mace of the House of Representatives. Designed by William Woodward. Uncirculated only.

1989-S Dollar	*	*	*	*	12.00

As preceding, Proof only.

Bicentennial of Congress half eagle

	MS-60	MS-63	MS-64	MS-65	PF-65
1989-W Half Eagle	—	—	110.	115.	107.

Obv. Capitol dome. Rev Spread eagle from old Senate Chamber. Designed by John Mercanti.

Eisenhower Birth Centennial

Eisenhower Birth Centennial dollar

	MS-60	MS-63	MS-64	MS-65	PF-65
1990-W Dollar .... (241,669)	11.00	12.00	13.00	13.50	*

Obverse by John Mercanti presents two busts of Dwight David Eisenhower facing left and right, first in five-star general's uniform as Allied commander in Europe and in civil dress as 34th President. The reverse depicts the Eisenhower home at Gettysburg, Pa., presented by the nation. This is the first appearance of the W Mint mark on a silver coin. Objections arose to another Eisenhower coin, after the 1971-78 circulating dollar and its controversial funding of the bankrupt Eisenhower College.

	MS-60	MS-63	MS-64	MS-65	PF-65
1990-P Dollar	*	*	*	*	16.00

As preceding, Proof only.

Mount Rushmore 50th Anniversary

Mount Rushmore half dollar

	MS-60	MS-63	MS-64	MS-65	PF-65
1991-D Half Dollar .... (172,754)	12.00	13.00	13.50	14.00	*

The obverse by Marcel Jovine presents a view of Gutzon Borglum's heroic Black Hills sculpture under a rising sun, no rim decoration. Mint sculptor T. James Ferrell's reverse bears a rather elongated American bison (a contrast to the short-bodied animal on Fraser's 1913 Nickel), italic GOLDEN ANNIVERSARY and outer border of stars.

	MS-60	MS-63	MS-64	MS-65	PF-65
1991-S Half Dollar .... (753,157)	*	*	*	*	13.00

As preceding, Proof only.

Mount Rushmore dollar

	MS-60	MS-63	MS-64	MS-65	PF-65
1991-P Dollar .... (133,139)	23.00	23.50	24.00	26.00	*

Obverse bears Marika Somogyi's interpretation of the heroic sculpture with incuse 1991 and wreath. Former Chief Engraver Frank Gasparro's reverse combines the Great Seal in circle and rays, a relief map of the U.S. merging with the formless clouds above it, below appears SHRINE OF DEMOCRACY.

Mount Rushmore continued

	MS-60	MS-63	MS-64	MS-65	PF-65
1991-S Dollar .... (738,419)	*	*	*	*	26.00

As preceding, Proof only.

Mount Rushmore half eagle

	MS-60	MS-63	MS-64	MS-65	PF-65
1991-W Half Eagle .... (31,959) .... (111,991)	—	—	130.	135.	124.

A stylized eagle holding mallet and chisel swoops on the monument on John Mercanti's obverse. Mint sculptor William Cousins engraved the all-inscription reverse designed by Robert Lamb. Half of the profit derived from the surcharges on the Mount Rushmore coins was applied to retiring the national debt, the remainder to restoration of the memorial after more than 50 brutal South Dakota winters and for completion of the Hall of Records originally planned by Gutzon Borglum.

Korean War 38th Anniversary

Korean War dollar

	MS-60	MS-63	MS-64	MS-65	PF-65
1991-D Dollar .... (213,049)	15.00	15.50	15.75	16.00	*

John Mercanti designed this crowded obverse, showing an advancing infantryman towering over minute warships, Saber jets flying toward eight stars. Precious space is wasted by the redundant word COMMEMORATIVE in the inscription. Reverse bears a relief map divided by the unidentified 38th Parallel. North Korea is shaded, South Korea's bears its national yin-yang emblem; an eagle head appears at r.

	MS-60	MS-63	MS-64	MS-65	PF-65
1991-P Dollar .... (618,488)	*	*	*	*	16.50

As preceding, Proof only.

Coin sales helped finance the long-awaited National Korean War Memorial in the nation's capital. It is fascinating to note that all publicity referred to the Korean "War," while the Truman Administration had irritatingly insisted on Korean "Conflict." The official explanation for celebrating the 38th anniversary was fear that fewer veterans would be alive for the 50th.

United Service Organizations 50th Anniversary

USO dollar

	MS-60	MS-63	MS-64	MS-65	PF-65
1991-D Dollar .... (124,958)	15.50	16.00	16.25	16.50	*

Robert Lamb used the pennant-like USO flag and script anniversary inscription for his obverse. John Mercanti's reverse placed a parrot-like eagle on globe holding a USO streamer dividing FIFTY YEARS SERVICE TO SERVICE PEOPLE.

1991-S Dollar .... (321,275)	*	*	*	*	15.00

As preceding, Proof only.

Half of the surcharges from this program went to USO programs, half to reduction of the national debt.

Games of XXV Olympiad, Albertville, Barcelona

XXV Olympiad half dollar

	MS-60	MS-63	MS-64	MS-65	PF-65
1992-P Half Dollar .... (161,619)	5.75	6.00	6.25	6.50	*

A girl gymnast leaps across a flag background on William Cousins' obverse. Olympic torch, laurel and motto CITIUS, ALTIUS, FORTIUS provide Steven Bieda's reverse.

1992-S Half Dollar .... (519,699)	*	*	*	*	8.00

As preceding, Proof only.

XXV Olympiad dollar

	MS-60	MS-63	MS-64	MS-65	PF-65
1992-D Dollar .... (187,562)	22.50	23.00	23.50	24.00	*

John R. Deecken chose a baseball pitcher throwing to home plate pointed out by sports card enthusiasts as a virtual copy of a popular baseball card portraying Texas Rangers player Nolan Ryan. Marcel Jovine's reverse presents the U.S. shield between laurel branches, Olympic rings enclose U/S/ A above, full national name legend. Edge on the Unc. Dollar shows fine reeding plus four reiterations of incuse XXV OLYMPIAD, two facing obv., two rev.

1992-S Dollar .... (504,544)	*	*	*	*	29.00

As preceding, Proof only.

Games of XXV Olympiad continued

XXV Olympiad half eagle

	MS-60	MS-63	MS-64	MS-65	PF-65
1992-W Half Eagle. .... (27,732) .... (77,313)	—	—	130.	135.	117.

A sprinter resembling the immortal Jesse Owens (1913-80) races along a track-like flag on James Sharpe's obverse, modeled by T. James Ferrell. Mint artist Jim Peed's reverse places the American eagle under Olympic rings, USA above.

The half dollar and dollar were sold in the usual sets and as singles and were also included in the Prestige Proof Sets with the regular 1992 coinage. Part of the profits went to the U.S. Olympic Committee.

White House Bicentennial

White House dollar

	MS-60	MS-63	MS-64	MS-65	PF-65
1992-D Dollar .... (123,803)	25.00	25.50	26.00	26.50	*

Edgar Z. Steever IV depicts the north portico, without John Adams' prayerful words, "May none but honest and wise men ever rule under this roof." Chester Y. Martin's reverse presents a half-length portrait of Irish-born architect James Hoban (ca. 1762-1831), who designed the "President's House" and directed its rebuilding after the British burned Washington in 1814. This was the first of the modern commemoratives to give an encouraging performance in the secondary market.

	MS-60	MS-63	MS-64	MS-65	PF-65
1992-W Dollar. .... (375,849)	*	*	*	*	27.50

As preceding, Proof only.

Columbus Discovery Quincentennial

Columbus Quincentennial half dollar

	MS-60	MS-63	MS-64	MS-65	PF-65
1992-D Half Dollar .... (135,718)	12.00	12.50	13.00	13.50	*

T. James Ferrell depicted Columbus landing on San Salvador on his obverse, the navigator's three ships on the reverse. Note the correct 500TH ANNIVERSARY OF COLUMBUS DISCOVERY.

	MS-60	MS-63	MS-64	MS-65	PF-65
1992-S .... (390,225)	*	*	*	*	13.00

As preceding, Proof only.

Columbus Discovery Quincentennial continued

Columbus Quincentennial dollar

	MS-60	MS-63	MS-64	MS-65	PF-65
1992-D Dollar .... (106,962)	18.00	18.50	19.00	20.00	*

John Mercanti's obverse depicts a standing discoverer holding banner and map, three ships above. The legend COLUMBUS QUINCENTENARY is incorrect, since the celebration is not of his birth or death but of his great discovery. Space shuttle *Discovery* and Columbus flagship *Santa Maria* divide the reverse by Thomas D. Rogers Sr.

	MS-60	MS-63	MS-64	MS-65	PF-65
1992-P Dollar .... (385,241)	*	*	*	*	26.50

As preceding, Proof only.

Columbus Quincentennial half eagle

	MS-60	MS-63	MS-64	MS-65	PF-65
1992-W Half Eagle .... (24,331) .... (79,734)	—	—	130.	135.	140.

Possibly the most imaginative design of the set shows the discoverer gazing at a New World map on T. James Ferrell's obverse. The reverse by Thomas D. Rogers Sr. depicts the Coat of Arms granted Columbus as *Almirante de Mar Oceano,*as recorded in the *Cronica de Oviedo*, with map and compass rose at right.

The Columbus coins are arguably the most successful in overall design quality. Coinage followed the 1992 Omnibus bill also authorizing the 1993 Bill of Rights-Madison and 1994 World Cup Soccer commemoratives, as well as silver medals for Gulf War veterans. Accompanying the celebration of the 500th anniversary of discovery was an undercurrent of anti-Columbus sniping from the trendy and politically correct.

Bill of Rights - James Madison

Bill of Rights/Madison half dollar

	MS-60	MS-63	MS-64	MS-65	PF-65
1993-W Half Dollar .... (193,346)	11.00	12.50	13.00	14.00	*

Seated James Madison inscribes the Bill of Rights, his home Montpelier appears in the right field on T. James Ferrell's obverse; a hand and torch dominate Dean McMullen's reverse. This is the only .900 silver half dollar since the 1982 Washington coin.

	MS-60	MS-63	MS-64	MS-65	PF-65
1993-S Half Dollar .... (586,315)	*	*	*	*	13.00

As preceding, Proof only.

Bill of Rights — James Madison continued

Bill of Rights/Madison dollar

	MS-60	MS-63	MS-64	MS-65	PF-65
1993-D Dollar .... (98,383)	14.50	15.00	15.50	16.00	*

A rugged James Madison appears on William Krawczewicz' obverse, modeled by Thomas D. Rogers Sr. James and Dolly Madison's stately Virginia home Montpelier graces Dean McMullen's reverse.

| 1993-S Dollar .... (534,001) | * | * | * | * | 16.00 |

As preceding, Proof only.

Bill of Rights/Madison half eagle

	MS-60	MS-63	MS-64	MS-65	PF-65
1993-W Half Eagle .... (23,266) .... (78,651)	—	—	165.	180.	117.

Scott R. Blazek's obverse shows a seated Madison holding his Bill of Rights; Joseph D. Pena's reverse bears a Madison quotation with eagle, torch and laurel. Obv. and Rev. were modeled by William C. Cousins and Edgar Z. Steever IV respectively.

Surcharge profits from this issue went to the James Madison Memorial Fellowship Trust Fund, founded 1986. In addition to the usual packaging options, Unc. silver half dollars were sold in a special Young Collector's Edition in a British-made holder and in tandem with a U.S. Mint Madison medal. The W half dollar and dollar were also included in the Prestige Proof set. Intense controversy was generated by American Numismatic Association's acquisition of some 10,000 Unc. half dollars, having Silvertowne of Winchester, Indiana, remove a section of reeding and impress a serial number, ANA lamp logo and initials of the Madison Fellowship.

World War II 50th Anniversary, Dual Dates 1991-1995

World War II half dollar

	MS-60	MS-63	MS-64	MS-65	PF-65
(1993) P Half Dollar .... (197,072)	9.00	9.50	10.00	10.50	*

George Klauba's obverse shows a GI, sailor and military nurse against a large V with a bomber and five stars above. Bill Leftwich placed a marine landing on a South Pacific island with fighter plane overhead on the reverse.

| (1993) S Half Dollar .... (317,396) | * | * | * | * | 12.00 |

As preceding, Proof only.

World War II 50th Anniversary continued

World War II dollar

	MS-60	MS-63	MS-64	MS-65	PF-65
(1993) D Dollar .... (107,240)	20.50	21.50	22.50	23.50	*

Thomas D. Rogers Sr. depicts a U.S. Army infantryman storming ashore on a Normandy beach. His reverse bears the emblem of the Supreme Headquarters, Allied Expeditionary Forces with a 7-line Eisenhower exhortation.

	MS-60	MS-63	MS-64	MS-65	PF-65
(1993) W Dollar .... (342,041)	*	*	*	*	25.00

As preceding, Proof only.

World War II half eagle

	MS-60	MS-63	MS-64	MS-65	PF-65
(1993) W Half Eagle .... (23,672) .... (67,026)	—	—	175.	190.	139.

An American GI giving a victory cry provides Charles J. Madsen's obverse. A large V for victory with Morse code equivalent appear on Edward Southworth Fisher's reverse.
Dating of these coins may offer a challenge to future numismatists. Coins bear the dual dates 1991-1995, but were actually struck in 1993. The silver dollar also bears the date June 6, 1944, as well. Some $3 million from coin sales went to the Battle of Normandy Foundation to fund educational programs and a Memorial Garden near the landing beaches. A former Foundation officer publicized charges of financial mismanagement, claiming that 90 percent of income went to administration only. The foundation counter-charged that the allegations were a cover-up of the officer's own "unauthorized and irregular use of funds."

Soccer World Cup

World Cup half dollar

	MS-60	MS-63	MS-64	MS-65	PF-65
1994-D Half Dollar .... (168,208)	6.50	7.00	7.50	8.50	*

Designed by Richard T. LaRoche and modeled by John Mercanti, this coin presents a charging soccer player and the common reverse by Dean McMullen with the World Cup logo, a stylized soccer ball, stripes suggesting the American flag between laurel branches.

	MS-60	MS-63	MS-64	MS-65	PF-65
1994-P Half Dollar .... (609,354)	*	*	*	*	11.50

As preceding, Proof only.

Soccer World Cup continued

World Cup dollar

	MS-60	MS-63	MS-64	MS-65	PF-65
1994-D Dollar .... (81,524)	21.50	22.00	22.50	23.00	*

Designed by Dean McMullen and modeled by T. James Ferrell, this coin presents two muscular contending players attempting to kick the ball.

| 1994-S Dollar .... (577,090) | * | * | * | * | 27.50 |

As preceding, Proof only.

World Cup half eagle

	MS-60	MS-63	MS-64	MS-65	PF-65
1994-W Half Eagle .... (22,447) .... (89,614)	—	—	145.	150.	135.

The World Cup graces the obverse by William J. Krawczewicz, mottoes and date completing the simple design.

This issue was a serious embarrassment to the Mint, since many more coins were struck than were actually sold. Nonetheless, the Organizing Committee awarded its director a startlingly large bonus out of its general revenue, including Treasury money.

Thomas Jefferson 250th Anniversary of Birth

Jefferson dollar

	MS-60	MS-63	MS-64	MS-65	PF-65
1993-P Dollar .... (266,927)	29.50	30.00	30.50	31.00	*

Produced and sold in 1994, but backdated to 1993. T. James Ferrell's designs presents head of the Architect of Democracy I., after a medallion portrait by Gilbert Stuart, original in Harvard University's Fogg Art Museum. This likeness is a bold contrast to the more idealized Houdon bust on the Jefferson nickel. Plaster models by Dutch artist Frans Karel Hejda using this same portrait for the 1938 Jefferson nickel design competition were discovered by Stack's in early 1994. The reverse presents a far more attractive view of Monticello than that on the adopted design of the Jefferson 5 cents.

| 1993-S .... (332,891) | * | * | * | * | 28.00 |

As preceding, Proof only.

In addition to the usual packaging options, the U.S. Mint assembled a highly unusual package consisting of the 1993-P Unc. Jefferson silver dollar, a Crisp Unc. 1976 Bicentennial $2 bill, and a specially prepared 1994-P Jefferson nickel, double struck from sandblast dies, in effect a Matte Proof!

Women in Military Service Memorial

Women in Military Service Memorial
dollar

	MS-60	MS-63	MS-64	MS-65	PF-65
1994-W Dollar .... (53,054)	26.00	26.50	27.00	27.00	*

T. James Ferrell's obverse presents five uniformed service-women three-quarters left, representing the
Army, Marine Corps, Navy, Air Force and Coast Guard. Reverse offers a perspective of the approved
design of the memorial as interpreted by Thomas D. Rogers Sr.

	MS-60	MS-63	MS-64	MS-65	PF-65
1994-P Dollar .... (213,201)	*	*	*	*	28.00

As preceding, Proof only.

Vietnam Veterans' Memorial

Vietnam Veteran's Memorial dollar

	MS-60	MS-63	MS-64	MS-65	PF-65
1994-W Dollar .... (57,317)	26.00	26.25	26.50	27.00	*

Thomas D. Rogers Sr. obverse shows a hand tracing the names on the black stone surface of the
memorial, Washington Monument in the background. The reverse presents three military decorations of
the Vietnam war, two U.S. and one of the vanished Republic of Vietnam.

	MS-60	MS-63	MS-64	MS-65	PF-65
1994-P Dollar .... (226,262)	*	*	*	*	29.00

As preceding, Proof only.

Prisoners of War Museum

Prisoner of War dollar

	MS-60	MS-63	MS-64	MS-65	PF-65
1994-W Dollar .... (54,790)	26.00	26.25	26.50	27.00	*

Tom Nielsen of the Department of Veterans Affairs designed this obverse, engraved by Alfred Maletsky, depicting an eagle breaking free through a circle of barbed wire, broken chains around its legs, FREEDOM at r. Edgar Z. Steever's reverse presents a rendering of the proposed National Prisoner of War Museum

1994-P Dollar .... (220,100)	*	*	*	*	29.00

As preceding, Proof only.

United States Capitol Bicentennial

Capitol Bicentennial dollar

	MS-60	MS-63	MS-64	MS-65	PF-65
1994-D Dollar .... (68,332)	25.50	26.00	26.25	26.50	*

A view of the Capitol dome by William C. Cousins dominates his obverse. Said to be taken from a stained glass window in the capitol's grand staircase is the eagle-flag-shield device on John Mercanti's reverse. At first glance this design suggests a Western sheriff's badge.

1994-S Dollar .... (279,579)	*	*	*	*	25.00

As preceding, Proof only.

Civil War Battlefields

Civil War Battlefields half dollar

	MS-60	MS-63	MS-64	MS-65	PF-65
1995-D Half Dollar .... (119,554)	10.50	10.75	11.00	11.50	*

Connecticut artist Donald Troiani created all obverses for this three-coin issue. The first bears a youthful drummer with shattered snake fence behind. T. James Ferrell's reverse bears a cannon, inscr. ENRICHING OUR FUTURE BY PRESERVING OUR PAST.

	MS-60	MS-63	MS-64	MS-65	PF-65
1995-S Half Dollar .... (330,519)	*	*	*	*	12.00

As preceding, Proof only.

Civil War Battlefields dollar

	MS-60	MS-63	MS-64	MS-65	PF-65
1995-P Dollar .... (45,879)	25.00	25.50	26.00	27.00	*

A wounded soldier receives battlefield aid on this obverse. John Mercanti's reverse bears an extensive quote from Joshua Chamberlain, spirits lingering on consecrated ground.

	MS-60	MS-63	MS-64	MS-65	PF-65
1995-S Dollar .... (330,457)	*	*	*	*	32.00

As preceding, Proof only.

Civil War Battlefields half eagle

	MS-60	MS-63	MS-64	MS-65	PF-65
1995-W Half Eagle .... (12,743) .... (55,264)	—	—	225.	260.	175.

A cavalry bugler dominates this obverse, Albert Maletsky's reverse presents a Civil War-era eagle on shield.

Special Olympics World Games

Special Olympics/Eunice Kennedy Shriver dollar

	MS-60	MS-63	MS-64	MS-65	PF-65
1995-W Dollar .... (89,298)	29.00	29.50	30.00	31.00	*

The concept of the Special Olympics as a participatory event for the developmentally challenged was originated by Anne Burke of the Chicago Park District in 1965. After the first few successful games, Ms. Burke requested and received a grant of $25,000 from the Joseph P. Kennedy Foundation in 1968. At this point, Eunice Kennedy Shriver became interested and took the concept nationwide. Although some debate centered on use of a living person on a U.S. coin, Treasury Secretary Robert E. Rubin approved the use of the Kennedy likeness on Feb. 3, 1995. This dollar honors the Special Olympics World Games as an adjunct event to the 1996 Games of the XXVI Olympiad in Atlanta, Ga.. James Wyeth submitted obverse design, portraying Eunice Kennedy Shriver as founder of the Special Olympics (an honor which excludes those working in this field before her arrival), and T. James Ferrell lent a hand with the modeling. Thomas D. Rogers Sr. supplied the reverse with its Special Olympics logo and rose spray. A storm of controversy erupted as both the Commission of Fine Arts and the Citizens Commemorative Coin Advisory Committee opposed portrayal of a living person on a commemorative issue.

1995-P silver dollar .... (352,449)	*	*	*	*	27.00

As preceding, Proof only.

Games of the XXVI Olympiad, Atlanta

This program commemorating the centennial of modern Olympic Games clearly marks the absurdity of recent trends in commemorative issues. The coins feature a common reverse for each of two dates for each of three denominations. There are two copper-nickel half dollar obverses, four silver dollar obverses, and two $5 gold half eagles in each of 1995 and 1996, for a total of 16 designs. Furthermore, each will be issued in both Proof and Uncirculated, for a 32-coin program, which could set back the completion-minded collector $2,000 or more. Ironically, the scope of this program approaches the doomed 53-coin proposal of Lazard Freres for the 1984 Los Angeles Olympics. Some of the designs shown are enhanced drawings. Mintages are not reported, as in an effort to salvage sales which failed to meet expectations by a wide margin, the coins were still being offered for sale in late 1997. The Atlanta Games were widely criticized for their blatant commercialism. In this sense, then, the behemoth program was appropriate for the event.

1995 Half Dollar Type I Basketball

	MS-60	MS-63	MS-64	MS-65	PF-65
1995-S Half Dollar .... (NR) .... (NR)	12.00	12.50	13.00	13.50	13.00

Copper-nickel clad. Proof and Unc. both struck with S Mint mark. Basketball obv. by Clint Hansen. Common rev. by T. James Ferrell superimposes Centennial Games logo over globe, USOA and HALF DOLLAR around.

Games of the XXVI Olympiad continued

1995 Half Dollar Type II Baseball

	MS-60	MS-63	MS-64	MS-65	PF-65
1995-S Half Dollar .... (NR) .... (NR)	12.00	12.50	13.00	13.50	13.00

Copper-nickel clad. Proof and Unc. both struck with S Mint mark. Baseball obv. by Edgar Steever depicts umpire, catcher and batter, who appears about to whack the motto. Common rev.

1995 Dollar Type I Gymnastics

	MS-60	MS-63	MS-64	MS-65	PF-65
1995-D Dollar .... (NR)	29.00	29.50	30.00	31.00	*

Gymnastics obv. Type I by James Sharpe, with Thomas D. Rogers, initials low at rim. Female gymnast 3/4 with arms wide behind male gymnast performing maneuver on the still rings. USA and Olympic rings to left. Common reverse, by William Krawczewicz, with T. James Ferrell. Clasped hands, legends above, E PLURIBUS UNUM, centennial games logo and ATLANTA above center, ONE DOLLAR below, designer's and engraver's initials left and right below arms.

1995-P Dollar .... (NR)	*	*	*	*	34.00

Same, Proof only.

1995 Dollar Type II Cycling

	MS-60	MS-63	MS-64	MS-65	PF-65
1995-D Dollar .... (NR)	29.00	29.50	30.00	31.00	*

Cycling obv. Type II by John Mercanti. Three cyclists advancing toward viewer. USA and Olympic rings left, XXVI OLYMPIAD and LIBERTY right. Motto and date below. Common reverse.

1995-P Dollar .... (NR)	*	*	*	*	34.00

Same, Proof only.

Games of the XXVI Olympiad continued

1995 Dollar Type III Track & Field

	MS-60	MS-63	MS-64	MS-65	PF-65
1995-D Dollar .... (NR)	29.00	29.50	30.00	31.00	*

Track and Field obv. Type III. John Mercanti's rendering of sprinters running right in track lanes numbered 2, 3, 4, 5 from top, USA and Olympic rings top center, LIBERTY and XXVI OLYMPIAD at left, motto and date below. Common reverse.

	MS-60	MS-63	MS-64	MS-65	PF-65
1995-P Dollar .... (NR)	*	*	*	*	34.00

Same, Proof only.

1995 Dollar Type IV Paralympic, blind runner

	MS-60	MS-63	MS-64	MS-65	PF-65
1995-D Dollar .... (NR)	29.00	29.50	30.00	31.00	*

Paralympic, blind runner obv. Type IV by Jim Sharpe, with Thomas Rogers.Depicting an event in the loosely associated Paralympics, wherein a blind runner is assisted by a sighted runner. TRIUMPH OF THE HUMAN SPIRIT PARALYMPICS around, motto and date between runners. Paralympic star logo at right, designer's and engraver's initials near logo. Just above the top point of the star, and just below the lead runner's free elbow, is the Braille phrase "spirit." Common reverse.

	MS-60	MS-63	MS-64	MS-65	PF-65
1995-P Dollar .... (NR)	*	*	*	*	35.00

Same, Proof only.

1995 Half Eagle Type I Torch Runner

	MS-60	MS-63	MS-64	MS-65	PF-65
1995-W Half Eagle .... (NR) .... (NR)	—	—	180.	195.	169.

Torch Runner obv. Type I by numismatic legend Frank Gasparro depicts the torch bearer with city skyline in background, LIBERTY above, games logo and ATLANTA 1996 at right, motto and date at lower left. Initials near trailing foot. Common rev. also by Gasparro shows a defiant standing eagle with banner proclaiming centennial years 1896-1996 in its beak. USOA and EPU above, FIVE DOLLARS below.

Games of the XXVI Olympiad continued

1995 Half Eagle Type II Atlanta Stadium

	MS-60	MS-63	MS-64	MS-65	PF-65
1995-W Half Eagle .... (NR) .... (NR)	—	—	180.	195.	179.

Atlanta Stadium obv. Type II by design veteran Marcel Jovine. Atlanta Stadium at lower left, site of opening and closing ceremonies and many track and field events.Games logo dominates at right. Funky distorted LIBERTY imitating curl of smoke and stars from the logo's torch at top with THE CENTENNIAL GAMES in three lines below it, motto at left, date below. Common rev.

1996 Half Dollar Type I Swimming

	MS-60	MS-63	MS-64	MS-65	PF-65
1996-S Half Dollar .... (NR) .... (NR)	12.00	12.50	13.00	13.50	13.00

Copper-nickel clad. Swimming obv. Type I by William Krawczewicz. Common rev. by Malcom Farley.

1996 Half Dollar Type II Soccer

	MS-60	MS-63	MS-64	MS-65	PF-65
1996-S Half Dollar .... (NR) .... (NR)	12.00	12.50	13.00	13.50	13.00

Copper-nickel clad. Soccer obv. Type II by Clint Hansen. Common rev.

1996 Dollar Type I Tennis

	MS-60	MS-63	MS-64	MS-65	PF-65
1996-D Dollar .... (NR)	30.00	31.00	31.50	32.00	*

Tennis player obv. Type I by Jim Sharpe depicts female tennis player about to hit a forehand volley. Common rev. by Thomas D. Rogers Sr. USOA and ONE DOLLAR around rim, large games logo at left, right field filled with EPU, ATLANTA 1996 and CENTENNIAL OLYMPIC GAMES.

	MS-60	MS-63	MS-64	MS-65	PF-65
1996-P Dollar .... (NR)	*	*	*	*	37.00

Same, Proof only.

Games of the XXVI Olympiad continued

1996 Dollar Type II Rowing

	MS-60	MS-63	MS-64	MS-65	PF-65
1996-D Dollar .... (NR)	30.00	31.00	31.50	32.00	*

Rowing obv. Type II by Bart Forbes depicts four-man crew at the pull, XXVI OLYMPIAD around top left Olympic rings logo centered in top field, motto small in lower field, with LIBERTY 1996 at rim below. Common rev.

1996-P Dollar .... (NR)	*	*	*	*	37.00

Same, Proof only.

1996 Dollar Type III High Jump

	MS-60	MS-63	MS-64	MS-65	PF-65
1996-D Dollar .... (NR)	30.00	31.00	31.50	32.00	*

High Jump obv. Type III. Calvin Massey's design shows a high jumper arched over the bar in the now-classic Fosbury Flop style, LIBERTY widely spaced around above, motto, Olympic rings logo and 1996 in lower field. Common rev.

1996-P High Jump silver dollar .... (NR)	*	*	*	*	37.00

Same, Proof only.

1996 Dollar Type IV Paralympic, wheelchair athlete

	MS-60	MS-63	MS-64	MS-65	PF-65
1996-D Dollar .... (NR)	30.00	31.00	31.50	32.00	*

Another design for the associated Paralympics, which received almost no media coverage, wheelchair athlete obv. Type IV depicts an athlete in a sport chair facing, arms raised in triumph, TRIUMPH OF THE HUMAN SPIRIT in two curved lines above, PARALYMPICS LIBERTY 1996 at rim below. Motto in left field, Paralympics logo in right field. IN upper right field near athlete's head is the Braille character "spirit," as on 1995 Paralympic obv. Common rev.

1996-P Dollar .... (NR)	*	*	*	*	37.00

Same, Proof only.

Games of the XXVI Olympiad continued

1996 Half Eagle Type I ceremonial Olympic Flame

	MS-60	MS-63	MS-64	MS-65	PF-65
1996-W Half Eagle .... (NR) .... (NR)	—	—	215.	220.	199.

Olympic flame lighting ceremony obv. Type 1. Common rev. depicts games logo flanked by laurel branches.

1996 Half Eagle Type II Flagbearer

	MS-60	MS-63	MS-64	MS-65	PF-65
1996 Half Eagle .... (NR) .... (NR)	—	—	215.	220.	199.

Flagbearer obv. Type II depicts US athletes in either opening or closing ceremony parade. Common rev.

National Community Service

National Community Service dollar

	MS-60	MS-63	MS-64	MS-65	PF-65
1996-S Dollar .... (23,463) .... (100,749)	31.00	32.00	33.00	34.00	37.00

Thomas D. Rogers Sr.'s obv. portrays standing allegorical figure holding lamp of knowledge and large starred and striped shield. LIBERTY above in rays from lamp. NATIONAL COMMUNITY SERVICE and 1996 at left, motto at right. Rev. by William C. Cousins, SERVICE FOR AMERICA in three lines with small EPU encircled by a wreath.

Smithsonian Institution 150th Anniversary

Smithsonian Institution 150th Anniversary dollar

	MS-60	MS-63	MS-64	MS-65	PF-65
1996-P Dollar .... (NR)	31.00	32.00	33.00	34.00	*

Obv. by Thomas D. Rogers Sr. depict the "Castle," the first Smithsonian building on the Mall in Washington, D.C. Large LIBERTY and smaller motto above, SMITHSONIAN and anniversary dates 1846-1996 below, laurel branches right and left. Rev. by John Mercanti shows a hooded and draped allegorical figure carrying the torch of knowledge, sitting on top of the world. USOA and ONE DOLLAR around, FOR THE / INCREASE/ AND/ DIFFUSION/ OF / KNOWLEDGE in right field. Portions of the proceeds of the sale of the coins is to help the Smithsonian expand and enhance its numismatic collections, housed in the Museum of American History.

1996-S Dollar .... (NR)	*	*	*	*	37.00

Same, Proof only.

Smithsonian Institution 150th Anniversary half eagle

	MS-60	MS-63	MS-64	MS-65	PF-65
1996-W gold half eagle .... (NR) .... (NR)	—	—	195.	210.	210.

Alfred Maletsky's obv. is a bust of James Smithson with his name spelled out below the truncation, FOR THE INCREASE AND DIFFUSION OF KNOWLEDGE around above, LIBERTY below. Anniversary dates 1846-1996 at left, motto at right. T. James Ferrell's reverse is the Smithsonian's sunburst logo, USOA, EPU and FIVE DOLLARS around, SMITHSONIAN below sunburst.

U.S. Botanic Garden

U.S. Botanic Garden dollar

	MS-60	MS-63	MS-64	MS-65	PF-65
1997-P Dollar ....(NR) ....(NR)	32.50	33.00	33.50	38.00	39.00

Like the Jefferson commem issued in 1993, the Botanic Gardens program gained the attention of coin collectors not so much for its commemorative offering, but for a packaging set which included a Matte Finish Jefferson 5-cent piece, this time limited to 25,000 Coinage & Currency Sets. The workaday obverse by Edgar Z. Steever depicts a far view of the Botanic Garden main conservatory, LIBERTY above, ONE DOLLAR, 1997, motto and USOA below. The medallic reverse styled by William C. Cousins depicts a large rose center, UNITED STATES / BOTANIC GARDEN / 1820-1995 and EPU below, with a garland of roses around the upper rim.

Franklin Delano Roosevelt

Franklin Delano Roosevelt half eagle

	MS-60	MS-63	MS-64	MS-65	PF-65
1997-W Half Eagle ....(NR) ....(NR)	—	—	—	—	—

Struck to more or less coincide with the dedication of the FDR Memorial in Washington, D.C., the half eagle obverse recreates one of FDR's favorite photographs showing the president on the bridge of the *USS Houston* reviewing the fleet in San Francisco Bay. Without the context of the ship, however, FDR's gleeful expression and windblown hair are reminiscent of the family dog out for a ride in the Studebaker. FRANKLIN DELANO ROOSEVELT encircles above, 1997 and motto at right, LIBERTY below. The reverse is a presidential eagle, wings spread emblazoned by stars. James Peed adopted the design from the presidential seal displayed at FDR's 1933 inaugural. USOA and EPU above, FIVE DOLLARS below, the eagle clutches a placard displaying the year 1933.

Jackie Robinson

Jackie Robinson dollar

	MS-60	MS-63	MS-64	MS-65	PF-65
1997-S Dollar .... (NR) .... (NR)	—	—	—	32.00	37.00

Al Maletsky's obv. features Robinson stealing home. LIBERTY above, motto at right, date below. T. James Ferrell's rev. depicts the 50th anniversary logo of the Jackie Robinson Foundation surrounded by USOA and ONE DOLLAR to the outside, ROOKIE OF THE YEAR 1947 HALL OF FAME 1962 and EPU in smaller letters in an inner circle. In a bizarre turn of politics, some of the surcharge revenues from this issue were diverted to the Botanic Gardens fund. In an interesting packaging twist, both the dollar and the gold half eagle were offered boxed with a reproduction of Robinson's rookie baseball card.

Jackie Robinson half eagle

	MS-60	MS-63	MS-64	MS-65	PF-65
1997-W gold half eagle .... (NR) .... (NR)	—	—	—	190.	190.

William Cousins designed the obv., which is a portrait of Robinson, his name above, LIBERTY below. Date 1997 is to the left, motto to the right. The rev. by Jim Peed has a baseball as the central image inscribed with 1919-1972 (Robinson's birth and death years) and Legacy of Courage. USOA, and FIVE DOLLARS around, with EPU in smaller letters below ball.

National Law Enforcement Officers Memorial

National Law Enforcement Officers Memorial dollar

	MS-60	MS-63	MS-64	MS-65	PF-65
1997-P Dollar .... (NR) .... (NR)	—	—	—	—	—

Al Maletsky designed the obv. which depicts a male and a female officer viewing the memorial to officers killed in the line of duty.. The reverse is the law enforcement shield draped with a rose, TO SERVE AND PROTECT below.

Pattern, Experimental & Trial Pieces

In numismatics as in history, "what might have been" holds a unique fascination for the thoughtful. For the student of U.S. or world coinage, few other areas equal the challenge provided by pattern, experimental and trial pieces. Since the beginning of organized American coin collecting in the first half of the 19th century, no other area has engendered as much controversy and debate as pattern and pattern-related issues.

First to catalog such coins was Philadelphia apothecary and numismatist R. Coulton Davis. Drawing on his inside connections in the Philadelphia Mint, Davis published a serial listing in the *Coin Collector's Journal* from 1885 to 1887. Building on this preliminary listing, Edgar H. Adams and William H. Woodin published their *United States Pattern, Trial and Experimental Pieces* through the American Numismatic Society in 1913, adding items featured in some of the great collections and auctions of that day.

Their work was far more complete, partly because Woodin was one of the great pattern collectors of all time, whose influence within the Mint had brought him such treasures as the two unique gold $50 pieces of 1877. Many coins listed in Adams-Woodin (or A-W, as the work was soon known) were exhibited in January and February 1914 at the American Numismatic Society museum in New York City.

The late Omaha ophthalmologist Dr. J. Hewitt Judd followed with *United States Pattern, Experimental and Trial Pieces* in 1959, which incorporated much of Walter Breen's early research in the U.S. Mint archives and the ideas of such pattern specialists as the late William Guild. Soon Judd numbers replaced A-W numbers in most numismatic writings and auction catalogs.

Part of the controversy in the pattern field has involved basic definitions. In the broadest sense, a **pattern** is a coin struck under official auspices to illustrate a new design or denomination, to try out a new size, alloy or type of planchet. Examples would include the billon 2 cents of 1836, medium size cents of 1854, gold $4 Stellas of 1879-80, or the 1872 Amazonian and 1879 Washlady silver coins.

The term **trial piece** has been proposed for pieces struck to literally test a die being developed by the engraver, letting him gauge his progress and giving an idea of how his design was progressing. This was a vital function in the days of direct engraving by eye into the die steel. Included in this definition would be essentially unique, non-collectible soft metal uniface impressions which frequently show incomplete designs.

Then there was the seemingly endless run of Proof pieces struck during the 19th century from the regular dies of nearly all denominations in other than normal metals. Seeking a convenient name for these **off-metal Proofs**, Dr. Judd called them **Regular Die Trial Pieces**. Included were the nickel-alloy, white metal, copper or aluminum Proofs struck each year from the regular dies largely for sale to collectors until Mint Director James Putnam Kimball put an abrupt end to the practice in 1887.

Experimental pieces presented less of a problem. For Adams-Woodin and Judd, experimental pieces were coins struck in novel alloys or in new shapes and formats to give tangible form to serious, if not always fully practical coinage proposals such as Dr. Wheeler W. Hubbell's goloid dollars, the 1883 5-cent coins containing varied proportions of nickel and copper, perforated 1852 gold ring dollars or holed 1885 copper-nickel cents and 5 cents.

Unfortunately, none of these terms provide totally exclusive meaning. All can and have been stretched to cover wider areas, often with the intention of disguising the actual origin of a given coin to aid its salability. Much past debate really involved judgment of the circumstances surrounding various pieces' birth. Exposing the sometimes colorful past of a particular coin was often more important than standardizing a definition.

Don Taxay's *Counterfeit, Mis-Struck and Unofficial U.S. Coins* explored some of the inner history of the 19th century U.S. Mint. In the 1971 edition of the *Comprehensive Catalogue and Encyclopedia of United States Coins*, Taxay drew on the counsel and extensive researches of veteran pattern student John J. Ford Jr. to attempt an across the board re-classification of all coins in this complex area.

Taxay introduced several terms that related to the historical background of patterns and associated coins. He advocated essay, from the French *essai*, pattern, for both engraver's die trials and for patterns actually intended to illustrate new designs or devices.

Cabinet coins would be the many pieces struck by the Mint for sale or trade to collectors. Normal and off-metal Proofs were included in this category. Another French term, *piece de caprice*, describes some pattern-like pieces which served no logical purpose related to development of new coin designs or denominations, but provided instead ready-made rarities for the collector market.

Taxay's terminology was elaborate yet precise, but failed to be adopted by the numismatic community. Collectors not possessing a copy of Taxay's earlier work will find his numbers included in Andrew W. Pollock III's listings in his *United States Patterns and Related Issues*, published by Bowers & Merena in 1994. For the present work, the following self-explanatory terms have been adopted: Metallurgical Trial Piece, Experimental Edge Trial Piece, Experimental Trial Piece, Experimental Size Trial Piece, Experimental Composition Trial Piece, Revised Design Trial Piece, Incomplete Die Trial.

Two terms most frequently used will be **Pattern Design Trial Piece**, any piece struck in any metal from a pattern die, and **Regular Design Trial Piece**, any product of a regular die in off-metal or other exceptional use.

Restrikes are pieces struck after the date they bear; **Fantasy Restrikes** are pieces struck after the date they bear, for which no original existed. More recently, writers such as Q. David Bowers have advocated a term originating in Russian numismatics, **Novodel,** for such items created within the walls of the U.S. Mint.

Mules combine unrelated obverses and reverses, occasionally contriving to bring together two obverses or two reverses. **Fantasy Mules** include several of the so-called transitional patterns, combining old and new obverse and reverse designs. Created for sale to collectors, these did not serve as patterns, nor did they legitimately record a change in design.

Private restrikes are pieces struck from salvaged dies, not always combining obverse and reverse proper for the coin they purport to represent and occasionally showing evidence of re-engraving in an attempt to improve detail. Joseph J. Mickley and Montroville W. Dickeson were makers of many of these well-known cobblings during the last century.

Three abbreviations are used to simplify this presentation. The nation's name United States of America is abbreviated **USOA**. The statutory motto E Pluribus Unum appears as **EPU**; In God We Trust as **IGWT**.

There are two basic methods for listing patterns, date order or denomination order. In this book, the simple and logical denomination order presents an unbroken panorama of the historical development of each denomination. Veteran numismatists will remember that this system was used by the late Wayte Raymond in the *Standard Catalogue of United States Coins* and in pattern guides of the Hewitt Brothers of Chicago, publishers of the late lamented *Numismatic Scrapbook Magazine*.

The *Coin World Encyclopedia*, or CWE, numbering system uses the prefix letter "E" to avoid conflict with the "P" used for pioneer gold pieces. Every piece listed here could in some manner be construed as *experimental*, hence the mnemonic.

The editors wish to express their gratitude to Q. David Bowers of Bowers & Merena Galleries of Wolfeboro, N.H., for permission to incorporate the numbers appearing in the seventh edition of Dr. J. Hewitt Judd's *United States Pattern, Experimental and Trial Pieces*, edited by the late A. Kosoff in 1982. We would also like to express our gratitude to David A. Novoselsky, President of the Pattern Collectors Society, for his tremendous contributions in the areas of historical commentary, pedigrees, auction results and pricing.

A note on the legality of owning modern patterns: For many years the Judd catalog carried a statement to the effect that patterns struck after 1916 were illegal to own. As the late Abe Kosoff was preparing to edit the seventh edition, one of the editors of this volume asked him why. Kosoff wrote to the Treasury Department and asked them why patterns made after 1916 were illegal to own. Their reply consisted of a photocopy of the comment in an earlier edition of Judd, and a letter saying that this book says they are! The comment was changed in the seventh edition of Judd, thereby hopefully legitimizing all patterns made after 1916.

However, the 1974 cent trial strikes in aluminum have been deemed illegal to own ever since (and because?) their existence proved to be an embarrassment to a U.S. Mint Director, and in 1994 a Mint spokesman made contradictory statements about a previously unknown 1974 cent trial strike in bronze-clad steel, first ruling them legal and then, after they were publicized, reversing this decision. Although we solicit additional information about modern patterns for inclusion in future editions, we advise and guarantee extreme discretion in their handling

A note on pricing: It is not the purpose of this catalog to act as a definitive price guide for all pieces listed. Pattern prices include what are believed to be reasonable estimates based on today's markets. Auction records are given for many pieces, since public auction performance is, after all, one of the clearest indications of value for such great rarities. However, because a pattern may have brought a record realization in a major sale such as Garrett, it does not follow that all succeeding examples will do as well. In this edition, auction realizations from Bowers & Merena sales are abbreviated BM, those from Stack's as ST, each followed by the date of sale with month and year, i.e. ST 3/92. **Please note: Bowers' reported prices include the 10% buyer's fee, Stack's prices do not include the 10%!** Other firm names are spelled out in full.

Some patterns are found in Uncirculated, others in Proof only. Estimated prices are for the method of manufacture most commonly encountered for each item listed. Most Regular Design Trial Pieces of 1861-1885 are normally found in Proof.

Auction records necessarily reflect the state of the auction market at the time of each sale. Market conditions of 1995 may necessitate lower or higher figures than some of the auction records cited. Certain series within the pattern field may show sharper price fluctuations than others, reflecting changing emphasis in collecting trends.

A note on notes: The following overview and many of the notes written after individual listings were written by David A. Novoselsky of Chicago, IL, one of the foremost pattern collectors in America and President of the Pattern Collectors Society. Other notes and the order of listing are the work of Thomas K. DeLorey, Research Director of the Pattern Collectors Society.

A note on the future: We have begun to record weights of known specimens for future reference now, before they are entombed in plastic. Eventually this may help determine if certain pieces are originals or restrikes. Additional information for our next edition may be sent to: Pattern Book, c/o Thomas K. DeLorey, P.O. Box 751, Blue Island, IL 60406. Either grams (used here) or grains are acceptable.

TKD, February 1995.

A note on the history or "pattern" of patterns

By David A. Novoselsky

At first glance, the thousands of different numbers assigned to patterns or experimental pieces may discourage one's inclination to find a forest in this sea of trees, particularly where even the trees themselves appear so different from one another. The sheer number and often shady reputation of the pattern series have discouraged efforts to show that these coins provide one the best methods of tracing the true history of United States coinage. Nonetheless, no real understanding of the history and development of American coinage is possible without a study and appreciation of how that coinage developed, which cannot be done without a study of patterns.

Unlike Topsy, our coins did not just grow or spring full-born as they now appear in the other parts of this book. The history of their design and post-adoption modification can be found in the patterns described *infra*. Unfortunately, the numismatic community has traditionally been reluctant to consider patterns in this light. Instead, this series has been viewed as a sea of contrasts, a bewildering compilation of the the freakish and the outcast, and dismissed out of hand without according them their proper place in the history of United States coinage.

This view has been encouraged not only by the bewildering number and variety of patterns, but also by the well-documented accounts by Taxay and others that have shown that many patterns were never intended as anything other than fantasies struck solely to provide something new and extremely rare to sell (at a tidy profit) to an ever-growing number of wealthy 19th century collectors. Earlier claims that these *pieces de caprice* were true prototypes or otherwise formed a part of the regular series have besmirched the reputation of the entire field of patterns. As a result, patterns have remained in the Outer Darkness of numismatics. They have been studied, if at all, as having only the occasional or most tenuous connection with mainstream United States coinage. This all-too common view is unfortunate even if it easily understood.

Some patterns are clearly a *piece de caprice*, and do not merit inclusion in any serious study of the development of our coinage. Some patterns are bizarre in appearance, and thus appear to have no relationship to normal coinage. Nonetheless, these coins are the foundation of the "normal" issues which are so avidly collected and studied today. Their exile to the Outer Darkness is unwarranted and unfortunate, since an unbiased study of "what might have been" can teach us quite a bit about what is and what was.

Part of the engine which has driven patterns into the fringes of numismatics has been the failure to bring order out of the chaos of apparently thousands of different patterns. Fortunately, a pioneering effort to change this was made by Don Taxay in the first edition of what has become the present work. He separated the true patterns from the off-metal strikes of regular issues, fantasy strikes, private patterns, and (in contrast to every other study up to the present) he carefully distinguished the off-metal strikes of otherwise legitimate patterns from the body of pattern development. This reduced the number previously known by the generic term "pattern" to a much more manageable figure by several orders of magnitude.

Taxay then simplified the method of reviewing patterns still further by linking the often-confusing die marriages for a single obverse or reverse (each marriage resulting in several different pattern numbers by virtue of the number of metals in which the resulting marriage had been struck) by using photographic diagrams. The number of true patterns was then reduced to a size lending itself to meaningful study. Looking at this sharply-reduced body of patterns as a group, an order emerges that places these coins in their proper place in U.S. coinage history.

Patterns were not struck at a whim. Far more often than not (with some glaring examples that will be discussed later) they were struck in response to the need to develop a new denomination or the need to replace a series of existing designs that were no longer satisfactory or were simply outdated. These needs are reflected in a period of several years in which the Mint concentrated on the production of a closely-related series of pattern focusing on the new denomination or design. All other work, including the production of patterns in other areas, was subordinated to this one task. This same concentration appears in the pattern series when the chosen design proved to be unsatisfactory. When this problem arose, as it did when the Flying Eagle cents were produced, the Mint continued to produce new patterns in the same area until an acceptable substitute was developed.

These periods of concentrated activity can often be traced by correspondence among the Mint, the Treasury Department, and Congress describing the efforts to obtain a satisfactory final design. Examples were provided by Taxay in his well-regarded history of the Mint and U.S. coinage. The tangible result of this activity can be found in the patterns struck at the same time, a variety all focused on a single denomination or design. This is the "pattern of patterns;" not a sea of chaos, but an orderly progression of work responsive to a particular need and concentrated in specific areas. If we want to trace the family tree of U.S. coinage, these are the true ancestors.

Recognizing this order also allows us to determine what was real and what was fantasy. The period of productivity in response to the need to develop new denominations or replace existing designs was followed by a period of idleness. As unfortunately happened all too often during these periods, patterns continued to be struck, but only to "snare a purse" or otherwise further the "workshop for their own gain" that characterized too much of the Mint's efforts during the 19th century. Such periods saw the design of patterns that were intended solely to be different. Other patterns that had been struck years or even decades before were struck once again. The intent of both was the same — create a rare prize for the unwary and support what was then a lucrative side business for those in power at the Mint and a select group of well-connected coin dealers.

With these principles in mind, we can easily separate the wheat from the chaff of patterns and view the design history of U.S. coinage that can be found in the patterns that remain. A few examples follow:

Quite obviously, the 1792 patterns fall outside of this practice since there was nothing that went before for the Mint to build upon. The real study of patterns begins with the appointment of Robert M. Patterson as the Director of the Mint in 1835 and the appointment of Christian Gobrecht as Second Engraver to assist (and effectively replace) the disabled Chief Engraver William Kneass soon thereafter. Called upon to develop a satisfactory design for the upcoming resumption of silver dollar coinage, Patterson concentrated the Mint's efforts on the task of developing the finest possible design, paying particular attention to artistic concerns that had been ignored in the haphazard development that preceded his appointment.

When asked by Congress to provide a sample of a 2-cent coin or a gold dollar during this same time period, the Mint responded with designs that were cobbled together as quickly as possible before returning their attention to the design for the silver dollar. These efforts continued through the initial adoption of the Seated Liberty series in 1837, and the production of patterns continued until it was stopped in 1839 when the final design modifications for the Seated Liberty series was found to be acceptable.

There were no new patterns struck in the following 10 years. Pattern production began again in 1849, when the Mint was asked to create three new denominations: the 3-cent silver coin, the gold dollar, and the double eagle. The latter two denominations were needed more urgently, and were hurriedly created. An annular design for the dollar was prepared by Longacre, who engraved a small number of these gold dollar patterns by hand rather than take the time to cut dies. They were quickly rejected and his non-perforated adopted design was accepted with no apparent pattern prototype, though dies were used to strike a handful of 1849 Proofs sent to various public officials. However, there were some modifications made to the head and wreath after regular issue production began. The double eagle pattern proved somewhat more troublesome, and had to be redesigned several times until dies satisfactory to the Chief Coiner could be delivered. Regular production began the next year.

Patterns for the 3-cent silver coin were given a lesser priority while the Mint completed the gold denominations. The first patterns were admittedly crude and never intended for actual use, unlike the gold dollar and double eagle pattern dies later used for regular issue coinage. While Franklin Peale tried to intervene in 1850 with a thrown-together design recalling his work with Gobrecht in 1836, the Mint followed its normal policy of concentrating its efforts on one denomination or design of patterns at a time, and waited until 1851 for Longacre to complete his work on the trime. Again, modifications to the design were made after production began, in 1854 and 1859.

Having concentrated its pattern efforts towards developing these three new denominations, the Mint turned to the problem of replacing the large copper cent. Beginning in early 1850s, the Mint turned out a bewildering variety of sizes, alloys and designs before eventually coming up with a pattern that is now known as the 1856 Flying Eagle cent, though it was actually just a temporary borrowing of two older designs to test a new size and composition. The replacement of that short-lived design by the Indian cent can be traced through the brief but intense flurry of pattern designs and modifications that followed. These resulted in adoption of the Indian cent and then in its several design modifications over the next few years.

The next burst of pattern activity came hard on the heels of the Flying Eagle/Indian efforts. In order to replace the unpopular but economically-vital fractional currency, a bronze 2-cent coin and copper-nickel 3-cent and 5-cent coins were developed during 1863-1866. Having spent an intense decade developing the new designs discussed above, the Mint was able to produce these three new denominations in a remarkably short time. In contrast to the diversity of designs for the Flying Eagle cent that were spread over the early and mid-1850s, the pattern "trail" left behind showing the development of 2-, 3- and 5-cent coins was remarkably short and concentrated in a series of closely-related patterns.

Both the Mint and its Chief Engraver Longacre had refined the task of developing new designs to a fine art. Both also recognized that production problems with new designs could be dealt with once the pressure of developing the initial design had been removed. This too can be seen by the series of patterns for 5-cent coins that Longacre continued to produce after the Shield 5 cents design was accepted in 1866 and then modified very slightly to remove the troublesome rays in 1867. He spent the remainder of the 1860s (and his life) developing pattern 5-cent pieces to be struck in aluminum or alternative designs in copper-nickel to find a solution to ongoing production problems caused by his earlier efforts.

This habit continued through the end of the pattern series in the early 1900s. With the death of Longacre, the speed of the process was slowed considerably when the Barbers brought their lesser skills to the Mint — and the designs of Morgan brought a rivalry to the fore that gave the series a unique and fascinating flavor. However, the pattern of pattern series can still be found in the coins that we have with us today. Placed in this perspective, the sea of patterns is not as vast as it may appear at first glance. The proper course through that sea is also quite easy to chart, with the reefs and rocks of restrikes and *pieces de caprice* obvious and easy to avoid. What we have prepared below should assist your efforts to chart your own particular course.

Rarity, Condition, Cachet and Value

There are three primary components that set the value of coins: **rarity**, both as to the number of coins struck as well as relative rarity within a particular type or design; **condition**, again weighed both as an absolute and in relation to the likelihood of obtaining a better-looking example; and the last and perhaps most elusive and subjective factor of all, **cachet**, the perceived importance or notoriety of the coin. The easiest way to define and demonstrate the latter is by a well-known example, the 1804 dollar. There are numerous other coins among the regular issues that are far rarer than the 1804 dollar — such as the 1802 half dime and the 1842 Small Date Proof quarter. Despite this, and also despite the fact that many of the 1804 dollars that turn up at auction with far more frequency than other "classic rarities" are circulated and (frankly) unattractive, they continue to command prices that cannot be justified when examined solely by the more objective criteria of rarity and condition.

Thus, the third leg of the value triad — cachet or fame — is clearly the most important factor of all when weighing the value of a coin. The other two may not be ignored, since condition within the spectrum of available specimens will always have to be factored into a determination of value, just as the overall number and likelihood of additional pieces being discovered plays an important role in the value equation. Nonetheless, a famous rarity is always valuable and relatively easy to sell even in a down market — presuming you are willing to take a loss from the price you paid if you bought it when the market was overheated. (Indeed, these coins sometimes bring a substantial price and widespread interest despite an otherwise lackluster market, as witnessed by the recent sale of the Reed Hawn specimen of the 1913 Liberty Nickel.)

These comments hold true for patterns with the addition of one factor unique to the pattern field — the metal in which the coin is struck. The alloy used to strike a pattern is a critical factor to be weighed in assessing the value of the specimen. Each of the factors that would normally be considered as setting the value of a particular coin need special and particular consideration when dealing with patterns.

To begin with, rarity has a completely different meaning when used in relation to any pattern. All patterns are rare in relation to other coins. Even the most common patterns, the 1856 Flying Eagle cents or the 1836-1839 Gobrecht dollars (which are considered by some experts not to be patterns at all), had a combined original and restrike mintage that did not exceed 2,000. Excluding those coins, the next most common pattern designs never saw a combined mintage of more than 100 or 200 pieces in all denominations. However, even these tiny mintages are an exception to the norm. The typical pattern mintage, including restrikes, is 30 or fewer.

Patterns struck in mintages of 12 or fewer would send collectors into a frenzy if they were part of any other series, but will hardly raise an eyebrow in pattern circles. Indeed, coins of which only two or three are known, even unique coins, are found with far greater regularity in the pattern series than in any other area of numismatics. This is something to keep in mind when someone offers an "ultra rare pattern, only one of six or eight known," and asks you to pay 15 times the actual value of the coin.

Condition is also an important factor in weighing the value of a given pattern. However, it must be remembered that unlike a coin that was capable of being spent (and even Proof gold was used to put food on the table during a depression), a pattern could not be spent at all because it was never "legal tender." No matter how pressed its owner may have been, a pattern could only be sold within numismatic circles, thereby ensuring that the pattern was less likely to be abused than an issue with a legally-recognized value.

As a result, with the exception of the most common patterns such as the 1858 and 1859 Indian cents with the next years' reverses, stray pieces that may have been given as a trinket to a child, or the occasional pocket piece, circulated patterns are a *rara avis*. Again, as with any other rarity, an MS-65 pattern will fetch a better price than the same pattern as an MS-63. It is not, however, worth the price multiplication that some claim is appropriate for coins with a similar divergence in grade in other areas of coinage. The mythical "finest known" pattern in a 65 holder is not worth twice the price of the second finest known in a 63 or 64 holder, particularly when they are two of only three or four pieces to begin with! Keep this in mind when you are offered a pattern as the "finest known" or the "finest of only two slabbed."

The next value factor to be considered is unique to the pattern field. Patterns were usually (but not always) struck in the "intended" metal (*i.e.* silver if the pattern design was for a half dollar or copper-nickel if intended as a pattern for a 5-cent coin.) At the same time, many (but once again, not all) were struck in copper, nickel, aluminum, or "white metal" (tin). One of the greatest difficulties in determining the value of patterns is evaluating the pricing of these off-metal strikes. A pattern struck in the intended metal is almost always worth substantially more than one struck in an off-metal, usually by a factor of several times the value of the off-metal piece. At the same time, there are patterns that are widely sought and quite difficult to obtain in the intended metal. Off-metal strikes of these patterns (which are themselves difficult to locate) therefore remain in demand whenever they turn up for sale. To confuse matters even more, several patterns were never struck in the intended metal but fetch a fairly substantial price, while others fetch little more than a yawn.

In some instances, understanding this phenomenon is quite simple — particularly where the Mint never struck the pattern in the "intended" metal. For example, in 1859, several patterns for a double eagle were struck (E.1815-1821). These patterns were never struck in gold. They are much sought after even though struck only in copper due to the scarcity of double eagle patterns and their connection to the "Paquet Reverse" briefly adopted by the Mint for this denomination soon after.

Even where the Mint did strike patterns in the intended metal, the value of off-metal strikes can remain quite high, the clearest example again being gold patterns. The value of gold patterns actually struck in that metal has remained extremely high because the Mint struck them in numbers that are minuscule even by pattern standards. With only a few exceptions, gold patterns struck in gold are either unique or show a mintage of four or fewer coins. When such coins come on the market they fetch prices well into six figures. As a result, the value of off-metal strikes has remained high since few collectors want to tie up their funds in a single coin.

The Mint struck two gold specimens of the Sailor Head eagle pattern in 1875 (E.1795). If one of these coins came onto the market today, the asking price would probably exceed $250,000. (The last sale with any significant number of gold patterns struck in gold was the Superior session of Auction '90.) The pattern was also struck in copper, aluminum and white metal (E.1796-1798) but again in numbers of eight or fewer for each of these metals. The so-called "finest known" E.1796 (in a PCGS PR-65 RB holder) was advertised in *Coin World* (February 6, 1995) as available for $12,500.

Quite a disparity in price? At first blush the answer would appear to be yes. But $12,500 is close to what the same example brought in Superior's Heifetz Sale in 1989, where all patterns in that sale brought strong prices. Since then, the market for all coins including patterns has cooled. Gold patterns even in off-metals continue to retain a significant portion of their value even in today's market.

Of course, even with regard to gold patterns, the rarity factor cannot be ignored. The most available gold pattern is the 1836 gold dollar, E.1535. This coin was struck in greater numbers than any other gold pattern, and restruck on at least one occasion. While prices (especially for the very few gem examples) remain strong, the prices for off-metal examples in any metal — including silver original strikes — have never been strong. Since the intended metal is relatively easy to find (with some patience) the off-metal strikes bring far less.

In many other instances, the off-metal strikes are substantially more rare than the coin in the intended metal — and few seem to care. Examples of 1866 pattern "nickels" struck in copper are more rare than their copper-nickel counterparts. The same can be said for off-metal strikes of the "Standard Silver" series and the 1873 pattern Trade dollars, a few of which are unique in some off-metals. These off-metal strikes bring only a fraction of the same coin in the intended metal, even if they are unique!

If all of this seems somewhat difficult to follow, consider these examples: The Mint struck a series of eight silver dollar patterns in 1876 (E.1433-1453). Two complete sets were struck in silver, with no other examples in silver turning up since that time. (An exception is E.1439, of which there appear to be at least four specimens in silver.) These "Centennial Dollars" have long been considered "classic rarities" within the pattern field, and are much sought after not only for their rarity, but for their beauty of design and their cachet. Because of the near impossibility of obtaining any examples of these bold 1876 designs in the intended metal, the demand and the prices for the off-metal strikes remains high.

This example also shows how supply has direct bearing on demand. There were approximately twice as many examples of E.1439 struck than the other seven coins in this set. When a specimen of E.1439 comes out on the market, it is eagerly sought after, but not to the extent that an appearance of one of its far rarer brethren would elicit. (The last appearance of a E.1439 was the example in the BM 3/94 Sunderland Sale.) The relative drop in value for this coin when compared to the others in the set is exacerbated by the fact that even off-metal examples are more readily available than off-metal examples of other members of the set.

Another pattern series always recognized for its cachet and perceived rarity is the 1877 half dollar. These coins were struck in silver in widely differing numbers, the most common having 10 or 12 silver examples (such as E.1164, which combines one of the Morgan obverse with the well-known Defiant Eagle reverse) while other die marriages are known to be unique in both the intended metal and in off-metal form (see E.1153). Any 1877 half dollar in silver will bring a substantial price whenever it is offered. Any 1877 half dollar in an off-metal is highly sought after, given the perceived rarity and cachet of this series.

The 1877 pattern half dollars are rare, though not extraordinarily rare when compared to some other patterns. For that reason, we have used the term "perceived rarity" to show how that perceived rarity tracks with the effect of cachet on value. The 1877 half dollar patterns may not be any rarer than other groupings within the pattern field, and turn up at auction with far more regularity than other highly significant patterns. They continue to bring prices in intended metal and off-metal form out of proportion to their true numbers and availability, assisted by actual numbers that keep them constantly before the collector's eye.

The Twisted Hair pattern half dollars of 1839 and the 1838 Seated Liberty half dollar patterns are listed in virtually every study of patterns as being equal in rarity to the 1877 pattern half dollars, the 1876 Centennial patterns, and the celebrated Amazonian, Washlady and Shield Earring patterns. The extreme rarity of these earlier patterns in any metal has affected their perceived value. Since they turn up so infrequently and are quickly snapped up when they do, their actual value has never been appreciated by most casual collectors. They are simply too rare to be touted for their true significance and value.

The 1877 pattern half series is considered to be the "sweepstakes" for the design of what is now known as the Morgan dollar. Their fame and importance are proven when these coins come on the market in any number, as they did in Bowers' Garrett Sale, Part I. The Garrett coins brought very high prices, with the unique examples within the series (such as E.1168, lot #386 and E.1153, lot #390) bringing absolutely record prices even in comparison to other pattern half dollars.

The same importance should be accorded the Gobrecht half dollar patterns of 1838 and 1839. The 1838 half dollar patterns with the Seated Liberty obverse and the Flying Eagle reverse differ in many important respects from the 1836-1839 Gobrecht dollars and provide a unique opportunity to study the development history of the Seated Liberty series. The 1839 Twisted Hair half dollar patterns are the only Gobrecht design that was fully executed but never used even in modified form on a regular issue silver coin, though its mirror image appeared on the 1838-39 $10 Liberty. Given the impact of Gobrecht's work on U.S. coinage, these half dollar patterns should be as famous as the far more available 1877 half dollar patterns in any metal. That they are not, and the fact that they remain off the market in long-standing pattern collections, shows that the old numismatic adage "you can't sell what you can't get" is quite apt when looking at patterns.

Again, the term "rare" needs to be further defined here. Only two examples of any Seated Liberty half dollar patterns in silver have turned up at auction in the last decade. An example of E.949 appeared as lot #3245 in Superior's Oct. 1989 Heifetz Sale, misattributed there as the equally-rare E.944. This same coin, originally misattributed as E.944, was lot #365 in Garrett I and (again misattributed) was lot #696 in Bowers & Merena's Jan. 1988 Higgins Sale. There was an example of E.950 in the Rarcoa session of Auction '90, lot #882. Before that, this particular coin was lot #448 in Superior's Crouch Collection Sale, June 13-16, 1977, and previously lot #3597, in Stack's 1976 ANA Sale. Have there been any other examples of this obverse on the market since the Witham collection was sold in 1981? No! Did they turn up in off-metal strikes? Only one or two examples of any off-metal strikes were available during this same time period.

Precisely two examples of Gobrecht's 1839 Twisted Hair half dollar have turned up at auction during the 15 years that followed the sale of the Witham collection of early half dollars in the Rarcoa portion of Auction '81. The only example in silver was the stunning and woefully undergraded E.958 that appeared as lot #3246 in Superior's 1989 Heifetz Sale. A copper strike of the same obverse married to a later reverse

(E.961) was lot #1250 in Superior's 10/92 sale. Only these have appeared since 1981.

The fact that only a tiny number of the early Seated Liberty or Twisted Hair half dollar patterns have ever been on the market, with Rarcoa's remarkable Witham collection an outstanding exception, shows that these coins are undeniably rare in the absolute sense and even in relation to other patterns. Why then have there been more 1877 half dollar patterns on the market in the last decade, more Amazonian patterns, and generally more of the later-dated patterns than these early half dollar patterns?

The answer is that these early patterns have never been promoted to the same extent as later and more available patterns by interested dealers. It is also much easier to sell something to a collector if it has some connection to an engraver or a series that is already popular and readily available. There are far more Barber collectors and Morgan dollar enthusiasts than those who collect earlier coinage. There are also more of the later patterns to promote and sell. As a result, specimens of the 1838 and 1839 Gobrecht pattern halves that have appeared on the market were quickly snapped up by sophisticated pattern buyers who appreciated their true rarity, did not need a dealer to hype their importance, and knew that few of these rarities were likely to appear in the foreseeable future.

Finally, sometimes the extreme rarity and cachet of a particular pattern sets its value at whatever the seller wants to charge. In those instances, it all comes down to what Q. David Bowers has called the "opportunity to acquire." This, once again, is demonstrated by example.

One of the most eagerly sought-after patterns is Morgan's famed Schoolgirl dollar of 1879. A silver example (E.1485) was lot #1465 in Bowers' 3/94 Sunderland Sale. That particular coin had been off the market since 1977. The only other Schoolgirl in this metal to appear at auction was the coin in the BM 1981 ANA Sale, a gap of 13 years! Before that, one was offered in the Garrett Sale.

Since this pattern only comes in the dollar denomination, was there any greater number of offerings in off-metals? There was an outstanding example in copper (E.1486) in BM 5/94 and another example in Superior's 1989 Heifetz Sale. Hardly an overwhelming number of pieces!

The Schoolgirl design is considered one of the most desirable of all patterns. It is undeniably rare in any metal, even in relation to other equally-desirable patterns of the same general era since, unlike them, it was only struck in one denomination. If one shows up for sale, it is clearly a seller's market. If you want one, pony up when it is offered, or it may take a decade or so for you to get another crack at the design.

The same can be said for the combination of absolute rarity and cachet that came together in E.1865, the only example ever struck of the Saint-Gaudens Indian Head in the double eagle denomination. A coin of incredible beauty and interest far beyond the pattern field, this coin was last on the market when it appeared in the Paramount section of Auction '84. Described as PR-67, this coin brought $467,500, a stunning price for any coin in that market. While the coin has not appeared in auction in a decade, what would it bring today? Whatever the seller is willing to accept for it!

Considering all of these points, the conclusion must be drawn that there is no more magic to determining the value of a given pattern than to determining the value of any other coin. There are recognized rarities within the pattern series. The presence of off-metal strikes within the series complicates the evaluation only to the extent noted above. When in doubt, the intended metal is to be preferred whenever possible. It is only where the intended metal is unavailable or too expensive that the off-metal alternative should be considered.

Half cents

E.1. 1854 Metallurgical Trial Piece. Reportedly oroide with a small quantity of silver, perhaps a continuation of the experiments with billon cents in 1850-53. Normal obv. and rev. dies (Breen-2). Plain Edge. J-155. Unique?

Metallurgical trial (Bowers & Merena)

E.2. 1856 Metallurgical Trial Piece. Copper-nickel, two alloys used, 90:10 and 88:12. Normal obv. and rev. dies (Breen-2). Plain Edge. J-177. Scarce, restrikes exist. Struck to test alloys for the new Flying Eagle cent. ST 3/92, Br. Proof $2,300; Eliasberg 5/96 Proof 63 .... $3,410

Large cents

Pattern Design Trial Piece of 1792 (Bowers & Merena)

E.3. 1792 Pattern Design Trial Piece. Obv. Female bust right with short, curly hair, 1792 below. Legend LIBERTY PARENT OF SCIENCE & INDUSTRY, beaded border. No name on truncation. Rev. ONE CENT and two sprigs within beaded circle, all within laurel wreath. UNITED STATES OF AMERICA. above, G * W. Pt. below, beaded border. White metal, tin or mostly tin. Plain Edge. J-6. Unique, Garrett IV $90,000.

    The first pattern U.S. cent struck, the design was not accepted but the position of the lettering greatly influenced early U.S. coin designs, especially the word LIBERTY above the bust which was used on every coin struck before 1807.

Pattern Design Trial Piece of 1792 (Bowers & Merena)

E.4. 1792 Pattern Design Trial Piece. Obv. Same die as preceding, but with the entire portrait hand-tooled deeper into the die. The forehead, chin and bust are stronger, and the curly hair has been elongated into flowing hair. Other curls draping the bust have been reworked, and a small BIRCH has been added on the truncation. The Birch cent, possibly work of William Russell Birch. Rev. Similar to preceding, but different wreath with fancier bow. Plain circle around ONE CENT, no sprigs above or below. 1/100 below bow, beaded border. Copper. Plain Edge. J-3. Very rare.

    This is a revision of the preceding design, presumably caused by objections to the hair styling and the reference to the incumbent president, which would have set a dangerous precedent.

E.5. Same, only edge inscribed TO BE ESTEEMED * BE USEFUL *. J-4. Extremely rare. Garrett IV $200,000.

E.6. Same, only edge inscribed TO BE ESTEEMED BE USEFUL (leaf) * (leaf). J-5. Extremely rare.

Large cent patterns continued

Silver plug in center

E.7. 1792 Metallurgical Trial Piece. Obv. Female bust right with flowing hair, 1792 below, legend LIBERTY PARENT OF SCIENCE & INDUST:. Rev. ONE CENT inside laurel wreath, 1/100 without fraction bar below bow, legend UNITED STATES OF AMERICA. Beaded border. Copper with silver plug in center. Reeded Edge. J-1. Very rare, Garrett IV $95,000. Struck to test the feasibility of a smaller coin containing one full cent's worth of metal. A unique copper example was discovered by a California dealer early in 1994, which had been struck without its silver plug in place. ST 3/95 Ch. Unc. $91,300.

E.8. Same, except struck in copper or billon, approximately 96% copper, 4% silver. Reeded Edge. J-2. Very rare, Garrett IV $28,000. Authentication recommended. Struck to demonstrate the results of mixing the two elements of the previous piece, and impossibility of distinguishing the billon strikes from copper counterfeits.

E.9. 1795 Experimental Edge Trial Piece. Normal obv. and rev. (Sheldon-79), copper with reeded edge. J-20. Six known.

Note: 1804: The pieces listed as J-28 are private restrikes ca. 1860, as are similar strikings in copper.

Note: 1806: The piece listed as J-38a is a private restrike.

Note: 1810: The pieces listed as J-41 are private restrikes.

Note: 1818: The piece listed as J-45 is a private restrike. The silver "cents" with engine-turned designs listed as Adams and Woodin-32 & 33 are not Mint products. They were probably made by Jacob Perkins of Newburyport, Massachusetts.

Note: 1823: The pieces listed as J-46 are private restrikes, as are similar strikings in copper.

Experimental size trial of 1850 (Smithsonian)

E.10. 1850 Experimental Size Trial Piece. Obv. U S A at top, ONE TENTH SILVER at bottom. Plain rim around outer edge and center hole. Rev. CENT at top, 1850 at bottom, rosettes flanking hole. Plain inner and outer rims. Billon, 10% silver, 90% copper. Perforated. Plain Edge. J-119. Rare. ST 3/92, P PF-64 $3,000; Eliasberg 5/96 Proof 65 2,090

E.11. Same, billon, unperforated restrike. Plain Edge. J-120. Rare $1,500

E.12. Same, copper, perforated. Plain Edge. J-121. Very rare. ST 3/92, AU $1.050

E.13. Same, copper, unperforated restrike. Plain Edge. J-122. Very rare $1,750

E.14. Same, copper-nickel, perforated restrike ca. 1853. Plain Edge. J-123. Rare $1,000

E.15. Same, copper-nickel, unperforated restrike ca. 1853. Plain Edge. J-124. Rare. ST 3/92, Ch. Br. Proof $4,400 ....

E.15a. Same, White-metal, Judd unlisted, ST 3/92, Ch. BU $5,250

E.16. (1850) Restrike Mule, ca. 1853. Obv. CENT/1850 die of 1850. Rev. Plain die with beaded border, copper. Plain Edge. Judd Appendix A, Very rare $800

E.17. Same, copper-nickel. Plain Edge. Judd Appendix A, Very rare; three pieces reported $1,000

E.18. (1850) Restrike Mule, ca. 1853. Obv. CENT/1850 die of 1850. Rev. ONE/CENT in olive wreath reverse of 1853. German silver, exact alloy unknown, perforated. Plain Edge. J-152. Very rare .. $900

E.19. Same, copper-nickel, unperforated. Plain Edge. J-152a. Very rare $950

E.20. Same, copper-nickel, perforated. Plain Edge. J-152b. Very rare, if it exists; may be a misdescription of E.18 ....

E.21. Same, white metal, perforated. Plain Edge. J-124a. Very rare, if it exists, may be a misdescription of E.18.

E.21a. Same, copper, perforated. Plain Edge. Unlisted in Judd. Unique?

Large cent patterns continued

Undated Pattern Design Trial Piece of 1851
(Bowers & Merena)

E.22. (1851) Pattern Design Trial Piece. Obv. USOA and wreath around hole, plain inner and outer rims. Rev. CENT at top, ONE TENTH SILVER at bottom. Thick ring inside legends, plain inner and outer rims. Billon, 10% silver, 90% copper. Perforated. Plain Edge. J-127. Rare. A piece with a larger perforation listed as J-127a may be a restrike $1,500

E.23. Same, billon, unperforated restrike. Plain Edge. J-128. Very rare $900

E.24. Same, billon, unperforated restrike. Reeded Edge. J-128a. Very rare $900

E.24a. Same, pure silver, unperforated restrike, Reeded Edge., Unlisted in Judd., Very rare, two known

E.25. Same, copper, perforated. Plain Edge. J-129. Rare $750

E.26. Same, copper, unperforated restrike. Plain Edge. J-130. Very rare $800

E.27. Same, copper-nickel, exact alloy uncertain, either 88:12 or 75:25 or possibly both. Unperforated restrike. Reeded Edge. J-131 and 131a. Rare $700

E.27a. (1851?) Mule. Obv. Same as preceding. Obv. The CENT/1850 die of 1850. Possibly a restrike c. 1853. Copper, perforated, Plain Edge. Unlisted in Judd. Unique?

E.28. (1851) Restrike Mule ca. 1853. Obv. CENT/ONE TENTH SILVER die of 1851. Rev. Plain die with beaded border, billon, unperforated. Plain Edge. Judd Appendix A, very rare $850

E.29. Same, copper, unperforated. Plain Edge. Judd Appendix A, very rare $900
  The Judd and Adams-Woodin listings of this die pair are contradictory as to which of the 1851 dies was actually used.

Metallurgical trial of 1853 (Smithsonian)

E.30. 1853 Metallurgical Trial Piece. Obv. Regular die of $2-1/2 gold. Rev. ONE/CENT in olive wreath, the ONE quite high, German silver, supposedly 40% nickel, 40% copper, 20% zinc. Reeded Edge. J-149. Rare. Eliasberg 5/96 Proof 64 .... $2,860

E.31. Same, German silver, 30% nickel, 60% copper, 10% zinc. (Observation: 3.75 grams, S.G. 8.72.) Reeded Edge. J-150. Rare. ST 3/92, Ch. Br. Proof $3,000

E.32. Same, copper-nickel, supposedly 60% copper, 40% nickel. Reeded Edge. J-151. Very rare. ST 3/92, BU, $1,500; Heifetz, 10/89, N, P-62 .... $2200
  Note: precise attribution of these three pieces is very difficult, even with X-ray testing. Results vary greatly.

E.33. (ca. 1853) Restrike Mule. Obv. ONE/CENT reverse of 1853. Rev. Plain die with beaded border. Billon, probably 10:90. Plain Edge. Judd Appendix A, very rare $900

E.34. Same, copper. Plain Edge. Judd Appendix A, very rare $900

E.35. Same, copper-nickel. Plain Edge. Judd Appendix A, very rare $950
  The ONE/CENT reverse was used again in 1857, muled with a $2-1/2 pattern obverse.

Metallurgical trial (Superior Galleries)

E.36. 1854 Metallurgical Trial Piece. Obv. Liberty Seated, 13 stars around, 1854 below with incomplete 4, appearing as 1851. Rev. 1 CENT in a thick wreath of oak leaves with acorns, tied with a bow. German silver, 40% nic8)l, 40% copper, 20% zinc. Reeded Edge. J-156. Rare. Approx. the color of modern copper-nickel Heifetz, 10/89, N, P-64 $2059; Eliasberg 5/96 MS-64 .... $2,420

E.37. Same, German silver, 30% nickel, 60% copper, 10% zinc. Reeded Edge. J-157. Rare. Somewhat darker than ordinary copper-nickel $1,000

E.38. Same, copper-nickel, 60:40. Reeded Edge. J-158. Rare. Light steel-gray in color, often found on cracked or defective planchets $1,000
  Precise attribution of these three is very difficult, even with X-ray testing. Plated coins reported.

E.39. Same, copper. Plain Edge. J-159. Very rare, frequently-seen electrotypes made at the Mint by William Dubois for collectors are worth less $700

Large cent patterns continued

Experimental weight trial of 1854
(Smithsonian)

E.40. 1854 Experimental Weight Trial Piece. Obv. Liberty head left, as on 1843-57 large cents, date below, no stars. Rev. ONE CENT in a small laurel wreath. USOA around, two leaves in cluster below E of STATES. Copper. Plain Edge. J-160. Scarce. Weight supposedly 100 grains, vs. 168 gr. of regular cent, but unreliable, as are following. 113.9 grains seen. BM 11/92, P P-65, $1,760; ST 3/92, BU $850

E.41. Same, bronze. Plain Edge. J-161. Scarce. Weight 96 gr. Restrikes exist. ST 3/92, Ch. BU $1800

E.42. Same, oroide. Plain Edge. J-162. Very rare $600

E.43. 1854 Pattern Design Trial Piece. Obv. Eagle flying left as on 1836-39 pattern dollars, 13 stars around, date below. Rev. Same as preceding. Copper. Plain Edge. J-163. Scarce. Weight 100 gr. Eliasberg 5/96 MS-65 .... $3,465

E.44. Same, bronze. Plain Edge. J-164. Scarce. Weight 96 gr. Restrikes exist $900

E.45. 1854 Pattern Design Trial Piece. Obv. Same as preceding. Rev. Similar to preceding but with medium laurel wreath, three leaves in cluster below E of STATES. Bronze. Plain Edge. J-165b. Very rare $1,500

Pattern Design Trial Piece of 1854
(Smithsonian)

E.46. 1854 Pattern Design Trial Piece. Obv. Same as preceding. Rev. Similar to preceding but with large laurel wreath, four leaves in cluster below E of STATES. Copper. Plain Edge. J-165. Very rare $1,500

E.47. 1855 Metallurgical Trial Piece. Obv. Same as preceding but dated 1855. Rev. Small laurel wreath reverse. Copper. Plain Edge. J-172. Rare $800

E.48. Same, bronze. Plain Edge. J-173. Rare. ST 3/92, Ch. Br. Proof $4,000

E.49. Same, copper-nickel. Plain Edge. J-174a. Very rare, alloy(s) uncertain $1,800

E.50. Same, oroide. Plain Edge. J-174. Very rare, if it exists.

Metallurgical trial piece

E.51. 1855 Metallurgical Trial Piece. Obv. Same as preceding. Rev. Large laurel wreath reverse. Copper. Plain Edge. J-167. Scarce. Originals ca. 100 gr.; heavier and lighter restrikes exist. 86.7 grains seen. ST 3/92, Br. Proof $2,000

E.52. Same, bronze. Plain Edge. J-168. Scarce. Originals about 96 gr.; heavier restrikes exist. ST 3/92, Ch. Br. Proof $2,100

E.53. Same, pure nickel. Plain Edge. J-167a. Very rare, if it exists. See next two.

E.54. Same, copper-nickel, supposedly 80:20. Plain Edge. J-170. Rare, difficult to tell from the next; some specimens have been tested by ANACS using X-ray analysis, revealing an actual composition of approximately 75% copper, 12% nickel and 13% zinc, commonly called German Silver. This composition is important as it may have determined the 12% nickel content of the 1856 Flying Eagle cents. Also reported with approx. 90% copper, 10% nickel and no zinc.This and the following may or may not exist as listed $1,000

E.55. Same, copper-nickel, supposedly 60:40. Plain Edge. J-171. Rare. Same comment. ST 3/92 Br. Proof $1,550

E.56. Same, oroide. Plain Edge. J-169. Very rare $1,000

Small Cents

Note: Because of the numerous mulings of the small cent designs, each obverse design will be designated by a Roman numeral and each reverse design by a letter. Design combinations will thus be designated as III-C or IV-D, etc. This system will be carried over several dates. Comments given as to individual working die varieties and die pairings based upon observations of actual coins. Other dies and die pairings possible. Continued research in this field is necessary.

Pattern Design Trial Piece of 1856

E.57. (1856?) Pattern Design Trial Piece. Obv. I: Flying eagle left as on preceding, though reduced to new coin size, no date, lettering. Rev. A: ONE CENT within wreath of corn, wheat, cotton and tobacco, copied from the $3 gold piece, the reverse design adopted in 1857. Copper. Plain Edge. J-179. Rare. Probably a restrike c. 1858 .... $2,600
Modern counterfeits exist.

E.58. Same, copper-nickel. Plain Edge. J-178. Very rare. Also reported in pure nickel; unlikely $3,000

Pattern Design Trial Piece of 1856

E.59. 1856 Pattern Design Trial Piece. Obv. II: Similar to preceding but with large USOA around, date below. Rev. A. This is the design combination adopted in 1857. Copper. Plain Edge. J-181. Very rare. Die varieties exist of this and following $5,000

E.60. Same, bronze. Plain Edge. J-182. Very rare $5,000

E.61. Same, copper-nickel, various alloys. Plain Edge. J-180, 183. Relatively common, and often collected as part of the Flying Eagle cent series, available in both Proof and Uncirculated. Many die varieties exist $6,000

Pattern Design Trial Piece of 1856, design III – B (Bowers & Merena)

E.62. 1856 Pattern Design Trial Piece. Obv. III: Similar to preceding but with smaller date and USOA. Rev. B: ONE CENT within an oak wreath; broad, fancy shield at top. Copper. Plain Edge. J-185. Very rare. This and following probably restrikes c. 1858 .... $3,000

E.63. Same, copper-nickel. Plain Edge. J-184. Very rare. Same rev. die and die state as E.88. Different rev. die from E.70 or E.77/84 or E.97. BM 11/92 P-62 .... $4,950

E.64. 1857 Regular Design Trial Piece. The Flying Eagle design, combination II-A. Copper. Plain Edge. J-187. Very rare $1,500

E.65. Same, copper-nickel, alloy composition 75:25. If 88:12, then a regular issue coin. Plain Edge. J-187a. Very rare, if it exists $1,500

Small cent patterns continued

Mule of 1857 (Bowers & Merena)

E.66. 1857 Mule. Obv. The die for a $2-1/2 pattern of this year, with a Liberty head later used on the copper-nickel 3-cent piece. Rev. ONE/CENT reverse of E.30-32. Copper-nickel. Plain Edge. J-186. Rare. ST 3/92, Ch. Br. Proof $6,250

    1. This pattern, and its companion quarter eagle in copper (E.1594) have unfortunately been overlooked by students of American coinage. They are of particular significance as they mark the first appearance of Longacre's Liberty Head obverse, which became a ubiquitous feature of Longacre's work from this point in his career until his death in 1869. Besides its appearance in the regular series as the obverse of the copper-nickel 3-cent design of 1865-1889, it appeared in this form (or with some minor variations such as a star added to the coronet, as may be seen on E.386) on numerous Longacre patterns for everything from this 1-cent pattern to his very last design, the eagle pattern of 1868 (E.1764).

    2. The rarity of this pattern and its companion quarter eagle has been significantly underrated. Auction appearances are few and far between, and both patterns are high R-7's with no more than 4-5 known. Like many of the early patterns, this one does not appear to have been restruck at a later date, presumably because of the availability of more recent patterns in the more-saleable larger denominations. The only obvious reuse of this obverse at a later date is the double-dated quarter eagle mule (E.1595) utilizing this obverse and a new reverse dated 1860.

E.67. (1858?) Fantasy Mule. Obv. I without date or inscription. Obv. II without date. Copper-nickel. Plain Edge. J-219. Unique?

E.68. 1858 Regular Design Trial Piece. Design II-A, dated 1858. Copper. Plain Edge. J-218. Very rare $1,000

E.69. Same, experimental copper-nickel alloy with higher nickel content. Plain Edge. J-218a. Very rare. Very difficult to distinguish from the regular issue $1,000

E.70. 1858 Pattern Design Trial Piece. Design II-B. Copper-nickel. Plain Edge. J-198. Very rare. Different rev. die from E.63/88 or E.77/84 or E.97. ST 3/92, Br. Proof $4,200

    Also listed as struck on broad planchet, J-199, rev. die variety(s) unknown, probably a restrike c. 1860.

E.71. 1858 Pattern Design Trial Piece. Obv. II. Rev. C: ONE CENT within laurel wreath. The design adopted in 1859 for one year only. Variations of this wreath, commonly attributed to Longacre, appear on various other pattern coins, the copper-nickel 3-cent pieces of 1865-89, the U.S. Mint Assay Medals of 1860, 1861 and 1867, and the ca. 1861 George Washington Time Increases His Fame medal, Julian PR-27, where it is attributed to Paquet! Copper-nickel. Plain Edge. J-196. Very rare $1,200

E.72. 1858 Pattern Design Trial Piece. Obv. II. Rev. D: ONE CENT within oak wreath. Copper-nickel. Plain Edge. J-197. Very rare $1,200

E.73. (1858?) Fantasy. Obv. II without date. Rev. A. Copper-nickel. Plain Edge. J-201. Very rare.

E.74. 1858 Regular Design Trial Piece. Design III-A, dated 1858. Copper. Plain Edge. J-217. Very rare. Eliasberg 5/96 MS-65 .... $7,920

E.75. Same, copper-nickel, alloy 75:25. If 88:12, then a Small Motto regular issue coin. Plain Edge. J-217a. Very rare, if it exists.

Pattern Design Trial Piece of 1858, design III – B (Smithsonian)

E.76. 1858 Pattern Design Trial Piece. Design III-B. Copper. Plain Edge. J-195. Unique?

E.77. Same, copper-nickel. Plain Edge. J-193. Rare. Same reverse die as E.84. Different rev. die than E.63/88 or E.70 or E.97. ST 3/92, Br. Proof $2,700; Eliasberg 5/96 Proof 65 .... $3,410

    Also listed as struck on broad planchet, J-194, rev. die variety(s) unknown, probably a restrike c. 1860.

Pattern Design Trial Piece of 1858, design III-C (Smithsonian)

E.78. 1858 Pattern Design Trial Piece. Design III-C, copper-nickel. Plain Edge. J-191. Rare. Same reverse die as E.85. Eliasberg 5/96 Proof 65 .... $3,300

Small cent patterns continued

Pattern Design Trial Piece of 1858, design III–D (Bowers & Merena)

E.79. 1858 Pattern Design Trial Piece. Design III-D, copper-nickel. Plain Edge. J-192. Rare. Eliasberg 5/96 Proof 64 .... $2,420

E.80. (1858?) Fantasy. Obv. III without date. Rev. D, copper-nickel. Plain Edge. J-200. Very rare.

E.81. 1858 Pattern Design Trial Piece. Obv. IV: Small, ugly eagle flying to left, USOA around, date below. Rev. A. Copper. Plain Edge. J-207. Very rare $1,200

E.82. Same, copper-nickel, various alloys. Some with same rev. die and die state as some E.87. Plain Edge. J-206, 207a. Scarce. Eliasberg 5/96 Proof 64 .... $1,980

E.83. 1858 Pattern Design Trial Piece. Design IV-B. Plain Edge. Copper. J-205. Very rare. ST 3/92, EF . $3300

E.84. Same, copper-nickel. Plain Edge. J-204. Rare. Same rev. die as E.77. ST 3/92, Ch. Br. Proof $2700
      E.84 is the earliest obv. die state of E.81 thru 86. All have top of second 8 recut. Late die pairings have minor die damage in denticles below 85 and above AT.

Pattern Design Trial Piece of 1858, design IV – C (Smithsonian)

E.85. 1858 Pattern Design Trial Piece. Design IV-C, copper-nickel. Plain Edge. J-202. Rare. Same rev. die as E.78 .... $700

E.86. 1858 Pattern Design Trial Piece. Design IV-D, copper-nickel. Plain Edge. J-203. Rare. Hollow outer leaves at 2 and 7 o'clock due to die polishing. Diff. rev. die than E.92. ST 3/92, Br. Proof $2,000; Eliasberg 5/96 Proof 65 $2,310

Pattern Design Trial Piece of 1858, design V – A (Smithsonian)

E.87. 1858 Pattern Design Trial Piece. Obv. V: Indian head left with raised LIBERTY on headband, USOA around, date below. The design adopted in 1859. Rev. A. Copper-nickel. Plain Edge. J-213. Scarce. Die varieties exist. One rev. same die and die state as E.82 .... $750
      Longacre's original wax model for this obverse survives in the Smithsonian collection.

Pattern Design Trial Piece of 1858, design V – B (Smithsonian)

E.88. 1858 Pattern Design Trial Piece. Design V-B, copper-nickel. Plain Edge. J-212. Rare. Obv. die diff. than E.87 or E.91 or E.92. Rev. same die and die state as E.63. ST 3/92, Br. Proof $2,000; Eliasberg 5/96 Proof 65 $2,860

Pattern Design Trial Piece of 1858, design V – C (Smithsonian)

E.89. 1858 Pattern Design Trial Piece. Design V-C, copper. Plain Edge. J-209. Very rare. The design combination adopted in 1859. Eliasberg 5/96 Proof 63 $5,060

Small cent patterns continued

E.90. Same, bronze. Plain Edge. J-210. Unique?

E.91. Same, copper-nickel. Plain Edge. J-208. Varieties exist, based on numbers of leaves in each cluster; one shows die rust above necklace and on bridge of nose. Scarce. Popularly collected as the "first" Indian Head cent. ST 3/92, Ch. Br. Proof $2,200

5 leaves ST 3/92, Proof $3,200

6 leaves ST 3/92 Br. Proof $3,200

E.92. 1858 Pattern Design Trial Piece. Design V-D, copper-nickel. Plain Edge. J-211. Same obv. die as E.91 but later die state. Diff. rev. die than E.86. Rare. ST 3/92, Br. Proof $2,300

E.93. 1858 Fantasy Mule. Obv. IV with Obv. V. Copper-nickel. Plain Edge. J-220. Unique?

E.94. (1858?) Fantasy. Obv. V without date. Rev. B. Copper-nickel. J-216. Very rare, struck on very broad planchet. Possibly struck c. 1860, along with next two.

E.95. (1858?) Fantasy. Obv. V without date. Rev. C. Copper. Plain Edge. J-215. Very Rare, struck on very broad planchet.

E.96. Same, copper-nickel. Plain Edge. J-214. Very rare. Struck on very broad planchet.

E.97. 1859 Pattern Design Trial Piece. Design V-B, dated 1859, copper-nickel. Plain Edge. J-227. Rare $1,500

E.98. 1859 Regular Design Trial Piece. Design V-C, copper. Plain Edge. J-230. Rare $1,000

E.99. Same, bronze. Plain Edge. J-231. Rare $1,000

E.100. Same, lead. Plain Edge. J-231a. Unique?

E.101. (1859?) Fantasy. Incuse impressions of the hubs for Obv. V (in the style of 1860-64) and Rev. C (the 1859 reverse), copper-nickel. Plain Edge. J-264 (as 1860). Unique.

Though the many and diverse fantasy pieces struck in the Mint in the 1860s suggest that this piece is just one more of them, it is possible that there was some official reason for this piece. In this era the Mint was experimenting with ways of making gold coins thinner in the centers so as to stop the practice of hollowing them out and replacing the gold with platinum, and it is theoretically possible that this piece was intended as a "fast and dirty" trial of the idea of making an incused gold coin that would be impossible to hollow out. This is impossible to prove, of course.

E.102. 1859 Pattern Design Trial Piece. Design V-D, copper-nickel. Plain Edge. J-226. Rare $800

E.103. 1859 Pattern Design Trial Piece. Obv. V. Rev. E: ONE CENT within oak wreath with narrow shield at top, the design adopted in 1860, copper. Plain Edge. J-229. Very rare $900

E.104. Same, copper-nickel. Plain Edge. J-228. Rare in Proof, but relatively common in Unc., often collected with regular series. Die varieties exist. ST 3/92, Proof $800

E.105. 1860 Regular Design Trial Piece. Copper. Plain Edge. J-265. Very rare $850

E.106. 1860 Incomplete Die Trial, the regular obverse paired with reverse without ONE CENT. Copper-nickel. Plain Edge. J-266. Very rare $1,000

E.107. 1861 Regular Design Trial Piece. Copper. Plain Edge. J-274. Very rare $850

E.108. 1862 Regular Design Trial Piece. Copper. Plain Edge. J-290. Very rare $850

E.109. Same, copper-nickel, alloy 75:25. If 88:12, then a regular issue coin. Plain Edge. J-291. Very rare, if it exists $900

E.110. Same, oroide. Plain Edge. J-292. Very rare $800

E.111. 1863 Metallurgical Trial Piece, regular dies without L on ribbon. Bronze. Plain Edge. J-299. Relatively common, often found with rotated dies. Rarely found on thick planchets. Die varieties exist. Some may be restrikes, especially those with radial die cracks at K-1 and K-4 on obv. and flat spot on upper left upright of N of ONE. Uniface strikes of that reverse on cent and dime blanks known. ST 3/92, Ch. Br. Proof $1,800

E.112. 1863 Experimental Edge, regular dies without L. Obv. die varieties exist. Copper-nickel, Reeded Edge. J-300. Rare. Proofs known. False pieces exist with reeding added to business strikes $1,000

E.113. 1863 Revised Design Trial Piece. Similar to regular obv., but L added on ribbon. Point of bust made thinner, more pointed. The revision adopted in 1864, and this is possibly a backdated fantasy. Bronze. Plain Edge. J-301. Very rare $1,500

E.114. Same, copper-nickel. Plain Edge. J-302. Very rare $1,500

E.115. Same, oroide. Plain Edge. J-303. Unique, if it exists.

E.116. Same, aluminum. Plain Edge. J-304. Very rare $2,000

E.117. 1864 Regular Design Trial Piece. The regular dies without L. Copper, thick planchet, 4.69 grams. Plain Edge. J-356a. Very rare. ST 3/92, Ch. BU Repunched 4 in date $3,800

E.118. Same, copper-nickel, thin planchet. Plain Edge. Unlisted in Judd. Unique?

E.119. 1864 Revised Design Trial Piece. Revised design with L on ribbon, copper. Plain Edge. J-357. Very rare, struck in Proof, and sometimes mistaken for the regular issue Proof $1,000

E.120. Same, copper-nickel, various alloys. Plain Edge. J-358, 359. Very rare $1,000

E.121. Same, oroide. Plain Edge. J-360. Very rare $1,000

E.122. Same, aluminum. Plain Edge. J-361. Very rare $1,000

Note: Also listed by Judd as "Composition Metal" without explanation.

E.123. 1864 Metallurgical Trial Piece. Regular dies without L, composition is copper 19: aluminum 1. Plain Edge. J-354. Very rare. Correct attribution very difficult on this and following $1,000

E.124. Same, copper 13: aluminum 1. Plain Edge. J-353. Rare $1,000

E.125. Same, copper 9: aluminum 1. Plain Edge. J-355. Rare $1,000

Small cent patterns continued

E.126. Same, copper 9: tin 1. Plain Edge. J-356. Rare $1,000

Note: Other compositions possible. Observed specimens include what may be oroide (copper and tin, a pale gold color) 2.525 grams, S.G. 7.436; copper-nickel with 1864/1864, 3.15 grams, S.G. 9.26; and German silver, 2.90 grams, S.G. 8.53. X-ray testing not available on these pieces at this time.

E.127. 1864 Fantasy Mule. Obv. Regular Indian obv. without L. Rev. Regular small-letter Flying Eagle obv. of 1858. Copper-nickel. Plain Edge. J-362. Very rare.

E.128. 1865 Regular Design Trial Piece. Copper. Plain Edge. J-403. Very rare. Thick or thin reported; 3.39 grams seen $1,000

E.129. Same, copper, thick or thin. Reeded Edge. J-403a. Very rare $1,000

E.130. Same, copper-nickel, various alloys, Plain Edge. J-404, 406. Rare. Thick or thin reported, 3.145 grams seen. Die varieties exist. St 3/92, Br. Proof $4200

Also reported in "nickel-silver" as J-406a. Unverified.

E.131. Same, copper-nickel. Reeded Edge. J-405. Very rare. Thick or thin reported $800

E.132. 1866 Regular Design Trial Piece. Copper. Plain Edge. J-455. Rare. Thick or thin reported $700

E.133. Same, copper-nickel, various alloys. Plain Edge. J-456, 457. Rare. Thick or thin reported. 4.57 grams seen $700

E.134. 1867 Regular Design Trial Piece. Copper. Plain Edge. J-550. Very rare. 2.94 grams seen $800

E.135. Same, copper-nickel, various alloys. Plain Edge. J-551, 552. Very rare $800

E.136. Same, oroide. Plain Edge. J-553. Very rare $1,000

E.137. 1868 Regular Design Trial Piece. Aluminum. Plain Edge. J-612. Rare, from one of at least five complete Proof sets, cent through $20, struck in aluminum on behalf of the Mint Director $1,750

Experimental size trial of 1868 (Smithsonian)

E.138. 1868 Experimental Size Trial Piece. Obv. Liberty head left, as on the 3-cent piece, USOA around, date below. Rev: Roman I within wreath of corn, wheat, cotton and tobacco, as on Type II & III gold dollars. Copper. Plain Edge. J-606. Very rare $1,200

    1. Part of set of patterns for minor coinage, identical except for diameter and denomination shown by the Roman Numeral I, III (E.263), and V (E.400). Whether this was intended by the Mint as a true effort to replace the then-existing patchwork of the Indian Head Cent, the 3-cent with the Liberty head as used on this pattern, and the Shield 5-cent piece, or simply another means to sell patterns to an ever-growing number of eager collectors is a matter of some debate among pattern scholars. These coins reappeared the next year, differing only as to the date (see E.148). These coins, and their 1869 counterparts, are among the most readily available patterns.

    2. Longacre was not the only 19th Century Mint Engraver who tried to develop sets of patterns to replace the mixture of design types that made up regular issue U.S. coinage. In addition to Longacre's effort reflected by these patterns, William Barber (who borrowed freely from Longacre after his death) developed his own version of Seated Liberty in 1870, begining with a proposed trime (E.527) and covering all of the remaining denominations through the dollar. The Barbers (it is sometimes difficult to be sure if some of the early efforts of Charles Barber were his own, or simply reworked versions of his father's designs) continued to propose pattern designs intended to replace a number of existing denominations ithroughout their tnure at the Mint. For example, although it is often grouped with the other 1877 half dollar patterns as part of the sweepstakes that eventually resulted in the Morgan dollar designs of 1878/79, the Barber Sailor Head half (E.1139) turns out to be nothing of the sort. It is actually part of a series of 1877 patterns with this same obverse that includes a 10-cent denomination (E.741) and a 25-cent pattern (E.915). Charles Barber submitted several other patterns for the 1877 half dollar series, as discussed in that section. Charles Barber finally reached his goal when his 1891 patterns (E.750, 929 and 1200) were accepted with minor modifications as what we now refer to as the Barber dime through half dollar of 1892.

E.139. Same, copper-nickel. Plain Edge. J-605. Rare $900

E.140. Same, aluminum. Plain Edge. J-607. Unique? $1,000

E.141. 1868 Experimental Size Trial Piece. Obv. Similar to preceding but from two different dies. Rev. Roman I within laurel wreath, as on 3-cent piece. Copper. Plain Edge. J-609. Very rare $1,000

E. 141a. Same, aluminum, J-unlisted. ST 6/94, Br. Proof $1,900

E.142. Same, copper-nickel. Plain Edge. J-608. Scarce. ST 3/92, Br. Proof $2600

Small cent patterns continued

Experimental size

E.143. 1868 Experimental Size Trial Piece. Obv. Regular large cent obv. of 1843-57, dated 1868. Rev. Regular large cent rev. of 1843-57. Copper. Plain Edge. J-611. Very rare. Popular as the "last of the large cents," though actually struck more as a fantasy while preparing large cent-sized dies for a proposed base metal 10 cents (q.v.) $8,000

    Although struck purely as a fantasy for collectors, and having no pretense as a legitimate pattern despite the later claims that it was struck to test the dies or as an experimental size trial, this pattern, particularly in higher grades, commands a price far beyond its true rarity and without regard for its questionable parentage. Even during the post-bull market of the early 1990s, this coin would bring $14,000 to $16,000 in Gem condition. These prices are in stark contrast to its legitimate half-brother, the real Experimental Size Trial Piece struck this same year in the intended metal, copper-nickel (E.636).

E.144. Same, copper-nickel. Plain Edge. J-610. Very rare $2,500

E.145. 1869 Regular Design Trial Piece. Copper. Plain Edge. J-668. Very rare $800

E.146. Same, copper-nickel, various alloys. Plain Edge. J-669, 670. Very rare. One known broad struck without collar, called "rude planchet" by A-W, broad planchet by Taxay. BM 11/91, MS-64 ... $1,540

E.147. Same, aluminum. Plain Edge. J-671. Very rare, from one of five complete aluminum Proof sets struck for the Mint Director $1,250

E.148. 1869 Experimental Size Trial Piece. Similar to E.141 but dated 1869. Copper. Plain Edge. J-667. Very rare $800

E.149. Same, copper-nickel. Plain Edge. J-666. Scarce. Obv. and Rev. die varieties exist. ST 3/92, Br. Proof.. $1800

E.150. 1870 Regular Design Trial Piece. Copper. Plain Edge. J-787. Very rare $1,000

E.151. Same, copper-nickel. Plain Edge. J-789. Very rare $1,250

E.152. Same, aluminum. Plain Edge. J-788. Very rare $1,000

E.153. 1871 Regular Design Trial Piece. Copper. Plain Edge. J-1041. Very rare $1,500

E.153a. Same, copper-nickel. Plain Edge. Unlisted in Judd. Unique?

E.154. Same, aluminum. Plain Edge. J-1042. Very rare $1,000

E.155. 1872 Regular Design Trial Piece. Copper. Plain Edge. J-1179. Very rare $900

E.156. Same, copper-nickel, various alloys. Plain Edge. J-1180, 1182. Very rare $1,000

E.157. Same, aluminum. Plain Edge. J-1181. Very rare $900

E.158. 1873 Regular Design Trial Piece. Copper. Plain Edge. J-1255. Very rare $950

E.159. Same, copper-nickel. Plain Edge. J-1257. Very rare $1,000

E.160. Same, aluminum. Plain Edge. J-1256. Very rare $900

E.161. 1874 Regular Design Trial Piece. Copper. Plain Edge. J-1346. Very rare $900

E.161a. Same, copper-nickel. Plain Edge. Unlisted in Judd. Unique?

E.162. Same, aluminum. Plain Edge. J-1347. Very rare $950

E.163. 1875 Regular Design Trial Piece. Copper. Plain Edge. J-1383. Very rare $850

E.164. Same, aluminum. Plain Edge. J-1384. Very rare $900

E.165. 1876 Regular Design Trial Piece. Copper-nickel. Plain Edge. J-1451. Very rare $1,200

E.166. Same, aluminum. Plain Edge. J-1450. Very rare $1,000

E.167. 1877 Regular Design Trial Piece. Copper-nickel, various alloys. Plain Edge. J-1495, 1496. Very rare $1,000

E.168. 1879 Regular Design Trial Piece. Copper-nickel. Plain Edge. J-1583. Very rare $1,000

E.169. 1881 Regular Design Trial Piece. Copper-nickel. Plain Edge. J-1664. Very rare $1,000

Pattern Design Trial Piece of 1881
(Smithsonian)

E.170. 1881 Pattern Design Trial Piece. Obv. Liberty head left wearing coronet incused LIBERTY, as on the 1883 Liberty 5 cents, USOA around, date below. Rev. Roman I in wreath of corn and cotton. Copper. Plain Edge. J-1666. Rare $900

Small cent patterns continued

E.171. Same, copper-nickel. Plain Edge. J-1665. Rare. ST 3/92, Ch. Br. Proof $3200
    1. This is the first appearance of the obverse later used in the 1883 Liberty 5-cent regular issue. The design went through several variations in placement of the stars, mottos, etc., resulting in a flurry of 5-cent patterns in 1882. (See the discussion of these patterns in that section.)
    2. Part of a proposed set of minor coinage, all with the same obverse, differing only in diameter and by the use of the appropriate designation on the reverse (III for the 3-cent pattern E.288 and V for the 5-cent pattern E.441. Only the 5-cent design continued to be developed.

E.172. Same, aluminum. Plain Edge. J-1667. Very rare $1,500

E.172a. 1884 Regular Design Trial Piece. Copper. Plain Edge., Unlisted in Judd. Unique? (Part of a complete 1884 set struck in copper, current whereabouts unknown.

E.173. 1884 Regular Design Trial Piece. Copper-nickel. Plain Edge. J-1723a. Unique?

Experimental trial of 1884 (Smithsonian)

E.174. 1884 Experimental Trial Piece. Obv. USOA around unbordered central hole, date at lower edge, denticled outer rim. Rev. ONE CENT at upper border, inverted shield at lower, laurel branch either side of shield, flanking hole. Copper-nickel. Plain Edge. J-1721. Rare. Thick and thin reported. Heifetz, 10/89, P P-67, $9,350;ST 3/92, Gem Br. Proof $3,800
    1. This pattern shows evidence of hasty preparation and lack of attention to the dies. As with its 5-cent counterpart (E.487), this pattern has the central hole punched out without regard for appearances, most of the coins seen having tiny spider cracks radiating out from the points of the perforation.
    2. The purpose for these perforated minor patterns as well as the perforated patterns of 1885 was probably the same as the so-called Blind Man's Nickels of 1882, to allow the visually handicapped to distinguish denominations by touch. Several members of Congress had sent letters to the Mint regarding the need for this type of coinage, with these perforated coins and the 5-cent with five evenly-spaced ridges on their otherwise plain edge providing the Mint's response.

E.175. Same, aluminum. Plain Edge. J-1722. Very rare $1,000

E.176. Similar, but struck from different dies with rims around hole. White Metal. Plain Edge. J-1723. Very rare $900

E.177. 1885 Regular Design Trial Piece. Aluminum. Plain Edge. J-1739. Very rare $1,000

Experimental trial (Bowers & Merena)

E.178. 1885/3 Experimental Trial Piece. Obv. USOA around central hole, blundered date below. Denticled inner and outer rims. Rev. ONE CENT at upper border, shield at lower border, olive branch either side of shield flanking hole. Denticled inner and outer rims. Silver. Holed. Plain Edge. J-1740. Very rare. BM 9/93 .... $5,000
    1. The overdate on this pattern is quite bold, with the 3 predominating over the 5.
    2. This pattern as well as its 5-cent companion (E.491) were clearly never intended as anything other than a general representation of how coinage for the blind might appear. Even though they appear to have a more finished look than their 1884 counterparts, they still show evidence of hasty workmanship. In the New Netherlands Sale 61 catalog (a must-have for anyone interested in patterns), John Ford states that the shield on the reverse has only "nine stripes" and finds there "are other various crudities of execution." The stripes on the shield are also bunched rather than laid out in a normal fashion. The reverse of the coin in the BM 9/93 Sale showed traces of compass marks used by the engraver in laying out the various elements of the design.
    3. John Ford in NN61 refers to these patterns as struck in "base silver," a reference to the metric alloy used in patterns struck a few years earlier.
    4. For some reason, most pattern references and auction catalogs say that there was no apparent purpose for the striking of these patterns. This is incorrect. As noted above with regard to the 1884 perforated patterns, the perforation and differences in the size of the central openings in these minor patterns was undoubtly intended to provide a solution for the problem of providing coinage for the blind. The central perforation would distinguish these minor coins from the other silver denominations already in use.
    5. The perforated patterns of 1885 are significantly rarer than their 1884 counterparts. Auction appearances even during the height of an active market were few and far between. Moreover, the 1-cent pattern appears to be harder to locate than its 5-cent companion. This pattern is either a high R-7 or a true R-8. (However, see the opposite view by Ford in New Netherlands Sale 61, lots #99 and 100.)

Small cent patterns continued

E.179. Same, silver but unperforated. Plain Edge. J-1740a. Unique?
E.180. 1890 Regular Design Trial Piece. Copper. Plain Edge. J-1757. Very rare $1,200
E.181. Same, copper-nickel. Plain Edge. J-1758. Very rare $1,000
E.182. Same, aluminum. Plain Edge. J-1759. Very rare $1,250

Pattern Design Trial Piece of 1896
(Smithsonian)

E.183. 1896 Pattern Design Trial Piece. Obv. Large shield overlaying two crossed poles, topped with liberty cap (l.) and eagle. Ribbon incused LIBERTY crosses the shield, EPU at upper border, date below. Seven stars lower left border, six lower right, large beaded border. Rev. Large 1 above small CENT, all within olive wreath, USOA around, large beaded border. Bronze. Plain Edge. J-1768. Scarce. Obv. and Rev. die varieties exist. BM 11/92, P P-64 .... $880
    1. This pattern and its 5-cent companion appeared in (relatively) large number after the Woodin/Mint trade in which Woodin returned the two gold half union ($50) patterns he had acquired from an "insider" dealer and was given "several crates" of patterns. This one rather hurried deal was the largest single source of a substantial number of the pattens now available. (See the notes under E.1873 for further comments on the Woodin–Mint swap.)
    2. Although readily available, many of these patterns (in various metals), as well as the matching 5-cent pattern of the same year, are found tarnished, spotted, or otherwise unsightly looking. Perhaps this appearance is the result of being stored without regard for preservation in a damp basement before packing them off as trade goods?
E.183a. Same, brass., alloy uncertain. Plain Edge. Unlisted in Judd. Unique?
E.184. Same, pure nickel. Plain Edge. J-1767a. Very rare. ST 3/92, Ch. Br. Proof $5,000
E.185. Same, copper-nickel. Plain Edge. J-1767. Rare $1,000
E.186. Same, aluminum. Plain Edge. J-1769. Rare $800
    Many other alloys were tested at this time, though the strikings are presumed to have been melted. For further information see Judd.
E.187. 1909 Regular Design Trial Piece. The Lincoln design, copper-nickel. Plain Edge. J-1780. Very rare.
    There also exists a uniface lead striking of an earlier version of the Lincoln cent obverse, with a taller bust and without IGWT.
Thomas L. Elder reported a 1915 cent in nickel, but he was not a reliable source.
E.188. 1942 Experimental Composition Trial Piece. Obv. Capped Liberty head right, adapted from a 1918 Colombia 2-centavos piece by John R. Sinnock. This head was used again in 1948 on a West German 20-mark note, Pick-9, printed by the U.S. Bureau of Engraving and Printing. LIBERTY at left border, JUSTICE at right, date below. Rev. UNITED STATES MINT inside laurel wreath previously used on an 1860 $2-1/2 (E.1595), an 1863 3-cents (E.251-2), several U.S. Mint George Washington medals, Julian PR-25&26 and MT-22, and an Abraham Lincoln medal, Julian PR-36. Bronze. Plain Edge. Not numbered in Judd. Very rare $2,000
E.189. Same, zinc-coated steel. Plain Edge. Very rare. ST 9/90, lot 53, $2750; ST 3/92, lot 1591, MS $2,100
E.190. Same, manganese. Plain Edge. Very rare $750
E.191. Same, plastic, various colors and textures. Plain Edge. Rare. Dark red, thick (approx. same as a Proof Jefferson nickel), 0.65 gms and thin (approx. same as a Proof Lincoln cent) 0.38 gms; ST 3/92, MS, $1,200. Black (glossy surfaces but crumbling, fibrous edges) 0.35 gms. BM 1/92 sale: Black $1,320; Brown $1,100; Red-Brown $1,100; Tan $231 and Brass-colored $1,100. Many exist broken to test durability. Typical nice specimen: $1,000
E.192. Same, Bakelite, various colors. Plain Edge. Very rare. Red: ST 9/90 sale, lot 54, $1,760; 3/92, lot 1592 (Same coin?) $1,200; Green-grey: Stacks 3/92, lot 1593, $600 .... $1,000
E.192a. Same, aluminum. Plain Edge. Very Rare $1,000
    Pressed glass and other compositions reported. Some varying reports may refer to duplicate sightings of the same piece due to different interpretations of colors and compositions. Regular design 1942 cents in brass and zinc-coated steel reported, unconfirmed. Some may be on foreign planchets.
1942, 1944 and 1945. Strikings of cents on thick planchets are known in white metal or similar alloy, copper and copper-aluminum alloys, though their reason for striking is unknown. There was no reason why the Mint would have used more copper rather than less in these years. ST 9/94: 2.7mm thick aluminum or white metal AU, $1,500; 2.6mm brass, EF, $850. BM 1/91: 1944 thick copper, MS-65, $715; 1945 thick copper, MS-65, $660; 1945, extra-thick copper, MS-63, $850.
A 1959-D cent with a Wheat Ears reverse is reported to exist, but the only one seen is a clever alteration from a 1958-D coin, not a die-struck counterfeit.

Small cent patterns continued

E.192b. (ca. 1962?) Experimental Trial Piece. Obv. Female head left with flowing hair to right and one lock of hair wrapped around the back of the neck and down over point of bust, similar to Dupre's Libertas Americana medal but without pole and cap. A similar design was later modeled by Mint Engraver Frank Gasparro for the mini-dollar that ultimately bore the image of Susan B. Anthony, possibly suggesting the engraver of this piece. No legend. Plain raised border. Rev. Laurel wreath with berries inside plain, raised border. 2358 in center. ACFLN curved upwards above, OPRSV curved downwards below. Composition, edge, purpose unknown. Illustrated in the May 1962 *Numismatic Scrapbook Magazine* with a request for information on it. Design linked to E.193 and E.194b below by the similar spellings of the gibberish inscriptions and the cryptic number 2358. Current whereabouts, if any, unknown.

Experimental trial piece (Thomas K. DeLorey)

E.192c. (1964-65) Experimental Trial Piece. Obv. Head of Lincoln as on the Lincoln cent, but poorly detailed. No inscriptions. Rev. STAFF in center, MANUFACTURING around upper border and DEVELOPMENT around lower border comparable to inscriptions USOA and ONE CENT on a normal cent. Struck in August 1964 and January 1965 at the General Motors Tech Center in Warren, Mich., on a prototype roller press using dies produced by Frank Gasparro of the U.S. Mint. 95% copper, 5% zinc. Plain Edge. Die varieties exist. The 1964 strikes are 20mm, observed weight 3.99 grams. The 1965 strikes are 21mm with a wider rim, observed weight 4.67 grams. Very Rare.

   A forerunner to this piece struck in June 1964 bears a block capital GM on one side and MD on the other. Narrow rims. 95% copper, 5% zinc. Plain Edge. 20mm. Observed weights 4.13 and 4.16 grams.

E.192d (1965?) Similar to E.192c except STAFF inside a heavy rectangle comparable in size to the Lincoln Memorial on the reverse of a normal cent. Copper, possibly plated afterwards. Plain Edge. Very Rare.

General Motors Roller Press trial piece ca. 1969 (Thomas K. DeLorey)

E.193. (ca. 1969) General Motors Roller Press Trial Piece. Obv. Draped female bust left, LYPPE ES MYSOR at upper border, SIKHTE in left field, ODI and G in right field. Plain, raised border. Rev. Laurel wreath with berries and flowers as on E.194b enclosing AUNHRB/ ACFH/ KOPRW/ 2358/ and G. Plain, raised border unlike E.194b. The design is a close overall approximation of the layout and relief of a Lincoln cent with Wheat Ears reverse, with the lady's hair bun simulating Lincoln's beard, etc., though one source connected to the earlier GM pieces calls this a "Young Queen Elizabeth (II)" design. Bronze. Plain Edge. Unlisted in Judd. Rare. BM ANA '89 MS-63 $357.50; 1/92 sale $192.50. Stacks 3/92 sale $300, $260 and $280 .... $300

   This piece was struck at the General Motors Tech Center in Warren, Mich., from dies prepared by the U.S. Mint to test a radically new roller press being developed by GM for the new Philadelphia Mint. The project was ultimately abandoned due to poor striking quality and excessive down-time resulting from breaking of any of 144 obverse and reverse dies. Such breakage would necessitate stopping and partly dismantling the entire press until repairs were complete. Most pieces show crude numbers and letters (L, M & R for left, middle and right banks) from a desperate attempt to salvage the project by catching the coins from each of 72 pairs of dies in different hoppers. Scarce. The owner of one specimen reported receiving it out of an entire cigar box full of them in a tavern near the Tech Center. These trial pieces are legal to possess as they were struck outside the Mint by private industry and do not bear adopted coin designs.

E.194. 1974 Metallurgical Trial Piece. Regular Lincoln cent dies, aluminum. Plain Edge. Very rare. One known, Smithsonian; others likely.

   Some 1.5 million aluminum cents dated 1974 were struck in 1973 to test the effect of aluminum on die life, in anticipation of a change in composition in 1974. A number of trial pieces were distributed to members of Congress, which failed to authorize the change. Approximately 12 pieces were not returned to the Mint.

E.194a. Same, bronze-clad steel. Plain Edge. Very rare. Five known.

   Some quarter-million 1974-dated trial strikes were made in 1973-74 to test this composition used successfully by West Germany for decades. Most melted. The five pieces known were salvaged by a lucky fellow who happened to be at the Alan Wood Steel Co. in Pennsylvania when about 40 bags of the pieces were being stuffed into a furnace. A bag burst and a few pieces blew off the chute. He reports that perhaps three others exist in "burnt" condition. The Treasury reports that this composition was also tested on nonsense dies, design unknown, but possibly related to E.194b below.

Small cent patterns continued

Experimental trial piece (Thomas K. DeLorey)

E.194b. (ca. 1962-74?) Experimental Trial Piece. Obv. Dupre's female head as on E.192b. Broad plain, raised border. Rev. Laurel wreath with berries and tiny flowers enclosing ACFH/KOPRW/2358. Anachronistic 19th Century denticled border similar to that found on the 1942 Experimental pieces, the leaves reminiscent of the engraving style of Charles Barber, but from no known work of Barber. Steel. Magnetic. Plain Edge. 2.795 gms; Specific gravity 7.657. Illustrated in the August 1979 and May 1980 *The Numismatist.* Design linked to E.192b by the common obverse and the similar spellings of the gibberish inscriptions and the cryptic number 2358. Has been attributed to the GM roller press project of E.193 solely on the basis of the similar legends, but as that project only used sheet bronze, this steel piece may rather have been related to the silver replacement experiments of 1964-65 or, more likely, the copper replacement experiments of 1973-4. *Coin World,* 9/26/94, in a story on a 1974 bronze-clad steel cent, quoted Treasury records as saying that bronze-clad steel pieces had been produced bearing "nonsense" designs. Further study necessary. Very rare.

Two cents

Pattern Design Trial Piece of 1836 (Bowers & Merena)

E.195. 1836 Pattern Design Trial Piece. Obv. Facing eagle on clouds, USOA around with A/E in STATES, date below with 3/6. Rev. TWO CENTS in laurel wreath. Billon, 10% silver, 90% copper. Plain Edge. J-52. Rare. Restrikes exist of this and following. ST 3/92, Br. Proof $5,500

    1. The possiblity of issuing a 2-cent coin was first raised in the Senate in 1806. It was successfully opposed by the Mint and nothing more was heard of the proposal until the idea was revived in Congressional discussions in 1835. Breen's *Secret History of the Gobrecht Coinages* states that Gobrecht and Peale were asked to take time off their efforts in creating what later became the Gobrecht dollar in order to execute the dies for this pattern. More detail can be found in Breen's History and in Taxay, but a glance at these patterns shows that Gobrecht and Peale did not spend a great deal of time on the project. The obverse is an eagle perched on two small clouds. That design is virtually identical to the reverse of the 1796 quarter, half dollar, and other denominations using what is now referred to as the small eagle design. The reverse is a simple wreath surrounding the words TWO CENTS. If one were to be charitable, it could be said that the design was Gobrecht's and Peale's homage to traditional Mint designs. However, as the thrust of their other work at the instruction of the Director of the Mint was to break away from existing designs and reach new heights of artistic achievement, the more likely explanation for a design that reached back nearly four decades was haste. If Congress wanted to see what a 2-cent coin might look like, but was not yet at the stage of approving its issue, then why waste time on a project that might very well go nowhere? Since much of the debate over the question of adopting this denomination was size and the metal to be selected, the fine points of the actual design were simply not important. Therefore, it is most likely that Gobrecht and Peale decided to simply dust off an old punch or rework an existing design, slap together the remaining design elements, and send it off for review as a representation of what a 2-cent coin would look like if the Mint were called upon to produce that denomination.

    2. This latter view is supported by a closer look at the resulting pattern. Evidence of the hasty workmanship has been pointed out in several auction catalogs, with the comments from the Rarcoa 4/72 Central States Sale, lot #971 quite correct in pointing out that "[e]ngraving errors show plainly — a 6 within the 3 of date and E under A of States."

    3. Restrikes outnumber originals. Restrikes can be readily identified as they are ususally struck in copper from buckled dies. The restrikes also show a die crack in a half moon shape running from the right upper obverse rim through the eagle's left wing tip and then back to the right, lower obverse rim. An example of an original billon pattern is the Garrett coin, Garrett II, 5/80, lot #974, now in a PCGS PR-64 slab and showing what the catalog aptly described as a look and "feel" typical of these patterns. (The billon strikes include those that were dipped in a weak acid solution at the Mint. This was done to show Congress that it would be easy to simulate silver, and used as a basis for rejecting the denomination for another 30 years. The coins treated in this fashion have the look of dull silver or even nickel.) The Rarcoa specimen described above (and now also entombed in a like fashion) shows all the characteristics of the copper restrikes.

Two cent patterns continued

4. The copper original strikes, although they do not appear to have been made in greater numbers than the billon examples, generally sell for less than the billon coins. This is because the copper originals and restrikes are not generally considered as distinct varieties and their combined number is far greater than the billon patterns.

E.196. Same, billon. Reeded Edge. J-53. Very rare $5,200
E.197. Same, copper. Plain Edge. J-54. Rare. BM 11/92, P P-63 .... $5,000
E.198. Same, copper. Reeded Edge. J-55. Very rare $5,000
E.199. Same, white metal. Plain Edge. J-56. Very rare $3,000
E.200. Same, white metal. Reeded Edge. J-56a. Very rare $3,000

Pattern Design Trial Piece of 1863
(Smithsonian)

E.201. 1863 Pattern Design Trial Piece. Obv. Washington bust right, GOD AND OUR COUNTRY above, date below. Rev. 2 CENTS (CENTS greatly curved) in wheat wreath tied with plain band, USOA around. Bronze. Plain Edge. J-305. Baker-37. Scarce, thick or thin planchet. ST 3/92, Proof $2,000
E.202. Same, copper-nickel. Plain Edge. J-306. Baker-37A. Very rare. BM 11/92, P-62 .... $3,520
E.203. Same, oroide. Plain Edge. J-307. Baker-37C. Very rare $1,800
E.204. Same, aluminum. Plain Edge. J-308. Baker-37B. Very rare $1,800
E.205. 1863 Pattern Design Trial Piece. Obv. Same as preceding. Rev. Similar to preceding except CENTS less curved and wreath tied with a bow, the reverse adopted in 1864. Bronze. Plain Edge. J-309. Baker-38. Rare, possibly a restrike first made in 1864 .... $1,200
E.206. Same, copper-nickel. Plain Edge. J-310. Baker-38B. Very rare $1,800
E.207. Same, aluminum. Plain Edge. J-311. Baker-38A. Very rare $1,800

Pattern Design Trial Piece of 1863 (Harlan J.
Berk Ltd.)

E.208. 1863 Pattern Design Trial Piece. Obv. National shield over crossed arrows, laurel branch hanging down at either side. GOD OUR TRUST in small letters on ribbon at top, date below. Rev. Die showing CENTS greatly curved. Copper. Plain Edge. J-312a. Rare, probably a restrike; 106 grains vs. theoretical 96 of following. ST 3/92, Ch. Br. Proof, $4,000
E.209. Same, bronze. Plain Edge. J-312. Scarce. 5.83 gms, or 89.97 gns. BM 11/92, P P-64 .... $2,585
E.210. Same, copper-nickel. Plain Edge. J-313. Very rare $1,600
E.211. Same, aluminum. Plain Edge. J-314. Very rare. Judd also lists a variety (J-314a) with a small motto, but as this design normally has a small motto it may be a misidentification of some other piece $1,800
E.212. 1863 Pattern Design Trial Piece. Obv. Same as preceding. Rev. The 1864 design. Bronze. Plain Edge. J-315. Very rare, possibly a restrike first made in 1864 .... $1,000

Pattern Design Trial Piece of 1863

E.213. 1863 Pattern Design Trial Piece. Obv. Similar to preceding, except IN GOD WE TRUST on ribbon in large letters. Rev. Same as preceding. The design combination adopted in 1864. Bronze. Plain Edge. J-316. Rare $1,000
E.214. Same, copper-nickel. Plain Edge. J-317. Very rare $1,200
E.215. Same, aluminum. Plain Edge. J-318. Very rare $1,500
E.216. 1864 Pattern Design Trial Piece. Obv. Same as preceding, dated 1864. Rev. Same as preceding. The design combination adopted for regular issues, die varieties exist. Copper. Plain Edge. J-370. Rare, easily confused with the regular issue $750
E.217. Same, copper-nickel, various alloys, some slightly magnetic. Plain Edge. J-371, 372a. Very rare $1,000

Two cent patterns continued

E.218. Same, aluminum. Plain Edge. J-372. Very rare $1,000

E.219. 1864 Pattern Design Trial Piece. Obv. Same as preceding. Rev. The 1863 style with CENTS greatly curved. Copper. Plain Edge. J-363. Rare, possibly a mule made for collectors $750

E.220. Same, copper-nickel. Plain Edge. J-364. Very rare $1,000

E.221. Same, aluminum. Plain Edge. J-365. Very rare $1,000

E.222. 1864 Revised Design Trial Piece. Obv: Similar to preceding except smaller IN GOD WE TRUST. Rev. The 1864 style. Copper. Plain Edge. J-373. Very rare, easily confused with the Small Motto regular issue coins made from at least one pair of dies of this design $1,000

E.223. Same, copper-nickel. Plain Edge. J-374. Very rare $1,000

E.224. 1864 Revised Design Trial Piece. Obv. Same as preceding. Rev. The 1863 style. Bronze. Plain Edge. J-366. Very rare, possibly a mule made for collectors. Eliasberg 5/96 Proof 65 $5,500

E.225. Same, copper. Plain Edge. J-367. Very rare $2,700

E.226. Same, copper-nickel. Plain Edge. J-368. Very rare $1,000

E.227. Same, aluminum. Plain Edge. J-369. Very rare $1,000

E.228. 1865 Regular Design Trial Piece. Copper. Plain Edge. J-408, 409b. Very rare. 6.21 gms. ST 3/92, Br. Proof. Some are silver plated. Some or all may be restrikes. See E.230, E.240 and E.240a $3,000

E.229. Same, copper-nickel, various alloys. Plain Edge. J-409, 409a. Very rare $1,600

E.230. 1865 Fantasy Planchet Strike. Regular dies, struck on planchet copper on one side and silver on the other. Plain Edge. J-407. Very rare, year of and reason for issue unknown; see 1869-70 listings $2,000

E.231. 1866 Regular Design Trial Piece. Copper-nickel, various alloys. Plain Edge. J-458, 459. Rare $800

E.232. 1867 Regular Design Trial Piece. Copper. Plain Edge. J-554. Very rare, die varieties exist $1,000

E.233. Same, copper-nickel, various alloys. Plain Edge. J-555, 556. Very rare $1,000

E.234. Same, oroide. Plain Edge. J-557. Very rare $800

E.235. 1868 Regular Design Trial Piece. Copper-nickel. Plain Edge. J-613. Very rare $800

E.236. Same, aluminum. Plain Edge. J-614. Very rare $800

E.237. 1869 Regular Design Trial Piece. Copper. Plain Edge. J-672. Very rare $800

E.238. Same, copper-nickel. Plain Edge. J-673. Very rare $800

E.239. Same, aluminum. Plain Edge. J-674. Very rare. Judd also lists J-674a, a bimetallic piece made of copper and aluminum without further explanation $1,250

E.240. 1869 Fantasy Mule. Obv. The regular 2 cents obverse. Obv. Standard Silver series 25 cents obverse die. Struck on planchet copper on one side and silver on the other. Plain Edge. J-675. Unique? See next two.

E.240a. 1870 Fantasy Mule. Rev. The regular 2 cents reverse. Rev. Standard Silver series 25 cents reverse die with cotton and corn wreath. Struck on planchet copper on one side and silver on the other. Unique? Ex-Farouk. See previous and following.

E.241. 1870 Regular Design Trial Piece. Bimetallic planchet, copper on one side and silver on the other. Plain Edge. J-793. Very rare $2,200

E.242. Same, copper. Plain Edge. J-790. Rare $800

E.243. Same, copper-nickel. Plain Edge. J-792. Very rare $900

E.244. Same, aluminum. Plain Edge. J-791. Very rare $900

E.245. 1871 Regular Design Trial Piece. Copper. Plain Edge. J-1043. Very rare. 5.97 gms $800

E.246. Same, aluminum. Plain Edge. J-1044. Very rare $800

E.247. 1872 Regular Design Trial Piece. Copper. Plain Edge. J-1183. Very rare $800

E.248. Same, aluminum. Plain Edge. J-1184. Very rare $800

E.249. 1873 Regular Design Trial Piece. Closed 3. Copper. Plain Edge. J-1258. Very rare $1,000

E.250. Same, aluminum. Plain Edge. J-1259. Very rare $1,000

Copper-nickel 3 cents

Experimental size trial of 1863 (Smithsonian)

E.251. 1863 Experimental Size Trial Piece. Obv. Coronet head left, as on 1843-57 large cents, 13 stars around, date below. Rev. 3 CENTS in laurel wreath previously used for a quarter eagle pattern design of 1860, E.1595, and used again on 1942 cents, E.188. USOA around. Bronze. Plain Edge. J-319. Rare, originals weigh 144 grains, restrikes approximately 119 grains. BM 11/92, P P-65, $3,300; Heifetz 10/89, P P-65, $4,840

E.252. Same, aluminum. Plain Edge. J-320. Very rare, restrikes possible. Eliasberg 5/96 Proof 66 $3,190, Proof 65 $3,630

    Intended as the companion piece to the bronze 1- and 2-cent pieces introduced in 1864, the bronze 3 cents was never approved. However, the need for a base metal coin to replace the paper 3-cent note then in circulation eventually resulted in the following.

E.253. 1865 Pattern Design Trial Piece. Obv. Liberty head left, incused LIBERTY on coronet. USOA around, date below. The adopted design. Rev. ribbed Roman III in laurel wreath tied with a bow. Similar to the adopted design except that the ribbon ends are longer and overlap the rim. Copper. Plain Edge. J-411. Very rare. ST 9/94 .... $1,850

E.254. Same, copper-nickel. Plain Edge. J-410. Very rare. ST 9/94, Ch. Br. Proof $1,800

E.255. Same, aluminum. Plain Edge. J-412. Very rare, if it exists.

    Because of the similarity between this variety and the revised reverse below, there has been much confusion in Judd and elsewhere as to the correct interpretation of the original Adams-Woodin numbers. Judd apparently mismatched AW-511 with J-410 and AW-512 with J-411, so it is possible that he was likewise in error when he listed AW-513 as J-412; thus J-412 may not exist.

E.256. 1865 Pattern Design Trial Piece. Obv. Same as preceding. Rev. Similar to preceding except ends of ribbons shortened to avoid the rim, the adopted design. Copper. Plain Edge. J-413. Very rare, thick (2.2 gm) and thin planchets. Heifetz 10/89, N P-64 .... $2,750

E.257. Same, oroide. Plain Edge. J-414. Very rare $1,000

E.258. Same, aluminum. Plain Edge. J-414a. Very rare $1,000

    Adams and Woodin were likewise confused on the 1865 3-cent pieces, listing as AW-511 a piece from normal dies on a "nickel" (i.e., copper-nickel) planchet, in other words a normal coin. This may have resulted from A-W confusion over a change in date position between two working dies.

E.259. 1866 Regular Design Trial Piece. Copper. Plain Edge. J-460. Rare, struck from a broken reverse die $500

E.260. 1867 Regular Design Trial Piece. Copper. Plain Edge. J-558. Very rare. Heifetz 10/89, N P-64 $2,750

E.261. Same, oroide. Plain Edge. J-559. Very rare $1,000

E.262. 1868 Regular Design Trial Piece. Aluminum. Plain Edge. J-621. Very rare $950

Experimental size trial of 1868 (Smithsonian)

E.263. 1868 Experimental Size Trial Piece. Obv. The regular 3 cents obverse with small date, set in a wider die with a wider rim. Rev: Smooth, unribbed Roman III within the corn, wheat, cotton and tobacco wreath of the Flying Eagle cent, normal Flying Eagle cent denticled rim. Copper. Plain Edge. J-616. Very rare. ST 3/92, Br. Proof $3,600

E.264. Same, copper-nickel, various alloys. Plain Edge. J-615. 615a. Scarce. ST 3/92, Ch. Br. Proof .. $2,100

E.265. Same, aluminum. Plain Edge. J-617. Very rare $950

    These and the following represent an unexplained attempt to increase the size of the 3 cents from that of the dime to that of the cent. This idea was repeated in 1869 and revived in 1881.

E.266. 1868 Experimental Size Trial Piece. Obv. Same as preceding. Rev. Similar to normal design but with smooth, unribbed III, normal-sized wreath set in larger field with denticled rim of normal width. Copper. Plain Edge. J-617b. Very rare, if it exists.

E.267. Same, copper-nickel. Plain Edge. J-617c. Very rare, if it exists.

Copper-nickel 3-cent patterns continued

E.268. Same, aluminum. Plain Edge. J-617a and J-620a. Very rare.
All of the above may exist, but because of the similarity between them and the following it is possible that certain pieces in either listing may be misdescriptions.

Experimental size trial (Superior Galleries)

E.269. 1868 Experimental Size Trial Piece. Obv. Similar to preceding, except head set in larger field with normal rim, large date. Rev. Same as preceding. Copper. Plain Edge. J-619. Very rare $900
E.270. Same, copper-nickel. Plain Edge. J-618. Scarce, die varieties exist. ST 3/92, Br. Proof, $1,700; Heifetz 10/89, P P-65 .... $2,310
Part of a set apparently intended by Longacre to replace the mix of existing designs for minor coinage with a uniform design, differing only by the designation on the reverse and the diameter. (See E.138 above and E.403 below.)
E.271. Same, aluminum. Plain Edge. J-620. Very rare $900
E.272. 1869 Regular Design Trial Piece. Copper. Plain Edge. J-678. Very rare $750
E.273. Same, aluminum. Plain Edge. J-679. Very rare $750
E.274. 1869 Experimental Size Trial Piece. Obv. & Rev. Same as 269 above, except for date. Copper. Plain Edge. J-677. Very rare $850
E.275. Same, copper-nickel. Plain Edge. J-676. Scarce, a reverse die variety with longer denticles is reported ST 3/92, Ch. Br. Proof $4,400
E.276. 1870 Regular Design Trial Piece. Copper. Plain Edge. J-794. Very rare $1,000
E.277. Same, aluminum. Plain Edge. J-795. Very rare $1,000
E.278. 1871 Regular Design Trial Piece. Copper. Plain Edge. J-1045. Very rare $1,000
E.279. Same, aluminum. Plain Edge. J-1046. Very rare $1,000
E.280. 1872 Regular Design Trial Piece. Copper. Plain Edge. J-1185. Very rare $1,000
E.281. Same, aluminum. Plain Edge. J-1186. Very rare $1,000
E.282. 1873 Regular Design Trial Piece. Copper. Plain Edge. J-1260. Very rare. ST 9/94, Ch. Br. Proof, ... $3,600
E.283. Same, aluminum. Plain Edge. J-1261. Very rare $900
E.284. 1874 Regular Design Trial Piece. Copper. Plain Edge. J-1348. Very rare $900
E.285. Same, aluminum. Plain Edge. J-1349. Very rare $850
E.286. 1875 Regular Design Trial Piece. Copper. Plain Edge. J-1385. Very rare $900
E.287. Same, aluminum. Plain Edge. J-1386. Very rare $850
E.287a. 1876 Regular Design Trial Piece. Copper. Plain Edge. Unlisted in Judd. Reported, not confirmed.

Pattern Design Trial Piece of 1881
(Smithsonian)

E.288. 1881 Pattern Design Trial Piece. Obv. Liberty head left with LIBERTY incused on coronet; wheat ears, cotton bolls and leaves behind coronet, USOA around, date below. Rev. Smooth, unribbed Roman III in wreath of corn and cotton. Copper. Plain Edge. J-1669. Rare. ST 3/92, Ch. Br. Proof $5,000
E.289. Same, copper-nickel. Plain Edge. J-1668. Rare $1,500
E.290. Same, aluminum. Plain Edge. J-1670. Very rare. ST 9/94, V. Ch. Br. Proof $3,800
Part of a proposed matched set of copper-nickel 1-, 3- and 5-cent coins by Charles E. Barber. Only the 5-cent pattern survived to be modified in a wide variety of ways in 1882 before emerging as the adopted design with (to all but the eye of the specialist) as only minor modifications in 1883.
E.290a. 1884 Regular Design Trial Piece. Copper. Plain Edge. Unlisted in Judd. Part of a complete 1884 set struck in copper. Present whereabouts unknown.
E.291. 1885 Regular Design Trial Piece. Aluminum. Plain Edge. J-1741. Very rare $1,000

Copper-nickel 5 cents

Because many 5-cent pattern designs were used repeatedly in different die combinations, each such design will be described in detail once and identified with a Roman numeral for an obverse and a letter for a reverse, after which only the number or letter will appear.

A Note on 5-cent Patterns:

As a denomination, the copper-nickel 5-cent coin was introduced relatively late. It was created, along with the copper-nickel 3-cent coin, to replace the financially-necessary, but unpopular fractional currency. Unlike its lesser companion, the "nickel" proved quite important and useful. The number and variety of patterns for this denomination reflect that importance, and the problems attendant to the compostion of these coins. The sheer number and variety of these patterns have held a special fascination for pattern collectors over the years, and many great collections have focused on these coins.

Backdated Fantasy (Harlan J. Berk Ltd.)

E.292. 1865 Backdated Fantasy. Design II-A (see 1866 listings): the normal design of 1866 With Rays. Copper. Plain Edge. J-417. Rare. 4.88 gms $3,000

E.293. Same, copper-nickel. Plain Edge. J-416. Very rare. Heifetz 10/89, P P-64 .... $9,900

1. Long considered to be the prototype for the Shield nickel or a transitional coin, this pattern appears to be a restrike from the 1868 era when such backdated fantasies were commonly produced. The obverse die is from the correct hub for this year, although the date was sunk from the logotype of the 1865 copper-nickel 3 cents. The reverse die is identical to the 1866 regular Proof, as per comparison of two examples of this pattern and several regular issue 1866 Proofs. This fact was noted in John Ford's comments on this pattern in the New Netherlands Sale 61, lot #16 and elsewhere. (For example, Breen in the LM 9/68 Sale lot#422, same pattern in copper, stated "Rev. from identical working die used on all 1866 regular Proof nickels, showing the center dot and recutting on 5." Further evidence of its fantasy status is a comparison of two example of this pattern and an example of E.295, the so-called No Rays prototype, but clearly a restrike of the 1868 era as that pattern uses a reverse hub that was not made until that date.

A side-by-side view of the obverse of two examples of this pattern and the E.295 showed that the E.295 was struck first as the two obverses are from the same die, and the die state for the obverse of this pattern (based on die polish marks at upper right tip of 5) prove it to be a later die state than the one used to strike E.295.

2. In addition to the extrinsic evidence that this pattern was not the prototype or a "transitional," to use the term adopted by Breen, the letter quoted by Taxay in his *U.S. Mint and Coinage* transmitting the group of pattern 5-cent coins for approval contains a description of what was later adopted as the Shield nickel of 1866 and various other patterns. Each of these other patterns are readily identifiable (such as E.325) and all of them bear a date of 1866. No mention is made of any of the patterns bearing an earlier date. Moreover, the enabling legislation and discussion of the need for this denomination in Congress took place too late for any prototypes to be struck in 1865. Thus, there was a pattern for the Shield nickel, but it was the dies later used to strike the 1866 With Rays regular issue Proofs, not this backdated fantasy.

Backdated Fantasy (Harlan J. Berk Ltd.)

E.294. 1865 Backdated Fantasy. Design II-B: the normal design of 1867 Without Rays. Copper. Plain Edge. J-419. Very rare $3,000

Copper-nickel 5-cent patterns continued

E.295. Same, copper-nickel. Plain Edge. J-418. Very rare. 5.02 gms $5,000
    Yet another pattern originally touted as a "transitional" coin, now known to be a backdated fantasy of the 1868 era. The pattern uses a reverse die used to strike regular issue Proofs of the 1868-69 period.

E.296. 1866 Pattern Design Trial Piece. Obv. I: National shield with cross at top, knob at bottom, crossed arrows behind base, laurel branch hanging down on either side. Date 18 66 below, divided by knob, very small IGWT at upper border. Rev. A: Large 5 within circle of 13 stars and 13 rays, USOA around, CENTS below. The reverse adopted in 1866. Copper. Plain Edge. J-498. Very rare. ST 3/92, Br. Proof $5,250

E.297. Same, bronze. Plain Edge. J-499. Very rare $2,000

E.298. Same, copper-nickel. Plain Edge. J-497. Very rare $1,200
    This obverse most nearly matches a drawing by Longacre showing his original proposal for this design with the date separated by a knob that has another, smaller knob attached to its bottom. The second knob did not appear on this first struck pattern of his design.

E.299. 1866 Pattern Design Trial Piece. Obv. I. Rev. B: Similar to preceding, but no rays between stars; the reverse adopted in 1867. Copper-nickel. Plain Edge. J-500. Very rare, probably a backdated fantasy $3,500

E.300. 1866 Pattern Design Trial Piece. Obv. I. Rev. C: Fancy 5 with bulbous serifs in delicate laurel wreath, USOA around. Copper. Plain Edge. J-490. Rare. ST 3/92, Ch. Br. Proof $3,400

E.301. Same, bronze. Plain Edge. J-491. Rare $1,000

E.302. Same, copper-nickel. Plain Edge. J-489. Rare $3,500

E.303. 1866 Pattern Design Trial Piece. Obv. I. Rev. D: Similar to preceding except 5 is taller, less fancy. Copper. Plain Edge. J-493. Very rare, if it exists.

E.304. Same, copper-nickel. Plain Edge. J-492. Very rare, if it exists.

E.305. 1866 Pattern Design Trial Piece. Obv. I. Rev. E: Short, wide 5 in heavy laurel wreath, USOA around in large letters. Copper. Plain Edge. J-495. Very rare $1,000

E.306. Same, bronze. Plain Edge. J-496. Very rare $1,000

E.307. Same, copper-nickel. Plain Edge. J-494. Very rare $3,500

E.308. 1866 Pattern Design Trial Piece. Obv. II: Similar to preceding except shield higher, date joined and IGWT larger. Rev. A, the adopted designs. Copper. Plain Edge. J-510. Very rare $1,000

E.309. Same, bronze. Plain Edge. J-511. Very rare $1,000

E.310. Same, steel. Plain Edge. J-512. Very rare $1,200

E.311. 1866 Pattern Design Trial Piece. Design II-B, as adopted in 1867. Copper. Plain Edge. J-508. Rare, but may be a backdated fantasy $3,000
    This coin is generally considered to be an off-metal strike of E.313 below. However, as stated in the notes under that pattern, E.313 used a reverse unique to that pattern with two center dots and not used again. Several comments on this pattern, including those of Breen, report examples of this pattern in this metal or bronze but lacking the distinctive, two center-dot reverse of E.313. If this is confirmed, then those coins may very well be backdated fantasies. If there are copper strikes of this coin with the two center dot reverse and with a later reverse, then two separate numbers should be assigned to these coins. The resolution to this question will have to wait for further evidence.

E.312. Same, bronze. Plain Edge. J-509. Rare $3,000

E.313. Same, copper-nickel. Plain Edge. J-507. Rare, widely touted as a "transitional pattern." $5,500
    For once, a true transitional, since the reverse die (unique to this pattern) does not appear to have been used before or after this pattern was struck. The matter was best summed up by John Ford in his discussion of J-416, -507, and -1690 as true transitional nickels in New Netherlands' Sale 61, 6/70. J-416 was lot #16, J-507 lot #24, and J-1690 was lot #86. His comments on J-507 were as follows:
    "Rarer than the 1867 with rays in Proof; about *five* examples said to be known ...The reverse die is apparently the initial attempt: Knob of 5 strongly recut, two center dots. Star points aim, atypically, at upright of first T of STATES (rather than A), at A and E of AMERICA (rather than between AM and R), and at left corner of N and between TS of CENTS (rather than E and T). Point of 5 aims at middle of a star. This reverse is unknown on any 1867-69 Proofs or business strikes. Some copper pieces of the same design (Judd 508 or 509) come with a different rev. die, one without center dot and with star points aiming at alternative positions given above. That particular reverse is also found on nickel Proofs of 1867-69 of regular design and on 1865 Judd 418, suggesting that the latter is an anachronistic piece of caprice."(NN, Sale 61, Lot #24, pp 4-5, emphasis in original.)
    In light of the fact that the other so-called "transitionals" are now believed to be fantasy restrikes of the 1868 era, this should be considered of special interest.

E.314. Same, white metal. Plain Edge. J-509a. Very rare $1,000

E.315. 1866 Pattern Design Trial Piece. Design II-D. Copper. Plain Edge. J-502. Very rare $1,000

E.316. Same, bronze. Plain Edge. J-503. Very rare $1,000

E.317. Same, copper-nickel. Plain Edge. J-501. Very rare. ST 6/94, Br. Proof $4,600

E.318. 1866 Pattern Design Trial Piece. Design II-E. Copper. Plain Edge. J-505. Very rare $900

E.319. Same, bronze. Plain Edge. J-506. Very rare $900

E.320. Same, copper-nickel. Plain Edge. J-504. Very rare. Eliasberg 5/96 Proof 66 $6,930

E.321. 1866 Mule. Obv. II. Rev. F: Short, thin 5 over CENTS slightly curved, all in heavy laurel wreath different from that of Rev. E, IGWT at upper border. Copper-nickel. Plain Edge. J-531. Very rare. Coin does not bear the legend UNITED STATES OF AMERICA, but presents legend IN GOD WE TRUST twice; may be a backdated fantasy $950

Copper-nickel 5-cent patterns continued

E.322. 1866 Fantasy Mule. Obv. II muled with the obverse die of a $3 gold piece. Copper-nickel. Plain Edge. J-531a. Unique?

Pattern Design Trial Piece of 1866, design III – A (Bowers & Merena)

E.323. 1866 Pattern Design Trial Piece. Obv. III: Washington bust right, attributed to James B. Lomgacre and resembling the 2-cent Washington pattern with IGWT at upper border, date below. Rev. A. Copper. Plain Edge. J-474, Baker 40A. Rare $1,800

E.324. Same, bronze. Plain Edge. J-475, Baker 40B. Rare $1,800

E.325. Same, copper-nickel. Plain Edge. J-473, Baker 40. Rare $4,000

1. One of two distinct Washington obverses that appear in the 1866 pattern series. This particular obverse (and the specific die marriage) can be traced through letters to the original submission of a group of these patterns that resulted in the adoption of the Shield design. The second Washington obverse is discussed under the notes for E.362.

2. Although this and the other 1866 patterns are generally well struck (the Washington patterns particularly so) the planchets often show the problems typical of the regular copper-nickel strikes. There is also some evidence of a reverse die crack noted on three different examples of this pattern, which uses the same reverse as the adopted With Rays design. (The die is cracked from the upper left reverse rim to the outer edge of the rays.) These may well be restrikes from late 1866, period or simply a harbinger of the troubles that were to follow with this reverse.

E.326. 1866 Pattern Design Trial Piece. Design III-B. Copper. Plain Edge. J-477, Baker 39B, Very rare, probably a backdated fantasy.

E.327. Same, copper-nickel. Plain Edge. J-476, Baker 39. Unique?

E.328. Same, brass. Plain Edge. J-478, Baker 39C. Unique?

E.329. Same, white metal. Plain Edge. J-479, Baker 39A. Very rare $1,250

E.330. 1866 Pattern Design Trial Piece. Design III-C. Copper. Plain Edge. J-465, Baker 41A. Very rare $2,000

E.331. Same, bronze. Plain Edge. J-466, Baker 41C. Very rare $1,200

E.332. Same, copper-nickel. Plain Edge. J-464, Baker 41. Rare $4,000

E.333. 1866 Pattern Design Trial Piece. Design III-D. Copper. Plain Edge. J-468, Baker 41G. Very rare $1,500

E.334. Same, bronze. Plain Edge. J-469, Baker 41H. Very rare $1,500

E.335. Same, copper-nickel. Plain Edge. J-467, Baker 41F. Very rare $1,500

Pattern Design Trial Piece of 1866, design III – E (Smithsonian)

E.336. 1866 Pattern Design Trial Piece. Design III-E. Copper. Plain Edge. J-471, Baker 42A. Rare $1,250

E.337. Same, bronze. Plain Edge. J-472, Baker 42B. Rare $1,250

E.338. Same, copper-nickel. Plain Edge. J-470, Baker 42. ST 3/92, Br. Proof $4,000

E.339. 1866 Mule. Design III-F. Silver. Plain Edge. J-466a, Baker 41C. Very rare, may be a backdated fantasy.

E.340. 1866 Mule. Obv. III. Rev. G: Large 5 over CENTS in a straight line, all in thin laurel wreath close to border. Very small IGWT at upper border. Copper-nickel. Plain Edge. J-529. Very rare. Probably a backdated fantasy struck c. 1869, as are most or all of the fantasy mules that follow.

E.341. Same, white metal. Plain Edge. J-530. Very rare.

This obverse was also muled with the following obverse (see below) and with a No Motto $5 reverse (see section on half eagles).

E.342. 1866 Mule. Obv. IV: Similar to preceding except USOA replaces IGWT. Rev. A. Copper. Plain Edge. J-514. Very rare $1,000

E.343. Same, copper-nickel. Plain Edge. J-513. Very rare $1,000

E.344. Same, brass, wide planchet. Plain Edge. J-515. Very rare $1,600

E.345. 1866 Mule. Design IV-B. Silver. Plain Edge. J-518, Baker 46D. Very rare, if it exists; may be a backdated fantasy.

E.346. Same, copper. Plain Edge. J-517, Baker 46A. Very rare $1,200

E.347. Same, copper-nickel. Plain Edge. J-516, Baker 46. Very rare $1,100

E.348. Same, brass. Plain Edge. J-519, Baker 46C. Very rare $1,200

Copper-nickel 5-cent patterns continued

E.349. Same, lead. Plain Edge. J-520, Baker 46B. Very rare. Only one seen has appearance of a restrike, with the reverse die deeply broken from the last S of STATES to the E of CENTS $1,000

E.350. 1866 Mule. Design IV-D. Copper-nickel. Plain Edge. J-527. Very rare, bears USOA each side .. $1,000

E.351. 1866 Mule. Design IV-E. Copper-nickel. Plain Edge. J-528. Very rare, bears USOA each side ... $1,000

Pattern Design Trial Piece of 1866, design IV – F (Bowers & Merena)

E.352. 1866 Pattern Design Trial Piece. Design IV-F. Copper. Plain Edge. J-462. Rare. Eliasberg 5/96 Proof 64/66 $2,970

E.353. Same, copper-nickel, various alloys. Plain Edge. J-461, 463. Rare. ST 3/92, Proof $2,400

E.354. 1866 Fantasy Mule. Obv. III & Obv. IV. Silver. Plain Edge. J-521. Very rare $1,500

E.355. Same, copper. Plain Edge. J-522. Very rare $1,000

E.355a. Same, copper-nickel. Plain Edge. Unlisted in Judd. Unique?

E.356. Same, brass. Plain Edge. J-523. Very rare $1,500

E.357. Same, white metal. Plain Edge. J-524. Very rare $1,000

E.358. 1866 Fantasy Mule. Obv. IV & Obv. IV. Copper. Plain Edge. J-525, Baker Q-46A. Very rare $1,000

E.359. Same, white metal. Plain Edge. J-526, Baker Q-46. Very rare $1,500
This obverse was also muled with a No Motto $5 reverse (see section on half eagles).

E.360. 1866 Pattern Design Trial Piece. Obv. V: Large Washington head right with GOD AND OUR COUNTRY legend, date below. Rev. C. Copper-nickel. Plain Edge. J-480. Unique?

E.361. 1866 Pattern Design Trial Piece. Design V-D. Copper. Plain Edge. J-482, Baker 44A. Very rare. ST 6/94, Br. Proof $4,400

E.362. Same, copper-nickel. Plain Edge. J-481, Baker 44. Very rare. Eliasberg 5/96 Proof 64 .... $6,820
1. This obverse, known as the High Relief Washington Head, is substantialy rarer in any die marriage or metal than the 1866 patterns struck with the lower relief Washington bust obverse, such as E.325.
2. Usually found well struck, and the only one of the 5-cent patterns with this particular obverse that has appeared on the market in the intended metal in the last few years. There was a P P-64 coin in the 1989 Heifetz Sale, $5,720; another similarly graded coin in the BM "Cabinet of Rarities" FPL in 1990.

E.363. 1866 Pattern Design Trial Piece. Design V-E. Copper. Plain Edge. J-484, Baker 43A. BM 6/91, Dr. George Polis Collection. PR-65, $6,380. Very rare $6,500

E.364. Same, bronze. Plain Edge. J-485, Baker 43B. Very rare $6,500

E.365. Same, copper-nickel. Plain Edge. J-483, Baker 43. Very rare $7,200

Pattern Design Trial Piece of 1866

E.366. 1866 Pattern Design Trial Piece. Obv. VI: Lincoln head right, USOA around, date below. Rev. F. Copper. Plain Edge. J-487. Rare $6,500

E.367. Same, bronze. Plain Edge. J-488. Rare $6,500

E.368. Same, copper-nickel. Plain Edge. J-486. Rare $9,000
1. A classic rarity among patterns that is underrated only in the sense that these patterns, in any metal, show up only very rarely on the market and, when they do, they do not last long enough to be promoted. Longacre's Lincoln portrait is a generally unappreciated bit of 19th century art, quite startling in light of its origin so near to the death of the president. Compare this portrait with later works by other engravers and the skill of a mature Longacre becomes readily apparent. What also needs to be appreciated is his speed in execution. Within an incredibly short time, he designed and engraved the Shield nickel, the various Washington nickel patterns including the rare High Relief variety (see E.362), several variations on the adopted Shield design (such as E.302 above), and this delightful Lincoln portrait. Whatever problems Longacre may have had in die execution in the late 1840s were quite obviously no longer troubling him by this date.

Copper-nickel 5-cent patterns continued

2. Breen's comments in the Lester Merkin 10/66 Sale (lot #217) are quite apt in placing this pattern in its proper prospective, as well as for its observations on die characteristics, "not too sharply struck up on Lincoln's hair and beard (as on all four examined to date in this metal including the A-W and Judd plate coins)... Known as a great rarity since the 1870s... One of the most coveted designs in the U.S. Pattern series, never restruck, never controversial, and in the intended metal; the earliest pattern to bear the head of the martyred President."

Similar comments about this "coveted Lincoln Head nickel" abound in the literature and catalogs since the 1870s. This is called an underappreciated pattern only to those who do not know patterns. Those who do, and who are offered the chance to buy one, do not hesitate or the opportunity is quickly lost.

E.369. 1867 Regular Design Trial Piece. Design II-A. Copper. Plain Edge. J-572. Very rare. Heifetz 10/89, N P-64, $3,300

E.370. 1867 Pattern Design Trial Piece. Design II-G. Copper. Plain Edge. J-573a (misdescribed). Very rare. ST 3/92, Ch. Br. Proof $5,000

Pattern Design Trial Piece of 1867, Design VII – H

E.371. 1867 Pattern Design Trial Piece. Obv. VII: Liberty head left with four feathers at back of head, four stars on hair above forehead, ribbon inscribed UNION & LIBERTY between, tiny LONGACRE F. below truncation. USOA around, date at lower border. Rev. H: Large V superimposed on national shield with ornate frame, IGWT at upper border. Copper. Plain Edge. J-563. Very rare $4,750

E.372. Same, copper. Reeded Edge. J-564. Very rare $3,500

E.373. Same, aluminum. Plain Edge. J-561. Rare $3,700

1. The intended metal for this die marriage was aluminum, in the same weight (1.244 gms) as the silver half dime. Concerned with the extensive die failures resulting from the use of nickel, Longacre created this pattern to show how well coins in aluminum would strike up. At the time, aluminum was far more difficult to obtain than it would be a few years later and was actually semi-precious in value. Had this metal been adopted, the task of preparing numerous working dies to deal with nickel would have been avoided.

2. The design is a fine example of a mature Longacre, the familiar profile and head being graced with a delicate headdress and otherwise finely detailed.

3. This pattern and its reeded-edge twin naturally come very well struck. If the (unfortunately) common problem of corrosion does not appear, the coin frequently appears almost as bright as silver.

E.374. Same, aluminum. Reeded Edge. J-562. Rare. Heifetz 10/89, P P-65 .... $3,850

A review of several decades of catalogs and fixed price lists shows that this pattern is significantly more rare than the plain-edged version (E.373). This does not translate into any difference in value, but may simply indicate that there was no reason to strike a reeded-edge 5-cent coin. At the same time, examination of die states does not indicate that these patterns are restrikes. The most likely explanation is that the coiner was not too concerned with the type of collar he used and may have struck the reeded-edge variety on a whim or by accident. Either possibility would explain the far smaller number of these pieces when even the most naive 19th Century collector did not collect patterns by edge variety.

E.375. 1867 Pattern Design Trial Piece. Obv. VII. Rev. I: Roman V within heavy wreath of oak and olive branches, star at top flanked by scrolls, period below star. Copper-nickel. Plain Edge. J-565. Very rare $2,500

Although reverse die trials in this style exist in the I, III and V Cents denominations, this reverse is the only example of this style to appear in an official pattern. The Roman III die can be found on the so-called Merriam Lincoln $3 pattern, privately struck in various metals. The reverse die was reused in 1868 on E.398.

Pattern Design Trial Piece of 1867, obverse VIII

E.376. 1867 Pattern Design Trial Piece. Obv. VIII: Liberty head left with coronet bearing LIBERTY in raised letters, USOA around, date below; the copper-nickel 3 cents design enlarged. Rev. G. Copper. Plain Edge. J-567, 578a. Rare. ST 3/92, Proof $1,500

E.377. Same, copper-nickel. Plain Edge. J-566, 578. Rare. ST 3/92, Br. Unc. $1,800

Apparently the strikings of this design combination were listed in two different places by Judd, unless his attribution of the obverse of J-578 and 578a is incorrect.

Copper-nickel 5-cent patterns continued

E.378. 1867 Pattern Design Trial Piece. Obv. VIII. Rev. J: Similar to Rev. G except CENTS is slightly curved. Copper-nickel. Plain Edge. J-569. Unique?

E.379. 1867 Mule. Design VIII-A. White metal. Plain Edge. J-574. Very rare $900

E.380. 1867 Mule. Design VIII-B. Copper-nickel. Plain Edge. J-575. Very rare $860

E.381. 1867 Mule. Design VIII-C. Copper-nickel. Plain Edge. J-576. Very rare $850

E.382. 1867 Mule. Design VIII-F. Copper-nickel. Plain Edge. J-577. Very rare $850

E.383. 1867 Mule. Obv. VIII & Obv. III of 1866. Copper-nickel. Plain Edge. J-580. Very rare $1,000

E.384. Same, white metal. Plain Edge. J-581. Very rare $800

E.385. 1867 Mule. Obv. VIII & Obv. IV of 1866. Silver. Plain Edge. J-579. Very rare $1,500

E.386. 1867 Pattern Design Trial Piece. Obv. IX: Similar to preceding except star added on coronet below LIB. Rev. G. Copper. Plain Edge. J-568. Very rare $1,000

E.387. 1867 Pattern Design Trial Piece. Design IX-J. Copper. Plain Edge. J-571. Rare. Obv. die varieties exist. Heifetz 10/89, P P-65, $3,520

E.388. Same, copper-nickel. Plain Edge. J-570. Scarce, reportedly 50 struck, from two different obverse dies. Heifetz 10/89, N P-64 .... $2,420

E.389. 1867 Mule. Design IX-B. Silver. Plain Edge. J-583. Very rare $1,500

E.390. Same, copper-nickel. Plain Edge. J-582. Very rare $1,000

E.391. 1867 Mule. Obv. IX & Obv. III of 1866. White metal. Plain Edge. J-585. Very rare $1,000

E.392. 1867 Mule. Obv. IX & Obv. IV of 1866. Copper-nickel. Plain Edge. Unlisted in Judd. Unique? Garrett II, Lot 999.

E.392a. Same, silver. Plain Edge. Unlisted in Judd. Unique? Well worn, 5.38 grams, previously attributed as the Lohr white metal specimen, which may not exist in that metal.

E.393. Same, white metal. Plain Edge. J-584. Very rare, if it exists. See previous.

Note: Obv. IX was also muled with a No Motto $5 reverse (see section on half eagles).

E.394. (1867) Mule. Rev. B & Rev. B. Copper. Plain Edge. J-573 (misattributed). Very rare. Heifetz 10/89, N P-64, $3,300

E.395. 1868 Regular Design Trial Piece. Copper. Plain Edge. J-635. Very rare $900

E.396. Same, aluminum. Plain Edge. J-636. Very rare $850

Pattern Design Trial Piece of 1868, design VIII – H

E.397. 1868 Pattern Design Trial Piece. Design VIII-H. Copper-nickel. Plain Edge. J-630. Very rare $850

E.398. 1868 Pattern Design Trial Piece. Design VIII-I. Copper. Plain Edge. J-632. Very rare. Three known. Eliasberg 5/96 Proof 64 .... $6,380

E.399. Same, aluminum. Plain Edge. J-632a. Unique? Also reported in copper-nickel.
There is a very real question as to whether this coin exists in this metal.

Pattern Design Trial Piece of 1868, design VIII – J (Smithsonian)

E.400. 1868 Pattern Design Trial Piece. Design VIII-J. Copper. Plain Edge. Medium diameter (approximately 21.6mm, compared to 20.5mm of Shield 5 cents and 21.21mm of current Jefferson 5 cents). J-626. Very rare $950

E.401. Same, copper. Plain Edge. Large diameter (approximately 24mm). J-627. Very rare $1,600

E.402. Same, copper. Reeded Edge. Large Diameter. J-628. Very rare $900

E.403. Same, copper-nickel. Plain Edge. Medium Diameter. J-623. Scarce. Heifetz 10/89, P P-64 .... $2,200
Part of a set apparently intended by Longacre to replace the mix of existing designs for minor coinage with a uniform design, differing only by the designation on the reverse and the diameter. (See E.138 and E.270 above.) Additional information is needed as to diameters on all minor patterns of this era.

E.404. Same, copper-nickel. Plain Edge. Large Diameter. J-624. Very rare. Heifetz 10/89, N P-64 ...... $2,750

E.405. Same, copper-nickel. Reeded Edge. Large Diameter. J-625. Very rare $1,000

E.406. Same, aluminum. Plain Edge. Medium Diameter. J-629. Very rare. Large diameter reported $900

E.407. 1868 Pattern Design Trial Piece. Obv. VIII. Rev. K: Large V in laurel wreath connected at top with ribbon inscribed IGWT, small Maltese cross inside fold at top. Copper. Plain Edge. J-631. Very rare $1,000

Copper-nickel 5-cent patterns continued

E.408. 1868 Pattern Design Trial Piece. Design IX-K. Copper. Plain Edge. J-634. Very rare $800

E.409. Same, copper-nickel. Plain Edge. J-633. Scarce. Obv. die varieties exist. ST 3/92, Br. Proof $2,100; Eliasberg 5/96 Proof 65 .... $3,190

E.410. 1869 Regular Design Trial Piece. Copper. Plain Edge. J-687. Very rare $750

E.411. Same, aluminum. Plain Edge. J-688. Very rare $800

E.412. Same, steel. Plain Edge. J-689. Unique?

E.413. 1869 Pattern Design Trial Piece. Design IX-D. Copper-nickel. Plain Edge. J-690. Very rare.
The description of these dies given in Judd is unclear; either or both of these designs may be misattributed.

E.414. 1869 Pattern Design Trial Piece. Design IX-G. Copper-nickel. Plain Edge. J-686. Very rare $850

E.415. 1869 Pattern Design Trial Piece. Design IX-H. Copper-nickel. Plain Edge. J-683. Very rare $800

E.416. 1869 Pattern Design Trial Piece. Design IX-K. Copper. Plain Edge. J-685. Very rare $800

E.417. Same, Copper-nickel. Plain Edge. J-684. Scarce. ST 3/92, V. Ch. Br. Proof $2,400

E.418. 1869 Fantasy Mule. Obv. IX, dated 1869. Obv. IV, dated 1866. Copper-nickel. Plain Edge. Unlisted in Judd. Unique? Garrett II, Lot 1001.

Obv. IX was also muled with a No Motto $5 reverse. See section on half eagles.

E.419. 1869 Fantasy Mule. A regular 5 cents obverse and a regular Indian cent obverse, struck on a 5-cent planchet. Plain Edge. J-691. Unique.

E.420. 1870 Regular Design Trial Piece. Copper. Plain Edge. J-805. Very rare. ST 3/92, Br. Proof $3,200

E.421. Same, nickel alloy, exact composition unknown. Plain Edge. J-807. Very rare. Identical to the regular issue except always light in weight $1,000

E.422. Same, aluminum. Plain Edge. J-806. Very rare $600

E.423. Same, steel. Plain Edge. J-808. Unique?

E.424. 1871 Regular Design Trial Piece. Copper. Plain Edge. J-1056. Very rare $800

E.425. Same, aluminum. Plain Edge. J-1057. Very rare $800

E.426. Same, steel. Plain Edge. J-1058. Unique?

Pattern Design Trial Piece of 1871, design X – L (Smithsonian)

E.427. 1871 Pattern Design Trial Piece. Obv. X: Similar to Obv. VIII except head smaller and USOA more evenly spaced. Rev. L: Roman V set backwards, with heavier stroke at right, above CENTS in laurel wreath. Copper. Plain Edge. 22mm. J-1051. Scarce, known in silver plate. ST 3/92, Br. Proof, $2,600; Heifetz 10/89, P P-65 .... $3,080

E.428. Same, copper-nickel. Plain Edge. J-1050. Rare. ST 3/92, Ch. Br. Proof $3,000

E.429. Same, aluminum. Plain Edge. J-1052. Rare. Large diameter reported. ST 3/92, Br. Proof $5,000

Pattern Design Trial Piece of 1871, design XI–M (Smithsonian)

E.430. 1871 Pattern Design Trial Piece. Obv. XI: Similar to preceding except set in smaller, more crowded field. Rev. M: Similar to preceding except 5 replaces V and wreath is set in smaller field more crowded around border. Copper. Plain Edge. 20.5mm. J-1054. Scarce. ST 3/92, Ch. Br. Proof $3,700

E.431. Same, copper-nickel. Plain Edge. J-1053. Rare. ST 3/92, Br. Proof $3,200

E.432. Same, aluminum. Plain Edge. J-1055. Rare $750

E.433. 1872 Regular Design Trial Piece. Copper. Plain Edge. J-1189. Very rare $750

E.434. Same, aluminum. Plain Edge. J-1190. Very rare $750

E.435. 1873 Regular Design Trial Piece. Copper. Plain Edge. J-1264. Very rare $750

E.436. Same, aluminum. Plain Edge. J-1265. Very rare $700

E.437. 1874 Regular Design Trial Piece. Copper. Plain Edge. J-1350. Very rare $700

E.438. Same, aluminum. Plain Edge. J-1351. Very rare $700

E.439. 1875 Regular Design Trial Piece. Copper. Plain Edge. J-1387. Very rare $750

E.440. Same, aluminum. Plain Edge. J-1388. Very rare $750

Copper-nickel 5-cent patterns continued

Pattern Design Trial Piece of 1881, design XII – N (Smithsonian)

E.441. 1881 Pattern Design Trial Piece. Obv. XII: Liberty Head left wearing coronet inscribed LIBERTY; cotton leaves and wheat stalks in hair. USOA around, date below. Rev. N: Large Roman V within wreath of cotton and corn. Copper. Plain Edge. J-1672. Rare $1,500

E.442. Same, copper-nickel. Plain Edge. J-1671. Rare. ST 3/92, Br. Proof $2,900

E.443. Same, aluminum. Plain Edge. J-1673. Very rare $800
22mm, vs. 20.5mm for the regular issue and 21.21mm adopted for the new design of 1883.

E.444. 1881 Pattern Design Trial Piece. Obv. XII. Rev. P: Similar to preceding except small IGWT added at upper border. Copper-nickel. Plain Edge. Misdescribed in Judd as J-1674 with EPU rather than IGWT. Unique, Smithsonian.

E.445. 1882 Experimental Edge Trial Piece. The regular obverse and reverse dies. Copper-nickel. The otherwise Plain Edge shows five equally-spaced raised ridges, the imaginative Blind Man's Nickel
1. This is one of two patterns for nickels struck that year that used a special collar to place on the otherwise plain edge five regularly spaced bars. (See E. 450 below.) This pattern surfaced for the first time in an Addendum to Haseltine's March 1, 1883, Sale, where it was described as "designed for the use of the blind." (Lot #17) E.450 was not in that sale. After the Haseltine Sale, the one coin that has been traced (the other is in the CSL Collection) has the following pedigree: William Woodin, Waldo Newcomer, F.C.C. Boyd, James Curtis, 1958 ANA Sale, Dr. Judd, 1968 CSNS, Charles Neumoyer, Harmer Rooke 1969 Million Dollar Sale, lot #3752, Art Kagin, Sale of the 70s, Kagin's 1983 A.N.A. (researched and cataloged by David T. Alexander) and 1986 ANA Lot #3582, unidentified collector and now in a Midwest collection. Although there are three specimens listed in Judd, nos. two and three are the same coin. The "third coin" is the ex-Judd, ex-Neumoyer example.
2. These two patterns are another example of the unsung treasures of the pattern field. This coin appeared as lot #575 of the New Netherlands 9/53 Sale 41, aka Hillyer Ryder Large Cents, along with E.450 as lot #573. This coin was described by Ford and Breen there as follows: "Unlisted [in A.W.] Proof, almost fully brilliant and perfect. Only three said to have been struck. First published by Col. Curtis in the 1948 *Numismatic Scrapbook* as a Haseltine discovery. Extremely rare, and of considerable interest and value. RRRR."
The catalog estimate price was $45. The PRL shows that it brought $87.50, one of the highest prices for a single coin in the entire sale! This should be compared to lot #559, a Bickford Eagle (J-1374, E.1788), which brought $37.50 on an estimate of $45. and lot #563, a J-1468, E.1440 which brought $82.50 on an estimate of $100.
3. According to Michael Wescott's *The United States Nickel Five-Cent Piece*, the Blind Man's Nickel was struck "as suggested by Congressman (Major General) W.S. Rosecrans, who thought that the five bars on the edge would aid the blind in determining the denomination of the coin." Wescott also claims five of these coins were struck, although citing no authority for this claim. This may refer to five examples of E.450. A letter by reader Henry Hettger in the Bowers *Rare Coin Review* No.95, quotes from a letter of Dec. 22, 1882, in the Mint's correspondence files from Rosecrans and "Mr. Fisher, chairman of the Committee on Coinage" asking the Mint to prepare a "specimen coin... that could be distinguished by touch. This requirement was necessitated by the call to provide coinage that would serve the needs of the blind population, which had difficulty distinguishing the various denominations quickly." The article continues: "Rosecrans and Fisher had requested the preparation of a one-cent minor coin with a raised point in the center and concave sides. If such a specimen coin or pattern die trial was prepared, it has not survived to the present. However, an 1882 nickel is described by Judd (#1697), of the regular dies, but with five equally spaced bars on the edge, the so-called 'blind man's nickel.'"
4. As to the actual number of this pattern and E.450, it first surfaced in the Addendum to Haseltine's March 1, 1883, Sale, where it was called "[e]xcessively rare." Haseltine (who was in a position to know, if he bothered to tell the truth) stated that there were "[o]nly three struck, and not in the Mint Cabinet." (Addenda, p. 2, lot #17.) The coin there was described as a "[b]rilliant Proof" and brought $10 at the same time J-271, E.1680 in gold (lot#11) brought $53. Since that time, only one example other than the CSL coin has been traced, always with the same high prices paid whenever it has surfaced, either in auction or by private treaty.

E.446. 1882 Pattern Design Trial Piece. Design XII-N. Copper. Plain Edge. 22mm. J-1676. Very rare $900

E.447. Same, copper-nickel. Plain Edge. J-1675. Very rare $1,000

Copper-nickel 5-cent patterns continued

Pattern Design Trial Piece of 1882, design XII – O

E.448. 1882 Pattern Design Trial Piece. Design Obv. XII. Rev. O: Large Roman V within wreath of cotton and corn. Similar to Rev. N of 1881 and 1882 except wreath set low to make room for EPU at upper border. Copper. Plain Edge. 22mm. J-1681. Rare $3,500

E.449. Same, copper-nickel. Plain Edge. J-1680. Rare. ST 3/92, Br. Proof $4,000

E.450. Same, copper-nickel. Another imaginative pattern for the blind, its otherwise plain edge displaying five equally-spaced raised ridges. J-1683. Very rare $10,000

    1. See the notes to E.445 above for the background of this pattern. The "five coins struck" may refer to a combination of this pattern and E.445 (two of the former are known and at least three of this pattern) or five of this pattern, which would be consistent with more recent research. There is one coin impounded in the CSL Collection, one in a long-term Midwest collection, and at least two others.

    2. Auction appearances as follows: Lot #573 of New Netherlands' 9/53 Sale 41, aka Hillyer Ryder Large Cents; ST 5/60 Neumoyer Sale, lot #2311, bringing $520 on the then current estimate in Judd of $450. Harmer, Rooke 11/69 Million Dollar Sale, lot #3751. BR 6/75 Scott Sale as Lot #1251. BR 6/77 Fairfield Sale, Lot #13. ST 1/87 Sale, lot #508 (brought $4,840). BM 1/94 Lexington Collection Sale (FUN Sale), lot #1564, P P-64, $9,250 plus 10%.

    3. New Netherlands 9/53 Sale 41, aka Hillyer Ryder Large Cents Sale, Lot #573, where it was described as follows: "Called A-W. 1669a in the 1914 ANS Exhibition; Judson Brenner loan. Mostly brilliant Proof, slightly spotted upon the obverse, and tarnished upon the edges. Like lot 575, called a 'Nickel for the blind' and the alleged discovery of dealer J.W. Haseltine. Not often seen." The catalog estimate was $35, while the PRL shows that it brought $77.50! This price and the slightly higher price realized for the slightly rarer companion Blind Man's Nickel were among the highest pattern prices paid at this sale.

E.451. Same, aluminum. Plain Edge. J-1682. Very rare $1,500

E.452. 1882 Pattern Design Trial Piece. Design XIIa-Oa. Same as preceding except set in 21.21mm die with smaller denticles. Copper. Plain Edge. J-1685. Rare $1,000

E.453. Same, copper-nickel. Plain Edge. J-1684. Rare. Eliasberg 5/96 Proof 65 .... $3,190

E.454. Same, aluminum. Plain Edge. J-1686. Very rare $1,000

E.455. 1882 Pattern Design Trial Piece. Design XII-P. IGWT at upper border. Copper. Plain Edge. 22mm. J-1678. Rare $1,200

E.456. Same, copper-nickel. Plain Edge. J-1677. Rare $1,300

E.457. Same, aluminum. Plain Edge. J-1679. Very rare $1,200

Pattern Design Trial Piece of 1882, design XIII – Q (Smithsonian)

E.458. 1882 Pattern Design Trial Piece. Obv. XIII: Liberty head left as preceding; small IGWT at upper border, seven stars at left border, six at right, date below. Rev. Q: Smaller Roman V in reduced wreath, USOA around upper border, EPU at lower border. The design adopted in 1883. Copper. Plain Edge. J-1688. Existence uncertain.

E.459. Same, copper-nickel. Plain Edge. J-1687. Very rare $1,500

E.460. Same, aluminum. Plain Edge. J-1689. Very rare $1,250

Pattern Design Trial Piece of 1882, design XIV – Q

E.461. 1882 Pattern Design Trial Piece. Obv. XIV: Liberty Head left as preceding; 13 stars around border, date below. The design adopted in 1883. Rev. Q. The combination adopted in 1883. Copper. 21.21mm. Plain Edge. J-1691. Very rare $5,400

Copper-nickel 5-cent patterns continued

E.462. Same, copper-nickel. Plain Edge. J-1690. Scarce, often seen circulated, may have been released as a regular issue in 1883 .... $9,500

Another 'transitional' which is neither a backdated fantasy nor in the technical sense a prototype. Generally considered to be identical to the regular issue 1883 Proofs, there are some differences. Turning once again to NN #61, John J. Ford noticed something that escaped everyone else, including later 'specialists' — the reverse die for this coin is not the same as used on the 1883 regular issue Proofs. These comments appear under lot#86 in the New Netherlands Sale 61: "Reverse identical to the preceding [lot in the sale, a J-1687], not found on regular 1883s and only on one 1883 pattern (Judd 1714): S in motto [EPU] on reverse first cut too far to right, then corrected."

E.463. Same, aluminum. Plain Edge. J-1692. Very rare $5,400

E.464. 1882 Revised Design Trial Piece. Obv. XV: Similar to regular design except ball removed from bottom of shield and entire device set in a slightly smaller field. Rev. B. Copper. Plain Edge. 20mm vs. 20.5mm standard size. J-1694. Very rare $1,000

Note: A piece struck on a small, thin planchet, possibly that of a cent, is listed by Judd as J-1694a.

E.465. Same, copper-nickel. Plain Edge. J-1693. Rare $4,000

1. Since the planchet is smaller than normal, the designer had to use a date logotype smaller than normal for a regular issue shield nickel. Comparison with an 1882 copper-nickel 3-cent shows that the date logotypes are identical.

2. Just what this pattern was intended to be presents an interesting question. There is no rationale for the appearance of this design at this point. Barber was already engaged in refining what would eventually become the Liberty nickel, having started with the 1-, 3-and 5-cent patterns in 1881. A flurry of modifications to the original design followed in 1882. So why come out with this pattern, and who did it? Barber was too busy. Morgan would hardly be fooling around with an old Longacre design, and was tied up (as was Barber) in producing other patterns at this time known to be their work, such as the Shield Earring design. The only logical candidate would be one of the assistant engravers who was fooling around with a design that everyone knew would be replaced within a few months. The die was then used to run off a few pieces as a whim, which then was "accidently" released. It could also have been created as a made-to-order rarity for later sale to collectors. Yet another intriguing thought would be that this obverse could well have been a partly-completed hub or die which was done in 1865-67 by Longacre and then rejected in favor of the accepted design. It could have been taken from the Mint's store of these hubs/dies, had the date punched in using the 3-cent logotype, and then — an instant rarity. In other words, the die is a novodel, but in the same fashion as the E.950 and the 1801-03 Proof dollar novodels, started on one date, engraved (in part) at that time, but completed later. A fascinating numismatic whodunit.

E.466. Same, white metal. Plain Edge. J-1696. Unique?

E.467. Same, aluminum. Plain Edge. J-1695. Very rare $2,000

Metallurgical trial of 1883, design XII–R
(Smithsonian)

E.468. 1883 Metallurgical Trial Piece. Obv. XII. Rev. R: PURE/ NICKEL in wreath of cotton and corn, FIVE at upper border, CENTS at lower border. Seven stars at left border, six at right. Pure nickel (magnetic). Plain Edge. 22mm. J-1704. Very rare $3,750

1. Part of a series of metallurgical trials for 5-cent coinage including pure nickel, an alloy of 75% nickel, 25% copper (E.471), 50% nickel, 50% copper (E.474), and 33% nickel, 67% copper (E.476). All are plain edge. This pattern, and all of the other metallurgical trials of 1883, use the same obverse as Barber's original Liberty design of 1881 — E.442. As Ford notes in his comments on these particular trials in NN Sale 61, lot #95 (a set of the four patterns), all of these patterns are oversize at 22mm compared to 21.21mm for the adopted design (E.462) and 20.5mm for the Shield nickel design. Looking at one of these pure nickel coins side by side with the other metallurgical trials and other nickels in the regular alloy, the differences in color and texture are obvious. (This is discussed in some depth by Ford in NN #61 for the more technical-minded.) This coin has a perfect, bright, silver-looking appearance. Several of the pure nickel coins have mammoth planchet cracks and some have severe laminations all through it, typical of the problems experienced with pure nickel.

2. This coin, and the other metallurgical trials of this date, have a center dot on the reverse. This does not appear to have been noted in any prior publication.

E.469. Same, copper-nickel. Plain Edge. J-1705. Very rare $3,000

E.470. Same, aluminum. Plain Edge. J-1706. Very rare $1,500

Copper-nickel 5-cent patterns continued

Metallurgical trial, design XII – S

E.471. 1883 Metallurgical Trial Piece. Obv. XII. Rev. S: Similar to preceding except 75 N./ 25 C. in wreath. Pure nickel, magnetic. Plain Edge. J-1707. Very rare $3,750

E.472. Same, copper-nickel. Plain Edge. J-1708. Very rare $3,750

E.473. Same, aluminum. Plain Edge. J-1709. Very rare $1,500

E.474. 1883 Metallurgical Trial Piece. Obv. XII. Rev. T: Similar to preceding except 50 N./ 50 C. in wreath. Copper-nickel. Plain Edge. J-1710. Very rare $3,750

E.475. Same, aluminum. Plain Edge. J-1711. Very rare $1,500

E.476. 1883 Metallurgical Trial Piece. Obv. XII. Rev. U: Similar to preceding except 33 N./ 67 C. in wreath. Copper-nickel. Plain Edge. J-1712. Scarce $3,550

E.477. Same, aluminum. Plain Edge. J-1713. Very rare $1,200

E.478. 1883 Mule. Obv. XII. Rev. Q, the regular design without CENTS. Copper-nickel. Plain Edge. 22mm. J-1706a. Unique?

Pattern Design Trial Piece of 1883, design XIV – V (Smithsonian)

E.479. 1883 Pattern Design Trial Piece. Obv. XIV, the regular design. Rev. V: Similar to the regular design without CENTS, but with CENTS incused on a scroll across the V. The first attempt to insert CENTS onto the reverse, not adopted. Copper. Plain Edge. 21.21mm. J-1718. Rare $1,200

E.480. Same, copper-nickel. Plain Edge. J-1717. Rare $4,750

    1. This pattern has been said by many to be far more attractive than the design eventually adopted.

    2. Although listed as an R-6 in Judd, many including Bowers (in several of his catalogs) and Rarcoa feel that this pattern is no less rare than any of the other 1883 nickel patterns of that year which are listed as R-7s by Judd. Indeed, given the number of appearances of the 1883 metallurgical trials in the last decade, far more of each of these have surfaced than this pattern. Indeed the comment that appears in several of the excellent Rarcoa pattern sales catalogs of the 1970s which state that this pattern is an R-7 as it is seldom seen now appears to be absolutely correct. The rarity of this pattern has been grossly understated in the past.

E.481. Same, aluminum. Plain Edge. J-1719. Very rare $1,900

E.482. 1883 Pattern Design Trial Piece. Obv. XIV. Rev. W: Similar to the regular design without CENTS, but with EPU moved above wreath and replaced at lower border by CENTS flanked by two dots. The adopted "With Cents" reverse used in the latter part of this year. Aluminum. Plain Edge. 21.21mm. J-1720. Very rare $1,800

    Could also be considered a Regular Design Trial Piece if struck after the WITH CENTS reverse was adopted. A piece that appeared to be cleaned and discolored copper was listed in Auction '89, Lot #1856 as copper-nickel.

Pattern Design Trial Piece of 1883, design XVI – Q (Smithsonian)

E.483. 1883 Pattern Design Trial Piece. Obv. XVI: Liberty head left as preceding, but with plain coronet, small LIBERTY at upper border, date below. Six stars at left border, seven right. Rev. Q. Copper. Plain Edge. 21.21mm. J-1715. Very rare $2,200

E.484. Same, copper-nickel. Plain Edge. J-1714. Very rare. ST 3/92, Ch. Br. Proof $3,750

    This pattern differs from the adopted design as the word LIBERTY is above the head rather than on the diadem, which is plain on this design. The reverse is identical to the regular design but from a die used in patterns only on the E.459 and E.462

Copper-nickel 5-cent patterns continued

E.485. Same, aluminum. Plain Edge. J-1716. Very rare $2,200

As the muling of 5-cent dies was discontinued after 1883, the numbering system for obverses and reverses will not be used after this date.

E.485a. 1884 Regular Design Trial Piece. Copper. Plain Edge. Unlisted in Judd. Unique? Part of a complete 1884 set struck in copper. Current whereabouts unknown.

E.486. 1884 Regular Design Trial Piece. Aluminum. Plain Edge. J-1727. Very rare $1,500

Experimental trial of 1884 (Smithsonian)

E.487. 1884 Experimental Trial Piece. Obv. USOA around circle of 13 stars, date below, octagonal hole in center. Rev. Large FIVE above, CENTS below perforation, national shields at right and left sides. Copper-nickel. Plain Edge. J-1724. Very rare. Heifetz 10/89, P P-65 .... $5,060
　　See the comments on the companion 1-cent coin.

E.488. Same, aluminum. Plain Edge. J-1725. Very rare. Heifetz 10/89, P P-64 .... $3,750

E.489. Similar, but struck from different dies with rims around hole. White metal. Plain Edge. J-1726. Very rare, see similar cent $2,500

E.490. 1885 Regular Design Trial Piece. Aluminum. Plain Edge. J-1743. Very rare $2,000

Experimental trial of 1885 (Bowers & Merena)

E.491. 1885 Experimental Trial Piece. Obv. USOA around circle of 13 stars, date below center hole, denticled inner and outer rims. Rev. Huge FIVE CENTS at upper border, shield flanked by olive branches at lower border, denticled inner and outer rims. Silver. Plain Edge. J-1742. Very rare, see the comments on the companion 1-cent coin $5,000

Pattern Design Trial Piece of 1896 (Smithsonian)

E.492. 1896 Pattern Design Trial Piece. Obv. Large shield over crossed poles topped by Liberty cap and eagle. Ribbon incused LIBERTY crosses the shield, EPU at upper border, date below. Seven stars left, six right, large beaded border. Rev. Large 5 above small CENTS, all within olive wreath, USOA around, large beaded border. Pure nickel. Plain Edge. J-1771. Very rare. See matching cent. ST 3/92, Ch. Br. Proof $3,500

E.493. Same, copper-nickel. Plain Edge. J-1770. Rare. ST 3/92, Ch. Br. Proof $4,100

E.494. Same, aluminum. Plain Edge. J-1772. Rare, usually seen oxidized. P P-63 .... $2,420

Judd lists many other compositions reportedly tested at this time, all supposedly melted. Other alloys possible. These coins and the similar 1-cent patterns are from the "crates of patterns" traded to Woodin in exchange for the half union patterns in gold.

E.495. 1909 Pattern Design Trial Piece. Obv. Similar to preceding except EPU removed and stars spaced around plain border. Rev. Similar to preceding except very small EPU added at lower, plain border. Copper-nickel. Plain Edge. J-1781. Unique, Smithsonian.

Copper-nickel 5-cent patterns continued

Pattern Design Trial Piece of 1909
(Smithsonian)

E.496. 1909 Pattern Design Trial Piece. Obv. Shoulder-length bust of George Washington right, small LIBERTY at upper border, large date below. Seven stars left, six right. Rev. Same as preceding. Copper-nickel. Plain Edge. J-1782. Unique, Smithsonian.

E.497. 1909 Pattern Design Trial Piece. Obv. Similar to preceding except date is smaller. Rev. Same as preceding. Copper-nickel. Plain Edge. J-1783. Unique, Smithsonian.

E.498. 1909 Pattern Design Trial Piece. Obv. Similar to preceding except LIBERTY at right border and 13 stars around left and upper border in continuous line. Rev. Same as preceding. Copper-nickel. Plain Edge. J-1784. Unique, Smithsonian.

E.499. 1909 Pattern Design Trial Piece. Obv. Similar to preceding except LIBERTY and 13 stars interspersed as L**I**B* *E**R**T**Y*. Rev. Same as preceding. Copper-nickel. Plain Edge. J-1785. Unique, Smithsonian.

Pattern Design Trial Piece of 1909
(Smithsonian)

E.500. 1909 Pattern Design Trial Piece. Obv. Larger bust of Washington left, LIBERTY at right border, date in lower left field. Rev. Same as preceding. Copper-nickel. Plain Edge. J-1786. Unique, Smithsonian.

E.501. 1909 Pattern Design Trial Piece. Obv. Similar to preceding except head is slightly larger and the date and LIBERTY are in different type styles. Rev. Large, hollow 5 with CENTS across opening, flanked by two laurel branches. USOA around upper border, EPU below USOA. Copper-nickel. Plain Edge. J-1787. Two known, one in Smithsonian.

E.502. 1910 Pattern Design Trial Piece. Obv. Similar to preceding except truncation of bust separated from rim, LIBERTY at left border, date at right. Rev. Same as preceding. Copper-nickel. Plain Edge. J-1788. Very rare, one in Smithsonian.

An important series of uniface electrotypes was produced in 1911 and 1912 by James Earle Fraser showing proposed designs for Indian Head, Lincoln Head and Liberty Head 5-cent pieces. Although uniface impressions are not included in this listing, we do refer the reader to Judd Appendix A.

Pattern Design Trial Piece of 1913
(Smithsonian)

E.503. 1913 Pattern Design Trial Piece. Obv. Indian head right, LIBERTY at right border. Date on shoulder, no designer's initial F on shoulder. Rev. American bison standing to left on mound inscribed FIVE CENTS, USOA at upper border. Small EPU below AMERICA. These are the designs adopted, but with F later added to the shoulder. Copper-nickel. Plain Edge. J-1789. Rare, 11 reported. Auction '89, Lot #1857 (very coarse surface—typical?) $13,750.

E.504. 1913 Pattern Design Trial Piece. Similar to preceding but with round-topped 3 and bolder rims. Copper-nickel. Plain Edge. J-1789a. Very rare, three reported.

E.505. 1913 Revised Design Trial Piece. Obv. The regular design with designer's initial. Rev. Similar to preceding except base of mound recessed to protect FIVE CENTS. Experimental bronze alloy, 95% copper, 5% nickel and zinc. Plain Edge. J-1790. Unique?

Silver 3 cents

The very first attempt by Longacre at designing a silver 3-cent piece consisted of running a strip of low-grade silver through a dime blanking press, upsetting the edge like a dime planchet and hand-stamping it three times with a Roman I. Though Longacre presumably used the dime equipment to minimize effort, a dime-sized trime of the proper weight and fineness could have been both intrinsically correct and easier to handle than the "fishscale" size finally adopted.

The dime size was borrowed again for the copper-nickel 3-cent piece of 1865-1889, which ultimately brought about the latter's demise when the advent of modern vending machines made the size of the two coins more important.

Metallurgical trial of 1849 (Smithsonian)

E.506. 1849 Metallurgical Trial Piece. Obv. Normal Liberty Seated half dime obverse, Valentine-4. Rev. Large Arabic 3 in plain field with beaded border. 50% silver, 50% copper. Reeded Edge. J-111. Rare, originals weigh 22 grains. Restrikes ca. 1858-59 and possibly 1868 are from a different obverse die with 1 recut at top and 9 recut at bottom, not listed by Valentine, and vary in weight. Eliasberg 5/96 MS65 .... $4,180

Metallurgical trial of 1849 (Smithsonian)

E.507. 1849 Metallurgical Trial Piece. Obv. Same as preceding. Rev. Large Roman III in plain field with beaded border. 60% silver, 40% copper. Reeded Edge. J-112. Rare, originals 18.5 grains, restrikes as preceding $3,500

Mule of 1849 trial designs (Smithsonian)

E.508. (1849) Mule. The 3 and III reverses of the preceding. Silver and copper, exact alloy not known. Plain Edge. J-113. Very rare, some, possibly all, are restrikes $4,000
E.509. Same, copper-nickel. Plain Edge. J-114. Same comment per restrikes, also reported in copper and brass. BM 11/92, P P-63 .... $5,170

Pattern Design Trial Piece of 1850
(Smithsonian)

E.510. 1850 Pattern Design Trial Piece. Obv: Radiate Liberty cap with LIBERTY on band, date below. Rev: USOA at border around palm branch encircling a Roman III. Silver. Plain Edge. J-125. Scarce, originals 12.375 grains; overweight restrikes exist. BM 11/92, P P-62 $2,500; Eliasberg 5/96 Proof 64 .... $2,750
   Engraved by Chief Coiner Franklin Peale from punches originally prepared by Christian Gobrecht for a gold dollar (q.v.) in an attempt to discredit James Longacre as chief engraver. Perhaps because the Chief Coiner was proud of his efforts, this pattern is the most readily available of the early patterns with the exception of the Gobrecht dollars.
E.511. 1853 Revised Design Trial Piece. Obv. Six-pointed star with national shield, double border around star, USOA around. Rev. Roman III in ornamented C, olive branch above III and three arrows below. The revised designs used in 1854. Silver. Plain Edge. J-153. Unique, currently unknown in any collection and may not exist.
E.512. 1863 Regular Design Trial Piece. Copper. Plain Edge. J-321. Very rare $900
E.513. Same, aluminum. Plain Edge. J-322. Very rare $800
   Restrikes exist, Taxay lists a restrike in "Nickel."
E.514. 1864 Regular Design Trial Piece. Copper. Plain Edge. J-375. Very rare. 0.70 gms $800

Silver 3-cent patterns continued

E.515. Same, copper-nickel. Plain Edge. J-377. Very rare $900
E.516. Same, aluminum. Plain Edge. J-376. Very rare $800
    John J. Ford Jr. told the engaging story of finding a partial roll of 35 Brilliant Proofs in a
    Manhattan antique shop in 1938, a discovery which helped to launch his career as a
    professional numismatist. See the Spring 1990 issue of *Legacy,* Ivy Press Inc., Dallas TX. Silver
    restrikes are also rumored to exist. Do not confuse with modern counterfeits struck in silver.
E.517. 1865 Regular Design Trial Piece. Copper. PE J-415. Very rare $900
E.518. 1867 Regular Design Trial Piece. Copper. PE J-560. Very rare $900
E.519. 1868 Regular Design Trial Piece. Aluminum. PE J-622. Very rare $800
E.520. 1869 Regular Design Trial Piece. Copper. PE J-680. Very rare $950
E.521. Same, copper-nickel. PE J-681. Very rare $950
E.522. Same, aluminum. PE J-682. Very rare $800
E.523. 1870 Regular Design Trial Piece. Copper. PE J-802. Very rare $950
E.524. Same, copper-nickel. PE J-804. Very rare $800
E.525. Same, brass. PE J-804a. Very rare.
E.526. Same, aluminum. PE J-803. Very rare $750
E.527. 1870 Regular Design Trial Piece. Obv. Liberty seated to left, shield and ribbon with raised LIBERTY in
    right hand, olive branch in left hand, cap on pole behind. USA around, date below. Diameter
    15.5mm, a die intended for a half dime pattern. Rev. Regular silver 3 cents design (14.0mm) set in a
    larger die with a wider rim to match half dime obverse. Silver. PE J-796. Rare $5,750
    One of a series of patterns by Barber beginning with this denomination up through the dollar.
    Commonly believed to be available in some numbers, these coins now appear to be quite rare
    based on auction appearances. Of all these denominations, this is the hardest to locate.
E.528. Same, silver. Reeded Edge. J-797. Rare $5,850
    Substantially rarer than its plain-edged companion.
E.529. Same, copper. Plain Edge. J-798. Rare $2,800
E.530. Same, copper. Reeded Edge. J-799. Rare. BM 3/94, P-64 .... $2,800
E.531. Same, aluminum. Plain Edge. J-800. Rare $3,000
E.532. Same, aluminum. Reeded Edge. J-801. Rare $3,000
E.533. 1871 Regular Design Trial Piece. Copper. Plain Edge. J-1047. Very rare $800
E.534. Same, copper-nickel. Plain Edge. J-1048. Unique?
E.535. Same, aluminum. Plain Edge. J-1049. Very rare $750
E.536. 1872 Regular Design Trial Piece. Copper. Plain Edge. J-1187. Very rare $750
E.537. Same, aluminum. Plain Edge. J-1188. Very rare $750
E.538. 1873 Regular Design Trial Piece. Copper. Plain Edge. J-1262. Very rare $750
E.539. Same, aluminum. Plain Edge. J-1263. Very rare $750

Half dimes

Pattern Design Trial Piece of 1792

E.540. 1792 Pattern Design Trial Piece. Obv. Female bust to left with curly hair, date below, legend LIB. PAR.
    OF SCIENCE & INDUSTRY, beaded border. Rev. Flying eagle left, USOA and HALF DISME around.
    Silver. Reeded Edge. J-7. Stack's Jimmy Hayes coll. MS-67, Oct. 1985, $57,750; Pacific Coast Rare
    Coin Auctions, MS-65, $100,000, June 1988; ST 10/92, Floyd Starr, Ch. BU, $87,000 .... $100,000
E.541. Same, copper. Plain Edge. J-8. Unique.
    Whether the silver coins were struck as patterns or are the first circulating coins struck by the
    fledgling U.S. Mint is still a matter of numismatic debate. Approximately 1,500-2,000 pieces
    were struck in the cellar of John Harper's saw works before the new Philadelphia Mint was in
    operation. Some of the silver for the issue is believed to have been supplied by President
    Washington. Most survivors are circulated, bolstering the claim to be America's first regular issue
    coin.

Half dime patterns continued

Pattern Design Trial Piece of 1794
(Smithsonian)

E.542. 1794 Pattern Design Trial Piece. Obv. Female bust right with flowing hair similar to regular issue without stars, LIBERTY above, date below, beaded border. Rev. Standing eagle, wing tips pointed down, USOA around, HALF DISME below. Plain field, beaded border. Copper. Reeded Edge. J-14. Unique, Smithsonian.

E.543. 1794 Pattern Design Trial Piece. Obv. Similar to preceding but stars added in field. Rev. Similar to preceding except denomination omitted, wreath added and USOA more widely spaced, the adopted design. Copper. Reeded Edge. J-15. Two known, Valentine varieties 3 and 4 .... $6,000

E.544. Same, copper. Plain Edge. J-16. Unique? Valentine-2

E.545. 1795 Regular Design Trial Piece. Copper. Reeded Edge. J-21. Two known.

E.546. 1854 Metallurgical Trial Piece. The regular design, German silver, alloy of copper, nickel and zinc. Plain Edge. J-166. Very rare. Struck to show similarity of color to silver. See German silver cent patterns of this era $2,500

Mule of 1859 (Bowers & Merena)

E.547. 1859 Mule. Obv. The regular design with stars. Rev. HALF DIME within wreath of corn, wheat, cotton, tobacco, sugar cane and oak leaves. The design adopted in 1860. Silver. Reeded Edge. J-232. Rare, highly touted as a "transitional pattern" due to its lack of the legend USOA $10,000

Mule of 1860 (Superior Galleries)

E.548. 1860 Mule. Obv. The regular design of 1859, dated 1860. Rev. The new regular design. Silver. Reeded Edge. J-267. Scarce, 100 struck to satisfy collector demand seen for the "transitional pattern" struck the previous year $3,500

E.549. 1863 Regular Design Trial Piece. Copper. Reeded Edge. J-323. Very rare, restrikes exist $1,500

E.550. Same, aluminum. Reeded Edge. J-324. Very rare $1,250

E.551. 1864 Regular Design Trial Piece. Copper. Reeded Edge. J-378. Rare, restrikes exist. ST 3/92, Ch. Br. Proof $4,800

E.552. Same, copper-nickel. Reeded Edge. J-380. Very rare $1,000

E.553. Same, aluminum. Reeded Edge. J-379. Very rare $900

E.554. 1865 Regular Design Trial Piece. Copper. Reeded Edge. J-420. Very rare $800

E.555. 1867 Regular Design Trial Piece. Copper. Reeded Edge. J-586. Very rare. 1.10 gms $800

E.556. 1868 Regular Design Trial Piece. Copper. Plain Edge. J-637. Very rare $900

E.557. Same, copper-nickel. Plain Edge. J-638. Very rare. Eliasberg 5/96 P-65 .... $3,418

E.558. Same, aluminum. Reeded Edge. J-639. Very rare $800

E.559. 1869 Regular Design Trial Piece. Copper. Reeded Edge. J-692. Very rare $800

E.560. Same, copper-nickel. Reeded Edge. J-694. Very rare $1,500

E.561. Same, copper-nickel. Plain Edge. J-695. Very rare $1,500

E.562. Same, aluminum. Reeded Edge. J-693. Very rare $900

E.563. 1870 Regular Design Trial Piece. Copper. Reeded Edge. J-821. Very rare $850

E.564. Same, copper. Plain Edge. J-822. Very rare $900

E.565. Same, copper-nickel. Reeded Edge. J-824. Very rare $1,000

E.566. Same, aluminum. Reeded Edge. J-823. Very rare $800

Because of the numerous die pairings in the different denominations of the Standard Silver series, the obverse designs will be identified by Roman numerals and the reverse designs by letters. The identifications of similar designs may vary from one denomination to another.

E.567. 1870 Pattern Design Trial Piece. Obv. I: Liberty figure seated to left, shield and ribbon with raised LIBERTY in right hand, olive branch in left, Liberty cap on pole behind. USOA around, date below. The Barber design. Rev. The regular design. Silver. Reeded Edge. J-815. Rare. ST 3/92, V. Ch. Br. Proof $5,500

E.568. Same, silver. Plain Edge. J-816. Rare. ST 3/92, Br. Proof $2,700
E.569. Same, copper. Reeded Edge. J-817. Rare. ST 3/92 Ch. Br. Proof $3,600
E.570. Same, copper. Plain Edge. J-818. Rare. ST 3/92 Br. Proof $3,000
E.571. Same, aluminum. Reeded Edge. J-819. Rare $1,000
E.572. Same, aluminum. Plain Edge. J-820. Rare $1,000
E.573. 1870 Pattern Design Trial Piece. Obv. I. Rev. A: 5 above CENTS within wreath of cotton and corn, STANDARD in small letters at upper border. The Standard reverse was used in some form on patterns for all silver denominations higher than the trime in 1870 and 1871. Silver. Reeded Edge. J-809. Rare $2,000
E.574. Same, silver. Plain Edge. J-810. Rare. ST 3/92, Br. Proof $2,500
E.575. Same, copper. Reeded Edge. J-811. Rare. ST 3/92, Ch. Br. Proof $4,200
E.576. Same, copper. Plain Edge. J-812. Rare $900
E.577. Same, aluminum. Reeded Edge. J-813. Rare $900
E.578. Same, aluminum. Plain Edge. J-814. Rare $900
E.579. 1871 Regular Design Trial Piece. Copper. Reeded Edge. J-1071. Very rare $1,100
E.580. Same, copper-nickel. Reeded Edge. J-1073. Very rare $1,300
E.581. Same, aluminum. Reeded Edge. J-1072. Very rare $900
E.582. 1871 Pattern Design Trial Piece. Obv. II: Liberty figure seated to left wearing Indian headdress, right hand supports pole with cap, left hand rests on globe with raised LIBERTY. Two flags behind, date below, no stars in field. The posthumous Longacre design from an 1870 silver dollar, used on all silver denominations above the trime in this year. Rev. The regular design. Silver. Reeded Edge. J-1062. Very rare $1,500
E.583. Same, copper. Reeded Edge. J-1063. Very rare $1,200
E.584. Same, aluminum. Reeded Edge. J-1064. Very rare $1,200

Pattern Design Trial Piece of 1871, design II – A (Bowers & Merena)

E.585. 1871 Pattern Design Trial Piece. Design II-A. Silver. Reeded Edge. J-1059. Very rare $1,500
E.586. Same, copper. Reeded Edge. J-1060. Very rare $1,200
E.587. Same, aluminum. Reeded Edge. J-1061. Very rare $1,200
E.588. 1871 Pattern Design Trial Piece. Obv. III: Similar to preceding except 13 stars around. Rev. The regular design. Silver. Reeded Edge. J-1068. Very rare $1,200
E.589. Same, copper. Reeded Edge. J-1069. Very rare $1,000
E.590. Same, aluminum. Reeded Edge. J-1070. Very rare $1,000

Pattern Design Trial Piece of 1871, design III – A (Smithsonian)

E.591. 1871 Pattern Design Trial Piece. Design III-A. Silver. Reeded Edge. J-1065. Very rare. Eliasberg 5/96 P-65 .... $5,940
E.592. Same, copper. Reeded Edge. J-1066. Very rare $1,300
E.593. Same, aluminum. Reeded Edge. J-1067. Very rare $1,200
Note: also reported in copper-nickel, unverified.
E.594. 1872 Regular Design Trial Piece. Copper. Reeded Edge. J-1191. Very rare $900
E.595. Same, aluminum. Reeded Edge. J-1192. Very rare $850
E.596. 1873 Regular Design Trial Piece. Copper. Reeded Edge. J-1266. Very rare $900
E.597. Same, aluminum. Reeded Edge. J-1267. Very rare $900
Note: Judd lists under 1875 a half dime Regular Design Trial Piece, an unexplained error on his part.

Dimes

Pattern Design Trial Piece of 1792 (Bowers & Merena)

E.598. 1792 Pattern Design Trial Piece. Obv. Liberty head left with flowing hair, date below, legend LIBERTY PARENT OF SCIENCE & INDUS., beaded border. Rev. Flying eagle, head facing right, USOA around, DISME below. Silver. Reeded Edge. J-9. Very rare, three known.

E.599. Same, copper. Reeded Edge. J-10. Rare. Copper, vertically reeded edge, ST 10/90 Lovejoy Collection, ex Brand, Park, Robison. Ch. VF, $26,000 .... $30,000

E.600. Same, copper. Plain Edge. J-11. Very rare.

Fantasy Mule of 1859

E.601. 1859 Fantasy Mule. Obv. Regular 1859 design with stars. Rev. ONE DIME within wreath of corn, wheat, cotton and tobacco, the regular design of 1860. Silver. Reeded Edge. J-233. Rare. Eliasberg 5/96 P-65 .... $34,100

E.602. 1863 Regular Design Trial Piece. Copper. Reeded Edge. J-333. Very rare. ST 3/92, Br. Proof .. $1,600

E.603. Same, aluminum. Plain Edge. J-334. Very rare $900

Pattern Design Trial Piece of 1863

E.604. 1863 Pattern Design Trial Piece. Obv. National shield over two crossed arrows, laurel wreath suspended from ring above, EXCHANGED FOR at upper border, U.S. NOTES at lower. Rev. 10 CENTS 1863 in center, POSTAGE CURRENCY at upper border, ACT JULY 1862 at lower. Silver, probably 90%. Reeded Edge. J-325a. Very rare.

E.605. Same, silver. Plain Edge. J-325. Rare $5,500

E.606. Same, billon, 25% Silver, 75% Copper. Reeded Edge. J-326. Rare, thin (1.7 grams) and thick (2.5 grams) planchets $5,000

E.607. Same, billon. Plain Edge. J-326a. Very rare. ST 3/92, Br. Proof $6,100

E.607a. Same, 75% Silver, 25% Aluminum. 1.8 gms. Plain Edge. Unlisted in Judd. Unique? SI

E.608. Same, aluminum-silver, 97:3. Reeded Edge. J-328. Very rare $2,750

E.608a. Same, copper, Reeded Edge. Unlisted in Judd. Very rare.

E.608b. Same, copper, Plain Edge. Unlisted in Judd. Very rare.

E.609. Same, copper-nickel. Reeded Edge. J-330a. Very rare $2,000

E.610. Same, aluminum. Plain Edge. J-327. Rare. ST 3/92, Br. Unc $2,000

E.611. Same, tin. Plain Edge. J-329. Scarce. May exist with Reeded Edge. ST 3/29, Br. Unc $2,600

E.612. Same, tin & copper, 97:3. Plain Edge. J-330. Rare. May exist with Reeded Edge $2,750

Pattern Design Trial Piece of 1863

E.613. (1863?) Pattern Design Trial Piece. Obv. Regular design without date. Rev. Same as preceding. Silver-nickel. Reeded Edge. J-331. Very rare, possibly a restrike ca. 1868-69, see 1869 Metallurgical Trial Pieces. Only rarely offered and probably no more than three struck. ST 3/92, V. Ch Br. Unc ... $6,400

E.614. Same, copper. Reeded Edge. J-331a. Very rare. Last seen as lot #504 of the LM 9/20/67 Sale. Listed there as "unique."

E.615. Same, copper-nickel. Reeded Edge. J-331b. Very rare.

Dime patterns continued

E.616. (1863?) Pattern Design Trial Piece. Obv. Same as preceding. Rev. The regular design. Aluminum. Plain Edge. J-332. Very rare $1,000

E.617. 1864 Regular Design Trial Piece. Copper. Reeded Edge. J-381. Rare. Restrikes exist. One seen has same rev. die and die state as 1870 E.666. 2.11 gms $1,250

E.618. Same, copper-nickel. Reeded Edge. J-383. Very rare $1,250

E.619. Same, aluminum. Reeded Edge. J-382. Very rare $1,500

E.620. 1865 Regular Design Trial Piece. Copper. Reeded Edge. J-421. Very rare $1,500

E.621. Same, copper-nickel. Reeded Edge. J-422. Very rare $1,500

E.622. 1866 Regular Design Trial Piece. Silver-nickel. Reeded Edge. J-535. Very rare. Possibly a restrike ca. 1868-69. See 1869 Metallurgical Trial Piece $2,000

E.623. Same, copper-nickel. Reeded Edge. J-534. Very rare $1,500

E.624. 1867 Regular Design Trial Piece. Silver-nickel. Reeded Edge. J-589. Very rare. Same comment as to possible restrike $4,500

E.625. Same, copper. Reeded Edge. J-587. Very rare. ST 3/29, Ch. Br. Proof $5,000

E.626. Same, copper-nickel. Reeded Edge. J-588. Very rare $2,500

E.627. 1868 Regular Design Trial Piece. Aluminum. Reeded Edge. J-649. Very rare $2,500

E.628. 1868 Pattern Design Trial Piece. Obv. Similar to regular design except no date. Rev. Similar to regular design except star added above ONE and date added below DIME. Silver. Reeded Edge. J-640. Very rare $2,000

E.629. Same, copper. Reeded Edge. J-642. Very rare $1,500

E.630. Same, copper-nickel. J-641. Very rare. Eliasberg 5/96 P-65 .... $4,400

E.631. 1868 Pattern Design Trial Piece. Obv. The EXCHANGED FOR U.S. NOTES die of 1863. Rev. Same as preceding. Silver. Reeded Edge. J-643. Very rare $3,750

E.632. Same, copper. Plain Edge. J-645. Very rare $1,500

E.633. Same, copper-nickel. Reeded Edge. J-644. Very rare $1,500

E.634. Same, aluminum. Plain Edge. J-646. Very rare. Also reported with Reeded Edge $1,000

Experimental size trial

E.635. 1868 Experimental Size Trial Piece. Obv. The regular large cent design of 1843-57, dated 1868. Rev. TEN CENTS in laurel wreath different from that of the large cent, USOA around. Copper. Plain Edge. J-648. Scarce $5,000

E.636. Same, copper-nickel. Plain Edge. J-647. Scarce $5,000

This obverse also used with a large cent reverse. See CENTS.

E.637. 1869 Regular Design Trial Piece. Copper. Reeded Edge. J-718. Very rare $1,000

E.638. Same, copper-nickel. Reeded Edge. J-720. Very rare $1,000

E.639. Same, aluminum. Reeded Edge. J-719. Very rare $900

Probably the most extensive series of related patterns was that denominated STANDARD SILVER. These coins were planned as lighter-weight alternatives to normal-weight silver pieces that were no longer in circulation in the troubled times following the Civil War. Their denominations were expressed as 5, 10, 25 and 50 cents rather than the familiar half dime, dime, quarter and half dollar. Because of the numerous die pairings in the different denominations of the Standard Silver series, the obverse designs will be identified by Roman numerals and the reverse designs by letters. The identifications of similar designs may vary from one denomination to another.

Dime patterns continued

Pattern Design Trial Piece of 1869, design I – A (Smithsonian)

E.640. 1869 Pattern Design Trial Piece. Obv. I. Liberty head right with cap showing two stars above forehead, plain ribbon in hair, USOA around upper border. IGWT on scroll at lower border. Rev. A: 10 CENTS within small oak and laurel wreath. Date below, STANDARD SILVER at upper border. Silver. Reeded Edge. J-696. Scarce. ST 3/92, Br. Proof $2,200
E.641. Same, silver. Plain Edge. J-697. Very rare. ST 3/92, V. Ch. Br. Proof $3,800
E.642. Same, copper. Reeded Edge. J-698. Rare $1,250
E.643. Same, copper. Plain Edge. J-699. Rare $900
E.644. Same, aluminum. Reeded Edge. J-700. Rare $900
E.645. Same, aluminum. Plain Edge. J-701. Rare $800

Pattern Design Trial Piece of 1869, design II – A (Smithsonian)

E.646. 1869 Pattern Design Trial Piece. Obv. II: Somewhat similar to preceding except Liberty cap replaced by plain coronet or diadem. Hair is different, and is tied with a plain cord above the coronet. Rev. A. Silver. Reeded Edge. J-702. Scarce. ST 3/92, Ch. Br. Proof $2,200
E.647. Same, silver. Plain Edge. J-703. Very rare. ST 3/92 V. Ch. Br. Proof $2,700
E.648. Same, copper. Reeded Edge. J-704. Rare $750
E.649. Same, copper. Plain Edge. J-705. Rare $750
E.650. Same, aluminum. Reeded Edge. J-706. Rare $700
E.651. Same, aluminum. Plain Edge. J-707. Rare $700
E.652. 1869 Pattern Design Trial Piece. Obv. III: Similar to preceding except coronet removed and the ribbon supports a single star upon the brow. Rev. A. Silver. Reeded Edge. J-708. Scarce. ST 3/92, Br. Proof $1,900
E.653. Same, silver. Plain Edge. J-709. Very rare. ST 3/92, Br. Proof $1,700
E.654. Same, copper. Reeded Edge. J-710. Rare $800
E.655. Same, copper. Plain Edge. J-711. Rare $800
E.656. Same, aluminum. Reeded Edge. J-712. Rare $700
E.657. Same, aluminum. Plain Edge. J-713. Rare $700

Note: The following Metallurgical Trial Pieces are not included in the obverse-reverse numbering system for pattern designs.

Metallurgical trial of 1869 (Smithsonian)

E.658. 1869 Metallurgical Trial Piece. Obv. The regular design without date. Rev. SIL. NIC. COP. in three lines with date in exergue. Silver-nickel-copper, 26:33:41. Reeded Edge. J-716. Very rare. ST 3/92, Br. Proof $4,200
E.659. Same, silver. Reeded Edge. J-716a. Very rare $3,750
E.660. Same, copper. Reeded Edge. J-717. Rare $800
E.661. Same, copper-nickel. J-717a. Very rare $800

Metallurgical trial (Superior Galleries)

E.662. 1869 Metallurgical Trial Piece. Obv. Same as preceding. Rev. SIL. 9 NIC. 1 in two lines with date in exergue. Silver-nickel, 90:10. Reeded Edge. J-714. Rare. Eliasberg 5/96 P-65 .... $3,960

Dime patterns continued

E.663. Same, copper. Reeded Edge. J-715. Rare $1,500
E.664. 1870 Regular Design Trial Piece. Copper. Reeded Edge. J-873. Very rare $1,500
E.665. Same, copper-nickel. Reeded Edge. J-875. Very rare $1,250
E.666. Same, aluminum. Reeded Edge. J-874. Very rare. One seen has same rev. die and die state as 1864
    E.617. 0.81 gms $1,250

Pattern Design Trial Piece of 1870, design
I – A (Harlan J. Berk Ltd.)

E.667. 1870 Pattern Design Trial Piece. Design I-A. Silver. Reeded Edge. J-855. Rare $4,500
E.668. Same, silver. Plain Edge. J-856. Rare. ST 3/92, Ch. Br. Proof $5,400
E.669. Same, copper. Reeded Edge. J-857. Rare $2,500
E.670. Same, copper. Plain Edge. J-858. Rare $2,500
E.671. Same, aluminum. Reeded Edge. J-859. Rare. 0.65 gms $1,000
E.672. Same, aluminum. Plain Edge. J-860. Rare $1,000

Pattern Design Trial Piece of 1870, design I–
B (Smithsonian)

E.673. 1870 Pattern Design Trial Piece. Obv. I. Rev. B: 10 CENTS within wreath of cotton and corn, date
    below CENTS, STANDARD in small letters at upper border. Silver. Reeded Edge. J-837. Rare. ST 3/
    92, Ch. Br. Proof $1,900
E.674. Same, silver. Plain Edge. J-838. Rare. ST 3/92, Br. Proof $2,100
E.675. Same, copper. Reeded Edge. J-839. Rare $2,750
E.676. Same, copper. Plain Edge. J-840. Rare. ST 3/92, Ch. Br. Proof $5,200
E.677. Same, aluminum. Reeded Edge. J-841. Rare $1,000
E.678. Same, aluminum. Plain Edge. J-842. Rare $1,000

Pattern Design Trial Piece of 1870, design
II–A (Harlan J. Berk Ltd.)

E.679. 1870 Pattern Design Trial Piece. Design II-A. Silver. Reeded Edge. J-861. Rare. ST 3/92, Br. Proof
    $2,200
E.680. Same, silver. Plain Edge. J-862. Rare $2,000
E.681. Same, copper. Reeded Edge. J-863. Rare $1,500
E.682. Same, copper. Plain Edge. J-864. Rare. 2.03 gms $1,500
E.683. Same, aluminum. Reeded Edge. J-865. Rare $900
E.684. Same, aluminum. Plain Edge. J-866. Rare $900

Pattern Design Trial Piece of 1870, design
II – B (Smithsonian)

E.685. 1870 Pattern Design Trial Piece. Design II-B. Silver. Reeded Edge. J-843. Rare $3,500
E.686. Same, silver. Plain Edge. J-844. Rare $3,500
E.687. Same, copper. Reeded Edge. J-845. Rare $2,000
E.688. Same, copper. Plain Edge. J-846. Rare $2,000
E.689. Same, aluminum. Reeded Edge. J-847. Rare $1,000
E.690. Same, aluminum. Plain Edge. J-848. Rare $1,000

Dime patterns continued

Pattern Design Trial Piece of 1870, design
III–A (Harlan J. Berk Ltd.)

E.691. 1870 Pattern Design Trial Piece. Design III-A. Silver. Reeded Edge. J-867. Rare $4,500
E.692. Same, silver. Plain Edge. J-868. Rare $4,500
E.693. Same, copper. Reeded Edge. J-869. Rare. 2.07 gms. ST 3/92, Br. Proof $5,250
E.694. Same, copper. Plain Edge. J-870. Rare $4,000
E.695. Same, aluminum. Reeded Edge. J-871. Rare $1,500
E.696. Same, aluminum. Plain Edge. J-872. Rare $1,500

Pattern Design Trial Piece of 1870, design
III – B (Smithsonian)

E.697. 1870 Pattern Design Trial Piece. Design III-B. Silver. Reeded Edge. J-849. Rare. ST 3/92, Br. Proof
    $2,300
E.698. Same, silver. Plain Edge. J-850. Rare $2,250
E.699. Same, copper. Reeded Edge. J-851. Rare $1,500
E.700. Same, copper. Plain Edge. J-852. Rare $1,500
E.701. Same, aluminum. Reeded Edge. J-853. Rare $1,.000
E.702. Same, aluminum. Plain Edge. J-854. Rare $1,000
E.703. 1870 Pattern Design Trial Piece. Obv. IV: Liberty seated to left, shield and ribbon with raised LIBERTY in
    right hand, olive branch in left hand, Liberty Cap on pole behind. Date below. The Barber design. Rev.
    The regular design. Silver. Reeded Edge. J-831. Rare $5,500
E.704. Silver. Plain Edge. J-832. Rare $5.500
E.705. Copper. Reeded Edge. J-833. Rare. ST 3/92, V. Ch Br. Proof $5,000
E.706. Copper. Plain Edge. J-834. Rare $1,750
E.707. Aluminum. Reeded Edge. J-835. Rare $1,000
E.708. Aluminum. Plain Edge. J-836. Rare $1,000

Pattern Design Trial Piece of 1870, design
IV–C (Harlan J. Berk Ltd.)

E.709. 1870 Pattern Design Trial Piece. Obv. IV. Rev. C: Similar to Rev. B except no date below CENTS. Broad
    border. Silver. Reeded Edge. J-825. Rare $2,700
E.710. Same, silver. Plain Edge. J-826. Rare. ST 3/92, Proof $2,700
E.711. Same, copper. Reeded Edge. J-827. Rare $1,750
E.712. Same, copper. Plain Edge. J-828. Rare $1,750
E.713. Same, aluminum. Reeded Edge. J-829. Rare $1,000
E.714. Same, aluminum. Plain Edge. J-830. Rare $1,000
E.715. 1871 Regular Design Trial Piece. Copper. Reeded Edge. J-1087. Very rare $1,750
E.716. Same, copper-nickel. Reeded Edge. J-1089. Very rare $2,000
E.717. Same, aluminum. Reeded Edge. J-1088. Very rare $1,750
E.718. 1871 Pattern Design Trial Piece. Obv. V: Liberty figure seated to left wearing Indian headdress, right
    hand supports pole with cap, left rests on globe with raised LIBERTY. Two flags behind, date below, no
    stars in field. The posthumous Longacre design. Rev. The regular design. Silver. Reeded Edge. J-1077.
    Very rare $1,200
E.719. Same, copper. Reeded Edge. J-1078. Very rare $1,000
E.720. Same, aluminum. Reeded Edge. J-1079. Very rare $1,000
E.721. 1871 Pattern Design Trial Piece. Design V-C. Silver. Reeded Edge. J-1074. Very rare $1,300
E.722. Same, copper. Reeded Edge. J-1075. Very rare $1,000
E.723. Same, aluminum. Reeded Edge. J-1076. Very rare $1,000
E.724. 1871 Pattern Design Trial Piece. Obv. VI: Similar to preceding except 13 stars added around border.
    Rev. The regular design. Silver. Reeded Edge. J-1084. Very rare $1,300
E.725. Same, copper. Reeded Edge. J-1085. Very rare. BM 3/94, P-63 .... $2,200
E.726. Same, aluminum. Reeded Edge. J-1086. Very rare $1,000

Dime patterns continued

Pattern Design Trial Piece of 1871, design
VI-C (Smithsonian)

E.727. 1871 Pattern Design Trial Piece. Design VI-C. Silver. Reeded Edge. J-1080. Very rare. Eliasberg 5/96
P-65 .... $5,720
E.728. Same, copper. Reeded Edge. J-1081. Very rare. ST 3/92, Br. Proof $4,200
E.729. Same, copper-nickel. Reeded Edge. J-1083. Very rare $2,000
E.730. Same, aluminum. Reeded Edge. J-1082. Very rare. ST 3/92 Br. Proof $2,500
E.731. 1872 Regular Design Trial Piece. Copper. Reeded Edge. J-1193. Very rare $2,000
E.732. Same, aluminum. Reeded Edge. J-1194. Very rare $1,000
E.733. 1873 Regular Design Trial Piece. Closed 3, No Arrows. Copper. Reeded Edge. J-1268. Very rare
$1,500
E.734. Same, aluminum. Reeded Edge. J-1269. Very rare $1,000
E.735. 1874 Regular Design Trial Piece. Copper. Reeded Edge. J-1352. Very rare $1,500
E.736. Same, aluminum. Reeded Edge. J-1353. Very rare $1,000
E.737. 1875 Regular Design Trial Piece. Copper. Reeded Edge. J-1390. Very rare $1,500
E.738. Same, aluminum. Reeded Edge. J-1391. Very rare $1,000
E.739. 1876 Regular Design Trial Piece. Copper. Reeded Edge. J-1452. Very rare $1,500
E.740. Same, copper-nickel. Reeded Edge. J-1453. Very rare $1,800
E.740a. 1876-CC Regular Design Trial Piece. Copper. Reeded Edge. Possibly struck at Philadelphia Mint. Judd
and A-W unlisted, unique? Also reported in "nickel," unconfirmed, ST 9/94, Ch. BU $11,000
E.741. 1877 Pattern Design Trial Piece. Obv. Liberty head left wearing coronet inscribed LIBERTY, 13 stars
around, date below. The Sailor Head used on 1875 20 cents, $5 and $10 patterns, 1876 dollar
patterns and 1877 dime through dollar patterns. Rev. The regular design. Copper. Reeded Edge. J-
1498. Very rare, also known silver-plated, and may possibly exist in silver. PST 3/92, Br. Proof$7,500

Pattern Design Trial Piece of 1879,
Washlady (Smithsonian)

E.742. 1879 Pattern Design Trial Piece. Obv. Liberty head left with wavy hair piled up in back, ribbon above
forehead labeled LIBERTY, wheat ears and cotton plants behind, USA around, date below. Charles E.
Barber's Washlady design, also used on quarters, half dollars and dollars. Rev. ONE DIME in circle of
dots, tiny EPU inside fancy border at top with wreath of cotton and corn on either side, tied at the
bottom. Silver. Reeded Edge. J-1584. Very rare. Eliasberg 5/96 P-65 .... $10,120
E.743. Same, copper. Reeded Edge. J-1585. Very rare $2,000

Pattern Design Trial Piece of 1879
(Smithsonian)

E.744. 1879 Pattern Design Trial Piece. Obv. Liberty head left as on Morgan dollar, USA around, date below.
Rev. ONE DIME encircled by EPA above and 13 stars below, all within a circle of dots surrounded by
wreath of cotton, wheat, corn and tobacco. Silver. Reeded Edge. J-1586. Very rare $5,500
E.745. Same, copper. Reeded Edge. J-1587. Very rare $4,500
E.746. 1879 Pattern Design Trial Piece. Obv. Same as preceding. Rev. Similar to preceding except wreath
replaced by laurel branch. Silver. Reeded Edge. J-1588. Very rare $5,500
E.747. Same, copper. Reeded Edge. J-1589. Very rare $4,500
E.748. 1884 Regular Design Trial Piece. Copper. Reeded Edge. J-1728. Very rare $4,500
E.749. 1885 Regular Design Trial Piece. Aluminum. Reeded Edge. J-1744. Very rare $2,750

Dime patterns continued

Pattern Design Trial Piece of 1891
(Smithsonian)

E.750. 1891 Pattern Design Trial Piece. Obv. Liberty head right with cap and laurel wreath, tiny LIBERTY incused on headband, USA around. The design adopted in 1892. Rev. The regular design, retained with a few minor changes for the Barber series. Silver. Reeded Edge. J-1760. Two known, Smithsonian.

Pattern Design Trial Piece of 1916
(Smithsonian)

E.751. 1916 Pattern Design Trial Piece. Obv. Liberty head left wearing a winged cap, LIBERTY around, small date below, IGWT in lower left field, no designer's initials behind neck. The so-called "Mercury" design. Rev. Fasces and olive branch, as on the wall behind the Speaker's platform in the U.S. House of Representatives. USOA around upper border, ONE DIME at lower border, EPU in lower right field. Silver. Reeded Edge. J-1794. Rare, several minor die varieties exist. Often found circulated, due to a burglary at a Mint official's home by a thief who spent them! $3,750

Metallurgical trial of 1965

E.752. (1965) Metallurgical Trial Piece. Obv. Martha Washington bust in mob cap right. VIRGINIA around upper border, 1759 below, MARTHA WASHINGTON in lower right field. Rev. 3/4 perspective of Washington home, MOUNT VERNON below, HOME OF THE WASHINGTON FAMILY around. Struck in various alloys of silver and copper, copper and nickel, nickel and silicon, stainless steel, Columbium, Zirconium and Monel metal to test proposed replacements for 90% silver in U.S. coinage. Only one piece is reported to survive in the Smithsonian, embedded in a block of Lucite along with quarter-sized and half dollar-sized strikes of the same design.

E.753. (1965) Metallurgical Trial Piece. Obv. Paul D. Merica bust r. Rev. aerial view of International Nickel Company's Merica Laboratory, date 1964 below. Large bust only, struck by Medallic Art Co. and Franklin Mint in experimental alloys such as nickel-silicon, see similar piece in quarter dollar patterns section $750

Twenty cents

Pattern Design Trial Piece of 1874, design I – A (Smithsonian)

E.754. 1874 Pattern Design Trial Piece. Obv. I: Liberty seated to left on globe labeled LIBERTY, right arm supports pole with Liberty cap. Cotton bales and tobacco plant to left of leg, Wheat sheaf behind globe, 13 stars around, Date below. Rev. A: Facing eagle with partially raised wings, three arrows in eagle's right (viewer's left) claw, olive branch in left claw. (Heraldic *faux pas*, favoring the arrows of war over the olive branch of peace, copied from the Trade dollar.) USOA at upper border, TWENTY CENTS at lower, very similar to the adopted design. Silver. Plain Edge. J-1354. Rare. BM 3/94, P-63 $7,500

    1. This is the first pattern for a 20 cent coin. The obverse is a reduction of the 1873 Bailly-designed trade dollar pattern, E.1386. The reverse is a reduction of the eagle used on some of the other trade dollar patterns of that date as eventually adopted for the 1873-1883 trade dollar. The same eagle reverse, with minor variations as noted below, was adopted for the final version of the 20 cent issue. The history of this pattern and the origins of the 20-cent coinage was part of a fine commentary (presumably by Andrew Pollock) in a discussion of a copper piece (E.755) in the 11/93 BM Donovan and Hudgens Sale, lot#1400:

    "The obverse… is attributed to Joseph Alexis Bailly. This is essentially the same design as that employed on certain pattern trade dollars in 1873 (see Judd-1315). The reverse is similar to that adopted on regular-issue 20-cent pieces in 1875, except that the terminal leaves of the olive brach overlap on the pattern variety. Impressions from these 20-cent piece dies are said to have been forwarded by Mint Superintendent James Pollock to Director Linderman on August 7, 1874.

    "Sir: The issue of a 20-cent silver piece being under consideration I have to request that you will cause a pair of experimental dies to be prepared for the same.

    "As the difference in the weight between the proposed piece of 20 cents and the 25-cent piece will be quite small, it will be necessary to give the former such devices etx., as will render it easily distinguished from the latter, I should prefer the Bailey (sic) figure of 'Liberty' as shown on one of the specimen Trade dollars and the Barber eagle as it appears on the Trade dollar."

    2. Much rarer than commonly thought. Only one coin of this type in silver appeared on the market beween 1989 and early 1992. The next appearance was in BM 9/94, part of an almost complete run of 20-cent patterns. A review of the auction catalogs, both recent and over the past few decades, show relatively few appearances for this pattern in any metal other than copper. The comments in BM 11/93 may show why. This particular design was obviously a 'lashup', using an already-rejected obverse design and a reverse from a regular issue coin. Linderman, in a later letter noted in Taxay, expressed a liking for what was later called J-1392 or E.770, but then approved a minor variation on existing coinage (E.774) with a 'distingushing' feature (raised LIBERTY on the shield vs. incused on the quarter) which proved to be a disaster. The letter above was an accurate warning, unfortunately ignored. As to rarity, since this obverse was never intended to be anything more than an example of a different obverse to distingush this denomination from others, the latter-struck designs of 1875 were no doubt struck in larger numbers, as is evident from the number of those patterns which have appeared on the market during the same time period that this pattern was conspicuous by its absence. At the same time, it should be noted that, for a relatively late type of pattern, the number of 20-cent patterns in any metal is relatively small. At a time the Mint was turning out all kinds of patterns, why is the number of these coins so small given the fact that there was such a wide variety of these patterns done and, at the same time, no evidence of later restrikes? The relative scarcity may be explained by the lack of popularity of the denomination itself. Why turn out a restrike of a pattern of an unpopular coin when more profitable patterns of interest to collectors who collected the regular issue of a given denomination could be made available? The answer to all of these questions is then simple — greed.

E.755. Same, copper. Plain Edge. J-1355. Rare. One known silver plated; has been misattributed as copper-nickel $4,500

E.756. Same, aluminum. Plain Edge. J-1356. Rare $4,500

E.757. 1874 Pattern Design Trial Piece. Obv. I. Rev. B: 20 CENTS within laurel wreath, USOA around. Silver. Plain Edge. J-1357. Very rare $9,000

    1. Does this pattern exist in this metal? If so, it has not been seen in many years.

    2. The letter quoted in the notes to E.754 shows that the marriage of this obverse and the 20 CENT reverse is clearly a restrike. (See E.758)

Twenty cents patterns continued

E.758. Same, copper-nickel. Plain Edge. J-1358. Very rare $8,500

As noted above, there is a substantial question as to whether this die marriage in silver actually exists (the one I was shown turned out to be copper-nickel — *DN*). That fact is brought into sharp focus by this pattern. There are few demonstrable specimens of 20-cent patterns that can be shown to be restrikes. Since this reverse was clearly one made for the 1875 patterns, this pattern and the so-called silver or intended metal pattern (E.757) are restrikes. However, this pattern is extremely rare (perhaps 3 or so currently traced) and restrikes of any 20-cent pattern are controversial. Since silver planchets were precious metals that had to be accounted for, this die marriage may represent a late appearance of what others call the "Midnight Minter" (in this case, a later generation copycat) who struck off a few pieces in copper-nickel to make a quick profit. And, as the market for these 20-cent patterns was small, the entire run of this pattern may be the work of an hour or two. The risk of striking one in silver was not worth the bother, hence the absence of any example of this fantasy strike in the intended metal.

Pattern Design Trial Piece of
1875, design II – A

E.759. 1875 Pattern Design Trial Piece. Obv. II: Liberty seated to left on globe labeled LIBERTY, outstretched right arm holds olive branch. Ocean scene with combination sail/steam ship to left of leg, wheat sheaf and two flags behind globe, 13 stars around, date below. Rev. A. Silver. Plain Edge. J-1399. Rare. Eliasberg 5/96 P-65 .... $7,920

1. This is the "Liberty by the Seashore" obverse combined with what proved to be the as-adopted reverse but for a few minor variations as discussed under E.774. This obverse was used in some dollar patterns this same year (1875).

2. This obverse has caused much mirth because of the early steamship with sail assist shown in the background. The ship shows a paddlewheel, which was many decades outdated by this date, but the *faux pas* that caused the laughter is the sails billowing in one direction while the smoke from the stack and the flag are blowing in the other direction. This fact has been noted in many places. However, what has not been discussed is the fact that when this same obverse was used on some dollar patterns the next year (1876), the gaffe had clearly been discovered since the sails were polished off the die, leaving the ship on the 1876 patterns proceeding under steam power only.

E.760. Same, copper. Plain Edge. J-1400. Rare $4,000
E.761. Same, copper-nickel. Plain Edge. J-1402. Very rare $4,500
E.762. Same, aluminum. Plain Edge. J-1401. Very rare $4,250

Pattern Design Trial Piece of 1875, design
II – B (Smithsonian)

E.763. 1875 Pattern Design Trial Piece. Design II-B. Silver. Plain Edge. J-1403. Rare $6,500

For some reason, this die marriage has proven to be the most available of all 20-cent patterns. (There were several in silver and one or two in other metals in Superior's 1989 Heifetz Sale alone!) The apparent wealth of examples in the last few years may just be happenstance.

E.764. Same, copper. Plain Edge. J-1404. Rare $4,000
E.765. Same, aluminum. Plain Edge. J-1405. Very rare $4,500
E.766. Same, white metal. Plain Edge. J-1406. Very rare $4,250

Twenty cents patterns continued

Pattern Design Trial Piece of 1875, design
II – C

E.767. 1875 Pattern Design Trial Piece. Obv. II. Rev. C: 1/5 OF A DOLLAR within a laurel wreath, USOA at upper border, TWENTY CENTS at lower. Silver. Plain Edge. J-1396. Rare $6,500

    1. In contrast to the previous die marriage, this marriage appears to be substantially rarer than most other 20-cent patterns. For example, before the run of 20-cent patterns in the 1994 BM sale noted above, the last appearance of one of these coins was lot #1784 in the Heritage 1992 A.N.A. Early Spring Auction. (The coin sold for $5,800 plus 10% buyer's fee.) That was the first appearance in auction or by private treaty in at least five years.

    2. The appearance of what seems, at first glance, to be a heavy dose of hairlines on each of these patterns, particularly the obverse, should be considered in light of Q. David Bowers' very accurate observations on another example which appeared as lot #123 in the BR William R. Sieck 1981 ANA Sale:

    "What appear to be hairlines in the fields are simply stray die finishing marks, raised, and are the result of careless die preparation - a situation common to all known examples of J-1396 and its other metal counterparts J-1397 [copper] and J-1398 [aluminum]." These comments are very accurate. While there have been relatively few examples of this die marriage to examine, each coin has had these characteristics regardless of the metal.

E.768. Same, copper. Plain Edge. J-1397. Rare $4,000
E.769. Same, aluminum. Plain Edge. J-1398. Very rare $4,000

Pattern Design Trial Piece of 1875, design
III – D (Bowers & Merena)

E.770. 1875 Pattern Design Trial Piece. Obv. III: Liberty head left wearing coronet marked LIBERTY, hair tied at back of head with ribbon, 13 stars around, date below. A copy of Sailor Head design prepared by William Barber for a $5 gold pattern. Rev. D: National shield with fancy 20 incused in center, two arrows and olive branch at base; sunburst above, USOA around, CENTS below. Silver. Plain Edge. J-1392. Rare $7,000
E.771. Same, copper. Plain Edge. J-1393. Rare $4,750
E.772. Same, copper-nickel. Plain Edge. J-1395. Very rare $4,250
E.773. Same, aluminum. Plain Edge. J-1394. Very rare $4,250
E.774. 1875 Pattern Design Trial Piece. Obv. IV: The regular Seated Liberty, as reduced from the dollar of 1840-73. LIBERTY on shield incused, as on other Seated Liberty coins. Rev. A. Silver. Plain Edge. J-1411. Rare $7,500

    1. Listed in many sources and catalogs as the prototype of the 20-cent coin, this is the adopted design, but with several often-overlooked variations. The most obvious at first glance is the fact that the date logotype is smaller than on the as-adopted 20 cent coin. The leaves on the reverse wreath are slightly different (overlapping the NT). However, the most obvious distinction, and the change that the Mint though would help distinguish the 20 cent coin from the quarter (besides the use of a plain edge) was the change between the incuse LIBERTY on the shield on the obverse of this pattern to a raised LIBERTY on the regular issue. This fact has been overlooked by several prominent experts, which makes it difficult to see how the Mint could have expected the public to pick up on it as a distinguishing factor. In the end, putting LIBERTY in relief on the shield ensured nothing more than a high point to show wear. Expecting the public to distingush a denomination by checking the edge or stopping a transaction to check to see if the coin had an incuse or raised LIBERTY shows that governmental stupidity was alive and well in our 19th century institutions.

    2. Yet another one of the 20-cent patterns that has not appeared at auction or otherwise with a frequency that would match its supposed rating. This pattern, and its companions in the off-metals, has been difficult to find at any time. The coin (like many of the regular issue) is very difficult to locate in gem condition.

E.775. Same, copper. Plain Edge. J-1412. Rare $4,000
E.776. Same, aluminum. Plain Edge. J-1413. Very rare $4,500

Twenty cents patterns continued

Pattern Design Trial Piece of 1875, design IV – C

E.777. 1875 Pattern Design Trial Piece. Design IV-C. Silver. Plain Edge. J-1407. Rare. 5.01 gms. 5.03 gms. BM 3/94, P-63 $3,850; Eliasberg 5/96 P-63/65 .... $4,180
E.778. Same, copper. Plain Edge. J-1408. Rare $1,700
E.779. Same, copper-nickel. Plain Edge. J-1410. Very rare $2,000
E.780. Same, aluminum. Plain Edge. J-1409. Very rare $2,000
E.781. 1875 Pattern Design Trial Piece. Obv. V: Similar to preceding except LIBERTY on shield in raised letters. The adopted design. Rev. E: Similar to Rev. A except olive branch rearranged. The adopted design. Copper. Plain Edge. J-1414. Rare $1,800
E.782. Same, aluminum. Plain Edge. J-1415. Very rare $2,000
E.783. 1876 Regular Design Trial Piece. Copper. Plain Edge. J-1454. Very rare $2,200

Quarter dollars

Pattern Design Trial Piece of 1792 (Bowers & Merena)

E.784. 1792 Pattern Design Trial Piece. Obv. Female bust right, LIBERTY above, date below. Plain rim. Rev. Eagle with partially raised wings standing on a segment of a globe, UNITED STATES OF AMERICA around, border made out of 87 tiny stars. Copper. Reeded Edge. J-12. Two known, one in Smithsonian.
E.785. Same, White Metal. Plain Edge. J-13. Two known.
    1. This design has been identified at various times as being intended for a large cent, a quarter dollar and a gold half eagle. The current consensus is that it is a quarter dollar.
    2. The 87 stars on the border may refer to the year (1787) the Constitution was approved by Congress, just as the 94 stars on the reverse of one 1794 cent may refer to the year the die was engraved. Proof of these theories is lacking. A pair of white metal obverse and reverse die impressions in Garrett IV, EF and VF respectively, brought $12,000.
Note: The 1805 piece listed as J-35 is a private restrike.
Note: The 1806 piece struck from a quarter dollar obverse and a large cent reverse listed as J-38a is a private restrike.
Note: The 1818 piece struck from a quarter dollar obverse and a large cent reverse listed as J-45 is a private restrike.
E.786. 1827/3 Off-Metal Restrike. Obv. The regular design, dated 1827/3. Rev. The regular design of 1819, with a flat-based 2 in 25 C. Copper. Reeded Edge. J-48. Rare $5,000
    Not a pattern, this piece and its silver brother listed under regular issues are merely restrikes semi-officially made at the Mint to provide specimens of a rare date for trading purposes.
E.787. 1834 Regular Design Trial Piece. Copper. Reeded Edge. J-50. Very rare.

Quarter dollar patterns continued

Incomplete master dies trial (Thomas K. DeLorey)

E.788. (1840) Incomplete Master Dies Trial Piece. Obv. Seated Liberty of the With Drapery design adopted in 1840. Denticled border. No stars or date, small hole as from compass point in Liberty's right thigh, and corresponding tracing circle inside the denticles where the stars would be added later, uneven field. Rev. Similar to the new 1840 rev. with sharply curved claws and no tongue on the eagle, but no denticles on rim. Small compass hole at top of first vertical stripe in shield. Very uneven field, including tracing marks through UNITED STATES OF AMERICA and QUAR. DOL. Struck on large brass disc. Plain Edge. J-110. Unique.

The 1840 rev. has fewer but wider denticles than the 1839 rev. This piece was struck from a new master die before the denticles were added to it, possibly while Gobrecht was still considering what style to use.

Experimental trial (Superior Galleries)

E.789. 1857 Experimental Trial Piece. Obv. The regular design. Rev. Plain field with USOA around upper border, QUAR. DOL. lower, denticled rim. Copper. Reeded Edge. J-188. Very rare $2,000

This piece was presumably made to test a ring punch bearing all of the letters of the reverse legend. Such a punch would speed up the production of new master dies, which were prepared for most denominations in the late 1850s. An interesting uniface die trial shows concentric ring punch impressions for a dime, quarter and half dollar.

E.790. 1858 Revised Design Trial Piece. Obv. The regular design. Rev. Similar to the regular design except eagle is taller and thinner, different lettering style. Anthony C. Paquet design. Silver. Reeded Edge. J-221. Very rare $8,000

1. The same combination (i.e. regular obverse and this reverse) was repeated in 1859 (E.791, J-234), in 1864 as (E.799, J-384) in silver and (E.800, J-835) in copper, and in 1865 as (E.806, J-423) in silver, (E.808, J-424) in copper and (E.807, J-424a) in "silver and copper."

2. This pattern is quite difficult to locate. BM 9/90 Robert W. Rusbar Sale, lot #719 states there are five examples of this coin. An early appearance of this same pattern as lot #84 in the Bangs & Co. 6/90 Parmelee Sale agrees that the coin was "very rare," resulting in a sale price, substantial for the time, of $5.50. In the 1976 edition of this work, Don Taxay stated that there were "[o]nly 4 pcs. struck according to Cogan sale of May, 1860, and we can trace no more."

E.791. 1859 Revised Design Trial Piece. Obv. The regular design. Rev. Same as preceding. Silver. Reeded Edge. J-234. Very rare $8,000

E.792. 1860 Regular Design Trial Piece. Copper-nickel. Reeded Edge. J-268. Very rare $1,800

E.793. 1861 Regular Design Trial Piece. Copper. Reeded Edge. J-275. Very rare $1,800

E.794. Same, copper-nickel. Reeded Edge. J-276. Very rare $1,800

E.795. 1863 Revised Design Trial Piece. Obv. The regular design. Rev. Regular design of 1866-91 with motto IN GOD WE TRUST on scroll above eagle. Silver. Reeded Edge. J-335. Very rare. 6.25 gms ... $2,000

Although the various patterns with IN GOD WE TRUST have long been believed to be backdated fantasies, the firm of Harlan J. Berk, Ltd. recently discovered a letter on Treasury Dept. letterhead from Salmon P. Chase, Secretary of the Treasury, to James Pollock Esq., Director of the Mint, as follows:

"Oct. 22d, 1863. Sir: You will please to furnish to Hon. George Opdyke, Mayor of New York, a Proof set of the specimen pieces struck at the Mint for the years 1862 and 1863, as follows: Half dollars and Quarter dollars in silver, and the series of Gold coins struck in copper, all bearing the legend, "In God we trust," on his paying the expense of the same."

Though this would seem to have authorized a back-dated striking of the 1862 pieces, none are currently known with IGWT, and none of the gold pieces dated before 1865 are known with IGWT. The order may have been filled with various GOD OUR TRUST pieces. This is not to say that some or all of the pre-1865 pieces with IGWT may not have been struck in 1865 or later. All seen to date of this die pair show severe die rust and die polish lines typical of 1868-70 Proofs and patterns, specifically E.881 of 1870. Further study of die varieties and die states is necessary.

Quarter dollar patterns continued

E.796. Same, copper. Reeded Edge. J-336. Rare. BM 3/94, P P-63 .... $3,410
E.797. Same, aluminum. Reeded Edge. J-337. Very rare $1,700
E.798. 1864 Regular Design Trial Piece. Copper. Reeded Edge. J-390. Very rare $1,500
E.799. 1864 Revised Design Trial Piece. Obv. The regular design. Rev. The Paquet design. Silver. Reeded
    Edge. J-384. Very rare, possibly a restrike ca. 1865-70. Eliasberg 5/96 P-63 .... $6,380
        See the notes under E.790. These patterns were clearly fantasy restrikes, very probably struck
    at the direction of Paquet himself, who had a thriving business in the sale of medals and patterns
    to various wealthy collectors. Having his work appear only briefly in regular coinage, and
    having very little impact even in the area of patterns, this engraver took advantage of what little
    work he had done to strike these patterns for private sale. (These same comments apply to E.801
    and E.806-811)
E.800. Same, copper. Reeded Edge. J-385. Very rare $1,250
E.801. 1864 Revised Design Trial Piece. Obv. The regular design. Rev. With Motto reverse of 1866. Silver.
    Reeded Edge. J-386. Very rare. See comments under E.795. Eliasberg 5/96 P-62 .... $5,280
E.802. Same, copper. Reeded Edge. J-387. Very rare $1,500
E.803. Same, copper-nickel. Reeded Edge. J-389. Unique?
E.804. Same, aluminum. Reeded Edge. J-388. Very rare $1,000
E.805. 1865 Regular Design Trial Piece. Copper. Reeded Edge. J-428. Very rare $1,500
E.806. 1865 Revised Design Trial Piece. Obv. The regular design. Rev. The Paquet design. Silver. Reeded
    Edge. J-423. Very rare, possibly struck 1866-70. See following two. Eliasberg 5/96 P-64 .... $3,740
E.807. Same, silver on one side, copper on the other. Reeded Edge. J-424a. Unique? Possibly struck at same
    time as 1869-70 2 cents of similar bimetallic composition.
E.808. Same, copper. Reeded Edge. J-424. Very rare. Eliasberg 5/96 P-64 .... $5,720
E.809. 1865 Revised Design Trial Piece. Obv. The regular design. Rev. With Motto reverse of 1866. Silver.
    Reeded Edge. J-425. Very rare, possibly struck in 1866 or later to meet demand $4,000
E.810. Same, copper. Reeded Edge. J-426. Rare $1,500
E.811. Same, aluminum. Reeded Edge. J-427. Very rare $1,200
E.812. 1866 Regular Design Trial Piece. With Motto. Copper. Reeded Edge. J-537. Very rare $1,250
E.813. 1866 Fantasy Mule. Obv: The regular design. Rev: 1865 No Motto reverse. Silver. Reeded Edge.
    J-536. Unique, stolen from Willis H. DuPont in 1967 and never recovered. Proof. Beware low-grade
    alterations.
E.814. 1867 Regular Design Trial Piece. Copper. Reeded Edge. J-590. Very rare $1,000
E.815. 1868 Regular Design Trial Piece. Aluminum. Reeded Edge. J-650. Very rare $1,000
E.816. 1869 Regular Design Trial Piece. Copper. Reeded Edge. J-739. Very rare $1,000
E.817. Same, copper-nickel. Reeded Edge. J-741. Very rare $1,500
E.818. Same, aluminum. Reeded Edge. J-740. Very rare $1,000

As noted under dimes, the series inscribed STANDARD SILVER was intended to introduce silver coins of lesser weight than the now-vanished heavier-weight regular issues. The Standard Silver patterns in this denomination were inscribed 25 CENTS rather than QUARTER DOLLAR. Because of the numerous die pairings in the different denominations of the Standard Silver series, the obverse designs will be identified by Roman numerals and the reverse designs by letters. The identifications of similar designs may vary from one denomination to another.

*Pattern Design Trial Piece of 1869, design
I – A (Smithsonian)*

E.819. 1869 Pattern Design Trial Piece. Obv. I. Liberty head right with cap showing 2-1/2 stars above
    forehead, ribbon in lower hair inscribed LIBERTY in raised letters, USOA around upper border, IGWT
    on scroll at lower border. Rev. A. 25 CENTS in oak and laurel wreath, date below, STANDARD SILVER
    at upper border. Silver. Reeded Edge. J-721. Scarce. ST 9/94, Br. Proof $2,000
E.820. Same, silver. Plain Edge. J-722. Very rare $1,500
E.821. Same, copper. Reeded Edge. J-723. Scarce $1,250
E.822. Same, copper. Plain Edge. J-724. Rare $1,250
E.823. Same, aluminum. Reeded Edge. J-725. Rare $1,000
E.824. Same, aluminum. Plain Edge. J-726. Rare $1,000
Note: For a bimetallic mule of this obverse with an 1869 2 cents, see the 2 cents listings.

Quarter dollar patterns continued

Pattern Design Trial Piece of 1869, design
II – A (Smithsonian)

E.825. 1869 Pattern Design Trial Piece. Obv. II. Somewhat similar to preceding except Liberty cap replaced by plain coronet or diadem. Hair is different, and is tied with a ribbon inscribed LIBERTY in raised letters. Rev. A. Silver. Reeded Edge. J-727. Scarce. ST 6/94, Br. Proof $1,700
E.826. Same, silver. Plain Edge. J-728. Very rare. 4.99 gms $1,500
E.827. Same, copper. Reeded Edge. J-729. Rare $1,250
E.828. Same, copper. Plain Edge. J-730. Rare $1,250
E.829. Same, aluminum. Reeded Edge. J-731. Rare $1,000
E.830. Same, aluminum. Plain Edge. J-732. Rare $1,000

Pattern Design Trial Piece of 1869, design
III – A (Smithsonian)

E.831. 1869 Pattern Design Trial Piece. Obv. III. Similar to preceding except coronet removed and the ribbon supports a single star upon the brow. Rev. A. Silver. Reeded Edge. J-733. Scarce. St 9/94, Br. Proof $1,700
E.832. Same, silver. Plain Edge. J-734. Very rare $1,700
E.833. Same, copper. Reeded Edge. J-735. Scarce $1,250
E.834. Same, copper. Plain Edge. J-736. Rare $1,250
E.835. Same, aluminum. Reeded Edge. J-737. Rare $900
E.836. Same, aluminum. Plain Edge. J-738. Rare $900
E.837. 1870 Regular Design Trial Piece. Copper. Reeded Edge. J-924. Very rare $1,200
E.838. Same, copper-nickel. Reeded Edge. J-926. Very rare $1,500
E.839. Same, aluminum. Reeded Edge. J-925. Very rare $900

Pattern Design Trial Piece of 1870. design
I – A (Bowers & Merena)

E.840. 1870 Pattern Design Trial Piece. Design I-A. Silver. Reeded Edge. J-906. Rare $1,500
E.841. Same, silver. Plain Edge. J-907. Rare. Eliasberg 5/96 P-64 .... $4,840
E.842. Same, copper. Reeded Edge. J-908. Rare $1,250
E.843. Same, copper. Plain Edge. J-909. Rare $1,250
E.844. Same, aluminum. Reeded Edge. J-910. Rare $900
E.845. Same, aluminum. Plain Edge. J-911. Rare $900

Pattern Design Trial Piece of 1870, design
I – B (Smithsonian)

E.846. 1870 Pattern Design Trial Piece. Obv. I. Rev. B: 25 CENTS in wreath of cotton and corn, date below CENTS, STANDARD in small letters at upper border. Silver. Reeded Edge. J-888. Rare $1,000

Quarter dollar patterns continued

E.847. Same, silver. Plain Edge. J-889. Rare $1,000
E.848. Same, copper. Reeded Edge. J-890. Rare $900
E.849. Same, copper. Plain Edge. J-891. Rare $900
E.849a. Same, copper-nickel. Reeded Edge. Unlisted in Judd. Unique?
E.850. Same, aluminum. Reeded Edge. J-892. Rare $800
E.851. Same, aluminum. Plain Edge. J-893. Rare $800
Note: For a bimetallic mule of this reverse with a 2 cents reverse, see the 2 cents listings.

Pattern Design Trial Piece of 1870, design
II – A (Bowers & Merena)

E.852. 1870 Pattern Design Trial Piece. Design II-A. Silver. Reeded Edge. J-912. Rare $1,000
E.853. Same, silver. Plain Edge. J-913. Rare $1,000
E.854. Same, copper. Reeded Edge. J-914. Rare $900
E.855. Same, copper. Plain Edge. J-915. Rare $900
E.856. Same, aluminum. Reeded Edge. J-916. Rare $800
E.857. Same, aluminum. Plain Edge. J-917. Rare $800

Pattern Design Trial Piece of 1870, design
II – B (Smithsonian)

E.858. 1870 Pattern Design Trial Piece. Design II-B. Silver. Reeded Edge. J-894. Rare $1,250
E.859. Same, silver. Plain Edge. J-895. Rare $1,250
E.860. Same, copper. Reeded Edge. J-896. Rare $1,000
E.861. Same, copper. Plain Edge. J-897. Rare $1,000
E.862. Same, aluminum. Reeded Edge. J-898. Rare $800
E.863. Same, aluminum. Plain Edge. J-899. Rare $800

Pattern Design Trial Piece of 1870, design
III – A (Bowers & Merena)

E.864. 1870 Pattern Design Trial Piece. Design III-A. Silver. Reeded Edge. J-918. Rare $1,250
E.865. Same, silver. Plain Edge. J-919. Rare. Eliasberg 5/96 P-64 .... $4,620
E.866. Same, copper. Reeded Edge. J-920. Rare $1,000
E.867. Same, copper. Plain Edge. J-921. Rare $1,000
E.868. Same, aluminum. Reeded Edge. J-922. Rare. $800
E.869. Same, aluminum. Plain Edge. J-923. Rare $800

Pattern Design Trial Piece of 1870, design
III – B (Smithsonian)

E.870. 1870 Pattern Design Trial Piece. Design III-B. Silver. Reeded Edge. J-900. Rare $2,500

Quarter dollar patterns continued

E.871. Same, silver. Plain Edge. J-901. Rare. ST 9/94, Ch. Br. Proof $2,600
E.872. Same, copper. Reeded Edge. J-902. Rare $1,000
E.873. Same, copper. Plain Edge. J-903. Rare $1,000
E.874. Same, aluminum. Reeded Edge. J-904. Rare $800
E.875. Same, aluminum. Plain Edge. J-905. Rare $800

Pattern Design Trial Piece of 1870, design IV (Harlan J. Berk Ltd.)

E.876. 1870 Pattern Design Trial Piece. Obv. IV: Liberty seated to left, shield and ribbon inscribed LIBERTY in right hand, olive branch in left, cap on pole behind, 13 stars around, date below. The Barber design. Rev. The regular design. Silver. Reeded Edge. J-882. Rare. Eliasberg 5/96 P-65 ....$4,620
  These patterns are far more difficult to locate than the rarity rating would indictate.
E.877. Same, silver. Plain Edge. J-883. Rare. Eliasberg 5/96 P-63/65 ....$5,280
E.878. Same, copper. Reeded Edge. J-884. Rare $1,400
E.879. Same, copper. Plain Edge. J-885. Rare $1,400
E.880. Same, aluminum. Reeded Edge. J-886. Rare $1,400
E.881. Same, aluminum. Plain Edge. J-887. Rare. 1.77 gms $1,400

Pattern Design Trial Piece of 1870, design IV – C (Superior Galleries)

E.882. 1870 Pattern Design Trial Piece. Obv. IV. Rev. C. Similar to Rev. B but no date. Silver. Reeded Edge. J-876. Rare $1,800
E.883. Same, silver. Plain Edge. J-877. Rare $1,800
E.884. Same, copper. Reeded Edge. J-878. Rare $1,000
E.885. Same, copper. Plain Edge. J-879. Rare $1,000
E.886. Same, aluminum. Reeded Edge. J-880. Rare $1,000
E.887. Same, aluminum. Plain Edge. J-881. Rare $1,000
E.888. 1871 Regular Design Trial Piece. Copper. Reeded Edge. J-1102. Very rare $800
E.889. Same, copper-nickel. Reeded Edge. J-1104. Very rare $1,000
E.890. Same, aluminum. Reeded Edge. J-1103. Very rare $800
E.891. 1871 Pattern Design Trial Piece. Obv. V. Liberty seated to left wearing Indian headdress, right hand supports pole with cap, left rests on globe inscribed LIBERTY. Two flags behind, date below, no stars in field. James B. Longacre design. Rev. Regular design. Silver. Reeded Edge. J -1093. Very rare . $3,000
  With all due respect to the Barber collectors, the creativity of these engravers (father and son) should be judged by contrast to their predecessor, Longacre. This pattern is merely one of the many that the elder Barber appropriated on Longacre's death, just as he did with the majority of the Standard Silver designs. With rare exception (such as the Amazonian designs and some of the 1877 pattern halves that he may have shared with his son), William Barber was not the most inspired of engravers; Charles Barber was a worthy successor to his father.
E.892. Same, copper. Reeded Edge. J-1094. Very rare $1,200
E.893. Same, aluminum. Reeded Edge. J-1095. Very rare $1,200

Pattern Design Trial Piece of 1871, design V – C (Superior Galleries)

E.894. 1871 Pattern Design Trial Piece. Design V-C. Silver. Reeded Edge. J-1090. Very rare $2,500
E.895. Same, copper. Reeded Edge. J-1091. Very rare $1,200

Quarter dollar patterns continued

E.896. Same, aluminum. Reeded Edge. J-1092. Very rare $1,200
E.897. 1871 Pattern Design Trial Piece. Obv. VI. Similar to Obv. V but 13 stars added around border. Rev. Regular design. Silver. Reeded Edge. J-1099. Very rare $2,500
E.898. Same, copper. Reeded Edge. J-1100. Very rare $1,200
E.899. Same, aluminum. Reeded Edge. J-1101. Very rare $1,200

Pattern Design Trial Piece of 1871, design VI – C (Smithsonian)

E.900. 1871 Pattern Design Trial Piece. Design VI-C. Silver. Reeded Edge. J-1096. Very rare. Eliasberg 5/96 P-65 .... $9,240
E.901. Same, copper. Reeded Edge. J-1097. Very rare $1,000
E.902. Same, aluminum. Reeded Edge. J-1098. Very rare $1,000
E.903. 1872 Regular Design Trial Piece. Copper. Reeded Edge. J-1198. Very rare $1,000
E.904. Same, aluminum. Reeded Edge. J-1199. Very rare $900

Pattern Design Trial Piece of 1872

E.905. 1872 Pattern Design Trial Piece. Obv. Liberty seated to left, her outstretched right arm seems to pat standing eagle on head. Left elbow rests on national shield, left hand holds sword that crosses shield. Date below, 13 stars around. Called William Barber's Amazonian design, even though sharp-eyed classicists will observe from Liberty's statuesque form that she is obviously not an Amazon. Rev. Standing eagle holding three arrows in right claw, left claw holds national shield and ribbon incused IGWT. USOA around, QUAR. DOL. below. Silver. Reeded Edge. J-1195. Very rare, this very beautiful and very popular design is repeated on half dollar and dollar patterns, but may have been rejected for its apparent heraldic militarism $18,500
　　One of the "big four" of patterns. (The others are Charles Barber's Washlady design of 1879 and Morgan's 1879 Schoolgirl and 1882 Shield Earring patterns.) The Amazonian patterns are hard to locate in the intended metal as they are in strong demand. It is interesting to note that the design does not appear to be quite finished, as the customary EPU and LIBERTY are missing.
E.906. Same, copper. Reeded Edge. J-1196. Very rare. A 3-piece Copper set of quarter, half dollar and dollar was sold in ST 6/94, see under dollars $7,500
E.907. Same, aluminum. Reeded Edge. J-1197. Very rare $5,000
E.908. 1873 Regular Design Trial Piece. Copper. Reeded Edge. J-1270. Very rare $1,500
E.909. Same, aluminum. Reeded Edge. J-1271. Very rare $1,000
E.910. 1874 Regular Design Trial Piece. Copper. Reeded Edge. J-1359. Very rare $1,500
E.911. Same, aluminum. Reeded Edge. J-1360. Very rare $1,000
E.912. 1875 Regular Design Trial Piece. Copper. Reeded Edge. J-1416. Very rare $1,500
E.913. Same, aluminum. Reeded Edge. J-1417. Very rare $1,000
E.914. 1876 Regular Design Trial Piece. Copper. Reeded Edge. J-1455. Very rare $1,500

Pattern Design Trial Piece of 1877 (Bowers & Merena)

E.915. 1877 Pattern Design Trial Piece. Obv: Liberty (or Sailor) head left in coronet inscribed LIBERTY, date below, Tiny IGWT at upper border. Seven stars left border, six right. Rev: Regular design. Silver. Reeded Edge. J-1499. Very rare $8,000
E.916. Same, copper. Reeded Edge. J-1500. Very rare $4,500

Quarter dollar patterns continued

E.917. 1879 Regular Design Trial Piece. White metal. Plain Edge. J-1595. Very rare. Part of an unusual set of plain edge white metal quarters struck this year.

Pattern Design Trial Piece of 1879,
Washlady (Smithsonian)

E.918. 1879 Pattern Design Trial Piece. Obv. Liberty head left with wavy hair piled up in back, ribbon inscribed LIBERTY supports wheat ear and cotton boll above forehead. Date below, small IGWT at upper border, seven stars left border, six right. Charles E. Barber's Washlady design. Rev. Eagle holds olive branch in right claw and three arrows in left. USOA and tiny IGWT curve around upper border, QUAR. DOLLAR at bottom. Silver. Reeded Edge. J-1590. Very rare $12,500
   Proof that competition brings out the very best in what was otherwise the pedestrian. The Barber duo (father and son) produced little of artistic note at the beginning of their 40 years of control of the Mint's engraving staff, with the exception of the Amazonian silver and gold patterns of 1872. With the arrival of Morgan, and a threat to their position by another Englishman, the creative juices flowed as never before, with the Barber contributions to the 1877 "sweepstakes" and coins such as this coming forth to match Morgan's offerings. Long thought to be the finest of the Barber designs, these patterns seem to be more readily available in all metals and denominations than the corresponding Morgan Schoolgirl patterns of this year and the Shield Earring patterns of 1882. Since there was a Barber sitting in the Chief Engraver's chair from Longacre's death in 1869 until the First World War, it is hardly a surprise that more Barber patterns happened to be struck than the designs of their talented Assistant Engraver. (On the other hand, Morgan's conduct in attempting to interfere with the production of the Peace dollar and other fits of temper show that he learned a lot from his obnoxiously long-lived compatriots.)

E.919. Same, copper. Reeded Edge. J-1591. Very rare $5,000
E.920. Same, white metal. Plain Edge. J-1592. Unique?
E.921. 1879 Mule. Obv. Same as preceding. Rev. Regular design. White metal. Plain Edge. J-1596. Unique?

Pattern Design Trial Piece of 1879 (Superior
Galleries)

E.922. 1879 Pattern Design Trial Piece. Obv. Liberty head left as on Morgan dollar, date below. E PLURIBUS at left border, UNUM at right, seven stars above head, six below. Rev. Facing eagle with olive branch and three arrows, USOA at upper border, QUARTER DOLLAR at lower. Tiny IGWT around lower half of eagle, inside other legends. Silver. Reeded Edge. J-1593. Very rare. BM 3/94, P P-64 .... $8,800
   This "miniature Morgan dollar" has been underappreciated because of its rarity. A superb example in the Heritage 1994 ANA Sale brought intense bidding and a substantial price.

E.923. Same, copper. Reeded Edge. J-1594. Very rare $4,000
E.924. Same, white metal. Plain Edge. J-1594a. Unique?

Pattern Design Trial Piece of 1882 (Superior
Galleries)

E.925. 1882 Pattern Design Trial Piece. Obv. Liberty head right with long flowing hair, headband inscribed LIBERTY, wearing small national shield as earring. Date below, EPU around upper border, seven stars lower left, six lower right. Rev. Defiant eagle to right, perched on olive branch and three arrows, USOA around, QUARTER DOLLAR below. Silver. Reeded Edge. J-1698. Very rare. BM 3/94, P P-64 $14,300; Eliasberg 5/96 P-65 .... $30,800

Quarter dollar patterns continued

Known as the Morgan Shield Earring design, this pattern is considered by many to be this engraver's *magnum opus*, while the dissenters prefer his Schoolgirl design on an 1879 dollar. The engraver placed the initial 'M' in a prominent manner on the truncation. Comparison of the profile of this pattern and the 1879 design shows that the head almost the same as the earlier design. Liberty's coiffure is quite different but both coins use a variation on the defiant eagle theme for the reverse. Many early catalogs state that 10 to 12 silver sets were thought to be made, which appears to be correct. The last time all three silver pieces appeared together at auction was in BR 1981 Sieck ANA Sale, one of the most comprehensive collections of patterns ever assembled for auction and a catalog on the must-have list if one is at all serious about collecting patterns. All described as Proof-67, the dollar brought $28,000, half dollar, $9,500; the quarter, $5,500.

E.926. Same, copper. Reeded Edge. J-1699. Very rare $4,000
E.927. 1884 Regular Design Trial Piece. Copper. Reeded Edge. J-1729. Very rare $4,000
E.928. 1885 Regular Design Trial Piece. Aluminum. Reeded Edge. J-1745. Very rare $3,000
E.929. 1891 Pattern Design Trial Piece. Obv: Barber's Liberty head right with cap and laurel wreath, date below, IGWT at upper border. Seven six-pointed stars left, six right. Rev. Heraldic eagle under clouds recalling rev. of 1804-07 quarters, QUARTER DOLLAR at lower border, five-pointed stars above eagle. Silver. Reeded Edge. J-1761. Two known, Smithsonian.

Note: Uniface electrotypes by James Fraser exist for a proposed 1915 Panama-Pacific quarter which was never authorized, bearing tree and farmer in field wielding sickle.

E.930. 1916 Pattern Design Trial Piece. Obv. Variant of Hermon MacNeil's semi-nude Liberty standing in motto- and star-bearing gate, outstretched right arm holding an olive branch, left arm holding a partially uncovered shield, LIBERTY at upper border, date below, dot-dash border. No designer's initial M to right of feet. Rev. Eagle flying to right, UNITED STATES at upper border, OF AMERICA below that, E PLURIBUS UNUM below that, QUARTER DOLLAR at lower border. Seven stars left border, six right. Silver. Reeded Edge. J-1795. Very rare $7,500
E.931. 1916 Pattern Design Trial Piece. Obv. Same as preceding. Rev. Similar to preceding except eagle higher in field, as on reverse of 1917, but with stars removed and a stylized laurel wreath at right and left border. Silver. Reeded Edge. J-1796a. Very rare $6,500
E.932. 1916 Pattern Design Trial Piece. Obv. Similar to preceding except designer's initial added to right of feet. The adopted design of 1916. Rev. Same as preceding. Silver. Reeded Edge. J-1796. Very rare $6,500

Additional minor changes were made to the obverse design before 1917 coinage began, most noticeably in the hair and the drapery to the left of the feet. Both sides were reworked later in the year to eliminate Liberty's classic toplessness.

Note: Uniface trial strikes exist for the reverse of the 1932 Washington quarter.

Metallurgical trial of 1965

E.933. (1965) Martha Washington Metallurgical Trial Piece. See 10 cents listing.

Metallurgical trial of 1965 (Thomas K. DeLorey)

E.934. (1965) Metallurgical Trial Piece. Obv. Paul D. Merica bust r. Rev. Aerial view of International Nickel Company (INCO) Merica Laboratory, date 1964 below. Struck in experimental alloys including copper-nickel clad copper and various nickel-silicon combinations, some pieces hand-engraved with their composition on obverse. Dies by Gilroy Roberts, struck by Medallic Art Company. BM 1/91 sale, Iron $495; Nickel (magnetic) $550 .... $650

Quarter dollar patterns continued

Metallurgical trial of 1965 (Thomas K.
DeLorey)

E.935. (1965) Similar to preceding but larger diameter with different, smaller style of bust and laboratory
view. Struck by Franklin Mint $500

It is ironic that INCO invented the copper clad alloy actually adopted by the U.S. Mint, but
spent most of its time in a vain effort to promote its favored mostly nickel silicon-bearing alloys.
INCO did, after all, produce and sell nickel.

Promotional trial of 1976 (Thomas K.
DeLorey)

E.936. 1976 Promotional Trial Piece. Obv. Bicentennial quarter design, without Mint mark. Rev. Bicentennial
quarter design, 40% silver. Reeded Edge. Proof. May no longer exist.

Several 40% silver three-piece Proof sets were struck at the Philadelphia Mint without Mint
marks on August 12, 1974, for display at the ANA convention and for presentation to the
designers of the three coins and a representative of just-inaugurated President Gerald R. Ford,
who understandably was too busy to attend the ceremony. Allegedly all were returned to the
Mint and replaced with regular Proof coins at a later date.

Half dollars

Note: Judd lists as J-17 two copper trial pieces for the 1794 half dollar cut down and struck as 1794 half cents for general circulation. Another piece used as a 1795 half dollar trial piece was cut down and used as a 1795 half cent, J-22.

Note: 1813 pieces listed as J-42, -42a and -43 are private restrikes using an 1810 reverse.

Metallurgical trial

E.937. 1814 Metallurgical Trial Piece. The regular design, O-107. Platinum, Lettered Edge. J-44. Three known, one in Smithsonian, another punched 33 times with a letter P, engraved PLATINA above the eagle. Reason for striking unknown.

Note: Copper 1823 pieces listed as J-47 are probably contemporary counterfeits.

Note: 1836 Reeded Edge halves listed as J-57 are regular issue coins of a revised design which was not struck in large numbers until the following year.

Note: Because of the numerous die pairings used for the pattern half dollars, the obverse designs will be identified with Roman numerals and the reverse designs with letters.

E.937a. 1838 Regular Design Trial Piece Copper. Reeded Edge. Unlisted in Judd. Unique?

*Pattern Design Trial Piece of 1838, obverse I
(Smithsonian)*

E.938. 1838 Pattern Design Trial Piece. Obv. I: Similar to the regular Capped Bust left design except cap replaced by coronet or diadem and ribbon labeled LIBERTY, date below, seven stars left, six right. Rev: The regular reverse of 1838-39. Silver. Reeded Edge. J-75. Two reported, originals only, unique today?

*Pattern Design Trial Piece of 1838, design
I – A*

E.939. 1838 Pattern Design Trial Piece. Obv. I. Rev. A: Facing eagle grasping olive branch and arrows, USOA and HALF DOLLAR around. Silver. Reeded Edge. J-72. Originals, c.13.36 gms., rare and restrikes, c.12.44 gms., scarce $6,500

Half dollar patterns continued

1. This obverse is said to the last work of William Kneass, although there is no paper trail to support this. The reverse is said to be the work of Gobrecht, with the same *caveat*. This coin, followed to a lesser degree by E.940, are easily the most available early half dollar patterns by a wide margin. For some reason now unknown, perhaps that the other pattern obverses were no longer suitable for use or did not last as long when tried, these coins were restruck in relatively large numbers in the late 1850s and possibly again in the 1868 time period. The restrikes can be told by the progressive weakness of the obverse, which was apparently hauled out and mated with the rapidly deteriorating reverse until the die polishing and fiddling becomes obvious even to the newest collector. Indeed, except for weights (whether restriking patterns or creating novodels such as the 1801-03 Proof dollars) there would appear to be a real question if more than a tiny number of originals exist. Nonetheless, the plethora of restrikes has kept the premium (if any) paid for an original at a minimum.

2. Despite the fact that this is one of the few "large" early patterns that can be located in the intended metal, it is remarkably difficult to locate in truly nice condition. Several of those that have been found are late restrikes, where the die polishing and other efforts to salvage the dies is plainly evident. These late examples also show excellent eye appeal and have brought surprisingly strong prices.

E.939a. Same, copper, Reeded Edge. Unlisted in Judd. Unique? Unverified.

Pattern Design Trial Piece of 1838, design I – B

E.940. 1838 Pattern Design Trial Piece. Obv. I. Rev. B: Flying eagle to left. USOA and HALF DOLLAR around. Silver. Reeded Edge. J- 73. Originals very rare, restrikes rare $7,500

1. Although clearly rarer than the preceding pattern, this pattern is far more available than any of the other 1838 and 1839 pattern half dollars. Many of the same comments that apply to E.939 apply to this pattern as well. The difference in the number available is a function of the condition of the reverse die, the real point of interest in this die marriage and a critical point in determining the design history of what later became the Liberty Seated regular issue coinage.

2. Originals can be distinguished from restrikes by weight, but also by the most casual inspection of the reverse. As will be discussed in more detail in the notes under E. 949, this reverse, even though first used after the Flying Eagle reverse was prepared for and used on the 1836 Gobrecht Dollars, is a slightly earlier version of the Flying Eagle design with several subtle, but important, differences. The reverse cracked when it was first used. The progression of the crack on this reverse and on other patterns which made use of it (until it presumably failed entirely) allows the "originals" to be quickly set apart from the restrikes — and also allows early restrikes to be set apart from the last examples, in which the massive cracks on the reverse reach a remarkable level.

E.941. Same, copper. Reeded Edge. J-74. Restrike only, Unique?
This obverse was used again in 1859 (q.v.).

E.942. 1838 Pattern Design Trial Piece. Obv. II: The No Drapery Seated Liberty design, but with LIBERTY on shield raised. Rev: The regular design of 1836-37 with 50 CENTS. Silver. Reeded Edge. J-82. Originals extremely rare, restrike unique? Die varieties exist $20,000

1. The 1838 and 1839 pattern half dollars are extreme rarities that are underappreciated by all but the more astute pattern enthusiasts, who snap up any of these coins as soon as they appear on the market. Although it is outside the scope of these brief notes, any student of U.S. coinage should be aware of the intense burst of concentrated effort that began at the Mint when Robert Patterson became its Director in 1835. Calling upon the services of Gobrecht, Peale, Hughes and others, Patterson attempted to create coinage that would satisfy even the most critical artistic demands and serve as an example of the very best that the then-young American Republic could produce in the face of European opinion that held us to be a brash collection of the boorish and the crude. This story is told in detail in Taxay's excellent history of the Mint. The role played by these patterns can be viewed in more detail in Breen's *Secret History of the Gobrecht Coinages.* The dies used to strike the 1836 dollars are the final versions of what came out of this period of development. These later-dated half dollar patterns are important as they use earlier versions of the final pattern designs and/or variations on these designs that provide the student with the only surviving examples of this critical period in the development of both the Seated Liberty series and the Mint itself.

2. The finest and most complete collection of these early pattern half dollars was the Witham Collection sold by Rarcoa in its session of Auction '81. The notes in that catalog provided important information that had been overlooked in Judd and earlier works as well as pointing out certain errors that could not be detected without close examination of these patterns. Some of those comments were picked up in later editions of Judd and elsewhere. The catalog still remains important for a more detailed study of these patterns.

Half dollar patterns continued

Pattern Design Trial Piece of 1838, obverse II (Smithsonian)

E.943. 1838 Pattern Design Trial Piece. Obv. II. Rev: The regular design of 1838-39 with HALF DOL. Silver. Reeded Edge. J-83. Originals only, extremely rare $20,000

Pattern Design Trial Piece of 1838, design II – B

E.944. 1838 Pattern Design Trial Piece. Design II-B. Silver. Reeded Edge. J-79. Originals and restrikes both extremely rare, die varieties exist $25,000
See E.949, below.

Pattern Design Trial Piece of 1838, design III – A

E.945. 1838 Pattern Design Trial Piece. Obv. III: Similar to preceding except LIBERTY on shield incused. The design adopted in 1839. Rev. A. Silver. Plain Edge. J-76. Originals and restrikes both extremely rare, die varieties exist $22,000
E.946. Same, silver. Reeded Edge. J-76a. Restrikes only, extremely rare $20,000
E.947. Same, copper. Plain Edge. J-77. Restrikes only, extremely rare $12,000
E.948. Same, copper. Reeded Edge. J-78. Restrikes only, extremely rare $12,000
E.949. 1838 Pattern Design Trial Piece. Design III-B. Silver. Reeded Edge. J-79a. Originals only, extremely rare $25,000

     1. This pattern and its almost identical brother E.944 have long been prized as 'baby Gobrecht dollars.' They fit that description only in the general sense, but their true importance as a physical link in the development of the Liberty Seated series has been overlooked in every work before these notes. The similarities and the differences between the earlier-dated 1836 dollar pattern coins (but later-struck 1836 dollar pattern dies) and these later-struck coins (but earlier-struck dies) requires close study. Once they are noted, they can be seen in many of the better photographs of their rare auction appearances. Taxay and Breen both discuss letters they found in the National Archives and elsewhere that show that Patterson, Gobrecht and the others involved in the creation of the Liberty Seated design had far more trouble producing a suitable and natural-appearing eagle for the reverse than they did in reaching a consensus on the obverse design. (Please see those works for the background of these notes.) There was some concern about depicting an eagle flying along with the obviously-contrived impediments of arrows and an olive branch. (See the notes to E.950 immediately below.) Indeed, the eagle did not look like it was flying at all, adopting a stance not dissimilar to the Morgan reverses of the late 1870s and later referred to as defiant. This was not what Patterson had in mind in his pursuit of a natural-appearing eagle. Once that problem was identified by review of some splashers and uniface strikes in brass made from the initial die that had been made for the reverse for this series (later used to create E.950), the reverse die was modified to remove the

Half dollar patterns continued

arrows and olive branch, resulting in the reverse used for this and the other 1838-39 pattern half dollars. The focus of the letters and discussions then turned to the appearance of the eagle's mouth and neck feathers on this reverse. The eagle's mouth is open on this reverse, and the neck feathers are ruffled and erect on the back of the bird's neck. There was quite a bit of writing up and back about these features, which were defended as conforming with nature since the neck feathers on a live eagle would only be ruffled when the mouth was open. A comparison of the reverse of any of the 1836-39 dollars and these coins show that the reverse die was altered to close the eagle's mouth and smooth the neck feathers, showing that Patterson refused to sacrifice accuracy for artistic license. Another change that has not been discussed before but which shows that these dies were struck before those used on the earlier-dated dollar patterns is the general appearance of the eagle and the positioning of the eagle in relation to the reverse itself. In keeping with an accurate depiction of what would appear in nature, on the screaming eagle (*i.e.* with the mouth open and the neck feathers ruffled) the eagle's neck is more curved and the bird itself slightly more compacted than the eagle which is depicted in more easy flight as used on the reverse for the dollar. The eagle on the dollar is also depicted as flying upwards. The beak of the eagle on the dollar patterns is between the I and T in UNITED. However, on the E.940, these patterns and all of the other 1838-39 pattern half dollars (which on the basis of their weights and other factors can be shown to have been struck in this period) with the very significant exception of the reverse eventually completed for E. 950, the beak is between the U and the N of UNITED, leaving the eagle flying level.

2. This latter distinction between this reverse die and the die used for the 1836-39 dollar coins is of critical importance not only in relation to these patterns but also with regard to some long-established notions regarding the method of distinguishing original strikes of the Gobrecht dollars and restrikes. Many experts have carefully separated original strikes of these dollars from restrikes by weight and die state, but most importantly by die alignment, including the distinction between those coins which have the eagle flying upwards (thought to be the mark of an original strike) and coins where the eagle is flying level — what has heretofore been considered to be the most telling mark of a restrike. The 1839 half dollar patterns, however, use a reverse in which the eagle (when struck after the 1836 original dollars patterns) was shown flying level. And, when the die for E.950 was indubitably completed in the 1858 period, and the lettering and other details added to the reverse, the eagle was depicted as flying upwards. (The eagle's beak on that die is positioned between the I and the T of UNITED, the same point as the beak on the original 1836 dollar patterns.) Whoever completed the reverse die for E.950 in the 1858 time period (or even in the next decade when it is suggested that the restriking of the Gobrecht dollars was in full swing) positioned the eagle on that die quite differently from the other restrikes supposedly created at this same time with the eagle flying level as either the intentional or accidental (but always consistent) mark of a restrike. There is then simply no way to square the "original equals upwards" and "level equals restrike" theory with the evidence reflected in the letters of the Mint and the physical fabric of these 1839 half dollar patterns, including the reverse for E.950, which was clearly one of the first (if not the first) Flying Eagle reverses created, but not completed until 1858 or later. The author does not claim to have the expertise possessed by others who have studied the 1836-39 Gobrecht dollars, but he does respectfully submit that the evidence provided by these 1839 patterns cannot be ignored. It may be that the numismatic community has erred in attributing a Gobrecht dollar as an original or a restrike based the orientation of the eagle as depicted on the reverse.

3. The problem of original or restrike cannot be resolved by simply concluding that all of the 1839 half dollar patterns are backdated restrikes (even if we were to ignore the anomaly of E.950.) For example, the coin in Superior's Heifetz Sale, lot #3245, attributed there as "J-79" (E.944) is correctly noted to be Garrett I lot #365. The color and black and white photos show distinct color and toning that cannot be questioned. The coin was attributed in Garrett as J-79 since the distinction between this obverse (E.949 with an incuse LIBERTY on the shield) and what is now recognized as J-79 or E.944 (with LIBERTY in raised letters on the shield) was not recognized in Judd until the comments on this error appeared in the Rarcoa section of Auction '81. The problem was corrected in the final edition of Judd that appeared in 1982. The misattribution of the Garrett coin has continued until this publication.) The pedigree of the Garrett coin was "ex-Ed. Frossard, May 6, 1882." After Garrett, this coin appeared as lot 696 in BM 1/88 Higgins Sale. In each of these sales, and in the Heifetz Sale, the coin was correctly noted as an original strike of 1839. The coin is now correctly attributed in a PCGS PR-65 holder and has been carefully examined by several experts. The condition of the coin (which is spectacular and which shows that the obverse was a very early die state), its weight, reed count, and the die state of both the obverse and the reverse (including the critical factor of the state and lack of progression of the reverse die crack) confirm that it was struck in 1839. A quick glance at any of the catalogs noted above will show that the eagle is flying level. At the same time, a glance at the photo of E.950 as Auction '90, lot #882, or before that as lot #448 in Superior's 6/77 Crouch Collection Sale, or before that as lot #3597 in Stack's 8/76 ANA Sale, will show that the eagle on that pattern is flying upwards, on what is plainly a die completed in 1858 or afterwards. In light of this, I suggest that using the die alignment theory to separate original and restrikes in the Gobrecht Dollar series needs to be reconsidered.

E.950. 1838 Fantasy Restrike. Obv. III. Rev. C: Flying eagle to left clutching olive branch and six arrows, USOA and HALF DOL. around. This design was a partly completed, early Gobrecht Flying eagle punch, finished on a newly created die by the addition of lettering and denticles some 20 years later and then used to create a fantasy restrike. Never used on a contemporaneous pattern so no originals could exist. Silver. Reeded Edge. J-80. Restrikes only, extremely rare $20,000

Half dollar patterns continued

    1. In addition to the significance of this pattern as shown by the notes to the preceding pattern (E.949), this coin has been misunderstood in every prior discussion. While this die marriage itself was not consummated until 20 years or more after the date on its obverse, the resulting union, as well as the reverse, is a vital link in any study of the Mint or the work of Christian Gobrecht.

    2. This pattern exists only as a restrike for the reasons discussed below. Its condition is a function of its creation. The centers of both obverse and reverse are always weakly struck and the central design elements are obscured. By the time the original obverse was used (and the obverse on at least one specimen examined proved to be a far later state of a die used to strike the Garrett E.949 many years before) it had been put to extensive use striking both originals and restrikes. Given the usage and the age of the obverse, and the fresh state of the newly-completed reverse, expecting the central elements of the design to strike up would be inconsistent with the mechanics of coin production. The strike on the design elements nearer to the rims of the specimen examined, particularly on the reverse, show that those portions of the die were newly-completed when the coin was struck. Since that specimen was as-struck, its grade in an early PCGS PR-63 holder would be consistent with its technical grade but too harsh in light of the history of the design. It is as good as it could be, and has remained in the same condition other than acquiring its toning, for the last century and a half. (See the photos of this coin for the typical die state and appearance as ex-Rarcoa, Auction '90, lot #882. See also lot #448, Superior's 6/77 Crouch Collection, and lot #3597 in Stack's 1976 ANA Sale.

    3. There has always been some lingering question as to the authenticity or legitimacy of this reverse. The fact that it was a very early Gobrecht reverse trial was made clear in an article in the 1991 ANA *Centennial Anthology*, by Elvira Clain-Stefanelli which discusses and provides photos of what is described there as an incomplete hub trial in brass for a half dollar pattern. The photo shows what would later become the reverse of this pattern before the lettering, including the denomination, and the denticles were added. The center is fully stuck and it is clear from its condition that it was struck many years before the hub was used to create this pattern die. The article also reproduces drawings obtained from the Gobrecht family, which includes a drawing that is unmistakably this reverse. Further evidence of the lineage of this reverse can be found in Mrs. Stefanelli's 1974 book, *The Beauty and Lore of Coins*, written with her late husband Vladimir Clain-Stefanelli, who were then the curators of the numismatic section of the Smithsonian. The book contains clear photographs of several patterns, hubs and the like from the National Numismatic Collections. On page 161, photo No. 200 is a large (apparently four-inch) bronze disk which is clearly the eagle, with arrows and a branch, eventually used to strike E.950 and 951. The photo also contains the bronze hub trial later pictured in the 1991 *ANA Anthology* as well as a photo of the completed pattern reverse.

    4. The lettering used for the reverse is very similar to that used on other patterns of the 1838-39 period. However, the pellets that flank the denomination are simple points, unlike the more elaborate pellets on the half dollar and dollar patterns struck from dies completed during the earlier period. The denticles are clearly those of the 1858 period and are far larger and more distinct than those of the obverse.

    5. No more than three to five examples of this pattern exist. Although the pattern was struck from a hub or die completed in the late 1850s, the fact that it provides the only physical evidence of the original concept for what later became the Flying Eagle reverse now so avidly sought by collectors makes this pattern far more important than previously thought. It not only provides the historical link noted above, but is mute testimony of the manner in which the Mint practice of creating fantasy restrikes was carried out. In this instance, the greed of 150 years ago has had the unforeseen but beneficial effect of preserving in a pattern that which would have been otherwise lost when this and other incomplete hubs were eventually destroyed. All that is necessary to complete this happy accident is give this pattern the recognition it so justly deserves without the stigma it has borne for too long.

E.951. Same, copper. Reeded Edge. J-81. Restrikes only, very rare $12,500

Restrike of 1839 (Bowers & Merena)

E.952. 1839 Restrike. Obv. The regular 1836-39 Capped Bust design. Reverse A. Silver. Reeded Edge. J-99. Restrikes only, extremely rare $18,000

E.953. 1839 Restrike. Obv. Same as preceding. Rev. B. Silver. Reeded Edge. J-100. Restrikes only, extremely rare $18,000

Half dollar patterns continued

E.954. 1839 Restrike? Obv. Same as preceding. Rev. D: Similar to the regular design of 1839-42 with small eagle and lettering, except with medium-sized lettering similar to that on 1838-39 Capped Bust halves. Letters AME in AMERICA touch, or nearly so. Silver. Reeded Edge. J-100a. Excessively rare ... $18,000
    This may be a transitional design with the new eagle but the old lettering, in which case it could be a Revised Design Trial Piece rather than a restrike. Only known in circulated condition, unlike other pieces with Rev. D which are Proof restrikes.

E.955. 1839 Restrike. Design III-A. Silver. Plain Edge. J-101. Restrike only, unique?

E.956. 1839 Restrike. Design III-B. Silver. Reeded Edge. J-102. Restrikes only, extremely rare. The Farouk sale listed a Plain Edge specimen, unconfirmed $18,000

E.957. 1839 Restrike? Design III-D. Copper. Reeded Edge. J-103. Probably Restrike only. extremely rare $8,000

Pattern Design Trial Piece of 1839, obverse IV (Smithsonian)

E.958. 1839 Pattern Design Trial Piece. Obv. IV: Liberty head right wearing coronet labeled LIBERTY, date below, 13 stars around. Rev. The regular design of 1839-42. Silver. Reeded Edge. J-93. Originals only, extremely rare. Eliasberg 5/96 P-65 ..... $19,800
    1. Known as the Twisted Hair obverse, this Gobrecht design is yet another of the extremely rare and highly significant early half dollar patterns that virtually never show up on the market. The Twisted Hair obverse should be recognized as what Gobrecht contemplated as a next step after the adoption of the Seated Liberty design or as a possible alternative for that design, which was still being criticized in some governmental circles. Had the final, With Drapery designs (which were adopted in 1840 on all other denominations) not been accepted, this obverse appears to be Gobrecht's answer to the problems raised as to his earlier work. Indeed, in light of the fact that Hughes and others had been brought in to change Gobrecht's original creation, this new design shows that Gobrecht was ready for a radical change in direction.
    2. Although there is no paper trail to show why this obverse was created, the preceding explanation conforms with the evidence we do have regarding the early changes made to the Seated Liberty design after Gobrecht finished with his efforts, as well as the physical evidence provided for by these patterns themselves. While it has been said that this obverse is very much like that which Gobrecht created for his gold coins or based on some of the elements of the contemporaneous large cents, there are certain design features that show this pattern was intended for silver coinage and not simply a rehash of a gold design struck as a pattern in silver. This design has LIBERTY on the coronet incuse, as never done on gold but always done on silver coins, with the exception of the adopted 20-cent design. The cords binding the hair on this pattern are plain, rather than beaded as on the gold coinage. This type of cord was last used on the 1837 Coronet large cents. The 1838 Coronet cents and the 1838 and later gold heads similar to this pattern used a beaded cord. This was clearly then a new design intended by Gobrecht as a viable alternative for the silver denominations he had originally designed but which were then under attack. In light of the fact that there was still a considerable question as to whether the Liberty Seated design would continue to enjoy official support, and also as an answer to the design's critics, Gobrecht created this design.
    3. This die marriage is considered by Breen in his *Secret History* to be "the only genuine pattern half-dollar of 1839 so far as I know, the others being restrikes or mules." The reason for this can be seen in the reverse itself. There are several die cracks in the reverse used on this pattern that continued to progress when the same reverse was used to coin the very small number of regular issue Proof half dollars of 1839. An example of this very rare Proof showed up in 1993 as lot #712 in Superior's 9/93 Worrell Collection Sale. Comparison of that coin and an example of this pattern before the sale showed that the regular issue Proof used the same die, except with die cracks that were far more pronounced than on this pattern. (These cracks are apparent in the catalog photographs.)
    4. The relatively mild cracking on this pattern reverse, and the more massive cracks that can be seen where this same reverse was used to coin the regular issue Proofs of the same year also provide a fascinating view of the wave of Mint restrikes of the 1850s. Given the fame of the early Gobrecht dollars, pattern half dollars with the Flying Eagle reverse were among the first patterns restruck during the 1850s as those most likely to bring a strong price. The massive (and additional) die cracks on the remaining Flying Eagle half dollar reverse were ignored as long as possible, as the progression of pattern restrikes with ever-growing and even new die cracks continued to be struck in an almost bewildering variety. (Those restrikes also included a few with this obverse, E.962-63.) When that reverse finally failed, after it was used over and over again despite its rapidly-developing cracks, the incomplete hub of an early version of the Flying Eagle

Half dollar patterns continued

reverse was pulled out of storage and completed with modern-style lettering and denticles, showing how and why E. 950 was born. When that die marriage proved to be a failure as the obverse was just too old and deteriorated, the search started for anything connected to Gobrecht that could be turned out to make a profit. Since the Twisted Hair obverse was relatively unused after striking between four and eight original patterns and then put aside when the 1840 Hughes design proved acceptable, the Mint turned to this die. As the original reverse had long ago failed, an even older reverse was tried first (the reverse from the Reeded Edge half dollars, resulting in E.964-65) and then the reverse from a then-current regular issue half dollar, producing E.960-61.

E.959. Same, copper. Reeded Edge. J-94. Very rare $14,000
E.960. 1839 Restrike. Obv. IV. Rev. The regular design of 1842-64. Silver. Reeded Edge. J-97. Restrikes only, very rare $22,000
E.961. Same, copper. Reeded Edge. J-98. Restrikes only, very rare $14,000
E.962. 1839 Restrike. Design IV-B. Silver. Reeded Edge. J-91. Restrikes only, very rare $22,000
E.963. Same, copper. Reeded Edge. J-92. Restrikes only, very rare $14,000
E.964. 1839 Restrike. Design IV-D. Silver. Reeded Edge. J-95. Restrikes only, very rare $22,000
E.965. Same, copper. Reeded Edge. J-96. Very rare $14,000
E.966. 1855 Regular Design Trial Piece. Aluminum. Reeded Edge. J-175. Unique, Princeton University coll.
E.967. 1858 Revised Design Trial Piece. Obv. The regular design. Rev. E: Similar to the regular design except eagle taller and thinner, lettering in different style, eagle's beak holds ribbon inscribed EPU. The Paquet design. Silver. Reeded Edge. J-222. Extremely rare $11,000
    This same reverse design was used for the 25-cent companion to this pattern, E.790. Unlike that die marriage, however, this combination was not repeated over the course of the next decade. It appears that only three or four of these coins may have been struck since, as rare as the 25-cent pattern may be, this pattern is even more difficult to locate.
E.968. Same, copper. Reeded Edge. J-223. Unique, defaced $2,400
E.969. (1838) Backdated Fantasy. Obv. I, dated 1838. Rev. E. Silver. Reeded Edge. J-254. Extremely rare, believed struck in 1859 .... $7,500
    For all of its undoubted rarity, even by pattern standards, this pattern's very obvious "bar sinister" and the generally poor condition of those coins that were struck has kept its value low.
E.970. Same, copper. Reeded Edge. J-255. Extremely rare $2,000
E.971. 1859 Mule. Obv. V: Liberty head right wearing wreath of oak and laurel, ribbon at neck incused LIBERTY, USOA around, date below. The Longacre Design. This head also used on the Assay Commission medals of 1860, 1861 and 1867. Rev. The regular design. Silver. Reeded Edge. J-243. Very rare $1,800
    1. The 1859 Longacre and Paquet are the most plentiful of the pre-Civil War patterns other than the Gobrecht dollars, the various 1-cent patterns, and the Peale trime (E.510). Although they were struck in large number, they are difficult to locate in Choice condition since they were given away as presents to children or otherwise treated as novelties. Still, even the finest do not fetch an overwhelming price.
    2. Many of the mules in this series are of extreme rarity — and elicit little more than a yawn when they appear infrequently on the market. Much like the mules and off-metal strikes of the Standard Silver series, these recognized rarities are worth a premium only to those working on completion of a set of the series in various die marriages or metals or both. (Not a bad idea for an interesting collection — just don't count on putting the kids through college on the profits when the collection is sold.)
E.972. Same, copper. Reeded Edge. J-244. Very rare $1,500

Mule of 1859, design V – E (Bowers & Merena)

E.973. 1859 Mule. Design V-E. Silver. Reeded Edge. J-245. Very rare. Reverse die varieties reported. Eliasberg 5/96 P-63 .... $4,070
E.974. Same, copper. Reeded Edge. J-246. Very rare $1,500
E.975. 1859 Pattern Design Trial Piece. Obv. V. Rev. F: HALF DOLLAR within wreath of corn, wheat, cotton, tobacco, sugar cane and oak leaves. Silver. Reeded Edge. J-237. Scarce $1,250
E.976. Same, copper. Reeded Edge. J-238. Scarce. Eliasberg 5/96 P-66 .... $3,190

Half dollar patterns continued

Pattern Design Trial Piece of 1859, design V–G

E.977. 1859 Pattern Design Trial Piece. Obv. V. Rev. G: Similar to preceding except large 1/2 DOLLAR within wreath. Silver. Reeded Edge. J-239. Scarce $900

E.978. Same, copper. Reeded Edge. J-240. Scarce. ST 6/94, Ch. Br. Proof $1,600; Eliasberg 5/96 P-65 $2,530

Pattern Design Trial Piece of 1859, design V – H (Smithsonian)

E.979. 1859 Pattern Design Trial Piece. Obv. V. Rev. H: Similar to preceding except 50 CENTS within wreath. Silver. Reeded Edge. J-241. Scarce $1,750

E.980. Same, copper. Reeded Edge. J-242. Scarce $1,250

Pattern Design Trial Piece of 1859, design VI – E (Smithsonian)

E.981. 1859 Pattern Design Trial Piece. Obv. VI: Liberty Seated to left, right hand supports fasces; left hand rests on national shield. Olive branch and three arrows at base of shield. 13 stars around, date below. The Paquet design. A similar design with an eagle partly behind the shield was used on a $20 pattern, E.1820-21a. Rev. E. Silver. Reeded Edge. J-235. Scarce. Reverse die varieties reported of this and next. Eliasberg 5/96 P-65 .... $4,400

E.982. Same, copper. Reeded Edge. J-236. Scarce. BM 3/94, P-63 .... $1,540

E.983. 1859 Mule. Design VI-F. Silver. Reeded Edge. J-247. Very rare. ST 9/94, Proof $1,400

E.984. Same, copper. Reeded Edge. J-248. Very rare $1,200

E.985. 1859 Mule. Design VI-G. Silver. Reeded Edge. J-249. Very rare. ST 9/94, Proof $1,600

E.986. Same, copper. Reeded Edge. J-250. Very rare $1,200

E.987. 1859 Mule. Design VI-H. Silver. Reeded Edge. J-251. Very rare. ST 9/94, Br. Proof $2,300

E.988. Same, copper. Reeded Edge. J-252. Very rare $1,200

E.989. 1859 Mule. Obv. V and Obv. VI. Silver. Reeded Edge. J-253. Very rare. Eliasberg 5/96 MS-65 $10,780

E.990. 1860 Experimental Trial Piece. The regular obverse and reverse designs. Copper. Reeded edge, with lettered edge applied over reeding. J-269. Very rare, one piece defaced.

E.991. 1861 Revised Design Trial Piece. Obv. The regular design. Die varieties exist. Rev. I: Similar to the regular design, except GOD OUR TRUST added on a ribbon above the eagle. Silver. Reeded Edge. J-277. Very rare. Some may be restrikes $2,000

E.992. Same, copper. Reeded Edge. J-278. Very rare. Obverse die varieties exist. Some may be restrikes $1,000

Half dollar patterns continued

Revised design trial (Superior Galleries)

E.993. 1861 Revised Design Trial Piece. Obv. The regular design. Rev. J: Similar to preceding, except GOD OUR TRUST in field above eagle. Silver. Reeded Edge. J-279. Very rare. Some may be restrikes. Eliasberg 5/96 P-63 .... $3,520

E.994. Same, copper. Reeded Edge. J-280. Very rare. Some may be restrikes. Eliasberg 5/96 P-66 .... $5,060

Revised Design Trial Piece of 1862 (Smithsonian)

E.995. 1862 Revised Design Trial Piece. Obv. The regular design. Rev. I. Silver. Reeded Edge. J-293. Scarce. 12.42 gms. Some may be restrikes $1,750

E.996. Same, copper. Reeded Edge. J-294. Scarce. Some may be restrikes $1,000

E.997. 1862 Revised Design Trial Piece. Obv. The regular design. Rev. J. Silver. Reeded Edge. J-295. Scarce. Some may be restrikes. ST 6/94, Ch. Br. Proof $2,900

E.998. Same, copper. Reeded Edge. J-296. Scarce. Some may be restrikes. ST 6/94, Br. Proof $2,300; Eliasberg 5/96 P-66 .... $4,400

E.999. 1863 Revised Design Trial Piece. Obv. The regular design. Rev. I. Silver. Reeded Edge. J-338. Rare. 12.43 gms. Eliasberg 5/96 P-64 .... $4,070

E.1000. Same, copper. Reeded Edge. J-339. Scarce $800

E.1001. 1863 Revised Design Trial Piece. Obv. The regular design. Rev. J. Silver. Reeded Edge. J-340. Rare. Eliasberg 5/96 P-64 .... $3,740

E.1002. Same, copper. Reeded Edge. J-341. Scarce. ST 9/94, Br. Proof $1,400; Eliasberg 5/96 P-64 $2,750

E.1003. 1863 Revised Design Trial Piece. Obv. The regular design, from different die than preceeding. Rev. With Motto regular design of 1866-91 with IGWT added on scroll above eagle. Silver. Reeded Edge. J-342. Very rare. 12.46 grams. See letter quoted under 1863 With Motto Quarter, E.795, concerning the striking of pre-1865 With Motto issues. Die rust below beak and tail. Additional study of die states and comparisons to regular Proof coins of 1863-70 important $2,500

E.1004. Same, copper. Reeded Edge. J-343. Rare $1,000

E.1005. Same, aluminum. Reeded Edge. J-344. Very rare $800

E.1006. 1864 Regular Design Trial Piece. Aluminum. Reeded Edge. J-395. Very rare $1,200

Revised Design Trial Piece (Superior Galleries)

E.1007. 1864 Revised Design Trial Piece. Obv. The regular design. Rev. With Motto reverse of 1866. Silver. Reeded Edge. J-391. Very rare. Same comment as E.1003 .... $2,000

E.1008. Same, copper. Reeded Edge. J-392. Very rare $1,600

E.1009. Same, copper-nickel. Reeded Edge. J-394. Unique? $4,000

E.1010. Same, aluminum. Reeded Edge. J-393. Very rare $2,000

Half dollar patterns continued

E.1011. 1865 Regular Design Trial Piece. Copper. Reeded Edge. J-432. Very rare $2,000
E.1012. Same, aluminum. Reeded Edge. J-433. Very rare $2,000
E.1013. 1865 Revised Design Trial Piece. Obv. The regular design. Rev. With Motto reverse of 1866. Silver. Reeded Edge. J-429. Very rare, possibly struck in 1866. Eliasberg 5/96 P-63 .... $7,040
E.1014. Same, copper. Reeded Edge. J-430. Rare $1,500
E.1015. Same, aluminum. Reeded Edge. J-431. Very rare $2,000

Regular Design Trial Piece of 1866 (Superior Galleries)

E.1016. 1866 Regular Design Trial Piece. With Motto. Copper. Reeded Edge. J-539. Very rare $1,000
E.1017. 1866 Fantasy Mule. Obv. The regular design. Rev: No Motto reverse of 1865. Silver. Reeded Edge. J-538. Unique, stolen from Willis DuPont in 1967, never recovered. Proof. Beware of alterations. Also reported in copper, unverified.
E.1018. 1867 Regular Design Trial Piece. Copper. Reeded Edge. J-591. Very rare $1,000
E.1019. 1868 Regular Design Trial Piece. Aluminum. Reeded Edge. J-651. Very rare $900
E.1020. 1869 Regular Design Trial Piece. Copper. Reeded Edge. J-760. Very rare $1,000
E.1021. Same, copper-nickel. Reeded Edge. J-762. Very rare $1,000
E.1022. Same, aluminum. Reeded Edge. J-761. Very rare $900

Pattern Design Trial Piece of 1869, design VII – L (Smithsonian)

E.1023. 1869 Pattern Design Trial Piece. Obv. VII: Liberty head right with cap showing two stars above forehead, ribbon in lower hair inscribed LIBERTY in raised letters. Engraver's initial B (for W. Barber) in folds of ribbon, USOA around upper border, IGWT on scroll at lower border. Rev. L: 50 CENTS in oak and laurel wreath, STANDARD SILVER at upper border, date below. Silver. Reeded Edge. J-742. Scarce, reported to exist with one or both revised obverses of this design, J-742a and/or J-747a, unconfirmed $3,000
E.1024. Same, silver. Plain Edge. J-743. Very rare $2,250
E.1025. Same, copper. Reeded Edge. J-744. Scarce $1,000
E.1026. Same, copper. Plain Edge. J-745. Rare $1,200
E.1026a. Same, brass. Reeded Edge. Unlisted in Judd. Unique?
E.1027. Same, aluminum. Reeded Edge. J-746. Rare $900
E.1028. Same, aluminum. Plain Edge. J-747. Rare $900

Pattern Design Trial Piece of 1869, design VIII – L (Harlan J. Berk Ltd.)

E.1029. 1869 Pattern Design Trial Piece. Obv. VIII: Somewhat similar to preceding except Liberty cap replaced by plain coronet or diadem. Hair different, tied with a ribbon inscribed LIBERTY in raised letters. Rev. L. Silver. Reeded Edge. J-748. Scarce $900

Half dollar patterns continued

E.1030. Same, silver. Plain Edge. J-749. Very rare $2,500
E.1031. Same, copper. Reeded Edge. J-750. Scarce. 8.40 gms $1,000
E.1032. Same, copper. Plain Edge. J-751. Rare $2,500
E.1033. Same, brass. Reeded Edge. J-753a. Unique?
E.1034. Same, aluminum. Reeded Edge. J-752. Rare $900
E.1035. Same, aluminum. Plain Edge. J-753. Rare $900
E.1036. 1869 Pattern Design Trial Piece. Obv. IX: Similar to preceding except coronet removed and the ribbon
        supports a single star upon the brow. Rev. L Silver. Reeded Edge. J-754. Scarce $1,500
E.1037. Same, silver. Plain Edge. J-755. Very rare $1,200
E.1038. Same, copper. Reeded Edge. J-756. Scarce $1,000
E.1039. Same, copper. Plain Edge. J-757. Rare. ST 9/94, Proof $1,050
E.1040. Same, brass. Reeded Edge. J-759a. Unique?
E.1041. Same, aluminum. Reeded Edge. J-758. Rare $900
E.1042. Same, aluminum. Plain Edge. J-759. Rare $900
E.1043. 1870 Regular Design Trial Piece. Copper. Reeded Edge. J-993. Very rare $1,000
E.1044. Same, copper-nickel (Various alloys?) Reeded Edge. J-995 & 995a. Very rare $1,200
E.1045. Same, aluminum. Reeded Edge. J-994. Very rare $900
E.1046. 1870 Pattern Design Trial Piece. Design VII-L of 1869. Silver. Reeded Edge. J-975. Very rare . $1,000
E.1047. Same, silver. Plain Edge. J-976. Very rare $1,000
E.1048. Same, copper. Reeded Edge. J-977. Very rare $1,000
E.1049. Same, copper. Plain Edge. J-978. Very rare $1,000
E.1050. Same, aluminum. Reeded Edge. J-979. Very rare $900
E.1051. Same, aluminum. Plain Edge. J-980. Very rare $900

Pattern Design Trial Piece of 1870, design
VIIa – L (Superior Galleries)

E.1052. 1870 Pattern Design Trial Piece. Obv. VIIa: Similar to preceding except no initial B in ribbon fold.
        Rev. L. Silver. Reeded Edge. J-969. Very rare $1,500
E.1053. Same, silver. Plain Edge. J-970. Very rare $1,500
E.1054. Same, copper. Reeded Edge. J-971. Very rare $1.,000
E.1055. Same, copper. Plain Edge. J-972. Very rare $1,200
E.1056. Same, aluminum. Reeded Edge. J-973. Very rare $900
E.1057. Same, aluminum. Plain Edge. J-974. Very rare $900
E.1058. 1870 Pattern Design Trial Piece. Obv. VIIa. Rev. M: 50 CENTS within wreath of cotton and corn,
        date below CENTS, STANDARD in small letters at upper border. Silver. Reeded Edge. J-945. Very
        rare $2,500
E.1059. Same, silver. Plain Edge. J-946. Very rare $2,500
E.1060. Same, copper. Reeded Edge. J-947. Very rare $1,000
E.1061. Same, copper. Plain Edge. J-948. Very rare $1,000
E.1062. Same, aluminum. Reeded Edge. J-949. Very rare $900
E.1063. Same, aluminum. Plain Edge. J-950. Very rare $900

Pattern Design Trial Piece of 1870, design
VIIb – L (Bowers & Merena)

E.1064. 1870 Pattern Design Trial Piece. Obv. VIIb: Similar to preceding except LIBERTY on ribbon in incused
        letters. Rev. L. Silver. Reeded Edge. J-963. Rare $1,500
E.1065. Same, silver. Plain Edge. J-964. Rare. Eliasberg 5/96 P-62 .... $3,300
E.1066. Same, copper. Reeded Edge. J-965. Rare $1,000

Half dollar patterns continued

E.1067. Same, copper. Plain Edge. J-966. Rare $1,000
E.1068. Same, aluminum. Reeded Edge. J-967. Rare $900
E.1069. Same, aluminum. Plain Edge. J-968. Rare $900

Pattern Design Trial Piece of 1870, design
VIIb – M (Smithsonian)

E.1070. 1870 Pattern Design Trial Piece. Design VIIb-M. Silver. Reeded Edge. J-939. Rare $1,500
E.1071. Same, silver. Plain Edge. J-940. Rare. Obverse die varieties exist for this and following. Eliasberg 5/
96 P-65 .... $3,960
E.1072. Same, copper. Reeded Edge. J-941. Rare $1,000
E.1073. Same, copper. Plain Edge. J-942. Rare $1,000
E.1074. Same, aluminum. Reeded Edge. J-943. Rare $800
E.1075. Same, aluminum. Plain Edge. J-944. Rare $800

Pattern Design Trial Piece of 1870, design
VIII – L (Bowers & Merena)

E.1076. 1870 Pattern Design Trial Piece. Design VIII-L. Silver. Reeded Edge. J-981. Rare $1,500
E.1077. Same, silver. Plain Edge. J-982. Rare. Eliasberg 5/96 P-65 .... $7,260
E.1078. Same, copper. Reeded Edge. J-983. Rare $1,000
E.1079. Same, copper. Plain Edge. J-984. Rare $1,000
E.1080. Same, aluminum. Reeded Edge. J-985. Rare $900
E.1081. Same, aluminum. Plain Edge. J-986. Rare $900

Pattern Design Trial Piece of 1870, design
VIII – M

E.1082. 1870 Pattern Design Trial Piece. Design VIII-M. Silver. Reeded Edge. J-951. Rare $1,500
E.1083. Same, silver. Plain Edge. J-952. Rare $1,500
E.1084. Same, copper. Reeded Edge. J-953. Rare $1,000
E.1085. Same, copper. Plain Edge. J-954. Rare $1,000
E.1086. Same, aluminum. Reeded Edge. J-955. Rare $900
E.1087. Same, aluminum. Plain Edge. J-956. Rare $900
E.1088. 1870 Pattern Design Trial Piece. Design IX-L. Silver. Reeded Edge. J-987. Rare $1,500
E.1089. Same, silver. Plain Edge. J-988. Rare. Eliasberg 5/96 P-65 .... $5,060
E.1090. Same, copper. Reeded Edge. J-989. Rare $1,200
E.1091. Same, copper. Plain Edge. J-990. Rare $1,000
E.1092. Same, aluminum. Reeded Edge. J-991. Rare $800
E.1093. Same, aluminum. Plain Edge. J-992. Rare $800

Half dollar patterns continued

Pattern Design Trial Piece of 1870, design IX – M (Smithsonian)

E.1094. 1870 Pattern Design Trial Piece. Design IX-M. Silver. Reeded Edge. J-957. Rare $1,000

E.1095. Same, silver. Plain Edge. J-958. Rare $1,000

E.1096. Same, copper. Reeded Edge. J-959. Rare $900

E.1097. Same, copper. Plain Edge. J-960. Rare $900

E.1098. Same, aluminum. Reeded Edge. J-961. Rare $800

E.1099. Same, aluminum. Reeded Edge. J-962. Rare $800

Pattern Design Trial Piece of 1870, obverse X (Smithsonian)

E.1100. 1870 Pattern Design Trial Piece. Obv. X: Liberty figure seated to left, shield and ribbon incused LIBERTY in right hand, olive branch in left hand, Liberty cap on pole behind, 13 stars around, date below. The Barber design. Rev. The regular design. Silver. Reeded Edge. J-933. Rare. Eliasberg 5/96 P-62/64 .... $3,740

E.1101. Same, silver. Plain Edge. J-934. Rare. Eliasberg 5/96 P-62/65 .... $4,620

E.1102. Same, copper. Reeded Edge. J-935. Rare $1,800

E.1103. Same, copper. Plain Edge. J-936. Rare $1,800

E.1104. Same, aluminum. Reeded Edge. J-937. Rare $1,500

E.1105. Same, aluminum. Plain Edge. J-938. Rare $1,500

E.1106. 1870 Pattern Design Trial Piece. Obv. X. Rev. N: Similar to Rev. M except no date. Silver. Reeded Edge. J-927. Rare $2,400

E.1107. Same, silver. Plain Edge. J-928. Rare $2,400

E.1108. Same, copper. Reeded Edge. J-929. Rare $1,800

E.1109. Same, copper. Plain Edge. J-930. Rare $1,800

E.1110. Same, aluminum. Reeded Edge. J-931. Rare $1,500

E.1111. Same, aluminum. Plain Edge. J-932. Rare $1,500

E.1111a. 1870 Pattern Design Trial Piece. Obv. Xa. Similar to preceding except LIBERTY on ribbon in raised letters. Rev. N. Silver. Reeded Edge. J-927a. Excessively rare $3,000

E.1111b. Same, copper. Reeded Edge. J-929a. Excessively rare $2,000

E.1112. 1871 Regular Design Trial Piece. Copper. Reeded Edge. J-1117. Very rare $1,000

E.1113. Same, copper-nickel. Reeded Edge. J-1119. Unique?

E.1114. Same, aluminum. Reeded Edge. J-1118. Very rare $1,000

E.1115. 1871 Pattern Design Trial Piece. Obv. XI: Liberty figure seated to left wearing Indian headdress, right hand supports pole with cap, left hand rests on globe inscribed LIBERTY, two flags behind. Date below, no stars in field. The Longacre design, used posthumously. Rev: The regular design. Silver. Reeded Edge. J-1108. Extremely rare $10,500

The No Stars Longacre Indian Princess coinage is rare in any metal, more rare in its intended metal (silver) than the reputed mintage figures would indicate, and decidedly more difficult to find in its No Stars form than the identical die marriage with stars. These coins have always brought a premium when they appear on the market, particularly in the larger denominations and when Choice. Part of this pattern's allure may be the unusually beautiful cameo effect of the high relief central figure without the distraction of the surrounding stars. This type of almost medallic beauty has been pointed out as a reason for the continued high value No Stars dimes and half dimes bring when they appear in Proof. The beauty of any design can be appreciated when the eye is not distracted by clutter.

E.1116. Same, copper. Reeded Edge. J-1109. Very rare $2,500

Half dollar patterns continued

E.1117. Same, aluminum. Reeded Edge. J-1110. Very rare $2,000

*Pattern Design Trial Piece of 1871, design
XI – N (Bowers & Merena)*

E.1118. 1871 Pattern Design Trial Piece. Design XI-N. Silver. Reeded Edge. J-1105. Very rare $8,000
E.1119. Same, copper. Reeded Edge. J-1106. Very rare. BM 3/94, P P-65 .... $6,875
E.1120. Same, aluminum. Reeded Edge. J-1107. Very rare $2,200
E.1121. 1871 Pattern Design Trial Piece. Obv. XII: Similar to Obv. XI except 13 stars added around border.
Rev. The regular design. Silver. Reeded Edge. J-1114. Very rare $2,500
E.1122. Same, copper. Reeded Edge. J-1115. Very rare $2,000
E.1123. Same, aluminum. Reeded Edge. J-1116. Very rare $2,000

*Pattern Design Trial Piece of 1871, design
XII – N (Smithsonian)*

E.1124. 1871 Pattern Design Trial Piece. Design XII-N. Silver. Reeded Edge. J-1111. Very rare. Eliasberg 5/
96 P-66 .... $9,680
E.1125. Same, copper. Reeded Edge. J-1112. Very rare. BM 3/94, P P-66 .... $6,050
E.1126. Same, aluminum. Reeded Edge. J-1113. Very rare $2,200
E.1127. 1872 Regular Design Trial Piece. Copper. Reeded Edge. J-1203. Very rare $1,200
E.1128. Same, aluminum. Reeded Edge. J-1204. Very rare $1,000

*Pattern Design Trial Piece of 1872, design
XIII – O*

E.1129. 1872 Pattern Design Trial Piece. Obv. XIII: Liberty seated left, outstretched right arm seems to pat
standing eagle on head. Left elbow rests on national shield, left hand holds sword that crosses shield,
date below, 13 stars around. William Barber's Amazonian design. Rev. O: Standing eagle holding
three arrows in right claw, left claw holds national shield, olive branch and ribbon incused IGWT.
USOA around, HALF DOL. below. Silver. Reeded Edge. J-1200. Very rare. See similar quarter and
dollar $28,000
Only the half dollar of this series has an olive branch on the shield.
E.1130. Same, copper. Reeded Edge. J-1201. Very rare. A Brilliant Proof copper set of quarter, half dollar and
dollar appeared in ST 6/94, bringing $39,000; half dollar alone, BM 3/94, P P-66 .... $20,900
E.1131. Same, aluminum. Reeded Edge. J-1202. Very rare $12,500
E.1132. 1873 Regular Design Trial Piece. Copper. Reeded Edge. J-1272. Very rare. Eliasberg 5/96 P-65
$5,060
E.1133. Same, aluminum. Reeded Edge. J-1273. Very rare $1,200
E.1134. 1874 Regular Design Trial Piece. Copper. Reeded Edge. J-1361. Very rare $1,300

Half dollar patterns continued

E.1135. Same, aluminum. Reeded Edge. J-1362. Very rare $1,300
E.1136. 1875 Regular Design Trial Piece. Copper. Reeded Edge. J-1418. Very rare $1,600
E.1137. Same, aluminum. Reeded Edge. J-1419. Very rare $1,600
E.1138. 1876 Regular Design Trial Piece. Copper. Reeded Edge. J-1456. Very rare $2,500

*Pattern Design Trial Piece of 1877, design
XIV – P (Smithsonian)*

E.1139. 1877 Pattern Design Trial Piece. Obv. XIV: Liberty head left wearing coronet labeled LIBERTY, date below, tiny IGWT at upper border, seven stars left border, six right. Rev. P: Heraldic eagle with wings raised, olive branch in right claw, eight arrows in left. EPU above eagle, USOA around upper border, HALF DOLLAR at lower. Silver. Reeded Edge. J-1501. Extremely rare, this and following by William Barber $28,000
    1. One of the Barber Sailor Head patterns struck in dime, quarter, half dollar, and one dollar denominations as what appears to be an effort by Barber to substitute one of his designs for the Gobrecht/Hughes Seated Liberty design that was getting a little long in the tooth by this time. Virtually impossible to locate in silver, this pattern has brought rather surprising prices on the infrequent occasions it has appeared at auction, as in the first part of the Garrett Sale. The central design is one of Barber's rare masterpieces, which undoubtedly accounts for its value. This coin is not one of Barber's entries into the 1877 pattern half dollar "sweepstakes" eventually won by Morgan. Those coins are discussed below.
    2. The reverse used on this pattern and several other Barber designs in the 1877 "sweepstakes" (see E.1143 & E.1149) is of special interest as it is clearly the basis of the reverse later adopted by Charles Barber for the regular issues of 1892 through the First World War. Comparison of this reverse, the reverse later adopted, and the design eventually adopted show only minor changes. Assuming that this reverse was (at least initially) the work of William Barber, his son's later adoption of his father's design appears to be more understandable than simple plagiarism.
E.1140. Same, copper. Reeded Edge. J-1502. Very rare $6,500
    The copper strikes of this pattern exist in greater number than the remaining 1877 half dollar patterns struck in this metal.

*Pattern Design Trial Piece of 1877, design
XV – Q*

E.1141. 1877 Pattern Design Trial Piece. Obv. XV: Liberty head left wearing cap with broad band inscribed LIBERTY, cotton and wheat plants behind band, 13 stars around, date below. Rev. Q: Facing eagle holding olive branch and arrows centered on a national shield, double ring around, inner one beaded, joined at four compass points; Gothic IGWT and EPU within upper and lower halves of rings. USOA and HALF DOLLAR around border. Silver. Reeded Edge. J-1524. Very rare. Obverse die varieties reported for this and next $22,000
    1. Since this is the first entry in the 1877 pattern half "sweepstakes," this is as good a point as any to introduce a series that has consistently been one of the most sought after series in patterns or in numismatics generally. In a bear market, these coins (especially in silver) bring good prices. In a bull market, the same coins bring staggering prices — with those that are recognized to be unique bringing astonishing prices.
E.1142. Same, copper. Reeded Edge. J-1525. Very rare $12,000

Half dollar patterns continued

Pattern Design Trial Piece of 1877, design
XVI – P (Bowers & Merena)

E.1143. 1877 Pattern Design Trial Piece. Obv. XVI: Liberty head left wearing ornate helmet in which is engraved a defiant eagle to left; LIBERTY incused on visor, tiny IGWT at upper border. Date below, 13 stars around. Rev. P. Silver. Reeded Edge. J-1528. Extremely rare $32,500

1. This is Barber's well-regarded Helmet Head obverse, an extraordinary design which is much sought after even within this already eagerly sought series. The design, according to ancient coin expert Harlan Berk is much like a "new style Athenian Tetradrachm" c. 166-88 B.C. Did Barber get his inspiration from that ancient coin? He may not have had to reach back that far, because the *A.N.A. Centennial Anthology*, p.90, has a sketch of a Gobrecht drawing very much like this design, wearing what the author of the article refers to as a Corinthian helmet. Did Barber then simply borrow yet another design from a predecessor, just as he did with so much of Longacre's work?

2. The last appearance of one of these patterns was the coin that appeared in the Superior section of Auction '89, lot #625. That coin was also lot #594 in Christie's 9/88 Sale.

3. This pattern is very difficult to locate because of its absolute rarity (most likely three coins, but no more than five) and because of the sheer beauty and impact of its design. At least two of these examples (the Superior/Christie's coin and the Judd plate coin) reside in longterm collections.

E.1144. Same, copper. Reeded Edge. J-1529. Very rare $15,000

Pattern Design Trial Piece of 1877, design
XVI – Q (Bowers & Merena)

E.1145. 1877 Pattern Design Trial Piece. Design XVI-Q. Silver. Reeded Edge. J-1526. Extremely rare $27,000

This pattern is a muling of the obverse of the preceding pattern and the reverse of E.1141. Since both the obverse and reverse dies have the motto IGWT, they were obviously not intended to be mated. Several of the Barber die marriages within this series of pattern halves are muled in this fashion, presumably to provide tidbits for sale to eager collectors.

E.1146. Same, copper. Reeded Edge. J-1527. Very rare $12,000

Pattern Design Trial Piece of 1877, design
XVI – R (Bowers & Merena)

E.1147. 1877 Pattern Design Trial Piece. Obv. XVI. Rev. R: Facing eagle holding olive branch and arrows and standing on a tablet inscribed EPU, USOA and HALF DOLLAR around. Silver. Reeded Edge. J-1530. Extremely rare $28,000

E.1148. Same, copper. Reeded Edge. J-1531. Very rare $12,000

Half dollar patterns continued

Pattern Design Trial Piece of 1877, design
XVII – P (Bowers & Merena)

E.1149. 1877 Pattern Design Trial Piece. Obv. XVII: Liberty head left wearing coronet labeled LIBERTY; cotton and wheat plants tucked into coronet. Tiny IGWT at upper border, date below, blundered with 8 punched over a 1. 13 stars around. Rev. P. Silver. Reeded Edge. J-1535. Extremely rare $32,500
Another beautiful and elusive Barber obverse, and a pattern that does not appear to be a muling unlike several of the other combinations. So rare that the blundered date apparently was not noticed until 1994. No more than three known, one in the Byron Reed collection and one in another long term collection. The third coin, the finest of the three, was lot #626 in the Superior section of Auction '89, bringing $37,400. Prior to that it was lot #391 in the Garrett I, $24,000. Listed in Garrett ex-Maris and (presumably) there ex-Mint.

E.1150. Same, copper. Reeded Edge. J-1536. Very rare $18,000

E.1151 [Deleted]
Formerly listed in silver as E.1151 (J-1532), but now believed to be just a copper piece that has been silver plated.

E.1152. 1877 Pattern Design Trial Piece. Design XVII-R. Copper. Reeded Edge. J-1533. Very rare $12,000

Pattern Design Trial Piece of 1877, design
XVII – S

E.1153. 1877 Pattern Design Trial Piece. Obv. XVII, with date blundered as 8/1. Rev. S: Similar to preceding except eagle hold olive branch and arrows in right claw and supports a national shield in left. Silver. Reeded Edge. J-1534a. Unique $37,500
1. This coin and another unique member of the 1877 pattern half series (E.1168) provide ample proof of their value in relation to other patterns and other coins. This pattern was lot #390 in Garrett I and sold for $32,500, a high for the 1877 half dollars in Garrett. While cynics might say many Garrett prices were an anomaly, the same coin was in the BM 8/87 Bebee-ANA Sale, lot #1503, bringing $23,100. This realization shows little difference even in a down market.
2. This coin is unique, despite the apparent appearance of several specimens all graded PR-64 in the PCGS population report, the result of multiple submissions of the same coin. (See the notes under E.1168.)

E.1154. Same, copper. Reeded Edge. J-1534. Very rare $18,000

Pattern Design Trial Piece of 1877, design
XVIII – R (Bowers & Merena)

E.1155. 1877 Pattern Design Trial Piece. Obv. XVIII: Liberty head left with large cap inscribed LIBERTY on band, tiny IGWT at upper border, date below, 13 stars around. Rev. R. Silver. Reeded Edge. J-1537. Unique? $32,500

E.1156. Same, copper. Reeded Edge. J-1538. Very rare $16,500

Half dollar patterns continued

Pattern Design Trial Piece of 1877, design
XVIII – S

E.1157. 1877 Pattern Design Trial Piece. Design XVIII-S. Silver. Reeded Edge. J-1539a. Extremely rare $28,000

E.1158. Same, copper. Reeded Edge. J-1539. Very rare $15,500

E.1159. 1877 Pattern Design Trial Piece. Obv. XVIII. Rev. T: Facing eagle with raised wings showing thin feathers standing on scroll incused IGWT, olive branch and arrows behind scroll. Circle of dots inside USOA and HALF DOLLAR at border. Copper. Reeded Edge. J-1541b. Very rare. May also exist in silver, J-1541a, if not silvered copper $14,000

Pattern Design Trial Piece of 1877, design
XIX – T (Bowers & Merena)

E.1160. 1877 Pattern Design Trial Piece. Obv. XIX: Liberty head left with cap and headband inscribed LIBERTY, cotton and wheat plants tucked into headband. The head adopted for the silver dollar in 1878. Circle of dots inside EPU at upper border, date lower, six stars left and seven stars right. Rev. T. Silver. Reeded Edge. J-1514. Very rare $23,000

    1. Obverse and reverse by George Morgan. The 1877 pattern half dollars mark this engraver's arrival at the Mint to shake-up the Barber dynasty that was not proving as creative as may have been hoped for. Despite winning the 1877 "sweepstakes," George Morgan remained the Assistant Engraver while Charles Barber got his father's job as Chief Engraver upon William's death.

    2. George Morgan's background and the history of the 1877 Morgan may be found in Pete Bischal's excellent chapter in the new edition of the Van Allen-Mallis silver dollar encyclopedia (VAM). For a more detailed history of the Morgan patterns, read that chapter in VAM for a job well done and a section very well written.

E.1161. Same, copper. Reeded Edge. J-1515. Very rare $10,000

Pattern Design Trial Piece of 1877, design
XIX – U (Bowers & Merena)

E.1162. 1877 Pattern Design Trial Piece. Obv. XIX. Rev. U: Similar to preceding except wing feathers fewer and thicker. Silver. Reeded Edge. J-1516. Very rare $23,000

E.1163. Same, copper. Reeded Edge. J-1517. Very rare $11,000

Half dollar patterns continued

Pattern Design Trial Piece of 1877, design XIX – V (Bowers & Merena)

E.1164. 1877 Pattern Design Trial Piece. Obv. XIX. Rev. V: Defiant eagle to left standing on scroll incused IGWT, arrows and longer olive branch behind scroll, circle of dots inside USOA and HALF DOLLAR at border. Silver. Reeded Edge. J-1512. Very rare $23,000

E.1165. Same, copper. Reeded Edge. J-1513. Very rare $11,000

E.1166. [Deleted]
  Formerly listed in silver as E.1166 (J-1518) but now believed to be just a copper piece that has been silver plated.

Pattern Design Trial Piece of 1877, design XIX – W (Bowers & Merena)

E.1167. 1877 Pattern Design Trial Piece. Obv. XIX. Rev. W: Facing eagle holding olive branch and arrows centered on national shield, olive branch around shield, except for IGWT on pleated ribbon above, USOA and HALF DOLLAR around. Copper. Reeded Edge. J-1519. Very rare, at least one known silver plated $14,000
  The difference in value compared to other copper pieces is a reflection of the doubtful existence of this pattern in its intended metal.

Pattern Design Trial Piece of 1877, design XIX – X (Bowers & Merena)

E.1168. 1877 Pattern Design Trial Piece. Obv. XIX. Rev. X: Similar to preceding except IGWT in raised letters on a band surrounding shield, and in turn surrounded by longer wreath. Silver. Reeded Edge. J-1520. Unique $35,000
  See the notes to E.1153 as to the prices brought by unique 1877 pattern halves in silver. This coin was Garrett I, lot #386. This pattern is unique, despite the fact that it appears several times in the current *PCGS Population Report* and also in the *NGC Population Report*. The same coin was sent in several times by one dealer, along with the unique E.1153 and one of the three existing E.1149s. This problem is not the fault of either grading service and is in the process of being corrected. Such population reports must not be used as a basis for revising the rarity of any of these patterns.

E.1169. Same, copper. Reeded Edge. J-1521. Very rare $18,000

E.1170. 1877 Pattern Design Trial Piece. Obv. XIX. Rev. Y: Similar to preceding except eagle small, shield more ornate and IGWT incused. Silver. Reeded Edge. J-1522. Very rare $22,000

E.1171. Same, copper. Reeded Edge. J-1523. Very rare $12,000

Half dollar patterns continued

E.1172. 1877 Pattern Design Trial Piece. Obv. XIX. Rev. Z: Facing eagle with raised wings holding olive branch and arrows, laurel wreath around lower part of eagle, Gothic IGWT above head, USOA and HALF DOLLAR around. Similar to the design adopted for the silver dollar in 1878. Silver. Reeded Edge. J-1523a. Unique? $30,000

E.1173. Same, copper. Reeded Edge. J-1523b. Extremely rare $17,500

Pattern Design Trial Piece of 1877, design
XX – Z (Bowers & Merena)

E.1174. 1877 Pattern Design Trial Piece. Obv. XX: Similar to preceding except head larger, no dotted circle and E PLURIBUS at left border, UNUM at right, seven stars above head and six below, flanking date. Rev. Z. Silver. Reeded Edge. J-1510. Extremely rare $24,000

    This Morgan reverse is very close (but not identical to) the adopted 1878 silver dollar. There also appear to be fewer 1877 Morgan patterns struck with this obverse than the other obverse designs. Similar obverses were used for quarters and halves in 1879.

E.1175. Same, copper. Reeded Edge. J-1511. Very rare $12,000

E.1176. 1877 Pattern Design Trial Piece. Obv. XXI: Similar to preceding except EPU at upper border, seven stars lower left, six lower right, date below. Similar to the design adopted for the silver dollar in 1878. Rev. T. Silver. Reeded Edge. J-1509c. Very rare, if it exists. May be a misdescription of E.1160.

E.1177. 1877 Pattern Design Trial Piece. Design XXI-V. Silver. Reeded Edge. J-1509a. Very rare, if it exists. May be a misdescription of E.1164.

E.1178. Same, copper. Reeded Edge. J-1509b. Very rare, if it exists. May be a misdescription of E.1165.

Pattern Design Trial Piece of 1877, design
XXI – W

E.1179. 1877 Pattern Design Trial Piece. Design XXI-W. Silver. Reeded Edge. J-1503. Very rare. Obverse die varieties exist for this and next four $24,000

    This die marriage is quite unusual as it was not struck in copper or any other off-metal. Since the problem of unauthorized striking was raised during the early part of Morgan's work on these patterns, this may account for the fact that it is one of the only non-mules not struck in copper.

Pattern Design Trial Piece of 1877, design
XXI – X (Bowers & Merena)

E.1180. 1877 Pattern Design Trial Piece. Design XXI-X. Silver. Reeded Edge. J-1504. Very rare $22,000

E.1181. Same, copper. Reeded Edge. J-1505. Very rare $12,000

E.1182. 1877 Pattern Design Trial Piece. Design XXI-Y. Silver. Reeded Edge. J-1506. Very rare $22,000

E.1183. Same, copper. Reeded Edge. J-1507. Very rare $12,000

Half dollar patterns continued

E.1184. 1877 Pattern Design Trial Piece. Design XXI-Z. Silver. Reeded Edge. J-1508. Very rare, similar to the design combination adopted for the silver dollar in 1878, for which it usually brings a substantial premium over related half dollar patterns $25,000

E.1185. Same, copper. Reeded Edge. J-1509. Very rare $13,000

Splasher of 1877, design XXII – AA (Smithsonian)

E.1186. 1877 Pattern Design Trial Piece. Obv. XXII: Liberty head left with plain hair tied by ribbon incused LIBERTY, 13 stars around, date below. Rev. AA: Facing eagle with national shield on breast clutching olive branch and arrows; head to left holding ribbon incused EPU, USOA and HALF DOLLAR around. Silver. Reeded Edge. J-1540. Very rare. This unusual, and rather unattractive, design by former Mint engraver Anthony Paquet did not include the required IGWT $18,000

Paquet wasn't really trying when he submitted this "old wine in a new bottle." If you compare this pattern with Paquet's 1868 International half eagle (E.1692-95) you will find that the reason the required IGWT is missing can be traced to the fact that this pattern is a mild reworking of the earlier design. The obverse of this pattern and the earlier Paquet design shows that the two versions of Liberty on the obverse of each are remarkably similar. The profiles are identical. The figures are both wearing a ribbon with a star at the front and the word LIBERTY incuse on the ribbon. There is an extra ribbon on the back of the head on E.1692 and the hair at the rear (the bun) is arranged in a slightly different fashion. This "new" 1877 pattern is a slightly simplified version of what was done a decade earlier by this same engraver — and not very well on either occasion.

E.1187. Same, copper. Reeded Edge. J-1541. Very rare $10,000

Pattern Design Trial Piece of 1879, design XXa – BB (Smithsonian)

E.1188. 1879 Pattern Design Trial Piece. Obv. XXa: Similar to Obv. XX except eight stars above head and five below. Rev. BB: Tall, facing eagle clutching olive branch and arrows, USOA and HALF DOLLAR around border, tiny IGWT around lower half of eagle inside legends. See similar reverses on 1878 $2-1/2 and $5 and 1879 dollars. Silver. Reeded Edge. J-1599. Very rare $16,000

E.1189. Same, copper. Reeded Edge. J-1600. Very rare $7,000

Pattern Design Trial Piece of 1879, design XXI – BB

E.1190. 1879 Pattern Design Trial Piece. Design XXI-BB. Silver. Reeded Edge. J-1601. Very rare $16,000

E.1191. Same, copper. Reeded Edge. J-1602. Very rare $6,000

Half dollar patterns continued

Pattern Design Trial Piece of 1879, design
XXIII – CC, Washlady (Smithsonian)

E.1192. 1879 Pattern Design Trial Piece. Obv. XXIII: Liberty head left with wavy hair piled up in back, ribbon above forehead labeled LIBERTY, behind which are wheat ears and cotton plants. Date below, tiny IGWT at upper border, seven stars left border, six right. The Washlady design by Charles Barber. Rev. CC. Facing eagle holding olive branch in right claw and three arrows in left, USOA around upper border, tiny EPU inside USOA, HALF DOLLAR at bottom. Silver. Reeded Edge. J-1597. Very rare. See matching dime, quarter and dollar $18,000
E.1193. Same, copper. Reeded Edge. J-1598. Very rare $8,000
E.1193a. Same, white metal. Reeded Edge. Unlisted in Judd. Unique?

Pattern Design Trial Piece of 1882, design
XXIV – DD (Smithsonian)

E.1194. 1882 Pattern Design Trial Piece. Obv. XXIV: Liberty head right with headband marked LIBERTY, wearing small national shield as earring. Date below, EPU at upper border, seven stars lower left, six right. Rev. DD: Defiant eagle to right, perched on olive branch and three arrows, USOA and HALF DOLLAR around border. Silver. Reeded Edge. J-1700. Very rare $22,000
E.1195. Same, copper. Reeded Edge. J-1701. Very rare $10,000
E.1196. 1884 Regular Design Trial Piece. Copper. Reeded Edge. J-1730. Very rare $1,500
E.1197. 1885 Regular Design Trial Piece. Aluminum. Reeded Edge. J-1746. Very rare $1,200
E.1198. 1891 Pattern Design Trial Piece. Obv. XXV: Liberty head right with cap and laurel wreath, tiny LIBERTY on headband above forehead, IGWT at upper border. Date below, six six-pointed stars at left border, seven right. Rev. EE: Heraldic eagle with national shield on breast, clutching olive branch in right claw, arrows in left and ribbon incused EPU in beak, 13 tiny five-pointed stars above and below ribbon, arch of clouds above stars. USOA and HALF DOLLAR around, similar to the Heraldic Eagle reverse of 1800-07. Silver. Reeded Edge. J-1762. Two known, Smithsonian.
    The reverse is very much like that used on certain 1877 pattern half dollars. (See E.1143.) The head and legs on the 1877 pattern reverse, and particularly the feathers on the "drumsticks," are very clearly the forerunners of this design and the other Barber 1891 patterns. This design reappeared on the regular issue coinage of 1892 onwards.
E.1199. 1891 Pattern Design Trial Piece. Obv. XXV. Rev. FF: Similar to preceding except eagle smaller and the ribbon bearing EPU passes over rather than under the eagle's neck. The olive branch has more leaves, and the arch of clouds is more curved. Silver. Reeded Edge. J-1764. Two known, Smithsonian.
E.1200. 1891 Pattern Design Trial Piece. Obv. XXV. Rev. GG: Similar to Rev. EE except clouds removed and stars enlarged and placed above the ribbon. The design adopted in 1892. Silver. Reeded Edge. J-1763. Two known, Smithsonian.
E.1201. 1891 Pattern Design Trial Piece. Obv. XXVI: Similar to preceding except seven five-pointed stars left, six right. Rev. HH: Similar to Rev. EE except eagle much smaller and enclosed in an oak wreath. Silver. Reeded Edge. J-1765. Two known, Smithsonian.

Half dollar patterns continued

E.1202. 1891 Pattern Design Trial Piece. Obv. XXVII: Standing liberty figure, head turned left, holding sword in right hand and liberty cap on pole in left, defiant eagle standing to right on a rock behind. Rays around upper half of figure, overlaid with IGWT in an arc near the figure and ****L*I*B*E*R*T*Y*** around the border, date below. Rev. II: Similar to Rev. HH except eagle smaller still and partially surrounded by rays. Silver. Reeded Edge. J-1766. Two known, Smithsonian, a third reported.

Commemorative fantasy of 1915 (Bowers & Merena)

E.1203. 1915 Commemorative Fantasy. Obv. & Rev: The regular Panama-Pacific half dollar designs, without Mint mark. Gold. Reeded Edge. J-1793. Very Rare, probably struck for the collection of the Secretary of the Treasury.

E.1204. Same, silver. Reeded Edge. J-1791. Very rare.

E.1205. Same, copper. Reeded Edge. J-1792. Very rare.

Pattern Design Trial Piece of 1916, design XXVIII – JJ (Smithsonian)

E.1206. 1916 Pattern Design Trial Piece. Obv. XXVIII: Liberty wearing an American flag walking towards rising sun at left. Right arm outstretched; left arm holds sheaf of oak and laurel, date below. LIBERTY in right field, IGWT below. Rev. JJ: Eagle with partially raised wings standing to left on rock with pine sapling, USOA around upper border, HALF DOLLAR curved beneath it, EPU at lower border. Silver. Reeded Edge. J-1797. Extremely rare $40,000

These patterns are highly sought after by collectors since there are only a handful of patterns available to the public struck after the early 1880s with the exception of the 1896 1-cent and 5-cent patterns from the Woodin swap. These high-denomination patterns have a crossover appeal for dedicated Walking Liberty enthusiasts as well. The last time these coins were on the market, the dealer who bought them at auction sold them quickly to just such an individual — who is now one of only two or three who could build the ultimate set of this design.

E.1207. 1916 Pattern Design Trial Piece. Obv. XXVIII. Rev. KK: Similar to preceding except eagle larger, EPU in left field and HALF DOLLAR below eagle. Similar to the adopted design, but without designer's monogram. Silver. Reeded Edge. J-1797a. Very rare $40,000

E.1208. 1916 Pattern Design Trial Piece. Obv. XXVIII. Rev: The regular design with designer's monogram. Silver. Reeded Edge. Very rare $40,000

E.1209. 1916 Pattern Design Trial Piece. Obv. XXIX: Similar to preceding except figure is smaller and LIBERTY is spaced around upper border. Similar to the regular design except date is smaller and IGWT lower. Rev. JJ. Silver. Reeded Edge. J-1798. Very rare $40,000

E.1210. 1916 Pattern Design Trial Piece. Design XXIX-KK. Silver. Reeded Edge. J-1799. Very rare $40,000

E.1211. 1916 Pattern Design Trial Piece. Obv. XXX: Similar to preceding except IGWT larger and higher. The normal design, but with smaller date. Rev. The regular design. Silver. Reeded Edge. J-1801. Very rare $40,000

E.1212. 1916 Pattern Design Trial Piece. Obv. XXXI: Similar to regular design except smaller, beaded border. Rev. LL: Similar to regular design except smaller, beaded border. Silver. Reeded Edge. J-1800. Very rare $40,000

These 1916 patterns are often found circulated, due to their similarity to regular coinage. Additional die varieties may exist.

E.1213. 1918 Commemorative Trial Piece. Obv. & Rev: The regular Lincoln-Illinois design. Copper. Reeded Edge. Very rare.

E.1214. Same, copper-nickel. Reeded Edge. Unique?

E.1215. Same, white metal. Reeded Edge. Unique?

Half dollar patterns continued

Metallurgical trial

E.1216. (1965) Metallurgical Trial Piece. Martha Washington design, dated 1759. See description under 10 cents.

E.1217. (1965) Metallurgical Trial Piece. Paul D. Merica - INCO designs, see descriptions under quarter dollar patterns $500

The search for a suitable alloy to replace silver resulted in other trial pieces including DuPont's Detclad and the widely marketed Franklin Mint Gardiner's Island pieces. These latter were sold in copper-nickel clad with sterling silver; pure nickel impregnated with Columbium, called Franklinium I; and Nicon, copper-nickel impregnated with Columbium. The Mint rejected all of these exotic patented alloys to avoid dependence on any coinage material it did not fully control.

Promotional trial of 1976 (Thomas K. DeLorey)

E.1218. 1976 Promotional Trial Piece. Obv: The Bicentennial half dollar design, without Mint mark. Rev: The Bicentennial design. 40% silver. Reeded Edge. Proof. May no longer exist.

Several 40% silver three-piece Proof sets were struck at the Philadelphia Mint without Mint marks on August 12, 1974, for display at the upcoming American Numismatic Association convention and for presentation to the designers of the three coins and a representative of newly-inaugurated President Ford, who was understandably too busy to attend the ceremonies. Allegedly all were returned to the Mint and replaced with regular Proof coins. Beware of alterations.

Silver and clad dollars

Pattern Design Trial Piece of 1794 (Bowers & Merena)

E.1219. 1794 Pattern Design Trial Piece. Obv. Liberty head right with flowing hair. LIBERTY at upper border, date below. Rev. The regular design. Copper. Lettered Edge. J-18. Unique $20,000

While this head resembles that on the obverse die used to strike the 1794 regular coinage, Michael J. Hodder's careful study has demonstrated that this pattern head is from a different punch, one never used for regular coinage. This No Stars pattern's reverse, however, was struck from the regular reverse die.

E.1220. 1794 Regular Design Trial Piece. Copper. Lettered Edge. J-19. Unique? Old electrotype copies exist $17,500

The unique copper Proof of this type was donated to the Smithsonian by Harvey G. and Lawrence R. Stack in 1993.

Note: Because of the numerous die pairings used on the silver dollar and trade dollar patterns, the obverse designs will be identified with Roman numerals and the reverse designs with letters.

Pattern Design Trial Piece of 1836, design I – A

E.1221. 1836 Pattern Design Trial Piece. Obv. I: Liberty figure seated to right on rock, right hand rests on national shield, across which is a ribbon with LIBERTY in raised letters, left hand supports pole with Liberty cap. No stars in field, small C. GOBRECHT F. in field below base, date at lower border. Rev. A: Eagle flying upwards to left, 26 stars in field, USOA and ONE DOLLAR around border. Silver. Plain Edge. J-58. Originals (dies reversed) excessively rare if they exist; Restrikes (dies rotated about 30 degrees) very rare. Eliasberg 5/96 P-64 .... $99,000

At the risk of starting a war, the existence of any so-called originals is one of those numismatic old wives tales that has unfortunately became accepted as fact. Nobody has ever seen an original. If originals did exist, none have been seen in more than 150 years, none have surfaced in any of the long-term early collections that were later sold, none could be found in Garrett, Norweb, Starr, Granberg, or anywhere else, and none have ever been seen by any numismatic scholar. The only "proof" of the existence of originals are apocryphal reports that coins were struck and then circulated. Early newspaper reports were then said to have criticized the "conceited German" for putting his name on so prominent a place on the new coin. Upset, Gobrecht was then said to have removed it, but was told by Patterson to replace it in a less-prominent position. Nonsense! Neither coins or newspapers moved that quickly in those days. Nobody has ever produced the paper trail to support this fanciful story. Most of the early trials for these coins were done on uniface splashers in lead or tin. These were then evaluated first at the Mint and then sent on to officialdom. The most likely explanation for the lack of originals is

Silver dollar patterns continued

something much akin to the history of E.950. This die was completed, and a few splashers or uniface trials evaluated and rejected in favor of the placement of Gobrecht's name on the base of the central figure. When the Mint launched its program of restrikes of every possible Gobrecht die it could find in the 1858 period, the restrikes were created, and even then in very small numbers. This theory should be viewed in light of the uniface trial of 1840, which bears the unmistakable workmanship of Gobrecht and has his name displayed below the base of the central figure. If that die was made after this die (and that appears to be the case, even if the 1840 date was an afterthought) it would appear that Gobrecht either did not learn his lesson or there was no lesson to learn.

E.1222. Same, copper. Plain Edge. J-59. Very rare, restrikes only $19,000

E.1223. 1836 Restrike. Obv. I. Rev. B: Similar to preceding except no stars in field. Silver. Plain Edge. J-63. Extremely rare, restrikes only $29,000

This pattern, and most of the following that are die marriages of an obverse without stars and a reverse without stars, or a combination with stars on both sides, are 1858 and later mulings of the Mint's collection of Gobrecht dies. These patterns were struck in very tiny numbers, often no more than two of each type in various metals. They are avidly sought after as part of the Gobrecht dollar series, but should not be viewed as representative of anything intended as true patterns for regular issue coinage. They are fantasy restrikes, pure and simple.

E.1224. Same, copper. Plain Edge. J-64. Extremely rare, restrikes only, two known $20,000

1. These two specimens illustrate how individual pattern tracking and pedigree can be done in this series. They were apparently struck within minutes as both coins have a small mark from a piece of lint on the reverse die that moved slightly between the impressions. It is possible to identify which of the two existing coins is depicted in a sale by the photographs, through the minor distinctions in toning on the obverse and the lint mark on the reverse below and between the F in OF and the A of AMERICA. Using this method, and physical examination of the coins, one specimen was identified as lot #880 in the Rarcoa session of Auction '90. Before that, it was lot #2072 in Session 3 of Kagin's 1977 ANA Sale. According to the Kagin's catalog, this same coin was lot #1860 in Kagin's M.A.N.A. sale, Nov. 1974, there described as a "lovely glittering Red and Bluish Proof, Choice! ONLY 2 KNOWN! This is the Parmelee specimen (sold 1890); Farouk collection (Palace Sale, 1954); Austin collection 1973." Realized $24,500 in the Austin sale. There was a different specimen (listed as A-W-49) as lot #1027 in Numismatic Gallery's 2/50 sale of the Col. James W. Curtis Collection of United States Patterns. The Parmelee specimen was lot #27 in that sale, bringing $27.00.

2. Physical comparison of the first specimen of this pattern and a well-struck and well-preserved example of E.1221 shows that this pattern was struck soon after the E.1221. Comparison to another E.1221 shows that the obverse die was in the same state. The obvious conclusion is that both specimens of this pattern and the better-known E.1221 were struck during a very short period of time, perhaps only a few days, during 1858.

E.1225. 1836 Pattern Design Trial Piece. Obv. II: Similar to preceding except C. GOBRECHT F. on base of rock. Rev. A. Silver. Plain Edge. J-60. Originals (1,000 struck 1836 with dies reversed and 600 struck 1837 with dies aligned) scarce. Often regarded as a regular issue coin despite its plain edge, which is highly unusual for any U.S. regular issue, but as no reeded edge dollar had been previously struck, not unlikely. Many are known well circulated, however (see under silver dollars in the regular listings). Restrikes very rare. Eliasberg 5/96P-62 .... $29,700

E.1226. Same, silver. Reeded Edge. J-61. Very rare, restrikes only $20,000

E.1227. Same, copper. Plain Edge. J-62. Very rare, restrikes only $7,000

E.1228. 1836 Restrike. Design II-B. Silver. Plain Edge. J-65. Extremely rare, restrikes only $29,000

E.1229. Same, copper. Plain Edge. J-66. Extremely rare. restrikes only $20,000

E.1230. 1838 Restrike. Obv. III: Similar to preceding except name of designer removed and 13 stars added around border. Rev. A. Silver. Plain Edge. J-88. Extremely rare, restrikes only. Also reported with Reeded Edge, Julian-25 .... $29,000

E.1231. Same, copper. Plain Edge. J-89. Extremely rare, restrikes only $20,000

E.1232. Same, copper. Reeded Edge. J-90. Extremely rare, restrikes only $20,000

E.1233. 1838 Pattern Design Trial Piece. Design III-B. Silver. Reeded Edge. J-84. Originals scarce, sometimes regarded as a regular issue coin. Restrikes very rare. Eliasberg 5/96 P64 .... $31,900

E.1234. Same, silver. Plain Edge. J-85. Extremely rare, restrikes only $23,000

E.1235. Same, copper. Reeded Edge. J-86. Extremely rare, originals only $8,000

Some pattern specialists question whether there were any off-metal original strikes of any of the Gobrecht series.

E.1236. Same, copper. Plain Edge. J-87. Extremely rare, restrikes only $8,000

E.1237. 1839 Restrike. Design III-A. Silver. Plain Edge. J-108. Extremely rare, restrikes only. Also reported with Reeded Edge, Julian-32 .... $29,000

E.1238. Same, copper. Plain Edge. J-109. Unique? Restrike only $10,000

E.1239. 1839 Pattern Design Trial Piece. Design III-B. Silver. Reeded Edge. J-104. Originals (300 struck with dies reversed) scarce, sometimes regarded as a regular issue coin. Restrikes (various alignments) rare. Eliasberg 5/96P-61 .... $15,400

E.1240. Same, silver. Plain Edge. J-105. Extremely rare, restrikes only $27,000

E.1241. Same, copper. Reeded Edge. J-106. Extremely rare, restrikes only $9,000

E.1242. Same, copper. Plain Edge. J-107. Extremely rare, restrikes only $9,000

E.1243. 1851 Restrike. The regular designs. Copper. Reeded Edge. J-132. Very rare, struck ca. 1859 $9,000

E.1244. Same, copper-nickel. Reeded Edge. J-133. Very rare $9,000

Silver dollar patterns continued

E.1245. 1852 Restrike. The regular designs. Copper. Reeded Edge. J-134. Very rare, struck ca. 1859 $8,000

E.1246. 1853 Restrike. The regular designs. Copper. Reeded Edge. J-154. Very rare, struck ca. 1859. Eliasberg 5/96P-64 .... $10,120

E.1247. 1863 Regular Design Trial Piece. Copper. Reeded Edge. J-348. Very rare $6,500

Revised Design Trial Piece (Superior Galleries)

E.1248. 1863 Revised Design Trial Piece. Obv. The regular design. Rev. C: With Motto design of 1866-73, with IGWT added on a ribbon above eagle. Silver. Reeded Edge. J-345. Very rare. See 1863 With Motto quarter, E.795, for letter and comments re pre-1865 With Motto patterns. Additional study of die varieties and die states of all Proofs of this era needed $14,000

E.1249. Same, copper. Reeded Edge. J-346. Rare $3,500

E.1250. Same, aluminum. Reeded Edge. J-347. Very rare $2,000

Revised Design Trial Piece (Superior Galleries)

E.1251. 1864 Revised Design Trial Piece. Obv. The regular design. Rev. C. Silver. Reeded Edge. J-396. Very rare. Same comment as E.1248 .... $14,000

E.1252. Same, copper. Reeded Edge. J-397. Very rare $3,500

E.1253. Same, copper-nickel. Reeded Edge. J-399. Very rare $5,000

E.1254. Same, aluminum. Reeded Edge. J-398. Very rare $5,000

E.1255. 1865 Regular Design Trial Piece. Copper. Reeded Edge. J-437. Very rare $3,500

E.1256. 1865 Revised Design Trial Piece. Obv. The regular design. Rev. C. Silver. Reeded Edge. J-434. Very rare. Same comment as E.1248 .... $14,000

E.1257. Same, copper. Reeded Edge. J-435. Rare. One seen silvered, 24.01 gms. Eliasberg 5/96 P-65 $7,920

E.1258. Same, aluminum. Reeded Edge. J-436. Very rare $8,000

E.1259. 1866 Regular Design Trial Piece. With Motto. Copper. Reeded Edge. J-541. Rare $4,000

E.1260. 1866 Fantasy Mule. Obv. The regular design. Rev. No Motto design of 1840-65. Silver. Reeded Edge. J-540. Two known, one stolen from Willis DuPont in 1967 along with matching quarter and half, never recovered $50,000

E.1261. 1867 Regular Design Trial Piece. Copper. Reeded Edge. J-592. Very rare $8,000

E.1262. Same, brass. Reeded Edge. J-593. Very rare $8,000

E.1263. 1868 Regular Design Trial Piece. Aluminum. Reeded Edge. J-652. Very Rare $4,000

E.1264. 1869 Regular Design Trial Piece. Copper. Reeded Edge. J-763. Very rare. ST 1/94, Gem Br. Proof $4,250

E.1265. Same, copper-nickel. Reeded Edge. J-765. Very rare $4,500

E.1266. Same, aluminum. Reeded Edge. J-764. Very rare $4,000

E.1267. 1870 Regular Design Trial Piece. Copper. Reeded Edge. J-1020. Very rare $4,000

E.1268. Same, copper-nickel. Reeded Edge. J-1022. Very rare $4,000

E.1269. Same, aluminum. Reeded Edge. J-1021. Very rare $4,000

Silver dollar patterns continued

E.1270. 1870 Pattern Design Trial Piece. Obv. IV: Liberty figure seated to left, shield and ribbon inscribed LIBERTY in right hand, olive branch in left hand, Liberty cap on pole behind. 13 stars around, date below. The Barber design, somewhat reminiscent of his 1869 Assay Medal. Rev. The regular design. Silver. Reeded Edge. J-1002. Very Rare $24,600

    Breen, in the LM 9/18/68 Sale, describes this pattern (lot #457) as "[a] true pattern, as all the necessary legends are present. Very rare, 6 or 7 now traced."

E.1271. Same, silver. Plain Edge. J-1003. Extremely rare $28,200

    These two patterns are far more difficult to locate than their official rarity ratings would otherwise indicate. Indeed, as discussed before, the 1870 Barber Seated Liberty series is far rarer than previously thought — and much sought after by collectors. For some reason, E.1271 is itself far rarer than its reeded edge brother, and brings a higher price as a result. There was an example of this pattern as lot #1043, Garrett II. A considerable time then passed until the next example surfaced in the Sunderland Sale 14 years later.

E.1272. Same, copper. Reeded Edge. J-1004. Rare. Eliasberg 5/96 P-62/65 .... $5,280
E.1273. Same, copper. Plain Edge. J-1005. Rare $3,000
E.1274. Same, aluminum. Reeded Edge. J-1006. Rare $3,500
E.1275. Same, aluminum. Plain Edge. J-1007. Rare $3,000

Pattern Design Trial Piece of
1870, design IV – D (Superior Galleries)

E.1276. 1870 Pattern Design Trial Piece. Obv. IV. Rev. D: 1 DOLLAR within wreath of cotton, wheat and corn, STANDARD in small letters at upper border. Silver. Reeded Edge. J-996. Rare $12,000
E.1277. Same, silver. Plain Edge. J-997. Rare $12,000
E.1278. Same, copper. Reeded Edge. J-998. Rare $4,800
E.1279. Same, copper. Plain Edge. J-999. Rare $4,800
E.1280. Same, aluminum. Reeded Edge. J-1000. Rare $4,400
E.1281. Same, aluminum. Plain Edge. J-1001. Rare $4,000

Pattern Design Trial Piece of 1870, design V
(Harlan J. Berk Ltd.)

E.1282. 1870 Pattern Design Trial Piece. Obv. V: Liberty figure seated to left wearing Indian headdress, right hand supports pole with cap, left hand rests on globe inscribed LIBERTY. Two flags behind, 22 stars on right one, date below, 13 stars around border. The Longacre design, engraved posthumously from his model, and signed LONGACRE at lower right. Rev. The regular design. Silver. Reeded Edge. J-1014. Very rare $14,500
E.1283. Same, silver. Plain Edge. J-1015. Very rare. Eliasberg 5/96 P-65 .... $15,400
E.1284. Same, copper. Reeded Edge. J-1016. Very rare. 24.35 gms $6,500
E.1285. Same, copper. Plain Edge. J-1017. Very rare $6,500
E.1286. Same, aluminum. Reeded Edge. J-1018. Very rare $6,500
E.1287. Same, aluminum. Plain Edge. J-1019. Very rare $2,500

Silver dollar patterns continued

*Pattern Design Trial Piece of 1870, design
V – D (Superior Galleries)*

E.1288. 1870 Pattern Design Trial Piece. Design V-D. Silver. Reeded Edge. J-1008. Very rare $14,500
E.1289. Same, silver. Plain Edge. J-1009. Very rare $14,500
E.1290. Same, copper. Reeded Edge. J-1010. Very rare $6,500
E.1291. Same, copper. Plain Edge. J-1011. Very rare $6,500
E.1292. Same, aluminum. Reeded Edge. J-1012. Very rare $6,000
E.1293. Same, aluminum. Plain Edge. J-1013. Very rare $6,000
E.1294. 1871 Regular Design Trial Piece. Copper. Reeded Edge. J-1151. Very rare $4,000
E.1295. Same, copper-nickel. Reeded Edge. J-1153. Very rare $5,000
E.1296. Same, aluminum. Reeded Edge. J-1152. Very rare $4,000
E.1297. 1871 Pattern Design Trial Piece. Obv. The regular design. Rev. E: Olive wreath tied at bottom with
ribbon reading GOD OUR TRUST; COMMERCIAL curved within upper wreath, above two
cornucopiae, DOLLAR below. 420 GRS and 900 FINE within lower wreath, USOA around upper
border. Silver. Reeded Edge. J-1160. Very rare $12,000

*Pattern Design Trial Piece of 1871 (Harlan J.
Berk Ltd.)*

E.1298. 1871 Pattern Design Trial Piece. Obv. Va: Similar to Obv. V except no name lower right. Rev. The
regular design. Silver. Reeded Edge. J-1145. Very rare $12,000
E.1299. Same, silver. Plain Edge. J-1146. Very rare $12,000
E.1300. Same, copper. Reeded Edge. J-1147. Very rare $4,200
E.1301. Same, copper. Plain Edge. J-1148. Very rare. 23.82 gms $4,200
E.1302. Same, aluminum. Reeded Edge. J-1149. Very rare $4,000
E.1303. Same, aluminum. Plain Edge. J-1150. Very rare $4,000
E.1304. 1871 Pattern Design Trial Piece. Design Va-D. Silver. Reeded Edge. J-1139. Very rare $12,000
E.1305. Same, silver. Plain Edge. J-1140. Very rare $12,000
E.1306. Same, copper. Reeded Edge. J-1141. Very rare $5,500
E.1307. Same, copper. Plain Edge. J-1142. Very rare $5,500
E.1308. Same, aluminum. Reeded Edge. J-1143. Very rare $5,500
E.1309. Same, aluminum. Plain Edge. J-1144. Very rare $5,500

Silver dollar patterns continued

Pattern Design Trial Piece of 1871, design Va – E (Bowers & Merena)

E.1310. 1871 Pattern Design Trial Piece. Design Va-E. Silver. Reeded Edge. J-1154. Only two known $28,500

E.1311. Same, silver. Plain Edge. J-1155. Only two known $28,500

    1. To quote from Ford's very astute comment in NN #61 regarding one of the rare appearances of any coin from this die marriage (an E.1310 in that sale): **"One of the most significant U.S. patterns!**... This pattern is the first of the 'Commercial' dollars struck... Being the 'first' it is therefore of extreme historical importance and value, and certainly is a prime candidate for a select collection of <u>authentic</u> U.S. pattern coins that can 'tell a story.' As probably every serious collector of American material knows, the idea expressed by this piece resulted in the ill-fated regular coinage of the trade dollar, 1873-78." (lot #43, p. 7, emphasis in original.)

    2. To add to the significance of these patterns, they are virtually impossible to locate. In addition to the E.1310 in NN #61, now off the market in a long term collection, there was a "toned Proof" in the 1/75 Kagin Sale, lot #967. The only example of E.1311 that has appeared recently was the coin offered by Bowers/ARCF as part of their 6/90 Cabinet of Rarities sale and priced at $26,500. Pedigree for that piece was the BM 1981 ANA-Sieck Sale, Lot #311 and then Kagin's 1983 ANA Sale, Lot #3033.

    3. The obverse die has a tiny flaw that appears on all of these patterns. Ford noted that the coin in NN #61 had a "tiny granular spot in the field immediately below the liberty cap on the obverse," but dismissed it as a matter of "no importance since it is a manufacturing flaw." The same spot appears on the 1981 ANA/1983 ANA E.1131.

E.1312. Same, copper. Reeded Edge. J-1156. Two known $14,000

E.1313. Same, copper. Plain Edge. J-1157. Two known $14,000

E.1314. 1871 Pattern Design Trial Piece. Obv. Vb: Similar to Obv. Va except only 13 stars on right flag. No name or initials at lower right. Rev: The regular design. Silver. Reeded Edge. J-1138a. Very rare $15,000

E.1314a. Same, silver. Plain Edge. Unlisted in Judd. Exceedingly rare, if it exists. Unverified.

E.1314b. Same, copper. Reeded Edge. Unlisted in Judd. Unique?

E.1314c. Same, copper. Plain Edge. Unlisted in Judd. Exceedingly rare, if it exists. Unverified.

E.1315. Same, aluminum. Reeded Edge. J-1138b. Very rare $7,000

Pattern Design Trial Piece of 1871, design Vb – D (Smithsonian)

E.1316. 1871 Pattern Design Trial Piece. Design Vb-D. Silver. Reeded Edge. J-1133. Very rare. Eliasberg 5/96 P-65 .... $16,500

E.1317. Same, silver. Plain Edge. J-1134. Very rare $14,000

E.1318. Same, copper. Reeded Edge. J-1135. Very rare $6,000

E.1319. Same, copper. Plain Edge. J-1136. Very rare $6,000

E.1320. Same, aluminum. Reeded Edge. J-1137. Very rare $6,000

E.1321. Same, aluminum. Plain Edge. J-1138. Very rare $6,000

E.1322. 1871 Pattern Design Trial Piece. Design Vb-E. Silver. Reeded Edge. J-1158. Very rare $14,000

Silver dollar patterns continued

E.1323. Same, copper. Reeded Edge. J-1159. Exceedingly rare, if it exists. Unverified.
E.1324. 1871 Fantasy Mule. Obv. VI: Similar to Obv. Vb except no stars around border, initials J.B.L. at lower
right. Rev: No Motto design of 1840-65. Copper. Reeded Edge. J-1132. Very rare $6,000
E.1325. Same, copper. Plain Edge. J-1132a. Very Rare $6,000
E.1326. 1871 Pattern Design Trial Piece. Obv. VI. Rev. The regular design With Motto. Silver. Reeded Edge. J-
1126. Very rare $15,000
E.1327. Same, silver. Plain Edge. J-1127. Very rare $15,000
E.1328. Same, copper. Reeded Edge. J-1128. Very rare $4,000
E.1329. Same, copper. Plain Edge. J-1129. Very rare $4,000
E.1330. Same, aluminum. Reeded Edge. J-1130. Very rare $4,000
E.1331. Same, aluminum. Plain Edge. J-1131. Very rare $4,000

*Pattern Design Trial Piece of 1871, design
VI – D (Bowers & Merena)*

E.1332. 1871 Pattern Design Trial Piece. Design VI-D. Silver. Reeded Edge. J-1120. Extremely rare ... $25,000
E.1333. Same, silver. Plain Edge. J-1121. Extremely rare $25,000
Very rare and very much sought after for its design and appearance. The Indian Princess, no
stars design in this denomination is a stunning example of the beauty of patterns that has lured
collectors for more than a century. As noted before, the No Stars obverse is far rarer than the
same design with the more traditional stars near the rim. The cameo effect of this obverse should
be seen by anyone interested in patterns whenever the opportunity presents itself.
E.1334. Same, copper. Reeded Edge. J-1122. Very rare $13,500
E.1335. Same, copper. Plain Edge. J-1123. Very rare $13,500
E.1336. Same, aluminum. Reeded Edge. J-1124. Very rare $13,000
E.1337. Same, aluminum. Plain Edge. J-1125. Very rare $13,000
E.1338. 1872 Regular Design Trial Piece. Copper. Reeded Edge. J-1210. Very rare $13,600
E.1339. Same, aluminum. Reeded Edge. J-1211. Very rare $12,500
E.1340. 1872 Pattern Design Trial Piece. Obverse: The regular design. Rev. E. Silver. Reeded Edge. J-1219.
Very rare $20,000
E.1341. Same, copper. Reeded Edge. J-1219a. Unique?

*Pattern Design Trial Piece of 1872 (Bowers
& Merena)*

E.1342. 1872 Pattern Design Trial Piece. Design Va-E. Silver. Reeded Edge. J-1212. Very rare $20,000
E.1343. Same, silver. Plain Edge. J-1213. Very rare $20,000
E.1343a. Same, copper. Reeded Edge. Unlisted in Judd. Exceedingly rare, if it exists. Unverified.
E.1344. 1872 Pattern Design Trial Piece. Obv. Vc: Similar to Obv. Vb but modeled by William Barber
from Longacre's design, differences trivial. Rev. The regular design. Silver. Reeded Edge. J-1208.
Very rare $17,000
E.1345. Same, silver. Plain Edge. J-1209. Very rare $17,000

Silver dollar patterns continued

Pattern Design Trial Piece of 1872,
design Vc – E (Smithsonian)

E.1346. 1872 Pattern Design Trial Piece. Design Vc-E. Silver. Reeded Edge. J-1214. Very rare $18,000

E.1347. Same, silver. Plain Edge. J-1215. Very rare $18,000

E.1348. Same, copper. Reeded Edge. J-1216. Very rare $6,000

E.1349. Same, copper. Plain Edge. J-1217. Very rare $6,000

E.1350. Same, aluminum. Reeded Edge. J-1218. Very rare $6,000

Pattern Design Trial Piece of 1872, design
Vc – F (Bowers & Merena)

E.1351. 1872 Pattern Design Trial Piece. Obv. Vc. Rev. F: Similar to Rev. E except TRADE replaces
COMMERCIAL, cornucopiae removed and IGWT replaces GOD OUR TRUST. Silver. Reeded Edge. J-
1220. Extremely rare. May be a restrike $20,000

> There is a debate among pattern scholars as to whether this pattern represents the first
> appearance of a reverse using the term "Trade dollar" or whether it is simply a muling of an
> 1872 pattern obverse and a reverse first used in 1873 for E. 1405.

E.1352. Same, copper. Reeded Edge. J-1221. Very rare. BM 3/94, P P-63 .... $9,350

E.1353. Same, aluminum. Reeded Edge. J-1222. Very rare $6,000

E.1354. 1872 Pattern Design Trial Piece. Obv. Vc. Rev. G: Standing eagle holding three arrows in right,
or dominant, claw. No olive branch, an oddly militant design. Left claw holds national shield and
ribbon incused IGWT, ribbon in beak labeled EPU. 420 GRAINS. 900 FINE in curved line below
eagle, USOA around upper border, TRADE DOLLAR lower. Silver. Reeded Edge. J-1223. Extremely
rare $20,000

> See the notes for the preceding pattern. Almost definitely a restrike or fantasy mule, created by
> using one of the many reverses designed for the pattern Trade dollars the following year. This is
> the classic example of the "delicacy created for the wealthy collector" that has shadowed the
> entire pattern series for years — and the type of mischievous nonsense that led to the Mint finally
> yielding to outside critics and curtailing the creation and sale of patterns. Having said that,
> however, these 1872 mules are particularly sought after by those interested in Trade dollar
> patterns as far more difficult to locate than the more common patterns of 1873.

Silver dollar patterns continued

The Amazonian Design Pattern Design Trial Piece of 1872

E.1355. 1872 Pattern Design Trial Piece. Obv. VII: Liberty seated to left. Outstretched right arm seems to pat standing eagle on head, left elbow rests on national shield, left hand holds sword that crosses shield. Date below, 13 stars around. William Barber's Amazonian design. Rev. H: Similar to preceding except eagle larger and weight, fineness and ribbon bearing EPU removed. Silver. Reeded Edge. J-1205. Very rare, and exceedingly popular $45,000

    The militant tone set by this design (two shields, a sword and arrows in the right claw of one of two eagles) may have been inspired by English-born William Barber's unease over the recent Franco-Prussian War and the political upheavals in Italy and Spain. The same motivation may have inspired the 1916 silver patterns.

E.1356. Same, copper. Reeded Edge. J-1206. Very rare $25,000

    A three-piece copper set of dollar, half dollar and quarter dollar was sold by ST 3/94, Br. Proof for $39,000.

E.1357. Same, aluminum. Reeded Edge. J-1207. Very rare. BM 11/93, P P-65 .... $31,900

E.1358. 1873 Regular Design Trial Piece. Copper. Reeded Edge. J-1274. Very rare $6,000

E.1359. Same, aluminum. Reeded Edge. J-1275. Very rare $6,000

E.1360. 1873 Pattern Design Trial Piece. Obv. VIII: Similar to Obv. Vc but completely remodeled, LIBERTY incused rather than raised, rock shorter, left leg more extended, pole more upright, etc. Rev. G. Silver. Reeded Edge. J-1308. Very rare $20,000

E.1361. Same, white metal. Plain Edge. J-1309. Very rare $2,000

E.1362. 1873 Pattern Design Trial Piece. Obv. VIII. Rev. I: Similar to Rev. G except EPU appears in the field above the eagle. White metal. Plain Edge. J-1307. Very rare $3,000

E.1363. 1873 Pattern Design Trial Piece. Obv. VIII. Rev. J: Small facing eagle clutching three arrows in right claw and olive branch in left, EPU on fancy scroll above eagle. 420 GRAINS/ 900 FINE below eagle, IGWT on fancy scroll below that, legend USOA and TRADE DOLLAR. Silver. Reeded Edge. J-1310. Scarce $8,000

E.1364. Same, silver. Plain Edge. J-1311. Very rare $12,000

E.1365. Same, copper. Reeded Edge. J-1312. Very rare $4,000

E.1366. Same, aluminum. Reeded Edge. J-1313. Very rare $4,000

E.1367. Same, white metal. Plain Edge. J-1314. Very rare $3,000

E.1368. 1873 Pattern Design Trial Piece. Obv. IX: Similar to Obv. VIII except Indian headdress replaced by coronet, rock to right of globe replaced by sheaf of wheat, two flags above globe replaced by two short plow handles, two cotton bales and ocean waves added to left of leg. Rev. G. Silver. Reeded Edge. J-1293. Scarce $8,000

E.1369. Same, silver. Plain Edge. J-1294. Very rare $14,000

E.1370. Same, copper. Reeded Edge. J-1295. Very rare $4,000

E.1371. Same, copper. Plain Edge. J-1296. Very rare $4,000

E.1372. Same, aluminum. Reeded Edge. J-1297. Very rare $4,000

E.1373. Same, white metal. Plain Edge. J-1298. Very rare $2,000

E.1374. 1873 Pattern Design Trial Piece. Design IX-I. Silver. Reeded Edge. J-1290. Very rare $14,000

E.1375. Same, silver. Plain Edge. J-1291. Very rare $14,000

E.1376. Same, white metal. Plain Edge. J-1292. Very rare $3,000

E.1377. 1873 Pattern Design Trial Piece. Obv. X: Similar to Obv. IX except plow handles longer, more slanted; wheat sheaf larger and cotton bales smaller and more numerous. Rev. F. Silver. Reeded Edge. J-1304a. Unique?

E.1378. Same, copper. Reeded Edge. J-1305. Very rare $6,000

E.1379. Same, white metal. Plain Edge. J-1306. Very rare $3,000

E.1380. 1873 Pattern Design Trial Piece. Design X-G. Silver. Reeded Edge. J-1300. Extremely rare ... $17,500

    This is a good example of the very rare (two to four struck) Trade dollar patterns whose true rarities are not commonly appreciated because of the relative availability of the better known, far more common patterns sold in sets by the Mint to the public during this time. The last one of these patterns to appear at auction was the P P-65 in BM's 3/94 Sunderland Sale, it brought one of the highest prices of any of the patterns, $16,500. If you are trying to complete a set of Trade dollar patterns, this is one of the true rarities that may take years to locate.

Silver dollar patterns continued

E.1381. Same, copper. Reeded Edge. J-1301. Very rare $7,000
E.1382. Same, copper. Plain Edge. J-1302. Very rare $7,000
E.1383. Same, aluminum. Reeded Edge. J-1303. Very rare $7,000
E.1384. 1873 Pattern Design Trial Piece. Design X-I. White metal. Plain Edge. J-1299. Very rare $9,000
E.1385. 1873 Pattern Design Trial Piece. Design X-J. White metal. Plain Edge. J-1304. Very rare $8,000
E.1386. 1873 Pattern Design Trial Piece. Obv. XI: Roughly similar to Obv. IX except globe smaller, wheat
    sheaf moved upwards to replace plow handles, tobacco plant atop cotton bales but no ocean to their
    left. Joseph A. Bailly's plump-faced Liberty design. Rev. K: Small, defiant eagle with upraised wings to
    right, standing on horizontal shield and clutching olive branch in right claw and arrows in left. EPU in
    field above, IGWT on ribbon below, 420 GRAINS/ 900 FINE in field below that. Legend USOA and
    TRADE DOLLAR. Silver. Reeded Edge. J-1315. Scarce. Eliasberg 5/96 P-66 .... $7,920
E.1387. Same, silver. Plain Edge. J-1316. Very rare $9,000
E.1388. Same, copper. Reeded Edge. J-1317. Rare $3,500
E.1389. Same, aluminum. Reeded Edge. J-1318. Very rare $3,000
E.1390. Same, white metal. Plain Edge. J-1319. Very rare $3,000

*Undated Pattern Design Trial Piece
design XII – L (Smithsonian)*

E.1391. (1873?) Pattern Design Trial Piece. Obv. XII: Liberty seated to left on two cotton bales, ocean waves to
    left, wheat sheaf to right. Outstretched right hand holds olive branch; left hand holds ribbon draped
    over bales, IGWT on ribbon at base of bales, 13 stars around border, no date. Similar to the adopted
    design, except wheat sheaf larger and ocean waves shorter. Rev. L: Fat, facing eagle clutching three
    arrows in right claw and olive branch in left, EPU on ribbon above eagle, 420 GRAINS. 900 FINE
    below eagle. Legend USOA and TRADE DOLLAR. Similar to the adopted design with reduced eagle.
    Silver. Reeded Edge. J-1320. Very rare $11,000
    It has been reasonably suggested that this pattern was not struck until 1876, and that either or
    both dies, particularly the reverse, were engraved by Anthony C. Paquet. There was no good
    reason for Paquet to be reinventing the wheel with an inferior rendition of an adopted design in
    1876. He might have had a slight chance with his own interpretation of it before the Barber
    version was adopted in 1873, but there is much about Paquet and his relationship to the Mint
    that is not understood. It is also remotely possible that the rendition is nothing more than an
    apprentice or would-be apprentice engraver's practice or "audition" essai, cut to demonstrate an
    applicant's potential engraving skills.
E.1392. Same, copper. Reeded Edge. J-1321. Very rare $5,000
E.1393. 1873 Pattern Design Trial Piece. Obv. XIII: Similar to Obv. XII except wheat sheaf smaller and ocean
    waves extend to denticled border. Very similar to the adopted design, which has minor differences in
    olive branch and ocean waves separated from the border. Rev. G. Silver. Reeded Edge. J-1326a.
    Extremely rare $14,000
E.1394. Same, white metal. Plain Edge. J-1326b. Very rare $3,000

Silver dollar patterns continued

Pattern Design Trial Piece of 1873, design
XIII – M (Superior Galleries)

E.1395. 1873 Pattern Design Trial Piece. Obv. XIII. Rev. M: Small, facing eagle clutching olive branch in right claw and three arrows in left, EPU on ribbon held in beak. 420 GRAINS. 900 FINE below eagle, legend USOA and TRADE DOLLAR. Silver. Reeded Edge. J-1322. Scarce $9,000

E.1396. Same, silver. Plain Edge. J-1323. Very rare $11,000

E.1397. Same, copper. Reeded Edge. J-1324. Rare $4,000

E.1398. Same, aluminum. Reeded Edge. J-1325. Very rare $3,000

E.1399. Same, white metal. Plain Edge. J-1326. Very rare $2,000

E.1400. 1873 Pattern Design Trial Piece. The designs ultimately adopted for the Trade dollar. Copper. Reeded Edge. J-1327. Very rare $3,000

E.1401. Same, aluminum. Reeded Edge. J-1328. Very rare $2,500

E.1402. Same, white metal. Reeded Edge. J-1329 & 1330. Very rare $2,700

E.1403. 1873 Pattern Design Trial Piece. Obv. XIV: Liberty head left wearing coronet labeled LIBERTY, from the head punch for the $20 gold piece. 13 stars around, date below. Rev. I. Copper. Reeded Edge. J-1289. Very rare $5,500

E.1404. 1873 Pattern Design Trial Piece. Design XIV-K. Copper. Reeded Edge. J-1288. Very rare $5,500

Pattern Design Trial Piece of 1873, design
XV – F

E.1405. 1873 Pattern Design Trial Piece. Obv. XV: Tall Liberty head left wearing coronet labeled LIBERTY; hair tied in a bun at back, 13 stars around, date below. Rev. F. Silver. Reeded Edge. J-1276. Scarce $7,500

E.1406. Same, silver. Plain Edge. J-1277. Very rare $10,000

E.1407. Same, copper. Reeded Edge. J-1278. Rare. BM 3/94, P P-64 .... $8,800

E.1408. Same, aluminum. Reeded Edge. J-1279. Very rare $2,000

E.1409. Same, white metal. Plain Edge. J-1280. Very rare $2,000

E.1410. 1873 Pattern Design Trial Piece. Obv, XVI: Liberty head left with garland of leaves and hair tightly coiled behind, 13 stars around, date below. Rev. G. Copper. Reeded Edge. J-1285. Very rare $3,000

E.1411. Same, aluminum. Reeded Edge. J-1286. Very rare $3,000

Silver dollar patterns continued

Pattern Design Trial Piece of 1873, design XVI – I

E.1412. 1873 Pattern Design Trial Piece. Design XVI-I. Silver. Reeded Edge. J-1281. Scarce. Eliasberg 5/96 P-66 .... $9,020

E.1413. Same, silver. Plain Edge. J-1282. Very rare $10,000

E.1414. Same, copper. Reeded Edge. J-1283. Very rare $2,500

E.1415. Same, aluminum. Reeded Edge. J-1284. Very rare $2,500

E.1416. 1873 Pattern Design Trial Piece. Obv. XVII: Liberty head right wearing coronet labeled LIBERTY, 13 stars around, date below. Rev. F. White metal. Plain Edge. J-1287. Two known $8,000

E.1417. 1874 Regular Design Trial Piece. Trade Dollar. Copper. Reeded Edge. J-1363. Very rare $4,000

E.1418. Same, aluminum. Reeded Edge. J-1364. Very rare $3,000

E.1419. 1875 Regular Design Trial Piece. Trade Dollar. Copper. Reeded Edge. J-1430. Very rare $3,000

E.1420. Same, aluminum. Reeded Edge. J-1431. Very rare $3,000

E.1421. 1875 Pattern Design Trial Piece. Obv. XVIII: Liberty figure wearing coronet seated to left on globe labeled LIBERTY in relief, outstretched right arm holds olive branch. Ocean scene with combination sail/steam ship to left of leg, wheat sheaf and two flags without stars behind globe. IGWT on fancy scroll below base, date below, 13 stars around upper border. Rev: No Motto design of 1840-65, specifically a die last used to coin some 1859 Proof dollars. Silver. Reeded Edge. J-1420. Extremely rare, six struck. Eliasberg 5/96 P-65 .... $25,300

 1. These "Liberty by the Seashore" patterns in silver seem to never appear at auction. Most (and they were only struck this year and the following) are in long-held collections. While the copper strikes appear from time to time, they are occasionally held down in price by unsightly spotting. There have been too few aluminum examples on the market to judge their condition, although the one or two that have been seen were free of the corrosion problems that often plague patterns in this metal. Much sought after in any metal, the hunt becomes nearly impossible in silver.

 2. Although any 1870s die combination with this pre-1866 No Motto reverse has traditionally been called a fantasy mule, its usage is quite correct with this obverse which already has IGWT on it.

E.1422. Same, copper. Reeded Edge. J-1421. Very rare, eight struck $8,000

E.1423. Same, aluminum. Reeded Edge. J-1422. Excessively rare, two struck $9,000

E.1424. 1875 Pattern Design Trial Piece. Design XVIII-E. Silver. Reeded Edge. J-1423. Extremely rare, six struck $25,000

E.1425. Same, copper. Reeded Edge. J-1424. Very rare, eight struck $10,000

E.1426. Same, aluminum. Reeded Edge. J-1425. Excessively rare, three struck $10,000

E.1427. 1875 Pattern Design Trial Piece. Obv. XVIII. Rev: The regular Trade dollar design. Silver. Reeded Edge. J-1426. Very rare $10,000

E.1428. Same, copper. Reeded Edge. J-1427. Very rare $3,000

E.1429. Same, aluminum. Reeded Edge. J-1428. Very rare $3,000

E.1430. Same, white metal. Reeded Edge. J-1429. Very rare $3,000

E.1431. 1876 Regular Design Trial Piece. Trade dollar. Copper. Reeded Edge. J-1476. Very rare $3,000

Note: Judd also lists aluminum as J-1477. It is doubtful that it exists.

E.1433. 1876 Pattern Design Trial Piece. Obv. XIX: Similar to Obv. XVIII except no stars and IGWT in cartouche below base. Rev. No Motto design of 1840-65. Silver. Reeded Edge. J-1470. Two struck $40,000

 1. "Liberty by the Seashore" pattern in silver, has the reverse from the 1857-59 No Motto Proof Seated Liberty U.S. dollar. This particular reverse was last used before this die marriage on the 1875 version of this coin and before that for some of the 1859 Proof dollars. When it was brought out for reuse in the 1870s it had rust pits and die rust on the rims. The result can be seen as toning on the photos of these coins.

 2. There were two sets of eight pattern dollars (four with the Sailor Head obverse and four with this obverse) struck in silver for this Centennial year. These coins are among the most highly sought after in the pattern series. The last offering as a complete set was lot #1102 in BM 11/85 Abe Kosoff Estate Sale. This pattern was lot #1099 in the individual lot numbering, although the set sold as a group. At the time of our nation's Bicentennial, Kosoff had solicited donations

Silver dollar patterns continued

from the hobby so that the set might be purchased from himself and William Mitkoff of Pittsfield, Mass., and presented intact to the Smithsonian for our National Numismatic Collections. The effort was not successful.

E.1434. Same, copper. Reeded Edge. J-1471. Very rare $10,000

E.1435. 1876 Pattern Design Trial Piece. Obv. XIX. Rev. The regular Trade dollar design. Silver. Reeded Edge. J-1474. Two struck $40,000

E.1436. Same, copper. Reeded Edge. J-1475. Very rare $10,000

Pattern Design Trial Piece of 1876, design XIX – E

E.1437. 1876 Pattern Design Trial Piece. Design XIX-E. Silver. Reeded Edge. J-1472. Two struck $40,000

E.1438. Same, copper. Reeded Edge. J-1473. Very rare $6,000

Pattern Design Trial Piece of 1876, design XIX – N

E.1439. 1876 Pattern Design Trial Piece. Obv. XIX. Rev. N: ONE DOLLAR within laurel wreath, USOA and EPU around border. Silver. Reeded Edge. J-1467. Five struck $32,000

E.1440. Same, copper. Reeded Edge. J-1468. Very rare $7,500

E.1441. Same, copper. Plain Edge. J-1469. Very rare $3,000

Pattern Design Trial Piece of 1876, design XX – N

E.1442. 1876 Pattern Design Trial Piece. Obv. XX: William Barber's Sailor Head, Liberty left wearing coronet labeled LIBERTY in raised letters, hair tied back with a dangling ribbon, date below, no stars or mottoes. Rev. N. Silver. Reeded Edge. J-1457. Excessively rare, two known $40,000

This is the first of the four Sailor Head patterns in the ex-Judd/Kosoff Centennial set. The late Walter Breen, in one of his more outstanding flights of fancy, declared this head to be a portrait of Britain's Queen Victoria. It is one of the favorites of this book's editors.

E.1443. Same, copper. Reeded Edge. J-1458a. Very rare. 23.86 gms $8,000

E.1444. Same, copper. Plain Edge. J-1458. Very rare $8,000

Silver dollar patterns continued

Pattern Design Trial Piece of 1876, design XXI – N

E.1445. 1876 Pattern Design Trial Piece. Obv. XXI: Similar to preceding except head smaller with small IGWT below neck. Rev. N. Silver. Reeded Edge. J-1459. Excessively rare, two known $40,000

E.1446. Same, copper. Reeded Edge. J-1460. Very rare $8,000

E.1447. Same, copper. Plain Edge. J-1461. Very rare $8,000

E.1448. 1876 Pattern Design Trial Piece. Obv. XXII: Similar to Obv. XX except small IGWT above head and 13 stars around border. Rev. N. Silver. Reeded Edge. J-1462. Excessively rare, two known $40,000

E.1449. Same, copper. Reeded Edge. J-1463. Very rare $8,000

E.1450. Same, copper. Plain Edge. J-1463a. Unique?

Pattern Design Trial Piece of 1876, design XXIIa – N

E.1451. 1876 Pattern Design Trial Piece. Obv. XXIIa: Similar to Obv. XXII except beaded border added to top of coronet. Rev. N. Silver. Reeded Edge. J-1464. Excessively rare, two known $40,000

E.1452. Same, copper. Reeded Edge. J-1465. Very rare $8,000

E.1453. Same, copper. Plain Edge. J-1466. Unique?

Pattern Design Trial Piece of 1877, design XXIIb – O (Bowers & Merena)

E.1454. 1877 Pattern Design Trial Piece. Obv. XXIIb: Similar to Obv. XXII except dot-dash border added to top of coronet. Rev. O: 1 DOLLAR within wreath of cotton, wheat and corn, USOA and EPU around border. Similar to Rev. D of 1870. Copper. Reeded Edge. J-1542. Very rare $20,000

Silver dollar patterns continued

Pattern Design Trial Piece of 1877, design
XXIII – O

E.1455. 1877 Pattern Design Trial Piece. Obv. XXIII: Similar to Obv. XXII except long, wavy hair added at back of neck and ribbon hangs straight down. Rev. O. Copper. Reeded Edge. J-1544. Very rare $20,000

Pattern Design Trial Piece of 1877, design
XXIIIa – O

E.1456. 1877 Pattern Design Trial Piece. Obv. XXIIIa: Similar to Obv. XXIII except dot-dash border added to top of coronet. Rev. O. Copper. Reeded Edge. J-1543. Very rare $20,000

Pattern Design Trial Piece of 1878, design
XXIV – P

E.1457. 1878 Pattern Design Trial Piece. Obv. XXIV: Liberty head left wearing coronet labeled LIBERTY in raised letters, IGWT at upper border, date below, stars around. Rev. P: Standing, facing eagle with wings partially raised clutching olive branch in right claw and three arrows in left. Gothic EPU above eagle, USOA and ONE DOLLAR around border. Designed by William Barber, and loudly favored by contemporary numismatists over the adopted Morgan design. Silver. Reeded Edge. J-1554. Scarce. Three obv. and four rev. die varieties reported for this and next. Eliasberg 5/96 P-65 .... $5,720

E.1458. Same, copper. Reeded Edge. J-1555. Rare $2,000

E.1459. Same, aluminum. Reeded Edge. J-1556. Very rare, if it exists.

E.1460. Same, white metal. Reeded Edge. J-1556a. Very rare $2,000

Silver dollar patterns continued

Mule of 1878, design XXV – P (Superior Galleries)

E.1461. 1878 Mule. Obv. XXV: Liberty head left wearing cap with LIBERTY incused on the band, cotton and wheat plants tucked into band. EPU at upper border, date below, seven stars left border, six right. The Morgan design, for following. Rev. P. Copper. Reeded Edge. J-1565. Very rare $6,000

Pattern Design Trial Piece of 1878, design XXV – Q (Smithsonian)

E.1462. 1878 Pattern Design Trial Piece. Obv. XXV. Rev. Q: Standing, facing eagle with raised wings clutching three-leafed olive branch in right claw and three arrows in left. Seven tail feathers. Laurel wreath around lower part of eagle, Gothic IGWT above head between wings, USOA and ONE DOLLAR around border. Three obv. die varieties reported. The Morgan design. Silver. Reeded Edge. J-1550 and 1550a. Scarce. Eliasberg 5/96 P-65 .... $10,340
E.1463. Same, copper. Reeded Edge. J-1551. Rare. ST 10/94, N P-66 .... $11,000
E.1464. 1878 Pattern Design Trial Piece. Obv. XXV. Rev. R: Similar to preceding except nine leaves to olive branch. Similar to the first adopted design with eight tail feathers except no designer's initial on wreath bow. Silver. Reeded Edge. J-1552. Very rare $4,000
E.1465. Same, copper. Reeded Edge. J-1553. Very rare $4,000
There were many changes to Morgan's basic design both before and after it was adopted for regular use. See *The Comprehensive Catalogue of U.S. Morgan and Peace Silver Dollars* by Van Allen and Mallis for the history of these issues.

Pattern Design Trial Piece of 1878, design XXVI – S, Goloid (Smithsonian)

E.1466. 1878 Pattern Design Trial Piece. Goloid dollar. Obv. XXVI: Liberty head left wearing cap with wide band incused LIBERTY, cotton and wheat in band. EPU at upper border, date below, seven stars left border, six right. Rev. S: USOA and ONE DOLLAR around circle of 38 stars, representing the number of states. Within circle in five lines: GOLOID./ 1 G./ 24 S./.9 FINE./ 258 GRS. Goloid composition, Dr. Wheeler Hubbell's patented alloy composed of gold, silver and copper. Reeded Edge. J-1557. Rare, 13 struck. Eliasberg 5/96 P-64 .... $3,410
E.1467. Same, silver. Reeded Edge. J-1558. Scarce. Restrikes exist $1,000

Silver dollar patterns continued

E.1468. Same, copper. Reeded Edge. J-1559. Rare $1,000

Pattern Design Trial Piece of 1878, design XXVI – T, Goloid (Smithsonian)

E.1469. 1878 Pattern Design Trial Piece. Goloid dollar. Obv. XXVI. Rev. T: USOA and ONE DOLLAR around laurel wreath. Within wreath in five lines: GOLOID./ 1 GOLD./ 24 SILVER./.9 FINE./ 258 GRS. Goloid alloy. Reeded Edge. J-1560. Very rare $4,000

E.1470. Same, standard silver. Reeded Edge. J-1561. Very rare, if it exists. Should be distinguishable from the goloid alloy by very careful specific gravity test $2,000

E.1471. Same, copper. Reeded Edge. J-1562. Rare $1,500

Pattern Design Trial Piece of 1878, design XXVI – U, Goloid (Smithsonian)

E.1472. 1878 Pattern Design Trial Piece. Goloid dollar. Obv. XXVI. Rev. U: USOA and 100 CENTS around circle of 38 stars. Within circle in six lines: GOLOID./ METRIC./ 1-G./ 16.1-S./ 1.9-C./ GRAMS 14.25. Goloid composition. Reeded Edge. J-1563. Very rare. Eliasberg 5/96 P65 .... $5,720

E.1473. Same, silver. Reeded Edge. J-1564. Very rare. Restrikes exist $2,000

Pattern Design Trial Piece of 1879, design XXV – V (Smithsonian)

E.1474. 1879 Pattern Design Trial Piece. Obv. XXV. The Morgan design. Rev. V: Standing eagle with wings partially raised, clutching olive branch in right claw and three arrows in left, USOA and ONE DOLLAR around. The William Barber design. Silver. Reeded Edge. J-1611. Very rare. Eliasberg 5/96 P-65 $14,300

E.1475. Same, copper. Reeded Edge. J-1612. Very rare $6,000

E.1476. 1879 Pattern Design Trial Piece. Obv. XXV. Rev. W: Similar to preceding except ONE DOLLAR smaller, eagle set lower and IGWT added around upper part of eagle. Silver. Reeded Edge. J-1613. Very rare $7,000

E.1477. Same, copper. Reeded Edge. J-1614. Very rare $6,000

Silver dollar patterns continued

E.1478. 1879 Mule. Obv. XXV. The Morgan design, with its EPU. Rev. X: Standing, facing eagle with partially outstretched wings, clutching large olive branch in right claw and three arrows in left. USOA and ONE DOLLAR around border, EPU in field above eagle. A design not used on any other pattern, usually attributed to William Barber but possibly the work of Charles, who succeeded his father to the position in this year. See next reverse. Silver. Reeded Edge. J-1615. Very rare $7,000

E.1479. Same, copper. Reeded Edge. J-1616. Very rare $6,000

Pattern Design Trial Piece of 1879, design
XXVII – Y, Washlady

E.1480. 1879 Pattern Design Trial Piece. Obv. XXVII: Liberty head left with wavy hair piled up in back, ribbon above forehead labeled LIBERTY in incused letters, above which are wheat and cotton plants, date below. IGWT at upper border, seven stars left border, six right. Charles Barber's Washlady design. Rev. Y: Similar to preceding except eagle set lower and EPU spaced out around top half of eagle, olive branch and arrows slightly different. Designer uncertain, usually attributed to Charles. See previous reverse. Silver. Reeded Edge. J-1603. Very rare. 26.74 gms $25,000

The Washlady is particularly hard to find in this denomination.

E.1481. Same, copper. Reeded Edge. J-1604. Rare $8,000

E.1481a. Same, white metal. Reeded Edge. Unlisted in Judd. Unique?

Pattern Design Trial Piece of 1879, design
XXVIII – Z

E.1482. 1879 Pattern Design Trial Piece. Obv. XXVIII: Similar to preceding except hair not as full and foliage rearranged, LIBERTY incused on ornamented ribbon tied in a bow behind the neck. Designer uncertain, often attributed to William Barber but possibly the work of Charles. Rev. Z: Similar to Rev. X except eagle much smaller, partially surrounded by laurel wreath similar to that of the Morgan dollar reverse. Silver. Reeded Edge. J-1605. Very rare $24,000

E.1483. Same, copper. Reeded Edge. J-1606. Very rare $7,000

E.1484. Same, white metal. Reeded Edge. J-1607. Unique?

Silver dollar patterns continued

*Pattern Design Trial Piece of 1879, design
XXIX – AA, Schoolgirl*

E.1485. 1879 Pattern Design Trial Piece. Obv. XXIX: Liberty head with pearl necklace left with long, wavy hair tied with ribbon at top of head labeled LIBERTY, date below, E PLURIBUS at left border, UNUM at right, seven stars above head, six below. Morgan's popular Schoolgirl design. Rev. AA: Defiant eagle to left standing on scroll incused IGWT. Large olive branch and three arrows behind scroll, USOA and ONE DOLLAR around border. Similar to 1877 half, Rev. V (see E.1164). Silver. Reeded Edge. J-1608. Very rare. Eliasberg 5/96 P-64 .... $70,400

> The classic example of a coin where the opportunity to acquire comes along only once in a very long time. The last example in silver was lot #1465 in the BM 3/94 Sunderland Sale. Based on the description and (particularly) the color photo, that coin looks like lot #75 from the 10/77 BR Fairfield Sale. This coin was earlier lot #1262 in 1975 BR Scott Sale. The last time a Schoolgirl had appeared in auction before the Sunderland specimen was in the 1981 BR Sieck-ANA Sale — a gap of 13 years! The Sunderland specimen brought the high price for patterns in that sale, and was a very pleasing coin despite its certified grade of PR-62. In light of the fact that a so-called "Gem" specimen was being hawked privately for nearly four times the sale price of the Sunderland coin (and supposedly sold at or near that level just before that sale), the $32,500 price paid for the coin at auction (plus 10%) appears to have been a bargain during a down market.

E.1486. Same, copper. Reeded Edge. J-1609. Very rare $23,000

> Quite rare in this metal, as Ford stated in NN #61: **"Definitely rarer than the silver strikes;** certainly less often seen, This was lot 1537 of the Michael F. Higgy collection, sold by the Numismatic Gallery, Sept. 10-11, 1943... Long considered to be one of the most outstanding U.S. coinage proposals, this coveted pattern dollar has (on at least one occasion) been thought to be <u>unique</u> in this metal."

E.1487. Same, lead. Reeded Edge. J-1610. Very rare $9,000

*Pattern Design Trial Piece of 1879, design
XXVI – BB, Goloid Metric (Smithsonian)*

E.1488. 1879 Pattern Design Trial Piece. Goloid Metric dollar. Obv. XXVI, as in 1878, the Barber design. Rev. BB: Tight circle of 38 stars around 15.3-G./ 236.7-S./ 28-C./ 14 GRAMS. in four lines. Concentric double legend, GOLOID METRIC DOLLAR, DEO EST GLORIA/ USOA and 100 CENTS. Goloid composition (see 1878). Reeded Edge. J-1626. Rare. 14.055 gms, S.G. 10.53; 14.03 gms, S.G. 10.54. Eliasberg 5/96 P-66 .... $4,400

E.1489. Same, silver. Reeded Edge. J-1627. Relatively common, sometimes lighter than 14 grams of preceding issue. 14.00 gms, S.G. 10.33 .... $1,000

E.1490. Same, copper. Reeded Edge. J-1628. Very rare $1,500

E.1491. Same, aluminum. Reeded Edge. J-1629. Very rare $2,000

E.1491a. Same, white metal, Reeded Edge. Unlisted in Judd. Unique?

E.1492. Same, lead. Reeded Edge. J-1630. Very rare $2,000

Silver dollar patterns continued

Pattern Design Trial Piece of 1879, design XXX – BB, Goloid Metric (Bowers & Merena)

E.1493. 1879 Pattern Design Trial Piece. Goloid Metric Dollar. Obv. XXX: Liberty head left with hair tightly braided at back of head, ribbon around hair incused LIBERTY at top of head. EPU at upper border, date below, seven stars left border, six right. The Morgan design. Rev. BB. Goloid composition. Reeded Edge. J-1631. Very rare $8,000

E.1494. Same, copper. Reeded Edge. J-1632. Very rare $2,000

E.1495. Same, aluminum. Reeded Edge. J-1633. Very rare $2,000

E.1496. Same, white metal. Reeded Edge. J-1634. Very rare $2,000

Pattern Design Trial Piece of 1879, design XXI – CC

E.1497. 1879 Pattern Design Trial Piece. Metric silver dollar. Obv. XXXI: Liberty head left as on Obv. XXIV of 1878. EPU at upper border, date below, seven stars left border, six right. The Barber design. Rev. CC: Wreath of cotton, wheat and corn partially around tight, dotted circle enclosing 895.8 S./ 4.2-G./ 100-C./ 25 GRAMS in four lines. DEO EST GLORIA in cartouche above circle, legend USOA and ONE DOLLAR. Metric alloy, silver, gold and copper. Reeded Edge. J-1617. Rare $2,000

E.1498. Same, silver (90:10). Reeded Edge. J-1618. Relatively common, usually lighter than 25 grams of preceding issue $1,000

E.1499. Same, copper. Reeded Edge. J-1619. Very rare $2,500

E.1500. Same, aluminum. Reeded Edge. J-1620. Very rare $2,500

E.1500a. Same, white metal. Reeded Edge. Unlisted in Judd. Unique?

E.1501. Same, lead. Reeded Edge. J-1621. Unique?

Pattern Design Trial Piece of 1879, design XXXII – CC (Superior Galleries)

E.1502. 1879 Pattern Design Trial Piece. Metric Silver Dollar. Obv. XXXII: Liberty head left with hair tied back in a bun, ribbon across hair incused LIBERTY. EPU at upper border, date below, seven stars left border, six right. The Morgan design. Rev. CC. Metric alloy. Reeded Edge. J-1622. Very rare. Eliasberg 5/96 P-66 .... $12,100

E.1503. Same, copper. Reeded Edge. J-1623. Very rare $2,500

E.1504. Same, aluminum. Reeded Edge. J-1624. Very rare $2,500

E.1505. Same, white metal. Reeded Edge. J-1625. Unique?

Silver dollar patterns continued

Pattern Design Trial Piece of 1880, design
XXVI – BB (Superior Galleries)

E.1506. 1880 Pattern Design Trial Piece. Goloid metric dollar. Design XXVI-BB. Goloid composition. Reeded Edge. J-1651. Rare $2,000

E.1507. Same, copper. Reeded Edge. J-1652. Very rare $2,500

E.1508. Same, aluminum. Reeded Edge. J-1653. Very rare $8,000

Pattern Design Trial Piece of 1880, design
XXX – BB (Bowers & Merena)

E.1509. 1880 Pattern Design Trial Piece. Goloid metric dollar. Design XXX-BB. Goloid composition. Reeded Edge. J-1654. Very rare. Eliasberg 5/96 P-65 .... $12,100

E.1510. Same, copper. Reeded Edge. J-1655. Very rare $6,000

E.1511. Same, aluminum. Reeded Edge. J-1656. Very rare $6,000

Pattern Design Trial Piece of 1880, design
XXXI – CC (Superior Galleries)

E.1512. 1880 Pattern Design Trial Piece. Metric silver dollar. Design XXXI-CC. Metric alloy. Reeded Edge. J-1645. Rare. Eliasberg 5/96 P-66 .... $7,700

E.1513. Same, copper. Reeded Edge. J-1646. Very rare. ST 9/94, Ch. Br. Proof $4,600

E.1514. Same, aluminum. Reeded Edge. J-1647. Very rare $3,000

Silver dollar patterns continued

Pattern Design Trial Piece of 1880, Metric (Smithsonian)

E.1515. 1880 Pattern Design Trial Piece. Metric silver dollar. Design XXXII-CC. Metric alloy. Reeded Edge. J-1648. Very rare $3,500

E.1516. Same, copper. Reeded Edge. J-1649. Very rare $3,500

E.1517. Same, aluminum. Reeded Edge. J-1650. Very rare $3,000

E.1518. 1882 Regular Design Trial Piece. Standard dollar. Copper. Reeded Edge. J-1703a. Unique?

E.1519. 1882 Regular Design Trial Piece. Trade dollar. Copper. Reeded Edge. J-1703b. Unique?

Pattern Design Trial Piece of 1882, design XXXIII – DD

E.1520. 1882 Pattern Design Trial Piece. Obv. XXXIII: Liberty head right with headband incused LIBERTY, wearing small national shield as earring, date below. EPU at upper border, six stars lower left, seven lower right. Rev. DD: Defiant eagle to right, perched on olive branch and three arrows, USOA and ONE DOLLAR around border. Silver. Reeded Edge. J-1702. Very rare. Eliasberg 5/96 P-67 .. $82,250
    Considered by many as the finest of Morgan's efforts. In NN #61, Ford expressed his thoughts on this coin (in contrast to the same designer's earlier Schoolgirl, as follows: "[T]his superior Morgan design with head to right [is in contrast to] his earlier work on the dollar pattern with head left (see lot 75, earlier.) The profile here is much the same as on its 1879 counterpart, though the coiffure greatly differs; presence of a 'defiant' eagle on both reverses is odd coincidence. Ten to twelve silver sets are believed to have been made." (Emphasis in original.)

E.1521. Same, copper. Reeded Edge. J-1703. Very rare $10,000

E.1522. 1883 Regular Design Trial Piece. Trade dollar. Copper. Reeded Edge. J-1720a. Very rare $4,000

E.1523. 1884 Regular Design Trial Piece. Standard dollar. Copper. Reeded Edge. J-1731. Very rare ... $5,000

E.1524. 1884 Regular Design Trial Piece. Trade dollar. Copper. Reeded Edge. J-1732. Two known, one silver plated $6,000

E.1525. 1885 Regular Design Trial Piece. Standard dollar. Copper. Plain Edge. J-1750a. Very rare $2,000

E.1526. Same, aluminum. Reeded Edge. J-1750. Very rare $6,000

E.1527. 1885 Experimental Edge Trial Piece. Obv. and Rev. The regular designs. Edge lettered E PLURIBUS UNUM in raised letters. Silver. Lettered Edge. J-1747. Very rare. Eliasberg 5/96 P-64 .... $8,140

E.1528. Same, copper. Lettered Edge. J-1748. Rare $4,000

E.1529. Same, aluminum. Lettered Edge. J-1749. Very rare $6,000

E.1530. 1964-D Trial Piece. Obv. and Rev. Similar to the Peace dollar of 1922-35, exact details uncertain. Struck to test the striking characteristics of new dies prepared for an expected regular issue. Sold at the cash window to Mint employees on the first day of striking, but recalled the following day and all said to have been melted. Reported to exist in private hands. The Mint's technical laboratory in Washington, D.C., held two specimens of this striking in its reference collection for many years, but eventually melted them despite an official request by the Smithsonian to include in the National Numismatic Collections.

Clad dollar patterns continued

Promotional trial of 1976 (Thomas K. DeLorey)

E.1531. 1976 Promotional Trial Piece. Obv. and Rev. The Bicentennial dollar design, without Mint mark. 40% silver. Reeded Edge. Proof. May no longer exist.

Several 40% silver three-piece Proof sets were struck at Philadelphia without Mint marks on August 12, 1974, for display at the upcoming American Numismatic Association convention and for presentation to the designers of the three coins and a representative of newly-inaugurated President Ford, who was understandably too busy to attend the ceremony. Allegedly all were returned to the Mint and replaced with regular Proof coins at a later date.

E.1532. (1976) Experimental Size Trial Piece. Obv. Bust right, VIRGINIA around upper border, 1759 below, MARTHA WASHINGTON in lower right field. Rev. Angle view of Washington home. MOUNT VERNON below. HOME OF THE WASHINGTON FAMILY around. 11-sided plain, raised rim. Composition and edge unknown. Prototype of what eventually became the Susan B. Anthony dollar, see April 1976 *COINage*.

E.1533. (1977) Experimental Size Vending Machine Trial Piece. Obv. and Rev. Blank except for low mound in center and 11-sided raised rim. Copper-nickel. Plain Edge. with 11 flat sides. 26.5mm. Distributed by the Mint to vending machine manufacturers as prototypes of a proposed smaller dollar eventually issued with the Susan B. Anthony design, to test new equipment for the smaller dollar. At least one specimen certified by ANACS $150

Note: Galvanos were prepared for a 10-sided, 27mm. 1977 Eisenhower dollar and an 11-sided, 26.5mm. Flowing Hair dollar by U.S. Mint Engraver Frank Gasparro. Gasparro told Coin World reporter Paul Gilkes in 1992 that trial strikes had been made at the Philadelphia Mint, but all were destroyed soon after. A Mint spokesman confirmed that trial strikings of the Flowing Hair design were made, all all destroyed. A photograph of a presumed trial strike indicates a round planchet with plain edge, although at the time Mint officials were still seriously considering the 11-sided planchet. Liberty is strongly a styled Flowing Hair Liberty with cap on pole, and the stars around the portrait are of an old style, with raised centers and ridges down the points of the stars. The reverse design is called "The Coming of A New Dawn," and shows a soaring eagle vaguely reminiscent of the one on the Saint-Gaudens double eagle type, although flying to right over a mountain sunrise. Gasparro's FG initials appear on both sides.

Gold half dollar

Experimental size trial (Bowers & Merena)

E.1534. (1852) Experimental Size Trial Piece. Obv. The regular reverse die for a half dime, struck on a holed planchet so that only UNITED STATES OF AMERICA and fragments of the wreath show. Rev. Blank die with beaded border. Gold. Reeded Edge. J-135. Very rare. Struck to test the feasibility of a gold half dollar of light weight with a large enough diameter to be easily handled. made unnecessary by adoption of the Arrows at Date silver of 1853. Paramount Auction '82 Gem Unc., $4,000; Ivy 5/83 Proof $7,000 .... $4,000

Gold dollars

Pattern Design Trial Piece of 1836

E.1535. 1836 Pattern Design Trial Piece. Obv. Liberty cap, radiant, with LIBERTY on headband. Rev. 1 D. in two lines within palm branch circle, USOA and date around border. Gold. Plain Edge. 14mm. J-67. Rare. Struck with dies aligned opposite each other. Restrikes exist, one over a cut-down 1859 gold dollar. Garrett II Proof, $17,000; BM 11/93, P P-65, $15,950; ST 3/95 Gem BU $15,500; Eliasberg 5/96 P-65 .... $18,700

    1. The only gold pattern struck in gold that is generally available — and available for less than a six-figure price. Hard to locate in Gem condition.

    2. Like the 2-cent pattern of this year, this pattern shows evidence of rather hasty die preparation. The C in AMERICA is struck over some other letter, with part of a serif of the underlying letter showing on the upper left curve of the C and what is left of the curved portion of the original letter or something else closing the mouth of the C. This is a very bold overstrike.

E.1536. Same, silver-alloyed gold. Plain Edge. J-68. Very rare. Struck with medallic die alignment $18,000

E.1537. Same, silver. Plain Edge. J-69. Very rare. Apparently all are restrikes. BM 9/84 Proof, $3,080 .... $3,000

E.1538. Same, copper. Plain Edge. J-70. Very rare. ST 10/83 Proof, $6,325 .... $2,000

E.1539. Same, oroide. Plain Edge. J-71. Very rare. Apparently all are restrikes $2,000

Experimental size trial of 1849 (Smithsonian)

E.1540. 1849 Experimental Size Trial Piece. Hand engraved. Obv. Laurel wreath around square central hole; U. STATES OF AMERICA around border. Rev. 1 DOLLAR and date within circle of 13 stars. Gold. Plain Edge. 16mm. J-115. Very rare. Hand-tooled to give an idea of what a larger gold dollar with a hole might look like. Minor variations in design between individual pieces. Heritage 6/87, $14,000 .... $21,000

    1. As noted in a letter from the Mint Director to Congress on 1/30/49, (quoted in the 1967 LM Sale discussed below) three gold and three silver-gilt examples were hand-engraved by Longacre over the period of a few days to show the proposed size and shape of a perforated gold dollar. Given Longacre's problems in sinking dies in general, and also because striking a few coins from a die that would not be used later made hand-engraving a realistic alternative, no dies were cut. These coins were intended to show only general size and configuration, including the center opening. They were not intended to represent anything like what would ever be struck as a gold dollar for circulation.

    2. These hand-tooled patterns are unique in numismatics — and a "sleeper" in either gold or gilded-silver. To quote Breen in the LM 9/20/67 Sale, lot#495: "One of the most fantastically desirable and historic of all patterns, of extreme interest not only because of the unique fabric but because it is something that was **actually worked on by Longacre's hands** rather than coming to us only indirectly via hubbed dies. A real museum piece. PLATE" (p.65, emphasis in original, this lot brought $2500 plus 10%). He continues: "[a]ll known specimens in gold or silver gilt differ slightly in details of execution; the present coin has OF smaller than in the Judd illustration. 'Three gold and three silver-gilt specimens... were enclosed in a letter from Mr. Patterson [Mint Director] to (Congressman) J.J. McKay, Jan 30, 1849.' Longacre had been engraving these six pieces during the preceding couple of days. No others are known to exist and no electrotype or other copies have ever been reported. One of the three silver-gilt pieces is in the Omaha City Library [Byron Reed Collection], a second in the Chase Manhattan Bank Money Museum, wt. 15-1/2 grains."

    3. Examing one silver-gilt specimen that appeared in a slab as a PR-60, and which appears to be the lot #3113 in the BM Lee F. Hewitt Sale, 11/84, the problem of grading these coins can be seen. This coin was "as made" and far better looking than the Garrett coin. The engraving process itself left all of these coins hairlined from the initial cleaning with a cloth that took place after each was individually engraved. The technical grade of PR-60 was then correct for a normal coin, while the PR-63 grade in the sale is more realistic.

E.1541. Same, silver gilt. Plain Edge. J-116. Very rare. Garrett II, $8,000 .... $20,000

Gold dollar patterns continued

Experimental size trial

E.1542. (1852) Experimental Size Trial Piece. Obv. USOA and outer portion of wreath from a normal Seated Liberty dime of the period, central hole. Rev. Blank die with beaded border. Gold. Reeded Edge. 17.9mm. J-136. Very rare. Struck from dies on hand to show the approximate size of the next piece, before its dies were engraved $5,000

Experimental size trial

E.1543. 1852 Pattern Design Trial Piece. Obv. USA above and date below central hole. Rev. Laurel wreath around central hole. Gold. Plain Edge. J-137. Very rare, two known, both restrikes struck over cut-down and holed quarter eagles of 1846 and 1859 .... $4,000

E.1544. Same, silver. Plain Edge. J-138. Very rare. Originals only, thick or thin planchets. ST 10/86 Unc., $2,090 .... $5,000

E.1545. Same, copper. Plain Edge. J-139. Very rare. Originals only. Eliasberg 5/96 P-64 .... $4,400

E.1546. Same, copper-nickel (various alloys). Plain Edge. J-140 & 140a. Very rare. Kagin's '86 ANA Proof, $1,320 .... $3,000

Pattern Design Trial Piece of 1852 (Bowers & Merena)

E.1547. 1852 Pattern Design Trial Piece. Obv. Same as preceding. Rev. DOLLAR above and laurel wreath below central hole. Gold. Plain Edge. J-141. Very rare. Garrett II Ch. Proof, $20,000 .... $11,000

E.1548. Same, silver. Plain Edge. J-142. Very rare $5,000

E.1549. Same, copper. Plain Edge. J-143. Very rare $3,000

E.1550. Same, copper-nickel. Plain Edge. J-144. Unique?

Pattern Design Trial Piece of 1852

E.1551. 1852 Pattern Design Trial Piece. Obv. USOA and fancy border around central hole. Rev. Same as preceding. Gold. Plain Edge. J-145. Rare, the thick pieces a little more so than the thin, Garrett II Choice Proof, $19,000 .... $11,000

E.1552. Same, silver. Plain Edge. J-146. Very rare $5,000

E.1553. Same, copper. Plain Edge. J-147. Very rare. ST 3/92, BU $3,800

E.1554. Same, copper-nickel (various alloys). Plain Edge. J-148 & 148a. Very rare. Superior Auction '83 Proof, $1,375 .... $2,000

E.1555. Same, brass. Plain Edge. J-148b. Very Rare $2,000

E.1556. 1855 Regular Design Trial Piece. White metal. Plain Edge. J-175a. Unique?

E.1557. 1858 Revised Design Trial Piece. Obv. and Rev. from the same device punches as the regular issue, but legends in different style basically taller than the regular lettering. A practice piece by Assistant Engraver Anthony Paquet. Gold. Reeded Edge. J-224. Unique, ANS collection.

E.1558. Same, copper. Reeded Edge. J-225. Very rare $3,000

E.1559. 1859 Revised Design Trial Piece. Obv. and Rev.: Similar to the regular design, but remodeled in a somewhat awkward style. Lettering style similar to preceding. Believed to be another practice piece by Paquet, though some have questioned its status as a Mint product. Copper. Reeded Edge. J-256. Very rare, Garrett II AU-55, $2,100 .... $2,000

E.1560. 1865 Regular Design Trial Piece. Copper. Reeded Edge. J-438. Very rare. BM 11/92, P P-64 $3,520

E.1561. 1867 Regular Design Trial Piece. Copper. Reeded Edge. J-594. Very rare $3,000

E.1562. 1868 Regular Design Trial Piece. Aluminum. Reeded Edge. J-653. Very rare. BM 9/84 Proof, $1,650 .... $2,000

E.1563. 1869 Regular Design Trial Piece. Copper. Reeded Edge. J-766. Very rare $2,000

Gold dollar patterns continued

E.1564. Same, copper-nickel. Reeded Edge. J-768. Very rare $2,500
E.1565. Same, aluminum. Reeded Edge. J-767. Very rare. Paramount Auction '86 Proof, $1,760 .... $2,000
E.1566. 1870 Regular Design Trial Piece. Copper. Reeded Edge. J-1023. Very rare $2,000
E.1567. Same, copper-nickel. Reeded Edge. J-1025. Very rare $2,500
E.1568. Same, aluminum. Reeded Edge. J-1024. Very rare $2,000
E.1569. 1871 Regular Design Trial Piece. Copper. Reeded Edge. J-1161. Very rare. ST 6/86 Proof,
   $1,320 .... $1,500
E.1570. Same, copper-nickel. Reeded Edge. J-1163. Very rare $2,000
E.1571. Same, aluminum. Reeded Edge. J-1162. Very rare $1,500
E.1572. 1872 Regular Design Trial Piece. Silver. Reeded Edge. J-1229. Unique?
E.1573. Same, copper. Reeded Edge. J-1227. Very rare. ST 1/87, Proof, $1,210 .... $2,000
E.1574. Same, aluminum. Reeded Edge. J-1228. Very rare $2,000

Pattern Design Trial Piece of 1872

E.1575. 1872 Pattern Design Trial Piece. Obv. William Barber's uniform design Liberty head left wearing cap
   incused LIBERTY, long curls behind and below neck. Date below, 13 stars around. Rev. Standing eagle
   similar to the Amazonian silver patterns holding three arrows in right claw, left claw holds national
   shield and ribbon incused IGWT. USOA and ONE DOL. around border. Gold. Reeded Edge. J-1224.
   Unique, sold in set of all six gold denominations in Kagin's 1983 San Diego ANA sale, $418,000,
   and in Superior's 10/90 sale at a reported $1,870,000.
      Note:This gold dollar is part of the only uniform design gold pattern set which included all six
   denominations from dollar to double eagle that were current in 1872. The complete set struck in
   gold was owned by such great numismatists as William H. Woodin and Dr. John E. Wilkinson;
   Egypt's King Farouk once owned all five denominations that are unique in gold. The set was
   consigned by Ed Trompeter to Superior Galleries for sale in October 1992 but withdrawn by his
   daughters after his death and still owned by them.
E.1576. Same, copper. Reeded Edge. J-1225. Very rare. Devonshire 7/82 Proof, $775 .... $5,000
E.1577. Same, aluminum. Reeded Edge. J-1226. Very rare $5,000
E.1578. 1873 Regular Design Trial Piece. Closed 3. Copper. Reeded Edge. J-1331. Very rare. Paramount
   Auction '86 Proof, $935 .... $2,000
E.1579. Same, aluminum. Reeded Edge. J-1332. Very rare $2,000
E.1580. 1874 Regular Design Trial Piece. Copper. Reeded Edge. J-1365. Very rare $2,000
E.1581. Same, aluminum. Reeded Edge. J-1366. Very rare $2,000
E.1582. 1875 Regular Design Trial Piece. Copper. Reeded Edge. J-1432. Very rare $3,000
E.1583. Same, aluminum. Reeded Edge. J-1433. Very rare $3,000
E.1584. 1876 Regular Design Trial Piece. Copper. Reeded Edge. J-1478. Very rare $2,000
Note: Judd also lists aluminum as J-1479. Doubtful.
E.1586. 1884 Regular Design Trial Piece. Copper. Reeded Edge. J-1733. Very rare $3,000
E.1587. 1885 Regular Design Trial Piece. Aluminum. Reeded Edge. J-1751. Very rare $4,000
E.1588. 1915 Fantasy. Obv. and Rev.: The regular Panama-Pacific designs without Mint mark. Gold. Reeded
   Edge. J-1793a. Rare, seven known. Thicknesses and die states vary from piece to piece. Struck for the
   collection of the Secretary of the Treasury. New England Rare Coin Galleries 1979 ANA Sale Proof-
   63, regular planchet $4,300; thick, $4,000, Aug. 1979 .... $8,000
E.1589. Same, gold. Plain Edge. J-1793a, die states two and three. Very rare, two known. NERCG 1979
   ANA sale, Proof-63, regular planchet $3,900; thick, $3,400 .... $8,000
E.1590. Same, Silver. Plain Edge. J-1793b. Very Rare, two known, NERCG Proof-60, thick planchet
   $2,300 .... $5,000
E.1591. 1916 Commemorative Design Off-Metal Strike. McKinley Memorial. Silver. Reeded Edge. Unique?
E.1592. Same, nickel alloy on broadstruck planchet. J-1802. NERCG MS-60, $3,400. Unique?
      Judd lists this piece struck from obverse and reverse dies in "nickel" as J-1802, the final
   numbered entry in the book; Taxay lists a uniface strike of the obverse die struck in "nickel."
   Either piece should be tested to determine the exact metallic composition.

Quarter eagles

E.1593. 1831 Regular Design Trial Piece. Silver. Reeded Edge. J-49. Unique? From the same dies as the Proofs
$17,500

Note: There exists a uniface die trial of the 1846 quarter eagle obverse on a copper disc, which was later
overstruck on the reverse with an 1846 half eagle obverse. J-110a. Unique.

Note: For the 1853 patterns with a $2-1/2 obverse and a 1-cent reverse, see cents.

E.1594. 1857 Pattern Design Trial Piece. Obv. Liberty head left wearing coronet incused LIBERTY. Date below,
13 stars around. The Longacre head ultimately used on the copper-nickel 3 cents of 1865. Rev.
Paquet's copy of the regular design, with characteristic skewed tail to left and bolder shield more
concave at the top. Copper. Reeded Edge. J-189. Very rare. This obverse die was also muled with a
small-sized cent reverse to form E.66 (see cents), and again in 1860 with a $2-1/2 pattern reverse to
form E.1595 .... $2,000

E.1595. 1860 Pattern Design Trial Piece. Obv. Same die as preceding, dated 1857. Rev. 2-1/2/DOLLARS/
1860 in laurel wreath. Copper. Reeded Edge. J-270. Very rare. ST 6/83 Proof, $2,500 .... $3,000
This laurel wreath was used again on several Mint medals of the 1860s, the 1863 large cent
sized 3-cent piece, and finally the 1942 experimental cents! (q.v.)

E.1596. 1861 Regular Design Trial Piece. Silver. Reeded Edge. J-281. Very rare $2,000

E.1597. Same, copper. Reeded Edge. J-282. Very rare. Garrett II Proof, $3,000 .... $1,500

E.1598. 1865 Regular Design Trial Piece. Copper. Reeded Edge. J-439. Unique? Mid-American 8/87 Proof,
$2,100. Also reported in silver $3,000

E.1599. 1866 Regular Design Trial Piece. Copper-nickel. Reeded Edge. J-542. Very rare $2,500

E.1600. 1867 Regular Design Trial Piece. Copper. Reeded Edge. J-595. Very rare. Proof dies.
2.52 gms $2,000

E.1601. 1868 Regular Design Trial Piece. Aluminum. Reeded Edge. J-654. Very rare. BM 9/84 Proof,
$2,200 .... $2,000

E.1602. 1869 Regular Design Trial Piece. Copper. Reeded Edge. J-769. Very rare. ST 1/87 Proof,
$852 .... $2,000

E.1603. Same, copper-nickel. Reeded Edge. J-771. Very rare. Superior 1/85 Proof, $1,500 .... $2,500

E.1604. Same, aluminum. Reeded Edge. J-770. Very rare. ST 6/84 Proof, $2,090 .... $2,000

E.1605. 1870 Regular Design Trial Piece. Copper. Reeded Edge. J-1026. Very rare $2,000

E.1606. Same, copper-nickel. Reeded Edge. J-1028. Very rare $2,500

E.1607. Same, aluminum. Reeded Edge. J-1027. Very rare $2,000

E.1608. 1871 Regular Design Trial Piece. Copper. Reeded Edge. J-1164. Very rare $2,000

E.1609. Same, copper-nickel. Reeded Edge. J-1166. Very rare $2,500

E.1610. Same, aluminum. Reeded Edge. J-1165. Very rare $2,000

E.1611. 1872 Regular Design Trial Piece. Copper. Reeded Edge. J-1233. Very rare $2,000

E.1612. Same, aluminum. Reeded Edge. J-1234. Very rare $2,000

Pattern Design Trial Piece of 1872

E.1613. 1872 Pattern Design Trial Piece. Obv. William Barber's Liberty head left wearing cap incused LIBERTY,
long curls behind and below neck. Date below, 13 stars around. Rev. Standing eagle holding three
arrows in right claw, left claw holds national shield and ribbon incused IGWT. USOA and 2 1/2 DOL.
around border, similar to Amazonian silver, see notes under E.1575. Gold. Reeded Edge. J-1230.
Unique, sold as part of six-piece set at Kagin's 1983 San Diego ANA sale, $418,000,and in
Superior's 10/90 sale at a reported $1,870,000.

E.1614. Same, copper. Reeded Edge. J-1231. Rare. Ivy 8/83 Proof, $3,000 .... $5,000

E.1615. Same, aluminum. Reeded Edge. J-1232. Very rare $5,000

E.1616. 1873 Regular Design Trial Piece. Closed 3. Copper. Reeded Edge. J-1333. Very rare $2,000

E.1617. Same, aluminum. Reeded Edge. J-1334. Very rare $2,000

E.1618. 1874 Regular Design Trial Piece. Copper. Reeded Edge. J-1367. Rare. Mid-American 1/87 Proof,
$1,300 .... $2,000

E.1619. Same, aluminum. Reeded Edge. J-1368. Very rare $2,000

E.1620. 1875 Regular Design Trial Piece. Copper. Reeded Edge. J-1434. Rare. Heritage 6/87 Proof,
$3,200 .... $2,500

E.1621. Same, aluminum. Reeded Edge. J-1435. Rare. Heritage 6/87 Proof, $3,000 .... $2,500

E.1622. 1876 Regular Design Trial Piece. Copper. Reeded Edge. J-1480. Very rare $2,000

Note: Judd also lists in aluminum as J-1481. Doubtful.

Quarter eagle patterns continued

Experimental size trial of 1878 (Bowers & Merena)

E.1624. 1878 Experimental Size Trial Piece. Obv. Liberty head left with hair combed back and tied in a small bun, two hair ribbons, the upper ornamented, lower (above forehead) incused LIBERTY. Date below. EPU around. Rev. Standing eagle clutching olive branch in right claw and three arrows in left. USOA and 2 1/2 DOLLARS around border. Designed by George T. Morgan. Gold. Reeded Edge. J-1566. Excessively rare, two known. 20.5mm, vs. 17.78mm standard size, struck to test a proposed wider but thinner coin less likely to be hollowed out and filled with platinum, a heavy but then inexpensive metal.

E.1625. Same, Copper. Reeded Edge. J-1567. Very Rare, some known gilt $2,500
E.1626. 1884 Regular Design Trial Piece. Copper. Reeded Edge. J-1734. Very rare $3,000
E.1627. 1885 Regular Design Trial Piece. Aluminum. Reeded Edge. J-1752. Very rare $4,000

Three dollars

Note: James Barton Longacre's original wax models for the $3 gold piece still exist in private hands. See *The Numismatist*, October 1985.

E.1628. 1864 Regular Design Trial Piece. Copper. Reeded Edge. J-400. Very rare $3,000
E.1629. Same, copper-nickel (various alloys). Reeded Edge. J-401 and 402. Very rare $3,000
E.1630. 1865 Off-Metal Restrike. First restrike, obv. of 1867-69 Proofs. Rev. Date level. Copper. Reeded Edge. J-442. Very rare, all are restrikes. Also reported in Bronze, J-444a $2,000
E.1631. Same, copper-nickel. Reeded Edge. J-443 and 444. Very rare $2,000
E.1632. 1865 Off-Metal Restrike. Second Restrike, obv. of 1872 regular issue coins. Rev. Date tilted to left. Silver? (Reported in silver, but may only exist as silver-plated copper.) Reeded Edge. J-441a. Unique, if it exists.
E.1633. Same, copper. Reeded Edge. J-441. Rare. ST 9/94, Br. Proof $4,300
Also restruck in gold, J-440.
E.1634. 1866 Regular Design Trial Piece. Copper-nickel. Reeded Edge. J-543. Very rare $2,000
E.1635. Same, aluminum. Reeded Edge. J-544. Very rare $3,000
Note: for the Fantasy Mule with a $3 obverse and an 1866 5 cents obverse, see E.322 in 5 cents section.
E.1636. 1867 Regular Design Trial Piece. Silver. Reeded Edge. J-598. Unique? $5,000
E.1637. Same, copper. Reeded Edge. J-596. Very rare. ST 9/94, Br. Proof $5,250
E.1638. Same, copper-nickel. Reeded Edge. J-597. Very rare $3,000
E.1639. 1868 Regular Design Trial Piece. Aluminum. Reeded Edge. J-655. Very rare. Dies aligned upright, as on the Proofs. BM 9/84 Proof, $2,200 .... $3,000
E.1640. 1869 Regular Design Trial Piece. Copper. Reeded Edge. J-772. Very rare. St 9/94, Br. Proof . $4,200
E.1641. Same, copper-nickel. Reeded Edge. J-774. Very rare $2,500
E.1642. Same, aluminum. Reeded Edge. J-773. Very rare $2,000
E.1643. 1870 Regular Design Trial Piece. Copper. Reeded Edge. J-1029. Rare. ST 9/94, Br. Proof $6,000
E.1644. Same, copper-nickel. Reeded Edge. J-1031. Very rare $2,500
E.1645. Same, aluminum. Reeded Edge. J-1030. ST 9/94, Ch. Br. Proof $8,500
E.1646. 1871 Regular Design Trial Piece. Copper. Reeded Edge. J-1167. Very rare. ST 9/94, Br. Proof $4,800
E.1647. Same, copper-nickel. Reeded Edge. J-1169. Very rare $2,500
E.1648. Same, aluminum. Reeded Edge. J-1168. Very rare $2,000
E.1649. 1872 Regular Design Trial Piece. Copper. Reeded Edge. J-1238. Very rare $2,500
E.1650. Same, aluminum. Reeded Edge. J-1239. Very rare. ST 9/94, Ch. Br. Proof $7,000

Three dollar patterns continued

Pattern Design Trial Piece of 1872

E.1651. 1872 Pattern Design Trial Piece. Obv. William Barber's uniform design Liberty head left wearing cap incused LIBERTY, long curls behind and below neck. Date below, 13 stars around. Rev. Standing eagle holding three arrows in right claw, left claw holds national shield and ribbon incused IGWT. USOA and THREE DOL. around border, similar to Amazonian silver design. Gold. Reeded Edge. J-1235. Unique, see notes under E.1575. Kagin's 1983 San Diego ANA sale, as part of six-piece set, $418,000,and in Superior's 10/90 sale at a reported $1,870,000.

    The $3 coin may have been an afterthought to this set, as the head and eagle punches used were the same as those for the smaller $2-1/2, making them seem proportionately smaller on the larger $3 coin. Then again, Barber may have just been trying to save himself a bit of work on the reducing lathe.

E.1652. Same, copper. Reeded Edge. J-1236. Very rare. ST, 9/94, Ch. Br. Proof $10,000
E.1653. Same, aluminum. Reeded Edge. J-1237. Rare. ST 9/94, Ch. Br. Proof $12,500
E.1654. 1873 Regular Design Trial Piece. Closed 3. Copper. Reeded Edge. J-1335. Very rare $5,000
E.1655. Same, aluminum. Reeded Edge. J-1336. Very rare $5,000
E.1656. 1874 Regular Design Trial Piece. Copper. Reeded Edge. J-1369. Very rare $4,000
E.1657. Same, aluminum. Reeded Edge. J-1370. Rare. Vintage 10/88 Proof, $3,900 .... $4,000
E.1658. 1875 Regular Design Trial Piece. Copper. Reeded Edge. J-1436. ST 9/94, V. Ch Br. Proof..... $8,500
    Some gilt.
E.1659. Same, aluminum. Reeded Edge. J-1437. Some gilt. Heritage 6/87 Proof, $6,750 .... $5,000
E.1660. 1876 Regular Design Trial Piece. Copper. Reeded Edge. J-1482. Very rare $4,000
E.1661. Same, aluminum. Reeded Edge. J-1483. Very rare $4,000
E.1662. 1884 Regular Design Trial Piece. Copper. Reeded Edge. J-1735. Very rare $3,000
E.1662a. 1885 Regular Design Trial Piece. Copper. Reeded Edge. Unlisted in Judd. Unique?
E.1663. 1885 Regular Design Trial Piece. Aluminum. Reeded Edge. J-1753. Very rare $4,000
E.1663a. 1889 Regular Design Trial Piece. Copper. Reeded Edge. Unlisted in Judd. Unique?

Four dollars or Stella

Pattern Design Trial Piece of 1879, Flowing Hair

E.1664. 1879 Pattern Design Trial Piece. Obv. Liberty head left with long, wavy hair behind and below neck, headband incused LIBERTY, the TY disappearing into the hair; small ornamental ball at upper end of ribbon, date below. *6*G*.3*S*.7*C*7*G*R*A*M*S* around border. Rev. Large five-pointed star with dotted outline, inscribed ONE/ STELLA/ 400/ CENTS incused in four lines. Small EPU around upper half of star, small DEO EST GLORIA around lower half, USOA and FOUR DOL. around border. Charles Barber design. Gold (.900 fine?). Reeded Edge. J-1635. Originals rare, restrikes more common. The 15 originals are generally well struck on the center of the head; the 400 restrikes are weakly struck as a rule, and planchet striations from the drawing bench tend to show on the head and star. Carter Gem Proof, $57,750, Jan. 1984; Superior 5/93, P-65, $66,000 .... $67,500
    It is possible that the 15 originals were actually struck in the .857 fine alloy listed in the inscription, though all restrikes are assumed to be standard .900 fine gold. Data as to weights and specific gravities would be helpful.

E.1665. Same, copper. Reeded Edge. J-1636. Rare. Obv. die variety reported. Superior 9/88 Proof, $4,620; Copper gilt, BM 11/93, N P-63, $8,800; Eliasberg 5/96 P-66 .... $28,600
E.1666. Same, aluminum. Reeded Edge. J-1637. Rare. BM 8/87 Proof, $7,975 .... $5,000
E.1666a. Same, white metal. Reeded Edge. Unlisted in Judd. Unique?

Four dollar patterns continued

Pattern Design Trial Piece of 1879, Coiled Hair (Stack's)

E.1667. 1879 Pattern Design Trial Piece. Obv. Liberty head left with hair braided atop back of head, band incused LIBERTY, *6*G*.3*S*.7*C*7*G*R*A*M*S* around border, date below. George T. Morgan design. Rev. Same as preceding. Gold. Reeded Edge. J-1638. Very rare, perhaps 15 struck. Superior 2/92, Trompeter, P-65 .... $198,000

E.1668. Same, copper. Reeded Edge. J-1639. Rare. BM 8/87 Proof, $17,600 .... $15,000

E.1669. Same, aluminum. Reeded Edge. J-1640. Rare. Harmer-Rooke 12/88 Proof, $19,000 .... $25,000

E.1670. Same, white metal. Reeded Edge. J-1641. Very rare $20,000

E.1671. 1880 Pattern Design Trial Piece. The Barber design. Gold. Reeded Edge. J-1657. Scarce, perhaps 25 struck; Superior 5/92, N P-65 .... $91,850

E.1672. Same, copper. Reeded Edge. J-1658. Rare. ST 1/88 Proof, $7,700;BM 11/88 AU $7,040; Copper gilt, BM 11/93, N P-63, $8,250 .... $8,500

E.1673. Same, aluminum. Reeded Edge. J-1659. Very rare $15,000

E.1674. 1880 Pattern Design Trial Piece. The Morgan design. Gold. Reeded Edge. J-1660. Rare, probably 10 struck. Eliasberg Proof-65, $99,000, Oct. 1982. Superior 2/92, Trompeter, P-65 .... $264,000 $90,000

E.1675. Same, copper. Reeded Edge. J-1661. Rare. Copper gilt, BM 11/93, N P-62 .... $12,100

E.1676. Same, aluminum. Reeded Edge. J-1662. Very rare $15,000

Half eagles

E.1677. 1795 Regular Design Trial Piece. Copper. Reeded Edge. J-23. Very rare, two known, one mutilated. NASCA 6/86 Unc., $2,500 .... $5,000

E.1678. 1797 Regular Design Trial Piece. Copper. Reeded Edge. J-24. 2 known, mutilated, NASCA Oct. AU, $4,000; BM 6/88 Unc., $2,310 .... $2,300

Note: The pieces listed by Judd for 1803 as J-27 are private restrikes. Copper or brass game counters (similar in function to modern poker chips) similar to 1803 $5 with KETTLE to left of date were struck in England in the early 19th Century. Beware removed name.

Note: The pieces listed by Judd for 1804 as J-29 thru 32 are private restrikes.

Note: The pieces listed by Judd for 1805 as J-36 thru 38 are private restrikes.

Note: The pieces listed by Judd for 1808 as J-39 & 40 are private restrikes.

E.1679. 1834 Pattern Design Trial Piece. Obv. & Rev. The new Classic Head design adopted this year. Copper. Plain Edge. J-51. Very rare $4,000

Note: A piece purporting to be J-51a, the above design in copper with a reeded edge, was determined by ANACS to be merely a contemporary counterfeit of an 1854 Liberty Head $5 in copper, badly worn with a damaged date. Actual existence of J-51a doubtful.

Pattern Design Trial Piece of 1860 (Superior Galleries)

E.1680. 1860 Pattern Design Trial Piece. Obv. Liberty head right wearing cap with 2-1/2 large stars above forehead. Ribbon across back of neck labeled LIBERTY, date below, 13 stars around. Designed by James B. Longacre, similar head used on 1869-70 Standard Silver. Rev. Facing eagle with tail feathers skewed to the left with olive branch in right claw and three arrows in left. Ribbon in beak reads EPU, USOA and FIVE DOLLARS around border. Paquet's style, though usually attributed to Longacre. Gold. Reeded Edge. 27mm. J-271. Excessively rare, three known. Large diameter and minimal thickness meant to foil practice of sawing gold coins in half and replacing center with less expensive platinum.

E.1681. Same, copper. Reeded Edge. J-272. Rare, some are gilt, Garrett II Ch. Proof, $7,500 .... $3,500

Half eagle patterns continued

Pattern Design Trial Piece of 1861 (Bowers & Merena)

E.1682. 1861 Pattern Design Trial Piece. Obv. and Rev. As preceding except for date. Copper. Reeded Edge. J-283. Some gilt. Heritage 2/86 Proof, $4,840 .... $4,000

E.1683. 1865 Regular Design Trial Piece. Copper. Reeded Edge. J-447. Very rare $3,500

E.1684. Same, aluminum. Reeded Edge. J-448. Very rare $5,000

E.1685. 1865 Pattern Design Trial Piece. Obv. The regular design. Rev. With Motto reverse adopted in 1866. Gold. Reeded Edge. J-445. Excessively rare, two known, one SI. From second die state of copper strikes below, suggesting the gold strikes were an afterthought.

E.1686. Same, copper. Reeded Edge. J-446. Rare. 4.91 gms & 4.97 gms. Two die states seen. Second has raised wedge from small dent in die on rim above star 8. Also reported in silver, but not currently known. ST 3/92, Ch. Br. Proof $8,250
   See comments under 1863 With Motto Quarter, E.795, for an interesting letter suggesting that earlier dates may have been struck with IGWT.

E.1687. 1866 Regular Design Trial Piece. Copper. Reeded Edge. J-546. Top of extra 8 shows on flat part of rim below date. Very rare. Two known. 4.79 gms $3,000

Two obverse dies for 1866 5-cent pieces, Obv. III and Obv. IV, were muled with a No Motto $5 Liberty reverse. The pieces were crudely struck without collars on white metal discs, and are listed by Judd as J-545 and J-547. As they were probably struck outside the Mint, they are not included in this listing. See 1867 and 1869 listings.

E.1688. 1867 Regular Design Trial Piece. Copper. Reeded Edge. J-599. Very rare $3,000

E.1689. Same, copper-nickel. Reeded Edge. J-600. Very rare $4,000

E.1690. 1867 Fantasy Mule. Obv. No Motto Obv. IX. Rev. No Motto $5 Liberty reverse. Silver. Plain Edge. Listed in Judd as J-601 in "nickel." Excessively rare, two known, probably clandestine strike at the Mint. See 1866 and 1869 listings. ST 6/88 Proof, $6,875; Garrett II Choice Proof, $6,500 ... $6,000

E.1691. 1868 Regular Design Trial Piece. Aluminum. Reeded Edge. J-660. Rare. BM 9/84 Proof, $1,375 .... $2,500

Pattern Design Trial Piece of 1868 (Smithsonian)

E.1692. 1868 Pattern Design Trial Piece. Obv. Rather homely Liberty head left with hair tied by two ribbons, the lower bearing a star above the brow and incused LIBERTY, date below, USOA around. Rev. 5/ DOLLARS/25/ FRANCS in four lines in wreath of oak and laurel. Copper. Reeded Edge. J-656. Rare. Prepared by Paquet for Congressional consideration of the U.S. joining the Latin Monetary Union, whose unit was the French franc. Akers 7/88 Proof, $4,620 .... $8,500
   1. The French counterpart of this pattern appeared with a copper-gilt specimen of this pattern in the Champa Sale. The French pattern had the head of Napoleon III on the obverse and the same denominations on the reverse, except for the 25 francs listed above the 5 dollars.
   2. This obverse design was reused, with minor changes only, as a pattern for a half dollar in 1877.

E.1693. Same, copper. Plain Edge. J-657. Rare $8,500

E.1694. Same, aluminum. Reeded Edge. J-658. Rare. ST 6/94, Proof, $4,200 .... $8,500

E.1695. Same, aluminum. Plain Edge. J-659. Rare. Garrett II Ch. Proof, $9,500 .... $8,500

E.1696. 1869 Regular Design Trial Piece. Copper. Reeded Edge. J-775. BM 6/88 Proof, $1,375 .... $2,000

E.1697. Same, copper-nickel. Reeded Edge. J-777. Very rare $2,500

E.1698. Same, aluminum. Reeded Edge. J-776. Very rare $2,000

E.1699. 1869 Fantasy Mule. Obv. 1869 5 cents Obv. IX. Rev. No Motto $5 Liberty reverse. Brass. Reeded Edge. J-778. Unique, Garrett II Proof, $8,000 .... $8,000

E.1700. 1870 Regular Design Trial Piece. Copper. Reeded Edge. J-1032. Rare. ST 1/87 Proof, $1,760 .... $2,000

E.1701. Same, copper-nickel. Reeded Edge. J-1034. Very rare $2,500

E.1702. Same, aluminum. Reeded Edge. J-1033. Very rare $2,000

Half eagle patterns continued

E.1703. 1871 Regular Design Trial Piece. Copper. Reeded Edge. J-1170. Very rare $2,000
E.1704. Same, copper-nickel. Reeded Edge. J-1172. Very rare $2,500
E.1705. Same, aluminum. Reeded Edge. J-1171. Very rare $2,000
E.1706. 1872 Regular Design Trial Piece. Copper. Reeded Edge. J-1243. Very rare $2,000
E.1707. Same, aluminum. Reeded Edge. J-1244. Very rare $2,000

Pattern Design Trial Piece of 1872

E.1708. 1872 Pattern Design Trial Piece. Obv. Liberty head left wearing cap incused LIBERTY. Long curls behind and below neck, date below, 13 stars around. Rev. Standing eagle holding three arrows in right claw. Left claw holds national shield and ribbon incused IGWT, USOA and FIVE DOL., around border. Designed by William Barber. Gold. Reeded Edge. J-1240. Unique, see notes under E.1575. Kagin's 1983 San Diego ANA sale, as part of a six-piece set, $418,000,and in Superior's 10/90 sale at a reported $1,870,000.
E.1709. Same, copper. Reeded Edge. J-1241. Very rare $5,000
E.1710. Same, aluminum. Reeded Edge. J-1242. Very rare $5,000
E.1711. 1873 Regular Design Trial Piece. Copper. Reeded Edge. J-1340. Very rare $2,000
E.1712. Same, aluminum. Reeded Edge. J-1341. Very rare. ST 6/84 Proof, $2,310 ....$2,000
E.1713. 1873 Pattern Design Trial Piece. Obv. Liberty head right wearing coronet labeled LIBERTY, long hair partly tied back with fancy bow. Date below, 13 stars around. Designed by William Barber. Rev. Same as E.1708. Gold. Reeded Edge. J-1337. Very rare, two known.
E.1714. Same, copper. Reeded Edge. J-1338. Very rare. ST 6/84 Proof, $3,960 ....$5,000
E.1715. Same, aluminum. Reeded Edge. J-1339. Very rare. ST 6/83 Proof, $3,750 ....$5,000
E.1716. 1874 Regular Design Trial Piece. Copper. Reeded Edge. J-1371. Very rare $2,000
E.1717. Same, aluminum. Reeded Edge. J-1372. Very rare. Krueger 7/84 Proof, $1,050 ....$2,000
E.1718. 1875 Regular Design Trial Piece. Copper. Reeded Edge. J-1441. Very rare. Heritage 6/87 Proof, $1,525 ....$4,000
E.1719. Same, aluminum. Reeded Edge. J-1442. Very rare. Heritage 6/87 Proof, $2,500 ....$6,000

Pattern Design Trial Piece of 1875

E.1720. 1875 Pattern Design Trial Piece. Obv. Liberty head left wearing coronet labeled LIBERTY, hair tied back in a bun with a dangling ribbon, date below, 13 stars around. Similar Sailor head by William Barber used on silver patterns 1875-77. Rev. Standing, facing eagle with three arrows in right claw and olive branch in left, same design and heraldic error as on the 20 cents and Trade dollar. EPU in field above eagle, IGWT on ribbon below, USOA and FIVE DOLLARS around border. Gold. Reeded Edge. J-1438. Excessively rare, two known.
E.1721. Same, copper. Reeded Edge. J-1439. Very rare $4,000
E.1722. Same, aluminum. Reeded Edge. J-1440. Very rare. BM 11/85, $1,320 ....$5,000
E.1723. Same, white metal. Reeded Edge. J-1440a. Very rare $5,000
E.1724. 1876 Regular Design Trial Piece. Copper. Reeded Edge. J-1484. Very rare $2,000
Note: Judd also lists in aluminum as J-1485. Doubtful.

Pattern Design Trial Piece of 1878

E.1726. 1878 Pattern Design Trial Piece. Obv. Liberty head left wearing cap with wide band incused LIBERTY, two wheat ears above cap. Long, curly hair below cap and neck, date below, tiny IGWT at upper border, seven stars left, six right. Rev. Standing eagle with oversized raised wings, clutching olive branch in right claw and three arrows in left. EPU in field above eagle between wings, USOA and FIVE DOLLARS around border. Believed to have been designed by William Barber, though reminiscent of the Morgan dollar design also used on the following. Gold. Reeded Edge. J-1575. Excessively rare, two known.

Half eagle patterns continued

E.1727. Same, copper. Reeded Edge. J-1576. Very rare $5,000

*Pattern Design Trial Piece of 1878
(Smithsonian)*

E.1728. 1878 Pattern Design Trial Piece. Obv. Liberty head left wearing a large cap, incused LIBERTY on the band. Date below, E PLURIBUS at left border, UNUM at right. Rev. Very similar to the Morgan dollar pattern Rev. Q of this year, three leaves on olive branch but wreath removed. FIVE DOL. at lower border. Designed by George T. Morgan. Gold. Reeded Edge. J-1577. Very rare, possibly unique?
E.1729. Same, copper. Reeded Edge. J-1578. Very rare. BM 8/87 Proof, $4,400 .... $5,000

1878 experimental size trial (Smithsonian)

E.1730. 1878 Experimental Size Trial Piece. Obv. Liberty head left, hair combed back and tied in a small bun, two ribbons in hair, upper ornamented, lower (above forehead) incused LIBERTY. Date below, EPU around, no periods between words. Rev. Standing eagle clutching olive branch in right claw and three arrows in left, USOA and FIVE DOLLARS around border separated by periods. Designed by George T. Morgan. Copper. Reeded Edge. J-1568. Very rare. Some are gilt. 25.4mm, vs. 21.54mm standard size, struck to test a proposed wider but thinner coin less likely to be hollowed out and filled with then-inexpensive platinum $5,000
E.1731. 1878 Experimental Size Trial Piece. Obv. As preceding. Rev. Similar to preceding except no periods between legends. Copper. Reeded Edge. J-1568a. Very rare $5,000
E.1732. 1878 Experimental Size Trial Piece. Obv. As preceding. Rev. Similar to preceding except eagle set lower over abbreviated FIVE DOL., and IGWT added around upper half of eagle. Copper. Reeded Edge. J-1569. Some gilt. ST 6/83 Proof, $3,000 .... $7,000
E.1733. 1878 Experimental Size Trial Piece. Obv. Similar to preceding except periods separate E. PLURIBUS. UNUM. Rev. Same as E.1730. Gold. Reeded Edge. J-1572. Unique.
E.1734. Same, copper. Reeded Edge. J-1573. Very rare $8,500
E.1734a. 1878 Experimental Size Trial Piece. Obv. As preceding. Rev. Same as E.1731. Copper. Reeded Edge. Unlisted in Judd. Two known, Smithsonian.
E.1735. 1878 Experimental Size Trial Piece. Obv. As preceding. Rev. Same as E.1732. Gold. Reeded Edge. J-1570. Unique.
E.1736. Same, copper. Reeded Edge. J-1571. Very rare $5,000

Experimental size trial

E.1737. 1878 Experimental Size Trial Piece. Obv. Liberty head left with long, curly hair wearing headband incused LIBERTY, date below, EPU around border. Rev. Standing eagle with olive branch in right claw and three arrows in left, as on 1879 dollar pattern Rev. Z. USOA and FIVE DOLLARS around border. Designed by William Barber. Copper. Reeded Edge. J -1574. Very rare. Some are gilt $7,500
E.1738. Same, brass. Reeded Edge. J-1574a. Unique, if it exists; may be a misdescription of a gilt specimen.
E.1739. 1880 Regular Design Trial Piece. Copper. Reeded Edge. J-1663. Unique?
E.1740. 1884 Regular Design Trial Piece. Copper. Reeded Edge. J-1736. Very rare $3,000
E.1741. 1885 Regular Design Trial Piece. Aluminum. Reeded Edge. J-1754. Very rare $4,000

Eagles

E.1742. 1797 Regular Design Trial Piece. Large eagle reverse. Copper. Reeded Edge. J-25. Very rare. $4,000

E.1743. 1799 Regular Design Trial Piece. Copper. Reeded Edge. J-26. Unique, mutilated $3,000

E.1744. 1804 Off-Metal Restrike. Struck from dies used in 1834-35 to make gold Proof 1804 eagles for inclusion in diplomatic presentation sets. Silver. Reeded Edge. J-34. Very rare $10,000

E.1745. Same, silver. Plain Edge. J-34a. Unique?

E. 1745a 1849 Pattern Design Trial Piece Obv. Liberty head left, narrow coronet or band with LIBERTY incused, 13 eight-pointed stars and date around border. BOUVET F. below the bust. Rev. Eagle with wings spread, shield on breast, olive branch in right claw, three arrows in left claw. What looks like a halo above eagle's head is a wreath, type unknown. USOA and TEN D. around border. The Bouvet design. Copper. Plain edge stamped with CUIVRE (copper in French) and Paris Mint hallmark.Two struck $12,000

  1. The circumstances behind the striking of this pattern are described in Appendix C of Judd and in the prior editions of this book by Taxay under "Semi Official Essays." The entry there stated: "EP 1408 Eagle. 1849. Dies by Louis Bouvet. Liberty head I., BOUVET F. below/Heraldic eagle, Copper. Plain Edge. R8. 1) White (Thick planchet); 2) Baldenhofer. Both are ex Farouk." Struck at the request of the Mint, it is properly included as an official pattern, as Taxay observed: "Despite the absence of documentation, the 1849 pattern for a gold eagle by French engraver Louis Bouvet was undoubtedly solicited by Director Patterson. At this time, Patterson was obsessed with the idea of removing the Mint's engraver J.B. Longacre, and was making overtures to various outside artists." (p. 199).

  2. Two only were struck. The better of the two coins was listed in BR "Empire Topics" Issue No. 3, Oct-Nov-Dec 1958, as lot#102: "UNIQUE PATTERN ITEM: 1849 Pattern Eagle by Bouvet. [Description]... Copper, plain edge: CUIVRE on edge. Proof. Originally from the Colonel Green collection as 'A.W.#106A' (cost him $750.00); later to King Farouk at $600.00. Later appeared in the Farouk sale. One specimen known, the piece offered here... That it is a [U.S.]pattern is absolutely certain, as the devices and legends conform to the Congressional requirements, and there is no attempt to copy any previous designs. That Bouvet signed his name is proof, to our minds, that he was submitting it for official approval; that it bears the Paris Mint stamp on the edge indicates that it was not a clandestine operation..." (p.20) The other coin is lot #1068 in the 11/11-12/55 Baldenhofer Sale by Stack's. The photo of the coin there shows a distinct mark on the cheek, showing that it is the same coin that was later offered in Bolt, noted as "cleaned and later lacquered" and graded there as "Extremely fine." The ex-Empire coin is Pr-63 or Pr-64, with no marks and excellent surfaces.

E.1746. 1855 Off-Metal Restrike from rusty dies, date and circumstances of striking unknown. Copper. Reeded Edge. J-176. Very rare.

Revised design trial of 1861 (Bowers & Merena)

E.1747. 1861 Revised Design Trial Piece. Obv. The regular design. Rev. Similar to regular design except GOD OUR TRUST added on ribbon above eagle. Gold. Reeded Edge. J-284. Very rare. Obv. die varieties exist of this and next three, suggesting some are restrikes.

E.1748. Same, copper. Reeded Edge. J-285. Very rare. Garrett II Ch. bronzed Proof, $8,000 .... $3,000

E.1749. 1861 Revised Design Trial Piece. Obv. The regular design. Rev. Similar to preceding except GOD OUR TRUST in field above eagle. Gold. Reeded Edge. J-286. Very rare.

E.1750. Same, copper. Reeded Edge. J-287. Very rare. ST 10/88 Proof, $2,530 .... $2,500

Eagle patterns continued

Regular Design Trial Piece of 1862
(Smithsonian)

E.1751. 1862 Revised Design Trial Piece. Same design as E.1747/8. Copper. Reeded Edge. J-297. Some bronzed. Very rare. Obv. die varieties exist of this and next, suggesting restriking. Kagin '86 ANA Proof, $1,650 .... $1,200

Regular Design Trial Piece of 1862
(Smithsonian)

E.1752. 1862 Revised Design Trial Piece. Same design as E.1749/50. Copper. Reeded Edge. J-298. Some bronzed or gilt. Very rare. ST 3/92, Proof, $28,000; BM 3/94, P P-64 .... $2,420

E.1753. 1863 Revised Design Trial Piece. Same design as E.1747/48. Gold. Reeded Edge. J-349. Very rare. Garrett II Proof, $57,500 .... $65,000

E.1754. Same, copper. Reeded Edge. J-350. Some are bronzed. Very rare. BM 6/88 Proof, $3,740 .. $1,600

E.1755. 1863 Revised Design Trial Piece. Same design as E.1749/50. Gold. Reeded Edge. J-351. Very rare. Garrett II Proof, $50,000 .... $65,000

E.1756. Same, copper. Reeded Edge. J-352. Some bronzed. Very rare. Mid-American 1/87 Proof, $1,040 .... $1,600

E.1757. 1865 Regular Design Trial Piece. Copper. Reeded Edge. J-451. Very rare $3,500

E.1758. 1865 Pattern Design Trial Piece. Obv. The regular design. Serif of an extra 1 in field above date. Obv. denticles weak, as though the entire die had been heavily polished to correct the blundered date. Rev. The With Motto reverse adopted in 1866. Gold. Reeded Edge. J-449. Very rare, two known.

E.1759. Same dies, copper. Reeded Edge. J-450. Rare. 9.32 gms., 9.41 gms., 9.42 gms., 9.44 gms. Garrett II Ch. Proof, $6,000 .... $5,000

    See comments under 1863 With Motto Quarter, E.795, for an interesting letter suggesting that earlier dates may have been struck with IGWT.

E.1760. 1866 Regular Design Trial Piece. Copper. Reeded Edge. J-548. Very rare $3,000

E.1761. 1867 Regular Design Trial Piece. Copper. Reeded Edge. J-602. Very rare $4,000

E.1762. Same, copper-nickel. Reeded Edge. J-603. Very rare $4,000

E.1763. 1868 Regular Design Trial Piece. Aluminum. Reeded Edge. J-664. Very rare. Superior 7/85 Proof, $2,530 .... $2,500

    Also reported in copper; not currently known.

Pattern Design Trial Piece of 1868

E.1764. 1868 Pattern Design Trial Piece. Obv. Liberty head left wearing coronet labeled LIBERTY in raised letters. Longacre's design as used on copper-nickel 3 cents and on other patterns, date below, 13 stars around. Rev. Paquet's revision of the regular design, smaller eagle with tail skewed to left. Gold. Reeded Edge. J-661. Paramount Auction '84 Proof, $39,600.

E.1765. Same, copper. Reeded Edge. J-662.Very rare. Obverse die varieties exist. BM 8/87 Proof, $4,620 .... $7,500

E.1766. Same, aluminum. Reeded Edge. J-663. Very rare. Garrett II Ch. Proof, $8,500 .... $7,500

Eagle patterns continued

E.1767. 1869 Regular Design Trial Piece. Copper. Reeded Edge. J-781. Very rare. BM 9/84 Proof,
$2,640 .... $2,000
E.1768. Same, copper-nickel. Reeded Edge. J-783. Very rare $2,500
E.1769. Same, aluminum. Reeded Edge. J-782. Very rare. Paramount Auction '86 Proof, $3,190 .... $2,000
E.1770. 1869 Pattern Design Trial Piece. Obv. The Longacre design of 1868. Rev. The regular design.
Copper. Reeded Edge. J-779. Some bronzed. Very rare. ST 6/88, Proof, $4,400 .... $4,500
E.1771. Same, aluminum. Reeded Edge. J-780. Very rare $4,000
E.1772. 1870 Regular Design Trial Piece. Copper. Reeded Edge. J-1035. Very rare. Heritage 9/87 Proof,
$2,250 .... $2,000
E.1773. Same, copper-nickel. Reeded Edge. J-1037. Very rare $2,500
E.1774. Same, aluminum. Reeded Edge. J-1036. Very rare. Akers 7/88 Proof, $4,840 .... $2,000
E.1775. 1871 Regular Design Trial Piece. Copper. Reeded Edge. J-1173. Very rare $2,500
E.1776. Same, copper-nickel. Reeded Edge. J-1175. Very rare $3,000
E.1777. Same, aluminum. Reeded Edge. J-1174. Very rare $2,500
E.1778. 1872 Regular Design Trial Piece. Copper. Reeded Edge. J-1248. Very rare $2,500
E.1779. Same, aluminum. Reeded Edge. J-1249. Very rare $2,500

Pattern Design Trial Piece of 1872

E.1780. 1872 Pattern Design Trial Piece. Obv. Liberty head left wearing cap incused LIBERTY, long curls
behind and below neck. Date below, 13 stars around. Rev. Standing eagle holding three arrows in
right claw, left claw holds national shield and ribbon incused IGWT, USOA and TEN DOL, around
border. Designed by William Barber. Gold. Reeded Edge. J-1245. Unique, see notes under E.1575.
Kagin's 1983 San Diego ANA sale, as part of a six-piece set, $418,000,and in Superior's 10/90
sale at a reported $1,870,000.
E.1781. Same, copper. Reeded Edge. J-1246. Very rare. ST 7/88 Proof, $3,960 .... $5,000
E.1782. Same, aluminum. Reeded Edge. J-1247. Very rare $5,000
E.1783. 1873 Regular Design Trial Piece. Copper. Reeded Edge. J-1342. Very rare $2,500
E.1784. Same, aluminum. Reeded Edge. J-1343. Very rare. Heritage 2/84 Proof, $2,800 .... $2,500
E.1785. 1874 Regular Design Trial Piece. Copper. Reeded Edge. J-1379. Very rare $2,500
E.1786. Same, aluminum. Reeded Edge. J-1380. Very rare. Paramount Auction '83 Proof, $2,970 ...... $2,500

Pattern Design Trial Piece of 1874

E.1787. 1874 Pattern Design Trial Piece. Obv. Liberty head left wearing coronet trimmed with six stars and
labeled LIBERTY, olive branch and ribbon at neck, date below, USOA around upper border. Rev. Six
segments outlined by rope borders around 16.72/ GRAMS/ 900 FINE/ UBIQUE. in four lines.
Segments read: DOLLARS 10, STERLING (pound sterling symbol) 2.1.1, MARKEN 41.99 (sic, proper
German plural is MARK), KRONEN 37.31, GULDEN 20.73, FRANCS 51.81 in two lines each. Gold.
Reeded Edge. J-1373. Excessively rare, two known.
Struck to illustrate a proposal by American world traveler Dana Bickford for an international
coin which could be spent in several major European countries, long before the advent of the
now-ubiquitous credit card.
E.1788. Same, copper. Reeded Edge. J-1374. Rare. Garrett II Ch. Proof, $15,500 .... $2,000
E.1789. Same, copper. Plain Edge. J-1375. Rare. ST 3/92, V. Ch. Br. Proof $13,000
E.1790. Same, copper-nickel. Reeded Edge. J-1377. Very rare. BM 11/92, P P-63 .... $7,425
E.1791. Same, copper-nickel. Plain Edge. J-1378. Very rare $3,000
E.1792. Same, aluminum. Reeded Edge. J-1376. Very rare $4,000
E.1793. 1875 Regular Design Trial Piece. Copper. Reeded Edge. J-1446. Very rare. Heritage 6/87 Proof,
$4,100 .... $5,000

Eagle patterns continued

E.1794. Same, aluminum. Reeded Edge. J-1447. Very rare $6,000

Pattern Design Trial Piece of 1875, Sailor Head

E.1795. 1875 Pattern Design Trial Piece. Obv. Liberty head left in coronet labeled LIBERTY, hair tied back in a bun with a dangling ribbon, date below, 13 stars around. Similar Sailor head used on silver patterns 1875-77 and 1875 gold $5. Rev. Standing eagle with three arrows in right claw and olive branch in left, same design and heraldic error as on the 20 cents and the Trade dollar. EPU in field above eagle, IGWT on ribbon below, USOA and TEN DOLLARS around border. Designed by William Barber. Gold. Reeded Edge. J-1443. Excessively rare, two known.

E.1796. Same, copper. Reeded Edge. J-1444. Very rare. Akers 7/88 Proof, $9,350; ST 9/94, Ch. Br. Proof $7,000

E.1797. Same, aluminum. Reeded Edge. J-1445. Very rare $8,000

E.1798. Same, white metal. Reeded Edge. J-1445a. Very rare $8,000

E.1799. 1876 Regular Design Trial Piece. Copper. Reeded Edge. J-1486. Very rare $2,500

E.1800. [Deleted]
    Judd lists this in aluminum as J-1487. Doubtful.

Pattern Design Trial Piece of 1877 (Smithsonian)

E.1801. 1877 Pattern Design Trial Piece. Obv. Liberty head left in large cap incused LIBERTY on the band, date below, E PLURIBUS at left border, UNUM at right. Rev. Similar to the Morgan dollar pattern Rev. Q of 1878 with three leaves on olive branch but with wreath removed, TEN DOL. at lower border. Designed by George T. Morgan. See matching 1878 $5, $10. Copper. Reeded Edge. J-1545. Very rare, some are gilt, Garrett II Ch. Proof, $19,000; Eliasberg 5/96 P-65 .... $13,750

Pattern Design Trial Piece of 1878

E.1802. 1878 Pattern Design Trial Piece. Obv. Liberty head left in cap with wide band incused LIBERTY. Two wheat ears above cap, long, curly hair below cap and neck, date below. Tiny IGWT at upper border, seven stars left, six right. Rev. Standing eagle with oversized raised wings, clutching olive branch in right claw and three arrows in left. EPU in field above eagle between wings, USOA and TEN DOLLARS around border. Believed to have been designed by William Barber, though reminiscent of the Morgan dollar design also used on the following. See matching $5. Gold. Reeded Edge. J-1579. Excessively rare, three known.

E.1803. Same, copper. Reeded Edge. J-1580. Some gilt. Very rare. BM 9/88 Proof, $8,580 .... $8,500

E.1804. 1878 Pattern Design Trial Piece. The Morgan design of 1877. Gold. Reeded Edge. J-1581. Excessively rare, four known.

E.1805. Same, copper. Reeded Edge. J-1582. Very rare $10,000

E.1806. 1884 Regular Design Trial Piece. Copper. Reeded Edge. J-1737. Very rare $3,500

E.1807. 1885 Regular Design Trial Piece. Aluminum. Reeded Edge. J-1755. Very rare $4,000

Note: a 1907-D Liberty $10 in copper is reported but unconfirmed.

Eagle patterns continued

E.1808. 1907 Pattern Design Trial Piece. Obv. Liberty head left wearing Indian headdress labelled LIBERTY on band, date below, 13 stars around upper border. Rev. Eagle standing to left upon a bundle of arrows, an olive branch overlapping same. EPU with periods before and after each word in upper right field, USOA and TEN DOLLARS around border. Gold. 46 stars on edge, weak rims. J-1774. Scarce, but very popular among serious collectors of $10 Indians $12,000

E.1809. Same, Gold. Plain Edge. J-1774a. Unique?

E.1810. 1907 Pattern Design Trial Piece. Obv. and Rev. Similar to preceding except remodeled dies with greater detail and more prominent, so-called rolled rims. Gold. Starred edge. J-1775. Rare, all but 42 pieces melted by Mint $30,000

Double eagles

E.1811. 1849 Pattern Design Trial Piece. Obv. Liberty head left, coronet inscribed LIBERTY, date below, 13 stars around border. Rev. Heraldic eagle clutching olive branch and arrows, with national shield on breast flanked by two fancy scrolls labeled E PLURIBUS and UNUM. Radiant arc and 13 stars in an oval above eagle, USOA and TWENTY D. around border. Gold. Reeded Edge. J-117. One known in Smithsonian; a second specimen is rumored, see next.

E.1812. Same, brass. Reeded Edge. J-118. A gilt restrike made ca. 1870, not currently known to exist.

E.1813. (1850) Pattern Design Trial Piece. Similar to preceding but from revised obv. hub. Relief slightly lower and stars repositioned, no date. Rev. The regular design adopted this year. Silver. Reeded Edge. J-126. Excessively Rare, two known $30,000
    All regular issue $20s 1850-58 descended from yet another obverse hub with LIBERTY misspelled as LLBERTY.

E.1814. (1857) Experimental Thickness Trial Piece. Copper. Reeded Edge. Uniface reverse impression run through an upsetting mill, struck and upset again, making the piece highly concave. This was Dr. J.T. Barclay's concept, intended to foil hollowing out or sawing coins in half to replace the interior with then-inexpensive platinum;. J-190. Unique.

E.1815. 1859 Regular Design Trial Piece. Copper. Reeded Edge. J-263. Very rare $5,000
    New obverse hub used this year with LIBERTY corrected, J.B.L. moved and other minor changes.

E.1816. 1859 Revised Design Trial Piece. Obv. Same as preceding, with 1859 date. Rev. Paquet's revision of the regular design, with added outline to shield, shorter rays in arc and taller letters in legend, the design briefly adopted in 1861. Copper. Reeded Edge. J-260. Very rare. Some are gilt $12,000

E.1817. 1859 Mule. Obv. Same as preceding, with 1859 date. Rev. Large oak and laurel wreath around border, USOA inside wreath, around 20 DOLLARS 1859. The Paquet reverse, intended for one of the following. This wreath was also used on numerous Mint medals. Copper. Reeded Edge. J-261. Some gilt. Very rare. ST 7/86 AU, $2,640 .... $12,000

E.1818. (1859) Mule. Obv. The regular design, without date, intended for use with the Paquet rev. (see next). Rev. The regular design. Copper. Reeded Edge. J-259. Very rare $12,000

Pattern Design Trial Piece of 1859 (Bowers & Merena)

E.1819. 1859 Pattern Design Trial Piece. Obv. Same as preceding, without date. Rev. The Paquet oak and laurel wreath rev. with date. Copper. Reeded Edge. J-258. Very rare. Some are gilt $12,000

E.1820. (1859) Mule. Obv. Liberty seated to left, right hand supports upright fasces; left hand rests on national shield. Olive branch and three arrows at base of shield. Small facing eagle partially behind shield, 13 stars around. The Paquet design, also used without eagle on pattern half dollars. Rev. The regular design. Copper. Reeded Edge. J-262. Very rare. Some gilt. Superior 1/85 Proof, $2,900 ..... $12,000

Double eagle patterns continued

Pattern Design Trial Piece of 1859

E.1821. 1859 Pattern Design Trial Piece. Obv. The Paquet seated design. Rev. The Paquet wreath design. Copper. Reeded Edge. J-257. Some are gilt; more are bronzed. 20.87 gms. Very rare. Garrett II Proof, $12,500; Kagin's 1983 ANA Proof, $8,000 .... $13,000

E.1821a. Same, Plain Edge. Unlisted in Judd. Unique?

E.1822. 1860 Pattern Design Trial Piece. Obv. The regular design. Rev. The Paquet revision of the regular design, with taller letters. Variety 1 with eagle set low, tip of left wing between T and E of UNITED, rays far from STATES OF. Gold. Reeded Edge. J-272a. Unique, Smithsonian.

This design combination used for some regular issue San Francisco Mint coins in early 1861.

E.1823. Similar, except Variety 2 reverse with eagle set high, tip of left wing beneath upright of E(D), rays close to STATES OF, copper. Reeded Edge. J-273. At least one gilt. Paramount Auction '82 Proof, $6,750 .... $10,000

This reverse used for some very rare 1861 Philadelphia strikes in gold.

Regular Design Trial Piece of 1861 (Harlan J. Berk Ltd.)

E.1824. 1861 Regular Design Trial Piece. Copper. Reeded Edge. J-289. 18.57 gms. Rims filed, perhaps while under the unenlightened ownership of King Farouk, or possibly related in some way to the following. Unique $10,000

E.1825. 1861 Experimental Thickness Trial Piece. Obv. and Rev. The regular designs. Copper. Plain Edge. J-288. Very rare, two known, one gilt. Struck without a collar, making piece very thin in center. See 1857 experimental piece. Very rare. Superior 9/86 Proof, $4,290; BM 11/85 Proof, $4,510 .... $10,000

E.1826. 1865 Regular Design Trial Piece. Copper. Reeded Edge. J-454. Very rare. BM 6/88 VF, $990 .... $3,000

Revised Design Trial Piece of 1865 (Harlan J. Berk Ltd.)

E.1827. 1865 Revised Design Trial Piece. Obv. The regular design. Rev. Similar to the regular design except eagle and shield remodeled and IGWT added within the oval of stars. IN of IGWT high and tilted to the left. This hub used on 1866-P and -S business strikes and 1867 Proofs, and possibly others. Corrected hub used on 1866 Proofs and most regular issues of this type. Gold. Reeded Edge. J-452. Excessively rare, two known, one Smithsonian.

Double eagle patterns continued

E.1828. Same, copper. Reeded Edge. J-453. Very rare. Some have heavy die crack left of date from rim up into bust. 18.32 gms. Some gilt, bronzed, or silvered. Silver and aluminum also reported, but unlikely. Garrett II "bronze," no die crack, Ch. Proof, $8,500 .... $8,000
    See comments under 1863 With Motto quarter, E.795, for an interesting letter suggesting that earlier dates may have been struck with IGWT.

E.1829. 1866 Regular Design Trial Piece. Copper. Reeded Edge. J-549. Very rare, some are gilt $3,500

E.1830. 1867 Regular Design Trial Piece. Copper. Reeded Edge. J-604. Very rare $3,500

E.1831. 1868 Regular Design Trial Piece. Aluminum. Reeded Edge. J-665.Very rare. BM 9/84 Proof, $2,640 .... $3,500

E.1832. 1869 Regular Design Trial Piece. Copper. Reeded Edge. J-784. Very rare $3,000

E.1833. Same, copper-nickel. Reeded Edge. J-786. Very rare $3,500

E.1834. Same, aluminum. Reeded Edge. J-785. Very rare. ST 7/86 Proof, $3,960 .... $3,000

E.1835. 1870 Regular Design Trial Piece. Copper. Reeded Edge. J-1038. Very rare. ST 1/87 Proof, $1,595 .... $3,000

E.1835a. Copper gilt. BM 11/93, N P-64, $16,500

E.1836. Same, copper-nickel. Reeded Edge. J-1040. Very rare $3,500

E.1837. Same, aluminum. Reeded Edge. J-1039. Very rare $3,000

E.1838. 1871 Regular Design Trial Piece. Copper. Reeded Edge. J-1176. Very rare $3,500

E.1839. Same, copper-nickel. Reeded Edge. J-1178. Very rare $4,000

E.1840. Same, aluminum. Reeded Edge. J-1177. Very rare $3,500

E.1841. 1872 Regular Design Trial Piece. Copper. Reeded Edge. J-1253. Very rare $3,000

E.1842. Same, aluminum. Reeded Edge. J-1254. Very rare $3,000

Pattern Design Trial Piece of 1872

E.1843. 1872 Pattern Design Trial Piece. Obv. Liberty head left in cap incused LIBERTY, long curls behind and below neck. Date below, 13 stars around. Rev. Standing eagle holding three arrows in right claw, left claw holds national shield and ribbon incused IGWT, USOA and TWENTY DOL. around border. Highest denomination in William Barber's uniform-design six-piece pattern set. Reeded Edge. J-1250. Unique, sold as part of the six-piece set in Kagin's 1983 San Diego ANA sale, $418,000, and in Superior's 10/90 sale at a reported $1,870,000. See note under pattern gold dollar, E.1575.

E.1844. Same, copper. Reeded Edge. J-1251. Very rare $6,000

E.1845. Same, aluminum. Reeded Edge. J-1252. Very rare $6,000

E.1846. 1873 Regular Design Trial Piece. Copper. Reeded Edge. J-1344. Very rare, One seen silver-plated through careless cleaning with used silver dip $3,000

E.1847. Same, aluminum. Reeded Edge. J-1345. Very rare $3,500

E.1848. 1874 Regular Design Trial Piece. Copper. Reeded Edge. J-1381. Very rare $3,000

E.1849. Same, aluminum. Reeded Edge. J-1382. Very rare $3,000

E.1850. 1875 Regular Design Trial Piece. Copper. Reeded Edge. J-1448. Very rare. Some gilt. Also reported in brass, possibly the gilt specimen. Heritage 6/87 Proof, $3,500 .... $3,500

E.1851. Same, aluminum. Reeded Edge. J-1449. Very rare. Superior 10/88 Proof, $8,250 .... $3,500

E.1852. 1876 Regular Design Trial Piece. Copper. Reeded Edge. J-1493. Very rare. BM 11/85 Proof, $3,630 .... $3,000

E.1853. [Deleted]
    Also reported in aluminum as J-1494. Doubtful.

E.1854. 1876 Revised Design Trial Piece. Obv. Similar to the regular design, but remodelled with stars more evenly spaced, design adopted in 1877. Rev. The regular design with TWENTY D. Gold. Reeded Edge. J-1488. Unique.

E.1855. Same, copper. Reeded Edge. J-1489. Very rare $5,000

Double eagle patterns continued

Revised Design Trial Piece of 1876 (Harlan J. Berk Ltd.)

E.1856. 1876 Revised Design Trial Piece. Obv. Similar to preceding but from different die. Rev. Similar to the regular design, but remodelled with EPU larger and TWENTY DOLLARS. Gold. Reeded Edge. J-1490. Unique. Superior Auction '86 Proof, $99,000.

E.1857. Same, copper. Reeded Edge. J-1491. Very rare $5,000

E.1858. Same, copper, gilt. Plain Edge. J-1492. From different obverse die than preceding, 1 very close to bust. Unique. 20.21 gms.

E.1859. 1879 Pattern Design Trial Piece. Metric Double Eagle. Obv. Similar to the regular design except *30*G*1.5*S*35*C*35*G*R*A*M*S* around border. Rev. Similar to the regular design except DEO EST GLORIA replaces IGWT. Copper. Reeded Edge. J-1642. Unique, rejected because engraving error omitted period in 3.5*C $25,000

Pattern Design Trial Piece of 1879, "3.5"

E.1860. Same dies as above with period added between 3 and 5 of 3.5*C. Gold. Reeded Edge. J-1643. Standard weight and fineness restrikes exist. Garrett II Proof, $90,000; ST 1/84 Proof, $93,500; Eliasberg 5/96 P-62/63 .... $214,500

E.1861. Same, copper. Reeded Edge. J-1644. Very rare. Mid-American 9/85 Proof, $7,250; BM 11/84 Proof, $7,700. Copper gilt and copper specimens were donated to the Smithsonian by Harvey G. and Lawrence R. Stack, 12/94 .... $15,000

E.1862. 1884 Regular Design Trial Piece. Copper. Reeded Edge. J-1738. Very rare, one gilt $3,800

E.1863. 1885 Regular Design Trial Piece. Aluminum. Reeded Edge. J-1756. Very rare $4,500

Pattern Design Trial Piece of 1906 (Smithsonian)

E.1864. 1906 Pattern Design Trial Piece. Obv. Liberty head left wearing cap with ribbon labeled LIBERTY, olive branch below ribbon. Date below, 13 five-pointed stars around border. Rev. Standing Liberty figure with head turned left, holding sword in right hand and liberty cap on pole in left. Defiant eagle to right standing on rock behind, rays around upper half of figure, overlaying IGWT in an arc. USOA and TWENTY DOLLARS around border, small fasces on base of rock. See similar half dollar pattern of 1891. Gold. Edge lettered *E*P*L*U*R*I*B*U*S*U*N*U*M. J-1773. Unique, Smithsonian.

Double eagle patterns continued

Pattern Design Trial Piece of 1907

E.1865. MCMVII (1907) Pattern Design Trial Piece. Obv. Liberty head left wearing Indian headdress, large LIBERTY below head, 13 stars around upper border. This is Saint-Gaudens' head adopted for the new eagle. Rev. Eagle flying upwards to left over sunrise, date on sun, USOA and TWENTY DOLLARS in two lines around upper border. Gold. Lettered Edge. J-1776. Unique, Paramount Auction '84, Proof-67, $467,500 .... $500,000

E.1866. Same, lead. Lettered Edge. J-1777. Unique, ANS coll.

E.1867. MCMVII (1907) Pattern Design Trial Piece. Obv. Standing, facing Liberty holding torch in right hand and olive branch in left. Sun rays behind gown, tiny U.S. Capitol building at lower left. 46 stars around border. LIBERTY inside upper border. Rev. Similar to preceding but no date on sun. Gold. Edge lettered E*PLURIBUS*UNUM ***********, appears facing either up or down. J-1778. Rare. The Ultra High Relief variety $250,000

E.1867a. Obv. and rev. same as preceeding. Gold. Edge lettered as on E.1864. Two known.

E.1867b. Obv. and rev. same as preceeding. Gold. Plain Edge., possibly a Mint error. Unique.

E.1868. Same, lead. J-1778a. Unique?

E.1869. MCMVII (1907) Pattern Design Trial Piece. Obv. and Rev. Similar to preceding except in less exaggerated relief, the High Relief variety without edge marking, as struck for circulation with Lettered Edge. Cracked reverse die. Gold. Plain Edge. J-1778c. Unique $500,000

E.1870. Same, lead. Lettered Edge. J-1778b. Very rare, two known.

Pattern Design Trial Piece of 1907
(Smithsonian)

E.1871. MCMVII (1907) Pattern Design Trial Piece. Obv. & Rev. Similar to preceding except reduced to size of gold eagle, struck on thicker planchet. Gold. Lettered Edge. J-1779. Very rare, supposedly all but two melted, both in Smithsonian.

E.1872. 1907 Regular Design Trial Piece. The regular issue with drastically reduced relief and Arabic date. Brass. Lettered Edge. J-1779a. Extremely rare, all seen have been mutilated by being passed through rollers.

Fifty dollars

Pattern Design Trial Piece of 1877

E.1873. 1877 Pattern Design Trial Piece. Obv. Large Liberty head left in coronet inscribed LIBERTY, as on 1878 dollar Obv. XXIV. Date and B for William Barber below head, 13 stars around border. Rev. Enlarged With Motto $20 reverse, FIFTY DOLLARS at lower border. Gold. Reeded Edge. J-1546. Unique, now in Smithsonian.

Large denomination gold coins of $100 and $50, to be called union and half union, had been urged 23 years earlier by California Senator William M. Gwin. It is not known why this idea was only implemented in 1877, but two obv. dies were prepared in 1877 and the unique gold striking of both large and small heads found their way into the collection of William H. Woodin. Woodin and co-author Edgar H. Adams called them "the most desirable coins ever issued by the United States Mint," in their 1913 pattern catalog. Adverse publicity forced the gold pieces' return to the Mint collection, although Woodin was compensated with trunks full of other pattern coins to console him in his loss.

E.1874. Same, copper. Reeded Edge. J-1547. Excessively rare, seven or so known, some gilt. Garrett II Choice Proof (gilt), $55,000, March 1980; ST 7/87 (gilt) Proof, $29,700: BM 8/87 Proof, $33,000; Kagin's 1983 ANA VF copper, $5000; Ivy 8/83 Proof, $29,500; Copper gilt, Heritage 1993 ANA Sale, lot #5882, PR-62, $75,000 .... $75,000

Pattern Design Trial Piece of 1877

E.1875. 1877 Pattern Design Trial Piece. Obv. Similar to preceding except head smaller, ornaments added along lower edge of coronet, whose point is just below a star. Rev. Same as preceding. Gold. Reeded Edge. J-1548. Unique, Smithsonian.

E.1876. Same, copper, some gilt. Reeded Edge. J-1549. Excessively rare, possibly seven. Kagin's 1983 San Diego ANA sale, (gilt), Proof-65, $34,000; ST 7/87 (gilt) Proof, $29,700; Paramount Auction '82 Proof, $26,000 .... $35,000

Judd Reference Concordance

To facilitate the use of the patterns section for those who are accustomed to using the Judd numbering system in *United States Pattern, Experimental and Trial Pieces*, the editors provide the following concordance. Numbers on the left are Judd numbers, with a corresponding CWE number following. Those pieces unnumbered in Judd are not included in the concordance. Pieces listed in Judd but omitted from the current work are followed by DEL. When a Judd number is referred to a CWE number ending in "n," the reference is to a note in the vicinity of the CWE listing.

Judd #	CWE #	Judd #	CWE #	Judd #	CWE #	Judd #	CWE #	Judd #	CWE #
1	7	53	196	106	1241	153	511	205	83
2	8	54	197	107	1242	154	1246	206	82
3	4	55	198	108	1237	155	1	207	81
4	5	56	199	109	1238	156	36	207a	82
5	6	56a	200	110	788	157	37	208	91
6	3	57	937n	110a	1593n	158	38	209	89
7	540	58	1221	111	506	159	39	210	90
8	541	59	1222	112	507	160	40	211	92
9	598	60	1225	113	508	161	41	212	88
10	599	61	1226	114	509	162	42	213	87
11	600	62	1227	115	1540	163	43	214	96
12	784	63	1223	116	1541	164	44	215	95
13	785	64	1224	117	1811	165	46	216	94
14	542	65	1228	118	1812	165b	45	217	74
15	543	66	1229	119	10	166	546	217a	75
16	544	67	1535	120	11	167	51	218	68
17	937n	68	1536	121	12	167a	53	218a	69
18	1219	69	1537	122	13	168	52	219	67
19	1220	70	1538	123	14	169	56	220	93
20	9	71	1539	124	15	170	54	221	790
21	545	72	939	124a	21	171	55	222	967
22	937n	73	940	125	510	172	47	223	968
23	1677	74	941	126	1813	173	48	224	1557
24	1678	75	938	127	22	174	50	225	1558
25	1742	76	945	127a	22	174a	49	226	102
26	1743	76a	946	128	23	175a	1556	227	97
27	1678n	77	947	128a	24	175	966	228	104
28	9n	78	948	129	25	176	1746	229	103
29	1678n	79	944	130	26	177	2	230	98
30	1678n	79a	949	131	27	178	58	231	99
31	1678n	80	950	131a	27	179	57	231a	100
32	1678n	81	951	132	1243	180	61	232	547
34	1744	82	942	133	1244	181	59	233	601
34a	1745	83	943	134	1245	182	60	234	791
35	785n	84	1233	135	1534	183	61	235	981
36	1678n	85	1234	136	1542	184	63	236	982
37	1678n	86	1235	137	1543	185	62	237	975
38	1678n	87	1236	138	1544	186	66	238	976
38a	9n	88	1230	139	1545	187	64	239	977
38a	785n	89	1231	140	1546	187a	65	240	978
39	1678n	90	1232	140a	1546	188	789	241	979
40	1678n	91	962	141	1547	189	1594	242	980
41	9n	92	963	142	1548	190	1814	243	971
42	937n	93	958	143	1549	191	78	244	972
42a	937n	94	959	144	1550	192	79	245	973
43	937n	95	964	145	1551	193	77	246	974
44	937	96	965	146	1552	194	77	247	983
45	9n	97	960	147	1553	195	76	248	984
45	785n	98	961	148	1554	196	71	249	985
46	9n	99	952	148a	1554	197	72	250	986
47	937n	100	953	148b	1555	198	70	251	987
48	786	100a	954	149	30	199	70	252	988
49	1593	101	955	150	31	200	80	253	989
50	787	102	956	151	32	201	73	254	969
51	1679	103	957	152	18	202	85	255	970
51a	1679	104	1239	152a	19	203	86	256	1559
52	195	105	1240	152b	20	204	84	257	1821

Judd reference concordance continued

Judd # .... CWE #	Judd # .... CWE #	Judd # .... CWE #	Judd # .... CWE #	Judd # .... CWE #
258 1819	326 606	391 1007	456 133	526 359
259 1818	326a 607	392 1008	457 133	527 350
260 1816	327 610	393 1010	458 231	528 351
261 1817	328 608	394 1009	459 231	529 340
262 1820	329 611	395 1006	460 259	530 341
263 1815	330 612	396 1251	461 353	531 321
264 101	330a 609	397 1252	462 352	531a 322
265 105	331 613	398 1254	463 353	534 623
266 106	331a 614	399 1253	464 332	535 622
267 548	331b 615	400 1628	465 330	536 813
268 792	332 616	401 1629	466 331	537 812
269 990	333 602	402 1629	466a 339	538 1017
270 1595	334 603	403 128	467 335	539 1016
271 1680	335 795	403a 129	468 333	540 1260
272 1681	336 796	404 130	469 334	541 1259
272a ... 1822	337 797	405 131	470 338	542 1599
273 1823	338 999	406 130	471 336	543 1634
274 107	339 1000	406a 131	472 337	544 1635
275 793	340 1001	407 230	473 325	545 1687
276 794	341 1002	408 228	474 323	546 1687
277 991	342 1003	409 229	475 324	547 1687
278 992	343 1004	409a 229	476 327	548 1760
279 993	344 1005	410 254	477 326	549 1829
280 994	345 1248	411 253	478 328	550 134
281 1596	346 1249	412 255	479 329	551 135
282 1597	347 1250	413 256	480 360	552 135
283 1682	348 1247	414 257	481 362	553 136
284 1747	349 1753	414a 258	482 361	554 232
285 1748	350 1754	415 517	483 365	555 233
286 1749	351 1755	416 293	484 363	556 233
287 1750	352 1756	417 292	485 364	557 234
288 1825	353 124	418 295	486 368	558 260
289 1824	354 123	419 294	487 366	559 261
290 108	355 125	420 554	488 367	560 518
291 109	355a 118	421 620	489 302	561 373
292 110	356 126	422 621	490 300	562 374
293 995	356a 117	423 806	491 301	563 371
294 996	357 119	424 808	492 304	564 372
295 997	358 120	424a 807	493 303	565 375
296 998	359 120	425 809	494 307	566 377
297 1751	360 121	426 810	495 305	567 376
298 1752	361 122	427 811	496 306	568 386
299 111	362 127	428 805	497 298	569 378
300 112	363 219	429 1013	498 296	570 388
301 113	364 220	430 1014	499 297	571 387
302 114	365 221	431 1015	500 299	572 369
303 115	366 224	432 1011	501 317	573 394
304 116	367 225	433 1012	502 315	573a 370
305 201	368 226	434 1256	503 316	574 379
306 202	369 227	435 1257	504 320	575 380
307 203	370 216	436 1258	505 318	576 381
308 204	371 217	437 1255	506 319	577 382
309 205	372 218	438 1560	507 313	578 377
310 206	372a 217	439 1598	508 311	578a 376
311 207	373 222	440 1632	509 312	579 385
312 209	374 223	441 1633	509a ... 314	580 383
312a 208	375 514	441a ... 1632	510 308	581 384
313 210	376 516	442 1630	511 309	582 390
314 211	377 515	443 1631	512 310	583 389
314a 211	378 551	444 1631	513 343	584 393
315 212	379 553	444a ... 1630	514 342	585 391
316 213	380 552	445 1685	515 344	586 555
317 214	381 617	446 1686	516 347	587 625
318 215	382 619	447 1683	517 346	588 626
319 251	383 618	448 1684	518 345	589 624
320 252	384 799	449 1758	519 348	590 814
321 512	385 800	450 1759	520 349	591 1018
322 513	386 801	451 1757	521 354	592 1261
323 549	387 802	452 1827	522 355	593 1262
324 550	388 804	453 1828	523 356	594 1561
325 605	389 803	454 1826	524 357	595 1600
325a 604	390 798	455 132	525 358	596 1637

Judd reference concordance continued

Judd #	CWE #	Judd #	CWE #	Judd #	CWE #	Judd #	CWE #	Judd #	CWE #
597	1638	664	1763	733	831	801	532	872	696
598	1636	665	1831	734	832	802	523	873	664
599	1688	666	149	735	833	803	526	874	666
600	1689	667	148	736	834	804	524	875	665
601	1690	668	145	737	835	804a	525	876	882
602	1761	669	146	738	836	805	420	877	883
603	1762	670	146	739	816	806	422	878	884
604	1830	671	147	740	818	807	421	879	885
605	139	672	237	741	817	808	423	880	886
606	138	673	238	742	1023	809	573	881	887
607	140	674	239	742a	1023	810	574	882	876
608	142	674a	239	743	1024	811	575	883	877
609	141	675	240	744	1025	812	576	884	878
610	144	676	275	745	1026	813	577	885	879
611	143	677	274	746	1027	814	578	886	880
612	137	678	272	747	1028	815	567	887	881
613	235	679	273	747a	1023	816	568	888	846
614	236	680	520	748	1029	817	569	889	847
615	264	681	521	749	1030	818	570	890	848
615a	264	682	522	750	1031	819	571	891	849
616	263	683	415	751	1032	820	572	892	850
617	265	684	417	752	1034	821	563	893	851
617a	268	685	416	753	1035	822	564	894	858
617b	266	686	414	753a	1033	823	566	895	859
617c	267	687	410	754	1036	824	565	896	860
618	270	688	411	755	1037	825	709	897	861
619	269	689	412	756	1038	826	710	898	862
620	271	690	413	757	1039	827	711	899	863
621	262	691	419	758	1041	828	712	900	870
622	519	692	559	759	1042	829	713	901	871
623	403	693	562	759a	1040	830	714	902	872
624	404	694	560	760	1020	831	703	903	873
625	405	695	561	761	1022	832	704	904	874
626	400	696	640	762	1021	833	705	905	875
627	401	697	641	763	1264	834	706	906	840
628	402	698	642	764	1266	835	707	907	841
629	406	699	643	765	1265	836	708	908	842
630	397	700	644	766	1563	837	673	909	843
631	407	701	645	767	1565	838	674	910	844
632	398	702	646	768	1564	839	675	911	845
632a	399	703	647	769	1602	840	676	912	852
633	409	704	648	770	1604	841	677	913	853
634	408	705	649	771	1603	842	678	914	854
635	395	706	650	772	1640	843	685	915	855
636	396	707	651	773	1642	844	686	916	856
637	556	708	652	774	1641	845	687	917	857
638	557	709	653	775	1696	846	688	918	864
639	558	710	654	776	1698	847	689	919	865
640	628	711	655	777	1697	848	690	920	866
641	630	712	656	778	1699	849	697	921	867
642	629	713	657	779	1770	850	698	922	868
643	631	714	662	780	1771	851	699	923	869
644	633	715	663	781	1767	852	700	924	837
645	632	716	658	782	1769	853	701	925	839
646	634	716a	659	783	1768	854	702	926	838
647	636	717	660	784	1832	855	667	927	1106
648	635	717a	661	785	1834	856	668	927a	1106
649	627	718	637	786	1833	857	669	928	1107
650	815	719	639	787	150	858	670	929	1108
651	1019	720	638	788	152	859	671	930	1109
652	1263	721	819	789	151	860	672	931	1110
653	1562	722	820	790	242	861	679	932	1111
654	1601	723	821	791	244	862	680	933	1100
655	1639	724	822	792	243	863	681	934	1101
656	1692	725	823	793	241	864	682	935	1102
657	1693	726	824	794	276	865	683	936	1103
658	1694	727	825	795	277	866	684	937	1104
659	1695	728	826	796	527	867	691	938	1105
660	1691	729	827	797	528	868	692	939	1070
661	1764	730	828	798	529	869	693	940	1071
662	1765	731	829	799	530	870	694	941	1072
663	1766	732	830	800	531	871	695	942	1073

Judd reference concordance continued

Judd #	CWE #	Judd #	CWE #	Judd #	CWE #	Judd #	CWE #	Judd #	CWE #
943	1074	1014	1282	1086	726	1155	1311	1226	1577
944	1075	1015	1283	1087	715	1156	1312	1227	1573
945	1058	1016	1284	1088	717	1157	1313	1228	1574
946	1059	1017	1285	1089	716	1158	1322	1229	1572
947	1060	1018	1286	1090	894	1159	1323	1230	1613
948	1061	1019	1287	1091	895	1160	1297	1231	1614
949	1062	1020	1267	1092	896	1161	1569	1232	1615
950	1063	1021	1269	1093	891	1162	1571	1233	1611
951	1082	1022	1268	1094	892	1163	1570	1234	1612
952	1083	1023	1566	1095	893	1164	1608	1235	1651
953	1084	1024	1568	1096	900	1165	1610	1236	1652
954	1085	1025	1567	1097	901	1166	1609	1237	1653
955	1086	1026	1605	1098	902	1167	1646	1238	1649
956	1087	1027	1607	1099	897	1168	1648	1239	1650
957	1094	1028	1606	1100	898	1169	1647	1240	1708
958	1095	1029	1643	1101	899	1170	1703	1241	1709
959	1096	1030	1645	1102	888	1171	1705	1242	1710
960	1097	1031	1644	1103	890	1172	1704	1243	1706
961	1098	1032	1700	1104	889	1173	1775	1244	1707
962	1099	1033	1702	1105	1118	1174	1777	1245	1780
963	1064	1034	1701	1106	1119	1175	1776	1246	1781
964	1065	1035	1772	1107	1120	1176	1838	1247	1782
965	1066	1036	1774	1108	1115	1177	1840	1248	1778
966	1067	1037	1773	1109	1116	1178	1839	1249	1779
967	1068	1038	1835	1110	1117	1179	155	1250	1843
968	1069	1039	1837	1111	1124	1180	156	1251	1844
969	1052	1040	1836	1112	1125	1181	157	1252	1845
970	1053	1041	153	1113	1126	1182	156	1253	1841
971	1054	1042	154	1114	1121	1183	247	1254	1842
972	1055	1043	245	1115	1122	1184	248	1255	158
973	1056	1044	246	1116	1123	1185	280	1256	160
974	1057	1045	278	1117	1112	1186	281	1257	159
975	1046	1046	279	1118	1114	1187	536	1258	249
976	1047	1047	533	1119	1113	1188	537	1259	250
977	1048	1048	534	1120	1332	1189	433	1260	282
978	1049	1049	535	1121	1333	1190	434	1261	283
979	1050	1050	428	1122	1334	1191	594	1262	538
980	1051	1051	427	1123	1335	1192	595	1263	539
981	1076	1052	429	1124	1336	1193	731	1264	435
982	1077	1053	431	1125	1337	1194	732	1265	436
983	1078	1054	430	1126	1326	1195	905	1266	596
984	1079	1055	432	1127	1327	1196	906	1267	597
985	1080	1056	424	1128	1328	1197	907	1268	733
986	1081	1057	425	1129	1329	1198	903	1269	734
987	1088	1058	426	1130	1330	1199	904	1270	908
988	1089	1059	585	1131	1331	1200	1129	1271	909
989	1090	1060	586	1132	1324	1201	1130	1272	1132
990	1091	1061	587	1132a	1325	1202	1131	1273	1133
991	1092	1062	582	1133	1316	1203	1127	1274	1358
992	1093	1063	583	1134	1317	1204	1128	1275	1359
993	1043	1064	584	1135	1318	1205	1355	1276	1405
994	1045	1065	591	1136	1319	1206	1356	1277	1406
995	1044	1066	592	1137	1320	1207	1357	1278	1407
995a	1044	1067	593	1138	1321	1208	1344	1279	1408
996	1276	1068	588	1138a	1314	1209	1345	1280	1409
997	1277	1069	589	1138b	1315	1210	1338	1281	1412
998	1278	1070	590	1139	1304	1211	1339	1282	1413
999	1279	1071	579	1140	1305	1212	1342	1283	1414
1000	1280	1072	581	1141	1306	1213	1343	1284	1415
1001	1281	1073	580	1142	1307	1214	1346	1285	1410
1002	1270	1074	721	1143	1308	1215	1347	1286	1411
1003	1271	1075	722	1144	1309	1216	1348	1287	1416
1004	1272	1076	723	1145	1298	1217	1349	1288	1404
1005	1273	1077	718	1146	1299	1218	1350	1289	1403
1006	1274	1078	719	1147	1300	1219	1340	1290	1374
1007	1275	1079	720	1148	1301	1219a	1341	1291	1375
1008	1288	1080	727	1149	1302	1220	1351	1292	1376
1009	1289	1081	728	1150	1303	1221	1352	1293	1368
1010	1290	1082	730	1151	1294	1222	1353	1294	1369
1011	1291	1083	729	1152	1296	1223	1354	1295	1370
1012	1292	1084	724	1153	1295	1224	1575	1296	1371
1013	1293	1085	725	1154	1310	1225	1576	1297	1372

Judd reference concordance continued

Judd #	CWE #	Judd #	CWE #	Judd #	CWE #	Judd #	CWE #	Judd #	CWE #
1298	1373	1367	1618	1440	1722	1509	1185	1569	1732
1299	1384	1368	1619	1440a	1723	1509a	1177	1570	1735
1300	1380	1369	1656	1441	1718	1509b	1178	1571	1736
1301	1381	1370	1657	1442	1719	1509c	1176	1572	1733
1302	1382	1371	1716	1443	1795	1510	1174	1573	1734
1303	1383	1372	1717	1444	1796	1511	1175	1574	1737
1304	1385	1373	1787	1445	1797	1512	1164	1574a	1738
1304a	1377	1374	1788	1445a	1798	1513	1165	1575	1726
1305	1378	1375	1789	1446	1793	1514	1160	1576	1727
1306	1379	1376	1792	1447	1794	1515	1161	1577	1728
1307	1362	1377	1790	1448	1850	1516	1162	1578	1729
1308	1360	1378	1791	1449	1851	1517	1163	1579	1802
1309	1361	1379	1785	1450	166	1518	DEL	1580	1803
1310	1363	1380	1786	1451	165	1519	1167	1581	1804
1311	1364	1381	1848	1452	739	1520	1168	1582	1805
1312	1365	1382	1849	1453	740	1521	1169	1583	168
1313	1366	1383	163	1454	783	1522	1170	1584	742
1314	1367	1384	164	1455	914	1523	1171	1585	743
1315	1386	1385	286	1456	1138	1523a	1172	1586	744
1316	1387	1386	287	1457	1442	1523b	1173	1587	745
1317	1388	1387	439	1458	1444	1524	1141	1588	746
1318	1389	1388	440	1458a	1443	1525	1142	1589	747
1319	1390	1390	737	1459	1445	1526	1145	1590	918
1320	1391	1391	738	1460	1446	1527	1146	1591	919
1321	1392	1392	770	1461	1447	1528	1143	1592	920
1322	1395	1393	771	1462	1448	1529	1144	1593	922
1323	1396	1394	773	1463	1449	1530	1147	1594	923
1324	1397	1395	772	1463a	1450	1531	1148	1594a	924
1325	1398	1396	767	1464	1451	1532	DEL	1595	917
1326	1399	1397	768	1465	1452	1533	1152	1596	921
1326a	1393	1398	769	1466	1453	1534	1154	1597	1192
1326b	1394	1399	759	1467	1439	1534a	1153	1598	1193
1327	1400	1400	760	1468	1440	1535	1149	1599	1188
1328	1401	1401	762	1469	1441	1536	1150	1600	1189
1329	1402	1402	761	1470	1433	1537	1155	1601	1190
1330	1402	1403	763	1471	1434	1538	1156	1602	1191
1331	1578	1404	764	1472	1437	1539	1158	1603	1480
1332	1579	1405	765	1473	1438	1539a	1157	1604	1481
1333	1616	1406	766	1474	1435	1540	1186	1605	1482
1334	1617	1407	777	1475	1436	1541	1187	1606	1483
1335	1654	1408	778	1476	1431	1541a	1159	1607	1484
1336	1655	1409	780	1477	DEL	1541b	1159	1608	1485
1337	1713	1410	779	1478	1584	1542	1454	1609	1486
1338	1714	1411	774	1479	DEL	1543	1456	1610	1487
1339	1715	1412	775	1480	1622	1544	1455	1611	1474
1340	1711	1413	776	1481	DEL	1545	1801	1612	1475
1341	1712	1414	781	1482	1660	1546	1873	1613	1476
1342	1783	1415	782	1483	1661	1547	1874	1614	1477
1343	1784	1416	912	1484	1724	1548	1875	1615	1478
1344	1846	1417	913	1485	DEL	1549	1876	1616	1479
1345	1847	1418	1136	1486	1799	1550	1462	1617	1497
1346	161	1419	1137	1487	DEL	1550a	1462	1618	1498
1347	162	1420	1421	1488	1854	1551	1463	1619	1499
1348	284	1421	1422	1489	1855	1552	1464	1620	1500
1349	285	1422	1423	1490	1856	1553	1465	1621	1501
1350	437	1423	1424	1491	1857	1554	1457	1622	1502
1351	438	1424	1425	1492	1858	1555	1458	1623	1503
1352	735	1425	1426	1493	1852	1556	1459	1624	1504
1353	736	1426	1427	1494	DEL	1556a	1460	1625	1505
1354	754	1427	1428	1495	167	1557	1466	1626	1488
1355	755	1428	1429	1496	167	1558	1467	1627	1489
1356	756	1429	1430	1498	741	1559	1468	1628	1490
1357	757	1430	1419	1499	915	1560	1469	1629	1491
1358	758	1431	1420	1500	916	1561	1470	1630	1492
1359	910	1432	1582	1501	1139	1562	1471	1631	1493
1360	911	1433	1583	1502	1140	1563	1472	1632	1494
1361	1134	1434	1620	1503	1179	1564	1473	1633	1495
1362	1135	1435	1621	1504	1180	1565	1461	1634	1496
1363	1417	1436	1658	1505	1181	1566	1624	1635	1664
1364	1418	1437	1659	1506	1182	1567	1625	1636	1665
1365	1580	1438	1720	1507	1183	1568	1730	1637	1666
1366	1581	1439	1721	1508	1184	1568a	1731	1638	1667

Judd reference concordance continued

Judd #	CWE #	Judd #	CWE #	Judd #	CWE #
1639	1668	1707	471	1774	1808
1640	1669	1708	472	1774a	1809
1641	1670	1709	473	1775	1810
1642	1859	1710	474	1776	1865
1643	1860	1711	475	1777	1866
1644	1861	1712	476	1778	1867
1645	1512	1713	477	1778a	1868
1646	1513	1714	484	1778b	1870
1647	1514	1715	483	1778c	1869
1648	1515	1716	485	1779	1871
1649	1516	1717	480	1779a	1872
1650	1517	1718	479	1780	187
1651	1506	1719	481	1781	495
1652	1507	1720	482	1782	496
1653	1508	1720a	1522	1783	497
1654	1509	1721	174	1784	498
1655	1510	1722	175	1785	499
1656	1511	1723	176	1786	500
1657	1671	1723a	173	1787	501
1658	1672	1724	487	1788	502
1659	1673	1725	488	1789	503
1660	1674	1726	489	1789a	504
1661	1675	1727	486	1790	505
1662	1676	1728	748	1791	1204
1663	1739	1729	927	1792	1205
1664	169	1730	1196	1793	1203
1665	171	1731	1523	1793a	1588
1666	170	1732	1524	1793a	1589
1667	172	1733	1586	1793b	1590
1668	289	1734	1626	1794	751
1669	288	1735	1662	1795	930
1670	290	1736	1740	1796	932
1671	442	1737	1806	1796a	931
1672	441	1738	1862	1797	1206
1673	443	1739	177	1797a	1207
1674	444	1740	178	1798	1209
1675	447	1740a	179	1799	1210
1676	446	1741	291	1800	1212
1677	456	1742	491	1801	1211
1678	455	1743	490	1802	1592
1679	457	1744	749		
1680	449	1745	928		
1681	448	1746	1197		
1682	451	1747	1527		
1683	450	1748	1528		
1684	453	1749	1529		
1685	452	1750	1526		
1686	454	1750a	1525		
1687	459	1751	1587		
1688	458	1752	1627		
1689	460	1753	1663		
1690	462	1754	1741		
1691	461	1755	1807		
1692	463	1756	1863		
1693	465	1757	180		
1694	464	1758	181		
1694a	464	1759	182		
1695	467	1760	750		
1696	466	1761	929		
1697	445	1762	1198		
1698	925	1763	1200		
1699	926	1764	1199		
1700	1194	1765	1201		
1701	1195	1766	1202		
1702	1520	1767	185		
1703	1521	1767a	184		
1703a	1518	1768	183		
1703b	1519	1769	186		
1704	468	1770	493		
1705	469	1771	492		
1706	470	1772	494		
1706a	478	1773	1864		

Philippine Coinage 1903-1947

American coinage is the most intensively studied in the numismatic world, yet includes one often-neglected area, the 40 year-long U.S. coinage for the Philippine Islands. This neglect may be a lingering reflection of America's ambivalent feelings toward this Far Eastern possession, acquired as a result of the Spanish-American war.

The U.S. never built the kind of colonial empire that Britain, France and other powers did in the 19th century. The Mexican War saw the last massive expansion of American territory until the War with Spain in 1898. Stumbling into the conflict without clear war aims, the U.S. found itself promoting independence for Cuba while annexing Puerto Rico, Guam and the Philippines.

America's Philippine adventure began with Commodore George E. Dewey's successful attack on Spanish naval forces in Manila Bay on May 1, 1898. On May 19, Gen. Emilio Aguinaldo, leader in the 1896 Katipunan uprising against Spain, returned and fought in August with the Americans to capture of Manila, though he had assumed leadership of the independence movement on June 12.

The Treaty of Paris, signed on Dec. 10, 1898, conveyed sovereignty over the 7,083-island chain to the U.S. in exchange for a $20 million payment to Spain. Ignoring the treaty, the Malolos Convention promulgated the constitution for the first Philippine Republic on Jan. 20, 1899.

U.S. forces now fought the long and costly Philippine Insurrection from Feb. 4, 1899 to April 1902. The U.S. had to create an archipelago-wide government in the midst of violent fighting. Military administration continued until William Howard Taft of Ohio was sworn in as first civil governor on July 4, 1901.

Coinage stabilization was an urgent task facing the new regime. Coins in daily circulation included Mexican silver pesos, countermarked Latin American silver and both gold and silver Philippine coins struck at the Manila Mint under Isabel II, Alfonso XII and Alfonso XIII.

Some Americans advocated introducing regular U.S. coins to the islands, while others argued for a distinctive Philippine coinage. The final decision followed the study and report of American economist Charles Arthur Conant (1861-1915).

Conant's November 1901 *Report on Coinage and Banking in the Philippine Islands*, showed the need for a strictly Philippine coinage. Existing U.S. denominations were simply too large for low Philippine pay scales and would not provide the small amounts needed for daily purchases.

The military administration exchange rate was set at US$1 for two Mexican pesos, but silver prices fluctuated wildly, causing cataracts of pesos to be exported to China, then back to the islands, where they soon dropped to less than 50 cents per peso.

The U.S. Congress passed a Philippine coinage bill in June 1902 but side-stepped the gold standard originally specified in the legislation. This standard was adopted in the Act of March 1903. The islands' theoretical unit would be a gold peso valued at 50 U.S. cents and freely convertible into U.S. money.

The largest coin actually struck was the 38 millimeter, .900 fine silver peso, with subsidiary silver coins of 50, 20 and 10 centavos. A copper-nickel five centavos, bronze centavo and half centavo completed the roster.

The Act required all designs to express both a Philippine identity and U.S. sovereignty. The designs adopted were the work of pre-eminent Filipino engraver Melecio Figueroa (1892-1903). Figueroa's common reverse featured an eagle atop a U.S. shield. His two obverse devices were a graceful Standing Lady and a Seated Worker, both posed with a hammer and anvil with the Mayon volcano smoking in the background.

A similar worker appeared on Figueroa's 45mm Manila Regional Exposition medal of 1895. His 10-year-old daughter Blanca was model for the Standing Lady. She lived on more than 80 years, known by her married name, Dona Blanca Vda. Figueroa de Opinion.

All obverses bore the islands' Spanish name FILIPINAS, a counterpoint to the reverse legend UNITED STATES OF AMERICA. All denominations were expressed in spelled-out English numbers ONE, FIVE, TEN, TWENTY and FIFTY.

Coinage dies were produced in the Philadelphia Mint, which struck some circulation coins and all Proofs from 1903 to 1908 without Mint mark. The San Francisco Mint struck circulation coins from 1904 until 1920 with the S Mint mark.

The first series coins of 1903-1906 were swept from circulation as silver prices surged to 13 percent over face value. Exported and melted by the millions, the first series was replaced by new coins of reduced size and fineness struck in 1907. The more stately first type shows small harmonious lettering around a Standing Lady far from the rims. The reduced size coins display lettering and lady disproportionately large and distinctly clumsy by comparison.

The U.S. government sent American engineer Clifford Hewitt create a new Manila Mint in the Intendencia building. Its inauguration on July 16, 1920 was commemorated by gold, silver and bronze medals with the bust of President Woodrow Wilson, coin-relief pieces eagerly collected as "Wilson Dollars." Coins struck at Manila bore no Mint mark in 1920 or 1921, but from 1925 through 1941 all bore the M Mint mark.

The Tydings-McDuffie Act of 1934 provided for self-rule, and legislation of May 1935 created the self-governing Commonwealth of the Philippines as a step toward independence. On November 15 1935, Manuel Luis Quezon took office as first Commonwealth President while Governor General Frank Murphy of Detroit, Mich., became the first U.S. High Commissioner.

The third series of U.S.-Philippine coins now appeared, still displaying the Figueroa obverses and UNITED STATES OF AMERICA but bearing the new Commonwealth Arms, three Katipunan stars around the castle and heraldic sea lion of Manila.

The charismatic Quezon began strengthening island defenses, appointing Gen. Douglas MacArthur field marshal of Commonwealth forces. Limited progress was made but war arrived on December 8, 1941 as the Japanese were also attacking Pearl Harbor. Manila fell on Jan. 2, 1942 as MacArthur and Quezon retreated to the rugged Bataan peninsula, on to the island of Corregidor and ultimately to Australia.

Despite the surrender of Fil-American forces by Gen. Jonathan M. Wainwright, a massive guerrilla insurgency was mounted against the Japanese. The monetary situation became chaotic as the invaders issued rapidly depreciating paper currency (JIM or Japanese Invasion Money).

Guerrilla units issued their own currency all over the archipelago, while the Philippine Republic proclaimed in 1943 under President Jose Paciano Laurel issued a series of bronze medals of purely Philippine design to assert its sovereignty. As Bataan fell, the Philippine treasury silver reserves of 350 tons of pesos were moved to Corregidor. To keep them from the Japanese, some 15,792,000 pesos were dumped in the deep waters of Caballo Bay off the island's southern tip. The coins were packed in bags of 2,000 pesos inside wooden boxes weighing 3,000 pounds. The Japanese attempted salvage using Filipino and U.S. Navy prisoners as divers.

After liberation, the U.S. Navy Seventh Fleet carried on salvage operations from May 1945 to April 1946, recovering 5 million pesos. The Philippine authorities later salvaged 6,533,297 pesos more, 75% of total having been recovered by 1958. MacArthur returned to Leyte with President Sergio Osmena Oct. 19, 1944 (Quezon had died at Lake Saranac, N.Y., that year). Fighting to dislodge the Japanese swept the islands, leaving Manila to rank with Warsaw as the most devastated capital of the world.

Commonwealth coinage resumed with the 1944-1945 issues struck by the Denver and San Francisco Mints. Despite the virtual destruction of the islands' infrastructure and the shabby refusal of the U.S. Congress to provide adequate reconstruction funds, independence was duly proclaimed on July 4, 1946. Amid the ruins of war the fledgling Republic of the Philippines struggled to begin a new national life.

Half centavo

17.8 mm Bronze, 30 grains.
95 Copper, 5 Zinc-Tin.

		VF-20	EF-40	MS-60	PROOF
1903 .... (12,084,000) .... (2,558)		1.00	2.25	10.00	37.50
1904 .... (5,654,000) .... (1,355)		1.25	2.50	15.00	50.00
One piece struck in silver was reported in the collection of Egypt's King Farouk.					
1905 .... (471 Proof only)		*	*	*	125.
1906 .... (500 Proof only)		*	*	*	85.00
1908 .... (500 Proof only)		*	*	*	85.00

The half centavo saw little circulation and was discontinued in early 1904 except for Proofs. Many were melted to reuse the bronze for coinage of 1-centavo pieces.

One centavo

FIRST TYPE

24 mm Bronze, 40 grs. 95 Copper,
5 Zinc-Tin. (Photo smaller than actual)

		VF-20	EF-40	MS-60	PROOF
1903 .... (10,790,000) .... (2,558)		1.25	1.75	15.00	37.50
1904 .... (17,040,400) .... (1,355)		1.25	1.75	15.00	55.00
1905 .... (10,000,000) .... (471)		1.50	2.00	20.00	100.

Philippines 1 centavo continued

	VF-20	EF-40	MS-60	PROOF
1906 .... (500)	*	*	*	75.00
Proof only				
1908 .... (500)	*	*	*	75.00
Proof only				
1908-S .... (2,187,000)	2.00	5.50	30.00	*
1909-S .... (1,737,612)	5.50	12.00	75.00	*
1910-S .... (2,700,000)	1.50	5.50	27.50	*
1911-S .... (4,803,000)	1.50	5.50	20.00	*
1912-S .... (3,001,000)	1.50	6.00	25.00	*
1913-S .... (5,000,000)	1.00	5.00	20.00	*
1914-S .... (5,000,500)	1.25	5.00	20.00	*
1915-S .... (2,500,000)	17.50	45.00	200.	*
1916-S .... (4,330,000)	10.00	20.00	100.	*
1917/6-S	5.00	10.00	75.00	*
1917-S .... (7,070,000)	1.50	4.50	25.00	*
1918-S .... (11,660,000)	1.50	3.00	20.00	*
1918-S Large S	27.50	70.00	250.	*
1919-S .... (4,540,000)	1.50	4.50	20.00	*
1920-S .... (2,500,000)	7.50	15.00	80.00	*
1920 (M) .... (3,552,259)	1.50	2.00	20.00	*
1921 (M) .... (7,282,673)	1.00	2.50	22.50	*
1922 (M) .... (3,519,100)	1.00	2.50	22.50	*
1925-M .... (9,325,000)	1.00	2.50	22.50	*
1926-M .... (9,000,000)	1.00	2.50	22.50	*
1927-M .... (9,270,000)	1.00	2.50	22.50	*
1928-M .... (9,150,000)	1.00	2.50	22.50	*
1929-M .... (5,657,161)	1.50	2.75	25.00	*
1930-M .... (5,577,000)	1.50	2.75	25.00	*
1931-M .... (5,659,355)	1.50	2.75	25.00	*
1932-M .... (4,000,000)	2.25	3.00	25.00	*
1933-M .... (8,392,692)	0.75	2.50	20.00	*
1934-M .... (3,179,000)	1.75	3.00	25.00	*
1936-M .... (17,455,463)	0.75	3.00	12.50	*

SECOND TYPE, COMMONWEALTH

		Same specifications		
	VF-20	EF-40	MS-60	PROOF
1937-M .... (15,790,492)	1.00	1.50	10.00	*
1938-M .... (10,000,000)	0.75	1.25	10.00	*
1939-M .... (6,500,000)	1.00	1.75	15.00	*
1940-M .... (4,000,000)	0.75	1.00	7.50	*
1941-M .... (5,000,000)	1.00	2.00	15.00	*
1944-S .... (58,000,000)	0.20	0.25	0.75	*

Sometimes called the Victory coins, the 1944-45 pieces were struck in substantial numbers but collectors have often thought that most returned to the U.S. to reside in dealers' junk boxes.

Five centavos

FIRST TYPE

21.2 mm, 77.16 grains Copper-Nickel 75:25

	VF-20	EF-40	MS-60	PROOF
1903 .... (8,910,000) .... (2,558)	1.25	2.50	15.00	65.00
1904 .... (1,075,000) .... (1,075)	1.50	3.50	27.50	70.00
1905 .... (471)	*	*	*	135.
Proof only				
1906 .... (500)	*	*	*	125.
Proof only				
1908 .... (500)	*	*	*	125.
Proof only				
1916-S .... (300,000)	22.50	55.00	275.	*
1917-S .... (2,300,000)	2.25	5.50	50.00	*
1918-S .... (2,780,000)	2.25	5.50	50.00	*
1918-S Mule	250.	450.	1750.	*
20 centavos reverse with tiny date, wing tips near rim.				
1919-S .... (1,220,000)	3.25	5.75	65.00	*
1920 (M) .... (1,421,078)	3.75	7.50	85.00	*
1921 (M) .... (2,131,529)	3.75	7.50	90.00	*
1925-M .... (1,000,000)	4.00	8.00	85.00	*
1926-M .... (1,200,000)	4.25	10.00	70.00	*
1927-M .... (1,000,000)	4.00	8.00	75.00	*
1928-M .... (1,000,000)	4.25	10.00	85.00	*

SECOND TYPE, REDUCED SIZE

19 mm, 75.16 grains Copper-Nickel

	VF-20	EF-40	MS-60	PROOF
1930-M .... (2,905,182)	2.50	4.00	50.00	*
1931-M .... (3,476,790)	2.50	4.00	50.00	*
1932-M .... (3,955,861)	2.50	4.00	50.00	*
1934-M .... (2,153,729)	3.50	5.50	55.00	*
1935-M .... (2,754,000)	2.50	4.50	45.00	*

THIRD TYPE, COMMONWEALTH

same specifications

	VF-20	EF-40	MS-60	PROOF
1937-M .... (2,493,872)	1.75	3.50	17.50	*
1938-M .... (4,000,000)	1.50	2.50	12.50	*
1941-M .... (2,750,000)	2.00	3.00	17.50	*

"WARTIME ALLOY" 5 CENTAVOS

Copper-Nickel-Zinc 65:12:23

		VF-20	EF-40	MS-60	PROOF
1944	(21,198,000)	0.25	0.50	1.50	*
1944-S	(14,040,000)	0.25	0.50	1.00	*
1945-S	(72,796,000)	0.20	0.35	0.50	*

Ten centavos

FIRST TYPE

18 mm, 41.15 grains .900 Silver.

		VF-20	EF-40	MS-60	PROOF
1903	(5,102,658) ... (2,558)	2.25	3.25	25.00	75.00
1903-S	(1,200,000)	10.00	27.50	180.	*
1904	(10,000) ... (1,355)	12.50	30.00	125.	90.00
1904-S	(5,040,000)	2.25	3.25	45.00	*
1905	(471)	*	*	*	150.
Proof only					
1906	(500)	*	*	*	135.
Proof only					

SECOND TYPE, Reduced Size

16.7 mm .30.86 grains .750 Silver

		VF-20	EF-40	MS-60	PROOF
1907	(1,500,781)	3.00	5.00	50.00	*
1907-S	(4,930,000)	2.25	3.50	45.00	*
1908	(500)	*	*	*	160.
Proof only					
1908-S	(3,363,911)	2.00	3.50	45.00	*
1909-S	(312,199)	22.50	45.88	225.	*
1910-S					
Possibly five struck, none may exist today.					
1911-S	(1,100,505)	4.00	8.00	45.00	*
1912-S	(1,010,000)	4.25	8.00	55.00	*
1913-S	(1,360,693)	5.00	9.00	55.00	*
1914-S	(1,180,000)	5.25	12.50	155.	*
1915-S	(450,000)	17.50	32.50	225.	*
1917-S	(5,991,148)	2.00	2.50	22.50	*
1918-S	(8,420,000)	1.50	2.00	20.00	*
1919-S	(1,630,000)	2.00	3.75	32.50	*
1920 (M)	(520,000)	5.50	12.50	70.00	*
1921 (M)	(3,863,038)	1.75	2.75	25.00	*
1929-M	(1,000,000)	1.75	2.75	27.50	*
1935-M	(1,280,000)	1.50	2.75	25.00	*

THIRD TYPE, COMMONWEALTH

same specifications

	VF-20	EF-40	MS-60	PROOF
1937-M .... (3,500,000)	1.50	3.25	17.50	*

Mint mark appears as in inverted W with slanting sides on at least some examples of this date. A unique pattern struck in aluminum appeared in the collection of Egypt's King Farouk.

	VF-20	EF-40	MS-60	PROOF
1938-M .... (3,750,000)	1.25	2.25	12.50	*
1941-M .... (2,500,000)	1.50	2.75	17.50	*
1944-D .... (31,592,000)	0.50	0.75	1.50	*
1945-D .... (137,208,000)	0.35	0.50	1.00	*

Twenty centavos

FIRST TYPE

23.2 mm, 83.10 grains .900 Silver

	VF-20	EF-40	MS-60	PROOF
1903 .... (5,350,231) .... (2,558)	3.25	4.25	32.50	80.00
1903-S .... (150,000)	20.00	35.00	175.	*
1904 .... (10,000) .... (1,355)	27.50	45.00	185.	95.00
1904-S .... (2,060,000)	3.25	4.25	37.50	*
1905 .... (471)	*	*	*	225.
Proof only				
1905-S .... (420,000) 8.50	17.50	85.00	*	
1906 .... (500)	*	*	*	200.
Proof only				

SECOND TYPE, Reduced Size

20.8 mm, 61.72 grains .750 Silver

	VF-20	EF-40	MS-60	PROOF
1907 .... (1,250,651)	4.00	6.25	55.00	*
1907-S .... (3,165,000)	3.25	5.50	37.50	*
1908 .... (500)	*	*	*	175.
Proof only				
1908-S .... (1,535,000)	3.25	5.50	37.50	*
1909-S .... (450,000)	8.25	22.50	190.	*
1910-S .... (500,259)	9.00	22.50	200.	*
1911-S .... (505,000)	9.00	22.50	175.	*
1912-S .... (750,000)	5.50	12.50	125.	*
1913-S .... (948,565)	5.50	12.50	110.	*
1913-S/S..	17.50	27.50	175.	*

This is a repunched Mint mark, frequently called S/S.

Philippines 20 centavos continued

	VF-20	EF-40	MS-60	PROOF
1914-S .... (795,000)	3.25	7.50	80.00	*
1915-S .... (655,000)	3.25	15.00	125.	*
1916-S .... (1,435,000)	3.25	12.50	95.00	*
1917-S .... (3,150,656)	2.25	4.50	27.50	*
1918-S .... (5,560,000)	2.25	4.50	27.50	*
1919-S .... (850,000)	2.50	7.50	50.00	*
1920 (M) .... (1,045,415)	3.35	10.00	95.00	*
1921 (M) .... (1,842,631)	2.25	3.50	27.50	*
1928-M .... (100,000)	12.50	60.00	325.	*
Mule, 5 centavos reverse showing large date, wing tips in from the rim.				
1929-M .... (1,970,000)	2.25	3.50	27.50	*

THIRD TYPE, COMMONWEALTH

same specifications.

	VF-20	EF-40	MS-60	PROOF
1937-M .... (2,665,000)	1.50	2.50	15.00	*
Mint mark appears as an inverted W with slanting legs on at least some examples of this date.				
1938-M .... (3,000,000)	1.50	2.25	10.00	*
1941-M .... (1,500,000)	1.50	2.50	10.00	*
1944-D .... (28,596,000)	0.75	1.25	2.50	*
1945-D .... (82,804,000)	0.35	0.50	1.25	*

Fifty centavos

FIRST TYPE

30.8 mm, 208 grains .900 Silver

	VF-20	EF-40	MS-60	PROOF
1903 .... (3,099,061) .... (2,558)	7.00	12.50	80.00	150.
1903-S				
Possibly a pattern or trial strike.				
1904 .... (10,000) .... (1,355)	27.50	37.50	127.50	175.
1904-S .... (2,160,000)	7.00	15.00	127.50	*
1905 .... (471)	*	*	*	350.
Proof only				
1905-S .... (852,000)	8.50	22.50	175.	*
1906 .... (500)	*	*	*	300.
Proof only				

SECOND TYPE, Reduced Size

	VF-20	EF-40	MS-60	PROOF
1907 .... (1,200,625)	6.00	12.50	80.00	*
1907-S .... (2,112,000)	4.50	8.50	70.00	*
1908 .... (500)	*	*	*	300.
Proof only				

Philippines 50 centavos continued	VF-20	EF-40	MS-60	PROOF
1908-S .... (1,601,000)	4.50	8.50	75.00	*
1909-S .... (528,000)	6.50	12.50	140.	*
1917-S .... (674,369)	6.50	12.50	130.	*
1918-S .... (2,202,0000	4.50	7.00	70.00	*
1919-S .... (1,200,000)	4.75	7.75	75.00	*
1920 (M) .... (420,000)	4.50	7.00	60.00	*
1921 (M) .... (2,316,763)	4.00	6.50	35.00	*

THIRD TYPE, COMMONWEALTH

27.5 mm, 154,32 grains .750 Silver

	VF-20	EF-40	MS-60	PROOF
1944-S .... (19,187,000)	1.00	2.50	5.00	*
1945-S .... (18,120,000)	1.00	2.50	5.00	*

Peso

FIRST TYPE

38 mm, 416 grains .900 Silver

	VF-20	EF-40	MS-60	PROOF
1903 .... (2,788,901) .... (2,558)	12.50	35.00	175.	300.
1903-S .... (11,361,000)	12.00	30.00	125.	*
1904 .... (10,000) .... (1,355)	70.00	130.	300.	350.
1904-S .... (6,600,000)	12.50	30.00	125.	*
1905 .... (471)	*	*	*	900.
Proof only				
1905-S .... (6,056,000) 12.50	35.00	160.	*	
1906 .... (500)	*	*	*	525.
Proof only				
1906-S .... (201,000) .... 725.	1500.	5000.	*	

SECOND TYPE, Reduced Size

35.7 mm, 308.64 grains .800 Silver

	VF-20	EF-40	MS-60	PROOF
1907-S .... (10,278,000)	7.00	12.50	85.00	*
1908 .... (500)	*	*	*	525.
Proof only				
1908-S .... (20,954,944)	6.00	12.50	80.00	*
1909-S .... (7,578,000)	6.00	12.50	85.00	*
1910-S .... (3,153,559)	6.50	15.00	110.	*
1911-S .... (463,000)	17.50	65.00	550.	*
1912-S .... (680,000)	17.50	65.00	650.	*

Proof sets

1906 7-piece set, half centavo through peso.
    BM 03/94, lot #2646 P Proof-65 through -67, $3,190.

Commemorative coinage

Manila Mint Inauguration Medals, 1920

Struck from dies by U.S. Mint Engraver George T. Morgan, these 38mm medals bear a civil bust of Woodrow Wilson l. with title PRESIDENT OF THE UNITED STATES. The reverse depicts Roman coinage goddess Juno Moneta and a small child operating a coining press with legend TO COMMEMORATE THE OPENING OF THE MINT, MANILA P.I./ 1920. These plain edge pieces are not coins but medals. Low relief and silver dollar size led to their inclusion among So-Called Dollars cataloged by Richard D. Kenney in 1953 and by Harold E. Hibler and Charles Kappen in 1963. The existence of only one gold Wilson Dollar is certain today.

	Mintage	Unc.
1920 (M) Wilson 'Dollar.' Gold. HK-1031. .... (5 pcs.)		$3,000.
1920 (M) Wilson 'Dollar.' Silver, HK-449. .... (2,200)		$250.
1920 (M) Wilson 'Dollar.' Bronze. HK-450. .... (3,700)		$150.

One known with a Matte finish, others with bright coin finish.

COMMONWEALTH INAUGURATION COMMEMORATIVES

Specifications of 1907.

	Mintage	Unc.
1936-M One Peso .900 Silver .... (10,000)		$125.

Conjoined busts Franklin D. Roosevelt and Manuel Luis Quezon l., date NOV. 15 1935 over, legend COMMONWEALTH OF THE PHILIPPINES, ONE PESO. Reverse of circulating Commonwealth coins. Designed by Ambrosio Morales, Professor of Fine Arts at the University of the Philippines.

	Mintage	Unc.
1936-M One Peso .900 Silver .... (10,000)		$125.

Conjoined busts High Commissioner Frank Murphy, President Manuel Luis Quezon l., NOV 15/ 1935 in right field. Reverse of preceding.

	Mintage	Unc.
1936-M 50 Centavos .750 Silver .... (20,000)		$75.00

Facing busts of Murphy and Quezon, rising sun bears date NOVEMBER/ 15/ 1935. Reverse of preceding.

Between 3,000 and 4,000 three-piece sets of these coins were included in the silver reserve submerged in Caballo Bay.

COMMEMORATIVE COINS, 1947

Specifications as last.

	Mintage	Unc.
1947-S One Peso .900 Silver .... (100,000)		$12.50

Unif. bust Gen. Douglas MacArthur r. DEFENDER AND LIBERATOR OF THE PHILIPPINES. Reverse Arms of Republic between orchids, PHILIPPINES, value below. By Laura Gardin Fraser, sc.

	Mintage	Unc.
1947-S 50 Centavos .750 Silver .... (200,000)		$4.50

Uniformed bust 3/4 r. Reverse as preceding.

These coins were actually struck for the infant Republic of the Philippines, but are closely allied to the Commonwealth coinage in size, alloy and denomination. Intended for sale to American collectors, they are included here for the sake of completeness. No circulating coins of the Republic would appear until 1958 when Figueroa's Standing Lady and Worker returned once more.

Hawaiian Coinage 1847-1883

The Hawaiian islands were unified by King Kamehameha I, called the Great, after 1810. As commerce expanded, a medley of European and Latin American silver and gold coins came into circulation, along with several early varieties of private scrip and tokens. The Spanish-colonial 8 reales and its fractions became the most widely used, and when King Kamehameha III (1825-1854) instituted a unified legal code in 1846, the monetary unit of the kingdom was declared the *dala* of 100 *keneta* (cents).

The new law specified the denominations, the silver *dala; hapalua* or half dollar; *hapaha*, quarter dollar; *hapawalu*, eighth dollar or bit (equal to the real or 12 ½ cents) and a 1/16 *dala* or 6 1/4 *keneta*. The keneta or cent was to be struck in copper. The keneta was struck on contract by the Attleboro, Mass., firm of H.M. & E.I. Richards, a famous maker of Hard Times Tokens, American political medalets and store cards.

Throughout Hawaiian numismatic history, the islands' beautiful Polynesian language would be a source of confusion to foreign die sinkers. The new copper keneta was a case in point. The obverse bore a somewhat inelegant facing uniformed bust with legend KAMEHAMEHA III KA MOI "the King," with date 1847 below. The reverse bore a wreath, national name APUNI HAWAII. The denomination was supposed to appear as HAPA HANELE, but the second word was misspelled HANERI.

There are two obverse date varieties, the crosslet 4 or plain 4 . Six reverse varieties are identified by the number of berries in the wreath. Full red Uncirculated examples of all varieties are rare, as the kegs of coins were shipped as hold ballast and immersed in salt water over much of their journey. The cent was unpopular, and of 100,000 struck, some 88,000 were melted in 1885.

Kamehameha's dynasty ended with the death of Kamehameha V in 1872 and the House of Nobles elected Prince William C. Lunalilo as king. This young monarch died in 1874 and the nobles then elected the flamboyant Prince David Kalakaua, who reigned until as Kalakaua I until his death in 1891. The Hawaiian people and nobility were dwindling in numbers as a result of disease and alcohol introduced from the mainland. The new king was determined to assert his sovereignty and to reinforce the Hawaiian character of his kingdom. He became the first reigning monarch to tour the world, increasing Hawaii's diplomatic and commercial contacts. The king also strove to protect the rights and increase the educational opportunities of native Hawaiians.

American settlers and developers opposed the king, and much of the "bad press" he received in subsequent history reflects their prejudices. Kalakaua is remembered in numismatics for his medals, the richly ornate Orders and Decorations he instituted and for the silver coinage of 1883. The coinage was authorized in negotiations between Kalakaua's agent, sugar baron Claus Spreckles, and the Department of State in Washington. Chief Engraver Charles E. Barber prepared the designs, the dies were made and 26 Proofs were struck at the Philadelphia Mint. All business strikes were then made at the San Francisco Mint.

All coins were struck in .900 silver to the same standards as contemporary U.S. denominations. A 19mm *hapawalu* or 1/8 dollar was originally planned and 20 Proofs struck before it was decided to substitute a dime (UMI KENETA or 10 cents) in its place. Obverses bore the bare head of the king in mutton-chop whiskers facing right with title KALAKAUA I KING OF HAWAII, the date 1883 appearing below with squared-crosspiece or block 8's. Reverse legends included the kingdom's motto, UA MAU KE EA O KA AINA I KA PONO, "The Life of the Land is Preserved in Righteousness."

The dime bore a crowned laurel wreath enclosing ONE DIME, UMI KENETA below. The quarter presented an ornate shield under tiny crown flanked by 1/4 D, HAPAHA below. The half dollar reverse is essentially the same as the quarter, but the dollar's large diameter gave Barber an opportunity to present the full royal Arms on a crowned mantle. The shield is quartered with first and fourth quarters bearing the red-white-blue stripes of the national flag; second and third quarters present the *kapu* or tabu stick; the escutcheon of pretense at center bears the arms of the dynasty. Supporters are two chiefs from the saga of Kamehameha the great, Kamanawa holding a spear, Kameeiamoku holding a ceremonial *kahili*. The distinctive royal crown tops both shield and ermine mantle.

Pattern 5-cent pieces were struck in Paris by a French nickel mine owner of New Caledonia . The king was styled KING OF SANDWICH ISLANDS, the name applied by Captain James Cook. An ornate 5 from the promoter's own private token appears in an oval Garter bearing the royal motto with the first word AU misspelled AU. Struck in copper-nickel and inscribed *Maillechort* on the rim, original patterns are very rare. Less so are Canadian-made restrikes of later date on thin planchets and lacking the cross on the orb that forms the top of the royal crown.

Eighteen regular-dies Proof sets were struck in copper including the dollar, half, quarter and eighth dollar. Clandestine strikes of the eighth dollar exist with fancy (curved-crosspiece) 8's struck in copper-nickel, bronze, gold and platinum. Quarters and half dollars exist dated 1884 struck in platinum, gold, copper and brassy oroide. None of these were struck with official authorization.

What are undoubtedly the most beautiful "patterns" related to Hawaii are the private issues struck by the British medallic firm of John Pinches for numismatist Reginald Huth. Huth honored several dethroned queens by creating sumptuously designed pieces struck in a remarkable array of precious and exotic metals including gold, platinum and iridium. Huth commissioned dala and 20 dala pieces of Queen Liliuokalani, struck after this sister of Kalakaua was dethroned in the revolution that led to the proclamation of Sanford Dole's usurping Hawaiian Republic. Pieces of similar elegance honored the youthful Princess Kaiulani, the queen's niece and heir apparent. Because of their unofficial nature, the Huth pieces are not listed here.

Kamehameha III

ONE CENT

One cent of Kamehameha III

	VF-20	EF-40	AU-50	MS-60	MS-63	MS-64	MS-65
1847 .... (100,000) .... 425.		650.	900.	1550.	2500.	3500.	5500.
Crosslet 4. Rev. 18 berries.							
1847 .... 325.		475.	675.	1100.	1550.	2225.	3250.
Crosslet 4. Rev. 15 berries.							
1847 .... 350.		500.	700.	1250.	1750.	2500.	3750.
Plain 4. Rev 17 berries.							
1847 .... 350.		500.	700.	1250.	1750.	2500.	3500.
Plain 4. Rev 15 berries, arranged 8 and 7.							
1847 .... 275.		475.	675.	1250.	1750.	2500.	3500.
Plain 4. Rev. 13 berries.							
1847 .... 350.		550.	750.	1500.	2500.	3500.	4500.
Plain 4. Rev . 15 berries, arranged 7 and 8.							

Kalakaua I silver coinage

DIME, UMI KENETA

Dime of Kalakaua I

	VF-20	EF-40	AU-50	MS-60	MS-63	MS-64	MS-65
1883 .... (250,000) 65.00		220.	600.	1000.	1500.	2500.	3500.

QUARTER DOLLAR, HAPAHA

	VF-20	EF-40	AU-50	MS-60	MS-63	MS-64	MS-65
1883 .... (500,000) 50.00		125.	175.	225.	450.	900.	2500.

HALF DOLLAR, HAPALUA

Half dollar of Kalakaua I

	VF-20	EF-40	AU-50	MS-60	MS-63	MS-64	MS-65
1883 .... (700,000)	100.	250.	750.	1000.	2000.	3000.	4500.

DOLLAR, AKAHI DALA

Dollar of Kalakaua I

	VF-20	EF-40	AU-50	MS-60	MS-63	MS-64	MS-65
1883	300.	675.	1000.	3250.	8500.	9500.	12000.

Kalakaua I pattern coins

5 CENTS, COPPER-NICKEL

Original, cross on crown

	MS-60	MS-63	MS-65
1881	10000.	17500.	25000.

EIGHTH DOLLAR, HAPAWALU, SILVER

	Prf-60	Prf-63	Prf-65
1883...................................(20)	20000.	25000.	35000.

Confederate States of America

Civil War emergency conditions had a far greater effect on the history of American paper money than on metallic coinage. The North issued paper money that was not redeemable in specie under the 1862 Legal Tender Act in defiance of the Constitution. This currency was issued under the direction of Treasury Secretary Salmon P. Chase, who as Supreme Court Justice later called the Act unconstitutional.

The new Confederate States of America relied heavily on paper, although attempts were made in 1861 to launch a separate coinage of half dollars and cents. In 1861 the South took over three Mints: Dahlonega, Ga.; Charlotte, N.C., and New Orleans, La.

Dahlonega struck an unknown number of 1861-dated Union type gold dollars with small D Mint mark solely for the Confederacy and some quarter eagles of this same date; Charlotte issued a small number of 1861-C quarter eagles from rusted dies (see under respective denominations).

Remarkably little new information has been added to our knowledge of Confederate pattern coinage since the 1870's, but in 1994-95, P. Scott Rubin (writing in the Numismatic Bibliomania Society journal, *The Asylum*) and Michael J. Hodder have made major discoveries and broken new ground in this long-static area.

At the order of Confederate Treasury Secretary Christopher G. Memminger, the New Orleans Mint struck four Proof patterns by combining an 1861 Union Seated Liberty die with a new Confederate obverse die cut by New Orleans diesinker August H.M. Petersen. This obverse bears a shield with seven stripes and stars flanked by cotton and rice with a liberty cap above.

This distinctive die was retired after four pieces were struck, although enough silver was on hand to allow striking of a number of Union-type halves with the same Seated Liberty die, its more advanced die crack showing that it was used after the Confederate coins had been struck.

These four coins enjoyed many adventures. Coiner Benjamin F. Taylor's own coin was sold with the obverse and reverse dies to Philadelphia dealer Ebenezer Scott Mason in 1879. Mason sold them to the New York dealer J.W. Scott, whose use of them is described below. The Taylor coin and reverse die came into the possession of famed numismatist J. Sanford Saltus, who later presented the coin to the American Numismatic Society.

Dr. Edward Y. Ames had the second coin, which passed through the hands of Thomas L. Elder, H.O. Granberg, William H. Woodin, Waldo Newcomer, Col. E.H.R. Green and Burdette G. Johnson before entering the collection of Eric P. Newman of St. Louis. Dr. John Leonard Riddell (often misreported as a "Professor Biddle"), former melter and refiner at the New Orleans Mint, had a third example, placed almost a century later in another private collection by New York numismatist Lester Merkin.

The fourth coin was in the possession of Confederate President Jefferson Davis when he was was captured by Union forces at Irwinville, Ga. He was not wearing female attire, as long-discredited myth would have it, but had thoughtfully placed his valuables in his wife's steamer trunk in the touching belief that no officer and gentleman would ransack a lady's effects.

Rifling through all the Davis baggage, Union soldiers stole the half dollar, the President's example of the rare Sabine Pass Medal and other memorabilia. The coin's disappeared for almost a century, reappearing at a 1961 New York coin convention, sold to numismatist John J. Ford Jr., who at first assumed it to be a restrike of the type now to be described. The specimen was consigned to Stack's of New York to be offered for private sale, and was on display at the American Numismatic Association's Early Spring Convention in Atlanta, Ga., in March 1995.

Philadelphia numismatist Mason sold the Taylor half dollar with the obverse and reverse dies to the go-getting New York firm of J.W. Scott & Co., derided by the cantankerous numismatist Ed Frossard as "the Fulton Street postage stamp dealers."

Working with the amiable David Proskey, described by Frossard as "the nice-looking young man with the big India-rubber conscience," Scott bought 500 1861-O half dollars to restrike with the Confederate die. Two coins had their normal Union reverse overstruck with the Confederate die. The remainder had their reverses planed off and the Confederate design impressed on their now-smooth surfaces.

A unique piece once owned by William A. Philpott Jr. showed a dramatically double-struck Union obverse with the date at both top and bottom as if the planchet had been turned 180 degrees while it was still in the die and then struck again.

All of these restrikes show some degree of obverse flattening, although a disc of soft brass protected them to some extent during restriking. All are underweight, around 185-187 grains vs 192 grains of an unaltered coin. Proskey confessed later that only half the issue actually sold in 1879, but the pieces are very popular today.

Generally mentioned with these restrikes is the white metal Scott business card featuring the Confederate reverse plus a statement that only four originals were struck. Two uniface brass strikes are said to exist, struck after Scott had softened and cancelled the die. The die itself was donated to the Louisiana Historical Society on April 25, 1922, but the society today has no record of it.

No Southern Mint had ever struck copper-nickel cents, but to begin cent coinage, Confederate agents contacted Philadelphia manufacturing jewelers Bailey & Co. about a contract coinage. This firm was well connected with medalists and diesinkers, and supplied dies for the private gold coinage of Clark, Gruber & Co. of Denver, Colo., in this very year.

Bailey asked noted diesinker Robert Lovett Jr. to cut the necessary dies. Lovett used his stock Liberty head with legend CONFEDERATE STATES OF AMERICA for his obverse, the reverse bearing the denomination in wreath of rice, wheat, tobacco and cotton.

Many influential Northern voices advocated "let them go," preferring peaceful secession to civil war. However, after striking 12 pieces, Lovett saw the winds of war blowing, feared prosecution by a Federal government which had no intention of "letting them go," and hid his coins and dies until 1873, save for a single cent he carried as a pocket piece.

The saga of the Confederate cent was long accepted as told by flamboyant Philadelphia numismatist Capt. John Haseltine, who never let mere dates and facts impede the broad flow of his narrative. Haseltine's story was that the bibulous Lovett inadvertently spent his pocket piece in a Philadelphia saloon. Hearing of this mysterious coin, Haseltine sought it out and acquired it. Recognizing Lovett's work, he hounded the unfortunate diesinker until he agreed to sell Haseltine both the 11 remaining copper-nickel coins and the dies.

In early 1995, however, researcher P. Scott Rubin published some important facets of this story conveniently overlooked by the colorful Haseltine. In point of fact, it was not Haseltine but the "kindly old Quaker Doctor," Edward Maris of New Jersey copper fame who found and acquired all the cents Lovett still possessed along with the dies in mid-1873. A Confederate cent specifically attributed to Maris was lot 665 in Haseltine's Jan. 13, 1874, sale; others appeared in the June 21, 1886, Harlan P. Smith sale and in the Nov. 16, 1900 S.H. and Henry Chapman auction of Maris pieces.

Haseltine's major involvement came soon after the first sale of a Confederate original. Using the dies bought by Maris, Haseltine worked with Philadelphia medalist Peter L. Krider to produce restrikes in gold, silver and copper. Small but significant variations in the numbers struck appear in the several retellings of Haseltine's tale over the next few decades.

Numismatist Fred L. Reed III was one of the few historians ever to read the entire *Journal of the Confederate Congress* in search of documentary clues to proposed Confederate coinage. Reed found tantalizing mention for an all-copper emergency coinage, but no mention of Bailey & Co. nor of Lovett. Michael J. Hodder has discovered a concrete Confederacy-Lovett tie is the form of the Washington Light Infantry Captain Simonton Medal, named for the officer charged with preventing the supplying of Fort Sumter at the very start of the war.

In the excitement of the Civil War Centennial, brash young Robert Bashlow obtained the cancelled Confederate cent dies, had transfer dies made by the Philadelphia medallic firm of August C. Frank and struck thousands of pieces ballyhooed as the "Second Restrike." These are easily distinguished from the Haseltine pieces by their crumbled edges and high, raised die-cancellation file marks crisscrossing the surfaces.

The silver "Confederate dimes" portraying a bearded Jefferson Davis and Gen. P.G.T. Beauregard are medalets allied to the political pieces of the time. Interestingly, however, their edges are reeded like those of coins.

[The editors wish to thank numismatist William T. Gibbs, researcher of the Confederate half dollar, for his contributions to this section.]

Half dollars

Original (American Numismatic Society)

1861 .... (4)
Originals as described above, all show fine die crack from rim past star 7 to bridge of Liberty's nose.

Confederate patterns continued

Scott restrike

1861 .... (500)
   Scott restrike, figure incl. two overstruck on unaltered half dollars, rest on pieces with original Union reverse removed.. Stack's Sutcliffe Coll., 9/94, Unc., $3,600; Eliasberg 4/97 MS-65 $17,600.

Double-struck restrike (David T. Alexander)

   The William A. Philpott coll. included a unique coin with double-struck rev., "1861" appearing at both top and bottom. The extra date was a secondary impression from the brass plate which cushioned the blow of the Confederate die, which gradually acquired an impression on it of the Seated Liberty design on the coins being struck against it. Other restrikes were carefully fitted into the impression before the Confederate die was applied to the other side, but this coins was inadvertently (?) rotated 180 degrees.
1861 .... (500)
   J.W. Scott store card in white metal, Confederate rev. muled with Scott legend. Stack's Sutcliffe Coll., 9/94 Ch. Unc. $1,000.

Cents

Confederate cent pattern

1861 .... (12)
   Copper-nickel, struck in Philadelphia workshop of engraver Robert Lovett. BM 1/88, Unc., $13,530
1861 .... (7)
   Gold; Haseltine variously reported three or seven struck in gold. Stack's cataloger of the Stanley Simon sale traced six pieces in Jan. 1989. Stack's 7/89, Brilliant Proof, $33,000, Stack's Sutcliffe Coll., 9/94, ex Farouk, Brilliant proof, $27,000; Eliasberg 4/97 Pf-64 $55,000.
1861 .... (12)
   Silver, ST 1/94, Brilliant Proof, $7,500; Eliasberg 4/97 Pf-62 $14,300.
1861 .... (55)
   Copper, ST 3/95 Ch. Proof $6,050; Eliasberg 4/97 Pf-60 $8,250.

Bashlow restrike

Bashlow Restrikes were made in at least 11 compositions, including three each in platinum and gold, 5,000 silver, 20,000 bronze and 5,000 "goldine." Their value today is best described as dubious.

Pioneer Gold

Although a few other countries boasted private gold coins, this type of pioneer coinage is typically American in its variety of makers and designs, duration and historical interest. Such coins were struck to meet the needs of miners, merchants and bankers during the gold rushes that shaped national and local history in Southern Appalachia, California, Oregon, Utah and Colorado from 1830 to 1850. While serving urgent community needs, private gold added a rich element to American numismatics.

Private coinage was the solution to coin shortages, avoiding risky shipping of precious metals to the far-away Mint. While the Constitution denied states the right to coin money, it did not deny this right to private individuals, as long as forthright copying of Federal designs did not raise the question of counterfeiting.

Pioneer issues are known in round, rectangular and octagonal shape. The early California octagonal $50 slugs were officially called ingots, but collectors think of ingots as pieces of refined gold or silver, cast with or without stated values though always bearing a statement of weight, and not intended for ordinary circulation. Generally they are found in large denominations.

A bar, on the other hand, usually has an odd value, and simply represents the amount of a miner's deposit after it had been assayed, refined, and cast into a convenient form, and stamped with its weight, fineness and value, often with a serial or deposit number. Bars saw limited circulation; when used as money, their values were rounded off to the nearest convenient figures. Sometimes large bars were also cast in even values, such as $100, to facilitate their handling by banks and bullion brokers.

Most surviving bars occupy a peripheral area of numismatics and are omitted from the present catalog unless they express a coinage equivalent such as $100, $20 or $16, official value of the Spanish colonial doubloon. Auction records for bars indicate a keen collector interest, however, and bars recovered from shipwrecks such as the *S.S. Central America* may expect a lively market when questions of ownership are finally resolved.

The first opportunity for private gold coinage followed the discovery of major gold deposits on the remote frontier of Georgia and North Carolina in 1830. At that time, U.S. gold coins were seldom seen in commerce because of their artificial official valuation in relation to silver. The appearance of substantial amounts of Appalachian gold and the very real hazards of transporting it over the mountains or up the Atlantic seaboard to the Philadelphia Mint opened the door for the first private gold coinage of Georgia's Templeton Reid.

A short history of each issuer accompanies the listing of known gold pieces and patterns. Unless otherwise specified, all coins listed are struck in gold.

A note on pricing: It is not the purpose of this catalog to provide a definitive price guide for each piece listed. Significant auction realizations are included for major pieces appearing in public sales within the last decade or so. Pieces which have made no such appearance are not priced. Most unpriced coins are excessively rare, but this may not be true in every case. Post-1989 Stack's listings appear as ST, without the 10% buyer's fee; Bowers & Merena listings as BM with the buyer's fee included.

Appalachian gold rush

TEMPLETON REID

Georgia inventor, gunsmith and cotton gin builder Templeton Reid set up the first private mint in the summer of 1830, striking $10, $5 and $2.50 coins from crudely refined native gold in his hometown, Milledgeville. He then moved to Gainesville in the center of the mining district for the rest of his brief and controversial career. Viciously attacked in the newspapers for supposedly violating the Constitution and accused of overvaluing his coins, Reid ceased coining and returned to gun and cotton gin manufacture.

The late Reid researcher Dexter C. Seymour concluded that no more than 1,500-1,600 pieces of all three denominations were struck. Reid's downfall resulted from ignorance, not greed. A self-taught assayer, he did not understand that his crude refining techniques left copper and tin with the "fluxed" gold, lowering its overall fineness below the 22 carats he tried to attain. His later career was clouded by bad debts, lawsuits, and bankruptcy. Too old and infirm to go to California, the unforgetting Reid struck a few coins from California gold brought to him in Georgia to vindicate his local reputation as a coiner.

1830 $2.50

P.1.   **1830 $2.50 :** Obv. Legend T. REID ASSAYER, 2.50 at center. Rev. GEORGIA GOLD, 1830 at center. Mid-American 1987 FUN Sale VF-30, $37,000.

1830 $5 (Bowers & Merena)

P.2.   **1830 $5:** Obv. TEMPLETON REID ASSAYER around $5. Rev. GEORGIA GOLD 1830 around $5. 1983 ANA Sale EF-40, $130,000; Brand VF, $63,250.

Templeton Reid continued

1830 $10

P.3. **1830 $10:** Obv. Legend TEMPLETON REID ASSAYER around TEN/DOLLARS. Rev. Legend GEORGIA GOLD around 1830. Brand EF, $90,750.

Undated $10 of 1830

P.4. **(1830) $10:** Similar obv. Rev. GEORGIA GOLD inscription at center, border of stars. Excessively rare.

1849 $10 (Harlan J. Berk Ltd.)

P.5. **1849 $10:** Obv. Legend TEMPLETON REID ASSAYER around 1849. Rev. CALIFORNIA GOLD around TEN DOLLARS. Copper, struck for Philadelphia dealer Stephen K. Nagy, two known, one on holed Draped Bust large cent, Kagin's 1983 ANA MS-60, $2,000.

P.6. **1849 $25:** Copper, possibly same dies as unique gold piece stolen from the Mint cabinet in 1858. Kagin's 1983 ANA AU-55, $2,200.

Note: A few other pieces bearing the names Reid and California, struck in copper and nickel are believed to be fantasies.

THE BECHTLERS

Emigrating to the U.S. from Baden, Germany, the Bechtler family of jewel and watch makers settled in Rutherfordton, N.C., and launched a 20-year career as private coiners of Georgia and North Carolina gold. Christopher Bechtler Sr., his son August, and nephew Christopher Jr. produced the longest-lasting private coinage in American history. By stating fineness and later weight on each $2.50 and $5 they struck, the Bechtlers avoided the negative publicity which had ruined Templeton Reid.

Christopher Sr. was in charge of the Bechtler coinage from July 1831 until his death in 1842. During the first few months, his output consisted of quarter and half eagles, struck on a standard of 30 grains per dollar at 20 carats, yielding a theoretical bullion value of a few cents per coin more than federal standard.

The first series bore no mark of weight. Similar issues that followed bore weights of 75 and 150 grains respectively. Both are very rare, since most are believed melted after 1834 (along with federal old-tenor gold) as worth more than face value. Christopher Sr. struck the first gold dollar in the U.S. in 1831, minted at 30 grains. Christopher Sr. and August were painfully honest and went to great effort to assure a coinage of consistent quality.

August Bechtler continued the coinage after his father's death. After August Bechtler retired, the mint was run by the nephew, called Christopher Jr. It remained in operation until 1852, but the younger, alcoholic Christopher did not maintain the same meticulous care for consistent fineness.

The Bechtlers' gold dollars, anticipated those of the U.S. Mint by 17 years. When the Federal government prepared to revalue its gold coinage in 1834, it announced that the new coins would bear the date Aug. 1, 1834. No Philadelphia coin actually bore such a specific date, but the Bechtlers revaluated their coinage to the new standard, and added this exact date to their dies.

With the equipment at hand, the Bechtlers could not fully refine their gold, and the coins vary somewhat in weight. The designations Carolina, Georgia or North Carolina, were added to the coins to show the origin of the metal, which varied in natural purity from place to place. Georgia gold was very pure, and with the addition of silver alloy, produced bright yellow coins. North Carolina gold, being generally less pure, resulted in coins of a duller hue.

CHRISTOPHER BECHTLER SR.

First Series: "Weightless," July-September 1831

First Series $2.50 (Bowers & Merena)

P.7. **$2.50:** Obv. Legend C. BECHTLER, ASSAYER, RUTHERFORD in circle at center. Fine beads. Rev. Legend NORTH CAROLINA GOLD., center 250. over 20.C. Coarse beads. Six to nine known. ST 5/92, EF, $20,000.

P.8. **$2.50:** Similar, fine beads on obverse, coarse beads reverse. Vars. in legend positioning. Possibly six of each var. known. Garrett VF-30, $4,500.

P.9. **$5:** Obv. C. BECHTLER, ASSAYER., inner circle RUTHERFORD COUNTY. Rev. NORTH CAROLINA GOLD. legend, 5/DOLLARS./20. CARATS. curving, star below. Possibly three known.

Second Series: Weights added to first series dies. 30 grains per dollar, 20 carats

Second Series $2.50 (Bowers & Merena)

P.10. **$2.50:** Similar obv. Rev. NORTH CAROLINA GOLD. legend, 250./20 C./75.G. at center. Rarcoa Auction '82, Gem Unc., $9,250; ST 3/95 AU $12,650; Eliasberg 5/96 AU-50 $42,000.

P.11. **$5:** As preceding series, tiny 150.C. added above star on rev. ST 3/95 VF $6,325; Eliasberg 5/96 EF-45 $15,950.

Third Series: Same standard, new dies

Third Series $1 (Bowers & Merena)

P.12. **$1:** Obv. C. BECHTLER. RUTHERF. legend, 30 G over star at center. Rev. N: CAROLINA GOLD DOLLAR legend, ONE at center Fine serrations. Norweb AU-55, $2,750; Eliasberg 5/96 AU-50 $5,720.

P.13. **$2.50:** Obv. C. BECHTLER ASSAYER. legend, star over 75 G at center. Rev. NORTH CAROLINA GOLD. legend, 250.20.C. at center. Wide edge reeding instead of previous fine. Norweb EF-40/VF-20, $18,700.

Fourth Series: 28 grains per dollar, 20 carats, August 1, 1834

P.14. **$1:** Obv. C BECHTLER. RUTHERF:, 28.G high in field. Rev. N:CAROLINA GOLD.DOLLAR, ONE at center. Excessively rare.

Fourth Series $1 (Bowers & Merena)

P.15. **$1:** Obv. As preceding, 28.G centered. Superior Heifetz I AU-50, $3,300.

P.16. **$5:** Obv. C.BECHTLER.AT RUTHERFORD, no period after D. Rev. Concentric legend CAROLINA GOLD., 20. CARATS./ AUGUST 1, 1834. 140 G. at center. R.E. Stack's "New England Museum" sale, Oct. 1988 EF, $3,740.

Note: All of the following have plain edge unless noted.

P.17. **$5:** As preceding, period after RUTHERFORD. P.E. ST 3/95 Ch. AU $7,700; Eliasberg 5/96 MS-63 $8,360.

P.18. **$5:** Similar but RUTHERF:, CARATS. near 20. Excessively rare.

P.19. **$5:** As preceding, CARATS far from 20. far from 20. Kagin's 1983 ANA VF-20, $2,900.

Fifth Series: 26.8 grains per dollar, 21 carats

Fifth Series $2.50

P.20. **$2.50:** Obv. BECHTLER. RUTHERF:, 250 at center. Rev. CAROLINA GOLD., legend, 67.C./ 21.CARATS at center and bottom. Kagin's 1983 ANA, MS-60, $5,250.

Fifth Series $5

P.21. **$5:** Obv. C: BECHTLER. AT RUTHERF: Rev. CAROLINA GOLD. legend, 134.G., at center, 21.CARATS at bottom. Star at lower center, one example shows lump of native gold at center. ST 3/95 Ch. AU $7,975.

P.22. **$5:** As preceding, no star on rev., two known. Excessively rare Transitional piece with Rev. of A. Bechtler coinage.

Sixth Series: GEORGIA GOLD, 25.6 grains per dollar, 22 carats.

Sixth Series $2.50 (Bowers & Merena)

P.23. **$2.50:** Obv. BECHTLER RUTHERF:, 250 at center. Rev. GEORGIA GOLD legend, CARATS, 64.G, 22 CARATS at center, bottom, first 2 low. A's missing crossbars. Garrett EF-40, $3,800; Eliasberg 5/96 AU $6,380.

P.24. **$2.50:** As preceding but 22 even. Kagin's 1983 ANA VF-20, $5,200; ST 3/95 Ch. EF $9,075.

Sixth Series $5

P.25. **$5:** Obv. C. BECHTLER. AT RUTHERFORD. star, 5 DOLLARS. at center. Rev. GEORGIA: GOLD 22 CARATS legend, 128.G:, star at center. Heritage Dec. 1988 EF-40, $4,700.

P.26. **$5:** As preceding, no colon after GEORGIA. Garrett EF-45, $4,000; ST 3/95 Ch. EF $12,650; Eliasberg 5/96 MS-63 $41,800.

P.27. **$5:** Obv. of 4th series, worn die, rev. of preceding. Garrett VF-30, $3,600.

Seventh Series: Name Bechtler, no initial, C. and A. Bechtler working together, 1840-42.

Seventh Series $1

P.28. **$1:** Obv. BECHTLER RUTHERF: star, 28:G: at center. Rev. CAROLINA DOLLAR, star, ONE at center with backwards N. Superior Heifetz I PCGS MS-61, $3,740.

P.29. **$2.50:** Obv. BECHTLER RUTHERF:, 250 at center, cracked and buckled dies common. Rev. CAROLINA GOLD CARATS, 70.G: 20 low in center. Rarcoa Auction '82 Choice BU, $4,750; Eliasberg 5/96 EF-45-AU-50 $8,580.

AUGUST BECHTLER, 1842-46

August Bechtler $1

P.30. **$1:** Obv. A. BECHTLER. star, tall 1, DOL: below. Rev. CAROLINA GOLD. 21.C. legend, 27.G. at lower center. R.E. Excessively rare. Eliasberg 5/96 AU050 $4,620.

P.31. **$1:** As preceding, P.E. Later strikes from rusty dies show lighter weight, beware brass counterfeits. Kagin's 1983 ANA MS-60, $2,200.

P.32. **$5:** Obv. A. BECHTLER. AT RUTHERFORD. legend, 5 DOLLARS. in center. Rev. CAROLINA GOLD. legend, CARATS legend, 128.G. at center, 22.CARATS below. Very rare. Kagin's 1983 ANA VF-20, $5,500; Eliasberg 5/96 Ef-45 $13,200.

P.33. **$5:** Obv. As preceding. Rev. CAROLINA GOLD. legend, 134.G: at center, 21. CARATS. below. R.E. Norweb VF-35, $3,520; Eliasberg 5/96 EF-45 $9,900.

P.34. **$5:** Similar obv. Rev. CAROLINA GOLD legend, 141.G:, 20 CARATS at center, bottom. Kagin's 1983 ANA VF-30, $3,600; Eliasberg 5/96 VF-20 $4,400.

P.35. **$5 Proof Restrike:** Obv. As preceding, heavy die crack rim to second A in CARATS. Five struck at Philadelphia Mint for numismatist Henry Chapman, 1922. Stack's Coles Sale, 10/83, Brilliant Proof, $5,500; Kagin's 1983 ANA Proof-60, $10,000.

P.36. **$5 Proof Restrike Fantasy:** Series Four obv. C: BECHTLER. AT RUTHERF:. Rev. As preceding; no original strikes exist of this die marriage. Five struck in 1922 for Henry Chapman. Excessively rare, Stack's Coles Sale, 10/83, Gem Brilliant Proof, $7,500.

California gold rush

FIRST PERIOD, 1849-1850

The greatest boom in pioneer gold coinage began in mid-1849, a year and a half after James Marshall, a worker in Sutter's Mill, struck it rich at Coloma, Calif. Almost overnight, an extravagant economy sprang up. The backweard territory that had used hides and cattle for money, and whose annual imports had employed but a dozen ships in 1847, now required a thousand vessels docking at San Francisco to supply those who had come for the diggings.

The only drawback was that all customs duties had to be paid in U.S. coin, of which there was but little in circulation. As a result, the merchants began to import foreign coins, which were more obtainable than those of the Philadelphia Mint some 3,000 miles away. However, they lost heavily on the exchanges, and in July 1848, leading San Francisco citizens petitioned military governor R. B. Mason for the right to issue private coins. Mason at first consented, but fearing to provoke the federal government on the eve of California's statehood, withdrew his permission.

NORRIS, GREGG & NORRIS

The business community took matters into their own hands, and on May 31, 1849, the San Francisco newspaper *Alta California* described what is believed to be the first California pioneer piece, a "Five Dollar gold coin, struck at Benicia City, though the imprint is San Francisco. In general appearance it resembles the United States coin of the same value, but it bears the private stamp of Norris, Grieg (sic) & Norris".

The coiners, Thomas H. Norris, Charles Gregg, and Hiram A. Norris, were members of a New York engineering firm, which manufactured and dealt in iron pipes and fittings. Since the only known half eagles of this firm differ radically in design from their U.S. counterparts, the above reference may actually be to an earlier issue which has not survived. This is also suggested by die sinker Albert Kuner's claim that he engraved the dies for the known Norris, Gregg & Norris issue. Kuner did not arrive in San Francisco until July 16, 1849.

1849 $5 With Period

P.37. **1849 $5:** Obv. Dropped-wing eagle with 5 on shield, legend CALIFORNIA GOLD WITHOUT ALLOY, no period after ALLOY Rev. FULL WEIGHT OF HALF EAGLE legend, circle of 22 stars, inner N.G.& N., SAN FRANCISCO, 1849 at center. P.E. Stack's Auction '85, prooflike AU, $5,500; Mid-American FUN Sale 1990, MS-60, $15,000.

P.38. **1849 $5:** Same, R.E. Stack's Auction '82 EF, $8,750.

P.39. **1849 $5:** As preceding, period after ALLOY. P.E. Garrett prooflike MS-60, $37,500.

P.40. **1849 $5:** As preceding, R.E. Rarcoa Auction '82 Unc., $10,000.

P.41. **1850 $5:** As preceding, but 16 stars and STOCKTON. P.E. Unique. Kreisberg-Schulman 10th Anniv. Sale, April 1967, retooled at Y of ALLOY, Fine, $18,500.; donated to the Smithsonian Institution by Willis Dupont, Dec. 1994.

MOFFAT & COMPANY

During the summer, a number of other private Mints began operations. The foremost of these was established by John Little Moffat, a New York assayer who, in association with Joseph R. Curtis, Philo H. Perry and Samuel Ward, opened an assay office at San Francisco. Moffat's first issues were assay bars and $16 ingots, or ounces. In early August, the firm began to strike coins, first eagles and then half eagles, from dies by Albert Kuner. The designs resemble those on U.S. coins, but on the reverse the legend S.M.V.; (Standard Mint Value) CALIFORNIA replaced UNITED STATES OF AMERICA. The Moffat coins always maintained a high standard, and those assayed at the U.S. Mint showed an average value of $9.98 per eagle.

Ingot of 1849

P.42. **(1849) Ingots:** Uniface rectangle, three-line inscription MOFFAT & CO., next lines for carat and dollar value. Three known of varying weights and values. Garrett sharp rectangle VF-30, $20,000; Rarcoa Auction '89 EF, concave right side, $17,600; Eliasberg 5/96 EF-45 $18,700.

1849 $5 (Bowers & Merena)

P.43. **1849 $5:** Obv. Similar to regular U.S. coin, MOFFAT & CO. on coronet. Rev. S.M.V. CALIFORNIA GOLD, Standard Mint Value, denomination below. Minor die varieties exist. Garrett AU-55, $10,000.

P.44. **1849 $10:** As preceding but for size, thinner Liberty head S.M.V. CALIFORNIA GOLD TEN DOL. on rev. Rarcoa Auction '89 AU, $5,225.

1849 $10 (Bowers & Merena)

P.45. **1849 $10:** As preceding, denomination as TEN D. Rarcoa Auction '79 VF, $2,600.
P.46. **1850 $5:** As 1849. Rev. Small eagle. Rarcoa Auction '79 Choice AU, $5,000.
P.47. **1850 $5:** As preceding but large eagle. Garrett MS-60, $21,000.

1852 $10

P.48. **1852 $10:** Obv. Different head. Rev Charles Cushing Wright's eagle on shield, 880 THOUS. on ribbon, legend 264 GRS. CALIFORNIA GOLD TEN D. Wide and close date vars., very rare. Rarcoa Auction '82 Proof, $16,000.

Note: For 1853 $20, see under United States Assay Office of Gold, Curtis, Perry & Ward.

J.S. ORMSBY

Around this same time, a firm opened in Sacramento under the name of Ormsby & Co., operated by Dr. John S. Ormsby and Major William M. Ormsby. The Ormsbys are said to have had an extensive business, despite the crudity of their planchets, hammer striking of their coins and the 20 percent they charged depositors of the value of the coins they made. An independent assay revealed a value of only $9.37 for Ormsby's $10 pieces.

Undated $5 of 1849

P.49. **(1849) $5:** Obv. J.S.O. in center, UNITED STATES OF AMERICA legend, CAL. at bottom. Rev. circle of 13 stars around 5/DOLLS. P.E. Unique.

P.50. **(1849) $5:** As preceding but R.E. Unique. Superior Auction '89, VF $125,000.

P.51. **(1849) $10:** As preceding but for size and denomination. Five known. Garrett F-12, $100,000.

P.52. **(1849) $10:** As preceding, silver trial piece struck on 1815 Mexico 2 reales. Unique, Garrett VG-8, $14,000.

MINERS BANK

Stephen A. Wright and Samuel W. Haight of Wright & Co., San Francisco exchange brokers, struck coins under the name of the Miners Bank. Their $10 pieces exist alloyed with native silver, with a greenish tinge, struck on narrowly constricted planchets. Red-gold pieces with normal rims were alloyed with copper, possibly back East where the dies were cut. These coins were denounced as seriously debased and helped trigger the 1850 coin panic, ending their life with discounts of 20 percent.

Undated $10 of 1849

P.53. **(1849) $10:** Obv. MINERS BANK SAN FRANCISCO around TEN D. Rev. Raised-wing eagle. CALIFORNIA, 13 stars around. Greenish gold, constricted rims. R.E. Kagin's 1983 ANA EF-40, $9,500; ST 3/94, AU, $8,000; ST 3/95 Unc. $38,500.

P.54. **(1849) $10:** As preceding but copper trial piece. Very rare. Clifford EF, $2,100.

P.55. **(1849) $10:** Similar but red gold alloyed with copper, normal rims. R.E. Garrett MS-65, $135,000; ST 9/90, AU, $16,500.

ITHACA MINING COMPANY

A single trial piece recalls this firm, composed of Elijah White, Jonas Olmstead, I.N. Thorne and others from Ithaca, N.Y. These adventurers purchased and probably tried out their coining press near home, accounting for the trial piece below. Arriving six months late from their arduous overland journey to San Francisco, they found their goods had arrived, but had been sold to pay freight charges by the ship captain who transported them.

Undated $10 trial of 1849 (Bowers & Merena)

P.56. **(1849) $10:** Obv. Large X. Rev Raised-wing eagle, CALIFORNIA, stars, GOLD. Copper trial piece struck over 1849 large cent. Unique. Clifford EF, $3,000.

THE PACIFIC COMPANY

Although many trial pieces exist with this name, the identity of the issuing company is not known. It may have been Bostonian John W. Cartwright's group which planned to live aboard the ship *York* after its arrival in San Francisco in autumn 1849.

Researchers believe that the controversial David C. Broderick and Frederick D. Kohler may have actually struck the Pacific Company pieces by the ancient sledgehammer method. Kohler was later appointed California state assayer.

1849 $5 (Stack's)

P.57. **1849 $5:** Obv. Liberty cap on pole in sunburst of rays and stars. Rev Thin-wing eagle, PACIFIC COMPANY CALIFORNIA around, date below. Three known. R.E. Garrett VF-30, $180,000.
P.58. **1849 $10:** As preceding except for size and denomination. Brand AU, $132,000.

Trial Pieces:

P.59. **1849 $1:** As preceding but for size and denomination. Silver, known overstruck on U.S. half dime, uniface on Spanish real, Brand silver gilt EF, $5,225.
P.60. **1849 $1:** As preceding, white metal, Clifford Good-VG, ex Levick, $1,000.
P.61. **1849 $2.50:** As preceding, silver. Garrett VF-20, $9,000.
P.62. **1849 $5:** As preceding, silver, struck over 1842-O Seated Liberty quarter. Unique. Bowers Taylor coll. EF-45, $7,480.
P.63. **1849 $5:** As preceding, copper, three known.
P.64. **1849 $5:** As preceding, thick copper planchet, some known gilt, very deceptive as they weigh about the same as the gold impressions. Excessively rare.
P.65. **1849 $10:** As preceding, copper pattern. Unique, Lilly coll., Smithsonian.

CINCINNATI MINING & TRADING COMPANY

Led by Cincinnati pioneer J.H. Levering, 50 members of this company journeyed overland to California. A *Cincinnati Gazette* letter published June 7, 1849, tells how they were forced to abandon most of its equipment 300 miles west of Independence, Mo., and almost left behind its coin press. The Cincinnati dies may have been engraved in that city, then a center of die sinking, but Broderick and Kohler may have had a hand in striking the known examples.

1849 $5

P.66. **1849 $5:** Obv. Indian bust in feather headdress left, legend CINCINNATI MINING & TRADING COMPANY. Rev. Eagle and shield, CALIFORNIA FIVE DOLLARS above. Unique, Smithsonian.

P.67. **1849 $5:** As preceding, copper pattern, some known gilt.

P.68. **1849 $10:** As preceding, gold. R.E. Garrett EF-40, $270,000.

P.69. **1849 $10:** As preceding but struck over a J.S. Ormsby $10, Brand EF-40, $104,500.

P.70. **1849 $20:** As preceding except for size and denomination. Copper pattern. Two known.

MASSACHUSETTS & CALIFORNIA COMPANY

Detailed information concerning this company appeared in the *New York Tribune* for March 2, 1849, which stated that it had been organized at Northampton, Mass., by Josiah Hayden, S. S. Wells, Miles G. Moies and others. The Rev. F. P. Tracy and W. Hayden had taken coining machinery, since "It is the intention of the Company to establish a private Mint in California, and with the approbation of the Government, to make coins of the same denomination as the coins of the United States, and of equal, if not a little higher, value."

Only a few of its gold pieces survive, heavily alloyed with copper and most likely struck in the East as patterns. Most of the many copper and silver examples, as well as types inscribed 5/ DOLLARS are believed to be the work of Philadelphia dealer Stephen K. Nagy in the early 20th century.

1849 $5 (Harlan J. Berk Ltd.)

P.71. **1849 $5:** Obv. Arms in circle of stars, vaquero throwing lasso on shield supported by bear and deer. The crest is an arm hurling a spear, ALTA (Upper California) appears on ribbon. Rev. Company name legend, FIVE/D. in wreath, date below.

P.72. **1849 $5:** As preceding, copper pattern, see introductory remarks. Clifford EF, $850.

P.73. **1849 $5:** As preceding, silver. Garrett VF-30, $6,000. Clifford gilt AU, $850; silver EF, $1,100.

P.74. **1849 $5:** Similar obv., but with wreath closed at top. Smaller letters 16 berries. Possibly six known. Superior Auction '80 EF-40, $4,500.

P.75. **1849 $5:** As preceding, silver.

P.76. **1849 $5:** As preceding, open wreath rev. without denomination. Garrett VF-20, $5,000.

P.77. **1849 $5:** Similar obv., small continuous wreath inside starry circle, copper. Brand EF, $1,870. Specimens also exist from false dies showing denomination as numeral 5.

P.78. **1849 $10:** Similar to 1849 FIVE D. but for size and denomination. Brass, two known, one struck over a button. Clifford Fine, $3,400.

Ephemeral companies

A number of firms are represented only by rare patterns, never progressing into full coining operation. Most struck only a pattern or two, such as J. H. Bowie of Maryland, who struck at least one half eagle and a copper dollar pattern. As rare are patterns of the Pelican Company, of Louisiana origin, whose assayer Dr. Pearson was recommended by the coiner and assistant superintendent of the New Orleans Mint.

Other such firms included Ohio's Columbus Company; Sierra Nevada Mining Company; Heinrich Schaeffer, former employee and executor for Christopher Bechtler Sr. The rare copper patterns of Moran & Clark are inscribed "San Francisco," which would indicate that this firm planned to coin gold there.

J. H. BOWIE COMPANY

P.79. **1849 $5:** Obv. Pine tree, CAL. GOLD above, date below. Rev. J.H. BOWIE at top, 137 GRS. at bottom, 5/DOLLARS/1849 at center. Two known.

1849 $1 pattern (Bowers & Merena)

P.80. **1849 $1:** Similar, as preceding except for size. Rev. J.H. BOWIE, 24 G. 24 C. legend, 1/ DOL. at center. Copper, Unique. Garrett VF-20, $12,000.

THE PELICAN COMPANY

P.81. **1849 $1:** Obv. Six pointed star, PELICAN CO. above, date below. Rev. ONE at center, CALIFORNIA DOL. around. Silver trial piece struck on U.S. half dime. Unique.

1849 $2.50 (Bowers & Merena)

P.82. **1849 $2.50:** Obv. As preceding but for size. Rev. CALIFORNIA 2 1/2 DOLLS legend, 21 CARATS at center. Brass. Unique. Garrett MS-60, $20,000.

1849 $10 (Bowers & Merena)

P.83. **1849 $10:** Obv. Pelican vulning, wounding self to feed young, Louisiana state emblem, PELICAN CO. above, date below. Rev. CALIFORNIA 10 DOLLARS around six-pointed star and 21 1/4 CARATS, 10 Dwt 23 Grs. Brass. Unique. Clifford VF, $8,250.

COLUMBUS COMPANY

1849 $5 pattern (Smithsonian)

P.84. **1849 $5:** Obv. COLUMBUS * COMPANY *, date at center. Rev. CALIFORNIA GOLD * DOL:S around double ring enclosing 5. Feb. 15 scratched in obv. field. Silver. Unique. Smithsonian.

P.85. **1849 $5:** As preceding, copper gilt, Unique. Copper, Garrett EF-40, $18,000.

SIERRA NEVADA MINING COMPANY

P.86. **(1849) $2.50:** Obv. Small Liberty head right, 10 stars and date. Rev. SIERRA NEVADA MINING CO. 2 1/2 DOL. around eagle. Silver trial piece struck over U.S. dime, last two digits of undertype's date are illegible. Unique.

HEINRICH SCHAEFFER

Undated $5 trial ca. 1849 (Bowers & Merena)

P.87. **(1849) $5:** Trial impression on U.S. large cent, H. SCHAEFFER and seven stars around 5/DOLLARS. Rev. CALIFORNIA GOLD, CARATS around 134 GR./21 at center. Typical Bechtler design for California-bound former associate. Unique. Clifford VF, $6,000.

MORAN & CLARK

$10 ca. 1849-50 (Harlan J. Berk Ltd.)

P.88. **(1849-50) $10:** Obv. Legend CALIFORNIA GOLD, MORAN & CLARK around curving WARRANTED 10 DOLLS. MINT VALN. Rev. Legend SAN FRANCISCO CALIFORNIA, wreath around 11 DWT 8 GR/20 1/2 CARAT (punched over error CARET). Copper pattern, not known in gold, most are struck off center and appear worn. Six to eight known. Garrett VF-20, scratches, $3,500; Brand EF, $2,640.

F. MEYERS & COMPANY

1/2 ounce trial ca. 1849 (Bowers & Merena)

P.89. **(1849?) 1/2 Ounce:** Uniface copper trial piece, legend U.S. STANDARD WARRENTED (sic), small MEYERS & CO. curving above, large 1/2/OZ/TROY at center. Struck over U.S. Large cent, Unique. Garrett Good-4, $4,750.

P.90. **(1849) $16 Ingot:** Obv. MEYERS & CO./1 OZ. TROY/$18.00. Rev Incuse U.S STANDARD/ WARRANTED. Unique. Clifford, no grade, $21,000.

California gold rush

SECOND PERIOD 1850-1851

DUBOSQ & COMPANY

After the flurry of ephemeral issues, the new year saw additional coining firms come into existence. Dubosq & Co. was owned by Theodore Dubosq Sr. and Jr. and Henry Dubosq, Philadelphia jewelers. Some 1849-dated Dubosq patterns exist, but no gold strikes are known until 1850. The devices on these coins are extremely similar to those of regular U.S. gold coins, and a pair of trial pieces for an 1849 Dubosq eagle and half eagle were among U.S. Mint engraver Longacre's personal effects. It is unlikely that he actually engraved this California private coinage, however. Dubosq coins were among the most reliable in circulation, widely trusted and accepted at par without question. The issues were large, perhaps 10,000 of each denomination.

1849 $2.50 pattern (Bowers & Merena)

P.91. **1849 $2.50:** Obv. circle of 13 stars over T. DUBOSQ/1849. Rev. S.M.V. CALIFORNIA GOLD, 2 1/2 DOL. around eagle. Copper pattern, one known gilt, Smithsonian. Garrett EF-45, $11,000; Clifford VF, $2,700.

P.92. **1849 $5:** As preceding but for size, denomination.

P.93. **1850 $5:** Obv. Coronet Liberty left, 13 stars and date. Rev. As preceding but for denomination. Three known, two in museums, extant piece described as plugged.

P.94. **1850 $5:** Uniface obv. white metal splasher. Two known. Clifford Unc., $850.

P.95. **1850 $5:** Uniface rev. white metal splasher. Two known. Clifford Unc., $750.

California 1850-51 continued

1850 $10

P.96. **1850 $10:** As preceding but for size, denomination. Eight known. Carter Fine, $38,500.
P.97. **1850 $10:** Uniface obv. white metal splasher. Two known. Clifford Unc., $1,500.
P.98. **1850 $10:** Uniface rev. white metal splasher. Two known. Clifford Unc., $550.

BALDWIN & COMPANY

Early in 1850, Frederick Kohler planned his own coinage, known from a single copper pattern for a Vaquero or horseman-type $10. He was appointed state assayer by the legislature on April 20, 1850, and produced the highest quality gold bars as a state officer.

After Kohler abandoned his own coinage scheme, the Broderick and Kohler machinery was sold to Baldwin & Co., San Francisco jewelry firm owned by George C. Baldwin and Thomas S. Holman. From the beginning, Baldwin's output was enormous, and it is recorded that during the first three months of 1851 the company struck over a half million dollars' worth of gold coins. The dies for the Baldwin coins, like those of several other companies, were engraved by Albert Kuner.

Baldwin & Co. struck Liberty head $5, $10 and $20, but is best remembered for the beautiful Vaquero or horseman $10, whose obverse is virtually identical to the Kohler pattern. This company was ruined by James King of William, failed banker and self-anointed guardian of the public weal, who publicized Augustus Humbert's critical assay of several private gold pieces in March 1851.

Although the Baldwin coins were only found to be 3 percent underweight, the resulting uproar induced Baldwin and partner Bagley to leave San Francisco on the next outward-bound ship. "Baldwin's trash" was then bought up at enormous discounts by bankers who sold the coins at full bullion value for recoinage into Humbert's $50 slugs.

Precursor

P.99. **1850 $10:** Obv. Vaquero (horseman or cowboy) with lasso, CALIFORNIA GOLD, TEN DOLLARs (sic), date around. Rev. Eagle in circle of 21 stars, KOHLER & CO., SAN FRANCISCO around. Copper, struck over 1844 large cent, ST 3/94, VF, $5,500.

1850 $5

P.100. **1850 $5:** Obv. Coronet Liberty left in circle of stars, BALDWIN & CO. on coronet. Rev. S.M.V. CALIFORNIA FIVE DOL. around eagle. Another die by Kuner. Paramount Auction '83 AU-55, $12,100; Eliasberg 5/96 AU-55 $23,650.

California 1850-51 continued

1850 $10

P.101. 1850 $10: Obv. Vaquero resembling Kohler pattern. Rev. 10 stars flank large eagle, BALDWIN & CO. above, SAN FRANCISCO below. Rarcoa Auction '84 Gem BU, $71,500.
White metal and other pieces with tall letters were struck from copy dies in early 20th century. Garrett Proof, $3,500 Silver P.E., BM 3/90, MS-60, $2,200.

P.102. 1851 $10: As preceding Liberty design but for denomination and date. Garrett EF-40, $32,500; Eliasberg 5/96 VF-30 $15,400.

P.103. 1851 $20: Obv. Coronet Liberty head left. Rev. As preceding but for size, denomination. Garrett VF-30, $110,000.

H.M. NAGLEE & COMPANY

Another California firm that went into the coin business in 1850 was H. M. Naglee & Co., successor to Naglee & Sinton, which opened a banking house on Jan. 9, 1849. Naglee & Co. struck $100 ingots, but nothing of smaller value. It dissolved in September 1850 after a severe run on the bank. Gen. Naglee was hero of the pivotal battle of Fair Oaks during the Civil War.

Undated $100 ingot of 1850
(Smithsonian)

P.104. (1850) $100 Ingot: Obv. Incuse curving H.M. NAGLEE/ & /CO./$100. Rev. 100.DOLL./IN CAL.M./COIN 880/2640 GR.THO. Unique. Smithsonian.
Note: While the lettering in the photograph appears to be raised, a different photograph of this specimen appearing in the 1976 Catalogue & Encyclopedia of U.S. Coins shows it to be incused, an important caveat to those who would attempt to identify varieties by photographs only.

UNITED STATES ASSAYER AUGUSTUS HUMBERT

It seemed for a time in 1850 that Congress would establish the much-needed San Francisco Mint. When it did not, the California delegation pressed for an interim measure, creation of a U.S. Assay Office in San Francisco. On Sept. 30, Congress directed the Secretary of the Treasury "to contract upon the most reasonable terms with the proprietor of some well established assaying works now in successful operation in California to perform under the supervision of the United States Assayer, such duties in assaying and fixing the value of gold in grains and lumps, and in forming the same into bars, as shall be prescribed by the Secretary of the Treasury."

On learning of this act, Moffat & Co. immediately offered their services, and received a contract to undertake the duties of the United States Assay Office. Augustus Humbert, a New York watch case maker was appointed U.S. Assayer. The state abolished its assay office on Jan. 28, 1851, and on the following day Moffat & Co. announced the opening of the U.S. Assay Office.

Humbert arrived in California a day or two later, and on Jan. 31 struck his first octagonal coin-ingots, which entered Western lore as "slugs." Humbert had brought with him hubs and dies prepared by the great New York medalist Charles Cushing Wright. The reverse of the coins featured an embossed surface known to mechanics as "engine turning," and similar to the web-like engraving in the vignettes on paper currency or on watch cases. This design was apparently impossible to duplicate, since the machine which produced it was said to be the only one in the country.

The new office was in full operation by Feb. 14. An article in the *San Francisco Prices Current* illustrated the octagonal $50 gold piece, announced the issue of $100 and $200 ingots similar in design to the former, but of double and quadruple thickness. $500 and $1,000 ingots were apparently also contemplated, shaped as "parallelograms about five inches in length, one and three-quarters inches in breadth, and ranging in thickness - the smaller being three tenths of an inch and the larger six tenths."

That at least some high-denomination ingots were actually struck is proven by the following reference, in a letter of Mar. 31, 1851, from Moffat & Co.; to Treasury Secretary Thomas Corwin:

> "The amount of ingots to this time issued is about $530,000 and of this not more than $15,000 have been of denominations above fifty Doll, thus conclusively showing that small denominations are more adapted to the wants of the people than the larger ones. The former, in the absence of a sufficient supply of coins, are required for a currency. For the latter there is no demand because bankers & merchants do and will for a long time to come make their remittances in gold dust instead of ingots or coin. And as they do not deem the ingots as legal tender, but believe the U.S. Assay Office to be adverse [to their] interests, they countenance its issuance no further than they are compelled to do by the convenience & wants of the community. They can give a preference to private coining establishments."

There were sound reasons why bankers looked askance at the Assay Office. They feared it would increase the price of gold, which they purchased from miners at the modest rate of $16 per ounce. They knew it would force them to increase their rates of exchange. Finally, the Assay Office was bound to destroy the private mints which bought large quantities of gold to the banks' profit.

On Jan. 7, 1852, Secretary Corwin had sent new authority for the Assay Office to strike coins of $10 and $20. Although this directive reached Moffat & Co. on the 17th, no public acknowledgment was made until the following month. On Feb. 14, John L. Moffat withdrew from the company which then reorganized as the United States Assay Office of Gold under Curtis, Perry & Ward.

Another problem was created in early Autumn by an unexpected Treasury Department directive. On Sept. 4, Acting Secretary Hodge told San Francisco Customs collector T. Butler King that Congress had prohibited him from receiving the issues of the U.S. Assay Office. Congress had done no such thing, but only insisted that all payments of public dues be made in coins of standard fineness. Accordingly, new dies were made, and the U.S. Assay Office began refining its deposits to make .900 fineness possible.

One unsolved mystery is the issue of 1853 Assay Office of Gold coins of .884 fineness. These included a number of experimental pieces struck from dies for .900 fine coins, but with an actual fineness ranging (of those tested) from .888 to .910. Possibly related to these are the white metal trial pieces for an eagle and half eagle struck from dies with the fineness intentionally omitted.

Since only .900 fine coins were acceptable at the Customs House, it is possible that the assay Office hoped to economize on its supply of parting acids (which were very difficult to obtain in California) by issuing lower-fineness coins which could be redeemed upon demand for .900 fine specie. This is confirmed by the 1853 double eagles with the Moffat name, a specimen of which has been recently assayed at only .863 fineness.

This issue is attributable to Curtis, Perry & Ward, since Moffat had already given up his minting activities and allowed his former partners to continue using his name. The U.S. Assay Office continued in operation until Dec. 14, 1853, when it closed its doors to make way for the newly established San Francisco Mint.

Edges with incuse lettering: AUGUSTUS HUMBERT UNITED STATES ASSAYER OF GOLD CALIFORNIA 1851.

P.105. 1851 $50: Obv. Eagle with shield on rock, label above inscribed 880 THOUS. legend UNITED STATES OF AMERICA, incuse 50, relief D, C. Rev. Engine-turned field, tiny target center inscribed 50. Very rare, the first octagonal "slug." Stack's Auction '82 Choice EF, $22,000.

1851 $50, "No 50" (Bowers & Merena)

P.106. 1851 $50: As preceding, no 50 on rev. Stack's Auction '79 BU, $51,000; Eliasberg 5/96 AU-55 $40,700.

P.107. 1851 $50: As preceding, but 880 THOUS obv., 12-pointed star at center rev. Unique. Proof, Kagin coll.

1851 $50, "887" (Superior Galleries)

P.108. 1851 $50: As preceding, but 887 THOUS, 50 at center rev. Kagin's 1983 ANA EF-45, $13,000; ST 12/94, Unc. $23,000.

P.109. 1851 $50: As preceding, without 50 at center rev., Stack's Reed Hawn Coll. AU, $21,000.

Reeded edges:

1851 $50 (Bowers & Merena)

P.110. 1851 $50: Obv. Legend AUGUSTUS HUMBERT UNITED STATES ASSAYER OF GOLD CALIFORNIA 1851 around edge, .880 THOUS., denomination in relief as FIFTY DOLLS. Rev. target design. Rarcoa Auction '83 Choice BU, $26,400.

P.111. 1851 $50: As preceding obv., 887 THOUS. Rev. Much larger central target. Humbert's personal Proof, Garrett, $500,000.

P.112. 1852 $50: Obv. Reworked eagle by Kuner, longer ends on label. 887 THOUS. Kagin's 1983 ANA, VF-30, $8,500.

1852/1 $20 (Superior Galleries)

P.113. 1852/1 $20: Obv. Similar eagle, legend UNITED STATES OF AMERICA TWENTY DOLS. .884 THOUS. Rev. engine-turned field with rectangle inscribed AUGUSTUS HUMBERT./UNITED STATES ASSAYER/ OF GOLD. CALIFORNIA./1852. 7,500 struck in a single day's run in Spring. Two Proofs known, Humbert's personal Proof, Garrett, $325,000; Eliasberg 5/96 MS-60 $31,900.

1852/1 $10

P.114. 1852/1 $10: As preceding but for size, denomination. Heavy diagonal rev. die crack. One var. has obverse die crack making legend appear as IINITED. BM 9/92, AU-50, $6,325.

California 1850-51 continued

1852 $10 (Bowers & Merena)

P.115. 1852 $10: As preceding, .884 fineness. Close and wide date vars. Rare with heavy obv. die crack making UNITED appear IINITED, more common than unbroken obv.

UNITED STATES ASSAY OFFICE OF GOLD, Curtis, Perry & Ward

1852 $50, "887" (Bowers & Merena)

P.116. 1852 $50: Obv. As preceding, 887 THOUS. legend UNITED STATES ASSAY OFFICE OF GOLD SAN FRANCISCO CALIFORNIA. 1852 follows outer rim. Rev. Medium target design. Carter AU, $29,700.

P.117. 1852 $50: As preceding but .900 THOUS. Rev. Medium target.

P.118. 1852 $50: As preceding but small target. Rarcoa Auction '79 Choice BU, $24,000.

P.119. 1852 $10: Obv. of preceding, .884 THOUS. rev. engine-turned field with rectangle inscribed UNITED STATES ASSAY/OFFICE OF GOLD/SAN FRANCISCO/CALIFORNIA 1852. O of OFFICE is positioned under I in UNITED. Garrett Unc., $18,000.

P.120. 1852 $10: As preceding, but O in OFFICE is under N in UNITED. Two vars, rarer bold and fine beads. Bold, Rarcoa Auction '82 Gem BU, $4,500.

1853 $20 (Superior Galleries)

P.121. 1853 $20: As preceding date, .884/880 THOUS. Garrett EF, $23,000.

California 1850-51 continued

1853 $20 (Bowers & Merena)

P.122. 1853 $20: As preceding, .900 /880 THOUS., minor vars. in spacing. Two Proofs known, possibly later Philadelphia Mint restrikes, ex Farouk, Smithsonian. Superior Auction '89 PCGS MS-60, $11,110.

P.123. 1853 $10: As preceding date but .884/0 fineness. One var. shows no line at left end of label. Rarcoa Auction '79 Choice EF, $19,000.

P.124. 1853 $10: As preceding but .900 THOUS. Garrett Unc., $35,000.

1853 $20 (Bowers & Merena)

P.125. 1853 $20: Obv. Coronet Liberty head left, MOFFAT & CO. on coronet. Rev. Design of Federal double eagles, legend SAN FRANCISCO CALIFORNIA TWENTY D. Struck by USAOG using old Moffat dies to meet urgent need for $20 gold pieces. Rarcoa Auction '82 Choice BU, $7,500.

PATTERNS AND TRIAL PIECES

P.126. 1851 $50: Obv. 880 THOUS, 50 on rev. P.E. Struck in pewter. Last reported in J. Schulman sale, March 1930.

P.127. 1851 $50: As preceding, incuse DWT. GRS, punched on lower rim, no 50 on rev. Copper. Two known, both in Garrett. Choice AU-55, $24,000 and $38,000. Another without incuse marks, design rotated so that D. C. is above a point. Unique, Garrett AU-55, $32,000.

P.128. 1852 $10: Obv. as issued, .884 THOUS., TEN DOLS. Rev. Rectangle inscribed UNITED STATES ASSAY/OF GOLD.CALIFORNIA/1852. Copper. Unique. Garrett Proof, $12,000.

P.129. 1853 $5: Uniface obv. trial piece in white metal, Wright's eagle, UNITED STATES OF AMERICA 5 D, THOUS without stated fineness. Connecticut State Library, Mitchelson coll. Unique.

P.130. 1853 $5: Uniface rev. trial piece in white metal, eagle of regular U.S. gold coins. Same coll. Unique.

P.131. 1853 $10: Uniface obv. in white metal. Same general design, THOUS. without fineness stated. Same coll. Unique.

P.132. 1853 $10: Uniface rev. in white metal, eagle as on $5 above. Same coll. Unique.

P.133. 1853 $200: Uniface, irregularly rectangular bar bearing circular impression of Wright's eagle, UNITED STATES OF AMERICA $200 (incuse) D. Below three rectangular stamps inscribed 1] GRS. 5162; 2) UNITED STATES ASSAY/OFFICE OF GOLD/SAN FRANCISCO/CALIFORNIA 1853.; A.HUMBERT/U.S. ASSAYER. Unique.

P.134. 1853 $50: Type of round USAOG round $20, .900 THOUS. Planchet of double eagle diameter and extra thickness. Two known, including Lilly coin in Smithsonian. Clifford prooflike Unc., $19,000, Mar. 1982.

P.135. 1853 $50: Similar but larger planchet. Smithsonian (Lilly) coll. R.E. on oversize planchet, Clifford prooflike Superb Unc., $22,000.

P.136. 1853 $50: Thin uniface obverse impressions are known with bold KUNER F. under eagle, said to have been struck from a die salvaged from the San Francisco earthquake ruins. Silver, Garrett MS-65, $7,000; Clifford brass EF, $825.

P.137. 1853 $20: As regular issue, but octagonal planchet. 900 THOUS, weight 421.25 grains, indicating planchet clipped after striking as circular coin. Unique. Clifford prooflike Unc., $9,000.

P.138. 1853 $20: As regular issue but struck in experimental alloys ranging from .880 to .917, eight known. One inscribed .905 gold with 170 reeds, Clifford Gem prooflike, $7,000.

P.139. 1853 $20: As preceding, struck in silver. Ford coll.

California 1850-51 continued

P.140. 1853 $20: As preceding, no fineness stated, white metal. Ford coll., others of varied shape and weight included piece with reverse legend MOFFAT & CO., Clifford EF, $900.

P.141. 1853 $20: As preceding, copper trial strike on 1852 large cent. Ford coll.

P.142. 1853 $20: Restrike for Stephen K. Nagy, 1908. Combines two variants of USAOG-engine turned reverses. Weakly struck on round planchet, nickel alloy. Unique. Kagin's 1983 ANA EF-45, $950.

P.143. 1853 $20: Copper uniface impression of engine-turned rev. on thick, concave disc. Another Nagy restrike, unique. Kagin's 1983 ANA MS-63, $950.

P.144. 1853 $20: As preceding, white metal. Unique. Connecticut State Library, Mitchelson coll.

P.145. 1852 $20: As preceding, die privately altered to read 1852. Restrikes on irregularly square silver planchets. Kagin's 1983 ANA, EF-45 $1,250. Reported also in copper and lead on square or round planchets.

The Ford, Clifford/Kagin and Smithsonian (Lilly) collections also contained target types in odd values. One piece, stamped A. HUMBERT U.S. ASSAY, has a value of 44.77. Another, without engine turning on the rev., has a value of 28.62 and .999 fineness. Another has value of 32.25, and an ingot of similar design is stamped 83.71.

Paul Franklin - John Ford Discovery Pieces

During the 1950s, gun collector Paul Franklin found these unique pieces on an Arizona ranch. Their discovery led to much heated controversy, though Ford demonstrated their authenticity through meticulous scientific testing. The pieces may have been struck in preparation for the change to .900 fine gold in March 1853.

P.146. 1853 Ounce: Round uniface disc, rectangle inscribed UNITED STATES ASSAY/OFFICE OF GOLD/ SAN FRANCISCO/CALIFORNIA 1853, large incuse 1 above, 900 below. Unique. Clifford EF, $8,500.

P.147. 1853 $20: Obv. Circular legend A. HUMBERT U.S. ASSAYER at center, COIN/GOLD at bottom, large incuse 900, small relief THOUS., large incuse 20 below. Rev. Engine turned field, USAOG rectangle as preceding, large incuse 3 above, 516 below.

P.148. 1853 $20: As preceding, no reverse numbers.

P.149. 1853 $20: As preceding, large incuse 900, 21.06 on obv., inverted 540 on rev. Clifford Choice Unc., $8,500.

P.150. 1853 $20: As preceding, 999 and 28.62 incuse on obv., no engine-turning around rev. rectangle. Planchet clip at right.

P.151. $20 1853: As preceding but stamped 32.25.

P.152. $20 1853: As preceding but stamped 44.77.

P.153. 1853 $20: Several lead trial pieces bear variations of 000/0000; three different appeared in Clifford, two at $850, one at $1,000.

SCHULTZ & COMPANY

Although the U.S. Assay Office was in operation, 1851 witnessed the emergence of two new private coiners. The first was Schultz & Co., whose partners Judge G. W. Schultz and William T. Garratt operated a brass foundry in the rear of Baldwin & Co.'s establishment. Schultz coinage was struck only until April, and its half eagles are today excessively rare. The dies, which were engraved by Albert Kuner, show the misspelling "Shults & Co."

1851 $5

P.154. 1851 $5: Obv. Liberty head left, SHULTS & CO. on coronet. Rev. PURE CALIFORNIA GOLD 5 D. around eagle. Possibly 12 known. Stack's Auction '84 Choice EF, $36,300; Eliasberg 5/96 EF-45-AU-50 $31,900.

P.155. 1851 $5: As preceding, trial strike on Mexico 1847-RM Durango Mint 8 reales. Unique. Clifford EF, $8,250.

DUNBAR & COMPANY

Despite James King of William's denunciation of private gold coins, pieces in smaller denominations than the Assay Office $50 slugs were still needed in commerce. To alleviate the situation, Edward E. Dunbar, owner of the California Bank in San Francisco, advertised to redeem Baldwin's coins. He purchased the machinery of the defunct firm and issued his own $5 pieces. Dunbar's coins were actually overweight, but were still affected by the anti-private coin hysteria.

1851 $5

P.156. 1851 $5: Obv. Liberty head left, DUNBAR & CO. on coronet. Rev. S.M.V. CALIFORNIA GOLD, FIVE 5 around eagle. Rarcoa Auction '79 EF, $72,500.

JAMES KING OF WILLIAM

King's malice toward private coiners resulted from his frustrated ambition to be a coiner himself. A single copper trial piece which may have been King's and a unique gold ingot are the only numismatic reminders of his stormy career. Active as a yellow journalist, King was assassinated in May 1856 by County Supervisor James P. Casey, whose criminal record in New York he had publicly exposed.

Half ounce trial ca. 1850 (Bowers & Merena)

P.157. (1850?) Half Ounce: Obv. J.A. KING MINT in circle of stars. Rev. PURE/GOLD/HALF/ OUNCE/ CALIF. Unique, double struck and extremely crude. Clifford VF, ex Thomas L. Elder, F.C.C. Boyd, $2,400.

P.158. 1851 $20 Ingot: Obv. JAS. KING/ornament OF ornament/WILLIAM & CO. in recessed rectangle. Rev. CALIFORNIA/ornament GOLD ornament/20 DOLLARS. Unique.

WASS, MOLITOR & COMPANY

Although the Humbert Assay Office ingots were accepted by the Customs House, and considered legal tender by Californians, they were not recognized as coins by the Mint. So long as a few private coiners were still operating, the issue of lower denominations by the Assay Office was not absolutely essential. By the end of the year, the "torrent of cumbrous slugs" from the Assay Office had become a nuisance, and were discounted 3 to 5 percent in making change.

Appeal after appeal was made by Moffat & Co.; for authority to issue smaller denominations, and then, when permission was finally granted on Dec. 9, it was revoked the following day. On Dec. 31, Moffat reported that "several of our most influential merchants and Banks, as a matter of absolute necessity, not choice, have been urging somebody to make small coin with a private stamp and I understand the dies are already in the hands of the engravers."

The firm that had taken this initiative was owned by Count Stephen C. Wass (modern spelling Vas) and Agoston P. Molitor, two Hungarian patriots of the 1848 struggle for independence. Trained in German mining schools, the Hungarians operated a most advanced gold smelting and assaying plant. The *San Francisco Herald* praised the new firm Nov. 19, 1851, as "almost the only one in California capable of making those delicate assays which are so much needed just at this time."

On November 25th, the *Herald* announced the opening of the firm, which was said to receive and assay gold dust and make a return "in any coin that may be current at the banks" within 48 hours. Since the Assay Office took eight days for the same service, Wass, Molitor & Co. were greatly appreciated by the community. Their coins first appeared Jan. 8, 1852, and were highly praised by the *Herald* because of their workmanship and their value was 4 percent higher than the Mint's own coins.

Goaded by this competition, Moffat & Co. resumed striking its own eagles, ostensibly to prevent "less reputable firms" from doing so. It has been stated that $300,000 worth of these coins were struck, but Moffat's own correspondence gives a face value of $86,500. Wass, Molitor coinage continued in 1855 in $10, $20 and the spectacular $50 denominations. Although their scientific skill was of the highest order, none of the Hungarian partners possessed the business skills that would have assured deserved financial success. Wass donated a virtually complete set of Wass, Molitor coins to the Hungarian National Museum in Budapest, and he ended his life in his native country's service after the Compromise of 1867 restored Hungarian autonomy.

1852 $5, "Small Head" (Superior Galleries)

P.159. 1852 $5: Obv. Small Liberty head left. Rev. Eagle, legend IN CALIFORNIA GOLD FIVE DOLLARS. All 1852 Wass, Molitor coins are softly struck. Garrett VF-30, $5,000; Eliasberg 5/96 VF-35 $5,720.

1852 $5, "Large Head" (Bowers & Merena)

P.160. 1852 $5: Obv. Large, crude Liberty head left. Rev. As preceding. Carter AU, $9,350.
P.161. 1852 $10: Obv. Long-neck Liberty head in fine style left. Date shows 2 on circular mound from drilling out the original 1. Rev. from recycled Dubosq & Co. die with eagle, S.M.V. CALIFORNIA GOLD TEN D. Garrett VF, $5,000.

1852 $10 pattern (Bowers & Merena)

P.162. 1852 $10: As preceding, copper pattern, does not show plug at date. Unique. Clifford EF, $388.
P.163. 1852 $10: Obv. Short-neck, crude Liberty left, die breaks linking stars. Rev. As preceding. Rarcoa Auction '82 BU, $8,250.
P.164. 1852 $10: Obv. Different head with close date. Rev. As preceding. Possibly struck in 1855. Garrett VF-20, $11,000.

California continued

1855 $10 (Bowers & Merena)

P.165. 1855 $10: Obv. As preceding, but last 5 in date on circular mound created by drilling out the earlier 2. ST 3/94, EF, $9,500; Eliasberg 5/96 EF-40 $9,900.

1855 $20, "Small Head" (Bowers & Merena)

P.166. 1855 $20: Obv. Same head as preceding in wide field. Rev. Similar eagle, label with 900 THOUS above, legend SAN FRANCISCO CALIFORNIA TWENTY DOL. Garrett EF, $16,000; Eliasberg 5/96 EF-40 $15,950.

1855 $20, "Large Head"

P.167. 1855 $20: Obv. Large head resembling that of U.S. double eagle. Rev.As preceding. Excessively rare, Carter VF, $40,700.

P.168. 1855 $20: As preceding, white metal pattern. Unique. Clifford VF-EF, $2,200.

1855 $50 (Bowers & Merena)

P.169. 1855 $50: Obv. Head as last, without company name on coronet. Rev. Laurel wreath around 50 DOLLARS, label with 900 THOUS above. Legend SAN FRANCISCO CALIFORNIA, WASS MOLITOR & Co. Garrett MS-65, $275,000; ST 3/95 Ch. EF $22,000; BM 5/92, EF-40, $12,100.

KELLOGG & COMPANY

The San Francisco Mint got off to a very slow start, particularly hampered by lack of parting acids. Private coinage continued to provide for California's needs even after the Mint was officially open for business. A new company formed in 1854 under the name of Kellogg & Co. The proprietors were John Glover Kellogg, once cashier, and G.F. Richter, once assayer for Moffat & Co. Reorganized late in the year, and Richter was replaced by none other than Augustus Humbert. Kellogg & Humbert, Melters, Assayers & Coiners, continued in partnership until 1860. The output of $20 pieces was phenomenal, probably 1,000 per day, or $300,000 in all. The legendary Kellogg $50 pieces were struck as Proofs, and never entered circulation.

1854 $20

P.170. 1854 $20: Obv. Liberty head left as U.S. double eagle, KELLOGG & CO. on coronet. Rev. SAN FRANCISCO CALIFORNIA TWENTY D. around eagle copied from U.S. coinage. Short arrow heads, Garrett, Augustus Humbert's own Proof, $230,000; Rarcoa Auction '82 Gem BU, $28,000. Long arrow heads, Stack's Auction '85 BU, $5,500.

P.171. (1854) $20: As preceding but without date. Copper pattern, three known. Garrett bronzed Proof, $8,000.

P.172. 1854 $20: As regular issue, but copper-gilt pattern with date. Unique.

P.173. 1855 $20: As preceding regular issue, long and short arrow head vars. Kagin's 1983 ANA, MS-60, $7,250.

1855 $50

P.174. 1855 $50: Obv. Distinctive Liberty head left, KELLOGG & CO. on coronet. Rev. SAN FRANCISCO CALIFORNIA FIFTY DOLLS. around eagle of Wright's design, ornate double label above inscribed 1309 GRS/887 THOUS. 11 known. Garrett Brilliant Proof, $300,000; Stack's Greater New York Proof, $180,400, May 1984.

P.175. 1855 $50: As preceding, copper pattern. Two known.

BLAKE & COMPANY, BLAKE & AGRELL

Among the most controversial private gold pieces are those bearing the names of firms associated with Gorham Blake of Vermont, who arrived in California in 1852. He formed a brief partnership with John Agrell in Sacramento in 1855 before taking the name Blake & Co. with W.R. Waters. A Unique ingot strip exists, divided into three small squares, each inscribed BLAKE/&/ AGNELL, a misspelling of interest.

The name Blake & Co. appears on a unique white metal bar struck from cancelled dies, but most famous are pieces bearing a coining press and the name Blake & Co. The $20 of this type exists in thousands of cheap pot-metal reproductions, used as advertising novelties in the late 1960s. These noxious pests have colored many a numismatists' outlook on the supposed originals, but genuine Blake bars were among those first recovered from the wreck of the *S.S. Central America* in the 1990s.

P.176. 1855 Ingot: Obv. Three squares inscribed BLAKE/&/ AGNELL/ASSAYERS/SAC. CAL. Rev. Three panels inscribed DOLLS./900THOUS/1855. Unique, Bank of California coll.

P.177. 1856 Ingot.: Obv. Curving and straight lettering, CALIFORNIA/1856 /BLAKE & CO./GOLD/ THOUS. FINE/VALUE/DOLLS. CTS. Rev. BLAKE & CO. five times in curving lettering. White metal pattern, cancelled twice on obv. Unique.

P.178. 1855 $50: Obv. Oblong bar impressed with circular dies, SAC. CALIFORNIA 50 DOLLS. around coining press with SMV .900, date below. Rev. BLAKE & AGNELL ASSAYERS around target with incuse 50 at center. Unique, Bank of California coll.

P.179. 1855 $20: Obv. As preceding. Rev. As preceding but 20 at center. Two known, Smithsonian, Bank of California colls.

1855 $20 trial strike (Bowers & Merena)

P.180. 1855 $20: As preceding, copper trial strike on 1848 large cent. Unique.

P.181. 1855 $20: Obv. As preceding. Rev. Curving BLAKE & CO. at top, rest blank.

P.182. 1855 $50: Obv. As preceding. Rev. As preceding. Octagonal white metal trial strike. Unique.

1856 $20 pattern (Bowers & Merena)

P.183. 1856 $20: Obv. Liberty head left, BLAKE & CO. on coronet. Rev. SACRAMENTO CALIFORNIA 20 D. around U.S. coinage-style eagle. Copper pattern. Garrett EF-40, 11,000.

DIANA GAMBLING HOUSE

An unusual double eagle, the exact date of which is unknown, was struck by James William, D. Webster and Stephen Whipple, owners of the large and elaborate Diana gambling house in San Francisco. The coins were issued in return for gold dust and nuggets in order to facilitate the play, or possibly for use in gaming.

Undated $20 of 1851 (Smithsonian)

P.184. (1851) $20: Obv. Legend DIANA SAN FRANCISCO CAL. around CLAY/TO/COMMERCIAL / STREETS/DRINKs (sic). Rev. GAMES/OF/CHANCE/CAL./COIN/GOLD, TWENTY DOLLARS below. Two known, Smithsonian and Ford colls.

SAN FRANCISCO STANDARD MINT; SAN FRANCISCO STATE OF CALIFORNIA

The exceptionally well designed pieces bearing the names San Francisco State of California and San Francisco Standard Mint and dated 1851 have intrigued numismatists. Bearing denominations from $2.50 to $20, they present a Liberty head facing left, values in wreaths for the smaller pieces, a seated Minerva from the California state emblem on the two highest denominations. A steel hub survives for the $10. None are known actually struck in gold.

While cataloging the 1983 Kagin's ANA sale, numismatist David T. Alexander identified the maker as Birmingham die sinker William Joseph Taylor (1802-85). Taylor's signature WJT appears on truncation of the San Francisco Standard Mint $5. This was not Taylor's only association with pioneer gold; he also engraved the dies for Australia's Fort Philip Kangaroo Assay Office pieces of 1853.

P.185. 1851 $5: Obv. Liberty head left in circle of stars, date below. Rev. Laurel wreath, 5/DOLLARS/SAN FRANCISCO/STANDARD MINT/22 CARATS/FINE. Copper-nickel. Kagin's 1983 ANA, MS-63, $1,750; BM 3/90, Prooflike MS-63, $3,300.

1851 $2.50 (Bowers & Merena)

P.186. 1851 $2.50: Obv. As preceding, no date. Rev. Laurel wreath encloses 2 1/2/DOLLARS, legend SAN FRANCISCO STATE OF CALIFORNIA, date below. Silver. Garrett Choice Proof, $10,000; BM 3/90, MS-63/64, $2,420.

P.187. 1851 $2.50: As preceding, copper. Kagin's 1983 ANA EF-45, $900.

P.188. 1851 $2.50: As preceding, white metal. Clifford AU, $375.

P.189. 1851 $5: As preceding but for size, denomination. Silver. Garrett Choice Proof, $10,000.

P.190. 1851 $5: As preceding, copper. Clifford Proof $525.

P.191. 1851 $5: As preceding, white metal. Clifford BU, $600.

California continued

1851 $10 (Bowers & Merena)

P.192. 1851 $10: Obv. As preceding but for size. Rev. Minerva seated with spear, shield, grizzly bear, Golden Gate behind, SAN FRANCISCO STATE OF CALIFORNIA above, 10 D in exergue. Silver. Garrett Choice Proof, $15,000.

P.193. 1851 $10: As preceding, copper. Clifford Proof, $650.

P.194. 1851 $10: As preceding, white metal. Clifford EF, $500.

1851 $20 (Bowers & Merena)

P.195. 1851 $20: Obv. As preceding but for size. Rev. As preceding, 20 D in exergue. Silver. Garrett Choice Proof, $17,000.

P.196. 1851 $20: As preceding, copper. Kagin's 1983 ANA Proof-63, $1,250.

P.197. 1851 $20: As preceding, white metal. Clifford AU, $600.

Four-piece set of $2.50, $5, $10 and $20 in silver, Eliasberg 5/96 Pr-63 or finer $27,500.

Model Coins, Counters, Other Eccentricities

The vast popularity of private gold, even among collectors who cannot afford such material, has caused a number of game counters and novelty items to be attached to the series. In this category are the Model Coins dated 1849, tiny pieces in denominations of 25 and 50 cents, $1, $2.50 and $5. These are another English import, probably made around 1860 by Joseph Moore of Birmingham and related to his equally tiny Model Coins of Queen Victoria.

Other pieces seen are the Dancing Bears, Liberty and flag, Eagle and flag, Pacific Currency doubloon of Mexican design, Liberty and kneeling prospector counters which appear on the market from time to time. While interesting, these were in all likelihood gaming counters and are properly cataloged with exonumia. Their inclusion with the gold coins and patterns tends to trivialize the more significant series.

Fractional gold tokens

A great many California gold coins of quarter dollar, half dollar and dollar denominations were issued in 1852-53 by San Francisco jewelers for use as emergency small change. Early researchers such as R.H. Burnie and Kenneth Lee attempted to separate genuine circulating small-denomination from later souvenir issues, but Walter Breen (with Ronald J. Gillio) made great progress in this quest in his 1983 catalog of the great Lee collection.

Circulating pieces were struck by several jewelry firms owned by French immigrants and often bear the makers' initials. Some may be confused with the souvenirs made 1859-82 in heavily gold plated silver, silver gilt and the worthless brass imitations of later date. There are also a great number of varieties of these later issues, which omit DOLLAR, DOL., CENTS, expressing value only as 1/4 or 1/2. Beware also of counterfeits of the original issues.

Pieces inscribed Louisiana Gold are tokens made by Farran Zerbe for the Louisiana Purchase Exposition of 1903-04; other issues inscribed Alaska, Washington, Montana, Idaho or Oregon Gold were exposition souvenirs of the early 20th century struck by M.E. Hart Co.; of San Francisco. British Columbia, Manitoba and Ontario Gold pieces are back-dated issues sold by a leading Canadian coin dealer in the 1950s. All of these, especially the tokens made for the Alaska Yukon Exposition, are of great interest and some rarity today.

A complete catalog of the California types is beyond the scope of this book. For an exhaustive listing, see the Breen-Gillio reference cited in the bibliography.

Utah-Mormon gold coinage

One of the first private Mints was that set up in 1848 by the Church of Jesus Christ of Latter-Day Saints, the Mormons, in Salt Lake City. Mormons James Marshall and Sam Brennan made the actual discovery of gold at Sutter's Mill. The Mormon coins were struck from California dust under the personal supervision of the redoubtable church president Brigham Young.

Young understood that the real money makers of the gold rush would not be the miners, but the growers of food and suppliers of provisions to those digging for the ore. Steel coinage dies were forged by English immigrant John Mobourn Kay. Young and engraver John Taylor created an innovative design including the three-point Phrygian crown of Mormon priesthood over the All-Seeing Eye with quotation from the Book of Exodus, "Holiness to the Lord."

The reverse presented the clasped hands of mutual support over date and denomination. Not understanding that native California dust was not pure gold, the Mormon Mint marked the $10 pieces struck in December 184 9 Pure Gold, the abbreviation G.S.L.C.P.G. on the $2.50, $5 and $20 representing Great Salt Lake City Pure Gold.

The $20 was the first of this denomination struck in the U.S. Beginning with 25 of the $10 coins struck in December, the Mint struggled to produce coins in spite of the usual shortages and breaking of precious crucibles needed to melt the gold. Coinage resumed in late 1849 in the adobe home of dentist William Sharp, using 1850-dated $5 dies in higher relief by cut by Robert Campbell. Colorado gold alloyed with silver was used for the lion and beehive $5 of 1860 with legend in the Deseret alphabet, possibly from dies by Albert Kuner.

The downfall of the Mormon coinage can be traced to crudely refined alloy and the light weight of the coins themselves. U.S. Mint assay revealed the value of the $10 as only $8.52, and the coins were attacked as fraudulent impostures on the public.

Federal opposition to Mormon ambitions for an independent State of Deseret, "Land of the Honeybee," and widespread hostility to the practice of polygamy added to the controversy and the largest part of the Salt Lake coinage was undoubtedly melted.

1849 $2.50

P.198. 1849 $2.50: Obv. Phrygian crown All-Seeing Eye in legend HOLINESS TO THE LORD. Rev. Clasped hands, G.S.L.C.P.G. and value around. Kagin's 1983 ANA AU-50, $9,000.

1849 $5

P.199. 1849 $5: As preceding but for size and denomination. ST 3/95 AU $11,500; Eliasberg 5/96 AU-50 $11,000.

1849 $10

P.200. 1849 $10: As preceding but for size and denomination. Excessively rare, Carter Choice AU, $132,000.

1849 $20 (Stack's)

P.201. 1849 $20: As preceding but for size and denomination. Rare. Garrett EF-40, $50,000; Eliasberg 5/96 VF-35 $34,100.

1850 $5

P.202. 1850 $5: Obv. As preceding but finer style, higher relief. Rev. Smaller hands, date below. Rarcoa Auction '82, Choice BU, $8,500.

Utah-Mormon coinage continued

1860 $5

P.203. 1860 $5: Obv. Couchant lion of Judah, Deseret alphabet HOLINESS TO THE LORD. Rev Eagle and beehive, legend DESERET ASSAY OFFICE, 5 D. Kagin's 1983 ANA MS-60, $16,000; ST 3/95 AU $17,600.

1860 $5 pattern (Bowers & Merena)

P.204. 1860 $5: Obv. Reclining lion, legend of preceding. Rev Smaller eagle and beehive. Copper pattern. Excessively rare. Kagin's 1983 ANA, VF-30, $6,250.

No specimen is known of a supposed early Mormon gold issue with a seagull on the reverse. In 1898, uniface copper restrikes were made of the 1849 and 1850 Mormon coins. Gilt specimens were made with wire hangers soldered to their backs. All are rare.

Oregon

Oregon miners working the California fields sent large quantities of gold dust home by mid-1849. Since a state coinage was impossible under the Constitution, a group of eight public spirited citizens organized the Oregon Exchange Company at Oregon City to strike Oregon's own gold coins. Dies for the $5 piece were engraved by Rev. Hamilton Campbell, who transposed Oregon Territory's initials as T.O.

Company organizers William Kilborne, Theophilus Magruder, James Taylor, George Abernethy, William Willson, William Rector, James Gill Campbell and Noyes Smith are represented on the coins by means of their last initials. Campbell is designated by a "G," another engraver's error. The Oregon $10 dies were cut by Victor Wallace, and are of better workmanship. For unknown reasons the initials "A" and "W" are omitted on this larger coin.

The "Native Gold" referred to on the pieces is California gold, struck without serious refining into coins whose extra weight was intended to compensate for the .884-.887 natural fineness.

1849 $5

P.205. 1849 $5: Obv. Beaver on log, K.M.T.A.W.R.G.S. above, T.O./1849 flanked by laurel branches below. Rev. Legend OREGON EXCHANGE COMPANY, 130 G./NATIVE GOLD/5 D. at center. R.E. Rarcoa Auction '82, Gem BU, $29,000; ST 5/90, VF, $9,075.

Oregon coinage continued

1849 $10

P.206. 1849 $10: Obv. Somewhat similar, K.M.T.R.C.S. and seven stars over beaver, O.T./1849 between branches below. Rev. company name, 10.D20.G./NATIVE GOLD./TEN.D at center. Rarcoa Auction '79 AU, $57,500; ST 5/92, EF, $16,000.

P.207. 1849 $10: As regular issue, white metal die trial. 1973 ANA sale, $35,000.

P.208. 1849 $5: As preceding but for size and denomination, incuse WOODS MUSEUM punched on obverse. Souvenir restrike. Clifford F-VF, $700.

T'ien Yuan Chinese-Oregon gold

In the winter of 1853-54, Chinese miners presented Swiss-born Peter Britt of Jacksonville, Ore., with a 10 x 14 mm, 2.185 gram ingot of native gold in gratitude for his help and friendship. Britt was the first photographer to record sights and scenes of pioneer life in the region. He befriended the hard-working Chinese when they faced general hostility and occasional violence from American settlers. This unique, uniface ingot bears the four Chinese characters *T'ien Yuan P'o Chin,* "Pure Gold of T'ien Yuan," probably the name of one of the companies into which oriental laborers grouped themselves for mutual help. This ingot is the only pioneer gold piece not made by whites known today, and was sold by Britt's son Emil to numismatist Walter H. Jones of Medford, Ore., in the 1930s. For a complete history, see "Peter Britt, the Chinese and Oregon Gold," by David T. Alexander, *The Numismatist,* March 1987.

Ingot ca. 1853-54 (David T. Alexander)

P.209. (1853-54) Ingot: Uniface, T'ien Yuan P'o Chin in recessed square, 2.185 grams. Unique, Peter and Emil Britt, Walter H. Jones.

Colorado

CLARK, GRUBER & COMPANY

Possibly the most successful of all private Mints was that established by Austin M. Clark, Milton E. Clark and Emanuel Henry Gruber in Denver March 1859. Coinage began in June 1860, using dies probably engraved for Milton Clark in Philadelphia by the firm of Bailey, Banks & Biddle.

These coins depicted a mountain with legend PIKE'S PEAK GOLD. This conical peak, like the triangular version on rejected patterns, in no way resembled the imposing mountain which gave the district its name. A $20 coin with another stylized peak and eagle, $2.50 and $5 pieces of the Coronet Liberty type completed the roster.

The 1861 Clark, Gruber coinage included Liberty Head pieces of all four values from $2.50 to $20. The firm struck an array of copper, brass and white metal trial strikes of both dates. Most fascinating are the impressions of the 1861 $20 struck over an 1849 Philadelphia Mint $10 and an 1861-S double eagle. Both were found among gold turned in under the 1933 Executive Order and were retrieved by a thoughtful Mint employee.

The success of the Clark, Gruber coinage reflected the conscientiousness of the firm, which made its first coins almost without alloy, with the result that they abraded too easily.

With the new 1861 issue, the coins were alloyed according to the U.S. standard. Even so, this remarkably scrupulous firm made its coins heavier than the federal issues in order to protect holders from loss by abrasion. In April 1862, Clark, Gruber & Co. sold its equipment to the Government which was then planning to establish a branch Mint at Denver.

1860 $2.50
(American Numismatic Association)

P.210. 1860 $2.50: Obv. Liberty head left, for lack of space, coronet is inscribed Clark & Co. Rev PIKE'S PEAK GOLD DENVER 2 1/2 D. R.E. Norweb AU-55, $9,075; ST 9/94, AU, $5,100.

1860 $5 (American Numismatic Association)

P.211. 1860 $5: As preceding but for size and denomination. R.E. Garrett MS-63, $9,000.

1860 $10

P.212. 1860 $10: Obv. Stylized, naturalistic mountain, DENVER below, legend PIKES PEAK GOLD TEN D. Rev. Eagle, CLARK, GRUBER & CO., date. R.E. Kramer AU-50, $9,350.

P.213. 1860 $20: As preceding but different mountain. R.E. Superior Auction '89 AU-55, $57,750; Eliasberg 5/96 AU $90,200.

1861 $2.50 (Harlan J. Berk Ltd.)

P.214. 1861 $2.50: Obv. Liberty head left, PIKES PEAK on coronet. Rev. Eagle, legend CLARK, GRUBER & CO. DENVER 2 1/2 D. R.E. Rarcoa Auction '79 Choice BU, $6,750.

Colorado coinage continued

1861 $5 (Harlan J. Berk Ltd.)

P.215. 1861 $5: As preceding but for size and denomination. R.E. Kagin's 1983 ANA AU-50, $3,400l; Eliasberg 5/96 EF-45 $3,740.

1861 $10 (Harlan J. Berk Ltd.)

P.216. 1861 $10: As preceding but for size and denomination. R.E. Kagin's 1983 ANA, AU-50, $3,400; ST 3/95 Ch. AU $3,740; Eliasberg 5/96 AU-50 $5,940.

1861 $20 (Harlan J. Berk Ltd.)

P.217. 1861 $20: Obv. Liberty head left adapted from U.S. double eagle. Rev. Eagle from U.S. coinage, legend of preceding, TWENTY D. R.E. ST 3/95 EF $13,200; Eliasberg 5/96 EF-45 $19,800.

Patterns and Trial Pieces.

P.218. 1860 $2.50: As regular issue. Copper. P.E. Kagin's 1983 ANA, Proof-63, $3,400.
P.219. 1860 $5: As preceding. P.E. Garrett Bronzed Proof, $2,200.
P.220. 1860 $10: Similar to naturalistic mountain regular issue coin. Copper. R.E. Garrett MS-65, $2,600; Gilt, Kagin's 1983 ANA, $2,700; BM 6/91, Proof-60, $4,620.
P.221. 1860 $10: Obv. Triangular mountain with slightly concave sides, DENVER below. Rev. Eagle, CLARK, GRUBER & CO. 1860. Brass. Unique, 1983 Kagin's ANA sale VF-30, $2,600.

1860 $20 pattern (Harlan J. Berk Ltd.)

P.222. 1860 $20: Obv. Triangular mountain with straight sides, DENVER below, PIKE'S PEAK GOLD TWENTY D. around. Rev. Similar to preceding Copper. R.E. Garrett EF-40, $1,300.
P.223. 1860 $20: As preceding, silver-plated.
P.224. 1860 $20: As preceding, white metal. Kagin's 1983 ANA MS-65, $1,600.
P.225. 1860 $20: Obv. uniface die trial. Garrett AU-50, $10,000.

Colorado coinage continued

Copper $2-1/2 pattern (Superior Galleries)

P.226. 1861 $2.50: As regular issue. Copper. P.E. Kagin's 1983 ANA, MS-67, $600; Garrett Proof, $1,500.

P.227. 1861 $2.50: Similar. R.E. Garrett EF-40, $550.

P.228. 1861 $5: Similar, double-thick white metal. P.E. Kagin's 1983 ANA EF-45, $1,900.

P.229. 1861 $5: Similar, white metal. R.E.

P.230. 1861 $5: Similar, copper. P.E. Kagin's 1983 ANA Proof-63, $1,050.

P.231. 1861 $5: Similar, copper. R.E. Kagin's 1983 ANA MS-65, $1,350.

P.232. 1861 $10: As regular issue, double thick white metal. P.E. Kagin's 1983 ANA Proof, $2,200.

P.233. 1861 $10: Similar, copper. P.E. Garrett AU-55, $1,700.

P.234. 1861 $10: Similar, copper. R.E. Garrett Proof, $1,500.

P.235. 1861 $20: As regular issue, white metal. P.E. Kagin's 1983 ANA MS-60, $2,800.

P.236. 1861 $20: As preceding, copper. P.E. Garrett Proof, $2,400.

P.237. 1861 $20: Similar. R.E. Garrett Choice Proof, $3,300; Kagin's 1983 ANA copper gilt MS-67, $3,100.

P.238. 1861 $20: Struck over 1857-S gold double eagle. Unique, Kagin's 1983 ANA Choice BU, $27,500; another overstrike exists over an 1861-S double eagle.

P.239. 1861 $20/$10: Struck over 1849 Philadelphia gold eagle. Unique. Superior Auction '88 MS-65, $15,950.

JOHN PARSONS & COMPANY

Indiana native Dr. John Parsons, an assayer who operated in South Park at the Tarryall Mines, began to issue ingots of double eagle denomination. These were followed by a brief 1861 coinage of $2.50 and $5 coins depicting a quartz-stamping mill. The legend misspells his name as PARSON; ORO refers to short-lived Oro City in California Gulch.

Undated $2.50 of 1861 (Bowers & Merena)

P.240. (1861) $2.50: Obv. Quartz-stamping mill, JNO. PARSON & CO. around, ORO below. Rev. Eagle, PIKES PEAK GOLD 2 1/2 D. Stack's Auction '84 VF-20, $25,300.

Undated $5 of 1861 (Harlan J. Berk Ltd.)

P.241. (1861) $5: As preceding but for size and denomination. Garrett VF-20, $100,000.

Patterns & Trial Pieces

P.242. (1861) $2.50: As preceding. Brass. Kagin's 1983 ANA EF-40, $5,250.

P.243. (1861) $2.50: As preceding. Silver, struck over U.S. half dime or dime.

P.244. (1861) $2.50: As preceding. Silver, struck on 1855-O With Arrows half dollar. Unique, impression of dies made by sledgehammer. Garrett, without grade, $7,500.

P.245. (1861) $5: As preceding but for size, denomination. Brass. Excessively rare.

P.246. (1861) $5: As preceding. Bronze. Garrett EF-40, $10,000.

DENVER CITY ASSAY OFFICE

Another Denver mint which may or may not have gone into operation in 1860 was the Denver City Assay Office. To date, only copper patterns for a $5 and $20 have surfaced. The dies have been attributed to the jewelry firm of Cord Brothers. This enigmatic series is a prime target for modern research.

P.247. (1860) $5: Obv. Mountain peak, two birds DENVER CITY/ASSAY OFFICE Rev. Blank. Uniface copper with planchet clip. Brand VF, $2,090.

Undated $5 pattern ca. 1860 (Bowers & Merena)

P.248. (1860) $5: Obv. as preceding, rev. is a serpentine coil pattern. Garrett EF-40, $5,000.

P.249. (1860) $5: Obv. as preceding. Reverse spread eagle, bold, curving KRAATZ below. Clifford EF, $1,500.

1860 5 tokens pattern (Bowers & Merena)

P.250. 1860 5 Tokens: Obv. as preceding. Rev. crossed shovels, prospector's pan over 917/1000/1860 below. P.E. Copper. Clifford EF, $1,500.

P.251. 1860 5 Tokens: As preceding, rev. counterstamped with two small 5-point stars. Clifford VF, $1,400. Fineness expressed as 917/1000 and general fabric of these "token" denomination pieces strongly suggests a date later than 1860.

J.J. CONWAY & COMPANY

J.J. Conway & Co., bankers of Georgia Gulch in Summit County, also struck gold coins during 1861, and these were said to have enjoyed the same prestige as the Clark, Gruber & Co. issues. The issue was short-lived, dying out as fast as did the Georgia Gulch gold deposit.

P.252. (1861) $2.50: Obv. J.J. CONWAY BANKERS, & CO at center. Rev. PIKES PEAK, ornate 2-1/2 at center, DOLLS below. Stack's Wayman Sale AU, $42,000, Sept. 1981.

Undated $5 of 1861 (Bowers & Merena)

P.253. (1861) $5: Obv. As preceding but circle of stars inside obv. legend. Rev. As preceding but ornate 5 in center. Garrett EF-45, $100,000.

Colorado coinage continued

Undated $5 of 1861 over 1845 half eagle (David T. Alexander)

P.254. (1861) $5: As preceding but center of rev. blank. Struck over 1845 U.S. half eagle, Unique. American Auction Assn. (Q. David Bowers), Robert Marks Sale Part II Unc., $36,000, Nov. 1972.

P.255. (1861) $10: Obv. J.J. CONWAY BANKERS around raised circle, & CO. at center. Rev. PIKES PEAK TEN DOLLARS around circle of stars, ornate 10 at center. Three known, two in Smithsonian.

Goldine restrikes of 1956 (Bowers & Merena)

P.256. (1956): 200 three-piece goldine souvenir sets were struck, including an otherwise unknown Coronet Liberty obverse for the $5, in 1956, reportedly in connection with the Denver Mint 50th anniversary. Kagin's 1983 ANA MS-65, three piece set, $180. The 1862 $5 obverse with UNION on the headband is known only from this restrike and from a unique uniface lead splasher examined by ANACS. This style suggests a possible connection with the Clark, Gruber & Co. issues, and may have been intended for an 1862 emission from that company. The die is in the collection of the Colorado Historical Society, Denver, cataloged with the Conway dies but physically different from any of them.

Western Monetary and Assay Ingots

Among the rarest and least understood categories of Western Americana are the gold bars or ingots made by frontier assayers. Those bearing names such as F.D. Kohler and Moffat & Co. can be found under those issuers. Most surviving bars are excessively rare or unique. It is anticipated that hitherto unknown types will be found among the treasures salvaged from the *S. S. Central America*; listed here are two known examples which typify these rarities.

Anonymous Assayer

$10 ingot (David T. Alexander)

P. 257. **1849 $10:** Obv. Raised-letter inscription CAL/49/GOLD in recessed field. rev. Flat field, TEN/DOLLARS. Rounded-end rectangle, 22.5 X 16.3mm. Probable fineness 20-21 carats, giving an intrinsic value of some $9.92 in 1849. Unique. $10,000

John J. Ford Jr. and the late Walter Breen planned to include this unique ingot in the last edition of Wayte Raymond's *Standard Catalog of United States Coins*, but no editions appeared after Raymond's death. This ingot was listed in the *Guide Book of United States Coins* in the late 1950s. The assayer has not been identified but the general fabric and fineness are those of early Gold Rush pieces.

California & Sierra Co.

P.258. 1860 $36.57: Obv. Boldly raised rim encloses relief inscription 1860/ASSAY, at sides incuse VAL./$36.57. Rev. Incuse VALUE AT/U.S. MINT/$36.57 on surface rounded from the casting process. Each narrow side bears an incuse inscription, (ends) GOLD/896 FINE and SILVER/102 FINE; (long sides) CALIFORNIA &/SIERRA CO. and OZS./1, DWT./19/GRS./12. Roughly rectangular. 22 X 17 X 8mm. ——

This unique ingot was listed in several editions of the *Guide Book of United States Coins*, as was the preceding piece.

Specifications

Dates

The insertion of a chronological mark or word on coins was a practice known to the ancients, but carried out by them on their money in a different method from that pursued by more modern sovereigns.

As for the United States, the original Mint Act of 1792 established the requirement that the date appear on U.S. coins, and this legislation has remained unchanged since that time.

Actually, the date on U.S. coins serves a very useful purpose, in that with it on a coin, counterfeiting is made more difficult and enforcement authorities can isolate specific issues which may have been produced illegally.

Traditionally, all United States coins have been dated the year of their coinage, although this didn't always happen the first few years the Mint was in operation and in recent years. One commemorative coin, the Lafayette-Washington dollar, is considered by Mint officials to be undated. The date 1900 appears on the coin, but that refers to the Paris Exposition; the coin was actually struck in December 1899.

The policy of placing the date in which a coin is struck was interrupted because of the coin shortage and the speculation in rolls and bags of coins which took place in 1964. As a result, Congress passed legislation so that after the calendar year 1964 coinage was produced, the Mint could still use the 1964 date.

Starting in 1965, therefore, all denominations of United States coinage continued to be struck with the 1964 date.

When the Coinage Act of 1965 was passed, it became mandatory that the Mint continue to use the 1964 date on all 90 percent silver coins (halves, quarters, and dimes). Therefore, all the 90 percent silver coins which were manufactured in 1964, 1965 and 1966 bear the 1964 date.

The last of the 90 percent silver quarters were struck in January 1966, the last of the dimes in February 1966, and the last of the halves in April 1966.

The Coinage Act of 1965 also made it mandatory that the clad coins be dated not earlier than 1965. Therefore, all the clad coins actually made in 1965 bear the 1965 date. All the clad coins made through July 31, 1966, bear the 1965 date.

The first clad dime was struck in December 1965, the first clad quarter dollar in August 1965, and the first clad half dollar in December 1965.

In December 1965, the decision was made to change the 1964 date on the 5-cent pieces and the cents to 1965, as one step in catching up on normal coin dating. From December 1965 through July 31, 1966, all cents and 5-cent pieces struck bear the 1965 date.

Starting on Aug. 1, 1966, and through Dec. 31, 1966, all denominations of United States coins minted during that period carried the 1966 date. Commencing Jan. 1, 1967, the Mints resumed normal dating procedures.

The usual process of dating was interrupted again in December 1974, when Mint Director Mary Brooks announced the date 1974 would continue on dollars, half dollars and quarter dollars produced in the first half of 1975. The date of 1975 appeared, however, on cents, 5-cent and 10-cent coins.

All dollars, half dollars and quarters struck after July 4, 1975, bore the 1776-1976 Bicentennial dates. Normal dating was resumed in 1977.

The Mint Director attributed the date freeze decision to the necessity of building a sufficient coin inventory to conduct business affairs of the nation.

In 1973, the Mint struck 1974-dated aluminum cents in an experiment made necessary because of Mint worries over rising copper prices. When rising copper prices caused Mint officials to finally change the composition of the cent in 1982, the Mint began striking 1982 cents in late 1981 to build up inventories.

Recent special coinage programs have caused Mint officials to strike coins with dates of following or preceding years. Production of Olympic coinage of 1984 gold eagles and 1984 silver dollars began in 1983 to produce an inventory for collector sales in 1984. Striking of the 1986-dated Statue of Liberty commemorative coins began in late 1985, again to build inventory. Production of Proof 1986-dated American Eagle gold and silver bullion coins, however, did not begin until early 1987 in order to permit the Mint to strike sufficient quantities of the business strike versions.

Edge designs

Edge designs on U.S. coins are one of the more neglected aspects of the field of numismatics. Occasionally differences will be noted in the books, such as the change from lettered edge to reeded edge on 1836 Capped Bust half dollars, some distinctions on early large cents, and, most surprising, Dr. W.Q. Wolfson's discovery of the 1921 Morgan, Infrequently Reeded Edge dollars.

We say "surprising" because collectors generally take reeding for granted. About the only people who examine reeded edges are those trying to compare fakes with genuine coins. Otherwise, almost the only time somebody mentions the edge is when he discovers, accidentally, the words misspelled on early halves.

Mention became even rarer when the lettered edges gave place to reeding. The only published mention of reeding counts we know of was in "Bristles and Barbs" in April 1965, and "Coinology" in June 1969, both in *Coin World*, the first being instigated by Wolfson's aforementioned discovery published in *Coin World's* "Fair to Very Fine" column in December 1964.

"Coinology" for June 11, 1969, reports that the number of reeds on Winged Liberty Head and Roosevelt dimes varies from 104 to 118, an average of 111, so the statement is made that the number of reeds will probably vary also on all other denominations. It also states that "reeding counts are important in the study of any coinage and should be considered seriously." If the statement that the numbers of reed varies in a series is true, it would make reeding less useful in studying fakes.

Both ornamented and lettered edges on coins to 1836 were made on a Castaing machine, consisting of two edge strips, one moving, the other not. Planchets were rolled between the two strips before going to the coining press. Occasional errors were caused by either the planchets or the movable strip slipping. The strips are known as "edge dies."

The same machine was used to make reeded edges up to 1836, reeds or grooves being used instead of letters. From 1836, a grooved collar was used as it still is, with the edge receiving the reeding at the same instance as the coin is produced. If the grooves were not the same in all collars, then the reeding would vary with the collar used. No detailed study has been made of such variations except for the 1921 Morgan, Infrequently Reeded Edge dollar, and the mention of variations in readings on dimes. Grooved collars are called "collar dies."

Different strips were used on Castaing machines, also, resulting in differences or varieties of ornamentation, lettering and more. Edge varieties and edge errors are two different things, and always have been true whether the edges contain letters, ornamental devices, reeding or a combination of any two or all of them. We discuss varieties here, caused by changes in Castaing strips or collars as the case may be.

Half cents: Two leaf ornamentation in 1793; one leaf 1794 with both large and small lettering known; 1795, large letters or no letters (plain edges); 1796, plain edges only; 1797, medium and small letters, no leaf, and plain edge varieties, also a "Gripped" variety (rare); 1798 and after, plain edge only.

Large cents: 1793 Vine and bars; two leaves; one leaf pointing down; one leaf pointing up (leaves accompany lettered edges); 1794, one leaf up, one leaf down; 1795, lettered edge, plain edge, reeded edge; 1796 and 1797, plain and partially gripped edges; 1798, plain and reeded edges; 1799 and thereafter, all plain edges.

Five-cent pieces: 1882, normal plain edges, a few patterns known with five raised bars.

Half dimes: reeded from 1794 thereafter.

Dimes: reeded from 1796, with some changes in number of reeds from 1837 and possibly still varying through Winged Liberty Head and Roosevelt.

Quarters: Reeded from 1796 to now with probable variations over the years in number of reeds or spacing; from 1838 normal count is 119, but Walter Breen noted some 1876-CC with 153 reeds.

Half dollars: 1794 to 1806, lettered edge with words separated by stars, squares and circles, occasional lettering errors from slipping edge dies; 1807 to 1813, no star after DOLLAR: 1814-1831, with star; 1830 and 1831, varieties with diagonal reeding between words; 1830 to 1836, star after DOLLAR, varieties with vertical reeding between words; vertical reeding with no letters; 1837 and after, vertical reeding, with four different reeded collars used in 1837, and probably unstudied variations thereafter.

Silver dollars: Lettered edge through 1803 with small designs separating words; 1840-1935, reeded edge with varieties possible. Normal is 188 reeds. Only positively known variety is 1921 Morgan, P-Mint, with 154 reeds, known as 1921 Morgan, Infrequently Reeded Edge, discovered by Wolfson. See Van Allen-Mallis.

Trade dollars: Reeded edges with possibility of variations.

Gold dollars: Reeded edges with apparent variations between Mints and types, but not yet permanently identified.

Quarter eagles: Reeded edges from 1796; 1840 and after differ at branch Mints from P-Mint coins, the former having fewer reeds.

Three dollars: Reeded edges, with possible variations at branch Mints.

Half eagles: Same comment.

Eagles: To 1907, same comment. 1907-1911, 46 stars on edge; 1912-1933, 48 stars on edge (1912 with 46 stars possible but unknown as yet).

Double eagles: To 1907, reeded edge without important variations; 1907 Roman Numerals, large letters on patterns, medium letters on regular issue; 1907 Arabic Numerals, small letters.

American Eagle: silver, gold platinum bullion coins: Reeded edges, no studies done.

Mottoes

In the act establishing the Mint the devices and legends for the new coins were prescribed as follows: "Upon one side of each of the said coins there shall be an impression emblematic of liberty with an inscription of the word LIBERTY and the year of the coinage; and upon the reverse of each of the gold and silver coins there shall be the figure or representation of an eagle, with the inscription, 'United States of America,' and upon the reverse of the copper coins there shall be an inscription which shall express the denomination of the piece."

E PLURIBUS UNUM

Two legends have appeared on many of the coins of the United States, the one from almost the beginning of the national coinage, and the other since the Civil War. Neither, however, has had an uninterrupted history, nor has either been employed on all the denominations of the series.

The motto E PLURIBUS UNUM was first used on U.S. coinage in 1796, when the reverse of the quarter eagle ($2.50 gold piece) presented the main features of the Great Seal, on the scroll of which this inscription belongs. The same device was placed on certain of the silver coins in 1798, and so the motto was soon found on all the coins in the precious metals. In 1834, it was dropped from most of the gold coins to mark the change in the standard fineness of the coins. In 1837 it was dropped from the silver coins, marking the era of the Revised Mint Code.

The Act of Feb. 12, 1873, made this inscription a requirement of law upon the coins of the United States. A search will reveal, however, that it does not appear on all coins struck after 1873, and that not until much later were the provisions of this act followed in their entirety. From facts contained in Mint records it would appear that officials did not consider the provisions of the law mandatory, but rather, discretionary. The motto does appear on all coins currently being manufactured.

The motto as it appears on U.S. coins means "One Out of Many," and doubtless has reference to the unity of the early states. It is said that one Colonel Reed of Uxbridge, Mass., was instrumental in having it placed on the coins.

IN GOD WE TRUST

From the records of the Treasury Department it appears that the first suggestion of the recognition of the Deity on the coins of the United States was contained in a letter addressed to the Secretary of the Treasury, by the Rev. M.R. Watkinson, Minister of the Gospel, Ridleyville, Pa., dated Nov. 13, 1861.

This letter states:

"One fact touching our currency has hitherto been seriously overlooked. I mean the recognition of the Almighty God in some form in our coins.

"You are probably a Christian. What if our Republic were now shattered beyond reconstruction? Would not the antiquaries of succeeding centuries rightly reason from our past that we were a heathen nation? What I propose is that instead of the goddess of liberty we shall have next inside the 13 stars a ring inscribed with the words "perpetual union'; within this ring the all-seeing eye, crowned with a halo; beneath this eye the American flag, bearing in its field stars equal to the number of the States united; in the folds of the bars the words 'God, liberty, law.'

"This would make a beautiful coin, to which no possible citizen could object. This would relieve us from the ignomity of heathenism. This would place us openly under the Divine protection we have personally claimed. From my heart I have felt our national shame in disowning God as not the least of our present national disasters.

"To you first I address a subject that must be agitated."

Under date of Nov. 20, 1861, the Secretary of the Treasury addressed the following letter to the Director of the Mint:

"Dear Sir: No nation can be strong except in the strength of God, or safe except in His defense. The trust of our people in God should be declared on our national coins.

"You will cause a device to be prepared without unnecessary delay with a motto expressing in the fewest and tersest words possible this national recognition."

It was found that the Act of Jan. 18, 1837, prescribed the mottoes and devices that should be placed upon the coins of the United States, so that nothing could be done without legislation.

In December 1863, the Director of the Mint submitted to the Secretary of the Treasury for approval designs for new 1-, 2-, and 3-cent pieces, on which it was proposed that one of the following mottoes should appear: "Our country; our God"; "God, our Trust."

The Secretary of the Treasury, in a letter to the Director of the Mint, dated Dec. 9, 1863, states:

"I approve your mottoes, only suggesting that on that with the Washington obverse the motto should begin with the word 'Our,' so as to read: 'Our God and our country.' And on that with the shield, it should be changed so as to read: 'In God We Trust.'"

An act passed April 22, 1864, changing the composition of the 1-cent piece and authorizing the coinage of the 2-cent piece, the devices of which were to be fixed by the Director of the Mint, with the approval of the Secretary of the Treasury, and it is upon the bronze 2-cent piece that the motto IN GOD WE TRUST first appears.

The Act of March 3, 1865, provided that in addition to the legend and devices on the gold and silver coins of the United States, it should be lawful for the Director of the Mint, with the approval of the Secretary of the Treasury to place the motto IN GOD WE TRUST on such coins as shall admit of the inscription thereon. Under this act, the motto was placed upon the double eagle, eagle and half eagle, and also upon the dollar, half dollar and quarter dollar in 1866.

The Coinage Act of Feb. 12, 1873, provided that the Secretary of the Treasury may cause the motto IN GOD WE TRUST to be inscribed on such coins as shall admit of such motto.

When the double eagle and eagle of new design appeared in 1907, it was soon discovered that the religious motto had been omitted. In response to a general demand, Congress ordered it restored, and the Act of May 18, 1908, made mandatory its appearance on all coins upon which it had heretofore appeared. The motto appears on all gold and silver coins struck since July 1, 1908, except Barber dimes. It was not mandatory upon the cent and 5-cent coins, but could be placed thereon by the Secretary of the Treasury, or the Director of the Mint with the Secretary's approval.

The issuance of the cent in 1909 honoring the centennial of the birth of Abraham Lincoln brought the motto IN GOD WE TRUST to the smallest denomination U.S. coin. This was an appropriate tribute to Lincoln, one of the most spiritual presidents.

Almost another three decades were to go by before the motto was carried over to the one remaining coin in the U.S. series that did not carry it, the 5-cent piece. In 1938, a design for this coin was chosen as a result of a nationwide competition. The design selected, honoring Thomas Jefferson, was executed by Michigan sculptor Felix Schlag. A feature on the obverse is the motto, IN GOD WE TRUST.

The act approved July 11, 1955, makes appearance of the motto IN GOD WE TRUST mandatory upon all coins of the United States.

Symbols

Eagle

The eagle was a favorite device of the United States' founding fathers before it was placed on U.S. national coinage. It appears on the Great Seal of the United States which was adopted in 1782. At this time the states established their own Mints and Massachusetts saw fit to place on the reverse of its coins a spread eagle with arrows and an olive branch in the claws.

When the Mint was established the devices and legends for the new coins were prescribed. It was ordered that "upon the reverse of each of the gold and silver coins there shall be the figure or representation of an eagle." However, the act of Jan. 18, 1837, removed the legal requirement for the half dime and dime. Subsequent gold and silver coins — the silver 3-cent coin, the gold dollar and the gold $3 coin — were not required to have an eagle on the reverse.

The eagle was added almost as an afterthought on one recent U.S. coin. The eagle on the reverse of the Franklin half dollar, introduced in 1948, is very small. The story that Franklin preferred the wild turkey over the bald eagle as a symbol of American pride is well known among collectors. The Liberty Bell is the most prominent device on the reverse of the Franklin half, with a diminutive eagle to the right of the bell.

Portraits

With the exception of the great statesman, Benjamin Franklin, and the great feminist, Susan B. Anthony, the only individuals whose images appear on regular issue U.S. coins have been U.S. presidents. The Indian used on the 5-cent piece introduced in 1913 is not the image of any individual but is a composite of several Indians studied by the designer (identified as Iron Tail, Two Moons and Chief John Big Tree). One of the most popular designs has been the Goddess of Liberty who appears on many of U.S. coins.

Use of "V" in Trust

In medieval times the letters "u" and "v" were used interchangeably. These letters were not given separate alphabetical listings in English dictionaries until about 1800. In recent times many sculptors have used the "V" in place of "U" for artistic reasons, such as, to represent the permanence and long time significance of their work. Artists who design coins may choose to spell "Trust" with a "V." All of the dollars of the Peace dollar design have this characteristic. From 1921 through 1935 the United States Mints made more than 190 million dollars of this type.

It is interesting to note that sometimes the "V" is similarly used in wording on public buildings.

Initials

The custom of placing the signature of the engraver upon a coin die dates from remote antiquity. Many Greek coins, especially in the creations produced by the cities of Sicily and Magna Graecia, are signed with the initials of the artist, and in some cases his full name. The same practice prevailed generally in the European countries. There were no initials on United States coins until the gold dollar appeared in 1849 with the initial of Longacre, L, on the truncation of the bust.

Other symbols

Arrows were sometimes used on U.S. coins to symbolize preparedness. Olive branches or leaves are found often also. Symbolizing peace, the olive branch is the international emblem of friendship and accord. The fasces on the reverse of the Winged

Liberty Head dime has a bundle of rods with protruding ax as the central device. It has been since ancient times a symbol of official authority. Also on this dime, the winged cap on the Roman style Liberty Head symbolizes freedom of thought.

The newer Roosevelt dime bears some representative symbols also. In the center of the reverse is a torch signifying liberty bounded by an olive branch on the left and an oak branch signifying strength and independence on the right.

The Kennedy half dollar contains much symbolism. The presidential coat of arms forms the motif for the reverse. The coat of arms depicts the American eagle holding the olive branch in his right claw and arrows in the left. Symbolism derived from the 13 original states governs the number of olive leaves, berries, arrows, stars and cloud puffs. The upper part of the flag or shield upon the breast of the eagle represents the Congress binding the Colonies into an entity. The vertical stripes complete the motif of the flag of the United States. Each state of the nation is represented in the 50-star amulet which rings the whole.

Issue dates, designers, original engravers, models

Regular issue U.S. coins

Half cents

Type	Issue dates	Designers[1]	Engraver	Model or Source
Liberty Cap Left	1793	Obv: Eckfeldt	Eckfeldt	Dupre's Libertas Americana medal
		Rev: Eckfeldt	Eckfeldt	Original design
Liberty Cap Right (Large Head)	1794	Obv: Scot	Scot	Similar to previous, but reversed
		Rev: Scot	Scot	Similar to previous
(Small Head)	1795-1797	Obv: Scot-Gardner	Scot	Similar to previous
		Rev: Scot-Gardner	Scot	Similar to previous
Draped Bust	1800-1808	Obv: Stuart-Scot	Scot	Ann Willing Bingham (?)
		Rev: Scot-Gardner	Scot	Similar to previous
Classic Head	1809-1836	Obv: Reich	Reich	Unknown model
		Rev: Reich	Reich	Original design
Coronet Type	1840-1857	Obv: Scot-Gobrecht	Gobrecht	Coronet Type large cent
		Rev: Reich-Gobrecht	Gobrecht	Similar to previous

Large cents

Type	Issue dates	Designers[1]	Engraver	Model or Source
Flowing Hair Chain Rev.	1793	Obv: Voigt	Voigt	Unknown model
		Rev: Voigt	Voigt	Fugio cent (?)
Wreath Rev.	1793	Obv: Voigt-Eckfeldt	Eckfeldt	Similar to previous
		Rev: Eckfeldt	Eckfeldt	Original design
Liberty Cap	1793-1794	Obv: Wright	Wright	Dupre's Libertas Americana medal, reversed
		Rev: Wright	Wright	Similar to previous
(Modified)	1794-1796	Obv: Wright-Gardner	Scot	Similar to previous
		Rev: Wright-Gardner	Scot	Similar to previous
Draped Bust	1796-1807	Obv: Stuart-Scot	Scot	Ann Willing Bingham (?)
		Rev: Wright-Scot	Scot	Similar to previous
Classic Head	1808-1814	Obv: Reich	Reich	Unknown model
		Rev: Reich	Reich	Original design
Coronet	1816-1835	Obv: Scot	Scot	Unknown model
		Rev: Reich	Reich	Same as previous
	1835-1839	Obv: Scot-Gobrecht	Gobrecht	Similar to previous
		Rev: Reich	Reich	Same as previous
	1839-1857	Obv: Scot-Gobrecht	Gobrecht	Similar to previous
		Rev: Reich-Gobrecht	Gobrecht	Similar to previous

Small cents

Type	Issue dates	Designers[1]	Engraver	Model or Source
Flying Eagle	1856-1858	Obv: Gobrecht-Longacre	Longacre	Titian Peale's design for dollar reverse, c. 1836
		Rev: Longacre	Longacre	Reverse of $1 & $3 gold
Indian Head	1859-1909	Obv: Longacre	Longacre	Longacre family composite
		Rev: (Both) Longacre	Longacre	Original designs
Lincoln Head (Wheat Rev.)	1909-1958	Obv: Victor D. Brenner	C. Barber	Brenner's plaque
		Rev: Victor D. Brenner	C. Barber	Original design
Lincoln Head (Memorial Rev.)	1959-	Obv: Brenner	C. Barber	Same as previous
		Rev: Gasparro	Gasparro	Lincoln Memorial

Two cents

Type	Issue dates	Designers[1]	Engraver	Model or Source
Two cents	1864-1873	Obv: Longacre	Longacre	Original design
		Rev: Longacre	Longacre	Original design

Silver 3 cents

Type	Issue dates	Designers[1]	Engraver	Model or Source
Silver 3 cents	1851-1873	Obv: Longacre	Longacre	Original design (three varieties)
		Rev: Longacre	Longacre	Original design (two varieties)

Copper-nickel 3 cents

Type	Issue dates	Designers[1]	Engraver	Model or Source
Copper-nickel 3 cents	1865-1889	Obv: Longacre	Longacre	Longacre family composite
		Rev: Longacre	Longacre	Original design

Half dimes

Type	Issue dates	Designers[1]	Engraver	Model or Source
Flowing Hair	1794-1795	Obv: Scot	Scot	Unknown model
		Rev: Scot	Scot	Original design
Draped Bust				
(Small Eagle)	1796-1797	Obv: Stuart-Scot	Scot	Ann Willing Bingham (?)
		Rev: Scot-Eckstein(?)	Scot	Similar to previous
(Heraldic Eagle)	1800-1805	Obv: Stuart-Scot	Scot	Same as previous
		Rev: Scot	Scot	Great Seal of the United States
Capped Bust	1829-1837	Obv: Reich-Kneass	Kneass	Unknown model (similar to dime by Reich)
		Rev: Reich-Kneass	Kneass	Original design (similar to dime by Reich)
Seated Liberty (No Drapery)[2]	1837-1840	Obv: Gobrecht	Gobrecht	Drawing by Thomas Sully
		Rev: Gobrecht	Gobrecht	Original design
(With Drapery)	1840-1859	Obv: Gobrecht-Hughes	Gobrecht	Similar to previous
		Rev: Gobrecht	Gobrecht	Same as previous
(Legend Obv.)	1860-1873	Obv: Gobrecht-Hughes-Longacre	Longacre	Similar to previous
		Rev: Longacre	Longacre	Original design

Copper-nickel 5 cents

Type	Issue dates	Designers[1]	Engraver	Model or Source
Shield	1866-1883	Obv: Longacre	Longacre	Original design
		Rev: Longacre	Longacre	Original design (two varieties)
Liberty Head	1883-1912	Obv: C. Barber	C. Barber	Unknown model
		Rev: C. Barber	C. Barber	Original design (two varieties)
Indian Head	1913-1938	Obv: James E. Fraser	C. Barber	Composite of three Indians
		Rev: James E. Fraser	C. Barber	"Black Diamond," Central Park Zoo
Jefferson Head	1938-	Obv: Felix Schlag	Sinnock	Bust by Houdon, c. 1789
		Rev: Felix Schlag	Sinnock	Monticello

Dimes

Type	Issue dates	Designers[1]	Engraver	Model or Source
Draped Bust				
(Small Eagle)	1796-1797	Obv: Stuart-Scot	Scot	Ann Willing Bingham (?)
		Rev: Scot-Eckstein (?)	Scot	Similar to Scot's 1794 silver reverse
(Heraldic Eagle)	1798-1807	Obv: Stuart-Scot	Scot	Same as previous
		Rev: Scot	Scot	Great Seal of the United States
Capped Bust[3]	1809-1837	Obv: Reich	Reich	Unknown model
		Rev: Reich	Reich	Original design

Dimes continued

Type	Issue dates	Designers[1]	Engraver	Model or Source
Seated Liberty (No Drapery)[2]	1837-1840	Obv: Gobrecht	Gobrecht	Drawing by Thomas Sully
		Rev: Gobrecht	Gobrecht	Original design
(With Drapery)	1840-1860	Obv: Gobrecht-Hughes	Gobrecht	Similar to previous issue
		Rev: Gobrecht	Gobrecht	Same as previous issue
(Legend Obv.)	1860-1891	Obv: Gobrecht-Hughes-Longacre	Longacre	Similar to previous issue
		Rev: Longacre	Longacre	Original design
Barber	1892-1916	Obv: C. Barber	C. Barber	French medal designs
		Rev: Longacre	Longacre	Same as previous issue
Winged Liberty Head	1916-1945	Obv: Adolph A. Weinman	C. Barber	Elsie Kachel Stevens
		Rev: Adolph A. Weinman	C. Barber	Fasces and olive branch design on wall behind Speaker of the U.S. House of Representatives
Roosevelt Head	1946-	Obv: Sinnock	Sinnock	Original design
		Rev: Sinnock	Sinnock	Original design

Twenty cents

Type	Issue dates	Designers[1]	Engraver	Model or Source
Twenty cents	1875-1878	Obv: Gobrecht-Hughes-W. Barber	W. Barber	Seated Liberty dollar
		Rev: W. Barber	W. Barber	Original design

Quarter dollars

Type	Issue dates	Designers[1]	Engraver	Model or Source
Draped Bust (Small Eagle)	1796	Obv: Stuart-Scot	Scot	Ann Willing Bingham (?)
		Rev: Scot-Eckstein (?)	Scot	Similar to Scot's 1794 silver reverse
(Heraldic Eagle)	1804-1807	Obv: Stuart-Scot	Scot	Same as previous issue
		Rev: Scot	Scot	Great Seal of the United States
Capped Bust[4]	1815-1838	Obv: Reich	Reich	Unknown model
		Rev: Reich	Reich	Original design (c. 1807)
Seated Liberty (No Drapery)	1838-1840	Obv: Gobrecht	Gobrecht	Drawing by Thomas Sully
		Rev: Reich-Kneass-Gobrecht	Gobrecht	Similar to previous issue
(With Drapery)	1840-1891	Obv: Gobrecht-Hughes	Gobrecht	Similar to previous issue
		Rev: Reich-Kneass-Gobrecht	Gobrecht	Same as previous issue
Barber	1892-1916	Obv: C. Barber	C. Barber	French medal designs
		Rev: C. Barber	C. Barber	Great Seal of the United States
Standing Liberty	1916-1930	Obv: Hermon A. MacNeil	C. Barber	Dora Doscher (two varieties.)
		Rev: Hermon A. MacNeil	C. Barber	Original design (two varieties)
Washington Head	1932-date	Obv: John Flanagan	Sinnock	Bust by Houdon (1785)
		Rev: John Flanagan	Sinnock	Original design
Bicentennial	1976	Obv: Flanagan	Sinnock	Same as regular issue
		Rev: Jack L. Ahr	Gasparro	Original design

Half dollars

Type	Issue dates	Designers[1]	Engraver	Model or Source
Flowing Hair	1794-1795	Obv: Scot	Scot	Unknown model
		Rev: Scot	Scot	Original design
Draped Bust (Small Eagle)	1796-1797	Obv: Stuart-Scot	Scot	Ann Willing Bingham (?)
		Rev: Scot-Eckstein	Scot	Similar to previous issue
(Heraldic Eagle)	1801-1807	Obv: Stuart-Scot	Scot	Same as previous issue
		Rev: Scot	Scot	Great Seal of the United States
Capped Bust[5] (50 C. Rev.)	1807-1836	Obv: Reich	Reich	Unknown model
		Rev: Reich	Reich	Original design
(50 Cents Rev.)	1836-1837	Obv: Reich-Gobrecht	Gobrecht	Similar to previous issue
		Rev: Reich-Gobrecht	Gobrecht	Similar to previous issue
(Half Dol.)	1838-1839	Obv: Reich-Gobrecht	Gobrecht	Same as previous issue
		Rev: Reich-Gobrecht	Gobrecht	Similar to previous issue
Seated Liberty	1839-1891	Obv: Gobrecht	Gobrecht	Drawing by Thomas Sully
		Rev: Reich-Gobrecht	Gobrecht	Similar to previous issue
Barber	1892-1915	Obv: C. Barber	C. Barber	French medal designs
		Rev: C. Barber	C. Barber	Great Seal of the United States
Walking Liberty	1916-1947	Obv: Adolph A. Weinman	C. Barber	Roty's Sower design on French silver
		Rev: Adolph A. Weinman	C. Barber	Original design
Franklin	1948-1963	Obv: Sinnock	Roberts	Bust by Houdon (1778)
		Rev: Sinnock	Roberts	Sesquicentennial half
Kennedy	1964-date	Obv: Roberts	Roberts	U.S. Mint medal
		Rev: Gasparro	Gasparro	Seal of the president of the U.S.

Half dollars continued

Type	Issue dates	Designers[1]	Engraver	Model or Source
Bicentennial	1976	Obv: Roberts	Roberts	Same as regular issue
		Rev: Seth G. Huntington	Gasparro	Independence Hall

Silver dollars, clad dollars

Type	Issue dates	Designers[1]	Engraver	Model or Source
Flowing Hair	1794-1795	Obv: Scot	Scot	Unknown model
		Rev: Scot	Scot	Original design
Draped Bust				
(Small Eagle)	1795-1798	Obv: Stuart-Scot	Scot	Ann Willing Bingham(?)
		Rev: Scot-Eckstein (?)	Scot	Similar to previous issue
(Heraldic Eagle)	1798-1804	Obv: Stuart-Scot	Scot	Same as previous issue
		Rev: Scot	Scot	Great Seal of the United States
Gobrecht[6]	1836-1839	Obv: Gobrecht	Gobrecht	Drawing by Thomas Sully
		Rev: Gobrecht	Gobrecht	Drawing by Titian Peale
Seated Liberty	1840-1873	Obv: Gobrecht-Hughes	Gobrecht	Similar to pattern issue
		Rev: Reich-Gobrecht	Gobrecht	Reich's 1807 reverse for silver
Morgan's Liberty Head	1878-1921	Obv: Morgan	Morgan	Anna W. Williams
		Rev: Morgan	Morgan	Original design
Peace	1921-1935	Obv: Anthony DeFrancisci	Morgan	Teresa C. DeFrancisci
		Rev: Anthony DeFrancisci	Morgan	Original design
Eisenhower	1971-1978	Obv: Gasparro	Gasparro	Sketch by Gasparro (1945)
		Rev: Gasparro	Gasparro	Apollo 11 emblem
Bicentennial	1976	Obv: Gasparro	Gasparro	Same as regular issue
		Rev: Dennis R. Williams	Gasparro	Original design
Anthony	1979-1981	Obv: Gasparro	Gasparro	Original design
		Rev: Gasparro	Gasparro	Apollo 11 emblem
Trade dollar	1873-1883	Obv: W. Barber	W. Barber	Unknown model
		Rev: W. Barber	W. Barber	Original design

Gold dollars

Type	Issue dates	Designers[1]	Engraver	Model or Source
Liberty Head	1849-1854	Obv: Longacre	Longacre	Longacre family composite
		Rev: Longacre	Longacre	Original design
Indian Head[7]	1854-1889	Obv: Longacre	Longacre	Longacre family composite
		Rev: Longacre	Longacre	Original design

Quarter eagles

Type	Issue dates	Designers[1]	Engraver	Model or Source
Capped Bust Right	1796-1807	Obv: Scot	Scot	Martha Washington (apochryphal)
		Rev. Scot	Scot	Great Seal of the United States
Capped Bust Left	1808	Obv: Reich	Reich	Unknown model
		Rev: Reich	Reich	1789 Mott token (?)
Capped Head Left[8]	1821-1834	Obv: Reich-Scot	Scot	Similar to previous issue
		Rev: Reich	Reich	Same as previous issue
Classic Head	1834-1839	Obv: Kneass	Kneass	Reich's Classic Head cent
		Rev: Reich-Kneass	Kneass	Similar to previous issue
Coronet	1840-1907	Obv: Gobrecht	Gobrecht	Coronet type large cent
		Rev: Reich-Kneass-Gobrecht	Gobrecht	Similar to previous issue
Indian Head	1908-1929	Obv: Bela Lyon Pratt	C. Barber	Unknown model
		Rev: Bela Lyon Pratt	C. Barber	Original design

Three dollars

Type	Issue dates	Designers[1]	Engraver	Model or Source
Three Dollars	1854-1889	Obv: Longacre	Longacre	Longacre family composite
		Rev: Longacre	Longacre	Original design

Half eagles

Type	Issue dates	Designers[1]	Engraver	Model or Source
Capped Bust Right				
(Small Eagle)	1795-1798	Obv: Scot	Scot	Martha Washington (apochryphal)
		Rev: Scot	Scot	Original design
(Heraldic Eagle)	1795-1807	Obv: Scot	Scot	Same as previous issue
		Rev: Scot	Scot	Great Seal of the United States
Capped Bust Left	1807-1812	Obv: Reich	Reich	Unknown model
		Rev: Reich	Reich	1789 Mott token (?)
Capped Head Left[8]	1813-1834	Obv: Reich-Scot	Scot	Similar to previous issue
		Rev: Reich	Reich	Same as previous issue
Classic Head	1834-1838	Obv: Kneass	Kneass	Reich's Classic Head cent
		Rev: Reich-Kneass	Kneass	Similar to previous issue

Half eagles continued

Type	Issue dates	Designers[1]	Engraver	Model or Source
Coronet Type	1839-1908	Obv: Gobrecht	Gobrecht	Coronet type large cent
		Rev: Reich-Kneass-Gobrecht	Gobrecht	Similar to previous issue
Indian Head	1908-1929	Obv: Bela Lyon Pratt	C. Barber	Unknown model
		Rev: Bela Lyon Pratt	C. Barber	Original design

Eagles

Type	Issue dates	Designers[1]	Engraver	Model or Source
Capped Bust Right (Small Eagle)	1795-1797	Obv: Scot	Scot	Martha Washington (apochryphal)
		Rev: Scot	Scot	Original design
(Heraldic Eagle)	1797-1804	Obv: Scot	Scot	Same as previous issue
		Rev: Scot	Scot	Great Seal of the United States
Coronet Type	1838-1907	Obv: Gobrecht	Gobrecht	Coronet Type Large Cent
		Rev: Reich-Kneass-Gobrecht	Gobrecht	$2.50, $5 Rev.
Indian Head	1907-1933	Obv: Saint-Gaudens	C. Barber	Unknown model
		Rev: Saint-Gaudens	C. Barber	Original design

Double eagles

Type	Issue dates	Designers[1]	Engraver	Model or Source
Liberty Head	1849-1907	Obv: Longacre	Longacre	Longacre family composite
		Rev: Longacre	Longacre	Original design
Saint-Gaudens Type	1907-1933	Obv: Saint-Gaudens	C. Barber	Unknown model
		Rev: Saint-Gaudens	C. Barber	Original design

American Eagle bullion coins

Type	Issue dates	Designers[1]	Engraver	Model or Source
Silver bullion	1986-date	Obv: Robert A. Weinman	Steever	Walking Liberty half dollar
		Rev: John Mercanti	Mercanti	Great Seal of the United States
Gold bullion	1986-date	Obv: Saint-Gaudens	Peloso	Double eagle design of 1907-33[9]
		Rev: Miley Busiek	Winter	Original design
Platinum bullion[10]	1997-	Obv: John Mercanti	Mercanti	Statue of Liberty
		Rev: Thomas D. Rogers Sr.	Rogers	Original design

Notes

1. When two or more names appear hyphenated as the designers, the first person created the design and the others modified it for artistic and/or personal reasons. Modifications of design and/or relief solely for striking purposes are not included.
2. Stars are not on the obverse of 1837 and 1838-O coins.
3. Smaller size (1828-37) engraved by Kneass.
4. Smaller size without E PLURIBUS UNUM (1831-1838) engraved by Kneass.
5. Slight modifications made in 1809 by Reich and in 1834 by Kneass.
6. Some coins are patterns but some did circulate.
7. Small Head 1854-56; Large Head 1856-89.
8. Smaller size (1829-34) engraved by Kneass.
9. Saint-Gaudens' Liberty was "slimmed down" to meet modern standards of physical beauty, under the orders of Treasury Secretary James A. Baker III.
10. It is expected that the reverse design will change each year.

Specifications of U.S. coins

Half cents

COIN/ DATES	GRAMS WGT.	TOL.	GRAINS WGT.	TOL.	DIA. (mm)	COMPOSITION	SPEC. GRAV.
1793-1795	6.739		104.000		23.50*	Pure copper	8.92
1795-1837	5.443		84.000		23.50*	Pure copper	8.92
1837-1857	5.443	0.227	84.000	3.50	23.50*	Pure copper	8.92

Large cents

COIN/ DATES	GRAMS WGT.	TOL.	GRAINS WGT.	TOL.	DIA. (mm)	COMPOSITION	SPEC. GRAV.
1793-1795	13.478		208.000		28.50*	Pure copper	8.92
1795-1837	10.886		168.000		28.50*	Pure copper	8.92
1837-1857	10.886	0.454	168.000	7.00	28.50*	Pure copper	8.92

Small cents

COIN/ DATES	GRAMS WGT.	TOL.	GRAINS WGT.	TOL.	DIA. (mm)	COMPOSITION	SPEC. GRAV.
1856-1864	4.666	0.259	72.000	4.00	19.30*	88 Cu, 12 Ni	8.92
1864-1873	3.110	0.259	48.000	4.00	19.05	95 Cu, 5 Zn & Sn	8.84

Small cents continued

COIN/ DATES	GRAMS WGT.	TOL.	GRAINS WGT.	TOL.	DIA. (mm)	COMPOSITION	SPEC. GRAV.
1873-1942	3.110	0.130	48.000	2.00	19.05	95 Cu, 5 Zn & Sn	8.84
1943	2.689/ 2.754	0.130	41.500/ 42.500***	2.00	19.05	Zinc-plated steel	7.80
1944-1946	3.110	0.130	48.000	2.00	19.05	95 Cu, 5 Zn	8.83
1947-1962	3.110	0.130	48.000	2.00	19.05	95 Cu, 5 Zn & Sn	8.84
1962-1982	3.110	0.130	48.000	2.00	19.05	95 Cu, 5 Zn	8.83
1982-	2.500	0.100	38.581	1.54	19.05	97.5 Zn,2.5 Cu****	7.17

Two cents

COIN/ DATES	GRAMS WGT.	TOL.	GRAINS WGT.	TOL.	DIA. (mm)	COMPOSITION	SPEC. GRAV.
1864-1873	6.221	0.259	96.000	4.00	23.00*	95 Cu, 5 Zn & Sn	8.84

Copper-nickel 3 cents

COIN/ DATES	GRAMS WGT.	TOL.	GRAINS WGT.	TOL.	DIA. (mm)	COMPOSITION	SPEC. GRAV.
1865-1873	1.944	0.259	30.000	4.00	17.90*	75 Cu, 25 Ni	8.92
1873-1889	1.944	0.130	30.000	2.00	17.90*	75 Cu, 25 Ni	8.92

Copper-nickel 5 cents

COIN/ DATES	GRAMS WGT.	TOL.	GRAINS WGT.	TOL.	DIA. (mm)	COMPOSITION	SPEC. GRAV.
1866-1873	5.000	0.130	77.162	2.00	20.50*	75 Cu, 25 Ni	8.92
1873-1883	5.000	0.194	77.162	3.00	20.50*	75 Cu, 25 Ni	8.92
1883-1942	5.000	0.194	77.162	3.00	21.21	75 Cu, 25 Ni	8.92
1942-1945	5.000	0.194	77.162	3.00	21.21	56 Cu, 35 Ag, 9 Mn	9.25*
1946-	5.000	0.194	77.162	3.00	21.21	75 Cu, 25 Ni	8.92

Silver 3 cents

COIN/ DATES	GRAMS WGT.	TOL.	GRAINS WGT.	TOL.	DIA. (mm)	COMPOSITION	SPEC. GRAV.
1851-1853	0.802	0.032	12.375	0.50	14.00*	750 Ag, 250 Cu	10.11
1854-1873	0.746	0.032	11.520	0.50	14.00*	900 Ag, 100 Cu	10.34

Half dimes

COIN/ DATES	GRAMS WGT.	TOL.	GRAINS WGT.	TOL.	DIA. (mm)	COMPOSITION	SPEC. GRAV.
1794-1795	1.348		20.800		16.50*	900 Ag, 100 Cu	10.34
1795-1805	1.348		20.800		16.50*	892.427 Ag, 107.572 Cu	10.32
1829-1837	1.348		20.800		15.50*	892.427 Ag, 107.572 Cu	10.32
1837-1853	1.336	0.032	20.625	0.50	15.50*	900 Ag, 100 Cu	10.34
1853-1873	1.244	0.032	19.200	0.50	15.50*	900 Ag, 100 Cu	10.34

Dimes

COIN/ DATES	GRAMS WGT.	TOL.	GRAINS WGT.	TOL.	DIA. (mm)	COMPOSITION	SPEC. GRAV.
1796-1828	2.696		41.600		18.80*	892.427 Ag, 107.572 Cu	10.32
1828-1837	2.696		41.600		17.90*	892.427 Ag, 107.572 Cu	10.32
1837-1853	2.673	0.032	41.250	0.50	17.90*	900 Ag, 100 Cu	10.34
1853-1873	2.488	0.032	38.400	0.50	17.90*	900 Ag, 100 Cu	10.34
1873-1964	2.500	0.097	38.581	1.50	17.91	900 Ag, 100 Cu	10.34
1965-	2.268	0.091	35.000	1.40	17.91	75 Cu, 25 Ni on pure Cu	8.92

Twenty cents

COIN/ DATES	GRAMS WGT.	TOL.	GRAINS WGT.	TOL.	DIA. (mm)	COMPOSITION	SPEC. GRAV.
1875-1878	5.000	0.097	77.162	1.50	22.50*	900 Ag, 100 Cu	10.34

Quarter dollars

COIN/ DATES	GRAMS WGT.	TOL.	GRAINS WGT.	TOL.	DIA. (mm)	COMPOSITION	SPEC. GRAV.
1796-1828	6.739		104.000		27.00*	892.427 Ag, 107.572 Cu	10.32
1831-1837	6.739		104.000		24.26*	892.427 Ag, 107.572 Cu	10.32
1837-1853	6.682	0.065	103.125	1.00	24.26*	900 Ag, 100 Cu	10.34
1853-1873	6.221	0.065	96.000	1.00	24.26*	900 Ag, 100 Cu	10.34
1873-1947	6.250	0.097	96.452	1.50	24.26	900 Ag, 100 Cu	10.34

Quarter dollars continued

COIN/ DATES	GRAMS WGT.	GRAMS TOL.	GRAINS WGT.	GRAINS TOL.	DIA. (mm)	COMPOSITION	SPEC. GRAV.
1947-1964	6.250	0.194	96.452	3.00	24.26	900 Ag, 100 Cu	10.34
1965-	5.670	0.227	87.500	3.50	24.26	75 Cu, 25 Ni on pure Cu	8.92
1976	5.750	0.200	88.736	3.09	24.26	40% silver clad**	9.53

Half dollars

COIN/ DATES	GRAMS WGT.	GRAMS TOL.	GRAINS WGT.	GRAINS TOL.	DIA. (mm)	COMPOSITION	SPEC. GRAV.
1794-1795	13.478		208.000		32.50*	900 Ag, 100 Cu	10.34
1796-1836	13.478		208.000		32.50*	892.427 Ag, 107.572 Cu	10.32
1836-1853	13.365	0.097	206.250	1.50	30.61*	900 Ag, 100 Cu	10.34
1853-1873	12.441	0.097	192.000	1.50	30.61*	900 Ag, 100 Cu	10.34
1873-1947	12.500	0.097	192.904	1.50	30.61	900 Ag, 100 Cu	10.34
1947-1964	12.500	0.259	192.904	4.00	30.61	900 Ag, 100 Cu	10.34
1965-1970	11.500	0.400	177.472	6.17	30.61	40% silver clad**	9.53
1971-	11.340	0.454	175.000	7.00	30.61	75 Cu, 25 Ni on pure Cu	8.92
1976	11.500	0.400	177.472	6.17	30.61	40% silver clad**	9.53

Silver dollars, clad dollars

COIN/ DATES	GRAMS WGT.	GRAMS TOL.	GRAINS WGT.	GRAINS TOL.	DIA. (mm)	COMPOSITION	SPEC. GRAV.
1794-1795	26.956		416.000		39.50*	900 Ag, 100 Cu	10.34
1796-1803	26.956		416.000		39.50*	892.427 Ag, 107.572 Cu	10.32
1840-1935	26.730	0.097	412.500	1.50	38.10	900 Ag, 100 Cu	10.34
1971-1978	22.680	0.907	350.000	14.00	38.10	75 Cu, 25 Ni on pure Cu	8.92
1971-1976	24.592	0.984	379.512	15.18	38.10	40% silver clad**	9.53
1979-1981	8.100	0.300	125.000	5.000	26.5	75 Cu, 25 Ni on pure Cu	8.92

Trade dollars

COIN/ DATES	GRAMS WGT.	GRAMS TOL.	GRAINS WGT.	GRAINS TOL.	DIA. (mm)	COMPOSITION	SPEC. GRAV.
1873-1883	27.216	0.097	420.000	1.50	38.10	900 Ag, 100 Cu	10.34

Gold dollars

COIN/ DATES	GRAMS WGT.	GRAMS TOL.	GRAINS WGT.	GRAINS TOL.	DIA. (mm)	COMPOSITION	SPEC. GRAV.
1849-1854	1.672	0.016	25.800	0.25	13.00*	900 Au, 100 Cu & Ag	17.16
1854-1873	1.672	0.016	25.800	0.25	14.86*	900 Au, 100 Cu & Ag	17.16
1873-1889	1.672	0.016	25.800	0.25	14.86*	900 Au, 100 Cu	17.16

Quarter eagles

COIN/ DATES	GRAMS WGT.	GRAMS TOL.	GRAINS WGT.	GRAINS TOL.	DIA. (mm)	COMPOSITION	SPEC. GRAV.
1796-1808	4.374		67.500		20.00*	916.667 Au, 83.333 Cu & Ag	17.45
1821-1827	4.374		67.500		18.50*	916.667 Au, 83.333 Cu & Ag	17.45
1829-1834	4.374		67.500		18.20*	916.667 Au, 83.333 Cu & Ag	17.45
1834-1836	4.180	0.008	64.500	0.13	18.20*	899.225 Au, 100.775 Cu & Ag	17.14
1837-1839	4.180	0.016	64.500	0.25	18.20*	900 Au, 100 Cu & Ag	17.16
1840-1873	4.180	0.016	64.500	0.25	17.78*	900 Au, 100 Cu & Ag	17.16
1873-1929	4.180	0.016	64.500	0.25	17.78*	900 Au, 100 Cu	17.16

Three dollars

COIN/ DATES	GRAMS WGT.	GRAMS TOL.	GRAINS WGT.	GRAINS TOL.	DIA. (mm)	COMPOSITION	SPEC. GRAV.
1854-1873	5.015		77.400		20.63*	900 Au, 100 Cu & Ag	17.16
1873-1889	5.015	0.016	77.400	0.25	20.63*	900 Au, 100 Cu	17.16

Half eagles

COIN/ DATES	GRAMS WGT.	GRAMS TOL.	GRAINS WGT.	GRAINS TOL.	DIA. (mm)	COMPOSITION	SPEC. GRAV.
1795-1829	8.748		135.000		25.00*	916.667 Au, 83.333 Cu & Ag	17.45
1829-1834	8.748		135.000		22.50*	916.667 Au, 83.333 Cu & Ag	17.45
1834-1836	8.359	0.017	129.000	0.26	22.50*	899.225 Au, 100.775 Cu & Ag	17.14
1837-1840	8.359	0.016	129.000	0.25	22.50*	900 Au, 100 Cu & Ag	17.16
1840-1849	8.359	0.016	129.000	0.25	21.54*	900 Au, 100 Cu & Ag	17.16
1849-1873	8.359	0.032	129.000	0.50	21.54*	900 Au, 100 Cu & Ag	17.16
1873-1929	8.359	0.016	129.000	0.25	21.54*	900 Au, 100 Cu	17.16

Eagles

COIN/ DATES	GRAMS WGT.	TOL.	GRAINS WGT.	TOL.	DIA. (mm)	COMPOSITION	SPEC. GRAV.
1795-1804	17.496		270.000		33.00*	916.667 Au, 83.333 Cu & Ag	17.45
1838-1849	16.718	0.016	258.000	0.25	27.00*	900 Au, 100 Cu & Ag	17.16
1849-1873	16.718	0.032	258.000	0.50	27.00*	900 Au, 100 Cu & Ag	17.16
1873-1933	16.718	0.032	258.000	0.50	27.00*	900 Au, 100 Cu	17.16

Double eagles

COIN/ DATES	GRAMS WGT.	TOL.	GRAINS WGT.	TOL.	DIA. (mm)	COMPOSITION	SPEC. GRAV.
1850-1873	33.436	0.032	516.000	0.50	34.29	900 Au, 100 Cu & Ag	17.16
1873-1933	33.436	0.032	516.000	0.50	34.29	900 Au, 100 Cu	17.16

American Eagle bullion coins

DENOM.	GRAMS WGT.	OUNCES WGT.	MM DIA.	COMPOSITION	OUNCE ALLOY WGTS.
SILVER					
$1 one-ounce	31.103	1.000	40.1	.999 Ag	1.000 Ag
GOLD					
$5 tenth-ounce	3.393	0.1091	16.5	.9167 Au, .0300 Ag, .0533 Cu	0.100 Au 0.003 Ag 0.006 Cu
$10 quarter-ounce	8.483	0.2727	22	.9167 Au, .0300 Ag, .0533 Cu	0.250 Au 0.008 Ag 0.015 Cu
$25 half-ounce	16.966	0.5455	27	.9167 Au, .0300 Ag, .0533 Cu	0.500 Au 0.016 Ag 0.029 Cu
$50 one-ounce	33.931	1.091	32.7	.9167 Au, .0300 Ag, .0533 Cu	1.000 Au 0.033 Ag 0.058 Cu
PLATINUM					
$10 tenth-ounce	3.11	0.10	16.5	.9995 Pt	0.100 Au
$25 quarter-ounce	7.78	0.25	22	.9995 Pt	0.250 Au
$50 half-ounce	15.55	0.50	27	.9995 Pt	0.500 Au
$100 one-ounce	31.10	1.00	32.7	.9995 Pt	1.000 Au

*   Unofficial data.
**   Consists of layers of 800 Ag, 200 Cu bonded to a core of 215 Ag, 785 Cu.
***   Cents struck on steel planchets produced in 1942 weigh 41.5 grains, while those struck on planchets produced later in 1943 weigh 42.5 grains.
****   Consists of a planchet composed of 99.2 percent zinc and 0.8 copper, the whole plated with pure copper.
         Not specified by law, established instead by the Director of the Mint.
         Au=Gold; **Ag**=Silver; **Cu**=Copper; **Mn**=Manganese; **Ni**=Nickel; **Sn**=Tin; **Zn**=Zinc; **Pt**=Platinum.

Treasury Officials

Secretaries of the Treasury

President	Secretaries	Term
Washington	Alexander Hamilton, New York	Sept. 11, 1789 — Jan. 31, 1795
	Oliver Wolcott, Connecticut	Feb. 3, 1795 — Mar. 3, 1797
Adams, John	Oliver Wolcott, Connecticut	Mar. 4, 1797 — Dec. 31, 1800
	Samuel Dexter, Massachusetts	Jan. 1, 1801 — Mar. 3, 1801
Jefferson	Samuel Dexter, Massachusetts	Mar. 4, 1801 — May 13, 1801
	Albert Gallatin, Pennsylvania	May 14, 1801 — Mar. 3, 1809
Madison	Albert Gallatin, Pennsylvania	Mar. 4, 1809 — Feb. 8, 1814
	George W. Campbell, Tennessee	Feb. 9, 1814 — Oct. 5, 1814
	Alexander J. Dallas, Pennsylvania	Oct. 6, 1814 — Oct. 21, 1816
	William H. Crawford, Georgia	Oct. 22, 1816 — Mar. 3, 1817
Monroe	William H. Crawford, Georgia	Mar. 4, 1817 — Mar. 6, 1825
Adams, J.Q.	Richard Rush, Pennsylvania	Mar. 7, 1825 — Mar. 5, 1829
Jackson	Samuel D. Ingham, Pennsylvania	Mar. 6, 1829 — June 20, 1831
	Louis McLane, Delaware	Aug. 8, 1831 — May 28, 1833
	William J. Duane, Pennsylvania	May 29, 1833 — Sept. 22, 1833
	Roger B. Taney, Maryland	Sept. 23, 1833 — June 25, 1834
	Levi Woodbury, New Hampshire	July 1, 1834 — Mar. 3, 1837
Van Buren	Levi Woodbury, New Hampshire	Mar. 4, 1837 — Mar. 3, 1841
Harrison, W.H.	Thomas Ewing, Ohio	Mar. 6, 1841 — Apr. 4, 1841
Tyler	Thomas Ewing, Ohio	Apr. 5, 1841 — Sept. 11, 1841
	Walter Forward, Pennsylvania	Sept. 13, 1841 — Mar. 1, 1843
	John C. Spencer, New York	Mar. 8, 1843 — May 2, 1844
	George M. Bibb, Kentucky	July 4, 1844 — Mar. 4, 1845
Polk	George M. Bibb, Kentucky	Mar. 5, 1845 — Mar. 7, 1845
	Robert J. Walker, Mississippi	Mar. 8, 1845 — Mar. 5, 1849
Taylor	Wm. M. Meredith, Pennsylvania	Mar. 8, 1849 — July 9, 1850
Fillmore	Wm. M. Meredith, Pennsylvania	July 10, 1850 — July 22, 1850
	Thomas Corwin, Ohio	July 23, 1850 — Mar. 6, 1853
Pierce	James Guthrie, Kentucky	Mar. 7, 1853 — Mar. 6, 1857
Buchanan	Howell Cobb, Georgia	Mar. 7, 1857 — Dec. 8, 1860
	Philip F. Thomas, Maryland	Dec. 12, 1860 — Jan. 14, 1861
	John A. Dix, New York	Jan. 15, 1861 — Mar. 6, 1861
Lincoln	Salmon P. Chase, Ohio	Mar. 7, 1861 — June 30, 1864
	Wm. P. Fessenden, Maine	July 5, 1864 — Mar. 3, 1865
	Hugh McCulloch, Indiana	Mar. 9, 1865 — Apr. 15, 1865
Johnson, A.	Hugh McCulloch, Indiana	Apr. 16, 1865 — Mar. 3, 1869
Grant	Geo. S. Boutwell, Massachusetts	Mar. 12, 1869 — Mar. 16, 1873
	Wm. A. Richardson, Massachusetts	Mar. 17, 1873 — June 3, 1874
	Benjamin H. Bristow, Kentucky	June 4, 1874 — June 20, 1876
	Lot M. Morrill, Maine	June 7, 1876 — Mar. 3, 1877
Hayes	Lot M. Morrill, Maine	Mar. 4, 1877 — Mar. 9, 1877
	John Sherman, Ohio	Mar. 10, 1877 — Mar. 3, 1881
Garfield	William Windom, Minnesota	Mar. 8, 1881 — Sept. 19, 1881

President	Secretaries	Term
Arthur	William Windom, Minnesota	Sept. 20, 1881 — Nov. 13, 1881
	Charles J. Folger, New York	Nov. 14, 1881 — Sept. 4, 1884
	Walter Q. Gresham, Indiana	Sept. 25, 1884 — Oct. 30, 1884
	Hugh McCulloch, Indiana	Oct. 31, 1884 — Mar. 3, 1885
Cleveland	Hugh McCulloch, Indiana	Mar. 4, 1885 — Mar. 7, 1885
	Daniel Manning, New York	Mar. 8, 1885 — Mar. 31, 1887
	Charles S. Fairchild, New York	Apr. 1, 1887 — Mar. 3, 1889
Harrison, B.	Charles S. Fairchild, New York	Mar. 4, 1889 — Mar. 6, 1889
	William Windom, Minnesota	Mar. 7, 1889 — Jan. 29, 1891
	Charles Foster, Ohio	Feb. 25, 1891 — Mar. 3, 1893
Cleveland	Charles Foster, Ohio	Mar. 4, 1893 — Mar. 6, 1893
	John G. Carlisle, Kentucky	Mar. 7, 1893 — Mar. 3, 1897
McKinley	John G. Carlisle, Kentucky	Mar. 4, 1897 — Mar. 5, 1897
	Lyman J. Gage, Illinois	Mar. 6, 1897 — Sept. 14, 1901
Roosevelt, T.	Lyman J. Gage, Illinois	Sept. 15, 1901 — Jan. 31, 1902
	L.M. Shaw, Iowa	Feb. 1, 1902 — Mar. 3, 1907
	G.B. Cortelyou, New York	Mar. 4, 1907 — Mar. 7, 1909
Taft	Franklin MacVeagh, Illinois	Mar. 8, 1909 — Mar. 5, 1913
Wilson	W.G. McAdoo, New York	Mar. 6, 1913 — Dec. 15, 1918
	Carter Glass, Virginia	Dec. 16, 1918 — Feb. 1, 1920
	David F. Houston, Missouri	Feb. 2, 1920 — Mar. 3, 1921
Harding	Andrew W. Mellon, Pennsylvania	Mar. 4, 1921 — Aug. 2, 1923
Coolidge	Andrew W. Mellon, Pennsylvania	Aug. 3, 1923 — Mar. 3, 1929
Hoover	Andrew W. Mellon, Pennsylvania	Mar. 4, 1929 — Feb. 12, 1932
	Ogden L. Mills, New York	Feb. 13, 1932 — Mar. 4, 1933
Roosevelt, F.D.	William H. Woodin, New York	Mar. 5, 1933 — Dec. 31, 1933
	Henry Morgenthau, Jr., New York	Jan. 1, 1934 — Apr. 12, 1945
Truman	Henry Morgenthau, Jr., New York	Apr. 13, 1945 — July 22, 1945
	Fred M. Vinson, Kentucky	July 23, 1945 — June 23, 1946
	John W. Snyder, Missouri	June 25, 1946 — Jan. 20, 1953
Eisenhower	George M. Humphrey, Ohio	Jan. 21, 1953 — July 29, 1957
	Robert B. Anderson, Connecticut	July 29, 1957 — Jan. 20, 1961
Kennedy	Douglas Dillon, New Jersey	Jan. 21, 1961 — Nov. 22, 1963
Johnson, L.B.	Douglas Dillon, New Jersey	Nov. 23, 1963 — Apr. 1, 1965
	Henry H. Fowler, Virginia	Apr. 1, 1965 — Dec. 20, 1968
	Joseph W. Barr, Indiana	Dec. 21, 1968 — Jan. 20, 1969
Nixon	David M. Kennedy, Utah	Jan. 22, 1969 — Feb. 10, 1971
	John B. Connally, Texas	Feb. 11, 1971 — June 12, 1972
	George P. Shultz, Illinois	June 12, 1971 — May 7, 1974
	William E. Simon, New Jersey	May 8, 1974 — Aug. 9, 1974
Ford	William E. Simon, New Jersey	Aug. 10, 1974 — Jan. 20, 1977
Carter	W. Michael Blumenthal, Michigan	Jan. 23, 1977 — Aug. 4, 1979
	G. William Miller, Rhode Island	Aug. 7, 1979 — Jan. 20, 1981
Reagan	Donald T. Regan, Massachusetts	Jan. 22, 1981 — Feb. 2, 1985
	James A. Baker III, Texas	Feb. 3, 1985 — Aug. 17, 1988
	Nicholas F. Brady, New Jersey	Sept. 14, 1988 — Jan. 20, 1989
Bush	Nicholas F. Brady, New Jersey	Jan. 20, 1989 — Jan. 20, 1993
Clinton	Lloyd Bentsen, Texas	Feb. 1993 — Dec. 22, 1994
	Robert E. Rubin, New York	Jan. 10, 1995 —

Treasurers of the United States

Treasurer	Term
Michael Hillegas, Pennsylvania	July 29, 1775 — Sept. 11, 1789
Samuel Meredith, Pennsylvania	Sept. 11, 1789 — Oct. 31, 1801
Thomas T. Tucker, South Carolina	Dec. 1, 1801 — May 2, 1828
William Clark, Pennsylvania	June 4, 1828 — May 31, 1829
John Campbell, Virginia	May 26, 1829 — July 20, 1839
William Selden, Virginia	July 22, 1839 — Nov. 23, 1850
John Sloan, Ohio	Nov. 27, 1850 — April 6, 1852
Samuel Casey, Kentucky	April 4, 1853 — Dec. 22, 1859
William C. Price, Missouri	Feb. 28, 1860 — Mar. 21, 1861
F.E. Spinner, New York	Mar. 16, 1861 — June 30, 1875
John C. New, Indiana	June 30, 1875 — July 1, 1876

Treasurer	Term
A.U. Wyman, Wisconsin	July 1, 1876 — June 30, 1877
James Gilfillan, Connecticut	July 1, 1877 — Mar. 31, 1883
A.U. Wyman, Wisconsin	April 1, 1883 — April 30, 1885
Conrad N. Jordan, New York	May 1, 1885 — May 23, 1887
James W. Hyatt, Connecticut	May 24, 1887 — May 10, 1889
J.N. Huston, Indiana	May 11, 1889 — April 24, 1891
Enos H. Nebecker, Indiana	April 25, 1891 — May 31, 1893
D.N. Morgan, Connecticut	June 1, 1893 — June 30, 1897
Ellis H. Roberts, New York	July 1, 1897 — June 30, 1905
Charles H. Treat, New York	July 1, 1905 — Oct. 30, 1909
Lee McClung, Tennessee	Nov. 1, 1909 — Nov. 21, 1912
Carmi A. Thompson, Ohio	Nov. 22, 1912 — Mar. 31, 1913
John Burke, North Dakota	April 1, 1913 — Jan. 5, 1921
Frank White, North Dakota	May 2, 1921 — May 1, 1928
H.T. Tate, Tennessee	May 31, 1928 — Jan. 17, 1929
W.O. Woods, Kansas	Jan. 18, 1929 — May 31, 1933
W.A. Julian, Ohio	June 1, 1933 — May 29, 1949
Georgia Neese Clark, Kansas	June 21, 1949 — Jan. 27, 1953
Ivy Baker Priest, Utah	Jan. 28, 1953 — Jan. 29, 1961
Elizabeth Rudel Smith, California	Jan. 30, 1961 — April 13, 1962
Kathryn O'Hay Granahan, Pennsylvania	Jan. 3, 1963 — Nov. 20, 1966
Dorothy Andrews Elston Kabis, Delaware	May 8, 1969 — July 3, 1971
Romana Acosta Banuelos, California	Dec. 17, 1971 — Feb. 15, 1974
Francine Irving Neff, New Mexico	June 21, 1974 — Jan. 19, 1977
Azie Taylor Morton, Texas	Sept. 12, 1977 — Jan. 20, 1981
Angela Buchanan, Maryland	Jan. 21, 1981 — July 1, 1983
Katherine Davalos Ortega, New Mexico	Sept. 23, 1983 — June 30, 1989
Catalina Vasquez Villalpando, Texas	Dec. 11, 1989 — Oct. 29, 1992
Mary Ellen Withrow, Ohio	March 8, 1994 —

Directors of the U.S. Mint

The Director of the Mint is appointed by the President of the United States, by and with the advice and consent of the Senate. The length of the term of office was not fixed by law from 1792 to 1873. The Act of February 12, 1873, fixed the term of the Director at five years. However, there is no restriction on the reappointment of Directors.

Director	Term of service
David Rittenhouse, Pennsylvania	April 1792 — June 1795
Henry William de Saussure, South Carolina	July 1795 — October 1795
Elias Boudinot, New Jersey	October 1795 — July 1805
Robert Patterson, Pennsylvania	January 1806 — July 1824
Samuel Moore, Pennsylvania	July 1824 — July 1835
Robert Maskell Patterson, Pennsylvania	July 1835 — July 1851
George N. Eckert, Pennsylvania	July 1851 — April 1853
Thomas M. Pettit, Pennsylvania	April 1853 — May 1853
James Ross Snowden, Pennsylvania	June 1853 — April 1861
James Pollock, Pennsylvania	May 1861 — September 1866
William Millward, Pennsylvania	October 1866 — April 1867
Henry Richard Linderman, Pennsylvania	April 1867 — April 1869
James Pollock, Pennsylvania	May 1869 — March 1873
Henry Richard Linderman, Pennsylvania	April 1873 — December 1878
Horatio C. Burchard, Illinois	February 1879 — June 1885
James P. Kimball, Pennsylvania	July 1885 — October 1889
Edward O. Leech, District of Columbia	October 1889 — May 1893
Robert E. Preston, District of Columbia	November 1893 — Feb. 1898
George E. Roberts, Iowa	February 1898 — July 1907
Frank A. Leach, California	September 1907 — Nov. 1909
A. Piatt Andrew, Massachusetts	November 1909 — June 1910
George E. Roberts, Iowa	July 1910 — November 1914
Robert W. Wooley, Virginia	March 1915 — July 1916

Director	Term of service
F.J.H. von Engelken, Florida	September 1916 — Feb. 1917
Raymond T. Baker, Nevada	March 1917 — March 1922
F.E. Scobey, Ohio	March 1922 — September 1923
Robert J. Grant, Colorado	November 1923 — May 1933
Nellie Tayloe Ross, Wyoming	May 1933 — April 1953
William H. Brett, Ohio	July 1954 — January 1961
Eva Adams, Nevada	October 1961 — August 1969
Mary Brooks, Idaho	September 1969 — February 1977
Stella Hackel Sims, Vermont	November 1977 — April 1981
Donna Pope, Ohio	July 1981 — August 1991
David J. Ryder	Sept. 1992 — Nov. 1993

Ryder as Acting Director was nominated by President George Bush, but his nomination was never taken up by the Senate. A rare recess appointment by Bush made Ryder's title official, but it expired at the close of Congress in 1993.

Philip N. Diehl	1994-

Mint Superintendents

It was 80 years from the time David Rittenhouse took over as first director of the U.S. Mint until future directors were given an "assistant" via the office of the superintendent.

The Coinage Act of 1873 put all Mint and assay office activities under the newly-organized Bureau of the Mint in the Department of the Treasury and the director's headquarters were moved to the Treasury Building in Washington, D.C. The top officer at Philadelphia was thereafter designated as superintendent. In 1996, the positions of Superintedent were reclassified from presidential appointees to career professionals. Proper title since that time is "Deputy Superintendent."

Philadelphia

Superintendent	Term
James Pollock	1873-1879
Col. A. Loudon Snowden	1879-1885
Daniel M. Fox	1885-1889
Col. O.C. Bosbyshell	1889-1894
Dr. Eugene Townsend	1894-1895
Maj. Herman Kretz	1895-1898
Henry Boyer	1898-1902
John H. Landis	1902-1914
Adam M. Joyce	1914-1921
Freas Styer	1921-1934
A. Raymond Raff	1934-1935
Edward H. Dressel	1935-1953
Rae V. Biester	1953-1961
Michael H. Sura	1961-1969
Nicholas G. Theodore	1969-1977
Shallie M. Bey Jr.	1978-1981
Anthony H. Murray Jr.	1981-1988
John T. Martino	1989-1993
Augustine "Gus" Albino (acting)	1993-1996
Augustine "Gus" Albino (Deputy)	1996-

Denver

Superintendent	Term
Frank M. Downer	1904-1913
Thomas Annear	1913-1921
Robert J. Grant	1921-1923
Frank E. Shepard	1923-1933
Mark A. Skinner	1933-1942

Moses E. Smith	1943-1952
Gladys P. Morelock	1952-1953
Alma K. Schneider	1953-1961
Fern V. Miller	1961-1967
Marian N. Rossmiller	1967-1969
Betty Higby	1969-1978
Evelyn Davidson	1978-1981
Nora Hussey	1981-1987
Cynthia Grassby Baker	1988-1989
Barbara McTurk (acting)	1989-1996
Raymond "Jack" DeBroeckert (Deputy)	1996-

San Francisco

Superintendent	Term
L. A. Birdsall	1853-1855
P.G. Lott	1855-1857
C.H. Hempstead	1857-1861
R.J. Stevens	1861-1863
R.B. Swain	1863-1869
A.H. La Grange	1869-1877
H.L. Dodge	1878-1882
E.F. Burton	1882-1885
I. Lawton	1885-1889
W.H. Diamond	1889-1893
J. Daggett	1893-1897
F.A. Leach	1897-1907
E. Sweeney	1907-1912
F.A. Leach	1912-1913
T. W. Shanahan	1913-1921
M. J. Kelly	1921-1933

P. J. Haggerty 1933-1944
N. H. Callaghan 1945-1947
G. B. Gillin 1948-1951
J. P. McEnery 1952-1952
R. P. Buell 1953-1955
A. C. Carmichael 1955-1958
OFFICER IN CHARGE, U.S. ASSAY OFFICE
J. R. Carr 1958-1968
John F. Brekle 1968-1972
Bland T. Brockenborough 1972-1980
Thomas H. Miller 1980-1988
SUPERINTENDENT, U.S. MINT
Carol Mayer Marshall 1990-1992
Donald Butler (acting) 1993-1996
Dale D. DeVries (Deputy) 1996-

West Point

Superintendent	Term
Clifford M. Barber	1988-1990
Bert W. Corneby	1990-1993
James Edwards (acting)	1993-1996
Bradford E. Cooper (Deputy)	1996-

Charlotte

Superintendent	Term
John Hill Wheeler	1837-1841
Burgess Sidney Gaither	1841-1844
Greene Washington Caldwell	1844-1846
William Julius Alexander	1846-1849
James Walker Osborne	1849-1853
Greene Washington Caldwell	1853-1861

On April 20, 1861, the Charlotte Mint was seized by Confederate forces, who continued coining operations until May 20, 1861. The Mint was officially closed May 31, 1861. An Assay Office was authorized by an Act of the Confederate Congress approved Aug. 24, 1861, and Dr. J.H. Gibbon received appointment as Assayer. In May 1862, the facility was turned over to the Confederate Navy Department. Following the war, it was reopened as a U. S. Assay Office March 19, 1867.

OFFICER IN CHARGE, U.S. ASSAY OFFICE
Isaac W. Jones 1867-1869
Calvin Josiah Cowles 1869-1885
Robert P. Waring 1885-1889
Stuart Warren Cramer 1889-1893
W.E. Ardrey 1893-1897
W.S. Clanton 1897-1903
D. Kirby Pope 1903-1908
William S. Pearson 1908-1911
Frank Parker Drane 1911-1913
The Charlotte Assay Office was closed June 30, 1913.

Carson City

Superintendent	Term
Abraham Curry	1870-1870
H.F. Rice	1870-1873
Frank D. Hetrich	1873-1875
James Crawford	1875-1885
Theodore R. Hofer	(temporary)
William Garrard	1885-1889

Samuel Coleman Wright 1889-1892
Theodore R. Hofer 1892-1894
Jewett W. Adams 1894-1898
Roswell K. Colcord 1898-1899
The Carson City Mint became an Assay Office effective July 1, 1899.

Dahlonega

Superintendent	Term
Joseph J. Singleton	1837-1841
Paul Rossignol	1841-1843
James F. Cooper	1843-1849
Anderson W. Redding	1849-1853
Julius M. Patton	1853-1860
George Kellogg	1860-?
Coiner	
David H. Mason	1837-1848
John D. Field, Jr.	1848-1849
Robert H. Moore	1849-1853
John D. Field, Jr.	1853-?
Assayer	
Joseph W. Farnum	1837-1843
Isaac L. Todd	1843-1850
M.F. Stephenson	1850-1853
Isaac L. Todd	1853-?

The Dahlonega Mint was seized by Confederate forces April 8, 1861; continued in operation until May 14, 1861; and officially closed May 31, 1861. An Act of the Confederate Congress, approved Aug. 24, 1861, authorized the opening of an Assay Office and Lewis W. Quillian was appointed Assayer.

New Orleans

Superintendent	Term
David Bradford	1837-1839
Joseph M. Kennedy	1839-1850
Robert M. McAlpine	1850-1853
Charles Bienvenu	1853-1857
Logan McNight	1858-1858
John H. Alpuente (acting)	1858-1858
Howard Millspaugh (acting)	1858-1858
William A. Elmore	1858-1861
M.F. Bonzano (Assayer in Charge)	1874-1875
M.F. Bonzano (Custodian)	1875-1876
M.F. Bonzano (Assayer in Charge and Superintendent)	1876-1877
M.F. Bonzano (Assayer in Charge)	1877-1878
Michael Hahn	1878-1878
Henry S. Foote	1878-1880
Martin V. Davis	1880-1882
A.W. Smyth	1882-1885
Gabriel Montegut	1885-1893
Overton Cade	1893-1898
Charles W. Boothby	1898(?)-1902
Hugh S. Sithon	1902-1911
William M. Lynch	1911-1914
Leonard Magruder	1914-1932
Cecil Grey	1932-1933
Hugh T. Rippeto	1933-1941
Charles M. Miller	1941-1942

The New Orleans Mint closed June 30, 1942.

The State of Louisiana took possession of the Mint Jan. 31, 1861, and carried on all the operations with the same officers as under the U.S. until March 31. The Confederate States of America took possession April 1 and continued with the same officers and men. Operations were suspended May 14, 1861, and the facility was closed May 31, 1861. An Assay Office was established by an Act of the Confederate Congress approved Jan. 27, 1862. The facility reverted to federal control following the recapture of the city May 1, 1862, and M.F. Bonzano, under orders of Secretary of the Treasury Salmon P. Chase, dated May 16, 1862, returned to New Orleans and took possession of the Mint and its property.

Chief Engravers

Joseph Wright
> Named by Washington, but died before appointment became official

Robert Scot 1793-1823
William Kneass 1824-1840
Christian Gobrecht 1840-1844
James Barton Longacre 1844-1869
William Barber 1869-1879
Charles E. Barber 1879-1917
George T. Morgan 1917-1925
John Ray Sinnock 1925-1947
Gilroy Roberts 1948-1964
Frank Gasparro 1965-1981
Elizabeth Jones 1981-1990

> Jones tendered a pro forma resignation in December 1988 after the election of George Bush. The Bush admininistration, in a startling break from tradition, accepted the resignation in late 1990. Bush nominated Mint Sculptor-Engraver John M. Mercanti in September 1990. However, the Senate did not take up the nomination. Mercanti was renominated in January 1991, and in March he asked that his name be withdrawn. The legislation that ended presidential appointments for Mint Superintendents also elimated the office of Chief Engraver, although an administrative head does exist.

Foreign Coins

To facilitate collecting of foreign coins struck at the U.S. facilities, this format supplements the United States Mint charts.

Coins struck at United States Mint facilities 1977-87 are listed by country. United States Mint facilities have not struck foreign coins since the 1984-dated coinage for Panama.

Dominican Republic

1978 50 centavos .... Philadelphia	732,000
1979 50 centavos .... Philadelphia	300,000
1979 50 centavos .... San Francisco	5,015
1980 50 centavos .... Philadelphia	554,000
1981 50 centavos .... Philadelphia	1,000,000
1982 50 centavos .... Philadelphia	1,300,000
1978 25 centavos .... Philadelphia	995,000
1979 25 centavos .... Philadelphia	1,785,000*
1979 25 centavos .... San Francisco	5,015
1980 25 centavos .... Philadelphia	504,000
1981 25 centavos .... Philadelphia	2,600,000
1982 25 centavos .... Philadelphia	3,200,000
1978 10 centavos .... Philadelphia	6,490,000
1979 10 centavos .... San Francisco	5,015
1980 10 centavos .... Philadelphia	600,000
1981 10 centavos .... Philadelphia	4,400,000
1982 10 centavos .... Philadelphia	6,000,000
1978 5 centavos ...... Philadelphia	4,984,000
1979 5 centavos ...... San Francisco	5,015
1981 5 centavos ...... Philadelphia	5,300,000
1982 5 centavos ...... Philadelphia	4,500,000
1978 1 centavo .... Philadelphia	5,980,000
1979 1 centavo .... San Francisco	5,015
1981 1 centavo .... Philadelphia	200,000
1978 1 peso .... Philadelphia	80,000
1979 1 peso .... San Francisco	5,015
1981 1 peso .... Philadelphia	20,000

Haiti

1979 50 centime ...... San Francisco	2,000,000

Panama

1980 10 balboa ...... Philadelphia	5,000,000
1979 half balboa ..... Philadelphia	1,000,000
1980 half balboa ..... Philadelphia	1,000,000
1982 half balboa ..... Philadelphia	1,500,000
1984 half balboa ..... Philadelphia	350,000
1979 quarter balboa Philadelphia	2,000,000
1980 quarter balboa Philadelphia	2,000,000
1982 quarter balboa Philadelphia	3,148,000
1984 quarter balboa Philadelphia	5,000,000
1982 1/10 balboa .. Philadelphia	7,740,000
1984 10 centesimo .. Philadelphia	7,750,000
1982 5 centesimo .... Philadelphia	8,400,000
1983 5 centesimo .... Philadelphia	5,500,000
1984 5 centesimo .... Philadelphia	2,000,000
1977 1 centesimo .... West Point	10,000,000
1978 1 centesimo .... West Point	10,000,000
1979 1 centesimo .... West Point	10,000,000
1980 1 centesimo .... West Point	10,000,000
1981 1 centesimo .... West Point	10,000,000
1982 1 centesimo .... West Point	2,000,000
1983 1 centesimo .... Philadelphia	20,000,000
1984 1 centesimo .... Philadelphia	25,000,000

Peru

1977 1 sol .... Philadelphia	2,100,000

Philippines

1977 5 sentimo .... Philadelphia	1,088,000
*Struck in 1978, dated 1979.	

Summary of foreign coinage by U.S. Mints, by country

Argentina (blanks)	64,058,334
Australia	168,000,000
Belgian Congo	25,000,000
Belgium	25,000,000
Bolivia	30,000,000
Brazil (blanks)	406,249,266
Canada	85,170,000
China	39,720,096
China, Republic of (Taiwan)	428,172,000
Colombia	133,461,872
Costa Rica	131,798,820
Cuba	496,559,888
Curacao	12,000,000
Dominican Republic	105,474,297
Ecuador	214,451,060
El Salvador	226,695,351
Ethiopia	375,433,730
Fiji	4,800,000
France	50,000,000
Greenland	100,000

Guatemala	7,835,000
Haiti	90,324,000
Hawaii*	1,950,000
Honduras	115,929,500
Indochina	135,270,000
Israel	91,000
Korea	295,000,000
Liberia	56,744,679
Mexico	91,076,840
Mexico (blanks)	175,714,411
Nepal	195,608
Netherlands	562,500,000
Neth. E. Indies	1,716,368,000
Nicaragua	26,080,000
Panama (Republic)	268,409,191
Peru	761,067,479
Philippines	3,483,718,169
Poland	6,000,000
Saudi Arabia	124,712,574
Siam (Thailand)	20,000,000
Suriname (Netherlands Guiana)	21,195,000
Syria	7,350,000
Venezuela	306,762,944
Totals (42 countries)	**11,325,756,346**

* Coined prior to Aug. 21, 1959, when
Hawaii became the 50th State of the
Union.

Foreign coins manufactured by U.S. Mints

Calendar year	Number of pieces produced
July 1, 1875-Dec. 31, 1905	155,896,973
1906	10,204,504
1907	45,253,047
1908	29,645,359
1909	11,298,981
1910	7,153,818
1911	7,794,406
1912	6,244,348
1913	7,309,258
1914	17,335,005
1915	55,485,190
1916	37,441,328
1917	25,208,497
1918	60,102,000
1919	100,269,195
1920	99,002,334
1921	55,094,352
1922	7,863,030
1923	4,369,000
1924	12,663,196
1925	13,461,000
1926	14,987,000
1927	3,650,000
1928	16,701,000
1929	34,980,000
1930	3,300,120
1931	4,498,020
1932	9,756,096
1933	15,240,000
1934	24,280,000
1935	109,600,850
1936	32,350,000
1937	26,800,000
1938	48,579,644
1939	15,725,000
1940	33,170,000
1941	208,603,500
1942	307,737,000
1943	186,682,008
1944	788,498,000
1945	1,802,376,004
1946	504,528,000
1947	277,376,094
1948	21,950,000
1949	156,687,940
1950	2,000,000
1951	25,450,000
1952	45,857,000
1953	193,673,000
1954	19,015,000
1955	67,550,000
1956	38,793,500
1957	59,264,000
1958	152,575,000
1959	129,647,000
1960	238,400,000
1961	148,500,000
1962	256,485,000
1963	293,515,000
1964	—
1965	—
1966	7,440,000
1967	176,196,206
1968	416,088,658
1969	348,653,046
1970	483,988,392
1971	207,959,692
1972	392,723,895
1973	295,408,674
1974	373,293,733
1975	762,126,363
1976	562,372,000
1977	13,188,000
1978	30,846,000
1979	15,530,090
1980	19,658,000
1981	23,520,000
1982	37,788,000
1983	25,500,000
1984	45,600,000
Total	**11,325,756,346**

Select Bibliography

The following works, most of which were sources of data for this and earlier editions, are recommended to anyone seeking additional information on the areas of American numismatics which they cover. Commentary following some entries represents the personal opinion of the editors.

Adams, Edgar H. *Private Gold Coinage of California, 1849-55, its History and its Issues.* Brooklyn, N.Y., 1912.

Adams, Edgar H. and Woodin, William H. *United States Pattern, Trial and Experimental Pieces.* American Numismatic Society, New York, 1913. Long the basic reference on this series, introduced the denomination-order concept. Co-author Woodin assembled one of the greatest pattern collections and served as Secretary of the Treasury.

Adams, John W. *United States Numismatic Literature,* Volume I 19th Century; Volume II 20th Century. George Kolbe, Crestline, Cal., 1982 and 1990. In-depth review and history of auction firms, consignors and coins consigned with incisive commentaries of each sale. A master work by a master bibliophile and leader both in books and early copper coinage of the U.S.

Ahwash, Kamal. *Encyclopedia of United States Liberty Seated Dimes, 1837-1891.* Kamah Press, Media, Pa., 1977. Labor of love by a very sincere numismatist, received inadequate recognition and use from numismatists. Needs revision in view of later discoveries.

Akers, David W. *U.S. Gold Dollars, 1849-1889.* Paramount Publications, Englewood, Ohio, 1975. First of a series published 1975-82, a meticulous analysis of all U.S. gold coins by date of issue, Mint mark and auction appearance. An update through the 1990's would be of inestimable value.

—— *U.S. Quarter Eagles, 1796-1929.* (1976).

—— *U.S. Three Dollar Gold Pieces 1854-1889.* (1976).

—— *U.S. Half Eagles, 1795-1929.* (1979).

—— *U.S. Eagles, 1795-1933.* (1980).

—— *U.S. Double Eagles, 1849-1933.* (1982).

—— *A Handbook of 20th Century United States Gold Coins, 1907-1933.* Bowers and Merena Galleries, Wolfeboro, N.H., 1988.

Alexander, David T. *The Numismatic Literary Guild, a 25-Year History,* Numismatic Literary Guild, Glen Rock, N.J. 1993. A glimpse of the important organization and its colorful contributions to the larger world of American numismatics, 1968-1993.

ANACS, American Numismatic Association Certification Service, *Counterfeit Detection, A Reprint from the Numismatist,* Colorado Springs, Col., 1983.

American Numismatic Society. *An Exhibition of U.S. & Colonial Coins,* Jan. 17-Feb. 18, 1914, New York. Valued guide to pedigrees of many great American rarities.

Anton, William T. Jr. and Keese, Bruce. *The Forgotten Coins of the North American Colonies, a Modern Survey of Early English and Irish Counterfeit Coppers Circulating in the Americas.* Published by the senior author, Woodcliff, N.J., 1990; paperback edition by Krause Publications, Iola, Wisc. A profusely illustrated study of this important category of colonial coinage.

Baker, William S. *Medallic Portraits of Washington,* Philadelphia, Robert M. Lindsay 1885.

——, *Centennial Edition,* revised and enlarged by Russell Rulau and Dr. George Fuld, Krause Publications, Iola, Wis. 1985. A long-awaited addition to the fast-reviving field of Washingtoniana, although it is already in urgent need of revision and updating.

Basso, Aldo P. *Coins, medals and tokens of the Philippines 1728-1974,* Second edition, Bookman Printing House, Manila, Philippines, 1975. A remarkably complete treatment of all Philippine material other than paper money.

Beistle, Martin Luther. *A Register of U.S. Half Dollar Die Varieties and Sub-Varieties.* Published by the author, Shippensburg, Pa. 1929. Based on Col. E.R.H. Green coll., written by the real inventor of the coin album. Unfortunately this was possibly the most tedious and hard to use works on any U.S. series, happily replaced for 1794-1836 halves by the later work of Al C. Overton.

Bell, R.C. *Commercial Coins, 1787-1804.* Newcastle upon Tyne, Corbitt & Hunter, 1963. One of several British token works by a profound authority on this tangled series, which shed light on several American-associated items.

Betts, C. Wyllys. *American Colonial History Illustrated by Contemporary Medals,* 1894; reprint by Quarterman, 1972. One of the most valuable works on the wider field of early American numismatics, offering unmatched historical sidelights into the Colonial era by youthful creator of several famous fantasy coins.

Blythe, Al. *The Complete Guide to Liberty Seated Half Dimes.* DLRC Press, Virginia Beach, Va., 1992. Useful rarity and market analysis, terse on variety identification, first major work since Valentine's bare-bones 1931 effort. One of a high quality series featuring Tom Mulvaney photography, created by this innovative publisher.

Bolender, Milferd H. *The United States Early Dollars from 1794 to 1803.* Fifth Revised edition with rarity revisions by the greatest living variety attribution specialist, Delaware's Jules Reiver, Krause Publications, Iola, Wis. 1988. Bolender's clarity of thought and description makes this an exemplary reference. Reiver's additions are of tremendous value in updating this series.

Bowers, Q. David. *The History of United States Coinage as Illustrated by the Garrett Collection.* Bowers and Ruddy Galleries, Los Angeles, Cal. 1979. If there is such a thing as a biography of a great collection, this book is it.

—— *United States Gold Coins, an Illustrated History.* (1982). Based on the great Louis Eliasberg collection sold at auction in 1982.

—— *Virgil Brand, the Man and His Era.* (1983) Provides a rich feeling of the human interest and drama of this remarkable millionaire numismatist.

—— *Abe Kosoff, Dean of Numismatics.* (1985). Significant tribute to one of the greats of U.S. numismatics.

—— *The Norweb Collection, an American Legacy.* (1987). A highly readable tale of an outstanding family and its collecting.

—— *Commemorative Coins of the United States, a Complete Encyclopedia.* Bowers & Merena Galleries, Wolfeboro, N.H., 1991. Thorough investigation not only of the coins but of the world into which the coins were released, the sometimes murky circumstances of their birth and subsequent market adventures.

—— *The American Numismatic Association Centennial History.* Two Volumes, American Numismatic Association, Colorado Springs, Colo., 1991. Drawn from the pages of *The Numismatist,* this history offers remarkable insights into such events as the hotly contested 1910 ANA presidential election, where the author notes Farran Zerbe's voter roll padding and other administrative irregularities, ignored by most writers since that election.

—— *Silver Dollars & Trade Dollars of the United States, a Complete Encyclopedia.* Two Volumes, Bowers & Merena Galleries, Wolfeboro, N.H., 1993. These massive volumes provide 3,000 pages of information on all silver and clad dollar coins from 1794 through the Susan B. Anthony coinage. Although renumbered with Bowers-Borchard numbers, the section of early dollars includes the Bolender's basic work; the data on the Morgan and Peace dollars exceeds anything that has seen print since 1878.

Breen, Walter. *Major Varieties of U.S. Gold Dollars.* Hewitt's Information Series, Chicago, Ill., 1964. One of many Breen monographs that blazed new trails in understanding of neglected series, as also the following.

—— *Varieties of U.S. Quarter Eagles.* 1964.

—— *Major Varieties of the U.S. Three Dollar Gold Pieces.* Same publisher, 1965.

—— *Early U.S. Half Eagles 1795-1838.* 1966.

—— *Varieties of U.S. Half Eagle 1839-1929.* 1967.

—— *U.S. Eagles 1795-1933.* 1967.

—— *A Coiner's Caviar: Walter Breen's Encyclopedia of U.S. and Colonial Proof Coins.* FCI Press, Albertson, N.Y. 1977. Master listing which cuts through the guesswork and wishful thinking which plagued Proof collecting in the past.

—— *Walter Breen's Encyclopedia of United States Half Cents.* American Institute of Numismatic Research, South Gate, Cal. 1983. Innovative scientific study of this coinage made memorable by Jack Collins' photography, undoubtedly the finest study of this neglected series.

—— *Walter Breen's Complete Encyclopedia of United States and Colonial Coins.* Doubleday, New York, 1988. A massive undertaking and a massive result. Due to the sheer scope of the work, parts were already obsolescent in 1988. After the author's disgrace and death in prison, a revised and updated edition would re-emphasize Breen's numismatic contributions that are part of the total life story of this frequently controversial and extraordinarily complex individual.

Breen, Walter and Gillio, Ronald J. *California Pioneer Fractional Gold.* Santa Barbara, Pacific Coast Rare Coin Galleries, 1983. First really scientific investigation of this confused area, based on the great Kenneth Lee coll.

Briggs, Larry. *The Complete Encyclopedia of United States Liberty Seated Quarters.* Published by the author, Lima, Ohio, 1991. Format of DLRC books, contains exceptionally useful variety listings and photographs.

Browning, Ard W. *Early Quarter Dollars of the United States, 1796-1838.* Wayte Raymond, New York, 1925. Updated and revised by Walter Breen and Robert W. Miller Sr., with commentary by Q. David Bowers, edited and compiled by Michael J. Hodder. Bowers & Merena Galleries, Wolfeboro, N.H., 1991. An enduring classic of die variety identification.

Burnie, R.H. *Small California and Territorial Gold Coins, Quarter Dollars, Half Dollars, Dollars.* Published by the author, Pascagoula, Miss., 1955. Generally obsolete but still the most valuable reference for "State Gold" and later-date exposition pieces.

Carlson, Carl W. A. and Hodder, Michael J., editors. *The American Numismatic Association Anthology.* American Numismatic Association, Colorado Springs, Colo., 1991. An actually readable 'Festschrift' for the ANA Centennial consisting of important articles by a wide array of numismatic contributors.

Clifford, Henry H. *Pioneer Gold Coinage of the West, 1848-61.* Privately Printed, Los Angeles, 1961.

Cline, J.H. *Liberty Standing Quarters.* Second revised edition published by the author, Palm Harbor, Fla., 1988. Contains some very valuable background data on models for Liberty.

Cohen, Roger S. *American Half Cents, the Little Sisters.* Published by the author, Arlington, Va., 1982. Original version had input of Paul Munson, Ray Munde. The late author was widely known for his often immoderate and spirited correspondence on subject.

Crosby, Sylvester Sage. *The Early Coins of America and the Laws Governing their Issue.* Published by the author, Boston, 1873. Seminal volume for all American numismatic writing; more than a century would pass before much new information would be added to Crosby's findings.

Dalton, R. and Hamer, S.H. *English Provincial Token Coinage of the 18th Century.* London, England, 1910-22. Basic source on this voluminous series, which includes many items directly related to American numismatics, including the Washington issues.

Davis, David J.; Logan, Russell J.; Lovejoy, Allen F.; McCloskey, John W.; Subjack, William L. *Early United States Dimes, 1796-1837.* John Reich Collectors Society, Ypsilanti, Mich., 1984. One of the most valuable recent die variety catalogs, exploring a denomination inexplicably neglected in earlier times.

Dickeson, Montroville W. *The American Numismatic Manual.* Lippincott, Philadelphia, 1865. A major effort for the early years of American numismatics, triggered lively sparring with New York's Augustus Sage.

Doering, David (first ed. with co-author **Doering, Susan**). *California Fractional Gold.* Published by the author(s), Santa Monica, Cal., 1980, 1982. Interesting example of fantasy pricing and the results, second edition without reference to co-author.

Dowle, Anthony and Finn, Patrick. *The Guidebook to the Coinage of Ireland from 995 A.D. to the Present Day.* Spink & Son, London, 1969. Valuable for St. Patrick's and Voce Populi classification.

Dryfhout, John H. *The Work of Augustus Saint Gaudens.* Hanover and London, University Press of New England, 1982. Of highest value in tracing development of 1907 gold coin designs.

Eckfeldt, Jacob Reese and DuBois, William Ewing. *A Manual of Gold and Silver Coins of All Nations, Struck within the Past Century.* Assay Office of the Mint, Philadelphia, Pa., 1842. Key volume in 1804 dollar saga.

Fivaz, Bill and Stanton, J. T. *The Cherrypickers' Guide to Rare Die Varieties.* Third Edition, Bowers & Merena Galleries, Wolfeboro, N.H., 1994. Follows earlier editions published by the authors, a deliriously successful though sparsely worded compendium of little-known die varieties of nearly all U.S. coins.

Flynn, Kevin. *Getting Your Two Cents* Worth Published with Robert Paul, Ranocras, N.J., 1994. A new and complete study of Two-Cent coinage enhanced by outstanding variety photography.

Forrer, Leonard S. *Biographical Dictionary of Medallists.* Six volumes, two supplements, one recent index. Spink & Son, London, 1911-23, 1988. Indispensable world reference of tremendous importance to U.S. numismatists.

Frossard, Edouard. *Monograph of United States Cents and Half Cents Issued between the Years 1793 and 1857.* T.R. Marvin, Boston, 1879. Significant early contribution to copper literature by feisty European-born numismatist.

Fox, Bruce. *The Complete Guide to Walking Liberty Half Dollars.* DLRC Press, Virginia Beach, Va., 1993. Presents much market analysis with original variety data enhanced by variety photos by such experts as Allen Herbert, Bill Fivaz and J. T. Stanton.

Gengerke, Martin. *American Numismatic Auctions.* Eighth edition 1990. Published by the author, Woodside, N.Y., 1990. A brilliantly successful pioneer contribution to the history of American numismatic auctions since earliest times and a 'must' for any numismatic working library.

Gillilland, Cory. *Sylloge of the United States Holdings in the National Numismatic Collection of the Smithsonian Institution.* Volume One, Gold Coins, 1785-1834. Smithsonian Institution Press, Washington and London, 1992. This is the first in-depth examination of any segment of the Smithsonian's U.S. coin collection and will hopefully introduce a series.

Gould, Maurice M. and Bressett, Kenneth. *Hawaiian Coins, Tokens & Paper Money.* Whitman Publishing, Racine, Wis. 2nd Rev. Ed., 1961.

Greer, Brian. *The Complete Guide to Liberty Seated Dimes.* DLRC Press, Virginia Beach, Va., 1992. A closer look into varieties than the same series' half dime book, taking the field a step beyond the work of the lamented Kamal Ahwash.

Grellman, John R. and Reiver, Jules. *Attribution Guide for United States Large Cents, 1840-1857.* Published by the authors, Montgomery, Al., 1987. Originally published as two loose-leaf volumes, consolidated in hard cover 1987. A dream come true for those who had to contend with Newcomb's attributions and sometimes murky style.

Gilbert, Ebenezer. *The United States Half Cents, from the First Year of Issue in 1793 to the Year When Discontinued, 1857.* Elder Numismatic Press, New York, 1916. An old stand-by which still sees some use today.

Heaton, Augustus G. *Mint Marks, a Treatise on the Coinage of the United States Branch Mints.* Published by the author, Washington, D.C. 1893. A slim booklet with revolutionary effect on American collecting habits.

Hilt, Robert P. II. *Die Varieties of Early United States Coins.* RTS Publishing Co., Omaha, Neb. 1980. Attempt to apply statistical analytic method to earliest silver coins, effectiveness limited by sometimes incomprehensible technical vocabulary.

Hodder, Michael J. and Bowers, Q. David. *The Standard Catalogue of Encased Postage Stamps.* Bowers & Merena Galleries, Wolfeboro, N.H. 1989. The first modern study of this fascinating Civil War contribution to American monetary history with valuable historical sketches of issuers and the rarity of individual types and denominations.

Ivy, Steve and Howard, Ron. *What Every Silver Dollar Buyer Should Know.* Ivy Press, Dallas, Texas, 1984. Interesting publication released when co-authors represented competing firms, although this fact was not noted in book.

Judd, J. Hewitt M.D. *United States Pattern, Experimental and Trial Pieces.* Whitman Publishing, Racine, Wis. 1959, last ed. 1977. The definitive reference to the subject through the early 1990's, replacing Adams and Woodin.

Julian, R.W. *Medals of the United States Mint, the First Century, 1792-1892.* Token and Medal Society, 1977. One of the greatest contributions to the basics of American numismatics, shedding light on a long-ignored area of U.S. Mint history, much of it directly relevant to the coinage.

Kagin, Donald H. *Private Gold Coins and Patterns of the United States.* Arco, New York, 1981. Outgrowth of author's doctoral thesis, a highly readable narrative and scientific investigation, richly illustrated listing of this colorful material, its creators and their histories.

Kessler, Alan. *The Fugio Cents.* Colony Coin Co., Newtonville,Mass., 1976. Expands Eric P. Newman's earlier definitive work on this series.

Kimmel, Jerry. *Pioneer Gold Auction Analysis, 1991.* Published by the Author, Avon Lake, Ohio, 1990. A fascinating compilation of price realizations since 1878.

Kliman, Myron. *The Two-Cent Piece and Varieties.* Numismatic Enterprises, South Laguna, Cal., 1977. A remarkably detailed work which attracted little collector recognition.

Lange, David W. *The Complete Guide to Buffalo Nickels.* 1992, DLRC Press, Virginia Beach, Va.,
—— *The Complete Guide to Mercury Dimes.* 1993. Well illustrated commentaries on dates and Mint marks, but both books offer virtually none of the variety information sought by serious collectors nor any especially original historical data on either series.

Lawrence, David. *The Complete Guide to Barber Dimes.* 1991, DLRC Press, Virginia Beach, Va., 1991. Important modern studies which have helped expand interest in these increasingly popular series.

Lee, Edward M. *California Gold Quarters, Halves, Dollars.* Tower-Lee, Glendale, Cal., 1932. The most serious reference in use before 1983.

Legarda, Angelita Ganzon de, M.D. *Piloncitos to Peso, a brief History of Coinage in the Philippines.* Bancom Development Corp., Manila, Republic of the Philippines, 1976. Undoubtedly the finest general investigation of all Philippine coinage since the pre-colonial era.

Margolis, Arnold. *The Error Coin Encyclopedia.* Published by the author, first edition, 1991. A fascinating examination of this field by the publisher of *Error Trends coin Magazine.* Only the independent-minded Margolis could dub his work, "The Plaid Book."

Maris, Edward M.D. *Varieties of the Copper Issues of the United States in the Year 1794.* William K. Bellows, Philadelphia, 1870. Outstanding work by Quaker doctor noted for colorful nomenclature for major cent varieties.
—— *Historical Sketch of the Coins of New Jersey,* same publisher, 1881. Landmark work on New Jersey colonial and state coinages. Valuable reprint with foreword by Walter Breen, Quarterman, 1974.

Medcalf, Donald and Russell, Ronald. *Hawaiian Money.* The authors, Honolulu, 2nd ed. 1990.

Miller, Henry Clay and Ryder, Hillyer. *State Coinages of New England.* ANS, New York, 1920. Both authors' numbering systems are still standard more than 70 years later.

Miller, Wayne. *The Morgan and Peace Dollar Textbook.* Adam Smith Publishing, Metairie, La. 1982. In its day a useful expansion of author's earlier Analysis, made distinctly colorful by a hysterical attack against the then-active ANACS.

Mossman, Philip L. *Money of the American Colonies and Confederation, a Numismatic, Economic & Historical Correlation.* American Numismatic Society Numismatic Studies No. 20, New York, 1993. A numismatic-historic *tour de force,* boldly multi-faceted examination of Colonial money and its total environment. Winner of NLG's Best Book of the Year, 1994.

Nagengast, Bernard. *The Jefferson Nickel Analyst.* Published by the author, Sidney, Ohio, 1979. In-depth study of what the author regards as a sleeper series.

Newcomb, Howard Rounds. *The United States Copper Cents of the Years 1816-1857.* Numismatic Review, Stack's, New York, 1944. One of the great pioneer efforts in basic American numismatics, hand-lettered by the author during wartime austerity and published under wartime conditions by Stack's. Newcomb numbers remain the standard, though following the author's original text is often difficult even for the most dedicated cataloger.

Newman, Eric P. *Varieties of the Fugio Cent.* Coin Collectors Journal, New York, 1949. Still the definitive work after 40 years.
—— *The 1776 Continental Currency Coinage.* Same publisher, 1952.
—— *Coinage for Colonial Virginia.* ANS, New York, 1956.
—— *Secret of the Good Samaritan Shilling.* Same publisher, 1959.
—— *The Early Paper Money of America.* Whitman Publishing, Racine, Wis., 1976. Of the greatest value to all serious students of Colonial and early Independence era paper and metallic currency, a true perspective-bringer for those interested in both once-separated fields.
—— **and Bressett, Kenneth E.** *The Fantastic 1804 Dollar.* Whitman Publishing, Racine, Wis., 1962. Breakthrough in numismatic investigative reporting which reminded the world of many bizarre U.S. Mint activities of the last century.
—— **editor; Doty, Richard C. associate editor.** *Studies on Money in Early America.* New York, 1976. Newman's amazing and sometimes hilarious discussion of origin of the term 'Bungtown' is "worth the price of admission."

Noe, Sydney P. *The Silver Coinage of Massachusetts.* Quarterman Publications, Lawrence, Mass. 1973. Invaluable compendium of Noe's earlier writings in this important area, with biography by Ruth Noe Pistolese, amendations by Newman and Breen.

Noyes, William C. *United States Large Cents, 1793-1814 and 1816-1839.* Two volumes, published by the author, Monument Beach, Cal., 1991. A vital contribution to large cent literature, deluxe photograph liberates collectors from cumbersome Sheldon-Newcomb verbal descriptions. Noyes' Condition Census information has drawn predictable fire from other voices in this controversy-spiced numismatic specialty area.

Orosz, Dr. Joel J. *The Eagle that is Forgotten: Pierre Eugene Du Simitiere, Founding Father of American Numismatics.* Bowers and Merena Galleries, Wolfeboro, N.H., 1988. Powerful plea for recognition of Swiss-born pioneer numismatist, medallic artist of the infant U.S. as first American numismatist of note, who literally starved to death rather than sell his beloved collection.

Overton, Al C., with Parsley, Don, editor. *Early Half Dollar Die Varieties, 1794-1836.* Third edition, published by the editor, Escondito, Cal., 1990. Boldly updated version of one of the most lucid, usable guides to any American series, especially valued as it freed a series long clouded by the convolutions of Beistle.

Peck, C. Wilson. *English Copper, Tin and Bronze Coins in the British Museum, 1558-1958.* Trustees of the British Museum, London, 1960. Another priceless "bridge" book, linking long-segregated American Colonial coinage to its proper place in the larger world of numismatics.

Pollock, Andrew W. III. *United States Patterns and Related Issues.* Bowers & Merena Galleries, Wolfeboro, N.H., 1994. Here is the long-needed revision of the Judd work. Pollock offers his own numbering system as well as some new additions and re-examination of coins in the usual chronological listings.

Shafer, Neil. *United States Territorial Coinage for the Philippine Islands.* Whitman Publishing Co., Racine, Wis., 1961. Shafer's is the pioneer American work on this neglected series, rescuing the series from undeserved oblivion through scientific research and factual presentation.

Raymond, Wayte. *Standard Catalogue of United States Coins,* 19 editions, Wayte Raymond Inc., 1934-1957. The last widely distributed basic guide to include full spectrum of coins, tokens and patterns until Scott-Taxay, 1971.

Reiver, Jules. *Variety Identification Guide for United States Half Dimes, 1794-1837.*
—— *Variety Identification Guide for United States Quarter Dollars, 1796-1838.*
—— *Variety Identification Manual for United States Reeded Edge Half Dollars, 1836-1839.* All published by the author, Wilmington, Delaware, 1984, 1987, 1988. Invaluable aids to easy identification of die varieties of series covered with varying degrees of usefulness by Valentine, Browning and Beistle. True numismatics at its best.

Rust, Alvin M. *Mormon and Utah Coins and Currency.* Rust Rare Coin Co., 1984. Masterful work on issues of Utah and the Mormons, unhappily includes some subsequently identified forgeries by convicted forger-murderer Mark Hoffman.

Schilke, Oscar G. and Solomon, Raphael E. *America's Foreign Coins.* Coin and Currency Institute, New York, 1964. An illustrated catalog of all coins formerly enjoying legal tender status in the U.S., gives fascinating insights into an era which saw more foreign than American coins in daily use.

Seymour, Dexter C. *Templeton Reid, First of the Pioneer Coiners.* ANS Museum Notes, New York, 1974. Classic of numismatic research which illuminated many seemingly permanent mysteries of the Appalachian gold rush.

Sheldon, William H. *Early American Cents.* Harper & Bros., New York, 1945;
—— with **Breen, Walter, Pascal, Dorothy.** *Penny Whimsy.* Titles fundamental to modern numismatic and especially large cent literature, introduced Sheldon scale; readability of a high order, all too rare in numismatic field.

Slabaugh, Arlie. *United States Commemorative Coins.* Whitman Publishing Co., Racine, Wis., 1976. A basic necessity for understanding the commemorative coinage in all its aspects.

Smith, Pete. *American Numismatic Biographies.* Gold Leaf Press, Division of The Money Tree, Rocky River, Ohio. 1992. A remarkable compilation of data on American numismatic leaders since the 18th century, including collectors, writers, dealers, medal subjects. Published in a startlingly small first edition, a second edition is urgently needed!

Snow, Richard with Pilliod, Chris, editor. *Flying Eagle & Indian Cents.* Tucson, Ariz., Eagle Eye Press, 1992. Fascinating re-study of these series with a splendid biography of designer J. B. Longacre and outstanding photography.

Stack, Norman. *United States Type Coins, an Illustrated History of the Federal Coinage.* Stack's, New York, 1986. A richly color-illustrated compendium of all regular issue U.S. coins.

Stewart, Frank H. *History of the First United States Mint, Its People and Its Operations.* Published by the author, Camden, N.J., 1924. Colorful narrative by the Philadelphia electrician who failed in his efforts to find some agency to preserve the historic building of the first U.S. Mint.

Swiatek, Anthony and Breen, Walter. *Encyclopedia of United States Gold and Silver Commemorative Coins.* Arco, New York, 1981. Major achievement in numismatic publishing, based largely on Swiatek's years of research into every aspect of this subject. Book is marred by Breen's irritating, judgmental language, "corpus delecti, accessories, suspects," etc.

Swiatek, Anthony. *Commemorative Coins of the United States, Identification and Price Guide.* Coin World, Sidney, Ohio, 1993. This information-packed treatment is Swiatek at his best, freed of the distracting input of an unqualified co-author that impeded the earlier title.

Taxay, Don. *Counterfeit, Mis-Struck and Unofficial U.S. Coins.* Arco, N.Y., 1963. Represented return of "higher criticism" to numismatic writing, effective exposure of inner history of U.S. Mint chicanery of 19th century.
—— *United States Mint and Coinage.* Same publisher, 1966. Definitive history of the Mint and all of its facets. One of the building stones of scientific, non-adulatory modern numismatic literature.
—— *Illustrated History of United States Commemorative Coinage.* Same publisher, 1967. Source of much original data on rejected designs and unpublicized struggles over development of all 1892-1954 U.S. commemorative coins.

Tomaska, Rick Jerry. *Cameo and Brilliant Proof Coinage of the 1950 to 1970 Era.* R. & I. Publications, Encinitas, Cal., 1991. Specialized study of an area receiving much commercial attention, especially since the introduction of the "slab."

Travers, Scott A. *The Coin Collector's Survival Manual.* Third revised edition, Bonus Books, Chicago, Ill., 1994. originally released by Arco Publishing Inc., New York, 1988 (2nd ed.). A fearless examination of market realities first published in 1984, which plunged unhesitatingly into controversial areas ignored in tradition numismatic writing and modern promotional market literature.

—— *Travers' Rare Coin Investment Strategy.* Prentice Hall Press, New York, 1989 (2nd. ed.).

—— *The Investor's Guide to Coin Trading.* John Wiley & Sons, New York, 1990. An independent examination of the contemporary numismatic marketplace, including certified grading, slabbing and electronic trading . The insider's view of the gyrations of a major investment firms of the 1980's is alone worth the price of the book.

Valentine, Daniel W. *The United States Half Dimes;* with Additional Material by Kamal Ahwash, Walter Breen, David J. Davis, Will W. Neil, Harold P. Newlin. Quarterman Publications, Lawrence, Mass., 1975. Complete update through 1975 of Valentine original, published by ANS in 1931. Includes Walter Breen's 1958 supplement in which he referred to all commemorative coins as "speculators' trash."

Van Allen, Leroy C. and Mallis, A. George. *The Comprehensive Catalogue and Encyclopedia of U.S. Morgan and Peace Dollars.* Revised edition, DLRC Press, Virginia Beach, Va., 1993. An amazingly detailed look into the arcana of these popular series, originally an Arco title, again available through an independent publisher.

Van Ryzin, Robert R. *Striking Impressions, a Visual Guide to Collecting U.S. Coins.* Krause Publications, Iola, Wisc., 1992. An unusually thorough pictorial examination of hundreds of major American coin varieties in highly usable form.

Vermeule, Cornelius C. *Numismatic Art in America: Aesthetics of U.S. Coinage.* Harvard University Press, Cambridge, Mass., 1971. Another book that no serious numismatic library should be without, provides unique insights into all areas of coin design.

White, Weimar. *The Liberty Seated Dollar, 1840-1873.* Sanford J. Durst, New York, 1985. In-depth look at this little-studied series, with somewhat arbitrary survival estimates and collector commentary.

Wiley, Randy and Bugert, Bill. *The Complete Guide to Liberty Seated Half Dollars.* DLRC Press, Virginia Beach, Va., 1993. This is the deepest variety, rarity and market analysis of all DLRC books, keyed as well to the Breen *Complete Encyclopedia* listings.

Wilhite, Bob and Michael, Tom. *Auction Prices Realized, 1994.* Latest in a series pioneered by Bernard Rome in the early 1970's, an invaluable tool for researching the contemporary auction field.

Willem, John M. *The United States Trade Dollar: America's Only Unwanted, Unhonored Coin.* Marchbanks Press, New York, 1959. Close investigation into the peculiar history of this coinage fiasco; not a variety guide.

Winter, Douglas. *Charlotte Mint Gold Coins, 1838-1861.* Bowers and Merena Galleries, Wolfeboro, N.H. 1988. Numismatic history and analysis of North Carolina Branch Mint.

Yeoman, R.S. with **Bressett, Kenneth E., editor**. *A Guide Book of United States Coins.* Issued annually 1946 to present. The most familiar popular-level book after demise of Wayte Raymond's Standard Catalogue.

Auction catalogs

Numismatists today are more aware than ever of the valuable role auction literature has played in the development of the entire field. Since 1976, many important collections have been sold at auction, returning thousands of rarities to the numismatic market. These results are incorporated in this book. The following catalogs, from the 19th century until the present, have contributed to this and earlier editions. Where most of a company's known sales were used, individual citations may be omitted. Post 1990 sales by Bowers & Merena and Stack's are cited as BM, ST with abbreviated month-year dates. The Eliasberg COllection sales (gold, 1982; silver and minor coins, 1986, 1987) are cited as "Eliasberg."

American Numismatic Association, All ANA Convention Sales, 1941- 1988. Incl. **Ira Reed, Frank Katen, Kosoff, Federal Brand, Aubrey Bebee, New Netherlands, James Kelly, Jim Charlton, Leo Young, Al C. Overton, Kagin's, Superior, Stack's, Paramount, Bowers & Ruddy, NERCG, Ivy, Heritage, Bowers & Merena**.

Charles E. Anthon, New York, 1879-1882.

"Apostrophe Sales," all from *Auction '79* through *Auction '89*; includes **Stack's, Superior, Rarcoa, Paramount** and **Akers**.

E.J. Attinelli, New York, Jan. 1878.

Bangs, & Co., New York. *William L. Bramhall,* May, 1859; *Satterlee, Mason, Hewitt,* March 1862.

Bowers & Ruddy. *Matt Rothert,* Nov. 1973; *C.W. Newport,* Jan. 1975; *Krugjohann,* May 1976; *Roy Harte, Fairfield,* Nov. 1977; *Garrett Collection sales,* Nov. 1979-March 1981; *Henry H. Clifford,* March 1982; *U.S. Gold Coin Coll. (Eliasberg)* Oct. 1982; *New York Public Library Coll.,* Oct. 1982.

Bowers & Merena. *Connecticut Historical Society,* April 1983; *Virgil M. Brand,* Nov. 1983; *Arnold and Romisa Colls.,* Sept. 1984; *Emery & Nichols Colls.,* Nov. 1984; *Russell B. Patterson,* March 1985; *Abe Kosoff Estate,* Nov. 1985; *Bank of Hawaii,* Jan. 1986; *Julian Leidman,* April 1986; *Frederick B. Taylor,* Mar. 1987; *The Norweb Coll.,* Oct. 1987 to Nov. 1988; *Ebenezer M. Saunders,* Nov. 1987; *Lloyd M. Higgins,* Jan. 1988; *Byron Johnson Estate,* Jan. 1989, all subsequent sales, cited as BM, date.

Samuel H. and Henry Chapman. *Marshall Lefferts,* July 1881; *Charles I. Bushnell,* June 1882; *A. Dohrmann,* Dec. 1886; *Edward Maris,* Nov. 1900; *J.O. Stevens,* 1902; *John G. Mills,* April 1904; *John F. McCabe,* June 1905; *Harlan P. Smith,* June 1906.

Chapman, Henry. *Matthew A. Stickney,* June 1907; *Andrew C. Zabriskie,* June 1909; *George H. Earle,* June 1912; *Clarence S. Bement,* May 1916; *John S. Jenks,* Dec. 1921.

Edward Cogan. *J.N.T. Levick,* Dec. 1859 and June 1865; *Emil Cauffman,* May 1871; *Benjamin Betts,* June 1871; *Isaac F. Wood,* May 1873; *Col. Mendes I. Cohen,* Oct. 1875; *Lewis White, Isaac F. Wood,* April, 1876; *William S. Jenks,* Oct. 1876; *John S. Randall,* May 1878.

George Cogan. *J. Colvin Randall,* March 1882;.

Thomas L. Elder. *Peter Gschwend,* June 1908; *F.W. Doughty, Parts I-III,* 1909; *Peter Mougey,* Sept. 1910; *Ebenezer Gilbert,* Nov. 1910; *William H. Woodin,* March 1911; *Henry C. Miller,* 1917, 1920.

Eliasberg. Bowers & Ruddy "U.S. Gold Coin Collection," Oct. 1982; Bowers & Merena, in cooperation with Stack's, May 1996 and April 1997. All are cited as "Eliasberg" followed by month and year.

Edouard Frossard. Many sales under own name or through Bangs & Co., 1878-1901.

S.V. Hankels. *Edward Maris Coll.* June 1886.

John W. Haseltine. *J. Randall,* April 1870; *William Idler,* April, Dec. 1870; *Joseph J. Mickley,* Jan. 1879; *A.M. Smith* Nov. 1882; *Sylvester S. Crosby,* June 1883.

Kagin's. *Mail Bid sales* 1930s-1974; *MANA Sale,* Nov. 1973; *San Diego ANA Sale,* Aug. 1983; *GENA Sale,* Oct. 1983; *Long Beach Sale,* Feb. 1984; *Metropolitan New York Sale,* March 1984; *Long Beach Sale,* May 1984, *Ditto,* Oct. 1984; *1984 Gillispie sale* has distinction of being the only auction named for a cat.

Abe Kosoff. *Julius Guttag,* 1940-41; *Michael F. Higgy,* Sept. 1943; *"World's Greatest Collection," F.C.C. Boyd,* Jan. 1945-Jan. 1946; *Adolphe Menjou,* June 1950; *Thomas G. Melish,* April 1956; *James O. Sloss,* Oct. 1959; *Edwin M. Hydeman,* Mar. 1961; *Lee G. Lahrman,* Feb. 1963; *Alex Shuford,* May 1968.

Kreisberg & Cohen, *Quality Sales. John A. Beck,* Jan. 1975, Feb. 1976; *Herbert Bergen,* Oct. 1979; *Gainesborough,* Sept. 1980.

Kreisberg & Schulman. *Adolphe Menjou, King Farouk,* Jan. 1957; *Gustav Lichtenfels,* Feb. 1961; *Col. James W. Curtis,* March 1962, Jan. 1963.

George A. Leavitt. *William Leggett Bramhall,* March 1860; *Alfred S. Robinson,* Dec. 1865.

Lyman H. Low. *Henry R. Linderman,* June 1887; *Edward Groh,* May, June 1905.

Ebenezer Locke Mason. *J. Colvin Randall,* Nov. 1868; *Montroville W. Dickeson,* Oct. 1869-May 1870; *William A. Fewsmith,* Oct. 1870; *Joseph J. Mickley,* Nov. 1878.

B. Max Mehl. *H.O. Granberg Coll.* July 1913, Jul.-Nov. 1919; *Arthur C. Nygren,* Nov. 1914; *Elmer S. Sears,* July-Dec. 1918; *James Ten Eyck,* May 1922; *Charles Wellinger,* Oct. 1923; *William Forrester Dunham,* June 1941; *Belden E. Roach,* Feb. 1944; *Fred E. Olsen,* Nov. 1944; *William Cutler Atwater,* June 1946; *Will W. Neil,* June 1947; *"A Royal Sale," King Farouk,* March 1948.

Lester Merkin. *Louis Helfenstein,* Aug. 1964; *Al C. Overton,* Sept. 1974; this firm was master of the concise, high quality sale format.

Mid-American Rare Coin Auctions. Inc. Lexington, Ky. Founded by Jeff Garrett, included cataloger Ron Guth, premier coin photographer Tom Mulvaney. Conducted high quality sales 1984-1992.

NASCA. Many sales Dec. 1976 through Nov. 1983; valuable for cataloging by Douglas Ball, Carl W.A. Carlson, Martin Gengerke, latter catalogers with Herb Melnick Inc., HIM. .

New Netherlands Coin Co. Many catalogs, 1940-1977, incl. *Wayte Raymond, F.C.C. Boyd* series. Valuable for cataloging by **John J. Ford Jr., Breen**.

New York Coin & Stamp Co. *Robert Coulton Davis,* Jan. 1890; *Lorin G. Parmelee,* June 1890; *Francis W. Doughty,* April 1891; *George Woodside,* April 1892.

Numismatic Auctions of Florida Inc. Subsidiary of Numismatic Investments of Florida, South Miami. Cataloging by David T. Alexander, 1985-1986.

Paramount International Coin. Co. Many sales, incl. several *ANA, FUN* and other convention sales.

Pine Tree Rare Coin Auctions. *First Breen Gold Sale,* March 1974; *EAC Convention,* Feb. 1975; subsequent *"Breen"* and *Florida United Numismatists Convention* sales.

RARCOA. *N.M. Kaufman Coll.,* Aug. 1978;

Wayte Raymond. *Waldo Newcomer,* June 1932-39; *Charles P. Senter,* Oct. 1933; *Jascha Heifetz,* 1937-38; *Howard R. Newcomb,* Jan.-May 1945.

J.W. Scott. *Henry R. Linderman,* Feb. 1888; *"Paris"* Dec. 1894; *F.S. Winston,* Oct. 1897.

Sotheby & Co. *Palace Collections of Egypt, (Farouk Sale)* Feb. 1954.

Stack's. *George H. Hall,* May 1945; *Charles Deetz,* Nov. 1946; *Fred S. Guggenheimer,* Jan. 1953; *R.T. McPherson,* Feb. 1953; *Anderson-Dupont,* Oct.-Nov. 1954; *Maj. Lenox R. Lohr,* Oct. 1956; *Charles W. Neumoyer,* May 1960; *R.E. Cox,* April 1962; *Brobson* (fixed price list) 1963; *Samuel W. Wolfson,* May-Oct. 1963; *George O. Walton,* June-Oct. 1963; *George S. Ewalt,* Nov. 1965; *Dr. Conway Bolt,* Apr. 1966; *Charles Jay,* Oct. 1967; *Massachusetts Historical Society,* May-Sept. 1971; *Winner Delp,* Nov. 1972; *Reed Hawn,* Aug. 1973, Mar. 1977; *Essex Institute,* Feb. 1975; *TAD Coll.* Feb. 1976; *John Work Garrett,* Mar. 1976; *Frederick S. Knobloch,* May 1978, May 1980; *Harold S. Bareford,* Dec. 1978, Oct. 1981; *Charlotte Mint Museum,* Mar. 1979; *Martin F. Kortjohn,* Oct. 1979; *Robison,* Feb.-Dec 1982; *John L. Roper II,* May 1983, March 1984; *Amon G. Carter Jr.,* March 1984; *Floyd T. Starr,* June 1984; *Richard Picker,* Oct. 1984; *50th Anniv., Jimmy Hayes, Primary Bartle et al,* Oct. 1985; *Herman Halpern,* Mar. 1988, May 1989; *L.R. French,* Jan. 1989; *Gilbert Steinberg,* Oct. 1989 and all sales since Fall 1989, cited as ST with date.

William H. Strobridge. *William A. Lilliendahl,* May 1862, Dec. 1863; *George F. Seavey,* Sept. 1863; *Benjamin Haines,* April 1872.

Superior Galleries. *Clarke E. Gilhousen,* Feb.-Oct. 1973; *Charles L. Ruby,* Feb.-Oct. 1974; *Walter L. Crouch,* June 1977; *Hoagy Carmichael and Wayne Miller Colls.,* Jan. 1986; *Robinson S. Brown,* Sept. 1986; *Buddy Ebsen Coll.,* May 1987; *Bernard Shore,* Jan. 1988; *Moreira Coll.,* Jan. 1989; *Jack H. Robinson,* Jan. 1989; *Jascha Heifetz,* Oct. 1989 and later sales since that date.

United States Coin Co. *F.W. Doughty,* Jan. 1914; *H.O. Granberg,* May 1915; *George P. French,* June 1915, Dec. 1917; *W.G. Jerrems,* April 1916; *Judson P. Brenner,* June 1916

W. Elliott Woodward. *Jeremiah Colburn,* Oct. 1863; *John F. McCoy,* May 1864; *Bache, Levick, Colburn,* Dec. 1865; *Joseph J. Mickley,* Oct. 1867; *H.W. Holland,* Nov. 1878; *William H. Bowdoin,* March 1879; *O.A. Jenison,* June 1881; *J. Colvin Randall,* June 1885-Oct. 1886.

LAUS DEO

Index

Symbols

A

D

S

U

ϒ

Z